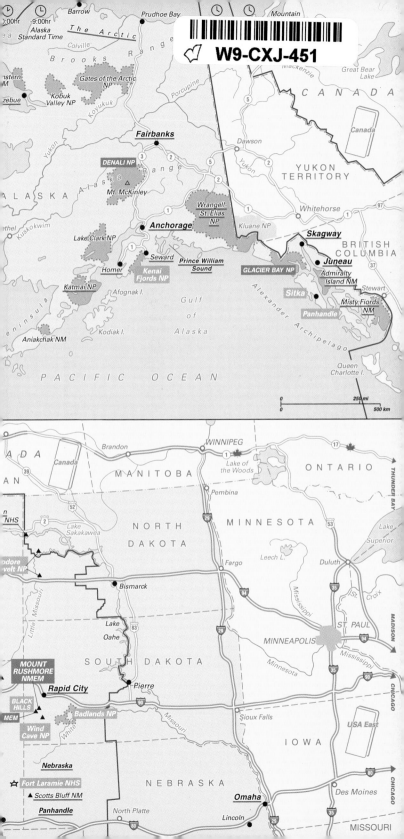

USA WEST

Editorial Director   Cynthia Clayton Ochterbeck

THE GREEN GUIDE TO USA WEST

Editor   Gwen Cannon
Contributing Writer   Eric P. Lucas
Production Coordinator   Natasha G. George
Cartography   GeoNova Publishing, Inc., Peter Wrenn
Photo Editor   Lydia Strong
Proofreader   Jonathan P. Gilbert
Layout & Design   Chris Bell, Ute Weber and Frank Ladd
Cover Design   Laurent Muller and Ute Weber

Contact Us: The Green Guide
                                Michelin Maps and Guides
                                One Parkway South
                                Greenville, SC 29615
                                USA
                                ☎ 1-800-432-6277
                                www.michelintravel.com
                                michelin.guides@us.michelin.com

                                Michelin Maps and Guides
                                Hannay House
                                39 Clarendon Road
                                Watford, Herts WD17 1JA
                                UK
                                ☎ (01923) 205 240
                                www.ViaMichelin.com
                                travelpubsales@uk.michelin.com

Special Sales: For information regarding bulk sales,
                                customized editions and premium sales,
                                please contact our Customer Service
                                Departments:
                                USA   1-800-432-6277
                                UK   (01923) 205 240
                                Canada 1-800-361-8236

Note to the Reader

One Team …
A Commitment to Quality

There's just one reason our team is dedicated to producing quality travel publications—you, our reader.

Throughout our guides we offer **practical information**, **touring tips** and **suggestions** for finding the best places for a break.

Michelin driving tours help you hit the highlights and quickly absorb the best of the region. Our descriptive **walking tours** make you your own guide, armed with directions, maps and expert information.

We scout out the attractions, classify them with **star ratings**, and describe in detail what you will find when you visit them.

Michelin maps featured throughout the guide offer vibrant, detailed and easy-to-follow outlines of everything from close-up museum plans to international maps.

Places to stay and eat are always a big part of travel, so we research **hotels and restaurants** that we think convey the essence of the destination, and arrange them by geographic area and price. We walk you through the best shopping districts and point you towards the host of entertainment and recreation possibilities available.

We **test, retest, check and recheck** to make sure that our guidebooks are truly just that: a personalized guide to help you make the most of your visit. And if you still want a speaking guide, we list local tour guides who will lead you on all the boat, bus, guided, historical, culinary, and other tours you shouldn't miss.

In short, we remove the guesswork involved with travel. After all, we want you to enjoy traveling with Michelin as much as we do.

The Michelin Green Guide Team

PLANNING YOUR TRIP

INTRODUCTION TO USA WEST

SYMBOLS

🛈 **Tourist Information**
🕐 **Hours of Operation**
🕐 **Periods of Closure**
😊 **A Bit of Advice**
😊 **Details to Consider**
👛 **Entry Fees**
Kids **Especially for Children**
🐾 **Tours**
♿ **Wheelchair Accessible**

CONTENTS

DISCOVERING USA WEST

HOW TO USE THIS GUIDE

Orientation

To help you grasp the "lay of the land" quickly and easily, so you'll feel confident and comfortable finding your way around the region, we offer the following tools in this guide:

- Detailed table of contents for an overview of what you'll find in the guide, and how the guide is organized.
- Map of USA West with the Principal Sights highlighted for easy reference.
- Detailed maps for major cities and villages, including driving tour maps and larger-scale maps for walking tours.
- Principal Sights organized alphabetically, by region, for quick reference.

Practicalities

At the front of the guide, you'll see a section called "Planning Your Trip" that contains information about planning your trip, the best time to go, different ways of getting to the region and getting around, and basic facts and tips for making the most of your visit. You'll find driving and themed tours, and suggestions for outdoor fun. There's also a calendar of popular annual events, information on shopping, sightseeing, kids' activities and sports and recreational opportunities.

WHERE TO STAY

We've made a selection of hotels and arranged them within the cities by price cate-gory to fit all budgets (*see the Legend on the cover flap for an explanation of the price categories*). For the most part, we've selected accommodations based on their unique regional quality, their regional feel, as it were. So, unless the individual hotel embodies local ambience, it's rare that we include chain properties, which typically have their own imprint. If you want a comprehensive selection of accommodations in San Francisco, Los Angeles and Las Vegas, see the red-cover **Michelin Guide San Francisco, Michelin Guide Los Angeles** and **Michelin Guide Las Vegas**.

WHERE TO EAT

We thought you'd like to know the popular eating spots, so we selected restaurants that capture the regional experience—those that have a unique regional flavor and local atmosphere. We're not rating the quality of the food per se: as we did with the hotels, we selected restaurants for many towns and villages, categorized by price, to appeal to all wallets (*see the Legend on the cover flap for an explanation of the price categories*).If you want a comprehensive selection of dining recommendations in San Francisco, Los Angeles and Las Vegas, see the red-cover **Michelin Guide San Francisco, Michelin Guide Los Angeles** and **Michelin Guide Las Vegas**.

Attractions

Principal Sights are arranged alphabetically. Within each Principal Sight, attractions for each town, village, or geographical area are divided into local Sights or Walking Tours, nearby Excursions to sights outside the town, or detailed Driving Tours—suggested itineraries for seeing several attractions around a major town. Contact information, admission charges and hours of operation are given for the majority of attractions. Unless otherwise noted, admission prices shown are for a single adult only. Discounts for children, seniors, students, teachers, etc. may be available; be sure to ask. If no admission charge is shown, entrance to the attraction is free.

If you're pressed for time, we recommend you visit the three and two-star sights first: the stars are your guide.

STAR RATINGS

Michelin has used stars as a rating tool for more than 100 years:

★★★	Highly recommended
★★	Recommended
★	Interesting

SYMBOLS IN THE TEXT

Besides the stars, other symbols in the text indicate sights that are closed to the public ⚬⟋; on-site eating facilities ✕; also see ⓒ; breakfast included in the nightly rate ⌇; on-site parking 🅿; spa facilities 𝐒𝐩𝐚; camping facilities △; swimming pool ⟍; and beaches ⌒.

See the box appearing on the Contents page and the Legend on the cover flap for other symbols used in the text.

See the Maps explanation below for symbols appearing on the maps.

Throughout the guide you will find peach-colored text boxes or sidebars containing anecdotal or background information. Green-colored boxes contain information to help you save time or money.

Maps

All maps in this guide are oriented north, unless otherwise indicated by a directional arrow. The term "Local Map" refers to a map within the chapter or Tourism Region. See the map Legend at the back of the guide for an explanation of other map symbols. A complete list of the maps found in the guide appears at the back of this book.

Addresses, phone numbers, opening hours and prices published in this guide are accurate at press time. We welcome corrections and suggestions that may assist us in preparing the next edition. Please send your comments to:

Michelin Maps and Guides
Hannay House
39 Clarendon Road
Watford, Herts WD17 1JA
UK
travelpubsales@uk.michelin.com
www.michelin.co.uk

Michelin Maps and Guides
Editorial Department
P.O. Box 19001
Greenville, SC 29602-9001
USA
michelin.guides@us.michelin.com
www.michelintravel.com

Manhattan Beach, California
© PhotoDisc, Inc

PLANNING YOUR TRIP

MICHELIN DRIVING TOURS

Now that you've got your car, it's time to hit the road. Outlined below are tours that take in highlights of the West, from Hollywood to Old Faithful, Mount St. Helens to The Alamo.

California Dreaming

15 days; about 1,800mi. Any season, but some parts of Sierra parks are closed in winter.
Anchoring the southwest coast, California has a bit of everything, from surf-washed beaches to alpine resorts, cosmopolitan cities to ghost towns. Our tour begins in **San Francisco**, keeper of the Golden Gate, its cable cars scaling the hills from **Fisherman's Wharf** to **Chinatown**. Drive south to **Monterey**, its aquarium anchoring Cannery Row. Highway 1 weaves a cliffside path along the wild **Big Sur** coast to emerge at eclectic **Hearst Castle**. From the charming mission town of **Santa Barbara**, boats provide access to Channel Islands National Park.
Stay long enough in sprawling **Los Angeles** to spy movie stars in **Hollywood** or **Beverly Hills**; spend an afternoon at the **Getty Center** or another renowned art museum. Revisit your childhood at **Disneyland**, the world's most famous amusement park. Subtropical **San Diego** is a delight for animal lovers with its world-famous zoo, wild animal park and **Sea World**. Loop back to L.A. via Pacific Coast Highway (Rte. 1) through Laguna Beach and **Long Beach**, permanent home of the **Queen Mary.** Northbound I-5 runs up the Central Valley, the richest farmland on earth, and lures outdoors lovers to the big trees of **Sequoia and Kings Canyon National Parks** and to the deep glacial valley and waterfalls of **Yosemite National Park**. Across the crest of the **Sierra Nevada**, year-round resorts surround deep-blue **Lake Tahoe**. A short drive from the casinos of **Reno**,

Nevada, is historic **Virginia City**, built in the 1860s and 70s on the fabulously rich Comstock Lode. West is the **Gold Country**, many of whose towns—like quaint **Nevada City** and bustling Auburn—date from the 1850s gold-rush era. Miners traveled upriver from **Sacramento**, now the state capital. In the **Wine Country** of Napa and Sonoma Counties, dozens of wineries welcome tasters. An easy drive down the Marin County coast, to rugged **Point Reyes National Seashore** and majestic **Muir Woods National Monument**, leads back to San Francisco.

Canyons and Casinos

15 days; about 1,800mi.
Best done in spring or fall.
Las Vegas is the gateway to the spectacular canyon country of the Southwest, but it is prudent to wait until this drive is over before investing in blackjack or roulette.
From **Las Vegas**, cross the great **Hoover Dam** and continue east via I-40 to the vast and colorful **Grand Canyon**. The largest chasm on earth is a mile deep, 10mi wide, 277mi long and nearly 2 billion years in the making. From Grand Canyon Village, touring roads extend east and west; dizzying trails descend to the canyon floor. Delightful **Sedona**, in **Red Rock Country** south of **Oak Creek Canyon** via Rte. 89A, is a magnet for artists and New Age spiritual seekers. National monuments preserve ruins of ancient civilizations. **Canyon de Chelly** and Navajo National Monuments are north and east on the broad Navajo Indian Reservation. Surrounded by Navajo lands, Hopi reservation residents pursue ancient cultural traditions. The landscape of **Monument Valley** is well-known from myriad Western movies. US-191 continues to **Moab**, a center for mountain biking and rafting, and gateway to **Canyonlands** and **Arches National Parks**—the former

a spectacular canyon wilderness, the latter preserving more than 2,000 sandstone arches. Southwest, drivers skirt the colorful backcountry of **Capitol Reef National Park** en route to **Bryce Canyon National Park**, a fairyland of rock spires and pinnacles. Two hours farther is **Zion National Park**, enclosing a steep canyon adorned with waterfalls and hanging gardens.

Returning to "Lost Wages," you now can gamble unspent cash in lavish casinos: On the world-famous **Las Vegas Strip**, you'll find the Eiffel Tower and Statue of Liberty, King Arthur's castle and King Tut's tomb.

The Heart of Texas

8 days; about 1,100mi.
Not suggested in summer.
Texas is the largest US state after Alaska. This tour, which starts and ends at the Dallas-Fort Worth airport, samples its cultural, historical and geographical diversity.

Begin in **Fort Worth**. The **Stockyards National Historic District** brings back to life the cowboy days of yore in western-wear stores, a rodeo arena and the world's largest honky-tonk. The **Kimbell Art Museum** is outstanding. South via I-35 in **Austin**, the state capital, is the nationally famous Sixth Street Entertainment District. The **Lyndon Baines Johnson Presidential Library and Museum** on the University of Texas campus pays homage to a native son further remembered at historical parks in the nearby **Hill Country**. Settled by Germans, **Fredericksburg** retains its Teutonic heritage.

San Antonio, rich in Hispanic tradition, is the cradle of Texas freedom. **The Alamo** canonizes 189 patriots who died in its defense. Gondolas cruise past the 2.5mi **River Walk**, lined with shops and cafes. Southeast via I-37, on the Gulf Coast, **Corpus Christi** is the gateway to **Padre Island National Seashore**, a favorite of birdwatchers.

East of San Antonio via I-10 is **Houston**, fourth largest city in the US and home to **Space Center Houston**, where US space research and astronaut training takes place. Oil wealth helps to supports Houston's superbMuseum District, highlighted by the Surrealist works of the **Menil Collection** and the energy exhibits of the **Houston Museum of Natural Science**. Seaside **Galveston** has a notable 19C historic district.

North via I-45 is **Dallas**. Shoppers love the Dallas Market Center, world's largest wholesale merchandise market. **The Sixth Floor Museum at Dealey Plaza** commemorates the life of President John F. Kennedy and analyzes his assassination here in 1963.

Peaks and Pueblos

13 days; about 1,500mi.
Best done in summer.
From the heights of the Rocky Mountains to the secrets of the ancient pueblo heritage, this tour highlights two states: Colorado and New Mexico. Start and finish in **Denver**, urban center of the Rockies. The **LoDo** district is a landmark of historic preservation; the **Denver Art Museum** has a renowned Native American collection. Climbaross the Continental Divide on I-70. Colorful Victorian architecture in the thin air of **Breckenridge** and **Leadville** bears testimony to a silver-mining heritage. The ski resort of **Vail** is a playground for high society; chic **Aspen**, which nestles near the beautiful **Maroon Bells**, has a delightful 19C downtown.

Continue west to the stark geology of **Colorado National Monument** and **Black Canyon of the Gunnison National Park**, then follow spectacular US-550 through the San Juan Mountains to **Durango**, with its fine historic railway. At nearby **Mesa Verde National Park**, visitors walk through five major cliff dwellings dated AD 750-1300. New Mexico's **Chaco Culture National Historical Park** embraces ruins that formed a 9-12C trade and political hub. South, off I-40, clifftop **Sky City at Acoma Pueblo** has been continually inhabited since the 11C. The **Indian Pueblo Cultural Center** at **Albuquerque** represents 19 communities; the **National Atomic Museum** details the nuclear age.

Enchanting **Santa Fe** begs a lengthy stay. See the **Palace of the Governors**, in use since 1610, and the **Georgia O'Keeffe Museum**, displaying the works of the great artist. Marvel at the spiral staircase in the **Loretto Chapel** and take in a show at **The Santa Fe Opera**. Meander north to the artists' colony of Taos, packed with galleries, historic homes, the remarkable **Taos Pueblo** and the adobe **San Francisco de Asis Church.**

En route back to Denver via I-25, pause in **Colorado Springs**. Take a railway to the 14,110ft summit of **Pikes Peak**, learn about broncos at the ProRodeo Hall of Fame, and say a prayer beneath the spires of the Cadet Chapel at the **US Air Force Academy**.

Rocky Mountain High

13 days; about 1,900mi.
Best done in summer.
Several of America's most famous national parks and historic sites are a part of this high-elevation tour, which begins in Salt Lake City and concludes in Denver.

Salt Lake City fascinates visitors intrigued by the religion and culture of the Mormons, who founded the Utah city in 1847. Take I-80 east to the historic mining town of **Park City**, site of many events in the 2002 Winter Olympics, then head north. US-89 leads through **Jackson**, renowned for its cowboy ambience and its **National Museum of Wildlife Art**, and **Grand Teton National Park**, embracing a dramatic range of craggy mountains reflected in morainal lakes. It continues into **Yellowstone National Park**, whose unparalleled natural attractions—geysers, hot springs, canyons and rich wildlife—demand more than an overnight stay.

Turning east on US-14, pause in **Cody** to explore **Buffalo Bill Historical Center**, then proceed directly across the Big Horn Mountains to the fluted monolith of **Devils Tower National Monument** and into the **Black Hills**. After paying homage to the stone images of US presidents at **Mount Rushmore National Memorial**, detour to **Wind Cave National Park** and the once-rowdy mining town of **Deadwood**. Swing east through the geological curiosities of **Badlands National Park**, then south across western Nebraska to pick up the **Oregon Trail** near Scotts Bluff National Monument.

The historic trail follows US-26 past **Fort Laramie National Historic Site**. Turn south through **Cheyenne**, a quintessential rodeo town; detour via US-34 to pristine **Rocky Mountain National Park.** The tour ends in **Denver**, described in "Peaks and Pueblos."

Northwest Passages

10 days; about 1,700mi.
Best done in summer.
This tour starts and ends in Seattle and takes in the volcanic peaks of the Cascade Range, great rivers, redwood forests and an unforgettable Pacific coastline.

The futuristic **Space Needle** towers above **Seattle**, home of Microsoft and Boeing, Nirvana and Starbucks Coffee. The maritime city invites exploration of its **Pike Place Market**, its **Seattle Center** cultural complex, museums and gardens. Visitors view 747 jets under construction at the **Boeing Everett Site**. Alpine roads wind southeast through magnificent **Mount Rainier National Park** and fascinating Mount **St. Helens National Volcanic Monument**, which offers perspective on the peak's 1980 eruption.

In the shadow of **Mount Hood** is **Portland**, Oregon's "Rose City." The International Rose Test Garden is one of several gardens in **Washington Park**, which sprawls across hills near downtown. Outside Portland is the

Distance Chart

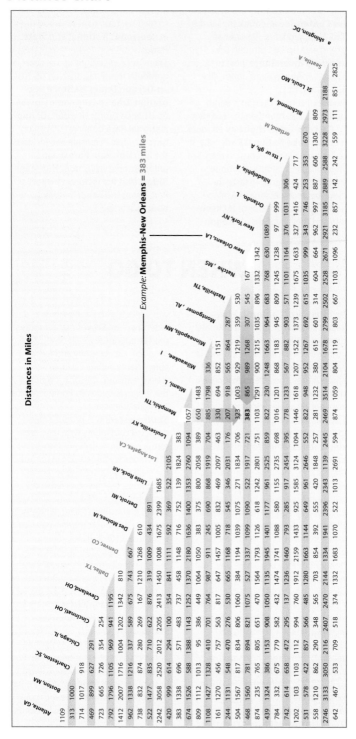

Distances in Miles

Example: Memphis–New Orleans = 383 miles

pinot-rich **Oregon Wine Country** and the End of the **Oregon Trail Interpretive Center**, documenting the journey of mid-19C pioneers. Panoramas extend east up I-84 through the **Columbia River Gorge**, host to myriad windsurfers and ribbon-like Multnomah Falls.

The hubof central Oregon is Bend, southeast of Portland on US-97. Drive the **Cascade Lakes Highway** en route to **Crater Lake National Park**, where a cobalt-blue lake, deepest in the US, fills a collapsed caldera. Continue southwest via Rte. 62 to taste the Shakespearean persona of Ashland, the 19C gold-rush flavor of **Jacksonville** and the labyrinths of **Oregon**

Caves National Monument. Slide into northwest California on US-199 to see forests of giant redwood trees in **Redwoods National and State Parks**.

Then proceed straight up the coast, a gorgeous three-day drive on US-101 via **Oregon Dunes National Recreation Area** and the noted Oregon Coast Aquarium in Newport. **Olympic National Park** dominates Washington's Olympic Peninsula and includes the lush **Hoh Rain Forest** and unforgettable views from **Hurricane Ridge.** Visit the Victorian seaport of Port Townsend before boarding a ferry back to Seattle.

WHEN TO GO

The diversity of **California**'s geographic regions promotes a dramatic variation in climatic conditions. Although coastal areas are subject to relatively little variation in seasonal temperatures, these tend to increase with distance from the coast, and drop quickly as elevation increases. Most rain falls between October and April. In the San Diego area, winter temperatures range from 60-70°F; summer temperatures average only 5-10°F more. The Los Angeles coastal area remains warm and pleasant year-round, while the inland areas are hot and hazy during the summer and fall. Average temperatures are 45-65°F in winter and 60-75°F in summer. San Francisco Bay Area weather can change suddenly in a single day, from warm and sunny to foggy and chilly. Thick fog is particularly characteristic of the summer months, and the same is true along much of the coast from Santa Barbara to Oregon. Inland Bay Area cities are warmer, with pleasant, sometimes hot, summer temperatures. Average temperatures are 40-55°F in winter and 55-70°F in the summer.

West of the Cascade Range, the **Pacific Northwest** experiences very wet winters with strong winds and extensive cloud cover that promotes mild temperatures—40-50∞F. Summers are usually sunny and rather comfortable with occasional heat waves reaching 90°F. The interior of the region is colder and drier in winter, hotter in summer.

Southwest winters produce mild days and cold nights with daytime temperatures typically in the 40s on the Colorado Plateau, 70s in the Sonoran Desert. Despite relatively mild conditions, heavy snows fall in the mountain areas. Mild winter days give way to long summer days of bright sunshine and hot temperatures that can exceed 100°F. In May, summers start out dry with little rain, but by mid-July the humidity increases and the area receives many thunderstorms as the summer progresses. Despite this rainfall, temperatures remain very hot. Winters in the **Rocky Mountain states** usually include large amounts of snow, and temperatures fluctuate between days of extreme cold to more mild days depending on air currents. In summer, with temperatures around 90°F, days are warm while the nights are cool, with temperatures between

40-50°F. Thunderstorms and hail are common in the summer months.
In the **Central and Southern Plains**, winters fluctuate between spells of warm, pleasant weather and bitterly cold snaps that bring snow and ice. Summers can be similarly unpredictable, often with severe thunderstorms and strong winds. Summer tempera-tures are typically hot, ranging from 90-100°F.

Winters in the **Northern Great Plains** are cold and dry, as polar air masses deliver extensive snow cover and sub-zero temperatures. Winter's extreme conditions are sometimes softened by chinook winds that bring warmer temperatures. Summer heat may invite

Temperature Chart

City	January			June		
	avg. high °F / °C	avg. low °F / °C	precip. in. / cm.	avg. high °F / °C	avg. low °F / °C	precip. in. / cm.
Albuquerque NM	47 / 8	22 / −6	0.4 / 1.1	90 / 32	58 / 14	0.6 / 1.5
Anchorage AK	21 / −6	8 / −13	0.8 / 2.0	62 / 17	47 / 8	1.1 / 2.9
Aspen CO	32 / 0	0 / −18	1.3 / 3.2	72 / 22	34 / 1	1.4 / 3.4
Billings MT	32 / 0	14 / −10	0.9 / 2.3	78 / 26	52 / 11	2.0 / 5.1
Boise ID	36 / 2	22 / −6	1.5 / 3.7	81 / 27	52 / 11	0.8 / 2.1
Dallas TX	54 / 12	33 / 1	1.8 / 4.6	92 / 33	70 / 21	3.0 / 7.6
Denver CO	43 / 6	16 / −9	0.5 / 1.3	81 / 27	52 / 11	1.8 / 4.5
El Paso TX	56 / 13	29 / −2	0.4 / 1.0	97 / 36	64 / 18	0.7 / 1.7
Grand Canyon AZ	42 / 5	18 / −8	1.4 / 3.7	78 / 27	45 / 7	0.5 / 1.3
Honolulu HI	80 / 27	66 / 19	3.6 / 9.0	87 / 31	72 / 22	0.5 / 1.3
Houston TX	61 / 16	40 / 4	3.3 / 8.4	90 / 32	71 / 22	5.0 / 12.6
Kansas City MO	35 / 2	17 / −8	1.1 / 2.8	83 / 28	63 / 17	4.7 / 12.0
Las Vegas NV	57 / 14	34 / 1	0.5 / 1.2	100 / 38	69 / 21	0.1 / 0.3
Los Angeles CA	66 / 19	48 / 9	2.4 / 6.1	72 / 22	60 / 16	0.0 / 0.1
Moab UT	42 / 6	18 / −8	0.6 / 1.4	93 / 34	50 / 14	0.4 / 1.1
Oklahoma City OK	47 / 8	25 / −4	1.1 / 2.9	87 / 31	66 / 19	4.3 / 10.9
Omaha NE	31 / −1	11 / −12	0.7 / 1.9	84 / 29	60 / 16	3.9 / 9.8
Phoenix AZ	66 / 19	41 / 5	0.7 / 1.7	104 / 40	73 / 23	0.1 / 0.3
Portland OR	45 / 7	34 / 1	5.4 / 13.6	74 / 23	53 / 12	1.5 / 3.8
Rapid City SD	34 / 1	11 / −12	0.4 / 1.0	78 / 26	52 / 11	3.1 / 7.8
Reno NV	45 / 7	21 / −6	1.1 / 2.7	83 / 28	47 / 8	0.5 / 1.2
Sacramento CA	53 / 12	38 / 3	3.7 / 9.5	88 / 31	55 / 13	0.1 / 0.3
Salt Lake City UT	36 / 2	19 / −7	1.1 / 2.8	83 / 28	55 / 13	0.9 / 2.4
San Antonio TX	61 / 16	38 / 3	1.7 / 4.3	92 / 33	73 / 23	3.8 / 9.7
San Diego CA	66 / 19	49 / 9	1.8 / 4.6	72 / 22	62 / 17	0.1 / 0.2
San Francisco CA	56 / 13	42 / 6	4.4 / 11.0	70 / 21	53 / 12	0.1 / 0.3
Santa Fe NM	47 / 8	14 / −10	1.1 / 2.8	82 / 28	47 / 9	4.4 / 11.1
Seattle WA	45 / 7	35 / 2	5.4 / 13.7	70 / 21	52 / 11	1.5 / 3.8
Tucson AZ	64 / 18	39 / 4	0.9 / 2.4	100 / 38	68 / 20	0.2 / 0.6
West Glacier MT	29 / −2	15 / −10	3.4 / 8.6	72 / 22	44 / 7	3.4 / 8.6

severe thunderstorms, hail and high winds.

Throughout the West, April and May, and September and October, are generally delightful months. The exception is the extreme southern part of the region, from Houston to Las Vegas, where unpleasant heat can occur in those months. Summer travelers to Texas, New Mexico and Arizona, and inland Californa, may experience the perverse discomfort of being too cold--indoors, where excessive air conditioning is common. Residents of these areas often bring sweaters to restaurants, museums and other public facilities.

Current weather conditions are online: www.weather.com or www.cnn. com/weather.

KNOW BEFORE YOU GO

Useful Websites

AIR TRAVEL

www.orbitz.com; www.travelocity. com; www.expedia.com. Most of the time, US airlines attempt to match the fares available on the search engine sites. Fare-tracking sites include www. kayak.com; www.farecast.com offers predictions on whether future fares will rise or fall.

CONSERVATION

The Sierra Club is the leading environmental advocacy organization and was founded in the West; www. sierraclub.org. The Nature Conservancy owns hundreds of private land preserves in the West; www.nature. org. Both organizations sponsor trips and tours.

DINING OUT

Lots of recommendations for the big cities can be found in the red-cover Michelin Guide San Francisco, the Michelin Guide Los Angeles and the Michelin Guide Las Vegas plus the Address Books of the Green Guide California as well as Must Sees Hawaii.

HISTORY

The best source for comprehensive, thoughtful information on Western history is www.academicinfo.net/ amwest.html.

SKI CONDITIONS

The two key sites to track ski conditions, updated each morning, are www.skireport.com and www. snocountry.com.

WESTERN POLITICS AND CULTURE

High Country News is a highly regarded, independent observer of the West: www.hcn.org. Another site, www.newwest.net, covers the North part of the Intermountain West, from Bend OR to Boulder CO.

WINE TRAVEL

A private site devoted to California is www.winecountry.com. Oregon's Willamette Valley is covered by www. oregonwinecountry.org. In Washington state, consult www.winecountry-washington.org.

SEARCHING SEARCHES

www.dogpile.com attempts to catalogue search engines of every description--travel, dining, accommodations, and so on.

Tourism Offices

In addition to state and regional tourism offices, visitors from outside the US may obtain information from the nearest US embassy or consulate in their country of residence (*see list below*). For a complete list of American consulates and embassies abroad, see the US State Department Bureau of Consular Affairs listing on the Internet at travel.state.gov.

US EMBASSIES AND CONSULATES

Australia
Moonah Place, Yarralumla, ACT 2600. ☎02 6214 5600. canberra. usembassy.gov.

Belgium
Regentlaan 27 Boulevard du Régent, B-1000 Brussels. ☎32-2 508-2111. belgium.usembassy.gov.

Canada
490 Sussex Drive, Ottawa, Ontario K1N 1G8. ☎613-688-5335. canada. usembassy.gov.

China
Xiu Shui Bei Jie 3, 100600. ☎86-10 6532-3831. china.usembassy.gov.

France:
2, avenue Gabriel, 75382 Paris Cedex 08. b33 1 43 12 22 22. france.usembassy.gov.

Germany:
Neustädtische Kirchstr. 4-5, 10117 Berlin, Federal Republic of Germany. ☎030 2385 174. germany. usembassy.gov.

Italy:
via Vittorio Veneto 121 - 00187 ROMA. ☎39 06.46741. rome. usembassy.gov.

Japan:
1-10-5 Akasaka, Minato-ku, Tokyo 107-8420 Japan. ☎03 3224-5000. tokyo.usembassy.gov.

Mexico:
Paseo de la Reforma 305, Col. Cuauhtemoc, 06500 Mexico, D.F. ☎01-55 5080-2000. mexico.usembassy.gov.

Netherlands:
Lange Voorhout 102, 2514 EJ The Hague. b31 70 310-2209. thehague.usembassy.gov.

Spain:
Serrano 75, 28006 Madrid. ☎91-587-2200. madrid.usembassy.gov.

Switzerland:
Jubilaumsstrasse 93, CH-3005 Bern, Switzerland. ☎031 357 70 11. bern.usembassy.gov.

United Kingdom:
24 Grosvenor Square, London, W1A 1AE, United Kingdom. ☎[44] (0)20 7499-9000. london. usembassy.gov.

STATE TOURISM OFFICES

State tourism offices (below) provide information and brochures on points of interest, seasonal events and accommodations, as well as road and city maps. Local tourist offices (*telephone numbers and Websites listed under each blue entry heading in the text*) provide additional information, free of charge, regarding accommodations, shopping, entertainment, festivals and recreation. Many countries have consular offices in major cities. Information centers are indicated on maps by the 🛈 symbol.

Alaska (AK)
Alaska Travel Industry Association 2600 Cordova St., Ste. 201 Anchorage, AK 99503. ☎907-274-7579. www.travelalaska.com.

Arizona (AZ)
Arizona Office of Tourism 1110 W. Washington St., Suite 155, Phoenix, AZ 85007. ☎602-364-3700 www.arizonaguide.com.

California (CA)
California Divison of Tourism P.O. Box 1499, Sacramento, CA 95812-1499. ☎916-444-4429. www.visitcalifornia.com.

Colorado (CO)
Colorado Travel and Tourism Authority
Denver, CO 80202. ☎303-892-3885. www.colorado.com.

Hawaii (HI)
Hawaii Visitors & Convention Bureau
2270 Kalakaua Ave., Suite 801, Honolulu, HI 96815. ☎800-464-2924. www.gohawaii.com.

Idaho (ID)
Idaho Travel Council, 700 West State St., P.O. Box 83720, Boise, ID 83720-0093. ☎208-334-2470. www.visitidaho.org.

Kansas (KS)
Kansas Travel and Tourism Development Division
1000 S.W. Jackson St., Suite 100, Topeka, KS 66612. ☎785-296-2009. www.travelks.com

Montana (MT)
Travel Montana
1424 9th Ave, Helena, MT 59601. ☎800-847-4868. www.visitmt.com

Nebraska (NE)
Nebraska Tourism Office
301 Centennial Mall South, P.O. Box 94666, Lincoln, NE 68509-4666. ☎800-426-6505. www.visitnebraska.org.

Nevada (NV)
Nevada Commission of Tourism
401 North Carson Street, Carson City, NV 89701. ☎800-638-2328. www.travelnevada.com.

New Mexico (NM)
New Mexico Department of Tourism
491 Old Santa Fe Trail, Santa Fe, NM 87501. ☎800-733-6396. www.newmexico.org.

North Dakota (ND)
North Dakota Tourism Division
Century Center, 1600 E. Century Ave. Suite 2 PO Box 2057, Bismarck, ND 58502-2057. ☎701-328-2525. www.ndtourism.com

Oklahoma (OK)
Oklahoma Tourism and Recreation Department
120 N. Robinson Avenue, 6th Floor, PO Box 52002, Oklahoma City, OK 73152-2002. ☎405-230-8400. www.travelok.com.

Oregon (OR)
Oregon Economic Development Department
Tourism Division
775 Summer St. NE, Suite 200, Salem OR 97301-1280. ☎800-547-7842. www.traveloregon.com.

South Dakota (SD)
South Dakota Department of Tourism
Capitol Lake Plaza, 711 East Wells Ave., c/o 500 East Capitol Ave., Pierre, SD 57501-5070. ☎605-773-3301. www.travelsd.com.

Texas (TX)
Texas Department of Economic Development
Tourism Division
PO Box 141009, Austin, TX 78714-1009. ☎512-936-0101. www.traveltex.com.

Utah (UT)
Utah Travel Council
Council Hall/Capitol Hill, Salt Lake City, UT 84114-1396. ☎801-538-1030. www.utah.com

Washington (WA)
Washington State Tourism
128-10th Avenue SW, PO Box 42525, Olympia, WA 98504-2525. ☎360-725-4000. www.experiencewashington.com

Wyoming (WY)
Wyoming Division of Tourism
I-25 at College Dr., Cheyenne, WY 82002. ☎307-777-7777. www.wyomingtourism.org

International Visitors

DOCUMENTS

All foreign visitors to the US must present a valid machine-readable passport for entry into the country. Citizens of countries participating in the Visa Waiver Pilot Program (VWPP) are not required to obtain a visa to enter the US for visits of fewer than 90 days. They will, however, be required to furnish a current passport, round-trip ticket and the customs form distributed in the airplane. Citizens of countries not participating in the VWPP must have a visitor's visa. For visa inquiries and applications, contact the nearest US embassy or consulate, or visit the US State Department Visa Services Internet site: travel.state. gov/visa.

CUSTOMS

All articles brought into the US must be declared at time of entry. The following items are exempt from customs regulations: personal effects; one liter of alcoholic beverages (providing visitor is at least 21 years old); either 200 cigarettes, 50 cigars (additional 100 possible under gift exemption) or 2 kilograms of smoking tobacco; and gifts (to persons in the US) not exceeding $100 in value. Prohibited items include firearms and ammunition (if not intended for legitimate sporting purposes); plant materials, and meat or poultry products. For other prohibited items, exemptions and information, contact any of the following before departure: a US embassy or consulate, Customs Headquarters (US Customs Service, 1300 Pennsylvania Ave. NW, Washington DC 20229; ☎202-927-1000) or the **US Customs Traveler Information** page on the Internet (www.customs. gov/travel) Note that most major cities have a local customs port; contact information is available from Customs Headquarters or from the Internet site.

HEALTH

The United States does not have a national health program; doctors' visits and hospitalization costs may seem high to most visitors. Check with your insurance company to determine if your medical insurance covers doctors' visits, medication and hospitalization in the US. If not, it is strongly recommended that you purchase a travel-insurance plan before departing. Prescription drugs should be properly identified and accompanied by a copy of the prescription.

Accessibility

Full wheelchair access to sights described in this guide is indicated in admission information by ♿. Federal law requires that existing businesses (including hotels and restaurants) increase accessibility and provide specially designed accommodations for the disabled. It also requires that wheelchair access, devices for the hearing impaired, and designated parking spaces be available at newly constructed hotels and restaurants. Many public buses are equipped with wheelchair lifts; many hotels have rooms designed for visitors with special needs. All national and most state **parks** have restrooms and other facilities for the disabled (such as wheelchair-accessible nature trails). Permanently disabled US citizens are eligible for a free **US national recreational lands pass** (see page 39) which entitles the carrier to free admission to all national parks and a 50 percent discount on user fees (campsites, boat launches). The pass is available at any national-park entrance fee area with proper proof of disability. For details, contact the National Park Service, Office of Public Inquiries, (*1849 C St. NW, Washington DC 20240; ☎202-208-4747, www.nps.gov*). Many attractions can also make special arrangements for disabled visitors. For information about travel for individuals or groups, contact the **Society for the Advancement of Travel for the**

Handicapped,(*347 5th Ave., Suite 610, New York, NY 10016;* ☎*212-447-7284; www.sath.org*).

Travel by Train

Train passengers who will need assistance should give 24hrs advance notice. Making reservations via phone is preferable to booking on-line since passenger's special needs can be noted on reservation by booking agent. The annual publication *Access Amtrak* providing detailed information on Amtrak's services for disabled travelers is available upon request (☎*800-872-7245 and 800-523-6590 TDD*) or may be viewed on Amtrak's Website: www.amtrak.com.

Travel by Bus

Disabled travelers are encouraged to notify Greyhound 48hrs in advance.

The annual publication *Greyhound Travel Policies* is available by request: ☎800-231-2222 or 800-345-3109 (TDD).

Rental Cars

Reservations for hand-controlled cars should be made well in advance.

SENIOR CITIZENS

Many hotels, attractions and restaurants offer discounts to visitors age 62 or older (proof of age may be required). Discounts and additional information are available to members of AARP, (*601 E St. N.W. Washington, DC 20094;* ☎*202-434-2277, www.aarp.org*), which is open to people over 50.

GETTING THERE AND GETTING AROUND

By Plane

Major US airlines serve most of the West's metropolitan areas. Airports with regular nonstop service to and from European cities include Denver, Dallas-Fort Worth, Houston, Las Vegas, Los Angeles, Phoenix, Portland, San Francisco, and Seattle.

MAJOR AIRPORTS

Albuquerque NM:
Albuquerque International Sunport (ABQ). ☎505-244-7700. www.cabq.gov/airport.

Anchorage AK:
Ted Stevens Anchorage International Airport (ANC). ☎907-266-2525. www.dot.state.ak.us.

Billings MT:
Billings Logan International Airport

(BIL). ☎406-247-8609. www.flybillings.com.

Boise ID:
Boise Airport (BOI). ☎208-343-8761. www.cityofboise.org/departments/airport.

Dallas/Ft. Worth TX:
Dallas/Ft. Worth International Airport (DFW). ☎972-574-8024. www.dfwairport.com.

Denver CO:
Denver International Airport (DEN). ☎303-342-2000. www.flydenver.com.

El Paso TX:
El Paso International Airport (ELP). ☎915-780-4700. www.elpasointernational airport.com.

Honolulu HI:
Honolulu International Airport

(HNL). ☎808-836-6413.
www.state.hi.us/dot/airports/
index.htm.

Houston TX:
Houston Intercontinental Airport
(IAH). ☎281-233-3000.
www.fly2houston.com.

Kansas City MO:
Kansas City International Airport
(MCI). ☎816-243-3000.
www.kansas-city-mci.com.

Las Vegas NV:
Las Vegas McCarran International
Airport (LAS). ☎702-261-5555.
www.mccarran.com.

Los Angeles CA:
Los Angeles International Airport
(LAX). ☎310-417-0439.
www.lawa.org.

Oklahoma City OK:
Oklahoma City Will Rogers World
Airport (OKC). ☎405-680-3200.
www.flyokc.com.

Orange County CA:
John Wayne Airport (SNA). ☎949-
252-5200. www.ocair.com.

Phoenix AZ:
Phoenix Sky Harbor International
Airport (PHX). ☎602-273-3300.
www.phoenix.gov/skyharbor
airport.

Portland OR:
Portland International Airport
(PDX). ☎503-944-7000.
www.flypdx.com.

Reno NV:
Reno/Tahoe International Airport
(RNO). ☎775-328-6789.
www.renoairport.com.

Sacramento CA:
Sacramento International Airport
(SMF). ☎916-874-0719.
www.sacairports.org.

Salt Lake City UT:
Salt Lake City International Airport

(SLC). ☎801-575-2400.
www.slcairport.com.

San Antonio TX:
San Antonio International Airport
(SAT). ☎210-207-3450.
www.sanantonio.gov/aviation.

San Diego CA:
San Diego International Airport
(SAN). ☎619-400-2400.
www.san.org.

San Francisco CA:
San Francisco International Airport
(SFO). ☎650-821-8211.
www.flysfo.com.

San Jose CA:
San Jose International Airport
(SJC). ☎408-501-7600.
www.sjc.org.

Seattle WA:
Seattle-Tacoma International
Airport (SEA). ☎206-433-5388.
www.portseattle.org.

Tucson AZ:
Tucson International Airport (TUS).
☎520-573-8000.
www.tucsonairport.org.

By Train

The Amtrak rail network offers a
relaxing alternative for travelers with
time to spare. Advance reservations
ensure reduced fares and availability
of desired accommodations. On some
trains, reservations are required;
smoking is not allowed on any Amtrak
trains. Passengers may choose from
first-class, coach, or cars with panoramic windows.
The **Explore America Rail Pass**
allows up to 45 days travel nationwide
(limited to three stops). The **North
America Rail Pass** links Amtrak train
routes with Canada's VIARail system
for 30 days with unlimited stops. The
USA RailPass (not available to US or
Canadian citizens) offers unlimited
travel within designated regions at
discounted rates; 15- and 30-day

passes are available. For schedule, prices and route information: ☎800-872-7245 or www.amtrak.com (*outside North America, contact a travel agent*). In the West, service is provided along the following routes:

California Corridor
Route: San Jose–Reno
Along the way: San Francisco, Sacramento

California Zephyr
Route: Chicago–San Francisco
Along the way: Denver, Salt Lake City, Sacramento

Cascades
Route: Vancouver–Eugene
Along the way: Seattle, Portland

Coast Starlight
Route: Seattle–Los Angeles
Along the way: Portland, San Francisco, Santa Barbara

Empire Builder
Route: Chicago–Seattle
Along the way: Minneapolis, Glacier Park

Southwest Chief
Route: Chicago–Los Angeles
Along the way: Kansas City, Santa Fe, Phoenix

The Alaska Railroad links Seward, Anchorage, Denali National Park and Fairbanks (mid-May–mid-Sept daily; in winter, weekends only); for schedule and reservations: Alaska Railroad Corp., P.O. Box 107500, Anchorage AK 99510, ☎907-265-2494 or 800-544-0552; www.akrr.com.

Travelers may relive the romantic era of travel aboard one of **Grand Luxe Rail Journeys** eight itineraries in the West, which cover national parks, southwest canyons, the ROckies and Sierra, and the Northwest. Each offers deluxe rail travel in large cabins with numerous sightseeing stops, and a dining car where meals prepared by expert chefs are served. For schedules and fares contact Grand Luxe at ☎303-962-5400 or 800-320-4206, www.americanorientexpress.com.

By Bus/Coach

Greyhound, the largest bus company in the US, offers access to most cities and communities. Overall, fares are lower than other forms of transportation. Some travelers may find long-distance bus travel uncomfortable owing to a lack of sleeping accommodations, and specific seat reservations are not allowed. Advance reservations are suggested. Greyhound offers various passes ranging from 7 days at $285 to 60 days at $650; discounted go-any-

Getting around in San Francisco

Brigitta L.House/MICHELIN

where fares (advance purchase) and other specials and promotions; visit Greyhound's Website (www.greyhound.com). Schedules, prices and route information: ☎800-231-2222 (*US only*) or Greyhound Lines, Inc., P.O. Box 660362, Dallas TX 75266-0362.

By Car

Limited-access **interstate highways** crisscross the US. North-south highways have odd numbers (I-15, I-25); east-west interstates have even numbers (I-40, I-80). Numbers increase from west to east (I-5 along the West Coast and I-95 on the East Coast) and from south to north (I-8 runs east from San Diego CA; I-94 connects Billings MT with Milwaukee WI). Interstate **beltways** encircle cities and have three digits: the first is an even number and the last two name the interstate off which they branch (I-410 around San Antonio TX branches off I-10). There can be duplication across states (there are I-405 beltways around Seattle WA, Portland OR and Los Angeles CA) and exceptions to this general rule. Interstate **spurs** entering cities also have three digits: the first is an odd number and the last two represent the originating interstate. .

A system of non-interstate highways and roads, predating the interstate system, includes US, state, county and Indian reservation routes. **US routes** and **state routes** range from major highways to winding two-lane roads. North-south roads have odd numbers (of one, two or three digits), east-west roads even numbers. County roads and **Indian reservation routes** typically are smaller local or connector roads. The US Forest Service and the Bureau of Land Management (BLM) manage a system of backcountry roads (generally unpaved) with their own route numbering.

RENTAL CARS

National rental companies have offices at major airports and downtown locations. Aside from the agencies listed on p 26, there also are local companies that offer reasonable rental rates. *See Yellow Pages for phone numbers.* Renters must possess a major credit card (such as Visa/Carte Bleue, American Express or MasterCard/Eurocard), a valid driver's license (international license not required). Minimum age for rental is 25 at most major companies. A variety of service packages offer unlimited mileage and discounted prices, often in conjunction with major airlines or hotel chains. Since prices vary from one company to another, be sure to research different companies before you reserve. (To reserve a car from Europe, it is best to contact one of the major US companies such as Hertz, Avis and so on, directly, or a travel agent.)

All rentals are subject to local taxes and fees which should be included in quoted prices. Liability insurance is not automatically included in the terms of the lease. Be sure to check for proper insurance coverage, offered at an extra charge. Most large rental companies provide assistance in case of breakdown.

Cars may be rented per day, week or month, and mileage is usually unlimited. Only the person who signed the contract is authorized to drive the rental car, but for an additional fee, and upon presentation of the required papers, additional drivers may be approved. If a vehicle is returned at a different location from where it was rented, drop-off charges may be incurred. The gasoline tank of the car should be filled before it is returned; rental companies charge a much higher price per gallon than roadside gas stations. Some companies offer a fuel-fill option in which you can "buy" a tank of gas at rental, often at advantageous prices, and return the car with any level of gas in the tank.

Rental car **information and reservations** across the US may be accessed on the Internet (www.bnm.com), or by calling one of the companies listed below.

Alamo:
☎800-462-5266.
www.alamo.com.

Avis:
☎800-331-1212. www.avis.com.

Budget:
☎800-527-0700.
www.budget.com.

Dollar:
☎800-800-3665. www.dollar.com.

Hertz:
☎800-654-3131. www.hertz.com.

National:
☎800-227-7368.
www.nationalcar.com.

Thrifty:
☎800-331-4200.
www.thrifty.com.

Enterprise:
☎800-261-7331.
www.enterprise.com.

Recreational Vehicle (RV) Rentals

One-way rentals range from a basic camper to full-size motor-homes that can accommodate up to seven people and offer a bathroom, shower and kitchen with microwave oven. Reservations should be made several months in advance. There may be a minimum number of rental days required. A drop fee is charged for one-way rentals. Cruise America RV ⓝ ☎800-671-8042, www.cruiseamerica.com) offers rentals with 24hr customer assistance. The **Recreational Vehicle Rental Association** (RVRA) lists a directory of RV rental locations in the US on their Website (☎703-591-7130; www.rvra.org). **RV America** (www.rvamerica.com) offers an on-line database of RV rental companies as well as information on campgrounds and RV associations.

ROAD REGULATIONS AND INSURANCE

The speed limit on most interstate highways in the western US ranges from 55mph (88km/h) to 75mph (120km/h), depending on the state and location. (Limits drop within urban areas.) On state highways outside populated areas the speed limit ranges from 55mph (88km/h) to 70mph (112kmh). Within cities, speed limits are generally 35mph (56km/h), and average 25-30mph (40-48km/h) in residential areas. Headlights must be turned on when driving in fog and rain. Unless traveling on a divided road, the law requires that motorists in both directions bring their vehicle to a full stop when the warning signals on a school bus are activated. Parking spaces identified with ♿ are reserved for persons with disabilities only. Anyone parking in these spaces without proper identification will be ticketed and/or their vehicle will be towed. The use of **seat belts** is mandatory for all persons in the car. Child safety seats are required in most states and are available at most rental-car agencies; indicate need when making reservations. In some states, motorcyclists and their passengers are required to wear helmets. Hitchhiking along interstate highways, except at entrance ramps, is forbidden by law. Auto liability insurance is mandatory in all states.

It is illegal to drink and drive and penalties are severe everywhere, including immediate surrender of car and driving license in some places. The maximum blood alcohol content is .08 percent. In California it is illegal to smoke in the car when minors are present.

IN CASE OF AN ACCIDENT

If you are involved in an auto accident resulting in personal or property damage, you must notify the local police and remain at the scene until dismissed. If blocking traffic, vehicles should be moved as soon as possible. Automobile associations such as the **American Automobile Association (AAA), Mobil Auto Club** *(☎800-621-5581)* and **Shell Motorist Club** *(☎800-355-7263)* provide their members with emergency road service. Members of AAA-affiliated automobile clubs overseas benefit from reciprocal services:

Australia

Australian Automobile Association (AAA) ☎02 6247 7311

Belgium

Royal Automobile Club de Belgique (RACB)
☎02 287 09 11
Touring Club de Belgique (TCB)
☎02 233 22 02

Canada

Canadian Automobile Association (CAA)
☎613 247 0117

France

Automobile-Club de France (ACF)
☎01 43 12 43 12
Fédération Française du Sport Automobile (FSA)
☎01 56 89 20 70

Germany

Allgemeiner Deutscher Automobil-Club E.V. (ADAC)
☎89 7676 0
Automobilclub von Deutschland E.V. (AvD)
☎69 6606 610

United Kingdom

The Automobile Association (AA)
☎800 444 999
The Camping & Caravanning Club (CCC)
☎203 694 995
The Caravan Club (CC)
☎01 342 326 944
The Royal Scottish Automobile Club (RSAC)
☎141 946 5045

Ireland

The Automobile Association Ireland Ltd. (AA Ireland)
☎01 617 9999

Italy

Automobile Club d'Italia (ACI)
☎06 49 98 1
Federazione Italiana del Campeggio e del Caravanning (Federcampeggio). ☎55 88 23 91
Touring Club Italiano (TCI)
☎02 85 26 1

Netherlands

Koninklijke Nederlandsche Automobiel Club (KNAC)
☎70 383 1612
Koninklijke Nederlandse Toeristenbond (ANWB)
☎088 269 22 22

Spain

Real Automóvil Club de España (RACE)☎91 594 74 00

Switzerland

Automobile Club de Suisse (ACS)
☎031 328 31 11
Touring Club Suisse (TCS)
☎022 417 27 27

WHERE TO STAY AND EAT

Where to Stay

For a listing of lodging recommendations for areas described in this guide, consult the **Address Book** sections in each chapter.

Luxury **hotels** are generally found in major cities and resort communities, **motels** in clusters on the edges of towns and along the interstate highways. **Bed-and-breakfast inns** usually are found in residential areas of cities and towns, and in more secluded natural areas. Many properties offer special packages and weekend rates that may not be extended during peak summer months (*late May–late Aug.*) and holiday seasons, especially near ski resorts. Advance reservations are recommended during these times. Rates tend to be higher in cities and near coastal and resort areas.

Many resort properties include outdoor recreational facilities such as ski areas, golf courses, tennis courts, swimming pools and fitness centers, as well as gourmet dining and entertainment. Activities such as hiking, mountain biking and horseback riding may be arranged by contacting hotel staff.

In most of the West, high season is June through August. In some very popular areas during this time, such as Yellowstone, Seattle and San Francisco, it is wise to make reservations months in advance. By contrast, high season in the desert resorts of Arizona and inland California is November through February.

Many cities and communities levy a hotel occupancy tax that is added to hotel rates. Contact local tourist offices to request free brochures that give details about area accommodations. (*Telephone numbers and Websites are listed under entry headings in each chapter.*)

HOTELS & MOTELS

Rates for hotels and motels vary greatly according to season and location, tending to be higher during holiday and peak seasons. For deluxe hotels, plan to pay at least $250 and up/night per room, double occupancy. Moderate hotels will charge $100–$250/night and budget motels range from $30–$100/night. In most hotels, children under 18 stay free when sharing a room with their parents. In-room efficiency kitchens are available at some hotels and motels. When reserving, ask about packages including meals, passes to local attractions and

Beverly Hills Hotel, Los Angeles, California

Allison Simpson/MICHELIN

weekend specials. Typical amenities at hotels and motels include television, alarm clock, Internet access, smoking/non-smoking rooms, restaurants and swimming pools. Always advise the reservations clerk of late arrival; unless confirmed with a credit card, rooms may not be held after 6pm. Contact state or local (*numbers under each blue entry in this guide*) tourism agencies for free information on accommodations.

Hotel & Motel Reservation Services

Hotel reservation services are abundant, especially on the Internet. Following is a brief selection.

Accommodations Express:
☎609-391-2100.
www.accommodationsexpress.com.

Central Reservation Service:
☎800-555-7555.
www.reservation-services.com.

Hotel Reservations Network:
☎214-369-1264.
www.hoteldiscount.com.
Hotels.com: www.hotels.com.

Quikbook:
☎800-789-9887. www.quikbook.com.

Major US Hotel/Motel chains
Best Western:
☎800-780-7234. www.bestwestern.com.
Choice Hotels International (Comfort Inn, Econo Lodge, Quality Inn):
☎877-424-6423, www.choicehotels.com.
Courtyard:
☎888-236-2427,
www.marriott.com/courtyard.
Days Inn:
☎800-329-7466, www.daysinn.com.
Embassy Suites:
☎800-560-7782,
embassysuites1.hilton.com.
Fairfield Inn:
☎800-228-2800,
www.marriott.com/fairfield-inn.
Four Seasons:
☎800-819-5053, www.fourseasons.com.

Hampton Inn:
☎800-560-7809,
hamptoninn1.hilton.com.
Hilton:
☎800-774-1500, www.hilton.com.
Holiday Inn:
☎800-315-2621,
www.holidayinn.com.
Howard Johnson:
☎800-446-4656,
www.howardjohnson.com.
Hyatt:
☎800-233-1234, www.hyatt.com.
La Quinta:
☎800-642-4271, www.laquinta.com
Marriott:
☎800-228-9290, www.marriott.com.
Motel 6:
☎800-466-8356, www.motel6.com.
Omni:
☎888-444-6664,
www.omnihotels.com.
Radisson:
☎888-201-1718, www.radisson.com.
Ramada:
☎800-272-6232, www.ramada.com.
Red Roof:
☎800-733-7663, www.redroof.com.
Residence Inn:
☎800-331-3131, www.marriott.com/residence-inn.
Ritz-Carlton:
☎800-241-3333, www.ritzcarlton.com.
Sheraton:
☎800-325-3535, www.starwood.com.
Super 8:
☎800-800-8000, www.super8.com.
Travelodge:
☎800-578-7878,
www.travelodge.com.
Westin:
☎800-598-1864, www.starwoodhotels.com/westin.

BED & BREAKFASTS AND COUNTRY INNS

Most B&Bs are privately owned historic residences. Bed-and-breakfast inns are typically cozy homes with fewer than 10 guest rooms; breakfast is usually the only meal provided. Country inns are larger establishments, often offering over 25 guest rooms; full-service dining is typically available. Both establishments include a breakfast ranging from continental fare to a gourmet repast; some offer afternoon tea and the use of sitting rooms with cozy fireplaces, or garden spots providing breathtaking panoramas of ocean shores or mountain vistas. Some lower-priced rooms may not have private baths. Especially during holiday and peak tourist seasons, reservations should be made well in advance. Minimum stay, cancellation and refund policies may be more stringent during these times. Most inns will accept major credit cards. Rates vary seasonally but range from $105 to $200 for a double room per night. Rates will be higher for rooms with such amenities as hot tubs, private entrances and scenic views.

Bed & Breakfast and Country Inn reservation services

Numerous organizations offer reservation services for B&Bs and country inns. Many services tend to be regional; following are some nationwide services. For a complete listing, consult the websites for CVBs in your destinations. Also, the **Select Registry** (☎269.789.0393 or 800.344.5244; *www.innbook.com*) publishes an annual register listing B&Bs and country inns by state.
Independent Innkeepers' Association:
☎269-789-0393. www.innbook.com.
The National Network of Bed & Breakfast Reservation Services (TNN):
www.go-lodging.com.
Professional Association of Innkeepers International:
☎800-468-7244. www.paii.org.
Wakeman & Costine's North American Bed & Breakfast Directory:
☎828-387-3697.
www.bbdirectory.com.

GUEST RANCHES

In the late 19C, working farms and livestock ranches welcomed big-city friends eager to help with chores, or paying guests to help them through tough economic times. The romanticization of the American West to an eastern audience lent a mystique to the cowboy and the open range that persists to this day. The "dude ranch," as it became known, provides a unique window on the Western lifestyle. Today's dude ranches, now usually called "guest ranches," vary in style from rustic to posh. Catering to as few as 12 or as many as 125 guests, they may be working ranches that involve guests in cattle drives and branding; outfitting ranches that emphasize horseback riding; or resort ranches, where relaxation is the order of the day. Many guests return to the saddle year after year for spectacular scenery, riding and family-style meals. Websites have made these Western vacations accessible to a global market intrigued by the cowboy lifestyle. Organizations that provide information on guest ranches include The Dude Rancher's Association (☎307-587-2339 or 866-399-2339, www.duderanch.org), and Guest Ranches of North America (*www.guestranches.com*).

SPAS

Modern spas offer a variety of programs—fitness, beauty and wellness; relaxation and stress relief; weight management, and adventure vacations. Guests are pampered with mud baths, daily massages, state-of-the-art fitness and exercise programs, cooking classes and nutritional counseling. Spas offer luxurious facilities in beautiful settings that may include championship golf courses, equestrian centers and even formal gardens. Most offer packages for stays ranging from 2 to 10 nights, which include health and fitness programs, golf and tennis, and image enhancement. Most facilities have age restrictions. Most spas are informal, but check when making reservations.
Prices range from $800/week to $3,500/week (price per person, double occupancy) depending on choice of program and season. All meals, including special diets, use of facilities, tax, gratuities and airport transportation, are usually included. **Spa Finders**

(☎212-924-6800; www.spafinders.com).

CONDOMINIUMS

Furnished apartments or houses are more cost-effective than hotels for families with children. Hawaii, in particular, has thousands of condos and rental homes available for visitors. Amenities include separate living quarters, fully equipped kitchen with dining area, several bedrooms and bathrooms, and laundry facilities. Most condos provide televisions, basic linens and maid service. Depending on location, properties may include sports and recreational facilities, patios and beach access. Most require a minimum stay of three nights or one week, especially during peak season. When making reservations, ask about cancellation penalties and refund policies. Chambers of commerce and convention-and-visitors bureaus have listings of local property management agencies that can assist with selection. A variety of private accommodations can be arranged through **Condo Vacation Concepts** (☎888-266-3653; *www.condoconcepts.com*).

HOSTELS

A simple, no-frills alternative to hotels and inns, hostels are inexpensive dormitory-style accommodations with separate quarters for males and females. Many have private family/couples rooms, which may be reserved in advance. Amenities include fully equipped self-service kitchens, dining areas and common rooms. Hostelling International members receive discounts on room rates and other travel-related expenses (Alamo car rentals, and local attractions). Hostels often organize special programs and activities for guests. When booking, ask for available discounts at area attractions, rental car companies and restaurants. Rates average $14 to $45 per night. For information and a free directory, contact **Hostelling International American Youth Hostels** (*733 15th St., NW, Suite 840, Washington*

Spa Accessories

DC 20005, ☎301-495-1240, www.hiayh. org). For more general information on hostels: www.hostels.com.

CAMPING & RECREATIONAL VEHICLE (RV) PARKS

National and state park listings p 39.
Campsites are located in national parks, state parks, national forests, along beaches and in private campgrounds. The season for camping in the high country usually runs from Memorial Day to Labor Day; in lower elevations, campgrounds are open year-round. Some offer full utility hookups, lodges or cabins, backcountry sites and recreational facilities. Advance reservations are recommended, especially during summer and holidays.

National park and state park campgrounds are relatively inexpensive, but fill quickly, especially during school holidays. Facilities range from simple tent sites to full RV hookups *(reserve 60 days in advance)* or rustic cabins *(reserve one year in advance)*. Fees vary according to season and available facilities (picnic tables, water/electric hookups, used-water disposal, recreational equipment, showers, restrooms): camping & RV sites $6–$21/day; cabins $20–$110/day. For all US national parks, national forests, BLM campgrounds and so on, contact the park you are visiting or the federal reservation site, recreation.gov (*☎518-885-3639 or 877-444-6777; recreation.gov*). For state parks, contact the state tourism office (*p 19*) for information.

Private campgrounds offering facilities from simple tent sites to full RV-hookups are plentiful. They are slightly more expensive (*$10–$16/day for tent sites, $20–$45/day for RVs*) but may offer more sophisticated amenities: hot showers, laundry facilities, convenience stores, children's playgrounds, pools, air-conditioned cabins and outdoor recreational facilities. Most accept daily, weekly or monthly occupancy. In winter (*Nov–Apr*), some campgrounds may be closed. Reservations are recommended, especially for longer stays and in popular resort areas. **Kampgrounds of America (KOA)** operates campsites for tents, cabins/cottages and RV-hookups throughout the United States. For a directory (*$10 by mail or view on line free at www.koakampgrounds.com*), contact KOA Kampgrounds, P.O. Box 30558, Billings MT 59114 (*☎406-248-7444*). Directories of campgrounds throughout the US are easily found on the Internet. Following is a sample of some Internet **campground directories** covering the US:

Camping USA
www.camping-usa.com

CIS' RV-America Travel & Service Center www.rv-america.com

Go Camping America Directory
www.gocampingamerica.com

RVing Campground Directory
www.rving.com

USA Campgrounds & RV Parks
usacampgrounds.net

Where to Eat

The culinary revolution begun by Alice Waters at Chez Panisse in Berkeley three decades ago has now spread to virtually all corners of the West. Even in smaller, more remote areas, restaurant cooks now incorporate local fresh ingredients in their cooking--sometimes to unique effect. Desert Southwest chefs, for instance, have taken up traditional Native American foods such as prickly pear and mesquite bean. Buffalo is widespread inland; travelers might even find buffalo hash in small roadside diners far from any cosmopolitan area. Game is common in the Rocky Mountains.

Brigitta L.House/MICHELIN

Fog City Diner, San Francisco

The most sophisticated dining experiences are still found in large cities and along the coast—especially Los Angeles, northern California, Portland and Seattle. Elsewhere in the vast rural expanses of the Western hinterland (and in big cities as well) daily cuisine still includes the ubiquitous hamburger, french fries and milkshake, as well as steaks, spaghetti, pizza, tacos, fried chicken, apple pie with ice cream. Modified ethnic cuisines such as Mexican, Italian, Southeast Asian and Chinese are readily available in nearly every large or medium-size town of the West. Fast-food teriyaki is as popular as hamburgers and french fries in Seattle; sushi holds the same regard in Los Angeles.

Regional differences persist. Seafood is the signature element along the coast--salmon, crab, oysters, clams and more exotic ingredients such as octopus, sea cucumber and seaweed. Diners seeking quality seafood should inquire about the freshness and origin of their meals; frozen fish is not as good (no matter what some may tell visitors), and some entrées that visitors often think are local are in fact not. With the exception of a very small fishery along the California central coast, for instance, lobster is flown thousands of miles to the West from New England or eastern Canada. Mexican influences pervade cuisine in Texas, New Mexico, Arizona and Southern California, with local distinctions in each of those places. Asian elements are strong along the coast:-

Thai-style curries find their way onto the most sophisticated menus.

Here is a brief synopsis of the signature dishes in a few areas:

Texas: barbecued beef shoulder, roasted plain (no sauce) over hot pecan or hickory smoke for 8-10 hours, served on butcher paper.

Oklahoma and Kansas: barbecued pork ribs with tomato-based sauce, smoked 4-6 hours.

Arizona: fajitas, sliced grilled skirt steak served with tortillas.

New Mexico: green chile, pork stew made with poblano or Anaheim chile peppers.

Southern California: sushi, particularly the California roll, which is crab, avocado and cucumber wrapped in rice and seaweed.

Northern California: Dungeness crab, fresh, grilled or steamed, served whole. Also common in Oregon and Washington.

Oregon and Washington state: grilled fresh king. silver or sockeye salmon, cooked just barely firm.

Summer and autumn travelers in the West would do well to watch for fruit and vegetable stands offering fresh local produce--oranges, grapefruits, strawberries in California; peaches, pears, apricots, apples and berries from Sacramento north through Washington state, and in Western Colorado and Idaho's Snake River Valley.

WHAT TO SEE AND DO

Outdoor Fun

ADVENTURE TRAVEL AND MULTI-SPORT EXCURSIONS

The varying geography of the western US provides unlimited opportunities for outdoor adventure—from snorkeling off the California and Hawaii coasts to cross-country skiing in search of bison herds in Yellowstone National Park. Contact state tourism offices (*p 19*) for information on activities in specific geographic areas, or consider an organized tour.

Gorp is an online site affiliated with *Outside* magazine that promotes and catalogues responsible adventure travel; gorp.away.com. REI also offers an extensive catalog of trips and adventures: www.rei.com.

Comstock, INC

Snowboarding

Following is a sampling of tour providers and programs available:

For exciting **all–inclusive vacations** involving activities such as bicycling, hiking and kayaking, contact **Backroads** (*801 Cedar St., Berkeley CA 94710-1800;* ☏*510-527-1555 or 800-462-2848, www.backroads.com*). Programs include destinations in Alaska, Arizona, California, Colorado, Hawaii, Idaho, Montana, New Mexico, Utah, Washington and Wyoming.

For adventures on **horseback** throughout the USA West, including riding tours, cattle drives and visits to working ranches, contact **Hidden Trails** (*202-380 West 1st Ave., Vancouver BC V5Y 3T7, Canada;* ☏*604-323-1141, www.bcranches.com*).

Multi-sport vacations are available from **The World Outdoors** (*2840 Wilderness Place, Suite F, Boulder CO 80301;* ☏*303-413-0938 or 800-488-8483, www.theworldoutdoors.com*). Destinations include Alaska, Arizona, California, Colorado, Hawaii, Montana, New Mexico, Utah, Washington and Wyoming.

Covering the western US from Alaska to Arizona, **Austin-Lehman Adventures** (*P.O. Box 81025, Billings*

MT 59108-1025; ☏*406-586-3556 or 800-575-1540, www.austinlehman.com*) provides multi-sport vacations for active travelers.

Cycling enthusiasts can see the US on tours listed on **America by Bicycle** (*P.O. Box 805, Atkinson NH 03811;* ☏*603-382-1662 or 888-797-7057, www.abbike.com*). Tours range from 5-11 day mini-tours to 52-day coast-to-coast programs.

Wilderness Inquiry, Inc. (*808 14th Ave. NE, Minneapolis MN 55414,* ☏*612–676–9400 or 800–728–0719, www.wildernessinquiry.org*) catalogs tours that include activities such as kayaking in Alaska's fjords, rafting in the Grand Canyon and horsepacking through the Rockies.

All but the most experienced **whitewater rafters and kayakers** book expert guides to lead them through rivers' perils. The following veteran outfitters know rivers not only in their home state but throughout the West: **All-Outdoors California Whitewater Rafting** (☏*925-932-8993 or 800-247-2387, www.aorafting.com*); **Dvorak's Kayak & Rafting Expeditions, Inc.** (☏*719-429-6851 or 800-824-3795, www.dvorakexpeditions.com*); **ECHO: The Wilderness Company** (☏*800-652-3246, www.echotrips.com*); **Nichols Expeditions** (☏*801-259-3999 or 800-648-8488, www.NicholsExpeditions.com*); **OARS** (☏*209-736-4677 or 800-346-6277, www.oars.com*); and **R.O.W.–River Odysseys West** (☏*208-765-0841 or 800-451-6034, www.rowinc.com*). In Hawaii: **Kayak Kaua'i** (☏*808-826-9844 or 800-437-3507, planet-hawaii.com/outbound*).

SKIING THE WEST

From the Rockies to the Cascades and Sierra Nevada, ski areas are abundant, ranging from small local hills to major international resorts. Most western states—except those of the southern Great Plains—boast at least one ski area; associations count 161 in all, including 31 in California and 27 in

Colorado. In **Hawaii**, intrepid skiers drive Jeeps to the summit of 13,796ft Mauna Kea, "The White Mountain," to play in winter snows. SkiTown (*www.skitown.com*) has details on every North American resort.

Major areas—with at least eight lifts and a 2,000ft vertical drop—include these:

Alaska: Alyeska Resort (☎907-754-1111, *www.alyeskaresort.com*).

California: Heavenly Valley (☎775-586-7000, *www.skiheavenly.com*), Kirkwood (☎209-258-6000, *www.kirkwood.com*), Northstar-at-Tahoe (☎530-562-1010, *www.northstarattahoe.com*), Sierra-at-Tahoe (☎530-659-7453, *www.sierraattahoe.com*), Squaw Valley (☎530-583-6985, *www.squaw.com*). June Mountain (☎760-648-7733, *www.junemountain.com*), Mammoth Mountain (☎760-934-0745, www.mammothmountain.com).

Colorado: Aspen/Snowmass (☎970-925-1220, *www.aspensnowmass.com*). Crested Butte (☎970-349-2323, *www.skicb.com*). Purgatory (☎970-247-9000, *www.durangomountainresort.com*), Telluride (☎970-728-6900, *www.tellurideskiresort.com*). Steamboat Springs: Steamboat (☎970-879-6111, *www.steamboat.com*). Breckenridge (☎970-453-5000, *breckenridge.snow.com*), Copper Mountain (☎970-968-2882, *www.coppercolorado.com*), Keystone (☎970-496-4111, *keystone.snow.com*). Beaver Creek (☎970-476-5601, *beavercreek.snow.com*), Vail (☎970-476-5601,

Golf: Hitting the Links

Following is a list of some top-rated public-access courses in the western US:

Course	Location	☎
Troon North	Scottsdale AZ	480-585-7700
Sedona	Sedona AZ	520-284-9355
Tahquitz Creek	Palm Springs CA	760-328-1005
Pebble Beach	Pebble Beach CA	800-654-9300
Meadows del Mar	San Diego CA	858-792-6200
Pasatiempo	Santa Cruz CA	831-459-9155
The Broadmoor	Colorado Springs CO	719-577-5790
The Prince	Kauai HI	808-826-5000
Mauna Kea Beach	Kohala Coast HI	808-882-7222
Coeur d'Alene	Coeur d'Alene ID	208-765-0218
Pumpkin Ridge	Cornelius OR	503-647-9977
Angel Park	Las Vegas NV	888-446-5358
Edgewood Tahoe	Stateline NV	775-588-3566
Piñon Hills	Farmington NM	505-326-6066
Del Lago	Conroe TX	409-582-7570
Horseshoe Bay	Burnet TX	830-598-2511
Las Colinas	Irving TX	972-717-2441
Entrada at Snow Canyon	St. George UT	435-674-7500
Teton Pines	Jackson WY	307-733-1733

Many websites list courses, including www.golflink.com.

vail.snow.com). Winter Park (☎970-726-5514, *www.skiwinterpark.com*).

Idaho: Schweitzer Mountain (☎208-263-9555, www.schweitzer.com). Sun Valley (☎208-622-4111, www.sunvalley.com).

Montana: Big Mountain (☎406-862-7669, *www.bigmtn.com*). Big Sky (☎406-995-5000, *www.bigskyresort.com*), Red Lodge Mountain (☎406-446-2610, *www.redlodge.com*).

New Mexico: Santa Fe Ski Basin (505-982-4429, www.skisantafe.com). Taos Ski Valley (☎505-776-2291, *www.skitaos.org*).

Oregon: Mt. Bachelor (☎541-382-7888, *www.mtbachelor.com*), Mt. Hood Meadows (☎503-337-2222, *skihood.com*).

Utah: Alta (☎801-359-1078, *www.alta.com*), The Canyons (☎435-649-5400, *www.thecanyons.com*), Deer Valley (☎435-649-1000, *www.deervalley.*

com), Park City (☎435-649-8111, *www.parkcitymountain.com*), Snowbasin (☎801-399-1135, *www.snowbasin.com*), Snowbird (☎801-742-2222, *www.snowbird.com*).

Washington: Crystal Mountain (☎360-663-2526, *www.skicrystal.com*), The Summit at Snoqualmie (☎425-434-7669, *www.summitatsnoqualmie.com*).

Wyoming: Grand Targhee (307-353-2300, www.grandtarghee.com). Jackson Hole (☎307-733-2292, *www.jacksonhole.com*).

GUIDES AND OUTFITTERS

A list of accredited **mountaineering organizations** can be obtained from the nonprofit **American Mountain Guides Association** (*710 Tenth St., Suite 101, Golden CO 80401; ☎303-271-0984, www.amga.com*). **America Outdoors** (*P.O. Box 10847, Knoxville TN 37939; ☎865-558-3595, www.americaoutdoors.org*) offers an outfitter database on its Website and a free publication available by mail, listing US outfitters.

Nature and Safety

WILDLIFE

In most natural areas, tampering with plants or wildlife is prohibited by law. Although the disturbance caused by a single person may be small, the cumulative impact of a large number of visitors may be disastrous. Avoid direct contact with wildlife; any animal that does not shy from humans may be sick. Some wild animals, particularly bears, may approach cars or campsites out of curiosity or if they smell food. *Do not ever offer food to wild animals--not only is this dangerous, in many places it is illegal.*
Food storage guidelines: hang food 12ft off the ground and 10ft away from a tree trunk, or store in a locking ice chest, in a car trunk or in lockers provided at many campgrounds.

Thunderstorm Safety Tips

If outdoors, take cover and stay away from trees and metal objects.

If riding in a vehicle, remain inside until the storm has passed.

Avoid being in or near water.

If in a boat, head for the nearest shore.

Do not use electrical appliances, especially telephones.

Tornado Safety Tips

If indoors, move to a predesignated shelter (usually a basement or stairwell); otherwise find an interior room without windows (such as a bathroom).

Stay away from windows.

Do not attempt to outrun the storm in a car. Get out of the automobile and lie flat in a ditch or low-lying area.

A Black Bear munching on dandelions, Alaska

Improper storage of food is a violation of federal law and subject to a fine. If a bear approaches, try to frighten it by yelling and throwing rocks in its direction. Never approach a mother with cubs, as she may attack to protect her young.

BEACH AND WATER SAFETY

In the strong sun of coastal areas where white sand and water increases the sun's intensity, visitors run the risk of sunburn, even in winter. Apply sunscreen even on overcast days, as ultraviolet rays penetrate cloud cover. During summer months, when temperatures may be extreme, avoid strenuous midday exercise and drink plenty of liquids.

Along public beaches warning flags may be posted: blue flags signify calm waters; yellow flags indicate choppy waters; **red flags** indicate dangerous swimming conditions such as riptides, strong underlying currents that pull swimmers seaward. Take precautions even when venturing into calm waters: never swim, snorkel or scuba dive alone; and supervise children at all times. Most public beaches employ lifeguards seasonally; take care when swimming at an unguarded beach. Stinging creatures such as jellyfish, Portuguese men-of-war and sea urchins can inhabit shallow waters. Although most jellyfish stings produce little more than an itchy skin rash, some can cause painful swelling. Treating the affected area with papain-type meat tenderizer will give relief. Stingrays and Portuguese men-of-war can inflict a more serious sting; seek medical treatment immediately. Before beginning any water-sports activity, check with local authorities for information on water and weather conditions. If you rent a canoe or charter a boat, familiarize yourself with the craft, obtain charts of the area and advise someone of your itinerary before setting out. **Life jackets** must be worn when boating. Many equipment-rental facilities also offer instruction. Be sure to choose a reputable outfitter. Boating while intoxicated is illegal.

EARTHQUAKE PRECAUTIONS

Although severe earthquakes are infrequent, they are also unpredictable, making earthquake preparedness a fact of life in California and other Pacific-coast states. If you are **outside** when a quake occurs, stay clear of trees, buildings and power lines. If you are in a **vehicle**, pull to the side of the road and stop. Do not park on or under bridges; sit on the floor of the vehicle if possible. If you are in a **building**, stand inside a doorway or sit under a sturdy table; stay away from windows and outside walls.

Be alert for aftershocks. If possible, tune to local radio or TV stations for advisories.

DESERT SAFETY

When traveling through desert areas, particularly in summer, certain precautions are essential. Before driving or hiking in remote areas, notify someone of your destination and your planned return time.

For Your Vehicle

Always stay on marked roads; most unpaved roads are suitable only for four-wheel-drive vehicles. As service stations may be far apart, it is wise to keep your gas tank at least half full, and carry extra radiator water. If the vehicle is running hot, turn off the air conditioning. Do not use your air conditioner while climbing long hills. If it overheats, pull to the side of the road, turn on the heater and slowly pour water over the radiator core (*do not stop the engine*). Refill the radiator after the engine has cooled. In the event of a breakdown, do not leave your vehicle to seek help; instead, stay with the vehicle and wait for passing traffic.

For You

Summer temperatures can reach above 120°F (48°C). It is imperative to carry plenty of water and drink it freely, at least once an hour. Do not lie or sit in the direct sunlight. Always wear loose-fitting clothes (preferably long-sleeved), a broad-brimmed hat and sunglasses.

Heat exhaustion is caused by over-exertion in high temperatures. Symptoms include cool, clammy skin and nausea. If experiencing either of these symptoms, rest in the shade and drink plenty of fluids. Symptoms of **heat stroke** include hot, dry skin, dizziness or headache; a victim may become delirious. To treat these symptoms, try to lower the body temperature with cold compresses (do not use analgesics) and seek medical assistance. Abandoned mines are common in desert areas, and all are potentially dangerous. Never enter a tunnel without a flashlight. Watch for loose rock and do not touch support timbers. Be watchful for sudden storms that may produce flash floods.

MOUNTAIN SAFETY

Take particular care if you are traveling at high altitudes, whether driving across Trail Ridge Road at 12,183ft in Colorado's Rocky Mountain National Park or taking the cog railway to the 14,110ft summit of Pikes Peak. Your body does not immediately acclimate to the reduced oxygen level and lowered atmospheric pressure. One to four days may be necessary to fully adjust. Restrict activity to moderate exertion, get plenty of rest, avoid large meals, and drink lots of water. Senior citizens, pregnant women and travelers with a history of heart problems should consult their physicians before climbing too high.

Especially if you are hiking or skiing above 8,000ft, you may suffer **altitude sickness** caused by overexertion. Symptoms include headache, shortness of breath, appetite loss or nausea, tingling in fingers or toes (which may progress to swelling in feet and legs) and general weakness. If experiencing any of these symptoms, rest and eat high-energy foods such as raisins, trail mix or granola bars; take a couple of aspirin and slow your pace. If symptoms become more severe, descend to a lower altitude; if they do not disappear in 2–5 days, seek medical attention.

As the sun's rays are more direct in the thinner atmosphere of higher elevations, they cause sunburn more quickly, especially in winter when they reflect off snow. A good sunblock is essential.

It is important to keep yourself warm and your clothing dry any time of year. Hypothermia poses the greatest threat in winter, but even midsummer temperatures can drop below freezing at high altitude.

National and State Lands

The United States has an extensive network of federal and state lands, including national and state parks, that offer year-round recreational opportunities such as camping (*p 31*), fishing, horseback riding, cross-country skiing and boating. US federal land-management agencies support a comprehensive on-line database (*www.recreation.gov*) that supplies information on all recreation areas through a variety of search options and Internet links. The National Park Service provides a listing of all lands under its jurisdiction on its Website (*www.nps.gov*).

Both national and state parks offer **season passes** (*disabled travelers p 21*). The **US national recreational lands pass** (*$80*) is good for one year and includes admission to all national parks and other federal lands that charge admission, parking fees and so on. The pass may be purchased at any park entrance area or online; www.nps.gov. Most parks have information centers equipped with trail maps and informative literature on park facilities and activities. Contact the following agencies for further information:

National Forests

US Department of Agriculture
Forest Service, National Headquarters
P.O. Box 96090
Washington DC 20090-6090
☎202-205-1680 or www.fs.fed.us

National Parks

US Department of the Interior
National Park Service
Office of Public Inquiries
1849 C St. NW
Washington DC 20240
☎202-208-6843 or www.nps.gov

State Park Divisions

Alaska Division of Parks & Outdoor Recreation:

550 W 7th Ave, Suite 1260, Anchorage, AK 99501-3557. ☎907-269-8400. www.dnr.state.ak.us/parks.

Arizona State Parks:

1300 W. Washington, Phoenix, AZ 85007. ☎602-542-4174 www.pr.state.az.us.

California Dept of Parks & Recreation:

P.O. Box 942896, Sacramento, CA 94296. ☎916-653-6995. www.parks.ca.gov.

Colorado Parks:

1313 Sherman Street, Suite 618, Denver, CO 80203. ☎303-866-3437. parks.state.co.us.

Hawaii Div of State Parks:

P.O. Box 621, Honolulu, HI 96809. ☎808-587-0300. www.hawaii.gov/dlnr/dsp.

Tips for Visiting Public Lands

Spray clothes with insect repellent (particularly around cuffs and waistline) and check for ticks every 3-4hrs when participating in outdoor activities.

Do not feed wild animals.

Do not litter; pack out everything you pack in.

Boil (5min) or chemically treat water from streams and lakes.

Cutting wood for fires is prohibited; only dead or fallen wood should be used. Campfires are limited to fire pits.

All plants and animals within the parks are protected.

Taking natural objects (antlers/horns, historical items, plants, rocks) is prohibited.

Idaho State Parks & Recreation Department:
5657 Warm Springs Ave., Boise, ID, 83716. ☎208-334-4199. www.idaho-parks.org.

Kansas Dept of Wildlife & Parks:
512 SE 25th Ave., Pratt, KS 67124. ☎620-672-5911. www.kdwp.state.ks.us.

Montana Parks Division:
PO Box 200701, Helena, MT 59620-0701. ☎406-444-2535. www.fwp.state.mt.us/parks/parks.htm.

Nebraska Game & Parks Commission:
2200 N. 33rd St., Lincoln, NE 68503. ☎402-471-0641. www.ngpc.state.ne.us/parks.

Nevada State Parks:
901 S. Stewart St., 5th Floor, Suite 5005 Carson City, NV 89701-5248. ☎775-684-2770. parks.nv.gov.

New Mexico State Parks Division:
1220 South St. Francis Dr., Santa Fe, NM 87505. ☎505-476-3200. www.emnrd.state.nm.us/main/index.htm.

North Dakota Parks & Recreation Department:
1600 E. Century Avenue, Suite 3, Bismarck, ND 58503-0649. ☎701-328-5357. www.ndparks.com.

Oklahoma Parks Division:
15 N Robinson, PO Box 52002, Oklahoma City, OK 73152-2002. ☎405-521-3411. touroklahoma.com.

Oregon State Parks & Recreation Department:
725 Summer St., N.E. Suite C, Salem, OR 97301. ☎503-986-0707. egov.oregon.gov/OPRD/index.shtml.

South Dakota Park & Recreation Division:
523 East Capitol Ave., Pierre, SD 57501. ☎605-773-3391. www.sdgfp.info/Parks/index.htm.

Texas Parks & Wildlife Department:
4200 Smith School Rd., Austin, TX 78744. ☎512-389-4800. www.tpwd.state.tx.us.

Utah Parks & Recreation Division:
1594 West North Temple, Salt Lake City, UT 84116. ☎801-538-7220. stateparks.utah.gov.

Park Avenue Pass, Arches National Park

Washington State Parks & Recreation Commission:
7150 Cleanwater Drive S.W., P.O. Box 42650, Olympia, WA 98504-2650. ☎360-902-8844. www.parks.wa.gov.

Wyoming Division of State Parks & Historic Sites:
2301 Central Ave., Cheyenne, WY 82002. ☎307-777-6323. wyoparks.state.wy.us.

HISTORIC AND SCENIC TRAILS

The National Park Service, US Forest Service and Bureau of Land Management administer national scenic and national historic trails in the US. Some are for hikers, others (historic) for car travelers. For information, obtain the *National Trails System Map and Guide ($1.25)* from the Consumer Information Center, US General Services Administration (*Pueblo CO 81009; ☎800-333-4636, www.pueblo.gsa.gov*) or contact agencies listed below.

National Trails System Branch of the National Park Service
1849 C St. NW, Washington DC 20240, ☎202-565-1177, www.nps.gov/nts.

Continental Divide National Scenic Trail
Continental Divide Trail Society, Northern Region, ☎406-329-3150. Rocky Mountain Region, ☎303-275-5350. www.cdtsociety.org.

Pacific Crest National Scenic Trail
Pacific Crest Trail Association, ☎916-349-2109. www.pcta.org.

Iditarod National Historic Trail
Iditarod Trail Committee, ☎907-376-5155. www.iditarod.com.

Juan Bautista de Anza National Historic Trail
National Park Service, ☎415-561-4700. www.nps.gov/juba.

Lewis and Clark National Historic Trail
Lewis and Clark Trail Heritage Foundation, ☎406-454-1234. www.lewisandclark.org.

Mormon Pioneer National Historic Trail
National Park Service, Long Distance Trails Office, P.O. Box 45155, Salt Lake City UT 84145, ☎801-539-4095, www.nps.gov/mopi.

Nez Percé (Nee-Me-Poo) National Historic Trail
Forest Service, Northern Region, ☎406-329-3590. www.fs.fed.us/r1.

Oregon National Historic Trail
Oregon Country Trails Assn., ☎816-252-2276. www.nps.gov/oreg.

Santa Fe National Historic Trail
Santa Fe Trail Assn., ☎620-285-2054. www.santafetrail.org.

Trail of Tears National Historic Trail
National Park Service, ☎505-988-6888. www.nps.gov/trte.

BASEBALL   Apr–Oct

MLB (Major League Baseball) *www.mlb.com*

Team	Venue	☏
Anaheim Angels	Edison International Field	714-634-2000
Arizona Diamondbacks	Bank One Ballpark, Phoenix	602-514-8400
Colorado Rockies	Coors Field, Denver	800-388-7625
Houston Astros	Minute Maid Park 713-259-8000	
Kansas City Royals	Kauffman Stadium	816-921-8000
Los Angeles Dodgers	Dodger Stadium	323-224-1448
Oakland Athletics	Network Associates Coliseum	510-762-2255
San Diego Padres	Qualcomm Stadium	619-881-6500
San Francisco Giants	Pacific Bell Park	415-972-2000
Seattle Mariners	Safeco Field	206-346-4001
Texas Rangers	The Ballpark in Arlington	817-273-5222

BASKETBALL   Oct–Apr

NBA (National Basketball Association) *www.nba.com*

Team	Venue	☏
Dallas Mavericks	American Airlines Center	877-316-3553
Denver Nuggets	Pepsi Center	303-405-1212
Golden State Warriors	Arena in Oakland	510-986-2200
Houston Rockets	Compaq Center	713-627-3865
Los Angeles Clippers	Staples Center	213-742-7500
Los Angeles Lakers	Staples Center	213-480-3232
Phoenix Suns	America West Arena	602-379-7867
Portland Trail Blazers	Rose Garden	503-231-8000
Sacramento Kings	ARCO Arena	916-928-6900
San Antonia Spurs	TSBC Center	210-554-7773
Seattle SuperSonics	KeyArena	206-281-5800
Utah Jazz	The Delta Center, Salt Lake City	801-355-3865

FOOTBALL   Sept–Jan

NFL (National Football League) *www.nfl.com*

Team	Venue	☏
Arizona Cardinals	Sun Devil Stadium, Tempe	602-379-0102
Dallas Cowboys	Texas Stadium	972-785-4800
Denver Broncos	Mile High Stadium	720-258-3333
Kansas City Chiefs	Arrowhead Stadium	816-920-9300
Oakland Raiders	Network Associates Coliseum	800-225-2277
San Diego Chargers	Qualcomm Stadium	619-220-8497
San Francisco 49ers	3Com Park	415-656-4900
Seattle Seahawks	Seahawks Stadium	888-635-4295

HOCKEY   Oct–Apr

NHL (National Hockey League) *www.nhl.com*

Team	Venue	☏
Colorado Avalanche	Pepsi Center, Denver	303-405-1111
Dallas Stars	American Airlines Center	214-467-8277
Los Angeles Kings	Staples Center	888-546-4752
Mighty Ducks of Anaheim	Arrowhead Pond	714-703-2545
Phoenix Coyotes	America West Arena	480-563-7825
San Jose Sharks	Compaq Center	408-287-9200

Professional Team Sports

See listings opposite
Tickets can be purchased at the individual venue or through the local Ticketmaster office.

Entertainment

The best source for entertainment, nightlife and events listings is the local newspapers in each city. Daily papers focus on mainstream offerings, while weekly papers include more offbeat and unorthodox arts and culture. Each paper maintains a website, though some require free registration by users for unlimited access. Consult each area's visitor information site for names of local papers.

The West's most notable symphonies are in Dallas, Houston, Los Angeles, San Francisco and Seattle. Opera companies of international renown are in Houston, San Francisco, Santa Fe (summer only) and Seattle (globally famed for its triennial Ring Cycle). Austin, San Francisco and Seattle are famous live-music locales; Portland is a national center for blues and jazz, as is Kansas City.

The most comprehensive events listings covering the US are available at www.citysearch.com.

Sightseeing & Tours

NATIONAL AND CITY TOURS

Several national tour companies provide all-inclusive packages for motor-coach tours of the US (*see opposite*). The scope of tours may vary among tour operators, but most offer packages of varying length, geographic coverage and cost. **TrekAmerica** (*P.O. Box 189, Rockaway NJ 07866; ☎973-983-1144 or 800-221-0596, www. trekamerica.com*) caters to travelers who prefer small groups, varied sightseeing/sporting activities and flexible itineraries. For those interested in more educational offerings, **Smithsonian Study Tours**, sponsored by the Smithsonian Institution, offer a variety of single- and multi-day thematic tour programs covering topics such as architecture, history, the performing arts and cuisine. Educators specializing in related fields lead tours. For more information: ☎202-633-1000 or www.si.edu.

Information on **city tours** can be obtained from convention and visitors bureaus in most large US cities. **Gray Line Tours** provides half- and full-day sightseeing motor-coach tours for more than 70 cities: Gray Line Worldwide (☎303-433-9800 or 866-866-9935, www.grayline.com).

NATIONAL TOUR COMPANIES

Brennan Tours:
5301 South Federal Circle, Littleton, CO 80123. ☎800-237-7249. www.brennantours.com.

Collette Tours:
162 Middle St., Pawtucket, RI 02860. ☎800-340-5158. www.collettetours.com.

GoGo Worldwide Vacations:
69 Spring St., Ramsey, NJ 07446-0507. ☎800-229-4999. www.gogowwv.com.

Globus and Cosmos:
5301 South Federal Circle, Littleton, CO 80123.☎877-245-6287. www.globusandcosmos.com.

Mayflower Tours:
1225 Warren Ave., P.O. Box 490, Downers Grove, IL 60515. ☎800-323-7604. www.mayflowertours.com.

Trafalgar Tours:
11 E. 26th St., Suite 1300, New York City, NY 10010. ☎800-854-0103. www.trafalgartours.com.

Tauck Tours:
10 Norden Place, Norwalk, CT 06855. ☎800-788-7885. www.tauck.com.

Kids Activities for Children

In this guide, sights of particular interest to children are indicated with a Kids symbol. Many of these attractions offer special children's programs. Most attractions offer discounted (if not free) admission to visitors under 12 years of age. In addition, many hotels and resorts boast special family discount packages, and some restaurants provide a special children's menu.

Calendar of Events

SPRING

late Mar: **Academy Awards**
Los Angeles CA
Cowboy Poetry & Music Festival
Santa Clarita CA
Mar or Apr: **Easter Pageant**
Phoenix AZ
Apr: **Houston International Festival**
Houston TX
Azalea Festival
Muskogee OK
Pole, Pedal, Paddle Triathlon
Jackson Hole WY
early Apr: **Merrie Monarch Hula Festival**
Hilo HI
mid-Apr: **International Wildlife Film Festival**
Missoula MT
Toyota Grand Prix
Long Beach CA
Orange Blossom Festival
Riverside CA
Cherry Blossom Festival
San Francisco CA
mid-late Apr: **Fiesta San Antonio**
San Antonio TX
late Apr: **Fiesta Broadway**
Los Angeles CA
Newport-Ensenada Yacht Race
Newport Beach CA
late Apr–early May: **Buccaneer Days**
Corpus Christi TX
Apple Blossom Festival
Wenatchee WA
late Apr–mid-May: **Ramona Pageant**
Hemet CA

May: **Molokai ka Hula Piko**
Molokai HI
Helldorado Days
Las Vegas NV
May 1: **Lei Day**
Honolulu HI
May 5: **Cinco de Mayo**
cities throughout the West
early May: **Mayfest**
Fort Worth TX
mid-May: **California Strawberry Festival**
Oxnard CA
Tejano Conjunto Festival en San Antonio
San Antonio TX
Kerrville Folk Festival
Kerrville TX
Bay to Breakers Foot Race
San Francisco CA
Calaveras County Fair & Jumping Frog Jubilee
Angels Camp CA
Elk Antler Auction
Jackson WY
late May: **Art Fest**
Dallas TX
Laguna Gloria Fiesta
Austin TX
Carnaval
San Francisco CA
Spring Festival of the Arts
Santa Fe NM
Sacramento Jazz Jubilee
Sacramento CA
Northwest Folklife Festival
Seattle WA
late May–early Jun: **Seattle International Film Festival**
Seattle WA
Jun: **El Paso/Juarez International Mariachi Festival**
El Paso TX
King Kamehameha Day
all islands HI
Portland Rose Festival
Portland OR
Mormon Miracle Pageant
Manti UT
The Great Cannery Row Sardine Festival
Monterey CA
early Jun: **Red Earth Native American Cultural Festival**
Oklahoma City OK

early–mid-Jun: **Austin Jazz & Arts Festival**
Austin TX

mid-Jun: **Juneteenth African-American Festivals**
major cities

Telluride Bluegrass Festival
Telluride CO

Smoky Hill River Festival
Salina KS

Cannon Beach Sand Castle Contest
Cannon Beach OR

La Jolla Festival of the Arts & Food Faire
La Jolla CA

SUMMER

Jun-Aug: **Black Hills Passion Play**
Spearfish SD

Medora Musical
Medora ND

Aspen Music Festival and School
Aspen CO

Cody Nite Rodeo
Cody WY

Jun–early Sept: **The Britt Festivals**
Jacksonville OR

late Jun: **Summer Solstice Celebration**
Fairbanks AK

Little Big Horn Days
Hardin MT

International Busker Fest
Denver CO

Lewis & Clark Festival
Great Falls MT

Lesbian/Gay/Bisexual/Transgender Pride Celebration
San Francisco CA

Boise River Festival
Boise ID

late Jun–early Aug: **Central City Opera**
Central City CO

late Jun–late Aug: **Santa Fe Opera**
Santa Fe NM

late Jun–early Sept: **Utah Shakespearean Festival**
Cedar City UT

Jul: **Cherry Creek Arts Festival**
Denver CO

Days of '47
Salt Lake City UT

Taos Pueblo Powwow
Taos NM

Green River Rendezvous
Pinedale WY

July 4: **Independence Day Celebrations**
every city and town

Independence Day Fireworks
Mt. Rushmore SD

early Jul: **Pikes Peak International Hill Climb**
Manitou Springs CO

World Championship Timber Carnival
Albany OR

early-mid-Jul: **North American Indian Days**
Browning MT

Venice Beach, Los Angeles, California

Allison Simpson/MICHELIN

ACT Theater, San Francisco

mid-Jul: **Cable Car Bell-Ringing Competition**
San Francisco CA

California Rodeo
Salinas CA

International Climbers Festival
Lander WY

mid-late Jul: **Cheyenne Frontier Days Rodeo**
Cheyenne WY

late Jul: **Golden Days & World Eskimo-Indian Olympics**
Fairbanks AK

Days of '76
Deadwood SD

Last Chance Stampede
Helena MT

US Open Surfing Championships
Huntington Beach CA

Oregon Brewers Festival
Portland OR

Gilroy Garlic Festival
Gilroy CA

Spanish Market
Santa Fe NM

July 24: **Pioneer Day**
Utah

Jul–Aug: **Colorado Music Festival**
Boulder CO

Flagstaff Festival of the Arts
Flagstaff AZ

Festival of Arts & Pageant of the Masters
Laguna Beach CA

Festival of the American West
Logan UT

Grand Teton Music Festival
Jackson WY

mid-Jul–mid-Aug: **Seafair Festival**
Seattle WA

Aug: **Hawaiian International Billfish Tournament**
Kailua-Kona HI

Kansas City Jazz Festival
Kansas City MO

World's Oldest Continuous Rodeo
Prescott AZ

Texas Folklife Festival
San Antonio TX

Fleet Week
San Diego CA

early Aug: **Sturgis Rally and Races**
Sturgis SD

Festival of the Arts
Bigfork MT

Old Spanish Days
Santa Barbara CA

Park City Arts Festival
Park City UT

Steinbeck Festival
Salinas CA

Hot August Nights
Reno NV

Burning Man
Black Rock Desert (near Reno) NV

Festival of Nations
Red Lodge MT

early-mid-Aug: **Inter-Tribal Indian Ceremonial**
Gallup NM
mid-Aug: **Indian Market**
Santa Fe NM
mid-Aug–mid-Oct: **State Fairs**
every state
late Aug: **World Body Surfing Championships**
Oceanside CA
Cherokee National Holiday
Tahlequah OK
Sept: **Grand Canyon Music Festival**
South Rim, Grand Canyon AZ
MoabMusic Festival
MoabUT
early Sept: **Fiesta de las Flores**
El Paso TX
A Taste of Colorado
Denver CO
All-American Futurity Race
Ruidoso NM
Pioneer Days
Fort Worth TX
Sausalito Art Festival
Sausalito CA
La Fiesta de Santa Fe
Santa Fe NM
Bumbershoot
Seattle WA
Virginia City International Camel Races
Virginia City NV
mid-Sept: **Mexican Independence Day**
cities near Mexican border
Navajo Nation Fair
Window Rock AZ
Fiestas Patrias
Houston TX
Pendleton Round-Up
Pendleton OR
United Tribes International Pow Wow
Bismarck ND
San Francisco Blues Festival
San Francisco CA
Monterey Jazz Festival
Monterey CA
Wooden Boat Festival
Port Townsend WA
National Championship Air Races
Reno NV
Jackson Hole Fall Arts Festival
Jackson WA

FALL

late Sept: G**athering of Indian Nations Festival**
Sedona AZ
River City Roundup & Rodeo
Omaha NE
Cabrillo Festival
San Diego CA
Sept–Oct: **Aloha Festival**
all islands HI
late Sept–early Oct: **Taos Fall Arts Festival**
Taos NM
late Sept–mid-Oct: **State Fair of Texas**
Dallas TX
Oct: **Festival of the Horse**
Oklahoma City OK
early Oct: **Albuquerque International Balloon Festival**
Albuquerque NM
Oklahoma International Bluegrass Festival
Guthrie OK
Oktoberfest
Fredericksburg TX
mid-Oct: **Alaska Day Festival**
Sitka AK
Canyonlands Fat Tire Festival
MoabUT
Helldorado Days
Tombstone AZ
late Oct: **Ironman Triathlon**
Big Island HI
Oct 31: **Halloween**
most cities and towns
Nov: **Kona Coffee Festival**
Kailua-Kona HI
Death Valley Fall Festival & '49er Encampment
Furnace Creek CA
early Nov: **Will Rogers Days**
Claremore OK
Wurstfest
New Braunfels TX
late Nov: **Hollywood Christmas Parade**
Hollywood CA
Doo Dah Parade
Pasadena CA
River Parade & Lighting Ceremony
San Antonio TX
Nov–Dec: Triple **Crown of Surfing**
North Shore, Oahu HI

late Nov–mid-Dec: **Feria de Santa Cecilia y Fiestas Navideñas**
San Antonio TX

late Nov–early Jan: **Red Rock Fantasy of Lights**
Sedona AZ

early Dec: **Bachelor Society Ball & Wilderness Women Contest**
Talkeetna AK

National Finals Rodeo
Las Vegas NV

Weinachsfest
Carmel CA

WINTER

Dec: **Christmas celebrations**
every city and town

La Mele o Maui
Maui HI

Festival of Poinsettias
Lawrence KS

Festival of Lights at the Grotto
Portland OR

Fiesta Bowl Events
Phoenix AZ

Yuletide in Taos
Taos NM

mid-Dec: **Our Lady of Guadalupe Fiesta**
Las Cruces NM

Christmas Boat Parade
Seattle WA, Newport Beach CA

Albuquerque International Balloon Festival, New Mexico

Dec 16–24: **Las Posadas**
Los Angeles CA

Jan: **Sundance Film Festival**
Park City UT

Seattle International Boat Show
Seattle WA

National Western Stock Show and Rodeo
Denver CO

Jan 1: **Tournament of Roses**
Pasadena CA

mid-Jan: **Winterfest**
Aspen CO

late Jan–Feb: **Chinese New Year Festival**
Asian communities (especially CA & HI)

Cowboy Poetry Gathering
Elko NV

Feb: **Flagstaff Winterfest**
Flagstaff AZ

Mardi Gras! Galveston
Galveston TX

San Antonio Stock Show and Rodeo
San Antonio TX

Cowboy Ski Challenge
Jackson WY

early Feb: **Winter Carnival**
Steamboat Springs CO

Whitefish Winter Carnival
Whitefish MT

Southwestern International Livestock Show
El Paso TX

Festival of Whales
Dana Point CA

mid-Feb: **Fur Rendezvous**
Anchorage AK

Race to the Sky Sled Dog Race
Helena MT

Whale Week
Maui HI

An Affair of the Heart
Oklahoma City OK

late Feb: **National Date Festival**
Indio CA

La Fiesta de los Vaqueros
Tucson AZ

Newport Seafood & Wine Festival
Newport OR

late Feb–end Oct: **Oregon Shakespeare Festival**
Ashland OR

early Mar: **Iditarod Trail Sled Dog Race**
Anchorage to Nome AK

©iStockphoto.com/Karen Gentry

Snowfest
Tahoe City CA
mid-Mar: **C.M. Russell Auction of Original Western Art**
Great Falls MT
Scottsdale Arts Festival
Scottsdale AZ
World Snowmobile Expo
West Yellowstone MT
Mar 17: **St. Patrick's Day**
many cities
Mar 19: **Return of the Swallows**
San Juan Capistrano CA

Books

Western Forests; Pacific Coast. Audubon Society. These two books are the best natural history guides to the landscapes and wild creatures of the West.
The Good Rain. Timothy Egan. The *New York Times* Northwest correspondent explains the delicate ecology of the Pacific Northwest.
Walt Disney: Triumph of the American Imagination. Neal Gabler. A complete and evenhanded look at the pioneer who created two key Western icons, Disneyland and animated film.
Lonesome Dove. Larry McMurtry. Widely considered the best fictional depiction of the cattle drive era. The TV movie based on it ranks high in most best-of lists.
Cannery Row, The Grapes of Wrath, East of Eden. John Steinbeck. These three novels, each an American treasure, portray the West in terms so real and human that they won Steinbeck a Nobel Prize.
Great Plains. Ian Frazier. A humane modern look at the vast high plains of the West.
Undaunted Courage. Stephen Ambrose. Prize-winning recounting of the Lewis & Clark expedition.
The Way West. A.B. Guthrie. A Pulitzer-prize novel about the Oregon Trail.
I Feel Earthquakes More Often Than They Happen. Amy Wilentz. A transplanted New Yorker looks at life in California in the Schwarzenegger era.

Films

Shane (1953), *The Ballad of Little Jo* (1993) George Stevens, Maggie Greenwald
Set amid incomparable mountain scenery, the tale of gunfighter Shane's epiphany is universally considered one of the best Westerns. By contrast, *Little Jo*, the fact-based story of a woman pioneer who masqueraded as a man, is a "stinging rebuke to the Hollywood myth of the Old West," in the words of one critic.
Cheyenne Autumn (1964) John Ford
Legendary director Ford's elegaic portrait of the tragedy of the Cheyenne is one of the earliest films to consider the Indian perspective.
High Plains Drifter (1971), *Unforgiven* (1992) Clint Eastwood
The iconic star's earliest directorial effort, and his two-decades-later Oscar winner, both offer unvarnished looks at a classic Western theme, vengeance.
Chinatown (1974), *Quinceanera* (2006) Roman Polanski, Richard Glatzer & Wash Westmoreland
Polanski's classic focuses on the water-grab that created Los Angeles; *Quinceanera* portrays the multicultural diversity of LA today.
Sometimes a Great Notion (1971), *Lonesome Dove* (1990)
Paul Newman, Simon Wincer

Shopping

Every city and medium-size town in the West now has a shopping mall in or near the population center; bigger cities have many. Outlet malls, which offer name-brand merchandise from manufacturers such as DKNY and Ralph Lauren, are ubiquitous; search for these at www.outletbound.com. The most famous shopping area in the West is Rodeo Drive, an ultra-high-end district in Beverly Hills, CA. Major cities still offer shopping districts downtown; many smaller cities are attempting to revive their historic centers by transforming them into tree-shaded, pedestrian-friendly districts with small boutiques and cafes. To find cities pursuing this revival visit www.main-street.org. Shoppers in three Western states enjoy an extra price advantage: Alaska, Montana and Oregon charge no state sales tax, though local taxes may be charged. In virtually all Western states there is no sales tax on groceries, not including food served in restaurants.

BASIC INFORMATION

Business Hours

Most businesses operate Mon–Fri 9am–5pm. Banking institutions are normally open Mon–Fri 9am–5:30pm, Sat 10am-1pm. Virtually all bank branches big and small, in cities and towns big and small, now have ATMs operating 24 hours. Most retail stores and specialty shops are open daily 10am–6pm. Malls and shopping centers are usually open Mon–Sat 10am–9pm, Sun 10am–6pm.

Electricity

Voltage in the US is 120 volts AC, 60 Hz. Foreign-made appliances may need AC adapters (available at specialty travel and electronics stores) and North American flat-blade plugs.

Emergencies

Except in remote areas where there is little or no telephone service, the emergency phone number through-out the West is 911, which can be dialed from any operating phone. Visi-tors in need of urgent non-emergency medical care can visit the emergency room at the closest hospital; or one of many urgent care clinics found in most cities. Patients may be required to demonstrate financial ability to pay. Most cities above 50,000 population have local clinics that provide urgent dental care; and 24 hours pharmacies.

Liquor Laws

The minimum age for purchase and consumption of alcoholic beverages is 21; proof of age may be required. Local municipalities may limit and restrict sales, and laws differ among states. In many states, liquor stores sell beer, wine and liquor. Beer and wine may also be purchased in pack-age-goods stores and grocery stores. Liquor is available at grocery stores in California. Beer may be purchased in gas station convenience stores in some states. However, in other states, wine and liquor are sold at state-operated shops and beer is sold by licensed distributors. Certain states, such as Utah, do not permit alcohol sales on Sundays, even in restaurants (exceptions usually apply in metro-politan and tourist areas). It is a serious offense for those over 21 to procure alcohol for minors.

Major Holidays

Banks and government offices are closed on the following legal holidays:

New Year's Day
January 1
Martin Luther King Jr.'s Birthday*
3rd Monday in January
President's Day*
3rd Monday in February
Memorial Day*
last Monday in May
Independence Day
July 4
Labor Day*
1st Monday in September
Columbus Day*
2nd Monday in October

Veterans Day*
November 11
Thanksgiving Day
4th Thursday in November
Christmas Day
December 25

*Many retail stores and restaurants stay open on these days.

Mail/Post

First-class postage rates within the US are: 41¢/letter (*up to 1oz*) and postcard. To Europe: 90¢/letter (up to 1oz), 90¢/postcard. Most post offices are open Mon–Fri 9am–5pm; some may open Sat 9am–noon. Companies such as UPS-Mail Boxes Etc. and FedexKinko's (*consult the Yellow Pages in the phone book under Mailing Services*) also provide mail service for everything from postcards to large packages. These companies also sell boxes and other packaging material. For photocopying, fax service and computer access, FedexKinko's has locations throughout the US (☎800-254-6567, www.kinkos. com) or consult the yellow pages in a local phone book under Copying Service for a listing of local companies.

Money

The American **dollar** ($1) is divided into 100 **cents**. A **penny** = 1 cent (1¢); a **nickel** = 5¢; a **dime** = 10¢; a **quarter** = 25¢. Most national banks and Thomas Cook (*locations throughout the US*, ☎800-287-7362, www.thomascook. com) **exchange foreign currency** at local offices and charge a fee for the service.
The simplest methods to obtain dollars are to use traveler's checks (*accepted in most banks, hotels, restaurants and businesses with presentation of a photo ID*) and to withdraw cash from **ATMs** (Automated Teller Machines) with a debit or credit card. Banks charge a fee (*$1–$3*) for non-members who use their ATMs. For more information on the ATM network, call MasterCard/Cir-

rus (*☎800-424-7787*) or Visa/Plus System (*☎800-843-7587*). In the event you lose your credit card: American Express, ☎800-528-4800; Diner's Club, ☎800-234-6377; MasterCard/Eurocard, ☎800-307-7309; Visa/Carte Bleue, ☎800-336-8472.
It is also possible to send and receive cash via **Western Union** (*locations in more than 100 countries, ☎800-325-6000, www.westernunion.com*).

Smoking

The US West, especially California, has led the world in restrictions on public smoking, inaugurating protections for nonsmokers so extensive that some airports in the Golden State greet travelers with signs that announce: "Welcome to America's non-smoking section." These restrictions have spread to most Western states; laws vary, but it is illegal to smoke in public areas in most places such as restaurants, airports, buses, offices open to the public such as banks and retail stores. All US airlines are completely nonsmoking.

In California, which continues to expand these policies, it is now illegal to smoke in a private car if children are present, and one California city has banned smoking in apartment buildings. Many beaches in California prohibit smoking, too (to curb litter). In Washington, smokers who head outside to practice their habit must keep away from doors and ventilation inlets. For a state-by-state list of restrictions, consult Action on Smoking and Health, www.ash.org.
Aside from legal restrictions, it is socially unacceptable to expose other individuals to tobacco smoke. Virtually all smokers voluntarily retire to locations where their habit will not affect others. If you are bothered by someone's smoke, it is quite all right to ask them to move, unless you are in a private residence or designated smoking area.

Tipping

In restaurants, it is customary to leave the server a gratuity, or tip, of 10–20 percent of the total bill (since it almost never is included otherwise). Taxi drivers are generally tipped 15 percent of the fare. In hotels, bellhops are tipped $1-$2 per suitcase and housekeeping $1-$2 per night.

Taxes and Tipping

In the US, with the occasional exception of certain food products and gasoline, sales tax is not included in the quoted price and is added at the time of payment. Sales taxes vary by state and range from 3 to 8.5 percent (except for Alaska, Montana and Oregon, which charge no sales tax). Sales tax may often be higher in major cities due to local taxes. In some states, the restaurant tax appearing on your bill when you dine out may be higher than the state tax; also, expect additional hotel and rental car taxes and surcharges.

Telephones

For **long-distance** calls in the US and Canada, dial 1 + area code (3 digits) + number (7 digits). Note: Many cellular phones, depending on the service provider, do not require the initial 1; just dial the 10-digit number you wish to call. To place **local calls**, dial the seven-digit number without 1 or the area code, unless the local calling area includes several area codes. To place an **international call**, dial 011 + country code + area code + number. To obtain help from an **operator**, dial 0 for local and 00 for long distance. For **information** on a number within your area code, dial 411. For long-distance information, dial 1 + area code + 555-1212. To place **collect calls**, dial 0 + area or country code + number. At the operator's prompt, give your name. For all **emergencies**, dial 911.

Since most **hotels** add a surcharge for local and long-distance calls, it is preferable to use your calling card or cell phone. Local calls from public telephones cost 50¢ unless otherwise posted. **Public telephones** accept quarters, dimes and nickels. You may also use your calling card or credit card

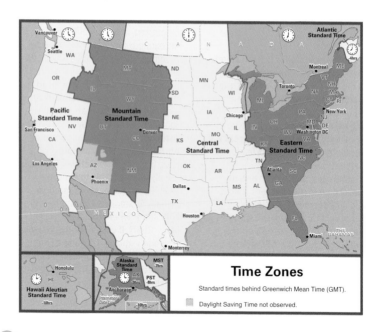

Time Zones

Standard times behind Greenwich Mean Time (GMT).

Daylight Saving Time not observed.

(recommended for long-distance calls to avoid the inconvenience of depositing large amounts of change). Instructions for using public telephones are listed on or near the phone.

Unless otherwise indicated, telephone numbers that start with **800**, **888**, **877** and **866** are toll-free within the United States, and often Canada. Numbers that begin with 900 charge extra fees, sometimes exorbitant; do not use these.

Time Zones

There are three standard time zones in the Western United States: Central, Mountain and Pacific, and additional Alaska and Hawaii time zones. Daylight Savings Time is observed in all states—except Arizona and Hawaii—from mid-March to mid-November; time is moved forward one hour, bringing an earlier dawn but also a later dusk. Pacific Standard Time (PST) is 8hrs behind Greenwich Mean Time (GMT), or Universal Time (UT); Pacific Daylight Time (PDT) is 7hrs behind GMT.

Rocky Mountains Landscape
© PhotoDisc, Inc

NATURE

The US West starts within the tier of Great Plains states west of the Mississippi—Texas, Oklahoma, Kansas, Nebraska and the Dakotas—-and includes all of the continent beyond to the Pacific Ocean, as well as the isolated states of Alaska and Hawaii.

Geologic Foundations

The easternmost part of the West is a broad swath of plains that rise gradually from the Gulf of Mexico and Mississippi Valley; the western two-thirds is a vast, corrugated expanse of mountains and plateaus interposed with canyons, valleys and basins of varying size. Although landforms have been more than 2 billion years in the making, the current uplift began 130 million years ago, after the Pacific Plate subducted the North American Plate. The tectonic collision brought island masses crashing into the continent and slowly raised vast uplands from what previously had been a shallow sea. Magma intruded through weakened parts of the earth's crust, welling over as volcanoes and volcanic plateaus. Faults (most aligned north-south) thrust mountain ranges sharply upward, creating abrupt escarpments; or dropped blocks of land to form grabens, typical of the Great Basin region. Streams, rushing from the rising highlands, cut deep canyons. Sediments flowing to lowlands deposited valley soils and built the Great Plains on the eastern side of the Rocky Mountains.

The subduction zone where the Pacific and North American Plates meet is part of the Ring of Fire, the geologically unstable zone that circles the Pacific Ocean. In the American West, its most volatile indicators are California's earthquake-prone San Andreas Fault, the volcanic Cascade Range and Alaska's Aleutian volcanoes; a bit farther east, Yellowstone National Park is the world's largest geothermal area.

During the early Pleistocene Epoch some 2 million years ago, alpine glaciers covered high-mountain expanses of the Rockies, Cascades, Sierra Nevada and Alaskan coastal ranges, sculpting glacial troughs, hanging valleys, cirques and other features, including Alaska's deep Pacific fjords. Enormous pluvial lakes covered thousands of square miles in the Great Basin. Cataclysmic floods periodically scoured the inland Pacific Northwest when glacial dams melted and broke. The continental ice sheets diminished the water level of the oceans, exposing a land bridge across the Bering Strait and spurring migration of animals and humans between Asia and North America.

Before about 5000 BC, cool, wet conditions prevailed in what is now the West. A drier, hotter climate subsequently began to dominate. Except for areas of high rainfall along Pacific Coast ranges and the Gulf Coast of Texas, the West today is characterized by aridity, a fact that has colored Western life in innumerable ways. An entirely new legal system called appropriation doctrine was created to manage water resources. The 100th meridian, which runs through the heart of the Great Plains, marks the approximate division between traditional farming and dryland ranching. East of the meridian, annual precipitation averages more than 20in per year; west, rainfall rapidly diminishes, making agriculture impractical without irrigation. Throughout the West today, farming and urban development depend on groundwater withdrawals or massive water-transfer schemes such as the aqueduct that brings Sierra Nevada snowmelt to Los Angeles.

Regions and Climates

COASTAL PACIFIC NORTHWEST

West of the **coastal ranges** of Oregon and Washington mild summers and wet, cool winters encourage the prolific growth of Douglas fir, spruce, hemlock and other evergreens. Broken only by the **Columbia River** and **Strait of Juan de Fuca** between California and Canada, the ranges are drained by short, swift streams. The western slope of the **Olympic Peninsula** receives more than 150in of annual rainfall, creating rain forests in the canyons beneath 7,965ft **Mt. Olympus**. East of the Olympics, the Strait of Juan de Fuca opens into the many-isled harbor of **Puget Sound**. On its eastern shore is Seattle, largest city of the region. The fertile and populous lowland that extends south between the Coast Ranges and Cascades encompasses the city of Portland and, below it, the pastoral **Willamette River Valley.**

THE CASCADES

This barrier of volcanic peaks, stretching over 600mi from Canada to California's **Lassen Peak**, is breached by the Colum-

bia—largest river in the West and a natural highway between the dry Columbia Plateau and the maritime regions to the west. Two dozen distinct peaks present a line of majestic domes, many capped by brilliant glaciers. Highest are Washington's **Mt. Rainier** (14,410ft) and California's **Mt. Shasta** (14,162ft). Snowy winters and mild summers, often doused with showers, keep slopes lush with evergreen forests, a boon to timber and recreation industries. The volcanoes are largely dormant, but scientists monitor signs of life that may escalate to explosive eruptions, as at Lassen in 1914 and **Mt. St. Helens** in 1980. Fewer than 8,000 years ago, the mere blink of an eye in geologic time, massive Mt. Mazama exploded, leaving a gaping crater that filled with snowmelt and rain to form Oregon's **Crater Lake.**

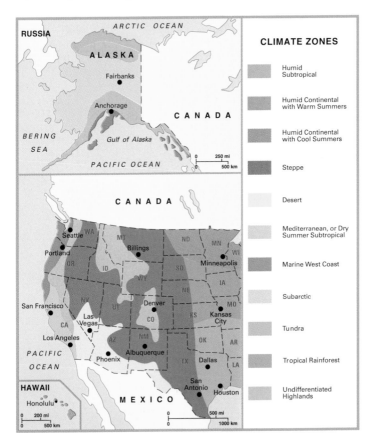

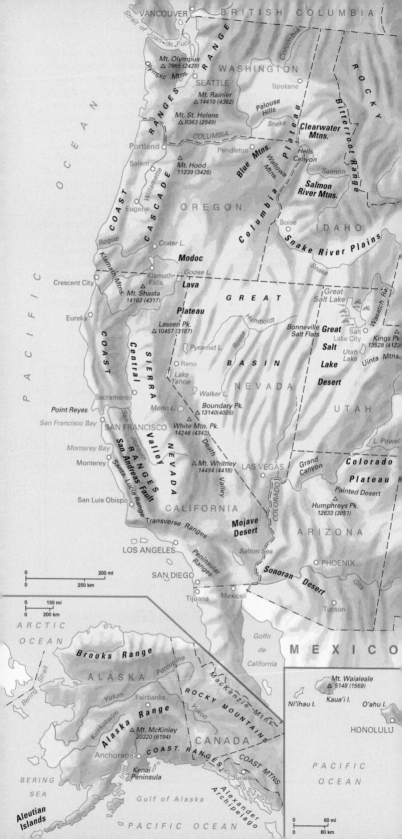

SASKATCHEWAN

ALBERTA

CANADA

MANITOBA

Lake Manitoba

Lake Winnipeg

WINNIPEG

Souris

Great Falls

Fort Peck L.

Missouri

L. Sakakawea

Mouse

Red

Red L.

MONTANA

NORTH DAKOTA

Helena

Crazy Mtns.

Billings

Yellowstone

Bismarck

James

Fargo

MINNESOTA

Powder

△ Granite Pk.
12799 (3901)

Absaroka Range

Big Horn Mtns.

Bighorn

GREAT

Badlands

SOUTH DAKOTA

Lake Oahe

Tetоn Range

Gannett Pk.
△ 13804 (4207)

Black Hills

Harney Pk.
7242 (2207) △

Rapid City

Pierre

Minnesota

WYOMING

Wind River Range

Great Divide Basin

Laramie Mtns.

North Platte

BADLANDS

Cheyenne

MISSOURI

Sioux Falls

Des Moines

Niobrara

NEBRASKA

IOWA

MOUNTAINS

Park Range

Front Range

Cheyenne

South Platte

Sand Hills

Platte

Omaha

Des Moines

Lincoln

Green

Colorado

DENVER

Mt. Elbert
14433 (4399) △

Pikes Pk.
14110 (4301) △

COLORADO

Gunnison

Sangre de Cristo Mtns.

San Juan Mtns.

San Juan

△ Wheeler Pk.
13161 (4014)

Santa Fe

Rio Grande

Albuquerque

Arkansas

KANSAS

Kansas

Kansas City

PLAINS

Wichita

Canadian

Oklahoma City

Espacado

Llano

Estacado

OKLAHOMA

Tulsa

MISSOURI

Jefferson City

MISSOURI

Springfield

Ozark Plateau

Boston Mtns.

Ouachita Mtns.

Little Rock

ARKANSAS

Red

NEW MEXICO

Chihuahuan Desert

Pecos

Lubbock

Odessa

El Paso

Ciudad Juarez

RIO GRANDE

TEXAS

Colorado

Abilene

Fort Worth

DALLAS

Brazos

Trinity

Sabine

LOUISIANA

MISSISSIPPI

Austin

Baton Rouge

Hill Country

SAN ANTONIO

HOUSTON

NEW ORLEANS

GULF COAST

Galveston I.

Matagorda I.

Corpus Christi

Padre I.

Shelf

Gulf of

Continental

Mexico

HAWAI'I

Moloka'i I.

Lana'i I.

Maui I.

Kaho'olawe I.

Hawai'i I.

Mauna Loa
13677 (4169) △

△ Kilauea
4091 (1247)

THE LAVA PLATEAUS

Extensive lava plateaus spread eastward in the rain shadow of the Cascades at 2,000-3,000ft elevation. The **Columbia Plateau** covers most of eastern Washington and parts of Oregon and Idaho. The **Modoc Lava Plateau** covers the northeastern corner of California and part of Oregon. Farther east rise several small ranges, including the Wallowas, which form the western wall of enormous, 8,000ft-deep Hells Canyon of the Snake River. Upstream, the **Snake River Plain** of Idaho and northern Nevada form yet a third extensive lava plateau, tracing its origins not to the Cascades but to clusters of spatter cones and volcanoes south of the Idaho Rockies. The Columbia Plateau and Snake River Plain have proven very fertile under irrigation from the Columbia and Snake Rivers.

COASTAL NORTHERN CALIFORNIA

The 600mi shoreline of northern and central California embraces a climate that varies from moist and mild (near Oregon) to semiarid Mediterranean. Washed by the Alaska Current, the rough, cold Pacific waters are rich in sea life but dangerous for shipping and swimming. The rugged **Coast Ranges** are breached only at the **Golden Gate**, entrance to **San Francisco Bay**. At several points, the coastal mountains yield to narrow strips of fertile lowlands—the agriculturally rich **Napa, Sonoma and Salinas Valleys.** Redwood forests grow profusely in the north and intermittently as far south as **Big Sur.** Drier chaparral, grasses and oaks predominate inland and to the south.

The **San Andreas Fault** parallels the coastline from Point Reyes (north of San Francisco) to Point Concepcion (northwest of Los Angeles), where it cuts inland.

COASTAL SOUTHERN CALIFORNIA

Shielded from the cold waters of the Alaska Current, the southern California coast is relatively warm and hospitable. Rainfall seldom exceeds 15in per year, giving Santa Barbara, Los Angeles and San Diego an enviable Mediterranean climate, free of winter snows except in nearby mountains. The **Los Angeles Basin**, California's largest and most heavily populated coastal plain, is hemmed on the north by the **San Gabriel Mountains**. These are a part of the **Transverse Ranges** that follow the San Andreas Fault eastward from the coast, rendering southern California one of the most seismically active regions of the US. East of the basin are the lower **Santa Ana Mountains**, part of the **Peninsular Ranges** that run south through Mexico's Baja Peninsula.

THE SIERRA NEVADA

Running southeasterly almost 400mi from the Cascades, 50-80mi wide, the fault-block Sierra Nevada rises in an abrupt escarpment on the east more than 2mi above the **Owens Valley** at **Mt. Whitney** (14,494ft)— highest peak in the contiguous US. The lofty range hinders weather systems, creating a rain shadow to its east. Westward slopes descend gradually through alpine high country, evergreen forests and rugged foothills. Streams and rivers run through great canyons to feed the Central Valley, a fecund plain with the richest agricultural land in the US. Remarkable **Yosemite Valley** is the best place to see the Sierra's sculpted peaks and U-shaped glacial valleys. Although it has prodigious winter snowfalls, providing excellent skiing, the Sierra also enjoys plenty of summer sun. **Lake Tahoe** is a year-round recreation center.

GREAT BASIN

East of the Sierra Nevada and west of the Rocky Mountains, the sagebrush-cloaked Great Basin is a high desert of hot, dry summer days, cool nights and cold winters. It is corrugated with parallel fault-block mountain ranges, some above 13,000ft, divided by valleys known as grabens. Escarpments of 5,000-6,000ft are common; below the 11,200ft Panamint Range, **Death Valley** falls to 282ft below sea level, lowest point in the Western Hemisphere. No streams that flow into the Great Basin drain to the sea; they evaporate or disappear into lakes or marshy sinks. Utah's **Great Salt Lake** is a remnant of prehistoric Lake Bonneville, which once covered some 20,000sq mi. For 150 years, mining towns have boomed and busted in this resource-rich, water-poor region. Except for cities at the foot of well-watered mountains—**Reno** in the west, **Salt Lake City** in the east—population density is the lowest of any region of comparable size in the contiguous US.

COLORADO PLATEAU

The nation's highest plateau region covers 130,000sq mi of Utah, Colorado, New Mexico and Arizona at a mile above sea level. Scattered mountain ranges reach as high as 11,000ft, but the most remarkable features are the myriad canyons carved by the **Colorado River** and its tributaries—thousands of feet deep, through eons-old rock strata. More than 25 national parks and monuments—including **Grand Canyon, Zion, Bryce Canyon** and **Canyonlands**—preserve arches, eroded pinnacles, natural bridges and immense gorges in rainbow hues, all carved by wind and water. With an arid climate and a dearth of fruitful soil, the area is home to such hardy plant species as sagebrush, juniper and piñon pine. The ruins of ancient Puebloan cliff villages may still be seen at **Mesa Verde** in Colorado, **Chaco Canyon** in New Mexico, and at the Betatakin and **Canyon de Chelly** ruins on the Navajo Indian Reservation.

THE DESERT SOUTHWEST

North America's largest arid region spreads east from California to Texas, containing three distinct deserts with vague transition zones. The mountainous **Mojave Desert**, which ranges into Death Valley, is home to the Joshua tree, a yucca that may grow 50ft tall. The Mojave fades into the Great Basin north of **Las Vegas** and meshes with the lower-elevation Sonoran Desert through the **Colorado Desert**, west

of the Colorado River. The **Sonoran Desert**, which extends through southern Arizona and northwestern Mexico, boasts a profusion of cacti—including the giant saguaro—dependent on intense monsoon cloudbursts that bring temporary relief from summer heat. Winters are mild and sunny, luring thousands of seasonal residents to Arizona. The large **Chihuahuan Desert** of southern New Mexico, west Texas and northeastern Mexico is a high-elevation desert of parched mountain ranges, extensive grasslands, cold winters and torrid summers. The **Rio Grande** flows through its heart, scribing the huge hook of **Big Bend National Park.**

ROCKY MOUNTAINS

Reaching from New Mexico to Canada, this vast mountain system comprises scores of subranges interposed with high basins, plateaus and plains. Modern resort villages, many founded as mining towns, nestle in broad valleys. A key area for timber, mining, grazing and recreation, the Rockies are perhaps most important as a source of water. Most major rivers of the western US, including the Snake, Columbia, Yellowstone, Missouri, Colorado, Rio Grande, Arkansas and Platte, originate here, flowing to the Pacific Ocean or the Gulf of Mexico from either side of the **Continental Divide**. The Northern Rockies are typified by the highly stratified, precipitous mountains of **Glacier National Park** in Montana, southern bulwark of the Canadian Rockies. Ranges like the Tetons rise above open plains or forested plateaus in the Middle Rockies of southern Montana and Wyoming. In the Southern (Colorado) Rockies are dozens of peaks above 14,000ft in elevation. The Rockies diminish in stature in New Mexico, growing generally more rounded and drier.

GREAT PLAINS

Built of sediment washed eastward from the Rocky Mountain slopes, the plains extend 1,000mi to the Mississippi. Semiarid high plains (the western third) naturally support short grass, ideal for bison and cattle; the tapping of aquifers permits more varied farming. Some areas are so flat that one can discern the curvature of the earth's horizon, but rolling landscapes are more typical. South Dakota's **Black Hills** and **Badlands**, and the Texas **Hill Country**, enhance an otherwise open landscape. Thunderstorms and tornadoes are frequent in summer; fierce blizzards mark the winters.

GULF COAST

Deep, rich soils extend along the Gulf of Mexico coast of Texas to Louisiana. High humidity and rainfall, and temperatures over 90°F, make summers muggy; winters are mild and snow-free. Numerous rivers—chief among them the **Rio Grande** on the US-Mexico border—water this naturally forested swath. Protecting most of the coast is a string of sandy barrier islands and peninsulas, including **Padre, Matagorda and Galveston Islands**, which support rich bird colonies, provide extensive recreational opportunities and help shield the mainland from hurricanes.

ALASKA

The largest US state contains more than 570,000sq mi of forests, mountains, glaciers and tundra. Bounded by the Pacific Ocean (south), Arctic Ocean (north) and Bering Strait (west), Alaska is a massive peninsula. The **Brooks Range** spans its northern tier, dividing oil-rich tundra from interior plains. The **Yukon River** flows through the center, bounded by the Alaska Range and North America's highest summit, 20,320ft **Mt. McKinley.** Southern coastal ranges curve west as the volcanic **Aleutian Islands** and arc east through the **Panhandle**, a fjord-strewn archipelago that shelters the Inside Passage from the heavy seas of the Gulf of Alaska. Although the interior is very cold and dry in winter, summer can bring high temperatures and clouds of insects that attract enormous bird migrations. The Panhandle is cool and wet year-round.

HAWAII

The world's most remote archipelago with a substantial population, Hawaii comprises 132 volcanic islands, of which the seven most southeasterly are largest. The earliest islands surfaced as volcanoes about 5 million years ago; the most recent (the "Big Island" of Hawai'i) is still growing from eruptions at Kilauea Volcano. The **Big Island** embraces the

© National Park Service

Colorado River on the Eastern Side of Grand Canyon National Park

world's largest volcano, 13,677ft Mauna Loa, while the huge dormant volcano of Haleakala dominates the eastern half of nearby Maui. Its tropical climate moderated by trade winds, Hawaii is diverse in weather, foliage and topography, with dramatic differences in rainfall between the wetter windward and drier leeward sides of each island. Mount Waialeale on **Kaua'i** receives as much as 500in of rain in a year, while the Big Island's Ka'u Desert is exceedingly arid. Fine beaches and lush foliage contribute to the islands' tourism fame.

HISTORY

Once a region traversed by nomadic settlers (perhaps 30,000 years ago), the US West was one of the last areas on earth exposed to European colonization. Its complex history of peoples in flux led to a frontier spirit that survives in both myth and reality. Those who live "out West," as the phrase goes in the US, pride themselves on their hardiness and adventurous spirit—and the region's colorful past explains why.

The Early Migrations

Archaeological sites throughout the Americas yield many clues about the origins of Native Americans, but controversy persists over when or by what route they arrived in the New World. Most scientists believe that the majority of ancestral Native Americans walked from northeastern Asia across the Bering land bridge during the Pleistocene Epoch. They would have moved south via an ice-free corridor that opened through Canada during a warming period. An intriguing newer theory postulates that some may have arrived from Siberia in skin boats—some settling in Alaska, most coasting around the maritime glaciers and quickly moving south to settle the more promising temperate coastal spots, then heading inland over succeeding generations.

The first Paleo-Indians apparently arrived 30,000 years ago, finding a land rich in mammoths, camels, large bison, mastodons, prehistoric horses and other big game. Whether the **Paleo-Indians** died out or were absorbed into later populations is unknown, but judging from the scant remains they left, they were anthropologically distinct from contemporary Native Americans. The oldest complete human corpse discovered in North America, the **Spirit Cave mummy** from central Nevada, was radiocarbon-dated to about 9,400 years ago and apparently has no direct descendants. The skeleton of 9,300-year-old **Kennewick Man**, found in a burial site near the Columbia River in Washington, indicates racial links nearer to southern Asian or Polynesian people than to modern Native Americans. Traces of Paleo-Indian flint projectile points have been found at Folsom and Clovis, New Mexico, and elsewhere.

The ancestors of most modern Native Americans began arriving about 15,000 years ago. Descended from northeastern Asian peoples, they also hunted big game, although larger mammals began to disappear as the climate warmed about 10,000 years ago. Succeeding generations of these **hunters and gatherers** fanned out across the Americas, adapting to specific territorial homelands.

A third migration about 9,500 years ago brought the **Athabascan** ancestors of the Navajo, Apache and peoples of the Alaskan and Canadian interior. Ancestors of the **Inuit and Aleut** people arrived in a fourth migration from Siberia about 4,500 years ago, occupying the frigid Arctic and stormy Aleutian Islands.

Hawaiians trace their ancestry to two distinct waves of Polynesian settlers who sailed northward in double-hulled canoes. The first wave arrived between AD 400 and 750, probably from the Marquesas Islands. The second migration, likely from Tahiti, arrived around

1100. These newcomers vanquished the earlier inhabitants and developed a society in which chiefs and hereditary priests held social ascendancy over large classes of farmers and fishermen.

Indian Nations

When Europeans arrived at the end of the 15C, scores of nations occupied America's West. Some were migratory hunters and gatherers; others lived in fixed villages. Erroneously assuming they had landed in the East Indies, the first Europeans called Native inhabitants "Indians." Though scholars may refer to Native Americans or Amerindians, the most common term used today, even among tribal leaders, is "American Indian."

Of the 54 million people that anthropologists estimate were living in the Americas at the time of Columbus' "discovery" in 1492, about 4 million dwelled north of Mexico. At least 300 distinct languages were spoken. West of the Mississippi River, anthropologists count 56 language families, although six predominated. **Uto-Aztecan** prevailed from central Mexico into Texas; it was spoken by the Comanche, Shoshone, Paiute, and the Pueblo cultures of New Mexico. **Siouan** was the dominant language of the Great Plains and Missouri River Valley. **Algonquian** was spoken by the Blackfoot, Cheyenne and Arapaho peoples who had migrated to the northern plains from northeastern woodlands. **Salish** was dominant in the Northwest coastal region. **Athabascan** was spoken in western (but not coastal) Canada and central Alaska, and by Navajo and Apache in the Southwest. **Eskimo-Aleut** was the tongue of the Inuit and Aleut people of Alaska. In California alone, there was a veritable Babel of 120 dialects (of seven separate language families).

Numerous migrations predated European contact in the late 17C. Eastern woodland farmers, including the **Mandan, Omaha, Osage, Pawnee** and **Wichita**, headed to the western prairies between 100 BC and AD 900. Later European settlement along the eastern seaboard spurred the **Lakota** and other nations to the Great Plains. Many tribes, like the Mandan, remained in permanent farming villages after their migration, while others abandoned villages once Spanish horses were introduced in the 17C, choosing a nomadic lifestyle following bison herds. Horses also brought greater leisure and a cultural renaissance to the **Lakota, Crow, Assiniboine, Cheyenne, Comanche, Blackfoot, Arapaho** and other tribes, all of whom developed elaborate religious rites and highly codified warrior rituals.

Mexican farming culture, based on corn, gourds, chiles, beans and squash spread by 300 BC into southern Arizona, where the **Hohokam** irrigated corn. Farming influenced the peoples of the southern Rockies and Colorado Plateau to settle in villages. The **Puebloans** in particular built cliff dwellings and sophisticated towns that maintained elaborate trade links as far distant as the Aztec cities. The **Puebloan** cities were abandoned by AD 1200, perhaps because of drought; they transformed into the modern **Hopi** and **Pueblo** cultures. Their lands were occupied by ancestors of the **Navajo** and **Apache** in the 14C.

The population of California on the eve of the Spanish conquests is estimated to have been over 300,000. With fish and shellfish, game, roots, seeds and acorns readily available, there was never a need for farming, except among **Yuman**-speaking desert tribes of the lower Colorado River. Coastal tribes, including **Ohlone, Chumash, Yurok** and **Pomo**, traded with inland tribes such as **Miwok, Maidu** and **Yokut** on the west side of the Sierra Nevada, who in turn traded eastward with Shoshonean tribes of the Great Basin.

The tribes of the Northwest coast, from northern California to Alaska—including **Chinook, Tillamook, Skokomish** and **Tlingit**—were likewise rich in resources, particularly fish and shellfish. They built sturdy homes, canoes and furniture of cedar, hemlock, spruce, bone and other resources, and cultivated highly refined notions of regarding material goods and social status. Acquisition of material wealth—especially its redistribution at a ceremony known as the potlatch—was a prime determinant of social status.

The inland tribes in the Columbia Basin, especially the Nez Percé, Cayuse and Flathead, migrated from the Pacific coast. They depended upon salmon runs for a major part of their diet, supplementing fish with game and plants, including the nutritious camas bulb. The arrival of the horse to this region in the 18C increased the tribes' mobility and trading contacts.

Despite the ubiquity of the American Indian tribes, new diseases brought by European contact swept the Americas and thinned Native populations as much as 90 percent. This was perhaps the most lethal pandemic ever visited upon human beings.

European Inroads

The conquest of the Aztec empire in 1521 by **Hernán Cortés** (1485-1547) enormously enriched the Spanish treas-ury and plunged the Spanish government into colonization of their vast new territories in the New World. Spanish exploration of North America followed rumors of gold carried back to Mexico in 1536 by **Alvar Núñez Cabeza de Vaca** (c.1490-1557), A succession of explorers penetrated the unknown land seeking treasures in the mythical Seven Cities of Cibola—most prominently the expeditions of **Hernando de Soto** (1496-1542), who entered Oklahoma from the east in 1541, and **Francisco Vásquez de Coronado** (1510-54). Coronado marched north from Mexico in 1540, wreaking mayhem among the Pueblos, pushing as far north as the Grand Canyon and possibly as far east as Kansas, but failing to find another Aztec or Inca empire.

Spain allowed its colonization of New Mexico and California to languish until **Sir Francis Drake** (c.1540-96) landed on California's north coast and claimed it for England in 1579. That sparked a northward expansion of Spanish frontiers. Throughout the 17C, expansion of Span-

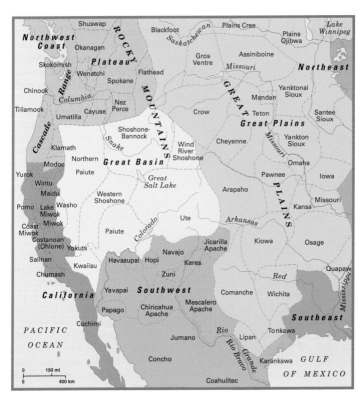

ish settlements—and with them, the forced conversion of Indians to Catholicism—progressed with checkered success throughout the Rio Grande Valley. The colonies survived despite periodic setbacks including the devastating **Pueblo Revolt of 1680**, when Indians drove the Spanish from New Mexico for more than a decade. Spanish policy thereafter was reformed to permit native religious practices to continue, and the culture of New Mexico developed into a blend of Spanish and Pueblo, with its capital at **Santa Fe.**

The French, meanwhile, were scouring the USA West for a different treasure: fur pelts. The French seized the key to the Great Plains in the 17C by building trading posts along the Mississippi River at St. Louis and other strategic points. They called the region Louisiana after King Louis XIV. By 1682, when **René-Robert Cavalier de la Salle** (1643-87) navigated the river to its mouth and claimed the Mississippi and its tributaries for France, the vast territory stretched from Canada to the Gulf of Mexico. Separating Florida from Mexico, it prompted a Spanish frenzy to colonize Texas.

Over the next half century, French traders explored every western tributary to the Rockies, even mounting an expedition to Santa Fe in 1739. The French did not pursue a vigorous colonization of Louisiana, however, so the tribes of the Great Plains remained unaffected by their paper affiliation with the French empire. Territorial settlements developed a Creole character born of French, African slave and Native American populations. Greater numbers of American adventurers arrived after 1763, when the **Treaty of Paris**—ending the French and Indian War—extended the borders of British colonies from the Atlantic Ocean to the Mississippi River. Neglected for more than a century, Spain's claims to Alta (Upper) California were revived by fears of foreign incursions. Under **Aleksei Chirikov** (1703-48) and Dane **Vitus Bering** (1681-1741), Russians began probing Alaskan waters in 1728, sparking an influx of fur hunters and fortified colonies along that coast. English ships also investigated the Pacific: **James Cook** (1728-79) claimed British Columbia for England in 1768. Cook subsequently visited the Pacific Northwest and Hawaii in 1778, and **George Vancouver** (1757-98) mapped the Canadian coast in 1792-94.

Goaded into action, a Spanish expedition organized by Padre **Junípero Serra** (1713-84) and **Gaspar de Portolá** (c.1723-86) pushed, by land and sea, to San Diego harbor, where Serra dedicated the first of California's 21 missions on July 16, 1769. Over the next decade, a string of missions, pueblos and presidios was erected along a coastal strip that stretched from San Diego to San Francisco Bay, with a provincial capital at Monterey.

Louisiana Purchase

The westward expansion of the US in the late 17C and 18C—both as a collection of British colonies and as an independent republic after 1776—inexorably progressed despite warfare with Native Americans and complex political and military maneuvering among European powers in North America. The rallying cry that justified and even glorified this expansion was **"Manifest Destiny,"** the idea that the US was ordained by divine right to push its borders to the

Annual Inter-Tribal Indian Ceremony, New Mexico

Courtesy of the New Mexico Tourism Department/Gary Romero

Pacific. European conflict enabled the single greatest stroke in this expansion when a shortage of funds convinced Napoléon to sell Louisiana to the US for about $15 million in 1803 to support his war against Great Britain.

Pressed as much by personal curiosity as national interest, President Thomas Jefferson selected his personal secretary, **Meriwether Lewis** (1774-1809), to head an exploratory expedition, and Lewis invited his boyhood friend, career soldier **William Clark** (1770-1838), as co-leader. Instructed to promote trade with the Indians, observe flora and fauna, map major rivers and their sources, and make records of soils, minerals and climate, the Corps of Discovery set course up the Missouri River on May 14, 1804, with a party of seasoned frontiersmen. Wintering at a Mandan village in what is now North Dakota, they enlisted a French Canadian trapper, Toussaint Charbonneau, as an interpreter for their journey. Charbonneau's Shoshone wife, **Sacagawea** (c.1786-1812), unexpectedly proved a far greater asset. The presence of a native woman signaled to western tribes that this was not a war party. Sacagawea was instrumental in obtaining horses when the expedition dramatically encountered a Shoshone tribe, led by her own brother, near the Continental Divide. After a strenuous descent from the Rockies, Lewis and Clark arrived at the Pacific Ocean on November 7, 1805. They wintered at the mouth of the Columbia River and returned to St. Louis in September 1806, having lost only one man to appendicitis.

The extraordinary success of Lewis and Clark overshadowed other government-funded forays into the West. After leading an expedition to the upper Mississippi in 1805-06, **Zebulon Pike** (1779-1813) investigated the Colorado Front Range headwaters of the Arkansas and Red Rivers; another party, led by Major **Stephen H. Long** (1784-1864), ascended the Platte River and looped back through the high plains; Long branded the region "the Great American Desert."

Others headed west without government support, seeking adventure and profit from the burgeoning fur trade. These "mountain men" sought buffalo robes, bear and deer hides, the pelts of otter and fox, and especially beaver furs, which earned high prices in Chinese and European markets. Among them was **John Colter** (c.1774-1813), who left the eastbound Lewis and Clark party and became the first person to describe the Yellowstone country. **Jedediah Smith** (1799-1831) was a Bible-toting teetotaler who blazed trails across the Great Basin to California and north to the Columbia River. Others included **Kit Carson** (1809-68), **Jim Bridger** (1804-81), **Jim Beckwourth** (c.1800-66) and **Joe Walker** (1798-1876). Living in extreme isolation and independence, these men became thoroughly acquainted with the West, blazing the first transcontinental trails or bringing long-established Indian trails to the attention of travelers. After Mexico overthrew Spanish rule in 1821, Santa Fe began welcoming American traders. **William Becknell** (c.1790-1865) became the first American to push wagons through the plains to the New Mexico outpost, opening the **Santa Fe Trail** and earning large profits by exchanging hardware and dry goods for livestock.

The fur trade heated up on the Pacific slope, too, after New Englander **Robert Gray** (1755-1806) made a fortune on a round-the-world voyage, gathering pelts along the Northwest coast in 1789 and selling them in China for vast profits. The name of his ship, *Columbia*, was bestowed upon the Northwest's great river. As New England merchants pushed deeply into the China trade, clipper ships called at San Diego, Santa Barbara, Monterey and San Francisco Bay, resupplying and trading for tallow and cowhides. California's enviable climate and excellent harbors became common knowledge along the Eastern seaboard after **Richard Henry Dana** published his best-seller, *Two Years Before the Mast* (1840).

Yankees also reaped great profits in the Pacific from hunting whales, the primary source of lamp oil in the mid-19C. A particularly rich hunting ground was the Hawaiian Islands. Soon after Captain Cook had introduced the remote archipelago (dubbed the "Sandwich Isles") to the world, **King Kamehameha I** (c.1758-1819) unified the islands in 1795. Whaling rapidly became the economic mainstay, increasing the kingdom's reliance on foreign advisers while enabling hundreds of sturdy Hawaiian sailors to ship out. The whalers' most insidious contributions to local culture were smallpox, syphilis and other epidemics that ravaged the indigenous population, hewing their numbers from 300,000 at the time of Cook's visit to 54,000 a century later.

The **Indian Removal Act of 1830** saw the Cherokee, Chickasaw, Choctaw, Creek and Seminole nations uprooted from their homelands in the South and forced to march to the **Indian Territory**, now Oklahoma. Ironically known as the Five Civilized Tribes for their adoption of American clothing and agricultural methods, the populations were decimated by the internment and grueling march, since referred to by the Cherokee tribe as the "Trail of Tears." Moved by a delegation of Flathead Indians that arrived in St. Louis in 1831 seeking information on Christianity, Methodist and Presbyterian missionaries set out for the isolated Oregon Country. A mission near modern Walla Walla, Washington, was built by **Marcus Whitman** (1804-47); in 1836, his wife, **Narcissa Whitman**, and her companion, **Eliza Spaulding**, became the first American women to cross the continent.

Pioneer Movement

The three Western destinations that most appealed to early pioneers were each claimed by a foreign nation. The promised land in the 1830s was Texas, then governed by Mexico. In the 1840s, new streams of pioneers set out for the Oregon Country, jointly (though sparsely) occupied by Britain and the US. Other pioneers set their sights on California, a neglected Mexican outpost.

Anglo-American traders and squatters had been unwelcome residents of Texas since the late 18C. Most Americans flooding into Texas had no intention whatsoever of respecting Mexican law or culture. Anglo Texans proved so

assertive of their independence that political tensions had degenerated to skirmishes, and Mexico resolved to put down the rebellion. In 1836, Mexican General **Antonio López de Santa Anna** (1794-1876) took 4,000 troops to San Antonio and slaughtered a party of insurrectionists at a former mission, the Alamo. Santa Anna then marched east to San Jacinto, near modern Houston, to dispatch another small Texas army, this one led by **Sam Houston** (1793-1863). Rallying under the battle cry "Remember the Alamo!" the Texans captured Santa Anna, defeating his troops and winning their independence. The new Republic of Texas elected Sam Houston as its president. Beset by debt, Indian hostilities and conflict with a Mexico unwilling to recognize its independence, Texas was steered by Houston toward statehood in 1845.

Oregon proved a less contentious acquisition. With its salubrious climate and soil, the Oregon Country's graces were well advertised in the East. Convoys of Conestoga wagons began journeying west from Independence, Missouri, in 1842, guided by scouts familiar with a route soon known as the **Oregon Trail**. Stretching some 2,000mi, the Oregon Trail followed the Platte River across Nebraska; surmounted the Continental Divide at broad South Pass, between Fort Laramie and Fort Bridger; then crossed the Snake River Plain and Blue Mountains to Whitman's Walla Walla mission. A final stretch down the Columbia River brought tired travelers to the lush Willamette River Valley. In 1843, the Oregon Country petitioned Congress for protection from British claims and marauding Indians. In 1846, the US and Britain compromised on the 49th parallel as their boundary. The slaughter of Whitman and his fellow missionaries by Indians in 1847 provoked another demand for federal protection, and in 1848 the Oregon Territory was formally established.

Some parties of transcontinental migrants left the Oregon Trail for California. The Mexican residents of California, known as **Californios**, were a self-sufficient lot; they received scant attention from Mexico's government, which

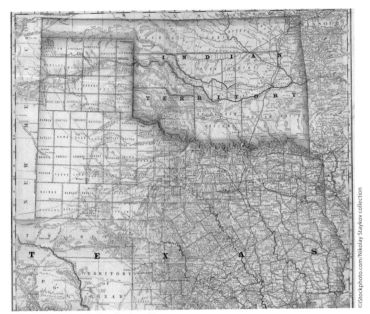
Nineteenth Century Indian Territory Map

©iStockphoto.com/Nikolay Staykov collection

was content to let the landholders rule themselves. A growing population of Yankees and other foreigners were living in Monterey and other settlements, having jumped ship, adopted the Catholic religion and become naturalized Mexican citizens. Many became prominent in Californio society.

Among the foreign residents was **John Augustus Sutter** (1803-80), a Swiss adventurer with vast land grants along the American River in the Sacramento Valley. Sutter entertained many travelers and immigrants at his walled fort, including US Army surveyor **John C. Frémont** (1813-90) after his exhausting 1844 winter crossing of the Sierra Nevada. Frémont's published report of his California journey became the standard guidebook for westbound travelers.

After Texas gained statehood, the resulting war with Mexico eventually brought the US the land that is today Arizona and New Mexico. A contemporaneous insurgent movement in California had declared the area an independent republic, but the rebels welcomed US help in the form of a military expedition led by General **Stephen Kearny** (1794-1848). By the end of hostilities in 1848, Texas was safely in US hands, along with the entire West all the way to Los Angeles, then a sleepy trading village, and San Diego.

The Mormons

Even before it was relinquished by Mexico, the Great Basin already had been proclaimed the State of Deseret by a sect of pioneers who called themselves Latter-day Saints, or Mormons. The Church of Jesus Christ of Latter-day Saints was founded in 1830 in New York by **Joseph Smith** (1805-44). His zealous missionary work reaped new members, but he antagonized many others with his determined espousal of Old Testament views on polygamy and by his adherence to the unorthodox *Book of Mormon*; attributed to divine revelation, it propounded that Jesus had taught in North America after his biblical resurrection. When the sect moved West to facilitate its missionary work, the Mormons were violently driven from Ohio to Missouri to Illinois, where Smith was murdered by an armed mob. **Brigham Young** (1801-77) assumed the role of prophet and leader.

Young led his people to the Great Salt Lake Valley in 1847. Young directed the construction of **Salt Lake City**; he returned East to bring more Mormon immigrants, encouraged others from Europe, and exhorted all to bring the tools, seeds and zeal they would need to establish a self-sufficient nation in a hard land. Thousands made the trek across the Plains and Rockies in ensuing decades, swelling the closely knit population and making the desert bloom with irrigation water from the Wasatch Mountains.

The Utah Territory was established in 1850, but friction soon developed over questions of loyalty. The institution of polygamy, and rumors of Mormon-inspired Indian uprisings, raised alarm in the East. Convinced of impending rebellion, the US government in 1857 ordered 2,500 troops to march to Utah to install a new governor to replace Young. Young portrayed the invasion as a tool of Mormon persecution. He declared martial law, mobilized a militia, recalled distant Mormon outposts, burned down Fort Bridger in Wyoming, fortified the west-ern boundary of the Utah Territory, and even ordered Mormons to be ready to torch their own settlements. Tensions peaked when zealots slaughtered a party of non-Mormon pioneers at the Mountain Meadow Massacre in south-ern Utah. But with both sides perched on the brink of disaster, common sense prevailed, and diplomats negotiated a peaceful resolution.

Gold and Silver Rushes

A few weeks before the formal peace with Mexico in 1848, flecks of gold were discovered in the sand at John Sutter's lumber mill on California's American River. The news spread like wildfire. The next year, **Forty-Niners** began pouring by land and sea into California from the eastern US, Europe, Australia, Asia, Mexico and South America. In just weeks, the port city of San Francisco grew from a sleepy village of 800 to a cosmopolitan hive of 90,000. In January 1849 alone, 61 vessels arrived at San Francisco Bay from the Eastern seaboard

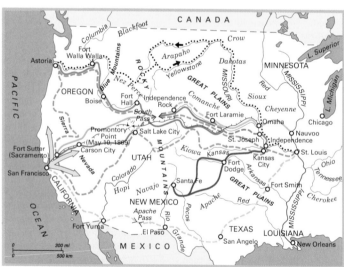

HISTORIC TRAILS

..... Lewis and Clark Expedition (1803-1806)	——— Oregon Trail	——— Pony Express
– – – Charles Frémont Expedition (1842-1844)	——— Mormon Trail	– – – Butterfield Overland Trail
⇨ The California Gold Rush (1848)	——— California Trail	–+–+– Union Pacific Railroad
	——— Santa Fe Trail	–†–†– Central Pacific Railroad

The boundaries shown between the United States, Mexico and Canada represent the present-day boundaries

©iStockphoto.com/Phil Morley

A Pile of Old Gold Pans

after sailing around stormy Cape Horn. As passengers and crews set off for the gold mines, abandoned ships rotted or were dragged ashore to serve as hotels, warehouses and offices. Meanwhile, thousands of prospectors—as well as tradesmen, money lenders, innkeepers, teamsters, preachers, gamblers, gunslingers and prostitutes—set out overland along the Oregon, California and Santa Fe Trails.

Mining camps with names like Rough and Ready, Hangtown, Poker Flat and Murderers Bar sprang up in the canyons and foothills, and California's Caucasian population mushroomed from 15,000 in 1848 to almost 100,000 in 1850, when California joined the Union as the 31st state. The frenetic activity died down toward the end of the 1850s with the decline of surface gold; individual gold miners gave way to mining corporations, companies with stockholders and the capital to build and operate hard-rock, dredging and hydraulic mining operations. Thousands of fortune hunters returned home or settled into new opportunities in California, where ranching, farming, construction, and other jobs became increasingly available.

The California gold rush was the archetype of a series of mining rushes that marked the West for the next 60 years, instantly peopling remote corners with makeshift towns. Strikes in Colorado and Nevada started new stampedes just as the California rush was settling down. The Pikes Peak gold rush hit pay dirt in 1858; the nearby city of **Denver** was platted by speculators that winter, and by spring 1859 a real rush was on. New lodes were discovered higher in the Rockies; Denver's first newspaper, *The Rocky Mountain News*, began publication in April, and a US mint opened the following year. Hostile confrontations with Indians increased; reservations were established deeper into the plains, and Indians were rounded up in campaigns that degenerated into the full-blown **Indian Wars**. Numerous smaller strikes flared up throughout the West, from Arizona to Montana and South Dakota.

The 1859 discovery of Nevada's vast **Comstock Lode** of silver and gold produced a very different kind of mining rush. The difficulties of mining ore required capital investment and sophisticated engineering. Speculators from California bought up stock in the richest mines, while San Francisco merchants, farmers and transport companies earned good profits shipping supplies, food and people to the town that grew atop the mines, Virginia City. As newly minted millionaires built elegant mansions atop Nob Hill in San Francisco, Virginia City emerged as the first truly industrialized city west of the Mississippi.

Linking East and West

The first overland transcontinental mail and passenger-coach service was contracted in 1857 to **John Butterfield, William G. Fargo & Associates**, who avoided the snows of the Rockies using a route from St. Louis and Memphis to El Paso, Tucson and Los Angeles. Faster service came with the **Pony Express**, which transported express mail by relays from St. Joseph, Missouri, to Sacramento, California, and by ship to San Francisco. Riding in 75mi increments, day and night, changing ponies at stations spaced every 10-15mi, a team of riders could transport the mail pouch in 10 days. The route grew shorter as telegraph lines edged across America; they joined in 1861.

The West escaped the ravages of the Civil War, save for a few small skirmishes. The US government, eager to ensure a steady flow of California gold and Comstock silver during the war, pushed for a transcontinental railroad that would link California and Nevada with the East Coast. As incentive, Congress offered land grants and subsidies to rail companies for every mile of track laid. Two companies formed to build lines from opposite ends: the **Central Pacific** eastward from California and the **Union Pacific** westward from Missouri.

Financiers **Collis P. Huntington** (1821-1900), **Mark Hopkins** (1814-78), **Charles Crocker** (1822-88) and **Leland Stanford** (1824-93)—who became known as "The Big Four"—established the Central Pacific in 1861. Construction over the most difficult sections of the Sierra's Donner Pass depended heavily upon 15,000 laborers from China, who laid the track. The Union Pacific, employing large numbers of Irish, set out across the Great Plains under chief engineer **Grenville Dodge** (1831-1916). Despite Indian resistance, the rolling terrain permitted faster progress than in the Far West. The project was known as "Hell on Wheels," both for its rambunctious crews and for the army of rascally camp followers, saloons, gambling dens and brothels that flourished in their wake. The two crews joined east and west with the **Golden Spike** at Promontory Point, Utah, on May 10, 1869.

The railroads prospered, and their boards and presidents acquired great political and economic clout. By deftly wielding their vast real-estate grants, these corporations could determine

A Herd of Bison

PhotoDisc, Inc

where cities and towns would be built, and which communities could prosper. The **Northern Pacific** opened the Dakota Territory and Montana to easier settlement by linking Minnesota with Portland, Oregon, in 1883, and with Seattle in 1887. The **Southern Pacific** extended a line from New Orleans to Los Angeles and San Francisco.

The Cattle Industry

The Great Plains obviously were ideal for livestock. Herds of **bison** numbered perhaps 50 million prior to the arrival of Europeans. However, the buffalo were nearly wiped out in an orgy of slaughter that climaxed in the 1870s, when animals were wantonly killed from passing trains or massacred en masse for their hides. Their extermination crushed the independence of the Indians, but it also opened the ranges for cattle. Ironically, three decades later US buffalo were saved from extinction partly through the efforts of former hunters such as Buffalo Bill (see p 459) and Theodore Roosevelt.

The **longhorn range cattle** of the Texas plains were descended from breeds brought north from Mexico in the late 17C. Most of the techniques of livestock husbandry used in 19C Texas likewise were developed from methods used in Spanish New Mexico: Cattle were grazed on open ranges, gathered by roping from horseback in annual roundups, branded and driven to market in herds. Even the clothing, saddle and lingo of the Anglo cattle industry were largely adapted from the *vaqueros*.

After the Civil War, with beef in Northern markets earning 10 times as much as on the Southern plains, enterprising Texans contrived a scheme to round up wild cattle. They were driven to railheads and shipped to stockyards and meat-packing plants in Chicago, Omaha and Kansas City, thence to the Northeast. Crews of cowboys branded and drove the cattle along what soon became well-established routes, including the **Chisholm, Goodnight-Loving,** **Sedalia** and **Western trails**. The drives were fraught with danger and discomfort. Rivers had to be forded; bandits, hostile Indians, wildfires, disease and extreme weather conditions took their toll.

After weeks in the saddle, cowboys were ecstatic to return to some semblance of civilization. The arrival of a cattle drive in a terminal town—among them Fort Worth, Texas; Cheyenne, Wyoming; Wichita, Abilene and Dodge City, Kansas—was marked by days and nights of frantic celebration and wild roughhousing by the pleasure-starved wranglers. The excitement and ready money in cow towns attracted saloon keepers, prostitutes, gamblers and various riffraff to service or fleece the cowboys. Gunplay was common, giving rise to a tough breed of lawmen who sometimes were hard to distinguish from hired gunslingers. Some names have become part of Western legend: **Wyatt Earp** (1848-1929), **William Barclay "Bat" Masterson** (1853-1921), **James Butler "Wild Bill" Hickok** (1837-76).

Many early Texas cattlemen—including **Jesse Chisholm** (1805-68), **John Chisum** (1824-84) and **Charles Goodnight** (1836-1929)—grew wealthy from the cattle drives and staked out huge ranches on the plains. Soon the introduction of barbed wire in the 1870s offered a practical method of fencing large, treeless areas. Consolidation of the cattle industry on large ranches encouraged the formation of cooperative organizations to fight rustlers, look after business interests and make rules governing roundups, quarantines, branding and mavericks (unbranded stray cattle). As the industry became more regulated, it attracted well-moneyed Eastern and European investors. Powerful organizations and cattlemen sometimes tried vigilantism to hinder "nesters" (homesteaders) and small ranchers from gaining footholds. Dangerous and widespread range wars, such as New Mexico's 1878 Lincoln County War, brought notoriety to gunmen like **William "Billy the Kid" Bonney** (c.1859-81).

The Indian Wars

As ever-growing numbers of miners, cattlemen, railroad builders, soldiers and pioneers pushed across the Great Plains and Rockies, overrunning what had been designated "Indian land," the federal government sought to redraw the boundaries of native homelands. Reservations for the Cheyenne, Arapaho, Blackfoot, Sioux, Crow and other tribes were reduced in size and placed as far as possible from railways and settlements. The Army set about enforcing the tribes' removal to the reservations. As buffalo herds dwindled, and with federal troops fighting the Civil War in the East, some tribes stepped up depredations against settlements in the high plains.

When one renegade band of Cheyenne sued for peace in 1864, a Colorado militia force led by Methodist minister John Chivington ambushed their camp, killing more than 300 men, women and children in what became known as the **Sand Creek Massacre**. Already angered by the decimation of bison herds, by countless trespasses on their hunting grounds and by broken treaties, the massacre further convinced Native Americans from Texas to Montana that they must fight to survive. The 1870s saw repeated insurrections. Among the bloodiest were the 1874-75 Red River War, staged by Comanche and Kiowa led by **Quanah Parker** (c.1845-1911); and the four-month, 1,200mi odyssey of the Nez Percé under **Chief Joseph** (c.1840-1904), who was determined not to be confined to a reservation.

The Sioux offered the most dogged resistance on the Great Plains. After the Bozeman Trail to Montana mines was cut through Sioux hunting grounds east of the Big Horn Mountains, **Red Cloud** (1822-1909) led the tribe in an 1866 campaign that forced the US Army to surrender and abandon Fort Phil Kearny. Red Cloud also secured guarantees for South Dakota's sacred Black Hills in exchange for his promise to never again go to war against the US. But when prospectors discovered gold in the Black Hills in 1874 and a full-blown gold rush ensued, the Sioux returned to war under **Crazy Horse** (c.1842-77) and **Sitting Bull** (1831-90).

Peace negotiations failed dismally. As the Sioux and their Cheyenne allies rode west toward the Big Horns, pursued by the Army, they established camp on the Little Bighorn River of Montana. When Lt. Col. **George Armstrong Custer** (1839-76) and his 7th Cavalry attacked without ascertaining the Indians' full force, he and all 225 of his troops, plus another 47 under command of other officers, were killed. A single horse survived what became known as "Custer's Last Stand." The nation was shocked. The Indians could not exploit their resounding victory, however. With winter they were forced to return to the reservation.

Another resilient people were the Apaches, who for centuries raided their Indian neighbors and played havoc with Spanish and Mexican settlers. Attacks continued against Americans in the 1850s and 1860s, growing more severe during the Civil War. Aided by familiar terrain and harsh climate, the Apaches—under such leaders as **Cochise** (c.1812-1874) and **Geronimo** (c.1829-1909)—for decades were able to evade Army campaigns by retreating into mountain strongholds.

In the 1880s, the messianic **Ghost Dance** religious movement swept from California to the Dakotas. Originating among the Paiutes, the cult exhorted followers to dance trance-like in a circle to commune with dead ancestors. The cult promised the resurrection of ancestors and old ways, a resurgence of the buffalo and the disappearance of the whites. In 1890, when they became alarmed by dances on the Pine Ridge Reservation in South Dakota, soldiers tried to disarm the Sioux, who fled into the nearby Badlands. In an ensuing melée, soldiers opened fire and killed about 250 men, women and children. The **Wounded Knee Massacre** was the last major conflict of the Indian Wars.

White settlers also pressured the government to open for settlement some former reservation lands of Oklahoma, seized from the Indians as Civil War reparation for their support of the Confederacy. In several government-organized land runs, the first in 1889, contenders for homesteads were assembled on the edge of each new tract and released en masse at an appointed hour. Numbering as many as 100,000 when the 6-million-acre **Cherokee Outlet** was opened in 1893, emigrants fanned out at full speed in wagons and buggies. They overran each new territory within hours, seizing farmsteads and city lots in Oklahoma City, Norman, Guthrie and other settlements that vaulted to life overnight.

The unsettled West provided ample space for criminals and unsociable elements to hide from the law. Known for robbing coaches, trains and banks, **Jesse James** (1847-82), the four **Dalton Brothers** (b.1861-71) and the Hole-in-the-Wall Gang of **Robert "Butch Cassidy" Parker** (1866-1909?) and **Harry "Sundance Kid" Longabaugh** (1870-1909?) were among the nefarious felons. As settlements grew, however, so did demand for law and order. The frontier sheriff or marshal enforced laws against carrying firearms in towns, an unglamorous and sometimes-risky task that contributed enormously to social order.

Acquisition of Alaska and Hawaii

Russia sold its vast North American territories to the US government for $7.2 million in 1867. Secretary of State **William Seward** (1801-72) negotiated the purchase, for which he was ridiculed by a handful of politicians and newspapermen. Few settlers ventured to Alaska until 1897-98, after gold was discovered on a tributary of the Klondike River in Canada's neighboring Yukon Territory, setting off the last of the West's gold rushes. Some 100,000 stampeding prospectors poured off steamships from Seattle and San Francisco, setting off on the Chilkoot Trail. Many were unprepared for the exertion, isolation or severe climate; fewer than half arrived at the gold fields. Hardy survivors—known thereafter as Sourdoughs for the starter they used to leaven camp bread—went on to strike gold in the Yukon and Tanana River Valleys, and in far-western Alaska at Nome.

Half an ocean away, Hawaii by the mid-19C boasted one of the world's highest English literacy rates, the fruit of New England missionaries. Enormous blocks of land were bought up by Americans and other foreigners and consolidated into sugar plantations. Thousands of contract laborers from China, and later from Japan, Korea, the Philippines and Portugal, met labor demands. When Hawaiian sugar was granted duty-free access to the US market in 1874, American business interests in Honolulu began to clamor for more power in the government.

In 1887, businessmen induced King **David Kalakaua** (1836-91) to adopt a constitution that reduced him to a figurehead. An attempted palace coup to replace the weakened king with his sister, **Liliuokalani** (1838-1917), was suppressed by US Marines. When Liliuokalani became queen by succession in 1891, her efforts to regain true power prompted a prominent newspaperman, Lorin Thurston, to lead the bloodless "Revolution" of 1893, establishing the **Republic of Hawaii.** Calls for US annexation were answered in 1898, and Hawaii achieved territorial status in 1900.

The Preservation Movement

The closing of the frontier brought some hard recognition that the resources of

A Tired Prospector, Alaska, 1905

©KLGO archives/NPS

the West, once seemingly boundless, were not inexhaustible. Water produced the longest and most intractable dispute; indeed, battles still rage today. The Mormons had shown that irrigation could accommodate a deficiency in rainfall and make the desert bloom. What's known as "appropriation doctrine" was created to govern water. Whoever first captured water and put it to use had the right to it, no matter where it originated; the individual (or organization) owns the right to the water, not the water itself. This system is often explained with the now-axiomatic phrases "Use it or lose it" and "First in time, first in right." As a result, vast networks of reservoirs and canals now distribute immense amounts of water hundreds of miles from its natural paths.

The dangers of unmanaged resource exploitation were pointed out early by **John Wesley Powell** (1834-1902). A naturalist who had lost his arm as an artillery battery commander in the Civil War, Powell achieved near-legendary status by twice leading wooden-boat expeditions through the rugged drainage of the Colorado River, including the Grand Canyon, the last major unexplored region of the continental US. Sponsored by the Smithsonian Institution, Powell's first expedition descended the Green and Colorado Rivers on dories in 1869. Powell was instrumental in creating the US Geological Survey, an agency he later headed. His respect for the miracles wrought by irrigation was tempered by warnings that the public lands of the West be rationally managed to conserve water and other resources.

The federal government vastly expanded water redistribution in the 20C by sponsoring massive "reclamation" projects, constructing dams, reservoirs, canals and irrigation systems that turned California's Central Valley into the richest agricultural region in the world. Large dams built on the Columbia, Snake, Colorado, Missouri, Arkansas and other Western rivers supply electricity and channel water for public consumption, agriculture and recreation. On the Great Plains, aquifers were tapped for irrigation; coupled with the development of dry-farming techniques in the late 19C, the plains states became major producers of wheat and other grains.

Reclamation projects, however, also enabled the sprawl of vast urban tracts on arid lands. The explosive growth of Los Angeles after the capture of Owens River water in the early 20C was later followed by the runaway expansions of Las Vegas and Phoenix, beginning in the 1970s.

Beginning in the late 19C, meanwhile, large natural areas came under the protective umbrella of the US government. The paintings and photographs of **Thomas Moran** and **William Henry Jackson**, which accompanied the first detailed descriptions of the wondrous Yellowstone Country, provoked public interest and spurred Congress to create the world's first national park in 1872. Protection for California's giant sequoias and peerless Yosemite Valley followed in 1890, inspired by the writings of **John Muir** (1838-1914). The conservation movement found a friend in President **Theodore Roosevelt** (1858-1919), whose own experiences on a North Dakota ranch had brought him joy and robust health. Though a Division of Forestry had been established in the 1870s, Roosevelt quadrupled the amount of national forest land, gave a boost to the creation of national parks and monuments in the early 20C, and created the vast federal system of wildlife refuges.

The National Park Service today manages 85 million acres (133,000sq mi) of parklands, while another 100 million acres (156,000sq mi) are protected by the US Fish and Wildlife Service as wildlife refuges. Managed for commerce, recreation and environmental purposes are 193 million acres (301,000sq mi) of national forest and 258 million acres (403,000sq mi) of public domain under the Bureau of Land Management (BLM). These lands lie, overwhelmingly, in western states.

The West Grows Up

As the percentage of women in the Western population increased, so did family life and the stability it represented. Drinking and gambling had been conspicuous features of the overwhelmingly male societies of mining settlements, lumber camps and cow towns. A scarcity of females has been cited as one reason the **women's suffrage movement** achieved its earliest successes in the Rocky Mountains, where male voters conceivably hoped enfranchisement might attract more women settlers. Wyoming Territory was the first US entity to grant women the vote, in 1869; it was followed by Utah in 1870, Colorado in 1893 and Idaho in 1896.

Government regulation and intervention transformed the West in the 20c. The Great Depression of 1929 and the 1930s coincided with one of the historically worst droughts on the Great Plains. As crops failed, winds blew away the parched topsoil and the region became known as the **Dust Bowl.** Thousands of farmers and ranchers faced bankruptcy. Foreclosures sent up to 400,000 migrant farmers, many from Oklahoma, in search of work to California (where they were labeled Okies). President **Franklin Roosevelt** (1882-1945) took revolutionary action with his New Deal, introducing bold programs to control erosion, regulate farm production to raise agricultural prices, provide drought relief, and fund huge reclamation and irrigation projects. The **Civilian Conservation Corps** (CCC) employed thousands in public construction projects. Federal and state governments spent millions building upgrading roads and bridges, a program that facilitated the growth of tourism throughout the West.

World War II heralded unprecedented growth and change. Burgeoning shipyards and war industries brought thousands of workers to Pacific Coast cities from other parts of the US. The Army and Navy established huge training bases and missile-testing ranges in the wide-open desert and plateau lands, while Alaska and Hawaii boomed with an influx of military personnel. The **aerospace industry** took root in southern California, Seattle and later Houston, bringing lucrative defense contracts, demands for labor, government jobs and subsidies for universities.

The booming post-war economy brought huge growth, especially in California, which overtook New York as the most populous state in the 1960s. Fueled by Asian and Latin American immigration, the demographic makeup of Western cities changed dramatically; Los Angeles and San Francisco became the most ethnically diverse regions of the US. Growth also brought many problems long associated with Eastern cities—scarce housing, urban blight, crime, poverty, traffic jams and pollution. Politically, the Pacific coastal areas became among the most liberal in the nation, while the Western hinterland has remained more politically conservative.

The **high-technology** revolution brought great wealth to California, major Northwest cities (at one time Seattle had 10,000 residents with at least $1 million of Microsoft stock) and other areas. It also created a trend that worries preservation-minded inland Westerners: Telecommuters now may live wherever they wish, instead of being concentrated where jobs dictate. Many scenic areas, especially near public recreation lands, have become highly desirable real estate: in 2007, the median asking price for a single-family residence in Jackson Hole, Wyoming was $2.5 million; and the Bend, OR, area grew an astounding 65 percent from 1996-2006. Ranchers find that subdividing their lands can be more profitable than agriculture. As new housing developments encroach upon diminishing wildlife habitats, they also crowd the sensibility of wide-open spaces that has always set the West apart from the Eastern US.

The new millennium has brought ever more intense battles over resource preservation, spurred by early 21C federal government proposals to expand logging and oil and gas exploration in undeveloped areas such as Grand Staircase-Escalante National Monument and the Arctic National Wildlife Refuge. Activists are starting to urge that dams be removed on Pacific Northwest rivers to help restore the region's rapidly disappearing salmon runs. Nonetheless, there are still many places where it's customary to raise a hand in greeting when vehicles pass on country roads--a custom adapted from similar traditions on horseback a century ago. Drivers can still be forced to wait along a Western road while a cattle drive goes by. Cougars and bears have become frequent visitors to Western suburbs, and the bald eagle, America's symbol, was removed from the endangered-species list in 2007. More than a dozen Indian tribes have begun restoring buffalo herds to their ancestral grounds. And the quintessential song of the West, the yipping cries of coyote packs, rings from foothills, rangelands and ridgetops throughout the region, an open range melody that has painted the evening air for thousands of years.

Time Line

c.30,000 BC Paleo-Indians begin arriving in North America, probably across the Bering Land Bridge.

c.300 BC Irrigated farming enters Arizona from Mexico.

c.AD 1200 Ancestral Puebloan cliff dwellings abandoned.

1492 Christopher Columbus lands in the Western Hemisphere.

1521 Hernán Cortés defeats the Aztecs and claims Mexico for Spain.

1540-42 Francisco de Coronado marches through the Southwest in search of the Seven Cities of Cibola.

1542 Juan Cabrillo explores the California coast.

1579 Sir Francis Drake lands in California, claiming it for England.

1609 Santa Fe is founded.

1680 Spanish colonists flee northern New Mexico after more than 400 are slaughtered in Pueblo Revolt; they return in 1692.

1682 René-Robert de la Salle sails down the Mississippi, claiming the river and its western drainage for France.

1728 Vitus Bering explores the coast of Alaska for Russia.

1762 France cedes Louisiana Territory to Spain to avoid losing it to England.

1763 Treaty of Paris extends British (American colonial) frontier west to the Mississippi River.

1768 Captain James Cook claims coastal Canada for Great Britain.

1769 Junípero Serra establishes first of 21 California coastal missions.

1776 The future San Francisco is founded at Mission Dolores.

1778 Captain Cook makes first landing in Hawaii.

1781 Los Angeles is founded.

1784 Russia establishes settlements at Kodiak and Sitka, Alaska.

1792-94 George Vancouver charts Pacific coast from San Diego to Alaska, leading to competing British and US claims to Oregon Country.

1800 Napoleonic France regains Louisiana Territory from Spain.

1803 US buys Louisiana Territory from France for $15 million.

1804-06 **Lewis and Clark** journey up the Missouri River, across the Rocky Mountains and down the Columbia River to the Pacific Ocean.

1811 Fur traders found Fort Astoria at mouth of Columbia River.

1812 Russians establish Fort Ross on northern California coast.

1818 Treaty with Great Britain establishes northern US territorial border.

1821 Mexico declares independence from Spain. Santa Fe Trail opens.

1824 US War Department creates Bureau of Indian Affairs.

1830 Indian Removal Act mandates relocation of Five Civilized Tribes from southeastern US to Indian Territory (now Oklahoma).

1834 Mexico secularizes California missions.

1836 Texas wins independence from Mexico six weeks after slaughter at The Alamo. Whitmans establish Walla Walla mission.

1842 First settlers leave Missouri on Oregon Trail.

1845 Republic of Texas becomes US state.

1846 US acquires Oregon Territory south of 49th parallel in negotiations with Great Britain.

1847 Brigham Young leads Mormons into Great Salt Lake Valley. Whitman missionaries slain by Cayuse Indians.

1848 US wins New Mexico and California in treaty ending **Mexican War.** Gold discovered in California, igniting gold rush of 1849.

1850 California enters Union.

1858-59 Gold discovered in Colorado; Comstock Lode (silver) revealed in Nevada.

1858-61 Butterfield stagecoaches run from St. Louis to Los Angeles.

1860-61 Pony Express.

1861-65 Civil War.

1861 First transcontinental telegraph line completed.

1866 Led by Red Cloud, Sioux eject Army from Wyoming's Fort Phil Kearny. First cattle drive on Goodnight-Loving Trail.

1867 US buys Alaska from Russia for $7.2 million.

1869 Transcontinental railroad joined in Utah. Wyoming gives women suffrage. John Wesley Powell charts Grand Canyon by boat.

1872 Yellowstone is established as first national park.

1876 Lt. Col. George Custer and his troops annihilated by Sioux and Cheyenne at **Battle of the Little Bighorn.**

1877 Chief Joseph and his band of Nez Percé are captured after a 1,200mi flight.

1878 "Billy the Kid" begins a short but notorious outlaw career by killing a sheriff during the Lincoln County War.

1883 "Buffalo Bill" Cody launches his renowned Wild West Show.

1887 Dawes Act redistributes reservation land to individual Indians.

1889-93 Land rushes bring 150,000 homesteaders to Oklahoma.

1890 Wounded Knee Massacre.

1892 Sierra Club founded with John Muir as president.

1893 US planters depose Hawaii's Queen Liliuokalani, establishing republic accepted in 1898 as US territory.

1896 Utah becomes state after Mormons de-sanction polygamy.

1897 Klondike gold rush begins, drawing prospectors to Alaska; oil gusher at Bartlesville, Oklahoma, signals start of industry.

1900 More than 6,000 people die in Galveston hurricane.

1902 Reclamation Act diverts funds from sale of public lands to construct dams and other irrigation projects in West.

1906 Great earthquake and fire devastate San Francisco.

1913 Los Angeles Aqueduct brings water from Owens Valley to L.A. Hollywood's first feature film, *The Squaw Man*, is released.

1916 William Boeing founds aircraft company in Seattle. National Park Service established in Washington DC.

1919 Grand Canyon National Park created.

1927-41 Mount Rushmore chiseled by sculptor Gutzon Borglum.

1936 Hoover Dam completed. Sun Valley resort opens.

1937 Golden Gate Bridge spans entrance to San Francisco Bay.

1941 Japanese bomb **Pearl Harbor,** Hawaii; US enters World War II.

1953 War hero Gen. Dwight Eisenhower, a Texas-born Kansan, succeeds Harry S Truman as US president.

©iStockphoto.com/Andre Nantel

The USS Arizona Memorial, the battleship sunk by the Japanese, at Pearl Harbor

1959 Alaska and Hawaii become 49th and 50th states.

1962 Cesar Chavez organizes United Farm Workers in California.

1963 President John Kennedy is assassinated in Dallas and succeeded by Lyndon Johnson, a native Texan.

1971 Alaska Native Land Claims Settlement Act distributes $1 billion and 44 million acres of land to indigenous tribes.

1975 Bill Gates and Paul Allen establish Microsoft in Albuquerque, New Mexico; four years later, they move it to a Seattle suburb.

1980 Washington's Mount St. Helens erupts, killing 57. California governor Ronald Reagan, a former actor, is elected US president.

1989 Tanker *Exxon Valdez* spills 11 million gallons of oil into Alaska's Prince William Sound.

1995 Terrorist bombing of Oklahoma City federal building kills 168.

2000 Former Texas governor George W. Bush becomes US president, winning second term in 2004.

2007 California's population passes 37 million: one in every eight Americans now lives in the Golden State. Devastating brush fires destroy homes in Malibu, California, before spreading south to San Diego, and even into Mexico.

ART AND CULTURE

The landscape of the West is big, distinctive, vividly colored and demanding; and so is the art it has engendered, from the huge, compelling canvases of Bierstadt and Moran to Georgia O'Keeffe's abstract personifications of nature. And the indigenous custom of storytelling finds expression in the modern art most dependent on story—film.

Art

Although US Indians created works of art, almost everything also had a utilitarian or religious purpose. Some of the finest baskets ever created were the work of Washoe artisans, of whom **Datsolalee**, of the late 19C, is the best known. Coastal California tribes also made baskets exceptional for their beauty and utility, some woven so tightly they could hold water. Peoples of the Northwest coast and Alaska excelled in the art of carving soapstone and walrus tusks, cedar masks and totem poles. Hawaiians created coral jewelry and finely decorated robes and helmets adorned with bird feathers.

All the tribes of the Southwest fashioned decorated pottery, although the art had slipped into a utilitarian mold by the early 20C. Potter **María Montoya Martínez** (c.1881-1980) of New Mexico's San Ildefonso Pueblo is credited with reviving the potter's art in the 1930s when she produced exquisite black-on-black ware. Southwest Indian artists also made names for themselves as painters, among them **Pablita Velarde** (1918-2006) and **Harrison Begay** (b.1917). Navajo women today weave rugs crafted in distinctive regional styles.

The Spanish decorated their missions with silver work and wood carvings, much of it made in Mexico and carried north by mule train. The Spanish probably also taught lapidary skills to the Pueblo Indians, who today produce some of the finest stone (especially turquoise) and silver jewelry in the US.

The American West provided an exceedingly rich canvas for artists and other chroniclers of frontier life and scenery. Early explorers often were accompanied by sketch artists, some of whom went on to become noted artists. **Karl Bodmer** (1809-93) and **George Catlin** (1796-1872) both recorded Indians and mountain men in the 1830s, while **John James Audubon** (1785-1851) made his own journey west to sketch birds and wildlife. Artist-photographer **Solomon Nuñes Carvalho** (1815-94) accompanied Frémont during a survey of the Far West. The paintings of **Thomas Moran** (1837-1926) and photographs of **William Henry Jackson** (1843-1942), part of the Hayden Expedition to Yellowstone in 1871, were crucial in swaying the public and Congress to create the first national park. **Alfred Jacob Miller** (1810-74), a Baltimore artist, made a trip west in the company of fur traders in 1837 and capitalized upon it in creating a series of paintings of great documentary value. German-born **Albert Bierstadt** (1830-1902) painted Western landscapes in a particularly Romantic style. Grittier and more lifelike are the sketches, paintings and sculptures of cowboys, Indians and other Western characters by **Frederic Remington** (1861-1909) and **Charles M. Russell** (1864-1926).

New Mexico, with its pueblos and unusual scenery, became a popular magnet for artists in the late 19C. Santa Fe, long the cultural center of the Southwest, is one of the largest art markets in the US after New York and Los Angeles; so is Scottsdale, Arizona. Taos boasted an artist colony in the very early 20C. **Georgia O'Keeffe** (1887-1986), an annual Taos visitor who later moved to the New Mexico desert, painted austere landscapes and decorated more than one famous painting with a parched cow skull against a bright Southwestern sky.

The stop-action photography of **Eadweard Muybridge** (1830-1904) preceded the invention of his zoopraxiscope, a landmark in pioneering the moving-

Ancient Puebloan Dwelling in Mesa Verde

picture industry. The haunting black-and-white shots of Western landscapes, particularly Yosemite, by **Ansel Adams** (1902-84) inspired generations of photographers and conservationists. Through her poignant portraits of farm migrants and photos of vast public-works projects rising amid arid landscapes, **Dorothea Lange** (1895-1965) dramatized the tragedies and triumphs of the Depression-era West. Photographers **Edward Weston** (1886-1958) and **Imogen Cunningham** (1883-1976) were among the more influential members of a West Coast coterie known as Group f.64.

The west coast of California also exerted a strong influence on 20C painting and sculpture. Artist colonies at Carmel, La Jolla and Laguna Beach spawned the California Impressionism and Plein-Air movements, including **Franz Bischoff** (1864-1929), creating landscapes inspired by the unique light and natural features of the area. During the 1930s, abstraction, surrealism and social realism came into play. In San Francisco, **Mark Rothko** (1903-70) and **Clyfford Still** (1904-80) inspired an explosion of abstract painting by their students, who included **Robert Motherwell** (1915-91). Painters such as **Richard Diebenkorn** (1922-93) and **David Park** (1911-60) responded with a representational movement known as Bay Area Figurative. An influential art scene that has developed in southern California since the 1950s includes **David Hockney** (b.1937). Tacoma, WA, native **Dale Chihuly** (b.1941) established a blown-glass art tradition, the Pilchuck School, now famed worldwide.

Architecture

Native Americans built homes to suit their environment and culture with available materials. Nomadic Plains tribes adopted buffalo skins spread over lean-to timber frames to build highly mobile **tepees**. Farming tribes of the Great Plains, like the Mandans and Pawnees, built permanent **earthen lodges**. Northwestern tribes erected sturdy **plank houses**, while the people of the

A Tepee

Great Basin and California lowlands preferred light summer lean-tos of thatch and brush, using more substantial materials in winter.

Most of the farming people of the Southwest built fixed houses. Ancient **cliff dwellings** and pueblos of dried mud or stone, some occupied for hundreds of years, still stand throughout the region. Raised on canyon shelves for protection from marauders, the cliff dwellings were abandoned in the late 12C. Latecomers to the Southwest, such as the Navajo, erected six-sided houses called **hogans**. The likely descendants of the cliff dwellers live today in **pueblos**. Some, like those of Taos, New Mexico, are stacked like apartment houses and are among the most remarkable buildings in America.

The Spanish built with sun-baked adobe bricks, made from wet clay and a binding material such as straw or horse hair. Structures were whitewashed and roofed with overhanging clay tiles to reduce rain damage. Adobe walls retain heat in winter and coolness in summer. Doors and windows could be carved from the sturdy walls with a minimum of effort. For their ecclesiastical buildings, Spanish architects tried to copy structures they knew from Spain or Mexico.

Most Western settlements in the American era were initially built of wood, the cheapest and most readily available material. A prominent exception was the **sod house** of the Great Plains which,

Spanish Influenced Ecclesiastical Architecture

though sturdy shelter, was dark and readily abandoned when wood became available. Rudimentary **log cabins** were usually superseded by **frame houses**, while commercial establishments achieved a tone of respectability by sporting facades of brick (often imported from the Midwest or East) or dressed stone, locally quarried. A characteristic feature of many towns was the **false front**, which served to make one-story shanties look larger and more reputable.

Large cities looked East for architectural inspiration in the 19C, often drawing upon the Greek Revival style for banks, or a hodgepodge of styles for the mansions and row houses of residential

Taliesin West created by Frank Lloyd Wright

districts. Romanticized throwbacks to the Old West have remained popular through the 20C, especially at dude ranches, resorts and national parks—a spectacular example being the **Old Faithful Inn** (1904, Robert Reamer) at Yellowstone National Park.

Widespread prosperity in the 20C enabled Westerners to experiment more with architectural style. In California, some builders put form before practicability, so that wealthier residential districts in some cities were imbued with a bewildering array of styles in close juxtaposition. In Los Angeles, one residential block might boast Tudor, Norman and Mission-style houses between a Japanese garden and Swiss chalet. The 1920s and 1930s popularized whimsical structures built to resemble extraneous objects (giant oranges, derby hats, even cartoon animals) to attract clientele.

More thoughtful architectural fashions of the 20C included the **Mission Style,** which resurrected the arched doorways and windows, red-tile roofs and white earthen walls of Spanish missions; **Art Moderne**, with streamlined contours and Art Deco detailing; and the **Prairie School**, emphasizing strong, horizontal lines and a lack of superfluous decoration. The latter, a creation of architect **Frank Lloyd Wright** (1867-1959), stressed organic architecture harmonizing with specific landscapes. Of hundreds of buildings designed by Wright in the West, the most important is **Taliesin West** (1937) in Scottsdale, Arizona. With its low-profile buildings of indigenous materials, uneven rooflines and deeply shaded entrances, Taliesin West remains a strong influence on design. The West Coast was a stronghold for **Craftsman** style, the American adaptation of the British Arts and Crafts movement, featuring simple decorative wood trim, built-in cabinetry and porches with broad pillars. San Diego and Oakland both have notable Craftsman neighborhoods.

Literature

Tall tales and colorful humor were popular on the frontier. Westerners were famous for telling tall tales—which is why John Colter's earliest descriptions of Yellowstone's geysers, hot pools and astringent streams were thought to be lies. Humorists like **Mark Twain** (né Samuel Clemens, 1835-1910) and **Edgar "Bill" Nye** (1850-96) carried on the tradition of exaggeration in print, writing satire that turned on common sense and droll humor. Twain's first break came with "The Celebrated Jumping Frog of Calaveras County" (1867). *Roughing It* (1872) is considered richest and funniest description of a dude's life in Virginia City, San Francisco, Hawaii and other parts of the Wild West.

More serious Western observations also were widely read in the East. Francis Parkman's exciting account of *The Oregon Trail* (1849) remains a standard today. John C. Frémont's reports of his forays to the West, scribed with governmental precision, were rewritten with dramatic flair by his wife, **Jesse Benton Frémont** (1824-1902); they were bestsellers in their day and made Frémont's guide, Kit Carson, into a great Western hero. The laconic Carson himself told his own story with less flamboyance in an autobiography not published until 1926. Other accounts of Western experiences embraced a wide range of views, including those of Indians (*Black Elk Speaks*, 1932) and homesteaders (the works of **Laura Ingalls Wilder**, 1867-1957). Historians like **Frederick Jackson Turner** (1861-1932), **Bernard De Voto** (1897-1955) and **Wallace Stegner** (1909-93) added heft and drama.

Sentimental stories, exemplified by the California gold-rush tales of **Bret Harte** (1836-1902), were popular throughout the 19C, but it was adventure and derring-do that gave the real impetus to a new brand of fiction, the Western. The first mass-market adventure fiction set in the Wild West appeared in the 1860s, and thousands of "dime novels" were enthusiastically embraced by the public—including several by Buffalo Bill featuring himself, and dozens more by other authors about him. The prototype of the modern Western is generally considered to be Owen Wister's *The Virginian* (1902), which combined a love interest with all the elements of frontier lore: chivalrous cowboys, treacherous Indians and a brooding bad man. Among the most enduring work is that of **Zane Grey** (1875-1939); his *Riders of the Purple Sage* appeared in 1912. The Western occasionally rose to high levels of literary complexity, as in the psychological narrative of a lynching in Walter Van Tilburg Clark's *The Ox-Bow Incident* (1940), Willa Cather's *Death Comes for the Archbishop* (1927) and Wallace Stegner's *Angle of Repose* (1971). Jack London's novel of man and dog in the Klondike gold rush, *The Call of the Wild* (1903), probably has been translated into more languages than any other novel set in the West. Few books have sparked so large a following as **Jack Kerouac**'s awakening call to the Beat Generation, *On the Road* (1957), a fictionalized account of aimless journeys through the contemporary West.

Other writers alerted public opinion to regional problems. John Muir's books and articles helped arouse Eastern support for greater protection of Western lands and resources. Helen Hunt Jackson's *Century of Dishonor* (1881) helped awaken sentiment to the mistreatment of Indians, a forerunner to Dee Brown's *Bury My Heart at Wounded Knee* (1971). **Frank Norris** (1870-1902) attacked the problem of greedy railroad barons in *The Octopus* (1901). Among the defenders of the deserts' fragile beauties were **Mary Austin** (1868-1934), whose *The Land of Little Rain* exalted the Owens Valley and Mojave Desert; and the irascible **Edward Abbey** (1927-89), author of *Desert Solitaire* (1968).

Another stalwart of Western fiction is the hard-boiled detective. **Dashiell Hammett** (1894-1961) created the tone with Sam Spade in *The Maltese Falcon* (1930), set in San Francisco. **Raymond Chandler** (1888-1959) followed suit in *The Big Sleep* (1939) by introducing Philip Marlowe, a cynical, self-sufficient but honorable detective who guarded the mean streets of Los Angeles. **Ross McDonald**'s books featuring detective Lew Archer succeeded Marlowe, painting a realistic but humane portrait of Southern California from 1949-1976. **Tony Hillerman** (b.1925) blends Western and detective fiction in his books, which recount the adventures of Navajo policemen Joe Leaphorn and Jim Chee in the Indian lands of the Southwest.

Music

Native Americans employed music and dance in all their ceremonies, both religious and social; these forms endure today at numerous annual **pow-wows**. The Spanish, who introduced the guitar to the West, also used music for sacred and social purposes, and took pains to instruct their mission neophytes in pla-

©iStockphoto.com/Norman Pogson

1960's Style Rock And Roll Electric Guitar

ying instruments. The bulk of popular music today, carried West in the folk music of pioneers and the hymns of missionaries, has roots in the British Isles. Fiddle, harmonica and banjo were the instruments of choice on wagon trains, where popular Oregon Trail tunes included "The Arkansas Traveler" and "Sweet Betsy from Pike." Accompanied by stomping feet, clapping hands and instructional dance calls, the fiddle gave life to capers, jigs and square dances at frontier gatherings, and entertained cowboys on cattle drives and soldiers in lonely barracks.

The archetype of contemporary Western music is a highly commercialized hybrid of cowboy songs, themselves descended from Scottish, English and Irish ballads by way of the rural South, and often incorporating elements of the Hispanic muwsic of Mexico. The genre was popularized on radio and in film by cowboy singers like **Roy Rogers** (1912-98) and **Gene Autry** (1907-98). Influenced by well-traveled singers like **Buck Owens** (1929-2006), several of whose songs were recorded by the Beatles, cowboy music began to absorb outside elements in the 1940s, picking up the tempo, heavier rhythms and twanging guitar that characterizes popular country-and-western music today. Texans **Bob Wills** (1905-1975), the "King" of Western swing; **Ernest Tubb** (1914-1984) and **Willie Nelson** (b.1933) broadened the genre's scope, incorporating popular music elements ranging from swing to rock and blues. National radio has eroded regional distinctions, but artists such as Texas' **Don Edwards** have revived traditional Western song. The West has made conspicuous contributions in the realm of rock music. In the early 1960s, as the Beatles emerged in England, southern California originated its own brand of lighthearted "surf" rock; its best-known ambassadors, **The Beach Boys,** sang in intricate harmony of waves, hot rods and surfer girls. Later in the decade, the social upheaval in San Francisco, culminating in 1967's "Summer of Love," drew numerous prominent singers and performers—including Texan **Janis Joplin** (1943-70) and Seattleite **Jimi Hendrix** (1942-70)—to

a local scene already celebrated for its "San Francisco Sound." The music of Jim Morrison's **The Doors,** Jerry Garcia's **Grateful Dead,** Grace Slick's **Jefferson Airplane**, John Fogarty's **Credence Clearwater Revival** and other top groups was characterized by driving guitar riffs and influenced by more traditional blues. In the early 1990s, Seattle became the center of a style termed "grunge rock," with bands like Kurt Cobain's **Nirvana** and Eddie Vedder's **Pearl Jam noted** for their raw, rough-edged music.

Theater and Film

Nineteenth Century miners were noted for their love of opera. They were so generous in supporting fine opera houses in remote towns that Eastern and European companies routinely toured San Francisco, Virginia City (Nevada), Central City (Colorado) and other thriving mining frontiers. Stage plays, running the gamut from Shakespearean excerpts to melodramas, were also popular. Among the famous actors who toured the Western mining camps were **Edwin Booth** (1833-93), **Helena Modjeska** (1840-1909) and the unconventional **Sarah Bernhardt** (1844-1923). Less exalted entertainment was offered by the scandalous exotic dancer **Lola Montez** (1818-61) and her comedic successor, **Lotta Crabtree** (1847-1924).

Today, San Francisco remains among the preeminent opera cities of the West, staging lavish productions with renowned casts. The Dallas Opera and Houston Grand Opera also are highly regarded, the latter known for its modern world premieres of John C. Adams' *Nixon in China* (1987) and *The Death of Klinghoffer* (1991). Since 1957, one of the brightest lights in the American opera scene has been the Santa Fe Opera Company, which offers outdoor summer performances. Live stage plays continue to attract tourists and local audiences in Los Angeles, San Francisco, Seattle and smaller cities like Ashland, Oregon, and Cedar City, Utah, both of which mount internationally recognized annual Shakespeare festivals.

Of all the Western-themed entertainment, nothing was more popular during the late-19C and early-20C than Buffalo Bill's Wild West Show, a commercial extravaganza. Theater on an epic scale, the show thrilled East Coast and European audiences with dramatized excepts from **William F. "Buffalo Bill" Cody** (1846-1917) himself. Drawing on Cody's remarkable life as a Pony Express rider, bison hunter, Army scout and soldier, the show re-created famous Western battles and presented feats of sharpshooting, an Indian attack on a stagecoach, trick riding and roping, bucking broncos, bull-riding, steer wrestling and other rodeo events. Among the most famous cast members were Sitting Bull sharpshooter **Annie Oakley** (1860-1926) and Cody himself.

Spectacular live shows continue to be a hallmark of the Western stage, particularly in resort centers like Lake Tahoe, Reno and especially Las Vegas. The prototypes of Las Vegas-style performers were stand-up comedians, torch singers and chorus-line Parisian showgirls like the Folies Bergères. Shows now embrace a mind-boggling array of magician acts, circuses, water choreography, and spectacles of electronic and pyrotechnic wizardry, as well as concerts by famous singers.

No other medium has propounded the myth of the Old West more successfully than the **Western movie.** Like Medieval morality plays, classic Westerns depict history selectively but irresistibly, winning audiences who root for heroes and boo villains without complicating ambiguities. Larger than life, Westerns helped to establish Hollywood as the world capital of film-making.

From the first silent Westerns in the early 20C through the 1950s, Westerns' cowboy heroes were chivalrous characters; Indians were usually villains, and other ethnic minorities were rarely depicted despite the prominent roles played by Chinese, black and Hispanic people throughout the American West. Some of these Westerns were undeniably powerful. Among the most emotionally satisfying, if conventional, were Red River (1948), starring **John Wayne;** High Noon (1952), starring **Gary Cooper;**

The Searchers (1956), starring Wayne; and many visually exciting works by director **John Ford**, beginning with Stagecoach (1939), also starring Wayne. Television Westerns of the 1950s and 1960s tended to reinforce the Western myth in shows like The Lone Ranger, Gunsmoke and Bonanza.

Since the 1960s, Hollywood has produced ever-greater numbers of offbeat, thoughtful, brooding Westerns that run against the grain of earlier productions. Protagonists are anti-heroes in Lonely Are the Brave (1962), starring **Kirk Douglas;** Hud (1963), starring **Paul Newman;** The Wild Bunch (1969), directed by **Sam Peckinpah;** and a series of "spaghetti westerns" (including The Good, the Bad and the Ugly, 1967) directed by **Sergio Leone** and starring **Clint Eastwood.** Another trend reversed old roles by placing Indians as heroes and soldiers as villains, as in Little Big Man (1970), starring **Dustin Hoffman,** and Dances with Wolves (1989), starring **Kevin Costner.** Film festivals throughout the West continue to influence the world and disseminate the medium. Among the most famous is Utah's Sundance Film Festival, the creation of actor-director **Robert Redford.**

Sports and Recreation

For exercise, entertainment, drama and fellowship, Americans love to play and watch sports. A year-round slate of professional ("pro"), collegiate and amateur competitions keeps the excitement high. College sports, especially football and basketball, attract the excited attention of fans and alumni nationwide, especially during the annual football "bowl game" series in December and January, and the "March Madness" championship basketball tournament.

TAKE ME OUT TO THE BALL GAMES

Often called the national pastime, **baseball** inspires legions of devoted fans who follow teams with religious intensity. Played on a diamond-shaped field with bases in each corner, the game

A football player in the ready stance.

tests the individual skills of batters, who try to strike a thrown ball, against pitchers and fielders, bearing some similarities to cricket. The game may appear slow-paced but can be fraught with suspense, the outcome often resting on a final confrontation between pitcher and batter. In March, when pro teams engage in their annual spring training in Arizona and Florida, seats at practice games are the hottest tickets in town. The Major League Baseball (www.mlb.com) season runs from April to October, culminating in the World Series, a best-of-seven-games matchup between the American League and National League champions.

Fast-paced **basketball** draws participants and spectators from every walk of life. In part because it requires a smaller playing area than most sports, the game is often played outdoors in crowded urban areas. Players score by throwing a ball through a suspended hoop. The 29 teams of the National Basketball Association (NBA) begin play in November, competing for a berth in the NBA Finals held in June. The 12-team Women's National Basketball Association (WNBA), founded in 1997, has inspired a new host of professional female players around the country. For information on both, visit www.nba.com.

With its unique combination of brute force and finely tuned skill, **American football** demands strength, speed and agility from players in their quest to pass, kick and run the football down a 100-yard field to the goal. The National Football League (NFL) oversees 32 teams in two conferences, the champions of which meet in late January in the annual Super Bowl, a game that draws more television viewers than any other event. Football season begins about September 1; visit www.nfl.com.

OTHER PROFESSIONAL SPORTS

Although **ice hockey** was born in Canada, the US has adopted the game in a big way. In this breakneck sport, skated players use sticks to maneuver a hard rubber puck into a goal at either end of an ice arena. The 29-team National Hockey League (NHL) pits professional Canadian and American teams in annual competition for the coveted Stanley Cup, with finals held in June.

The US may be the world's preeminent **golf** nation, attracting golfers from around the globe to its challenging, well-manicured courses. Public and private links abound throughout much of the West, especially California, Arizona, Las Vegas and Hawaii, where the climate permits year-round play. A yearlong slate of tournaments for men, women and senior men utilizes numerous championship courses in Arizona, California and Hawaii.

Descended from frontier horsemanship contests, **rodeo** celebrates the skills developed by generations of cowboys.

Members of the Professional Rodeo Cowboys Association (PRCA) compete for millions of dollars in bronc-riding, calf roping, steer wrestling and other events. Most dangerous is bull-riding, in which a cowboy tries to remain on the back of a rampaging bull for all of eight seconds; rodeo clowns distract the bull from goring the rider after he has been thrown. Hugely popular pro rodeos are held in Cheyenne (Wyoming), Pendleton (Oregon), Houston, Las Vegas, Oklahoma City, Fort Worth, Denver, Reno and other cities.

A RECREATIONAL PARADISE

Skiing in the Colorado Rockies; **surfing** the big waves on the north shore of O'ahu. Whitewater **rafting** down Idaho's Salmon River; backpacking the 2,550mi Pacific Crest Trail. **Mountain-biking** through Utah's slick-rock canyons; **fly-fishing** isolated lakes in Alaska's vast interior; riding horseback through aspen-clad mountainsides: Seekers of outdoor recreation and natural beauty take full advantage of the wealth of mountains, forests, lakes, rivers and oceanfront, as well as urban parks and biking/running paths.

In-line skating, snowboarding and mountain biking are recent additions to the panoply of popular recreational sports. **Sky-diving** and **mountain climbing** attract increasing numbers of mainstream participants. Adventure-travel agencies design vacations around bicycling, canoeing, wildlife viewing and other themes.

Hiking, **horseback riding** and river rafting provide the best access to thousands of square miles of Western backcountry and parkland. A vast network of trails probes remote corners of the Rockies, Sierra Nevada and Cascades. Undeveloped Alaska offers plenty of true wilderness for adventurers—even for comfort-loving anglers or hunters who hire bush pilots to find the perfect lake. Throughout the West, guest ranches offer room, board and riding opportunities to "city slickers"; some even sponsor working cattle-drive vacations. The Colorado River of Utah and Arizona might be the most celebrated rafting challenge, but most Western states offer white-water to match the skill level of any rafter or kayaker.

©iStockphoto.com/Rick Hyman

A Rodeo Rider Roping a Calf

THE REGION TODAY

The spirit of invention and adventure that has marked the West for centuries continues unabated today. The area remains one of the most culturally, politically and economically progressive regions on earth, from state governments to the innumerable startup companies that make Silicon Valley hum. Having absorbed ethnic influences from east, west and south, its cuisine is now finding new frontiers in supporting organic foods. Its builders call on the world's most innovative architects; its artists, musicians and filmmakers find new ways to practice their crafts. And the commitment to preserve the matchless natural landscape has never been stronger.

Government, Politics and Society

Though it has since been copied around the world, when the United States created its then-unique federated republic it was radical indeed. The national government consists of three branches--the executive, in the office of the president; the legislative, which consists of Congress's Senate and House of Representatives; and the judiciary, which consists of many types and levels of courts, culminating in the Supreme Court. These three bodies guide the vast federal government, which holds sway over national and foreign affairs, and all matters that involve relations between the states. This includes safeguarding the constitutional liberties Americans enjoy, such as freedom of speech and fair trial guarantees. A federal income tax brings in the bulk of the national budget.

The 50 states, including the 19 covered in this guide, govern themselves in internal affairs such as road construction, criminal and civil law such as requirements for marriage and inheritance standards. All the states are organized along lines very similar to the national government, with an executive, the governor; a legislature (Nebraska, uniquely, has a one-house assembly); and a multilevel judicial system culminating in some sort of supreme court. All 19 Western states are further subdivided into counties (some of which are larger than many European countries) and cities within those counties, divisions which likewise govern some aspects of life within their borders. Some rural Western counties, for instance, do not require building permits for residential home construction.

All these levels of government rely on popular vote to select their members, with the exception of judges, some of whom are elected and some appointed. Federal and state elections take place every two years; by and large, governors and senators serve four-year terms, representatives two years.

States, counties and cities raise revenue through various taxes and fees, usually including income and sales taxes. The differences here exemplify the colorful political and cultural diversity of this huge region: Washington state, like several other Western states, has no income tax, and its residents consistently reject any effort to create one. Its neighbor, Oregon, has no sales tax, and its residents consistently reject efforts to create one. In Alaska, there is no property tax, the mainstay of public school funds in every other state.

By and large, the three Pacific Coast states, Washington, Oregon and California, are more liberal (socially progressive) than interior states. California, for instance, has led the US (not to mention the world) in restrictions on public smoking. These three states evince an interesting internal dichotomy—the areas nearest the coast, especially the cities, are much more liberal than the inland regions beyond a dividing mountain range. San Francisco is world-famed—and has been for more than a century—as a community tolerant of nontraditional behavior. A gay couple walking down the street in San Francisco holding hands would be a common-

House Chamber, November 17, 1947

Library of Congress

place; the same sight would be unheard-of in small towns in far inland California, separated from the liberal coast by not one but two mountain ranges.

It is largely true that individualism and independence enjoy high regard in the Western states--but, as the old axiom has it, what's gospel in one place is heresy in another. Montana was famous during the '90s as the state with no daytime highway speed limit other than "reasonable and prudent." (Under pressure from the national government, the upper limit was made 75 mph in 1999.) Assisted suicide is legal in Oregon and illegal in every other US state. California allows medical marijuana use; in Alaska, citizens may possess small amounts of marijuana for personal use. Pot is strictly prohibited in most other Western states. A few counties in Nevada have made brothels legal; they are the only such places in the United States.

Innumerable other examples illustrate the great sociopolitical diversity of the West today. The thread of independence that runs through this theme had its birth in the settling of the West by adventurous pioneers, many of whom simply did not fit in elsewhere. Here, as throughout the US, the continuing political ferment over social issues is decided in the privacy of the voting booth, and despite their differences everyone would agree that's best. Alas, fewer than half of Americans vote in most elections.

The Economy

The Western economy thrives on the unique American system of free enterprise—a laissez-faire capitalism whereby individuals can create, own and control the production of virtually any marketable good, service or commodity they can conceive. In this arena of inventive enterprise the Western economy has given rise to enterprises of global significance, such as high technology and aerospace. Only public services, such as bus and subway systems, are government-owned.

The US has undergone a profound transformation over the last few generations, from one based on resource extraction to one based on service industries and manufacturing. Its 21C economy is complex and varied, and its premier example, California, is so large that considered by itself it would be the 8th-largest in the world.

Natural Resources

European settlers were first lured westward by an abundance of fur pelts, minerals, fossil fuels, grazing lands, fertile soil, fisheries and timber. Except for furs, these resources still underlie a substantial portion of the Western economy. Private companies engaged in timber harvesting, mining and grazing benefit from favorable contracts for the lease of public lands managed by the US Forest Service or Bureau of

An Oil Field, Central Valley, California

Land Management. Altogether, mining accounts for about $65 billion of the US GDP; Nevada is at the forefront of non-fuel production with $4.4 billion annual earnings, mostly from gold, silver and copper. Crude oil is concentrated in pockets along the Gulf of Mexico and in Texas, Oklahoma, California, Alaska and Wyoming, while a vast reserve of undeveloped oil shale underlies the central Rocky Mountains and Colorado Plateau. Fuels production, also largely a Western industry, contributes more than $250 billion to the US GDP.

Irrigation has allowed agriculture to thrive despite arid or semiarid conditions over much of the West. With over $26 billion in annual sales, California leads the nation in overall agricultural production, followed by Texas with more than $13 billion; Nebraska ranks fourth in the US, after Iowa.

The most diverse Western farmlands are valleys near the Pacific coast. These include Oregon's Willamette Valley, which lured pioneers after being acclaimed by Lewis and Clark. With more sunshine but greater need for irrigation, California's fertile valleys—particularly the Central and Salinas—yield some of the richest harvests in the world. Its Napa and Sonoma Valleys are famed for wine grapes, while elsewhere in the state, farmers produce artichokes, tomatoes, citrus, nuts and other vegeta-

bles and fruits. Washington is noted for apples and wine, Oregon for wine and berries, Idaho for potatoes, the Great Plains for wheat and grains. Livestock, especially sheep and cattle, are vital to the economies of several Western states, especially in the Rocky Mountains and Great Plains.

Once known for pineapples and sugar, Hawaii has had to downsize and diversify in the face of foreign competition. A broader threat to agriculture is urban growth and competition for water from burgeoning cities such as Las Vegas, Phoenix, Denver and Los Angeles.

Diversified Economies

All those classic Western industries—farming and ranching, mining, timber, oil and gas--today contribute less than a quarter of the total USA West GDP of $3.2 trillion. The growing Pacific coastal cities were the first to diversify from resource- and agricultural-based economies; San Francisco has always been a trade and banking center, and Seattle shifted quickly from timber to trade and manufacturing. During the 20C, manufacturing and service industries inexorably moved to other Western cities. Regional banking centers such as Denver and Reno grew from mining and railroad-supply settlements in the 19C.

Los Angeles has grown into the West's largest, wealthiest, most culturally

©iStockphoto.com/Ian Crockett

influential metropolitan area. With an artificial harbor, good railroad connections and ambitious engineering projects that delivered freshwater from the Sierra Nevada, Colorado River and northern California, L.A. set the example for other sprawling, prosperous and economically diversified Western cities such as Houston, Phoenix and Seattle. The high-technology revolution of the late 20C spread from successful beginnings in Silicon Valley (San Jose), California, to Seattle and other regional centers in Oregon, Texas, Colorado and Idaho.

Service industries are the fastest growing employers in the West. Government is responsible for much of this growth, especially in California, with more than 250,000 federal civilian employees, and Texas, with almost 200,000. Large military bases in Hawaii, California, Nevada, Texas and Washington employ thousands.

Tourism and travel-related services (lodging, restaurants, entertainment, transportation) account for an increasing proportion of US economic activity—$700 billion per year. Tourism engenders close to $100 billion annually in California, followed by Texas ($50 billion), Nevada ($21 billion) and Hawaii ($12 billion).

People of the West

The American West has always been perceived as a land of possibility, a place to start anew. Its population is largely composed of immigrants and their descendants, people who set out in quest of the American dream.

The West remains the fastest growing region of the US. The demographic trend is playing out dramatically in booming communities like Las Vegas, Tucson, Fresno, Santa Fe and Boise, as the largest cities—Los Angeles, San Diego, Houston, Dallas, Denver, Phoenix, San Antonio, Kansas City, and the San Francisco Bay and Puget Sound metropolitan areas—continue to drive the West's economic engines. Retirees account for large numbers of new residents here, although many of them are "sunbirds" who depart for cooler cli-

mates in summer. Denver, Seattle and Portland have all experienced huge growth as well, driven by jobs growth. Other parts of the West, particularly the Great Basin, the Chihuahuan Desert of west Texas and southern New Mexico, the northern Rockies and Alaska, still contain thousands of square miles that are very sparsely inhabited.

The centuries-old steady influx of migrants to the West brought a heady mix of cultural traditions. San Francisco, Oakland, Los Angeles and Seattle are among the most ethnically diverse cities in the world, with significant Chinese, Southeast Asian, Japanese, Filipino, Hispanic, Italian, Greek, Portuguese, Eastern European and African-American populations. The Texas Hill Country has strong ties to Germany. Alaska celebrates Russian heritage in Sitka and Kodiak. Basque sheepherders exert their influence on the hearty restaurants and small hotels of the Great Basin, Idaho and Wyoming. The ubiquitous Irish, who supplied so much of the labor force of the early West, have rendered St. Patrick's Day a nearly universal celebration. Mexico's Cinco de Mayo is equally popular, and so is Chinese New Year in coastal cities.

COWBOYS AND INDIANS

The mythical picture of the West casts settlement as primarily a contest between Indians and Americans of European heritage. It's a woefully incomplete picture. For instance, a high percentage of cowboys in the late 19C, and rodeo circuit riders of the early 20C, were black. Many others were Hispanic and Indian. And many parts of the West, from southern Texas and Colorado to California, were first settled by Europeans of Hispanic descent.

Chinese workers represented a large percentage of the miners in the early West, as well as fishermen, railroad workers, road builders and construction workers. Hispanic workers continue to dominate the ranks of migratory field laborers throughout the West.

Most Indians have adopted popular American dress and customs, and many have intermarried with other races and

Joanne DiBona/San Diego CVB

© Comstock, Inc

© Comstock, Inc

©New Mexico Tourism Department

Joanne DiBona/San Diego CVB

© Comstock, Inc

© Image DJ Corporation

© Comstock, Inc

moved to urban areas. But a highly visible segment still dwells on reservations throughout the West; many of these tribes are thriving cultural and economic nations. The most traditional are the Hopi, who still live in pueblos on high desert mesas, completely surrounded by the Navajo Reservation. Other tribes and the Navajo maintain a balance between old ways and new, operating dynamic industries that range from timber to tourism. The reservations of the Great Plains and the Pacific slope are less tied to the nomadic ways of the past, but likewise are less inclined to welcome tourism. The recent trend to open casinos on tribal lands has revitalized the economies of many such groups.

Food and Drink

The food and drink of the West is linked to the staples developed by its peoples during successive waves of immigration: the corn, beans, chiles, squash and tomatoes of MesoAmericans; the salmon and shellfish of coastal peoples; the beef cattle, stone fruits, potatoes and wheat of European immigrants. All these ingredients have been mainstays for centuries. Modern Western cuisine is colored most distinctively by the styles of Hispanic and Asian cooking.

The chief regional distinction arises from Hispanic settlement in the Mexican border states—Texas, New Mexico, Arizona and California—where traditional cooking was based on corn (maize) and chiles. The native cuisine of the Indians embraced corn in many colors, including blue, white and yellow. Dried kernels are ground and made into breads, baked in ovens or on hot stones, resulting in the ubiquitous tortilla (which can also be made from wheat). This cuisine is famed for its tacos, tamales and enchiladas, many of which include hot chiles to lend spice. In Texas, such foods are popularized as Tejano or Tex-Mex; one signature dish is chili, a spicy meat stew. Different versions of this cuisine are found throughout most of the West, especially now that immigrants of Hispanic descent have spread north to the Canadian border.

HISTORICAL FARE

Tomatoes, beans, squash, chiles and corn were all originally cultivated in Central America, but widely distributed throughout the Southwest and Great Plains when the first Europeans arrived. The dried meats of Plains Indian hunters and the carne seco of Southwestern farmers were forerunners of today's popular "jerky" snack. Foods such as prickly pears, sunflower seeds, wild berries, mushrooms, piñon nuts, wild game and fish were readily adapted--salmon remains the signature dish of Pacific Northwest cuisine.

The stampede of American settlers during gold and silver rushes depended initially upon game for food, but developed a taste for tinned foods and bread. Circumstantial invention produced novelties ranging from the Hangtown Fry (an omelet made from eggs, bacon rind and preserved oysters) to Caesar salad, now the most popular salad in the US. Immigrants brought such simple recipes as Cornish pasties, Irish stews, Southeast Asian curries and Japanese teriyaki, the latter now ubiquitous.

A scarcity of yeast prompted a method of leavening bread with a large pinch of the latest dough, left in a warm spot to ferment its own. The resultant sourdough bread, descended from the Cali-

A hamburger with a side of crispy onion rings

©iStockphoto.com/Kelly Cline

Economies of the Western United States

	*GSP (mil.$)	Principal Industries
California	$1,622,116	manufacturing, tourism, crops, oil, film
Texas	989,443	oil, livestock, cotton, manufacturing
Washington	267,308	fishing, timber, manufacturing, wheat
Colorado	216,537	tourism, manufacturing, mining, oil
Arizona	216,528	manufacturing, mining, tourism
Oregon	144,278	timber, fishing, fruit, manufacturing
Oklahoma	121,490	natural gas, oil, wheat, livestock
Nevada	111,342	gambling, tourism, mining, hydroelectric
Kansas	105,574	wheat, corn, livestock, oil, manufacturing
Utah	90,778	mining, oil, livestock, manufacturing
Nebraska	70,676	corn, wheat, livestock, manufacturing
New Mexico	68,870	mining, manufacturing, livestock
Hawaii	54,019	tourism, sugar, pineapple, military
Idaho	47,189	potatoes, wheat, timber, mining
Alaska	39,314	fishing, oil, natural gas, mining, timber
South Dakota	30,919	corn, wheat, mining, manufacturing
Montana	29,885	mining, wheat, forage crops, livestock
Wyoming	27,269	mining, oil, sheep, forage crops
North Dakota	24,397	wheat, potatoes, oil

*Gross State Product (2005), from US Bureau of Economic Analysis

fornia gold rush, is still baked from San Francisco to Alaska.

The era of the cowboy has associated beef with the West, though wranglers themselves were more likely to enjoy beans, stews and organ meats than the tough, stringy steaks. Well-fattened and far tastier beef emerged after a session in the stockyards at the end of the trail drives, to this day giving Kansas City and Omaha a reputation for steaks and barbecue. Barbecue has become a hallmark of Western dining, a staple of every ranch and resort, and a popular excuse for weekend gatherings. While grilling over gas fires has replaced using coals or mesquite as the most popular means, the traditional method in Texas is to bury a prepared carcass with the coals, allowing it to cook underground.

NATURE'S BOUNTY

Though over-fishing threatens wild stocks, commercial fisheries along the Gulf Coast are famed for shrimp catches, San Francisco and Seattle for Dungeness crabs, northern California for abalone, the Pacific Northwest for shellfish and salmon, Alaska for salmon and king crab. Western farms, particularly in the fine soils and climate of California's inland valleys, are world leaders in developing new crop strains. The world's most productive wheat fields, vegetable farms and livestock ranches are in the West, and its producers have led the way in the 21st century boom of organic farming. Westerners have long been known for their penchant for red meat. Some interesting culinary reactions developed in the 1960s. Chief among these was California cuisine, credited to Alice Waters and her Berkeley restaurant, Chez Panisse, which emphasized using fine local ingredients, lightly prepared and presented artistically. Shortly afterward, Seattle and Portland chefs adapted local ingredients to a style known as Northwest Contemporary, which blends seafood with Continental and Asian influences. Refined tastes for wine have encouraged the expansion of acreage planted with grapes, especially in California, Oregon and Washington state. Viticulture has expanded even into the Rockies, the desert Southwest, Texas and Hawaii. Demand for exceptional beer also has fueled the growth of small craft breweries across the West, their products called "microbrews." Portland is a center for this craft.

For the best little places,
follow the leader.

Looking for the latest news on today's best hotels and restaurants? Pick up the Michelin Guide and look for the Bib Gourmand and Bib Hotel symbols. With 45,000 addresses in Europe, in every category and price range, the perfect place to dine or stay is never far away.

A better way forward

Los Angeles, California
© Photodisc, Inc

DISCOVERING USA WEST

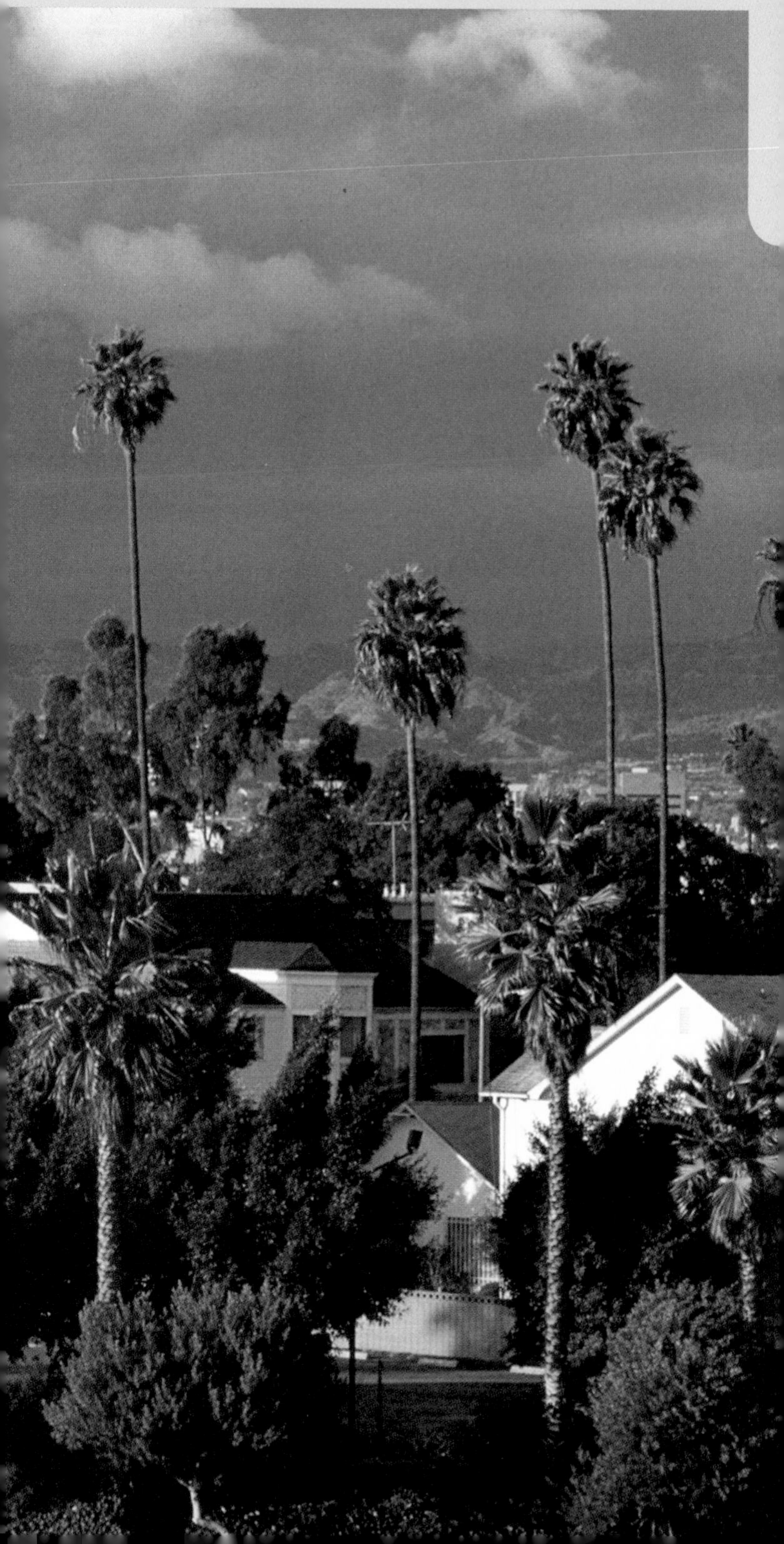

ALASKA

Alaska is more than twice the size of Texas, the next largest US state, and is bigger than all but 16 of the world's nations. It claims the 16 highest peaks in the US and far more wildlife and national parkland than any other state. A huge knob at the northwestern corner of North America, "The Great Land" spans 2,350mi from the border of Canada to the western tip of the Aleutian Islands in the Pacific Ocean. Separated from Siberia by a mere 51mi of water, Alaska lies 500mi northwest of the nearest US mainland state, Washington. Only 670,000 people live in this vast (570,000sq mi) state, ranking it last in population density.

Sometime between 15,000 and 30,000 years ago, nomadic bands crossed an exposed land bridge from Asia to America, Alaska thus becoming the gateway to this new world. Living along the coast and in the interior, Native groups were well established by the time Europeans arrived in the 18C. Driven by high prices for sea otter furs, the Russians developed a trade empire that stretched to California. As hunting hastened the decline of the otter population, the Russians withdrew, selling the vast Alaska territory to the US in 1867 for $7.2 million.

Though the lower 48 states were considered a frozen wasteland, the glitter of gold swelled settlement, with rushes to Juneau (1880), Skagway (1897-98), Nome (1899) and Fairbanks (1902). A much larger buildup occurred during World War II with military posts and construction of the Alaska Highway, linking Canada and the lower 48 to Fairbanks through 1,500mi of wilderness.

Statehood in 1959 brought recognition of the state's riches and strategic importance, as well as a need to grapple with a complex web of Native claims, developers' and conservationists' interests More than one-quarter of Alaska's land is protected as park, refuge and wilderness, from coastal mountains and fjords to tundra and bear-haunted forests.

Chilkoot Trail

© National Park Service

THE PANHANDLE★★

MICHELIN MAP 930 INSET
ALASKA STANDARD TIME

A complicated puzzle of land and water stretching north 540mi from Misty Fiords National Monument to Malaspina Glacier, the Panhandle reaches like an appendage from the body of Alaska toward the lower 48 states, separating Canada from the Gulf of Alaska. Constituting only 6 percent of the state's land area, the Panhandle (often called the Southeast) nevertheless totes up 10,000mi of shoreline with its irregular coast and its 1,000-island Alexander Archipelago.

- **Information:** ☎907-586-4777. www.alaskainfo.org
- ▶ **Orient Yourself:** Juneau, capital of Alaska, is two-thirds of the way up the nearly 600-mile stretch of fjords, islands and mountains that compose the Panhandle. The only roads in the area reach Skagway and Haines from Canada's Yukon.
- **Don't Miss:** Glacier Bay; Sitka
- **Organizing Your Time:** Cruise-line tours typically stop a full day in Juneau, Ketchikan, Skagway and Sitka. On-shore activities arranged through local visitor bureaus may be more affordable.

A Bit of History

For 6,000 years Tlingit (*KLINK-it*) Indians carved cedar canoes and harvested an easy living from the sea. They traded otter furs and dried salmon to Athabascans of the Interior for copper and caribou skins. When the Russians arrived in the late 18C, their capital in the New World, Sitka, acquired the look of a European enclave. For a time, it was the largest city on North America's west coast, until the Russians left in the mid-19C. Today ferries and cruise ships thread the island-sheltered Inside Passage on their way north from Ketchikan to Skagway. While fishing is still the main industry in most Panhandle areas, tourism and timber production also bolster the economy. Nearly half the old-growth forest of the Tongass had been clearcut before restrictions came to its rescue in the 1990s.

The island-strewn landscape is backed by coastal mountains that crest at more than 15,000ft, the highest maritime range in the world. Glaciers slip from the heights to deep fjords where seals bask on ice floes and seabirds nest on granite islands. The region receives some of the heaviest rainfall in the state, which, coupled with a sea-tempered climate, has created a lush covering of spruce-hemlock rain forest. The largest US national forest, the Tongass, contains some 75 percent of the Panhandle's land area.

Sights

Ketchikan
285mi south of Juneau. ☎*907-225-6166. www.visit-ketchikan.com.*
The southernmost town in Alaska (with 8,000 residents) and one of the wettest, Ketchikan bills itself as the salmon capital of the world. Its **Creek Street Historic District** preserves a boardwalk that until 1954 was a red-light district. Several attractions honor the Tlingit, Haida and Tsimshian cultures. The **Totem Heritage Center**★ (*601 Deermount Ave.;* ☎*907-225-5900*) displays nearly three dozen 19C totem poles salvaged from abandoned villages. The **Saxman Native Village**★ (*S. Stedman St.;* ☎ *907-225-4846*) offers tours that cover the tribal house, schoolhouse, carver's shed and a park punctuated with 28 totem poles. Visitors may watch master carvers at work and view native dance performances at the clan house.

Misty Fiords National Monument★
Headquarters, 3031 Tongass Ave., Ketchikan. ☎*907-225-2148. www.fs.fed. us/r10/tongass.*

Practical Information

GETTING THERE & GETTING AROUND

Main airports serving Alaska are **Anchorage International Airport (ANC)** (☎907-266-2526; www.anchorageairport.com), **Fairbanks International Airport (FAI)** (☎907-474-2500, www.dot.state.ak.us/faiiap) and **Juneau International Airport (JNU)** (☎907-789-7821; www.juneau.org/airport). **Alaska Airlines** (☎800-252-7522; www.alaskaair.com) offers most flights to and within Alaska. In-state airlines include **ERA Aviation** (☎907-266-8394 or 800-866-8394, www.flyera.com) and **Peninsula Airways** (☎907-771-2640 or 800-448-4226; www.penair.com). **Alaska Railroad Corp.** (☎907-265-2494 or 800-321-6518; www.alaskarailroad.com) links Seward, Anchorage, Denali National Park and Fairbanks. There is bus service between Anchorage, Fairbanks and Whitehorse, in Canada's Yukon Territory, via **Alaska Direct Bus Lines** (☎907-277-6652; www.alaskadirectbusline.com). Independent tour companies offer travel throughout Alaska by coach.

Scheduled **ferry** service from Bellingham WA to Juneau and several other ports in Alaska is provided by the **Alaska Marine Highway System** (*see page 103*). Reservations are required. For **cruise** companies, consult the Alaska Travel Industry Association (*below*).

ACCOMMODATIONS

Numerous lodges are located in and around national parks and in gateway cities. For more information, contact **Alaska Tour and Travel** (☎245-0200; www.alaskatravel.com). For **bed-**and-breakfast reservations:** Alaska Private Lodgings (☎907-235-2148; www.alaskabandb.com). For a list of public **campgrounds** and maps contact the Alaska Travel Industry Association (*below*).

Motels along highways usually have a cafe, gasoline and repair facilities. Call for availability, especially Oct–mid-May. Sights and services are listed in *The Alaska Milepost,* available in bookstores or directly from The Milepost (☎800-726-4707; www.themilepost.com).

SIGHTSEEING

Adventure Tourism: Alaska Travel Adventures (☎907-789-0052; www.alaskaadventures.com); Alaska Wildland Adventures (☎907-783-2928; www.alaskawildland.com). **Biking:** Alaskan Bicycle Adventures (☎907-245-2175; www.alaskabike.com). **Escorted tours:** Gray Line (☎888-452-1737; www.graylineofalaska.com). **Multi-sport excursions:** REI Adventures (☎253-437-1100; www.rei.com/travel).

For a list of ecotourism outfitters and more information on adventure travel, contact the **Alaska Wilderness Recreation & Tourism Association** (☎907-258-3171; www.awrta.org) or the Alaska Public Lands Information Center (☎907-271-2737; www.nps.gov/aplic).

VISITOR INFORMATION

For further information on points of interest, accommodations, sightseeing, tour companies and events, or to request the Official State of Alaska Vacation Planner, contact the **Alaska Travel Industry Association** (☎929-2200; www.travelalaska.com).

A 3,570sq mi preserve of lushly forested mountains, glacial fjords flanked by 3,000ft granite cliffs, and mist-enshrouded islands rich in wildlife, this park holds hidden waterfalls, spouting whales and spruce-top eagle aeries for visitors who boat its shores and hike its dense forests.

Sitka★★

136mi southwest of Juneau. ☎ 907-747-5940. www.sitka.org.

This historic town sits on the west side of Baranof Island. Tlingit life was uninterrupted for millennia until Russian traders in 1799 established a fortress and solicited Native help in fur trapping. But in 1802 Tlingits attacked the redoubt and killed nearly all the Russians. The Russians returned two years later, outfought

Alaska by Sea Bus

In Southeast Alaska, with few roads, planes and boats are the rule. Voyaging by water can be a memorable part of an Alaskan vacation in itself. The **Alaska Marine Highway System** (☎907-272-7116 or 800-642-0066; www.alaska.gov/ferry) is used by commuters and sightseers alike. The ferry system links 14 towns in the Panhandle; south-central Alaska and the Aleutian Islands; and Bellingham, Washington, with major stops along the Inside Passage—the 1,000mi waterway from Puget Sound to Skagway—making for a less expensive travel option than luxury cruises or commercial airlines. Naturalists often are on board in the summer to interpret marine mammal and bird life. Comfortable overnight cabins are available. Those planning to book a cabin, or to transport a car in summer, should reserve many months ahead. Port stops generally are brief; many travelers bring a kayak or bicycle aboard, adding an adventure option for a small fee.

the Tlingits and began displacing Native clan houses with fort-like dwellings. Upon the sale of Alaska to the US in 1867, Sitka became the new territorial capital. Juneau claimed that office in 1906. **St. Michael's Cathedral** (Lincoln & American Sts.; ☎907-747-8120), symbolizes Sitka's Russian heritage; it was rebuilt in 1976 on the site of the original 19C church, destroyed by fire. Now with a population of 9,000, Sitka holds all the charms of an old seaside village.

Sitka National Historical Park★

106 Metlakatla St.; Bishop's House at Monastery & Lincoln Sts. ☎ 907-747-6281. www.nps.gov/sitk.

This 107-acre park has two parcels. Exhibits at the visitor center, at the mouth of the Indian River, examine the cultural clash created by the arrival of Europeans. The adjacent **Fort Site** recalls the 1804 Battle of Sitka. A 1mi loop trail through a spruce forest passes the clearing where a Tlingit fort stood. Along the trail, nestled in the trees, is one of the finest collections of **totem poles★★★** in the US. The long, ocher **Russian Bishop's House★★** (1843), near downtown, was sturdily built by Finnish shipwrights.

Sheldon Jackson Museum★

104 College Dr. ☎907-747-8981. www.museums.state.ak.us.

The oldest museum in Alaska sits on the campus of Sheldon Jackson College, where author James Michener lived from 1984-86 while researching his novel Alaska. Bentwood baskets,

ivory tools, painted drums and other artfully executed pieces represent the major Native groups—Southeast and Athabascan Indians, Aleuts and Native Alaskans.

Alaska Raptor Center★

1000 Raptor Way (half mile east of Sitka). ☎907-747-8662. www.alaskaraptor.org. This rehabilitation/research facility is devoted to bald eagles. Here, visitors learn about them upclose.

Juneau★

650mi southeast of Anchorage. ☎907-586-1737. www.traveljuneau.com. Tucked along a slim strip of land between Gastineau Channel and high mountains,

© National Park Service

A Totem Pole

Alaska Address Book

For prices, see the Legend on the cover flap.

WHERE TO STAY

$$$$$ Great Alaska Adventure Lodge – *33881 Sterling Hwy., Sterling AK 99672.* ☎*907-262-4515 or 800-544-2261. www.greatalaska.com. 22 rooms. Open mid-Apr-mid-Sept.* The front door of this timber lodge swings open into Kenai National Wildlife Refuge. Package visits may include fishing, canoeing, kayaking, hiking and even bear-viewing. A seaplane delivers guests to wilderness camps where gourmet meals are flown in daily.

$$$$ Hotel Captain Cook – *4th Ave. & K St., Anchorage AK 99501.* ☎*907-276-6000 or 800-843-1950. www.captaincook.com. 547 rooms.* With spectacular vistas of Cook Inlet and the Chugach Mountains, this high-rise was Alaska's first luxury inn. **The Crow's Nest** (**$$$**) on the 20th floor serves fresh seafood amid nautical décor.

$$$ Glacier Bay Country Inn – *P.O. Box 5, Gustavus AK 99826.* ☎*907-697-2288 or 800-628-0912. www.glacierbay-alaska.com. 5 rooms, 5 cabins. (per person, meals inclusive). Open mid-May-mid-Sept.* Guests are rewarded by the solitude of this rambling inn, isolated in meadows of wildflowers. Guests spend days fly fishing, whale-watching or cruising Glacier Bay, and evenings dining on halibut or grilled salmon.

$$$ McKinley Chalet Resort – *Milepost 238.5, George Parks Hwy., Denali National Park AK 99755.* ☎*800-276-7234. www.denaliparkresorts.com. 350 rooms.* ⏰ *Open mid-May-mid-Sept.* The nearest hotel to Denali Park has rooms in cedar lodges beside the swift Nenana River, a magnet for rafting enthusiasts. Within are restaurants and a melodrama dinner theater. A sister hotel, **McKinley Village Resort** (**$$$**), has 150 units among spruce trees.

$$ The Oscar Gill House – *1344 W. 10th Ave., Anchorage, AK 99501.* ☎*907-279-1344. www.oscargill.com. 3 rooms.* This 1913 pioneer home was on the demolition block when Mark and Susan Lutz bought it for $1 in 1993 and moved it to a lot facing the Delaney Park Strip. The Lutzes offer guests free use of bicycles or cross-country skis. Two rooms share a bath; a larger room has a private bath.

$ Alaskan Hotel – *167 S. Franklin St., Juneau, AK 99801.* ☎ *907-586-1000 or 800-327-9347. www.thealaskanhotel.com. 42 rooms.* Stained-glass panels and oak shelves characterize this Victorian-style hotel, built in 1913. About half the rooms share baths, but all have phones or sinks.

WHERE TO EAT

$$$ The Marx Bros. Café – *627 W. 3rd Ave., Anchorage.* ☎ *907-278-2133. www.marxcafe.com. Dinner only. Closed Sun. and Mon.* **Regional.** This quaint, wood-frame house offers an intimate dining experience with a daily fresh menu of seafood (salmon, Kodiak scallops or marlin) as well as wild game and vegetarian options.

$$ The Pump House – *796 Chena Pump Rd. (Mile 1.3), Fairbanks.* ☎ *907-479-8452. www.pumphouse.com.* **Steak and Seafood.** This family-oriented restaurant abuts the Chena River. Riverboats and float planes cruise past the patio; inside are a mahogany bar and other 19C antiques. The menu features salmon, smoked ribs, and the "world's most northern oyster bar."

$$$ Ludvig's Bistro – *256 Katlian Dr., Sitka.* ☎*907-966-3663. www.ludvigs-bistro.com. Dinner only. Closed Sun. and Mon.* **Regional.** The best dining in Southeast offers Mediterranean-tinged seafood such as cioppino, paella and catch of the day with risotto.

the capital of 31,000 is accessible only by air or sea. Juneau has the look of a quaint European city, its narrow streets curving up from the waterfront. The discovery of gold in 1880 led to the establishment of a town site that became the territorial capital in 1906.

Near the cruise-ship terminal, the **Mt. Roberts Tramway**★ (*490 S. Franklin St.;* ☎*907-463-3412, www.mountroberts*

© National Park Service

Glacier Bay

tramway.com) ascends 1,880 vertical feet to views of town and harbor. A short stroll from People's Wharf, through the heart of the historic district on Franklin and Main Streets, brings visitors to the **Alaska State Capitol** *(4th & Main Sts.; ☎907-465-2479)*, ornamented with marble quarried on Prince of Wales Island.

Alaska State Museum★★

395 Whittier St. ☎ 907-465-2901. www.museums.state.ak.us.
This extensive facility holds more than 23,000 artifacts and works of art. The Alaska Native Gallery features splendid works such as ceremonial masks and sealskin kayaks. A life-size diorama of a treetop eagle's nest highlights the Natural History ramp, while the State History Gallery limns important events in the Russian period, the gold-mining era and other early chapters.

Admiralty Island National Monument★

Access by boat only: inquire at headquarters, 8465 Old Dairy Rd., Juneau. ☎907-586-8790. www.fs.fed.us/r10/tongass.
This pristine 1,709sq mi island is famous for brown bears. Some 1,500 inhabit the forest, mountains and rocky beaches, feeding on salmon and wild berries. Permits are required to visit Pack Creek Bear Preserve on the northeast shore.

Mendenhall Glacier★

Mendenhall Loop Rd., 13mi northwest of downtown Juneau via Egan Dr. ☎907-789-0097, www.fs.fed.us/r10/tongass.
An easily accessible wonder, this 1.5mi-wide glacier arcs 12mi from the Juneau Icefield down to Mendenhall Lake, where it calves into the water. A short trail leads to the water's edge, while the 3.5mi **East Glacier Loop** gets hikers close to the glacier's edge. The river of ice is retreating about 200ft per year.

Glacier Bay National Park and Preserve★★★

Gustavus, 65mi west of Juneau. ☎907-697-2230. www.nps.gov/glba.
Encompassing 4,297sq mi, Glacier Bay showcases views of ice-clad mountains, a rich variety of marine and land animals, and miles of wilderness. The original glaciers, however, have retreated more than 60mi in two centuries. UNESCO declared this natural kingdom a World Heritage Site in 1992.
When explorer George Vancouver sailed past in 1794, he saw only an icy shoreline, with barely an indentation to suggest a retreating glacier. The first person to seriously study the area and bring it to attention, naturalist John Muir traveled here in 1879. Inside Passage cruise ships first came calling in the 1970s.
Unforgettable day-long **cruises**★★★ depart Bartlett Cove each morning. In the lower bay, naturalists point out sea otters at play; humpback whales breach-

ing, their tails fanning as they dive; and pods of orcas rolling like black and white waves. Tours pause at **Marble Island**★★ where thousands of kittiwakes, puffins, cormorants, murres and other birds noisily commune on the rocks, and sea lions snort and nose each other for better places in the sun. At the head of the bay, spectacular glaciers rear up 200ft; tours venture close enough to witness tremendous splashes as chunks of ice calve into the water.

Skagway★

80mi north of Juneau. ☎907-983-2854. www.skagway.com.
Positioned at the northern end of the Inside Passage, Skagway was the rollicking frontier town through which gold seekers passed on their arduous way up the 33mi **Chilkoot Trail** to the Yukon goldfields in 1897-98. To prevent their perishing in the wilderness, prospectors were required to carry one ton of supplies over the pass, which meant 40 back-breaking ascents. Many fell prey to the dance halls and streetwalkers of Skagway.
Klondike Gold Rush National Historical Park★ *(2nd Ave. & Broadway; ☎ 907-983-2921; www.nps.gov/klgo)* preserves the Chilkoot Trail (now a recreational byway) and the historic district, with its false-fronted buildings and wooden sidewalks. Brothels and gambling dens are now shops and eateries. The narrow-gauge, 41mi **White Pass & Yukon Route Railway**★ *(2nd Ave. & Spring St.; ☎800-343-7373, www.whitepass-railroad. com)* takes tourists through scenery traversed by prospectors. *com)* takes tourists through scenery traversed by prospectors.

ANCHORAGE★

MICHELIN MAP 930 INSET
ALASKA STANDARD TIME
POPULATION 278,700

Sprawled over the one piece of flat ground between Cook Inlet and the sharp peaks of the Chugach Range, Alaska's largest city holds nearly half the state's population. As the state's center of commerce and culture, the city welcomes both business travelers and tourists.

🚹 **Information:** ☎907-276-4118. www.anchorage.net

A Bit of History

Starting as a tent city of pioneers and rail workers in 1914, Anchorage grew into a frontier city. Fort Richardson and Elmendorf Air Force Base helped push population over 30,000 by 1950. Cold War defense-system headquarters added to the city's problems: inadequate housing, vice crimes and heavy traffic. The earthquake of 1964 rocked Anchorage to its foundations. Rebuilding invigorated the skyline with new life. Late 1960s oil development in Prudhoe Bay provided another boost. Anchorage today offers fine restaurants, upscale galleries, parks and cultural events.

Sights

Anchorage Museum of History and Art★

Kids *121 W. 7th St. ☎ 907-343-4326. www.anchoragemuseum.org.*
Covering most of a city block, this repository of history, ethnography and art presents an in-depth look at Alaskan culture. The first-floor art collection highlights people and landscapes; included are **canvases**★ by Sydney Laurence (1865-1940), Alaska's most famous painter. Upstairs, the Alaska Gallery displays historical objects of Indian, Aleut and Native Alaskan lifestyles, proceeding into the era of European contact. A highlight is the life-size diorama of an

18C Aleut house of whalebone, grass and sod.

Alaska Aviation Heritage Museum★

Kids *4721 Aircraft Dr., Lake Hood Air Harbor.* ☎ *907-248-5325. www.alaskaairmuseum.org.*

The din of seaplanes on the lake outside—85,000 takeoffs and landings a year, the most of any air harbor on earth—adds realism to a compendium of history in a state that relies on aircraft to reach "the bush." Displays include vintage bush planes, a restoration room, photos and a theater.

Excursion

Girdwood Area★

37mi southeast of Anchorage via Seward Hwy. (Rte. 1).

A national scenic byway, the Seward Highway takes motorists from Anchorage along **Turnagain Arm**, whose 38ft bore tide in spring is the second-greatest in North America. Beluga whales sometimes spout and breach here. The road continues through Chugach National Forest to the Kenai Peninsula.

Less than an hour from the city, the **Alyeska Resort Tramway**★ *(Alyeska Hwy., 3mi east of Girdwood;* ☎ *907-754-1111, www.alyeskaresort.com)* whisks visitors 2,300ft above the valley to the top of Alaska's premier ski mountain for **views**★★ of Turnagain Arm and ice-bitten peaks. Nearby **Crow Creek Mine** Kids *(Crow Creek Rd., 2mi east of Girdwood;* ☎ *907-278-8060, www.crowcreekgoldmine.com)* harbors a clutch of weathered buildings from the gold-rush era. The **Portage Glacier Recreation Area**★ *(5.5mi east of Seward Hwy., Milepost 79;* ☎ *907-783-3242, www.fs.fed.us/r10/chugach)* offers a short course on glacial geology and a chance to grab chunks of ice in a glacial lake. On 1hr boat tours, visitors see and hear Portage Glacier calve.

SOUTH CENTRAL ALASKA★★

MICHELIN MAP 930 INSET
ALASKA STANDARD TIME

South of the Alaska Range, the land gentles into fertile valleys and rolling forests, then suddenly buckles into another cordillera of glacier-capped peaks along the Gulf of Alaska. Land, sea and sky meet in grand proportion in this diverse region where goats clamber on steep cliffs in sight of spouting whales, and fishing villages reap the bounty of tens of millions of spawning salmon.

🛈 **Information:** ☎907-262-5229. www.kenaipeninsula.org

▶ **Orient Yourself:** Most of the area is reached through Rte 1 south out of Anchorage, roughly a 4hr drive to Homer; but Valdez, at the northern tip of Prince William Sound, is 6hr in the other direction on Rte 1.

☺ **Don't Miss:** Homer, a haven for artists and free spirits.

A Bit of History

The ice-free ports of Valdez *(val-DEEZ)*, Cordova, Seward, Homer and Kenai were staging points for exploitation of copper, coal and gold. In the 1910s the railroad linked Seward with Anchorage, but not until the 1950s did a highway traverse the 225mi from Anchorage to Homer.

On the **Kenai Peninsula**, south of Anchorage, knife-ridged mountains seem to rise directly from the sea. Clouds accumulate in the moist sea air, saturating the coastline in summer with light but frequent rains.

The region continues to recover from the massive *Exxon Valdez* oil spill of 1989, which affected more than 1,500mi of shoreline from Prince William Sound to Kodiak Island.

Sights

Seward★

Seward Hwy. (Rte. 9), 130mi south of Anchorage. ☎907-224-8051. www.sewardak.org.

A spirited town of bright stucco-and-clapboard bungalows and fewer than 3,000 citizens, Seward rests at the head of mountain-rimmed **Resurrection Bay.** Starting in 1902 as the southern terminus of the Alaska Railroad, Seward became known as the "Gateway to Alaska". Visitors shop and eat at the picturesque **Small Boat Harbor,** watch fishermen returning with their catches, and take wildlife cruises into the bay.

Alaska SeaLife Center★

Kids *301 Railway Ave. ☎ 907-224-6300. www.alaskasealife.org.*

This modern research, rehabilitation and education facility was funded by a legal settlement from the *Exxon Valdez* spill. Viewing platforms allow visitors to gaze into pools for sea lions, seals and sea otters; marine birds have a rock pool and cliffs.

Kenai Fjords National Park★★

Visitor center at Small Boat Harbor on 4th Ave., Seward. ☎907-224-7500. www.nps.gov/kefj.

Covering 1,045sq mi of coastal fjords and glacier-clad mountains on the southeastern side of the Kenai Peninsula, this park preserves a wilderness where thousands of marine mammals and seabirds find sanctuary. More than 30ft of snow a year replenish the 300sq mi Harding Icefield, which feeds 30 glaciers. **Boat tours**★ vary from 2hr 30min cruises around Resurrection Bay to 9hr voyages down the coastline to Harris Bay and Northwestern Glacier. Wildlife sightings range from murres and horned puffins to sea otters and humpback whales. On the north side of the park, the **Exit Glacier**★ area *(Exit Glacier Rd., 9mi west of Seward Hwy.; first 4mi paved)* has a network of trails to bring visitors close to the 3mi-long river of ice. The **Glacier Access Trail** *(.5mi)* is an easy stroll to a glacial viewpoint. The more strenuous **Harding Icefield Trail**★ *(3.5mi one-way)* ascends 3,000ft to spectacular views of the vast icefield. From this frozen sea jut jagged *nunataks*, an Native Alaskan word meaning "lonely peaks."

Homer★

Sterling Hwy. (Rte. 1), 225mi southwest of Anchorage. ☎ 907-235-7740. www.homeralaska.org.

Guarding the entrance to Kachemak Bay in the lower Kenai Peninsula, the individualistic town of Homer is framed by Cook Inlet and the jagged graph of the Kenai Mountains. For decades it has attracted artists, retirees, fishermen and, more recently, tourists; the permanent population is 4,000. The 4.5mi **Homer Spit** harbors an extensive commercial and recreational fishing industry.

© National Park Service

Sea Lions

Dogsled Racing

A team of huskies mushing across a frozen landscape is a quintessential Alaska image. More than 4,000 years ago, nomadic Natives enlisted indigenous malamutes to help pull loads and reach hunting and fishing grounds. Their stamina and sense of direction made them invaluable to later explorers. Jack London's 1903 classic, *The Call of the Wild*, described gold seekers using dogs to haul equipment and provisions. In 1967, during Alaska's centennial celebration, a race was held to commemorate the Iditarod Trail, a route used in 1925 to relay diptheria serum to Nome. Today, Anchorage is the March starting point for the 1,049mi **Iditarod**. The route spans tundra, frozen rivers and icy mountain ranges, with winners typically reaching Nome in just over nine days. Improved equipment, trail conditions, breeding and training have whittled the course time from 20 days in 1973. First-place finishers win $70,000, a four-wheel-drive truck, and the accolades of the dogsledding world. Dogsled fans consider the 1,000mi Fairbanks-to-Whitehorse Yukon Quest in February an even tougher challenge.

Pratt Museum★

3779 Bartlett St. ☎ 907-235-8635. www.prattmuseum.org.

A first-rate collection of art and natural history, the Pratt offers a gut-wrenching exhibit on the Valdez spill, an interesting display about the ongoing spruce-beetle epidemic, and a hands-on video monitor for viewing nesting birds on nearby Gull Island via remote-control camera.

Halibut Cove★★

Access by Danny J ferry (4hr 30min tours) from the Homer Spit Marina. ☎ 907-235-7847. www.centralcharter.com.

A 32-person ferry takes locals and tourists to this tranquil curve of beach backed by a lagoon dotted with houses on stilts. Stroll the boardwalks, visit the handful of galleries, and absorb the beauty of a watery paradise.

Prince William Sound★

☎ 907-835-4636. www.valdezalaska.org.

Basking in the protective embrace of the Chugach Mountains on the north and the Kenai Peninsula on the west, Prince William Sound offers a quiet 15,000sq mi seascape for kayaking, cruising and studying marine wildlife. One road links the Sound with the Interior—the scenic Richardson Highway to **Valdez**, a port at the end of the Trans-Alaska Pipeline servicing the giant oil tankers.

Wrangell-St. Elias National Park★

Headquarters at Mile 105.5 Old Richardson Hwy. (Rte. 4), Copper Center, 10mi south of Glenallen. ☎ 907-822-5234. www.nps.gov/wrst.

A magnificent wilderness of glaciers, streams and towering snow-crowned peaks, the park's 20,600sq mi make it the largest US national park. Larger than Switzerland, it tops out at 18,008ft **Mt. St. Elias,** second-highest in the US.

Excursions

Lake Clark National Park and Preserve

Headquarters, 4230 University Dr., Suite 311, Anchorage. ☎907-644-3626. Field headquarters, Port Alsworth; 150mi southwest of Anchorage. ☎907-781-2218. www.nps.gov/lacl.

The stunning range of landscapes here varies from coastal wetlands rich in marine mammals, to alpine tundra thick with bears, to 50mi-long **Lake Clark,** host to an immense run of sockeye salmon.

Katmai National Park and Preserve★

Field headquarters, King Salmon; 290mi southwest of Anchorage. ☎ 907-246-3305. www.nps.gov/katm.

Katmai embraces 6,250sq mi at the head of the Alaska Peninsula. Volcanic eruptions in 1912 poured molten rock into a once-green valley, after which steam and gases emitted from thousands of vents. Four years later, a National Geographic Society team saw these fumaroles spewing smoke and steam and named the 40sq-mi area the **Valley of Ten Thousand Smokes**★. The smokes have trailed off, yet wisps are sometimes visible. Katmai is known for its Alaskan brown bears, which may exceed 1,400 pounds. Viewing platforms at Brooks Camp and **McNeil River State Game Sanctuary**★ enable visitors to observe bears up close. Human visitation is by lottery.

Aniakchak National Monument

Field headquarters, King Salmon. ☎907-246-3305. www.nps.gov/ania.
This isolated, otherworldly tract of volcanic land south of Katmai boasts an active volcano with a huge caldera, 6mi wide and 2,000ft deep. Reached by plane from Anchorage in three stages, the park is often raked by high winds and foul weather; visitors must wait for a break in the weather, then land on the lake or in the caldera.

INTERIOR AND THE ARCTIC★

ALASKA STANDARD TIME

MICHELIN MAP 930 INSET

A great rolling plain sandwiched between the Alaska and Brooks Ranges, the Interior has long been a haven for wildlife. Much in the landscape has remained the same for millennia. The taiga—a forest of spruce, alder and willow—supports a chain of mammalian life from bear and moose down to snowshoe hare and lynx. Birds in the millions migrate through as they have for thousands of years, wings drumming, responding to the call of the north.

- 🅘 **Information:** ☎907-465-2012. www.travelalaska.com.
- ▶ **Orient Yourself:** From Fairbanks, the hub of Alaska's interior, it's an 8hr drive to Anchorage; roughly 3 days on the Alaska Highway to Fort St. John, Canada; and 18hr on the Dalton Highway to Prudhoe Bay.
- 👁 **Don't Miss:** A flightseeing tour of Gates of the Arctic National Park. Muskox and caribou can be seen *(summer only)* at the Large Animal Research Station in Fairbanks *(Yankowich Rd., 2mi northwest of the airport;* ☎907-474-5724, www. uaf.edu/lars)*.
- 🄺🄸🄳🅂 **Especially for Kids:** In Fairbanks, Pioneer Park and Riverboat Discovery.

A Bit of History

The Interior surged in population during the 1890s gold rush as prospectors made their way to Canada's Klondike along the Yukon River. The grittiest stayed, turning log-cabin settlements into a few sparse towns. One of them, Fairbanks, grew into a small city that is now home to the University of Alaska.
North of the Interior sprawls the vast and forbidding Arctic, an alien region that occupies nearly a third of Alaska and claims very few human residents. In this land of extremes, the sun never sets in the summer, never rises in the winter. A major mountain range, largely unexplored, arcs across its midriff; frozen deserts dot the hinterlands; shimmering streams etch sinuous patterns across the tundra. In the brief summer wildflowers bloom bravely in chill winds and caribou thunder north to calving grounds.

Interior

Fairbanks★

Alaska Hwy. (Rte. 2) & George Parks Hwy. (Rte. 3), 358mi north of Anchorage. ☎907-456-5774. www.explorefairbanks.com.

Spread among rolling hills along the Chena River, Alaska's second-largest city (31,500 people) is the hub for the Interior. Beginning as a trading post for gold miners in 1901, the town prospered with the building of military installations in World War II and the Trans-Alaska Pipeline in the 1970s. A resourceful and often eccentric citizenry copes with brutal winters—tempered by the spectacle of the northern lights—and opens its arms to the nightless days of summer.

Pioneer Park★

Kids *Airport Way & Peger Rd.* ☎*907-459-1087. co.fairbanks.ak.us/ParksandRecreation.*
This 44-acre history theme park holds the National Historic Landmark SS *Nenana*, a restored sternwheeler that plied the Yukon River from 1933 to 1952. There are also historic wooden buildings, now gift shops and snack stands.

Riverboat Discovery★

Kids *Steamboat Landing, Discovery Rd.* ☎*907-479-6673. www.riverboatdiscovery.com.*
A 20mi (3hr30min) cruise down the Chena and Tenana Rivers is enlivened by sled-dog demonstrations, and a visit to a re-created Athabascan Indian village.

Museum of the North★★

907 Yukon Dr. ☎ *907-474-7505. www.uaf.edu/museum.*
Mounted animals, dioramas, hands-on objects, an art gallery and video programs survey the history and culture of five principal geographical regions of the state. The Rose Berry Gallery★ focuses on art by Alaskans, from historic to contemporary.

Denali National Park and Preserve★★★

George Parks Hwy. (Rte. 3), Denali Park; 125mi south of Fairbanks & 240mi north of Anchorage. ☎ *907-683-2294. www.nps.gov/dena.*
At 9,375sq mi, Denali offers an incomparable cross section of the untamed Alaska Range, including the highest peak in North America, 20,320ft **Mt. McKinley.** The park's geography varies from spruce forest to grassy tundra

to austere granite pinnacles mantled in snow and ice. Glaciers have scoured cirques, and chiseled ridges and steep valleys, to create a remote Olympian landscape that often appears to float in a world of its own above the clouds. Set aside as a refuge in 1917, the park harbors 37 mammal species and 157 bird species. Moose, wolves and grizzly bears roam. Caribou graze the tundra; Dall sheep dot the uplands.
McKinley is the single largest mountain and highest exposed mountain in the world. Rising 18,000ft above the lowlands of **Wonder Lake,** it is 7,000ft higher than Everest from base to summit. Early mornings provide the best chance to view the often cloud-covered peak. **Shuttle-bus tours★★** cross forested taiga and open tundra, offering opportunities for wildlife sightings. Few trails cross this wilderness park.

The Arctic★

Spreading from Canada 700mi to the Chukchi Sea, the Arctic's northern border is the frigid Beaufort Sea, while to the south runs the Yukon River. The dominating feature rises just north of the Arctic Circle—the ancient Brooks Range, with its 9,000ft peaks running east to west in endless, sharp spires. Access is mainly by air, but the Dalton Highway from Fairbanks to Prudhoe Bay is one of just two through roads in North America that cross the Arctic Circle.

Gates of the Arctic National Park★

Headquarters, 417 Geist Rd., Fairbanks. ☎ *907-457-5752. Field office, Bettles; 180mi northwest of Fairbanks.* ☎*907-692-5494. www.nps.gov/gaar.*
Bush pilots fly visitors to this sprawling (12,816sq mi) national park, with no formal trails or facilities, in the Brooks Range. Guided adventures, booked well in advance, begin either in the Inupiaq village of **Anaktuvuk Pass** or in the century-old trading village of **Bettles**.

Prudhoe Bay

380mi north of Fairbanks. ☎*907-659-2368. www.prudhoebay.com.*

This remote outpost harbors Pump Station One at the beginning of the 800mi Trans-Alaska Pipeline, and a wide variety of Arctic flora and fauna. Oil field facilities can be visited only through guided tours.

Barrow

500mi north-northwest of Fairbanks. ☎907-852-5211. www.cityofbarrow.org.
Northernmost town in the Western Hemisphere, this Inupiaq community of 4,500 citizens clings to a treeless tundra on the edge of the Arctic icepack. The Inupiaq have lived in these climes for 1,500 years; archaeologists are excavating an ancient village on a bluff near downtown. The **Wiley Post-Will Rogers Memorial** *(15mi southwest)*, marks the spot the pilot and humorist died in a 1935 small plane crash.

Kotzebue★

450mi west-northwest of Fairbanks. ☎907-442-3401. www.cityofkotzebue. com.
Alaska's most populous Native community with more than 3,100 residents, 70 percent Native, Kotzebue is a living cultural museum. Visitors can learn how humans have lived in this unrelenting environment for millennia. Kotzebue is headquarters *(☎907-442-3890)* for three remote, pristine park wildernesses.

Noatak National Preserve *(www.nps. gov/noat)* harbors the largest virgin river basin in the US; UNESCO has designated the river an International Biosphere Reserve. **Kobuk Valley National Park** *(www.nps.gov/kova)*, at the remote west end of the Brooks Range, has 100ft-high dunes, limpid streams and relict flora. **Cape Krusenstern National Monument** *(www.nps.gov/cakr)*, across Hotham Inlet from Kotzebue, has coastal landscapes of harsh beauty, its ridges rife with 6,000 years of Native Alaskan artifacts.

Nome

520mi west of Fairbanks. ☎907-443-6624. www.nomealaska.org.
With the discovery of gold here in late 1898, Nome's population soared to 20,000. Those rambunctious frontier days long gone, the town of about 3,500 is the commercial hub of northwestern Alaska, and is the finish line for the Iditarod Trail dogsled race in March.

Bering Land Bridge National Preserve

Visitor center, 240 Front St., Nome. ☎907-443-2522. www.nps.gov/bela.
Hot springs, extinct volcanoes, stunningly clear lakes and prehistoric camping sites dot the peninsula where Siberian nomads first crossed into Alaska.

Arctic Wildlife

The semi-aquatic **polar bear** is one of the most elusive. Living on ice floes in the far north, this fierce predator hunts walruses, seals and whales, sometimes waiting hours for prey to surface at a breathing hole. Unlike polar bears, **grizzly bears** eat food other than meat, often grazing on blueberries near Antigun Pass off the Dalton Highway. Though not as large as the brown bears of Alaska's south coast, Arctic grizzlies can top 900 pounds. The heaviest polar bears weigh about 1,200 pounds. Alaskan brown bears may exceed 1,400 pounds.

Re-introduced to the Arctic, **musk oxen** are exceptionally adapted to extreme cold. A layer of fat topped by thick skin, a heavy undercoat and silky hair 15-20in long keeps them comfortable at -80ºF. Their wool, or qiviut, is prized for its softness and warmth. Chief among their enemies, **wolves** hunt in packs on the dry alpine tundra. When under attack, the musk oxen herd will circle up like a wagon train, shaggy heads facing defiantly outward. Magnificent **caribou** migrate to the tundra in summer across cold rivers and through mountain passes, their herds sometimes running in the thousands..

BLACK HILLS REGION

Rolling hills seem to go on forever in the northern Great Plains, punctuated only by an occasional ranch house or barn. Here and there, a cowboy may ride over the crest of a hill, sheepdogs in the lead, to find 100 head of cattle in a draw. Multiple thunderstorms move through the expanse of sky like ships adrift in a deceptively placid sea. High buttes that once were landmarks for westbound pioneers interrupt these wide-open spaceslike ancient ruins.

The Black Hills of western South Dakota were forced 60 million years ago to heights of 14,000ft. Ravaged by inland seas and thundering upheavals, the domed range today stands 3,000ft–4,000ft above the surrounding plains.

From a distance, the heavily wooded hills appear dark: thus their name.

The Black Hills are renowned for their caves. The same geological forces that caused them to uplift 60 million years ago cracked the limestone layers deposited by a previous inland ocean. Water seeped in, slowly wearing down the rock into a maze of passages. The "racetrack" of limestone that circles the granite core is strewn with hundreds of miles of ancient caverns, constituting the second-longest cave system in the world. Eight caves are developed for public viewing.

East of the hills, across the Cheyenne River, the erosion of sedimentary stone in the past 500,000 years created the Badlands.

© PhotoDisc, Inc

Mount Rushmore National Memorial

BLACK HILLS★★

MAP P 116
MOUNTAIN STANDARD TIME

The Black Hills uplift, 125mi long and 65mi wide, has a rugged core of granite spires, knobs and mountains. It is flanked in the west by a limestone plateau, framed by the Cheyenne and Belle Fourche Rivers and the appropriately named Red Valley. The region's urban center, and Black Hills gateway, is Rapid City.

- **Information:** ☎605-355-3600, www.blackhillsbadlands.com
- **Don't Miss:** The Mt. Rushmore and Crazy Horse memorials. Deadwood is worth visiting.
- **Organizing Your Time:** Plan on a full day to visit Rushmore and Crazy Horse: the morning for the first and afternoon for the latter, which are about a half-hour apart.
- **Especially for Kids:** The Journey Museum.

A Bit of History

The area's human history goes back 11,000 years. Ancient mammoth hunters were followed by nomadic tribes. For centuries these ponderosa-clad hills have been sacred to Native Americans—they call them Paha Sapa, "hills that are black." The Lakota Sioux, having domesticated horses, ruled the northern plains until European fur-trading posts arose on the Red and Missouri Rivers. In the 1850s, homesteaders moved in; European immigrants and the railroad followed.

After a member of Lt. Col. **George Custer**'s expedition discovered gold in 1874 in the Black Hills, the Lakotas' sacred hunting ground, South Dakota's gold rush began. The treaty that had granted them this territory in perpetuity was ignored as prospectors rushed in to grab the earth's treasure. This inevitably led to conflict. The Sioux and Cheyenne prevailed at the Battle of the **Little Bighorn** in nearby Montana in 1876, but that was their final hurrah. The massacre at **Wounded Knee** in 1890 completed the subjugation of Native tribes. In 1897 President Grover Cleveland established the Black Hills Forest Reserve, later Black Hills National Forest. Until it closed at the end of 2001, the Homestake Gold Mine in Lead was the world's oldest continuously operated gold mine.

Sights

Rapid City★

US-16 & Rte. 79 at I-90. ✕⅏🅿 ☎800-487-3223. *www.visitrapidcity.com.*

The principal Black Hills community was established on a foundation of mining, lumber and ranching; trade and tourism now support its 62,000 people. In 1876, Frenchman Henri LeBeau began creating gold designs that remain a regional trademark. Free factory tours are offered at **Mt. Rushmore Black Hills Gold** *(2707 Mt. Rushmore Rd.; ☎605-343-2226).*

Downtown Rapid City launched a major urban art project whereby by 2012, life-size bronze sculptures of every US president will mark street corners.

A Berlin Wall exhibit stands in **Memorial Park** *(444 Mt. Rushmore Rd.),* just north of downtown. **Dinosaur Park** *(Skyline Dr. W. off Quincy St.; ☎605-343-8687)* features concrete replicas of prehistoric beasts, including a brontosaurus visible miles away. The **Stavkirke Chapel** *(Chapel Lane Dr. off Jackson Blvd.)* was built in 1969 as a replica of a 12C Norwegian stave church. **South Dakota Air and Space Museum** *(Ellsworth Air Force Base, I-90 Exit 66; ☎605-385-5189, www. ellsworth.af.mil)* displays stealth bombers and other aircraft.

The Journey Museum★★

222 New York St. ⅏🅿 ☎605-394-6923. *www.journeymuseum.org.*

Address Book Black Hills Region

For coin ranges, see the Legend on the cover flap.

WHERE TO STAY

$$$ The Hotel Alex Johnson – *523 6th St., Rapid City, SD.* ✕ ⅋ 🅿 ⌕ ☎*605-342-1210 or 800-888-2539. www.alexjohnson. com. 143 rooms.* When Alex Johnson built his seven-story hotel in 1928, he foresaw a showplace for Sioux culture, with hand-painted buffalo tiles and a chandelier of spears. Each floor today honors a tribe, from Black Spirit Horse to White Calf Buffalo. The **Landmark Restaurant** (**$$**) features such cuisine as trout and buffalo.

$$$ State Game Lodge & Resort – *US-16A, Custer State Park, SD.* ✕ ⅋ 🅿 ☎*605-255-4772 pr 888-875-0001. www. custerresorts.com. 69 units.* Built in 1920, this erstwhile presidential retreat has stately lodge rooms, motel units and intimate cabins. The **Historic Pheasant Dining Room** (☎*605-255-4541;* **$$$**) offers creative preparations of wild-game dishes: pheasant braised in peach brandy, antelope chops in a red-onion demi-glace.

$$ The Historic Franklin Hotel – *700 Main St., Deadwood, SD.* ✕ 🅿 ☎*605-578-3670. www.silveradofranklin.com. 81 rooms.* The Franklin has hosted a galaxy of stars since 1903. Rooms are dedicated to movie stars, presidents and rodeo riders. In the antiques-laden lobby is a hand-operated elevator; Durty Nelly's is Deadwood's oldest gaming hall.

$$ Missouri River Lodge – *140 42nd Ave. NW, Stanton, ND.* ⅋ 🅿 ☎*701-748-2023 or 877-480-3498. www.moriver-lodge.com. 7 rooms.* Lewis and Clark Trail enthusiasts love this 2,000-acre working ranch, which spreads from the Missouri into Badlands. Trails invite hiking, biking and horseback riding, while boaters and canoeists may launch vessels from the river banks. All rooms have private baths and TVs.

$$ River Place Inn – *109 River Place, Pierre, SD.* 🅿 ☎*605-224-8589. www. bbonline.com/sd/riverplace. 4 rooms.* Overlooking the Missouri River, this modern B&B inn has rooms with private or shared baths. The owners also operate a bird-hunting lodge nearby.

$$ Spearfish Canyon Resort – *US-14A, Latchspring Village. SD* ✕ ⅋ 🅿 ☎*605-584-3435 or 800-439-8544. www.spf-canyon.com. 54 rooms.* Soaring timbers rise above a river-rock fireplace in the great room of this classic lodge, 15mi south of Spearfish. Suites offer Jacuzzi tubs and decks with canyon views. The **Latchstring Village Restaurant** (**$$**) specializes in Black Hills trout: pan-seared, fried or almandine.

$ Rough Riders Hotel – *3rd Ave. & 3rd St., Medora, ND.* ✕ 🅿 ☎*701-623-4444 or 800-633-6721. www.medora.com. 9 rooms.* Teddy Roosevelt used to ride from his ranch into town to dine on bison and other game at this hotel, built in 1883 and restored in 1962. Every air-conditioned room has antiques and TV. Inexpensive off-season rates include meals and wine.

WHERE TO EAT

$$ La Minestra – *106 E. Dakota St., Pierre, SD.* ⅋ *Closed Sun.* ☎*605-224-8090. www.laminestra.com.* **Italian**. Mark Mancuso weaves his culinary spell in an open kitchen behind an antique mahogany bar. Old World flavor permeates the cafe; the building was constructed in 1896 as a funeral parlor: minestra means "destiny." The menu features homemade pastas, eggplant Parmesan, steaks and seafood.

$$ Peacock Alley Bar & Grill – *422 E. Main St., Bismarck, ND.* ⅋ ☎*701-255-7917. www.peacock-alley.com.* **American**. The floral décor doesn't quite mesh with the framed photos of early bucking champions, but contradictions are right at home among the politicians who frequent this 1930s hotel lobby near the state capitol. The eclectic menu ranges from burgers to roast duck, Cajun shrimp to Shanghai salad.

$$ Powder House – *US-16A, Keystone, SD.* ⅋ 🅿 *Open May–Sept.* ☎*605-666-4646. www.powderhouselodge.com.* **American**. The log-cabin Powder House once hid bootleg liquor under its tin roof in the 1930s. Today, spirits are served upon the tree-branch legs of big oak tables, along with breaded mushrooms, prime rib, and buffalo stew in a homemade bread bowl.

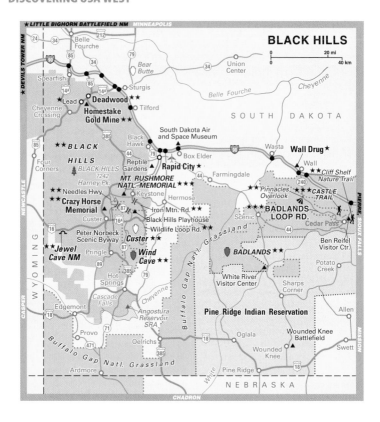

State-of-the-art multimedia techniques relate the 2.5-million-year history of the Black Hills region through collections of five museums, including the **Sioux Indian Museum**★★ of the US Department of the Interior; the **Duhamel Plains Indian Collection**, and the **Minnilusa Pioneer Museum**★★. Provocative displays offer insight into the minds of Indian warriors and the secrets of the Sioux's sacred Black Hills.

Located on the road toward Mt. Rushmore, **Reptile Gardens** Kids *(US-16, 6mi south of downtown; ☎605-342-5873; www.reptilegardens.com)* features amphibians, exotic birds, raptors, alligators and snakes. **Bear Country USA** Kids *(US-16, 9mi south of Rapid City; ☎605-343-2290; www.bearcountryusa.com)* is a drive-through, open-air zoo.

Mt. Rushmore National Memorial★★

Kids ⅢⅢ *Rte. 244, 3mi west of Keystone.* ✗♿⧠ *☎605-574-2523. www.nps.gov/moru.*

Carved in a granite cliff over 14 years (1927-41) by **Gutzon Borglum**, Mt. Rushmore is his "shrine to democracy." Borglum chose to depict four US presidents—George Washington, first president; Thomas Jefferson, author of the Declaration of Independence; Abraham Lincoln, who ended slavery; and Theodore Roosevelt, who led key reforms in conservation and business.

The **Avenue of Flags**, representing every US state and territory, leads 700ft to the **Lincoln Borglum Visitor Center**. Ten-foot historical photosand storyboards tell the story of the making of Mt. Rushmore. Six TV monitors flicker with vintage clips; The **Presidential Trail** *(.5mi)* takes walkers to the talus slope of the mountain and Borglum's own Sculptor's Studio.

Crazy Horse Memorial★★

US-16/385, 4mi north of Custer. ✕♿🅿
☎*605-673-4681. www.crazyhorse.org.*

The world's largest sculptural undertaking features the emerging 563ft-high image of Sioux Chief Crazy Horse (c1840-77), battle leader at the Little Bighorn. The warrior's face, higher than the Sphinx, was completed in 1998. The colossal carving-in-progress began in 1948 after sculptor Korczak Ziolkowski (1908-82) was invited by Sioux chiefs to create a work to complement Mt. Rushmore; the Sioux wanted "the white man to know the red man has great heroes, too." Ziolkowski's widow and children carry on the project. Ongoing blasting work is a big visitor draw.

Native artisans demonstrate their skills in the **Native American Educational and Cultural Center**★ at the foot of the mountain. The nearby **Indian Museum of North America** presents traditional crafts and historic sepia-tone photos.

Jewel Cave National Monument★★

US-16, 13mi west of Custer. ♿🅿 ☎*605-673-2288. www.nps.gov/jeca.*

Since prospectors discovered the cave in 1900, spelunkers have mapped more than 120mi of passages a mere 2 percent of what is estimated.

The 80min **scenic tour**★ starts with a 234ft elevator descent. Visitors then follow a concrete path and aluminum stairways to 370ft below the surface, where it is a constant, cool 49°F. Massive chambers glitter with elongated crystals of dogtooth spar and nailhead spor. A **candlelight Tour** and 4hr **spelunking tour** are offered also.

Custer★

US-16 & 385. ✕♿🅿 ☎*605-673-2244. www.custersd.com.*

Established during the 1870s gold rush near George Custer's original encampment, this hill-embraced town of 2,000 perpetuates the historic flair of the late 19C. A highlight is the **National Museum of Woodcarving** (*3mi west on US-16;* ☎*605-673-4404, www.blackhills.com/woodcarving/;* 🕒*closed Nov–Apr*), which displays humorous caricature scenes by more than 20 carvers.

Custer State Park★★

US-16A & Rte. 87. Park headquarters 23mi south of Mt. Rushmore. ⛺✕♿🅿 ☎*605-255-4464. www.sdgfp.info.*

This state park encompasses 114sq mi of grasslands, prairie swales, forest and granite peaks. Elk, deer, pronghorn, bighorn sheep and a bison herd of 1,400—are at home among wildflowers, cacti, pine and spruce.

Three scenic driving routes wind through the park, two of them segments of the 66mi **Peter Norbeck Scenic Byway** (*US-16A, Rtes. 87, 89 & 244*). The 18mi **Wildlife Loop Road**★★ runs south and west from the rustic, 1920 State Game Lodge to Blue Bell Resort, offering vistas of the park's resident "begging" burros. The 17mi **Iron Mountain Road**★★ (*US-16A*) includes pigtail bridges designed in the 1930s to span steep climbs in short distances. Three narrow tunnels frame Rushmore as drivers pass through. Granite peaks—including 7,242ft Harney Peak—flank the 14mi **Needles Highway**★★ (*Rte. 87*). Just off it is the long-established **Black Hills Playhouse** (*Rte. 753;* ☎*605-255-4141, www.blackhillsplayhouse.com*), offering Shakespeare to Andrew Lloyd Webber (*summer only*).

Wind Cave National Park★★

US-385, 10mi north of Hot Springs & 22mi south of Custer. ⛺♿🅿 ☎*605-745-4600. www.nps.gov/wica.*

Although Indian legends addressed holes that "blew wind," the cave's recorded discovery came in 1881.

Ranger-led tours range from the 1hr, 150-stair **Garden of Eden Tour** to the 4hr, lots-of-crawling **Caving Tour.** Unique honeycomb-like boxwork is Wind Cave's trademark; created by calcite left by dissolved limestone, boxwork was named for its resemblance to old postal sorters—a diagonal crisscross of fragile-looking lines of calcite protruding from walls.

The Mammoth Site★

1800 US-18 Bypass, Hot Springs. ♿🅿 ☎*605-745-6017. www.mammothsite.com.*

Some 26,000 years ago, the collapse of a sinkhole created a 60ft-deep death trap for Pleistocene mammals. The silt-filled hole was revealed again 1974. Today this trove of Ice Age fossils delights visitors, who get a primer on earth history during a 30min guided tour.

Deadwood★★

US-14A, 13mi west of Sturgis. ✕♿🅿 *800-999-1876. www.deadwood.org.*

By 1876, 25,000 people had swarmed to Deadwood Gulch. Fortune seekers, cavalrymen, Chinese laborers and gun-slinging gamblers established a main street of tents, banks, 53 saloons and 33 brothels.

Today the buildings are now shops, restaurants and, well, gaming halls—80 in all—lining **Main Street★★**. At the **information center** (*753 Main St.;* ☎605-578-2507), visitors can pick up a "Historic Deadwood Walking Tour" map. The **Adams Historical Museum★** (*54 Sherman St.; ☎ 605-578-1714, www.adamsmuseumandhouse.org*) holds a 7.75oz gold nugget found in 1929. The nearby **Adams House★** (*22 Van Buren St.*) is an 1892 Queen Anne-style mansion. In the **Old Style Saloon No. 10** (*657 Main St.;* ☎605-578-3346), the floor is still cloaked in sawdust. The **Broken Boot Gold Mine** 🄺🄸🄳 (*Upper Main St. & US-14A;* ☎605-578-1876) offers underground tours and gold panning.

Homestake Gold Mine★★

160 W. Main St., Lead, 3mi southwest of Deadwood. 🅿 ☎605-584-3110. *www.homestaketour.com.*

The world's oldest continuously operated gold mine, until it closed in 2001, lies uphill from Deadwood in the town of **Lead★** (pronounced LEED), whose old miners' homes crawl up steep hillsides. The mine extracted gold from one of the richest veins of gold ever discovered. By 1945, 40 million tons of ore had been taken out. Surface tours of the **Open Cut★★**, an enormous pit 1,800ft wide, 4,500ft long and 968ft deep, are still offered (*May–Sept*).

Spearfish★

US-14A at I-90, 50mi northwest of Rapid City. ✕♿🅿 ☎605-642-2626. *cvb.spearfishchamber.org.*

With a historic district centered on its 1906 opera house, Spearfish is one an enticing small town. Visitors may drive up **Spearfish Canyon★★** or attend the Black Hills Passion Play, a summer fixture here since 1939. The **High Plains Western Heritage Center** (*825 Heritage Dr.;* ♿🅿 ☎605-642-9378, www.western-heritagecenter.com*) boasts extensive in- and outdoor exhibits that honor Native Americans and early pioneers.

Excursions

Devils Tower National Monument★

Wyoming Rte. 110 off Rte. 24; 10mi south of Hulett WY & 52mi southwest of Belle Fourche SD via Rte. 34. ⚠♿🅿 ☎307-467-5283. *www.nps.gov/deto.*

Sacred to Native Americans, this fluted monolith rises 867ft; the top covers 1.5 acres. Devils Tower is the core of an igneous intrusion that became exposed as surrounding sedimentary rock eroded. The first ascent of the peak was made on July 4, 1893, as more than 1,000 spectators watched; today 5,000 climbers a year challenge its vertical rock walls. The butte is worth the bother, especially for

---

Wild Bill Hickok

US marshal and army scout James Butler Hickok confessed to having killed between 15 and 100 men before he was 27—"but I never, in my life, took any mean advantage of an enemy." Sharp-shooting Wild Bill was in Deadwood for only 67 days, but his legacy colors the city and, indeed, the Black Hills to this day. Hickok's murder is reenacted in a mini-drama at **Old Style Saloon No. 10** and in a diorama, complete with honky-tonk music and gunshots, at the **Journey Museum** in Rapid City**.** Wild Bill Hickok is buried in **Mt. Moriah Cemetery★**, Deadwood's "Boot Hill," next to Martha "Calamity Jane" Canary, America's most famous bullwhip-toting dame. One-hour trolley tours depart Main Street for the cemetery.

Sturgis Rally and Races

South Dakota is home to one of the largest motorcycle rallys in the world. Each August, 400,000 riders meet in Sturgis (population 6,442; www.sturgis.com), 27mi northwest of Rapid City. In 1938 motorcycle-shop owner J.C. "Pappy" Hoel held the first rally with 19 racers. Today poker runs, drag races, hill climbs, road tours and riding exhibitions are among events on a full seven-day schedule. Even non-bikers attend to see what's new in the motorcycle world and to view more than 100 antique bikes—including the oldest unrestored running 1907 Harley-Davidson and actor Steve McQueen's 1915 Cyclone—at the **Sturgis Motorcycle Museum & Hall of Fame** (2438 Junction Ave.; ☎605-347-2001, www.sturgismuseum.com).

Exhibits at the Sturgis Motorcycle Museum & Hall of Fame

those who hike the paved 1.3mi **Tower Trail**★ around its base.

Little Bighorn Battlefield National Monument★★

US-212, Crow Agency MT; 15mi south of Hardin MT & 201mi northwest of Belle Fourche SD. ♿ 🅿 ☎406-638-3204. www.nps.gov/libi.

Here on June 25-26, 1876, Lakota Sioux and Cheyenne warriors killed 272 US cavalrymen, including Lt. Col. George Custer. Natives know the conflict as the Battle of Greasy Grass; Americans refer to it as Custer's Last Stand. It was the last major victory for Native Americans in the western US. Visitors can peruse the maps, photos and dioramas in the **visitor center and museum**.

BADLANDS★★

MAP P 116

MOUNTAIN STANDARD TIME

The play of dawn's light tints the rock faces a gentle bluish-pink that warms to red, gradually covering existing layers of purple shale, chestnut sand, orange iron oxide and white volcanic ash. While the Badlands boast a remarkable geological history, it is the rare and not-so-subtle beauty of a landscape that changes seasonally, and even hourly, that visitors are compelled to see again and again.

- **Information:** ☎605-355-3600, www.blackhillsbadlands.com.
- **Don't Miss:** Badlands National Park.
- **Especially for Kids:** Wall Drug.

Badlands National Park

A Bit of History

The term "Badlands" was bestowed by the Lakota Sioux. French trappers referred to the country as *les mauvaises terres à traverser*—"bad lands to cross." Fossils as old as 77 million years have been unearthed here; of particular note are those of early mammals, such as the rhinoceros-like *brontotheres* from the Eocene era. The range of spires and sawtooth ridges—a sculpted mudstone wall roughly 1,000ft at its highest—runs 90mi from South Dakota into Nebraska, and is bounded on both sides by prairies.

Sights

Badlands National Park★★

Rte. 240 (Badlands Loop Rd.), 8mi south of I-90 Exit 110 at Wall, 51mi east of Rapid City. △✕*(summer only)* ♿🅿 ☎*605-433-5361. www.nps.gov/badl.*

Most visitors see only one strip of this 375sq-mi park—the most dramatic. The 39mi **Badlands Loop Road**★★★ traverses the northern rim of the Badlands, where prairie grasslands give way to buttes and hoodoos. Long blond grasses shimmer in the wind like a shaken sheet. Wildflowers speckle stream canyons, intricately carved slopes and tiny sodded buttes. **Pinnacles Overlook**★★ offers a sweeping viewpoint to the south. Formations are bleached white on top, then bleed pinkish to a tawny yellow. Tiny white Hood's phlox bloom in the broad expanse of gray. The **Castle Trail**★★★ *(4.5mi)* is spectacular in early morning when the moonscape valley and pointed spires get their first dose of light. The **Cliff Shelf Nature Trail**★★ *(.5mi)* is popular for its shady juniper trees. The boardwalk winds through a "slump," where water retention has created an oasis.

Park headquarters are at the **Ben Reifel Visitor Center** *(Cedar Pass, 8mi south of I-90 Exit 131)*, at the east end of the park road. The **White River Visitor Center** *(☎605-455-2878, 25mi north of Wounded Knee)* ⏲ *open Jun–Aug)* services the southern end.

Pine Ridge Indian Reservation

US-18 & connecting routes south of Badlands National Park. ☎*605-867-5301. www.pineridgechamber.com.*

The home of the Oglala Sioux tribe covers nearly 3,000sq mi of western South Dakota, southeast of the Black Hills. About 20,000 Oglala live on the reservation, established in 1878 and a landmark in American Indian history.

In late 1890, two weeks after Chief **Sitting Bull** was killed during a "precautionary" arrest farther north, Chief **Big Foot** and his band left Pine Ridge to hide in the Badlands. The cavalry intercepted them. On December 29, as troops searched the band for weapons, a rifle was fired, setting off a barrage that didn't stop until Big Foot and some 250 Oglala men, women and children were dead. Thirty soldiers also died, many from their own crossfire.

A mass grave, gray stone monument and wooden highway sign today mark the **Wounded Knee Massacre site** (*Tribal Rte. 27 just east of Rte. 28*).

The **Heritage Center in Red Cloud Indian School** (*100 Mission Dr., Pine Ridge; ☎605-867-5491, www.redcloud-school.org*) showcases Plains Indians arts and crafts. Renowned Chief **Red Cloud** is buried on a hilltop overlooking the Holy Rosary Mission. The **Wounded Knee Museum** (*207 10th Ave., in Wall; 605-279-2573; www.woundedkneemuseum.org*) has exhibits on the massacre and the debates about it that persist.

Wall Drug★

Kids *510 Main St., Wall; 51mi east of Rapid City off I-90 Exit 109 or 110.* ✗🅿 ☎605-279-2175. www.walldrug.com.

Wall Drug is the world's most famous "drug store," but not just a pharmacy. Behind a Western storefront is a 76,000sq-ft space with some 20 shops, filled with 1,400 historical photos, 6,000 pairs of cowboy boots, wildlife exhibits, a Western art collection displayed in five dining rooms, and more. In the backyard a children's play area has ice-water wells and a roaring 80ft **Tyrannosaurus** that sends toddlers running every 12min.

In the 1930s, Ted and Dorothy Hustead began offering free ice water to travelers; today the pharmacy is a tourist oasis greeting some 15,000 visitors a day during the busy summer season.

Excursion

Pierre

US-14, US-83 & Rte. 34. 188mi east of Rapid City. Central Time Zone. △✗🅿 ☎605-224-7361. www.pierre.org.

Seven other towns in South Dakota are larger than the quaint state capital, located near the geographical center of the state. Some 14,000 people live in Pierre (pronounced PEER). The town lies on the Missouri River just below meandering **Lake Oahe,** which extends 231mi upstream into North Dakota.

The four-story **South Dakota State Capitol** (*500 E. Capitol Ave.; 🅿 ☎605-773-3765*) is a modified Greek structure with Ionic columns. Built in 1910 of native fieldstone, Indiana limestone and Italian marble, it was restored in 1989.

The **South Dakota Cultural Heritage Center★** (*900 Governors Dr.; 🅿 ☎605-773-3458, www.sdhistory.org*) is built into a hillside a few blocks north of the Capitol. Constructed to resemble an Arikara earth lodge (1989, Blake Holman), the center is an archives and a museum that couples Native American and pioneer history.

NORTH DAKOTA★

MICHELIN MAP 491 I, J, K, 4, 5
CENTRAL & MOUNTAIN STANDARD TIMES

North Dakota typifies the Great Plains—from the small lakes and forested hills of the glaciated north, where every mile has a pair of mallards in a bulrush-buttressed pothole, to the rugged badlands of the Little Missouri and the rolling hills that cross into South Dakota. This is a land of climate extremes, of frigid winter blizzards and violent summer thunderstorms. But the wide-open spaces also boast a stark beauty. Outdoor recreation, prolific wildlife and vast fields of grain attract visitors from near and far.

Information: ☎701-328-2525, www.ndtourism.com
Don't Miss: Theodore Roosevelt National Park.
Kids **Especially for Kids:** Fort Abraham Lincoln State Park.

A Bit of History

Inhabited by Native Americans for at least 15,000 years, the state's high plains first drew European fur traders in the mid-18C. After the Louisiana Purchase in 1803, explorers **Meriwether Lewi**s and **William Clark** wintered with the Mandan tribe on the Missouri River, where they were joined by **Sacagawea**, the Shoshone woman who helped guide them to the Pacific. The region developed slowly until the 1870s, when the the railroad brought many wheat-farming homesteaders to the area. Statehood came in 1889. Since the late 1950s, oil derricks have dotted the landscape.

Sights

Theodore Roosevelt National Park★★

Off I-94 & US-85 between Medora & Watford City (3 units). ⚠ ♿ 🅿 ☏*701-623-4466. www.nps.gov/thro.*
The Little Missouri River links the 110sq mi park's South, Elkhorn Ranch and North Units, as does the 120mi Maah Daah Hey Trail. Erosion by wind, water and ice is the subtle artist, paring down softer rock, leaving behind the razor-sharp ridges and rugged buttes now called badlands. In the **North Unit**★★ *(US-85, 16mi south of Watford City)*, a 14mi scenic drive climbs to Oxbow Overlook, 500ft above the river. The **Achenbach Trail** *(16mi)* approaches **Sperati**

The Lewis and Clark Expedition

To lead a scientific expedition into the Louisiana Territory purchased from Napoleonic France in 1803, US President Thomas Jefferson chose **Meriwether Lewis**, his personal secretary, and **William Clark**, a career soldier. The Corps of Discovery set off from St. Louis on May 14, 1804. It returned 28 months later, after traveling more than 8,000mi up the Missouri River, across the Rocky Mountains, down the Snake and Columbia Rivers, and back again. Lewis and Clark succeeded in making the unknown known to a growing nation and in opening the land to settlement. Facilities along the **Lewis and Clark National Historic Trail** *(☏608-264-5610; www.nps.gov/lecl)* were improved in all 11 states (including North and South Dakota) along the explorers' route prior to the 200th anniversary of the trek. In the Dakotas, visitors can follow the Missouri River by car, boat or foot, stopping at interpretive signs, museums and visitor centers.

The explorers negotiated passage upriver with Sioux warriors near the site of modern Pierre, at the mouth of the Bad River, in September 1804. They camped near On-A-Slant Village (now in Fort Abraham Lincoln State Park), south of modern Mandan, in October and spent that winter beside the Missouri across from its confluence with the Knife River. Exhibits at the **North Dakota Lewis & Clark Interpretive Center** *(US-83 & Rte. 200-A, Washburn; ☏701-462-8535, www.fortmandan. org)* include artifacts of every tribe the party encountered between the Plains and Pacific. An art gallery contains a full set of Karl Bodmer's prints of upper Midwest Indian cultures and lifestyles. **Fort Mandan Historic Site** *(2mi west)* replicates the trapezoidal fort where the party wintered.

At **Knife River Indian Villages National Historic Site** *(Rte. 37, .5mi north of Stanton; ☏701-745-3309, www.nps.gov/knri)*, 3mi farther upriver, a 15min film describes the Hidatsa Mandan tribe that helped Lewis and Clark through that harsh winter. Eleven miles of trails weave past three buried villages and a re-created earth lodge. One village was the home of French interpreter Toussaint Charbonneau, who signed on with the expedition here, and his Shoshone wife, Sacagawea, who guided the Corps west and smoothed relations with Sioux and other tribes.

Visitors to the nearby **Missouri River Lodge** *(140 42nd Ave. NW off Rte. 37, 7mi north of Stanton; ☏701-748-2023, www.moriverlodge.com)* may climbto the same badlands overview from which Bodmer painted the river, visit ancient Mandan spiritual sites, ride horses, canoe and scout out eagles' nests.

Point★, the narrowest gateway in the badlands. The **South Unit**★★ *(Rte. 10 Bypass off I-94, Medora, 16mi west of Belfield)* is best seen on a paved 36mi scenic loop drive. **Scoria Point Overlook** and **Boicourt Overlook** offer panoramas of yellow, gray and burnt-red buttes. **Wind Canyon Trail** *(.2mi)* negotiates the steep edge of a ridge. Wild horses grazing upland plateaus are a vision to behold, but prairie dogs are the darlings of the park. Behind the **Medora Visitor Center** stands Roosevelt's Maltese Cross Cabin, restored and relocated here. At the site of **Elkhorn Ranch** *(35mi north of Medora),* foundation blocks are all that remain of Roosevelt's 1885 ranch.

Medora★

Rte. 10 Bypass off I–94. ✕ & 🅿 ☎701-623-4444. www.medora.com.
This delightful frontier-style village clings to its late-19C origins with pioneer facades and a "Hi, how are ya?" spirit among its townspeople. Broadway-style productions are presented in summer at Burning Hills Amphitheater. The 26-room Chateau de Mores, built in 1883, offers guided tours.

Fort Union Trading Post National Historical Site★

Rte. 1804 (Lewis & Clark Trail) 25mi southwest of Williston. & 🅿 ☎701-572-9083. www.nps.gov/fous.
Reconstructed, this palisaded fort sits near the confluence of the Yellowstone and Missouri Rivers. Inside, the **Bourgeois House** traces the history of the thriving trade of **John Jacob Astor**'s American Fur Company.

Bismarck

I-94 & US-83. ✕ & 🅿 ☎701-222-4308. www.bismarckmandancvb.com.
Established as a rail camp in 1872, Bismarck boomed as a Missouri riverboat port. Now this city of 58,000 is an agricultural center and nexus for water sports on nearby Lakes Oahe and Sakakawea. Its stark **North Dakota State Capitol** *(600 E. Boulevard Ave.;* ☎701-328-2471), a 19-story limestone structure, was built in 1933. On the grounds, the **North Dakota Heritage Center**★ 🄺🄸🄳🅂 *(612 E. Boulevard Ave.* & 🅿 ☎701-328-2666. www.state.nd.us/hist)* contains well-interpreted history and natural history exhibits that explore the Northern Plains. Outside is a statue of Sacagawea, *The Bird Woman* (Leonard Crunelle, 1910).

Fort Abraham Lincoln State Park★

🄺🄸🄳🅂 *4480 Ft. Lincoln Rd. (Rte. 1806), 7mi south of Mandan.* ⚠ 🅿 ☎701-667-5340. www.ndparks.com.
This 1,000-acre park holds the house from which Lt. Col. George Custer set out in 1876 for his "last stand" at the Little Bighorn. Costumed guides offer tours of the home and other structures in Fort Abraham Lincoln, abandoned in 1891 and later restored. The **On-A-Slant Indian Village** includes four reconstructed Mandan earth lodges used from the mid-16C to mid-18C.

NEBRASKA PANHANDLE★

MICHELIN MAP 491 I 7, 8

MOUNTAIN STANDARD TIME

Three easterly flowing rivers help define the Nebraska Panhandle, which extends 135mi from the Black Hills to the Colorado border. In the north, above the White River, the white cliffs and buttes of rugged Pine Ridge extend in a 100mi arc to South Dakota's badlands. Farther south, the Niobrara River slices past 19-million-year-old fossils and through the expansive ranch and dune country of the Sand Hills. Overlooking the North Platte River, the geological formations of Chimney Rock and Scotts Bluff were significant milestones for westbound travelers.

🄸   **Information:** ☎308-632-2133; www.westnebraska.com.
🄰   **Don't Miss:** Scotts Bluff National Monument
🄺🄸🄳🅂 **Especially for Kids:** Agate Fossil Beds

A Bit of History

Western Nebraska was an important 19C transition area from the Great Plains to the Rocky Mountains. The Oregon Trail followed the North Platte to Fort Laramie, Wyoming; fur merchants plied their trade farther north, on the White River. After the 1874 Black Hills gold strike, Fort Robinson was built to defend settlers and travelers from Indian attacks.

Sights

The Museum of the Fur Trade

US-20, 3mi east of Chadron. ♿ P ☎308-432-3843. *www.furtrade.org.*
Some 6,000 pieces represent objects exchanged by Indians and European-Americans in the fur trade, including 234 trade guns. Behind the museum is an earthbound trading post built in 1833.

Fort Robinson State Park★

US-20, 3mi west of Crawford. △✕♿ P ☎ 308-665-2900. *www.ngpc.state. ne.us.*
Nebraska's largest and most historic state park covers 34sq mi in the Pine Ridge region. Established in 1874, the fort was used until 1948. Pivotal events of the Indian Wars occurred here, including the 1877 killing of Chief **Crazy Horse** and the 1879 Cheyenne Outbreak, an abortive escape attempt by 149 imprisoned and starving Cheyenne men, women and children. In the late 19C–early 20C, this was home to the African-American garrison known as the **Buffalo Soldiers**.

The **Fort Robinson State Park Inn & Lodge** serves as a visitor center. The **museum** has exhibits on military history, including an unusual account of the war dogs trained to sniff out mines.

Kids Agate Fossil Beds National Monument★

River Rd. off Rte. 29, 44mi north of Scottsbluff. ♿ P ☎308-668-2211. *www.nps. gov/agfo.*
Some 3,000 acres near the Niobrara River preserve 19-million-year-old fossil remains of animals that roamed here 40 million years after dinosaurs disappeared. The **James H. Cook Collection**★ of Oglala Sioux artifacts includes a whetstone that once belonged to Crazy Horse. The **Fossil Hills Trail** *(2mi)* leads to what's left of an ancient waterhole.

Scotts Bluff National Monument★

Rte. 92, 5mi southwest of Scottsbluff. ♿ P ☎308-436-4340. *www.nps.gov/scbl.*
Sandstone and clay bluffs stand 800ft higher than the North Platte River. The Oregon Trail runs past the visitor center at their foot. Exhibits in the **Oregon Trail Museum** include works by pioneer photographer-artist William Henry Jackson. **Saddle Rock Trail** *(1.6mi)* treats hikers to **views**★★ of the North Platte Valley.

Chimney Rock National Historical Site

Rte. 92, 23mi east of Scottsbluff. ♿ P ☎308-586-2581. *www.nps.gov/chro.*
Westbound pioneers scrawled descriptions in their journals about this unique spire visible along both sides of the North Platte. Designated a national site in 1956, the grounds include a visitor center and museum.

CANYONLANDS

As far as the eye can see in southern Utah's Canyonlands region, undeveloped land extends in undulating contours and sharp angles, its vivid colors bent in whimsical and raw shapes. Earth, water and sky hold sway here. Visitors come for the experience of nature, and southern Utah delivers on an epic scale.

Most of this land is owned by the federal government, and much is protected for public recreational use. Canyonlands National Park is split into three areas by the confluence of the Colorado and Green rivers, its colorful rock strata witness to billions of years of geologic history. Arches National Park is a landscape of wind- and water-sculpted rocks, formed into freestanding arches and natural bridges spanning hundreds

of feet. Capitol Reef National Park's central feature is a 100mi-long rock form known as Waterpocket Fold. Bryce Canyon National Park features dizzying, multicolored rock spires and hoodoos. The canyons of Zion National Park are surrounded by cliffs as high as 3,000ft. At Natural Bridges National Monument, three mammoth stone spans are set in a network of narrow canyons. The Navajo tribe considers Rainbow Bridge National Monument a sacred place; it is reached via boat on Lake Powell, created in the 1960s when Glen Canyon Dam was built on the Colorado River. Grand Staircase-Escalante National Monument adjoins Glen Canyon.

Cities are few and far. St. George is the earliest Mormon colony in southern Utah. Cedar City hosts an annual Shakespearean festival. Moab is of national renown to river rafters and mountain bikers as an outdoor-recreation center.

Delicate Arch, Arches National Park

BRYCE-ZION AREA★★★

MAP P 128

MOUNTAIN STANDARD TIME

Considered by some the most appealing area in all of Utah, this region contains three national parks (Zion, Bryce Canyon and Capitol Reef), two national monuments (Grand Staircase-Escalante and Cedar Breaks), stunning state parks and national forests, accented by an annual dose of Shakespeare in Cedar City.

🛈 **Information:** ☎435-634-5747, www.utahstgeorge.com.

👁 **Don't Miss:** Zion and Bryce Canyon National Parks.

Sights

St. George★

I-15 Exit 8. ✕&🅿 ☎*435-628-1658. www.stgeorgechamber.com.*
Mormons sent south from Salt Lake City settled St. George during the Civil War. Today the city of 68,000 is one of Utah's fastest growing communities.
The red-sandstone 1876 **Mormon Tabernacle** *(Main & Tabernacle Sts.;* ☎*435-673-5181, www.lds.org/placestovisit)* is open to visitors (the nearby St. George Temple is not). **Brigham Young's Winter Home** *(67 W. 200 North;* ☎*435-673-5181)* was built in 1873 by the Mormon leader. The **Jacob Hamblin Home** *(US-91, 3mi west of St. George;* ☎*435-673-5181)* was the homestead of the first Mormon missionary; he gained a reputation for social skills with previously hostile Indians, converting many to Mormonism.
Snow Canyon State Park *(Rte. 18, Santa Clara, 10mi northwest of St. George;* ☎*435-628-2255, stateparks.utah.gov)* has eroded red-and-white sandstone formations, some coated with layers of lava.

Zion National Park★★★

Rte. 9, Springdale, 42mi east of St. George & 23mi west of US-89. △✕&🅿 ☎*435-772-3256. www.nps.gov/zion.*
Surrounding a 2,500ft-deep sandstone canyon decorated with waterfalls and damp hanging gardens, Zion is one of the oldest (1919) national parks. More than 65mi of hiking trails lead into its backcountry wilderness. Non-hikers can go on horseback or join shuttle-bus tours of the valley *(Apr–Oct).*
The massive sandstone features began forming 225 million years ago, when the park was an ancient sea floor. Later, it was a river delta and a lake bottom, and was covered in ash by volcanic eruptions. Shellfish flourished here; dinosaurs walked here. Around 170 million years ago, huge deposits of wind-blown sand left the region covered in dunes. Over time, the sand hardened into the 2,000ft-thick compacted sandstone that is now Zion's major geologic feature.
Over the last 15 million years, a short span of geological time, the forces of the Virgin River began carving **Zion Canyon.** Even today, the river continues its carving: A million tons of rocky sediment are washed out of Zion Canyon yearly. Zion Canyon—8mi long, .5mi wide and .5 mi deep—begins at the park's south entrance off Route 9. **Zion Scenic Canyon Drive** runs 8mi to the **Temple of Sinawava,** a natural sandstone amphitheater. (From April to November the road is closed to private vehicles beyond historic **Zion Lodge,** 1mi from Route 9.) From the Temple, a paved 1mi trail follows the Virgin River to **The Narrows,** barely 20ft wide in the river bottom, squeezed between rock walls rising 2,000ft above it.
Other sandstone monoliths include **The Watchman,** rising 2,555ft above the canyon floor; and the massive 7,810ft **West Temple,** standing more than 4,100ft above the river road. **The Great White Throne** is a prominent monolith that rises majestically 2,400ft behind a red-rock saddle. An attraction of a different sort is **Weeping Rock,** a cool rock niche carved over millennia by seeping water. Fertile hanging gardens thrive in the damp confines of its grotto.

Address Book Canyonlands Area

For price ranges, see the Legend on the cover flap.

WHERE TO STAY

$$$ Sunflower Hill B&BInn – *185 N. 300 East, Moab, UT.* 🅿 ☎*435-259-2974 or 800-662-2786. www.sunflowerhill. com. 11 rooms.* Wooded pathways, and flower gardens provide a quiet retreat from nearby downtown Moab. Guests relax on wicker chairs on the covered porch, savor the stone fireplace in the living room, or collapse into antique iron beds.

$$ Boulder Mountain Lodge – *Rte. 12 near Burr Trail Jct., Boulder, UT.* 🗙🅿 ☎*435-335-7460 or 800-556-3446. 20 rooms. www.boulder-utah.com.* Boulder was the last community in America to replace mule trains with postal trucks. This sandstone-and-timber building complex, surrounding a lake and bird sanctuary, still seems undiscovered.

$$ Bryce Canyon National Park Lodge – *Bryce Canyon National Park, UT.* 🗙🅿 ☎*435-834-5361. www.bryc-ecanyonlodge.com. 110 rooms (🕑 open Apr–Oct only).* A shingled roof, stone piers and green shutters reflect the restoration of this 1930s National Historic Landmark to its former rustic elegance. Its porch overlooks the brilliant colors of Bryce's famed hoodoos—tall, red-rock pinnacles.

$$ Desert Pearl Inn – *707 Zion Park Blvd. (Rte. 9), Springdale, UT.* 🗙🅿 ☎*435-772-8888 or 888-828-0898. www. desertpearl.com. 61 rooms.* Nestled along the Virgin River at the gateway to Zion Canyon, this lodge is built of fir and redwood from an old railroad trestle. Balconies and terraces give every room a river or cliff view.

$$ Lake Powell Resort – *100 Lakehore Dr., Page, AZ.* 🗙🅿 ☎*928-645-2433 or 888-896-3829. www.lakepowell.com. 350 rooms.* Overlooking the Wahweap Marina at the west (and most accessi-ble) end of Lake Powell, this full-service hotel is a great place from which to launch lake tours or houseboating (**$$$$$**) excursions.

$ Valley of the Gods B&B – *East of Rte. 261, 9mi north of Mexican Hat, UT.* 🅿 ☎*970-749-1164. www.zippitydodah. com/vog. 4 rooms.* Gary and Claire Dorgan's solar- and wind-powered stone ranch house is located in a mini-Monument Valley north of the San Juan River. Visitors enjoy the sights of Red Rock country from the long front porch, or relax in rooms with rock walls and wood stoves.

WHERE TO EAT

$$ Adriana's – *164 S. 100 West, Cedar City, UT.* ☎*435-865-1234.* **Continental.** Lodged in a 1916 Victorian manor near the Shakespearean theater, this Olde English eatery offers steaks, chicken and chops served by waitresses in Renaissance costume. Celtic music accompanies dishes like pork tenderloin with apricot-ginger sauce and grilled rainbow trout with roasted almonds.

$$ Cafe Diablo – *599 W. Main St., Torrey, UT.* ☎*435-425-3070. www.cafediablo. net.* **Southwestern.** Local trout gets a pumpkin-seed crust, poblano peppers are buried beneath hominy, rattlesnake cakes are topped with rosemary aioli: Everything here has a desert twist. Chef Gary Pankow's "painted chicken" is coated with honey, lime and tomatillo salsa, and the chipotle-fired ribs heat up diners' tongues.

$ Slick Rock Cafe – *5 N. Main St., Moab, UT.* ☎*435-259-8004. www.slickrockcafe. com.* **Southwestern.** This hip spot, with murals and petroglyph replicas on walls, is a hangout for mountain bikers and river rafters. Diners munch platters of "Macho Nachos" at tables facing Main Street activity, or dine inside on Utah red trout with herbed cornmeal or a chili verde burrito stuffed with pork, black beans and rice.

The **Kolob** area of Zion Park—accessible only by road from I-15 Exit 40, 20mi south of Cedar City—features a 5mi scenic drive along the Hurricane Fault, where twisted layers of exposed rock may be seen. Kolob's **Finger Canyons** extend southeast toward the main park area and are favored by backcountry hik-

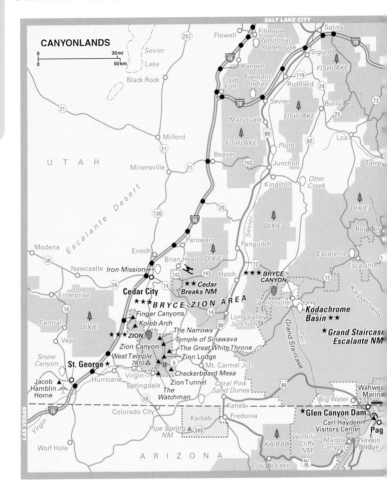

ers. A strenuous 7mi hike from Lee Pass, on La Verkin Creek, leads to **KolobArch,** one of the world's largest stone spans at 310ft across.

Route 9 east from Springdale to US-89, through 5,607ft-long **Zion Tunnel,** features six switchbacks; the tunnel was blasted out between 1927 and 1930. At the east end is **Checkerboard Mesa,** horizontal and vertical lines etched into the sandstone by geological fractures eroded by rain and snow.

Cedar City

Rtes. 14 & 56 at I-15 Exit 59. 51 miles northeast of St. George & 252mi southwest of Salt Lake City. △✕&🅿 ☎435-586-4055. *www.scenicsouthernutah.com.*

Cedar Breaks National Monument, Arch

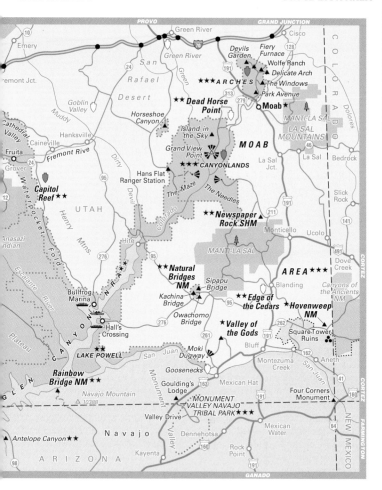

Known for its **Utah Shakespearean Festival**★ *(late Jun–early Oct;* ☎*435-586-7880; www.bard.org)*, this town of 22,000 was the site of the first iron foundry west of the Mississippi River. At **Iron Mission State Park** *(Rte. 91; b435-586-9290, stateparks.utah.gov)*, the old foundry (1851-58) has been converted into a museum of farm machinery.

Cedar Breaks National Monument★★

Rte. 14, 23mi east of Cedar City & 3mi south of Brian Head. △⛓♿🅿 ☎*435-586-9451. www.nps.gov/cebr.* ⏱*Facilities open late May–mid-Oct.*

A 3mi-wide sandstone amphitheater is rimmed by bristlecone pines, some of the oldest living plants on earth. Cedar Breaks' heavily eroded features are sculpted to a depth of 2,500ft below the 10,000ft rim in a series of rugged, narrow walls, fins, pinnacles, spires and arches that resemble Bryce Canyon. Mormon settlers misnamed the site for trees in the canyon bottom—they were junipers, not cedars.

In winter Cedar Breaks road is impassable. But that makes it more appealing to cross-country skiers, who easily ascend the unplowed road from **Brian Head Resort** *(Rte. 143;* ☎*435-677-2035, www.brianhead.com)*, just 3mi north. Brian Head is southern Utah's largest ski area, with six lifts and 53 runs; its base elevation of 9,600ft is the state's highest.

© National Park Service/Ray Mathis

Silent City Formation, Bryce Canyon National Park

Bryce Canyon
National Park★★★

▥ *Bryce Canyon, 24mi southeast of Pan-guitch & 77mi east of Cedar City.* ⛺✕♿🅿
☎*435-834-5322. www.nps.gov/brca.*

This 56sq mi park contains an array of rock spires, pinnacles, arches and hoodoos tinted in a palette of rich shades, considered by some to be the most brightly colored rocks on earth. Red, yellow and brown shades derive from iron content; purple and lavender rocks contain more manganese. The odd rocks rise from the floor of a series of vast horseshoe-shaped natural amphitheaters.

The sculpted rocks began forming during the Cretaceous Period, around the time dinosaurs disappeared and flowering plants appeared. Deposits of sand and minerals, uplifts forced out of the earth, and erosional effects of rain and running water combined with snowfall, freezing and thawing to gradually remove billions of tons of rocks from the amphitheater rim. Eventually this debris was washed away by the Paria River, a tributary of the Colorado. Southern Paiute Indians lived around Bryce Canyon for hundreds of years prior to white settlement in the late 1800s. Native Americans called this place "red rocks standing like men in a bowl-shaped canyon." Americans shortened it to Bryce Canyon after rancher Ebenezer Bryce, who grazed livestock in

the canyon bottoms in 1875 and called it "one hell of a place to lose a cow." President Warren Harding declared the area a national monument in 1923; it became a national park in 1928.

An 18mi (one-way) scenic drive leads along the pine-clad rim top to popular views and trailheads leading down into the maze-like amphitheaters. Rim spots such as Sunrise, Sunset, Rainbow and Inspiration Points, all around 8,000ft elevation, afford differing views of the crenellated and sculpted rocks.

Hiking into Bryce Canyon provides a very different perspective of the rock forms. The park has more than 50mi of trails for hiking and horseback riding. Winter visitors, for whom the park may be virtually empty, cross-country ski on park roads or borrow snowshoes (gratis) from the Bryce Canyon Visitor Center.

Grand Staircase-Escalante
National Monument★

Access from Rte. 12 between Cannonville & Boulder or US-89 west of Page. ⛺♿🅿
☎*435-826-5499 (Escalante visitor center) or 435-644-4680 (Kanab visitor center). www.ut.blm.gov/monument.*

This fairly new (1997) national monument occupies 1.9 million acres of southern Utah wilderness west of the Waterpocket Fold and north of Lake Powell. This was one of the last regions in the continental US to be mapped. High, rugged and remote, it rises 4,500ft above the Colorado River and Lake Powell, and is considered a geological sampler, containing a huge variety of sedimentary rock formations. It has also been the subject of much political controversy over cattle grazing and proposals to drill for oil within the monument.

The **Grand Staircase**—mammoth cliffs and miles-long ledges formed into natural steps of colored rock strata—dominates its western third. Stretching across the distant horizon for a distance of more than 100mi is layer upon layer of rock comprising the Pink, Gray, White, Vermilion and Chocolate Cliffs.

The area also includes the **Escalante River,** which flows from Boulder Mountain to Lake Powell in Glen Canyon National Recreation Area. The Escalante has carved deep canyons and gorges into an immense puzzle of sandstone mazes and slot canyons that offer extensive opportunities for self-sufficient and well-prepared backpackers and hikers. There are no services within the large and remote backcountry that comprises this park. Services are available only in the adjacent communities of Boulder, Escalante, Cannonville and Kanab.

Kodachrome Basin State Park★★

9mi south of Cannonville off Rte. 12. ☎435-679-8562. stateparks.utah.gov.
The primary characteristic of this park is the concentration of numerous tall sandstone chimneys—sand pipes—that rise from the desert floor. The spires appear white or gray in midday light. In low-angle sun of early morning or late afternoon, they begin to glow in unexpected shades of crimson, mauve and burnished orange.

Capitol Reef National Park★★

Rte. 24, 11mi east of Torrey. ⚠️♿🅿️ ☎435-425-3791. www.nps.gov/care.
This park displays an amalgam of rocks of numerous varieties and colors—great slabs of white, pink, gold, purple, orange and red rocks combined into immense, vividly colored 1,000ft-tall cliffs, stone arches and natural bridges. Primarily a backcountry park, it features miles of unpaved driving roads as well as hiking,

biking and Jeep trails leading toward remote wilderness. A visitor center is located in the heart of the park, 9mi east of the junction of Routes 12 and 24.

The park was named by 19C Mormon pioneers, whose travels across Utah were impeded by a huge, convoluted, eroded rock uplift known as the **Waterpocket Fold.** Stretching 100mi to Lake Powell, it blocked travel as a coral reef would a ship. This "reef" is crowned by white domed rock that reminded pioneers of the US Capitol in Washington DC. Waterpocket Fold itself is named for its eroded rock basins, also called pockets or tanks, that can hold thousands of gallons of water after a rainfall.

The fold is a classic monocline, thrusting the earth's crust upward, with one extremely steep side, in an area otherwise characterized by flat layers of horizontal rocks. The fold is 50 million to 70 million years old and the result of movement along an ancient fault line.

Around AD 700, the Fremont culture established farming communities in the area, drawn by the water reserves of the rock pockets, and by the **Fremont River,** which also attracted abundant game and nourished wild foods. Their residency lasted 600 years. Fremont cultural history is told in petroglyphs (rock carvings) and painted pictograph panels throughout the park.

In the 1880s, Mormon pioneers established farms and orchards along the Fremont River at **Fruita**, in the vicinity of today's park visitor center. Their descendants raised cattle and fruit here until 1969, two years before Congress declared Capitol Reef a national park. The orchards are still maintained, and visitors may pick fruit in season.

A 10mi (one-way) scenic drive from the visitor center leads to overlooks of remote canyon country, slick-rock terrain, arches and spires. Turnouts offer views of such geological features as Capitol Dome, Chimney Rock, Egyptian Temple and The Goosenecks. A short, moderately strenuous hike leads to Hickman Bridge, a natural stone bridge. A short, steep hike climbs to the Golden Throne and Capitol Gorge. Numerous other trails lead to a variety of overlooks and points of interest.

GLEN CANYON AREA★★

MAP P 128

MOUNTAIN STANDARD TIME

Environmentalists still lament damming the Colorado River to form Lake Powell in 1963. Glen Canyon, they say, was even more beautiful than its southerly neighbor, the Grand Canyon, though not as deep. But most visitors acclaim the 186mi-long lake, whose 1,960mi shoreline is longer than California's Pacific coast.

- **Information:** ☎888-261-7243. www.pagelakepowelltourism.com
- ▶ **Orient Yourself:** The gateway city of Page is in Arizona, but most of Lake Powell lies upstream in Utah.
- **Don't Miss:** Rainbow Bridge

A Bit of History

Lake Powell is the centerpiece of an area characterized by a relative lack of human intrusion throughout history. In places such as the remote Valley of the Gods or Natural Bridges National Monument, nature holds sway, not people. Even Rainbow Bridge National Monument—revered by the Navajo, whose reservation lands surround it, and visited by hundreds of tourists traveling by Lake Powell tour boats daily—retains its natural grandeur, arcing in a great curve over lake-lapped desert beaches.

In other places, however, man has produced obvious changes. The town of Page, Arizona, the primary gateway to Lake Powell, didn't exist before the Glen Canyon Dam was built. The dam, considered an engineering marvel, was constructed between 1956 and 1966 to store water for development of the desert Southwest. Nearby, the Four Corners Power Generating Station's tall stacks protrude into clear-blue sky.

Sights

Glen Canyon National Recreation Area★★

US-89 at Page, AZ; Rte. 276 at Bullfrog Marina & Hall's Crossing, 158mi southwest of Moab, UT; Rte. 95 at Hite UT, 155mi southwest of Moab. ⚠✕&🅿 ☎520-608-6200. www.nps.gov/glca.

This vast area extends from Canyonlands National Park southwest to Grand Canyon National Park, covering more than 1,900sq mi. **Lake Powell★★**, its center-

piece, is a huge recreational playground, whose watery fingers reach into sandy coves, inlets and slot canyons, coursing between towering red-rock cliffs to depths of 500ft. The waters, which took 17 years to fill to a surface elevation of 3,700ft above sea level, provide opportunities for houseboating and power boating, fishing and water skiing. On the lake are five marinas and several campgrounds.

Lake Powell occupies only one-eighth of the parkland's acreage. The surrounding lands, with their myriad inlets and coves, are fascinating as well. Side canyons protect ancient ruins and a full array of natural stone features, including arches and bridges, pinnacles, fins, towers and stone chimneys known as sand pipes. Extensive backcountry hiking, biking and Jeep trails may be found throughout. Food, water and gasoline services, however, are generally available only in small communities on the periphery of the national recreation area.

Page

US-89, 157mi east of St. George UT & 135mi northeast of Grand Canyon Village AZ. ✕&🅿 ☎928-645-2741. www. pagelakepowellchamber.org.

Established during construction of the Glen Canyon Dam in 1956, this Arizona town, at the northwest corner of the Navajo Indian Reservation, grew as the lake behind the dam began filling with water in 1963. The national recreation area has its headquarters here. The **John Wesley Powell Museum & Visitor Information Center★** (6 N. Lake Powell Blvd.;

☎928-645-9496, www.powellmuseum.
org) features artifacts from exploration
of the region about 130 years ago. The
museum describes the exploits of Major
Powell, a one-armed Civil War veteran
who first charted the waters of the Colorado River in a wooden boat in 1869. At
Navajo Village (Haul Rd.; ☎928-660-
0304, www.navajovillage.com), members
of the Navajoland Academy prepare a
traditional dinner, demonstrate crafts
and perform songs and dances.

Tours of **Antelope Canyon★★** (5mi
east of Page off Rte. 98) may be booked
through the Powell Museum. Here on
the Navajo Reservation is one of the
swirling, narrow slot canyons often seen
in photographs of the Southwest.Rain
and wind has sculpted the porous sandstone into a slender crevice, 130ft deep
and only 3ft wide in places. Tours are
permitted only with a licensed guide.

Glen Canyon Dam★

US-89, 2mi northwest of Page. ☎928-608-
6404. www.nps.gov/glca.
The dam produces more than 1.3 million
kilowatts of electricity, serving 1.7 million users in Utah, Colorado, Wyoming,
Arizona and New Mexico. With all eight
of its generators operating, 15 million
gallons of water pass through the dam
each minute. The **Carl B. Hayden Visitors Center** (US-89; ☎928-608-6404) has
displays on construction of the dam; free
tours of the dam are provided.

Rainbow Bridge National Monument★★

☎520-608-6200. www.nps.gov/rabr.
Rainbow Bridge stands 290ft above
the waters of Lake Powell, beside an
inlet just inside the Utah border with
Arizona. Higher than the US Capitol, it
spans 275ft, nearly the length of a football field. Called Nonnezoshi ("rainbow
turned to stone") by the Navajo, who
believe that passing beneath Rainbow
Bridge without offering special prayers
will bring misfortune. To respect these
beliefs, the Park Service asks visitors to
refrain from walking under the bridge.
Boat tours depart daily from **Wahweap
Marina,** north of the Glen Canyon Dam,
and cover the 50mi to Rainbow Bridge.
Tours also depart from **Bullfrog Marina**
and **Hall's Crossing** at mid-lake.
Hikers may reach the bridge by a 14mi
trail around Navajo Mountain from Tribal
Road 16 (85mi east of Page). Permission
must first be obtained from the Navajo
Tribe (Parks and Recreation Dept., ☎928-
871-6647, navajonationparks.org).

Natural Bridges National Monument★★

Rte. 275 off Rte. 95, 42mi west of Blanding UT. ⛺ ♿ 🅿 ☎435-692-1234. www.
nps.gov/nabr.
This remote parkland contains the
eroded stone networks of Armstrong
and White Canyons. Over centuries, erosion created three natural stone bridges
that are among the largest in the world.

Sipapu Bridge, Natural Bridges National Monument

© National Park Service

The three bridges may be seen from overlooks along a 9mi paved park road. Short hiking trails lead to each site, and an 8.5mi trail links all three bridges.

The bridges were given Hopi Indian names. **Sipapu Bridge** is the longest (268ft) and highest (220ft); it is thought to be the second-largest natural bridge in the world. **Kachina Bridge** is 204ft long, 210ft high and 93ft thick. **Owachomo Bridge** is the oldest and smallest of the park's natural bridges; it spans 180ft in length, but is only 9ft thick in spots and barely 27ft wide. Owachomo is considered a late-stage natural bridge.

Valley of the Gods★

Rte. 261, 10mi north of Mexican Hat UT & 35mi south of Natural Bridges National Monument. 🅿 ☏*435-587-1500. www. utah.blm.gov.*

Similar, though smaller in scale, to its southerly neighbor, Monument Valley, Valley of the Gods is far less crowded.

A rough 17mi dirt road passes through the valley. A four-wheel-drive vehicle is recommended, with plenty of gas for the car and water for its passengers. Hardy bike riders particularly enjoy the Valley of the Gods loop for its isolation and lack of motor traffic. There are no services whatsoever. The best view of Valley of the Gods is from the **Moki Dugway** *(Rte. 261),* where it descends in 1,000ft of steep switchbacks from Cedar Mesa to the valley floor. Just past Valley of the Gods, a side road leads 3mi to **Goosenecks State Park** *(Rte. 316; b435-678-2238, stateparks.utah.gov),* a clifftop aerie offering a view of the meandering San Juan, 500-1,000ft below.

MOAB AREA★★★

SEE MAP P 128
MOUNTAIN STANDARD TIME

A town of 4,900 that serves as gateway to the Arches and Canyonlands National Park areas, Moab is surrounded by breathtaking scenery of carved rock and powerful flowing water. It is the stage for a wide range of outdoor activities, particularly Colorado River rafting and "slick-rock" mountain biking.

A large number of expedition outfitters and guided-tour operators make their headquarters in Moab, which offers far more lodging and dining options than any other southeastern Utah community. Limited services may be found in the smaller towns of Monticello, Blanding and Bluff.

- 🛈 **Information:** ☏435-259-8825, canyonlands-utah.com.
- 😊 **Don't Miss:** Arches & Canyonlands National Parks
- ⚲ **Also See:** Newspaper Rock

Sights

Moab★

US-191, 244mi southeast of Salt Lake City. ⚠✕🅿 ☏*435-259-8825. www.discover moab.com.*

A 1950s uranium boomtown, Moab is the center of an adventure travel industry built around two national parks, Arches and Canyonlands; state parks; and adjacent public lands straddling the Colorado and Green Rivers.

Moab was settled in 1855 by Mormon colonists dispatched from Salt Lake City by Brigham Young. In subsequent decades, the eroded deserts around Moab have been a hideout for such outlaws as Butch Cassidy, a dock for a Colorado River boat company, and a setting for novels by Zane Grey.

Today mountain biking, golf, river rafting and kayaking, hiking and Jeep driving appear to be the primary pursuits of residents and visitors alike. Winter attracts cross-country skiers to the La Sal Mountains, which rise east of Moab to more than 13,000ft.

The town's **Dan O'Laurie Canyon Country Museum** (118 E. Center St.; ☎ 435-259-7985) displays artifacts of ancient Indians and exhibits on Moab's role in the uranium boom. The Nature Conservancy's **Scott M. Matheson Wetlands Preserve** (Kane Creek Blvd.; ☎ 435-259-4629) protects a riparian slough rich in bird and plant life.

Arches National Park★★★
Off US-191, 5mi northwest of Moab. ⚠ ♿ 🅿 ☎ 435-719-2299. www.npsgov/arch.

The greatest concentration of natural stone arches - more than 2000 - in the US is found in this rugged 120sq mi park's serpentine network of multicolored canyons, distinguished by enormous, narrow rock fins, slender spires and improbably balanced rocks.

Arches' unique terrain represents the effects of 150 million years of erosion on 5,000 vertical feet of rock, revealing a porous layer of 300ft-thick Entrada Sandstone, out of which today's arches were formed. Created as a national monument in 1929, Arches was upgraded to a national park in 1971. Previously, only Native Americans had lingered long in this daunting landscape. One rare settlement was established in the late 19C by Civil War veteran John Wesley Wolfe and his son Fred. They raised cattle for 20 years at **Wolfe Ranch;** the ruins of their log cabin and corrals remain today.

Many geological attractions may be seen from the park's 18mi (one-way) main road. Short hikes from the roadway offer more intimate perspectives on some of the most dramatic features.

Two miles from the visitor center, **Park Avenue** is the name given to a tapering red-rock canyon resembling a city skyline. Seven miles farther, a paved spur road leads 3mi to a clustered group of geological features, including numerous arches, in **The Windows** section. Short trails lead to the major features, which include the North and South Windows, Double Arch and Turret Arch.

Returning to the main road, another spur road (2.5mi farther) leads to Wolfe Ranch and the **Delicate Arch** viewpoint. Delicate Arch is perhaps the park's most recognizable feature. A steep hike (1.5mi) from Wolfe Ranch leads to the base of the 46ft-high, 35ft-wide arch, which frames the La Sal Mountains in the eastern distance.

At the end of the main road, the **Devils Garden** area contains numerous arches, including Skyline Arch and Landscape Arch—one of the world's longest, spanning 306ft although it is only 10ft thick in one spot. A mostly level trail (2mi one-way) reaches the Garden's highlights.

Edward Abbey

Author Edward Abbey (1927-89) gained fame in the late 20C as a champion of the pristine desert environment. A park ranger at the Arches in the 1950s, he immortalized his experiences in a book called Desert Solitaire (1968), now considered a classic of the ecology movement. Abbey, who called himself "a man with the bark still on," wrote of the seasonal changes in the then-largely deserted park. Living alone in a small, isolated trailer, he found time to note and describe subtleties in the rock formations as well as the interplay of weather conditions, plant and animal life and humans' place in it all.

The cynical Abbey considered humans insignificant but careless and short-sighted creatures. He felt man lacked the good sense to preserve the wilderness areas where primitive human urges could be expressed harmlessly.

Other books by the gruff philosopher include the nonfiction The Journey Home (1977), Abbey's Road (1979) and Down the River (1982). His best-known novels are The Monkey Wrench Gang (1975), a humorous but insightful look at environmental terrorism, and The Brave Cowboy (1956), made into a 1962 movie (starring Kirk Douglas) called Lonely Are the Brave. Other novels include Good News (1980), The Fool's Progress (1988) and Hayduke Lives! (1990).

The **Fiery Furnace** area contains a jumble of rock fins, towers, pinnacles and twisting canyons. It is considered so confusing to navigate that visitors are encouraged to walk only with a park ranger as a guide (Mar–Oct only).

Canyonlands National Park★★★

Island in the Sky District, Rte. 313, 35mi southwest of Moab via US-191. The Needles District, Rte. 211, 87mi south of Moab via US-191. The Maze District, Rec. Rd. 633, 136mi southwest of Moab via US-191, I-70, Rte. 24 & Lower San Rafael Rd. ⚠ 🅿 ☎435-719-2313. www.nps.gov/cany.

Trisected by the deep canyons of the Colorado and Green Rivers, Utah's largest national park Canyonlands' three main sections are reached via different routes.

It contains 527sq mi of deep canyons, characterized by sheer cliffs, outstanding mesas and all other varieties of bizarrely shaped hoodoos, balanced rocks, spires, pinnacles, fins and arches.

Below Moab, the Green River flows into the Colorado, which proceeds through the strong rapids of Cataract Canyon and empties into Lake Powell. The rivers are separated by the **Island in the Sky** District, a gigantic level mesa reached via a spur road that turns south off US-191 about 9mi north of Moab. At its tip, 3,000ft above the confluence, is **Grand View Point**, with panoramic views of 100mi of tiered canyons, changing colors in dramatic red, orange and pink layer-cake slices in the low-angle light of the late-afternoon or early-morning.

The Needles District, reached from a westbound turnoff 39mi south of Moab, is separated from Island in the Sky by more than 100 road miles, although their respective paved roads end just 10mi apart, the Colorado flowing between. Incredible rock forms protrude from the vast canyons, spires and arches. The Needles are a massive city-size formation of vertical standing rocks.

The road entrance to **The Maze** District is hours from the rest of the park. From Route 24, 90mi west of Moab via I-70 at the town of Green River, drivers must navigate the dirt Lower San Rafael Road, maintained by the Bureau of Land Management, another 46mi southeast to **Hans Flat Ranger Station.** Although most high-clearance vehicles can travel it with ease, the road may nonetheless be impassable in wet weather. Consid-

Mountain Biking

The diverse terrain and moderate desert climate of the Canyonlands make this region irresistible to mountain bikers. Two-wheel adventurers can be found from the river-carved red-rock canyons to the heights of 13,000ft mountains, in between tackling Moab's challenging, world-famous slick-rock hills.

The **Slickrock Bike Trail** is probably the best-known trail of its type anywhere. It stretches over 11 technically demanding miles on undulating slickrock, a form of eroded sandstone that takes on graceful curved shapes and swirls, becoming dangerously slippery when wet. Riders follow a track, indicated by dotted white lines painted on red rocks, that hugs cliff faces and potentially lethal drop-offs.

Other biking trails with international reputations include the 100mi **White Rim Trail** (also suitable for Jeeps) through Canyonlands National Park, and the shorter, off-road Hurrah Pass Trail and Poison Spider Trail. The paved roads through Arches National Park are likewise popular with bikers, although off-road biking is prohibited in Arches.

One of the most demanding bike trails anywhere, the **Kokopelli Trail,** begins at the Slickrock Trail and covers 128mi from Moab to Grand Junction, Colorado. Along the way, the multi-day route traces the route of the Colorado River, passing from the desert canyon country of Utah into the pine-and-aspen forests of neighboring Colorado.

Each year, Moab is host to several of the biggest mountain-biking events anywhere, luring riders from around the world. Numerous bicycle shops in Moab provide full retail and rental services, and link riders with specialized tour operators for group biking adventures.

© National Park Service

Mountain Biking, White Rim Trail, Canyonlands National Park

ered one of the most remote locations in the continental US, the 30sq mi Maze District contains a severely convoluted canyon network where innumerable rock fins, towers and mesas are found. Ancient Indian pictograph panels, depicting ghostly characters twice human size, are seen in the Great Gallery at **Horseshoe Canyon** *(Lower San Rafael Rd., 30mi north of Hans Flat).* These primitive paintings may be as old as 2,000 years. Relatively few visitors have passed since that time; hence the panels have remained intact. The dark grotto may be reached only after a steep 2mi hike down Barrier Creek Canyon.

Dead Horse Point State Park★★
Rte. 313, 32mi southwest of Moab via US-191. ⚠ ♿ 🅿 ☎435-259-2614. *stateparks. utah.gov.*
This park, en route to the Island in the Sky, was named for a herd of wild horses once corralled and left to die on this isolated point 2,000ft above the Colorado River. The sunset views from this point, light tracing across the multi-hued sandstone canyons and cliffs, are among the most dramatic in all the Canyonlands.

Newspaper Rock State Historical Monument★★
Rte. 211, 51mi south of Moab via US-191.
This small roadside park, 12mi west of US-191 on the route to The Needles District, contains a rock wall virtually covered in hundreds of Indian picto-

graphs and etched petroglyph carvings. Portrayed in or on the stone wall is nearly every figure found in ancient Indian art throughout the Southwest: the hunchbacked flute player Kokopelli, hunters with bows and arrows, horses and wild animals. Archaeologists believe the site was a message board for ancient people.

Edge of the Cedars State Park★★
660 W. 400 North, Blanding, 74mi south of Moab. ♿ 🅿 ☎435-678-2238. *stateparks. utah.gov.*
This small and very well done museum contains the remains of a pre-Columbian Ancestral Puebloan village, occupied from AD 700-1200. There is also a museum, which contains a fine collection, including pottery and weavings.

Hovenweep National Monument★
Square Tower Ruins, Hovenweep Rd. (County Rd. G), 46mi west of Cortez CO & 31mi east of US-191 south of Moab UT. ⚠ 🅿 ☎970-562-4282. *www.nps.gov/ hove.*
Founded in 1923 to preserve six Ancestral Pueblo villages, Hovenweep includes the unusual **Square Tower** Ruins, where a small visitor center offers exhibits. The unique square, oval, circular and D-shaped towers provided residents, as recently as 800 years ago, extensive views of their surroundings.

COLORADO ROCKIES

Climaxed by 53 peaks of 14,000ft elevation or higher, the Rocky Mountains—a series of north-south-running ranges—dominate the western two-thirds of the state of Colorado. Many of North America's most famous ski resorts are found here, along with fascinating pieces of mining and railroad heritage.

The Continental Divide winds through this mountainous domain, headspring of three of North America's six longest rivers. The Colorado, which begins as a trickle in Rocky Mountain National Park, flows southwesterly 1,450mi through Arizona's Grand Canyon to the Sea of Cortez. The Arkansas, whose modest source is beneath 14,433ft Mount Elbert, Colorado's highest summit, runs east 1,459mi and joins the Mississippi River. The Rio Grande, which rises in the San Juans, courses south through New Mexico and sculpts an international border before reaching the Gulf of Mexico, 1,900mi from its font.

Colorado Rockies
CO

Originally inhabited mainly by Ute tribes, Colorado's mountains were divided between Spain and France as the 19C opened. The US acquired the eastern flank of the Rockies in the Louisiana Purchase of 1803, the balance in 1848 by treaty from Mexico. But this elevated land was rarely visited; westbound pioneers followed the Oregon Trail through lower mountains to the north, or took the Santa Fe Trail to the south. Not until the discovery of gold in 1858, soon followed by an even larger silver boom, was there stimulation to settle here.

© Daniel Bayer

Maroon Bells in Fall

HIGH ROCKIES★★★

MAP PP 144- 145

MOUNTAIN STANDARD TIME

Spread across more than 20,000sq mi, crossed by highways that climb high passes, and dive into valleys, this lofty zone brings travelers scenic views around almost every turn. And it rewards the intrepid with a rich flora and fauna, evocative mining heritage, and unsurpassed recreational opportunities.

- **Information:** ☎800-265-6723, www.colorado.com.
- ▶ **Orient Yourself:** The Front Range applies to the easternmost flank of the Rockies, which embrace Pikes Peak, Mount Evans and Longs Peak. West of the Continental Divide, the region is called the Western Slope.
- **Don't Miss:** Trail Ridge Road in Rocky Mountain National Park.
- **Especially for Kids:** Glenwood Caverns and Hot Springs Pool.
- **Also See:** Steamboat Springs.

A Bit of History

The Utes were dominant from the 17C to mid-19C; Arapaho and Cheyenne also hunted in these mountains. After the US acquired the territory, Zebulon Pike explored rivers and valleys in 1806-07, Major Stephen Long ventured up the South Platte and Arkansas valleys in 1820, and John C. Frémont visited northern Colorado in 1842. It wasn't until the Civil War era that the promise of mineral wealth attracted permanent residents. The war had a sobering effect on the gold rush that began in 1859, but silver created another flurry of prospecting. The mountains were considered so formidable that the transcontinental railroad was routed through neighboring Wyoming in 1869. Narrow-gauge railroads began serving mining camps in the 1870s. When resources were exhausted, some settlements faded into ghost towns; others persisted. Central City, Georgetown, Breckenridge, Leadville, Aspen, Crested Butte and Telluride are survivors.

Hiking, golf and whitewater rafting are other popular summer activities. In winter, skiing turns the Rockies into America's leading recreational playground (visit www.coloradoski.com).

Driving Tours

Rocky Mountain National Park★★★

2–3 days, 205mi round-trip

- ▶ *From Golden, west of Denver, drive 13mi west on US-6 through Clear Creek Canyon to Rte. 119, then 5mi south.*

Black Hawk and Central City★

Rtes. 119 & 279. ✕&P ☎303-582-5251. Spawned by 1859 gold strikes, these once-forlorn foothills towns, a mile apart, are booming again, thanks to limited-stakes gambling, legalized in 1991, in some 50 casinos. The original excavation at Gregory Gulch marks the entrance to Central City, a few steep streets with narrow sidewalks. Brick masonry in the wake of a devastating 1874 fire resulted in sturdy Victorian buildings that still stand. Among them is the 1878 **Central City Opera**★ (*124 Eureka St.*), whose six-week summer season (*☎303-292-6700; www.centralcityopera.org*) was launched by silent-screen star Lillian Gish in 1932.

- ▶ *Return to Rte. 119 & continue north 65mi on the Peak to Peak Highway.*

Address Book Colorado Rockies

For price ranges, see the Legend on the cover flap.

WHERE TO STAY

$$$$$ The Home Ranch – *54880 Rte. 129, Clark, CO, 19mi north of Steamboat Springs.* ✕ ♿ 🅿 ⬛ ☎ *970-879-1780. www.homeranch.com. 6 rooms, 8 cabins.* Here is the best in Western hospitality: 80 horses, fly fishing, gourmet meals, elegant private cabins with wood-burning stoves and lofts. The minimum summer stay is one week; nightly rates are available in winter, as the ranch becomes a cross-country skiing mecca.

$$$$$ Hotel Jerome – *330 E. Main St., Aspen, CO.* ✕ ♿ 🅿 ⬛ ☎ *970-920-1000 or 877-412-7625. www.hoteljerome.com. 91 rooms.* Over a century ago, the rich mining crowd bellied up to the cherrywood bar to celebrate silver strikes. Aspen's elite still frequent the same terra-cotta brick landmark. Glass-cut doorknobs open to Victorian rooms decorated in raspberry and hunter green. Old mining maps and silver-etched lamps line the hallways.

$$$$$ The Lodge at Vail – *174 E. Gore Creek Dr., Vail, CO.* ✕ ♿ 🅿 ⬛ ☎ *970-476-5011 or 877-528-7625. www. lodgeatvail.com. 123 rooms.* Tyrol meets Rockies in an opulent mix 30 yards from Vail's chairlifts. Wide stairs lead to rooms of polished woods, high-backed leather chairs and private balconies. Enjoy Colorado lamb at the **Wildflower Restaurant ($$$)**, pasta in **Cucina Rustica ($$)** or a chilled martini in Mickey's piano bar.

$$$ The Stanley Hotel – *333 Wonderview Ave., Estes Park, CO.* ✕ ♿ 🅿 ⬛ ☎ *970-586-3371 or 800-976-1377. www. stanleyhotel.com. 135 rooms.* Ailing F.O. Stanley came to this valley for alpine air in 1903, and never left. His white-pillared Georgian hotel later became author Stephen King's setting for The Shining. Double fireplaces and staircases still grace the lobby, and Palladian windows provide spectacular views.

$$$ Strater Hotel – *699 Main Ave., Durango, CO.* ✕ ♿ 🅿 ☎ *970-247-4431 or 800-247-4431. www.strater.com. 93 rooms.* The Strater is a palace of red brick and white trim with a hint of the Wild West, furnished with a fabulous collection of Victorian walnut antiques, embellished with brass rails and brocaded settees. Rooms boast four-poster beds and ornate wallpaper.

$$$ New Sheridan Hotel – *231 W. Colorado Ave., Telluride, CO.* ✕ ♿ 🅿 ☎ *970-728-4351 or 800-200-1891. www.newsheridan.com. 32 rooms.* Had you visited a century ago, the New Sheridan would indeed have been "new." Today the fully restored inn is a classic of Victorian elegance, its rooms adorned with period furniture and photos of early Telluride. A historic bar and the gourmet **Chop House ($$$)** restaurant lure locals.

WHERE TO EAT

$$$$ Krabloonik – *4250 Divide Rd., Snowmass Village.* ☎ *970-923-3953. www.krabloonik.com. Lunch winter only; dinner year-round.* **Wild game.** Combining fine dining with a large dog-sledding kennel, Krabloonik may be one of a kind. By winter day, dog teams pull sledders on tours of the Maroon Bells Wilderness. Afterward, diners relax and enjoy a menu of wild-mushroom soup and home-smoked game, like pheasant, boar, caribou and moose.

$$$$ Mirabelle at Beaver Creek – *55 Village Rd., Avon.* ☎ *970-949-7728. mirabelle1.com. Dinner only.* **Contemporary.** Daniel Joly, who lives with his family above this restaurant in an 1898 farmhouse, is the only Master Chef of Belgium working in the US. Impeccable service matches the French-influenced cuisine, highlighted by Joly's signature lamb chops, grilled with garlic and rosemary. The menu changes every six weeks, but often features roasted elk and Dover sole.

$$$$ Old West Steakhouse – *11th & Lincoln, Steamboat Springs.* ☎ *970-879-1441. www.oldweststeakhouse.com. Dinner only.* **Western.** Owner Don Silva has been serving Steamboat visitors ranch-style meals since 1985, and though the menu has few surprises—mainstays are steaks, chops and roasts—the execution is reliably superb. The restaurant's walls feature top-quality Western art and ranch artifacts such as braided horse-hair bridles.

$$$ Sweet Basil – *193 E. Gore Creek Dr., Vail.* ☎ *970-476-0125. www.sweetbasil-vail.com.* **Contemporary.** The menu changes seasonally, but this bistro is always packed from wall to mustard-colored wall. Dishes include halibut with black-truffle risotto, seared duck with mango spring rolls, and saffron linguini with lobster. The main-floor wine bar is popular.

$$ The Hearthstone – *130 S. Ridge St., Breckenridge.* ☎ *970-453-1148. www.hearthstonerestaurant.biz.* **Regional.** A late-19C Victorian home one block off Main Avenue is the setting for this friendly restaurant. Upper-story windows offer views of nearby mountains. Generous portions of wild game, steaks and seafood are the fare, complemented by an award-winning wine list.

Peak to Peak Highway★★
Rtes. 119, 72 & 7. ⚠ ✕

This scenic route winds through pine woods that periodically open to offer tantalizing mountain views. In **Neder-land**★, *(b303-258-3936, www.nederland-chamber.org)* a small, lively, former mining-supply town, Route 119 branches east toward Boulder *(p 172)*. Proceed north on Route 72. After 14mi, look for a left turn to **Brainard Lake**★, surrounded by the soaring snow-cloaked summits of the Indian Peaks Wilderness.

▶ *Return to Route 72, continue north 9mi and turn left on Route 7 to Estes Park.*

Estes Park★
US-34, US-36 & Rte. 7. ⚠ ✕ ⬥ 🅿 ☎*970-577-9900. westesparkcvb.com.*

Estes Park nestles at the east edge of Rocky Mountain National Park. An **aerial tramway**★ *(420 E. Riverside Dr.;* ☎*970-586-3675, www.estestram.com)* climbs 8,900ft Prospect Mountain in summer, with fine views of adjacent summits.

▶ *Take US-36 west from the south side of Estes Park to the main national park entrance station and the Beaver Meadows Visitor Center.*

Rocky Mountain National Park★★★
US-34 & US-36. ⚠ 🅿 ☎*970-586-1206. www.nps.gov/romo.*

This magnificent landscape boasts craggy mountains, glaciated valleys, perpetual snowfields, small lakes and vast alpine tundra that covers one-third

of its 415sq mi. It features more than 100 mountains of 11,000ft or higher, reaching its apex at 14,255ft **Longs Peak,** whose distinctive flat-topped summit dominates the park's southeast corner. The **Beaver Meadows Visitor Center** has park maps and information on ranger-led tours and lectures. From here, 10mi **Bear Lake Road**★ runs south, providing access to trailheads.

Trail Ridge Road★★★
US-34, 50mi from Estes Park to Grand Lake. ⚠ ⬥ 🅿 🕐 *Open late May–Oct, depending upon weather conditions.*

This is the highest continuous paved highway in North America, ascending rapidly from coniferous and aspen forests to treeless tundra at 12,183ft, and offering outstanding mountain panoramas. Viewing areas include **Many Parks Curve**★★ and **Forest Canyon Overlook**★★. The **Tundra Trail at Rock Cut**★★ *(.5mi)*, an interpretive path with signs describing the geology, botany and wildlife of this harsh environment, is short and gentle, but at this elevation it may be exhausting for flatlanders. After passing its high point, the road curves downhill past the **Gore Range Overlook**★ and the **Alpine Visitor Center**, crossing the Continental Divide at 10,758ft Milner Pass.

Grand Lake★
Rte. 278 off US-34. ⚠ ✕ ⬥ 🅿 ☎*970-627-3402. www.grandlakechamber.com.*

A small town at the west entrance to the park, Grand Lake boasts Old West-style log buildings and boardwalks. It is named for its large glacial lake (1.2mi long, 1mi wide, 400ft deep), fed by the Colorado River. Below Grand Lake, the river is dammed twice to form **Shadow Mountain Lake** and large **Lake Granby**.

▷ *Continue south 15mi on US-34 from Grand Lake to Granby. Turn left (southeasterly) on US-40 and proceed 46mi to I-70 at Empire.*

Middle Park

Fraser River Valley, US-40 south of Granby. △✕⑤🅿 ☎970-726-4118. www.winter-park-info.com.
Cattle graze in this broad valley whose mountain-sheathed location renders it one of the coldest places in the continental US. **Cozens Ranch Museum**★ *(US-40 south of Fraser;* ☎*970-726-5488, www.grandcountymuseum.com)* displays pioneer and Ute artifacts in an 1870s ranch house, stagecoach stop and post office. **Winter Park**★ *(US-40;* ☎*970-726-5514)* is known for mountain biking and winter skiing on two mountains. The route crosses the Continental Divide at 11,315ft **Berthoud Pass** and swings through Empire, a 19C mining town.

▷ *Return 29mi via I-70 & US-6 to Golden.*

Denver-Vail-Aspen★★

3 days, 276mi one-way

Interstate 70 is Colorado's principal east-west thoroughfare. Between Denver and Glenwood Springs, it is one of America's most scenic highways. For early settlers here, wealth came from gold, silver and other minerals. Today's gold is white at ski areas, green at golf courses.

▷ *From Denver, drive west 32mi on I-70.*

Idaho Springs

I-70 Exit 241. △✕⑤🅿 ☎303-567-4660. www.clearcreekcounty.org.
Nineteenth-century commercial buildings line the main street of this old mining town of 2,000 citizens. The 1913 **Argo Gold Mine & Mill** *(2350 Riverside Dr.;* ☎*303-567-2421)* is an ore-process-ing mill open for self-guided tours and panning for gold. At the **Phoenix Gold Mine**★ *(right on Stanley Rd., left on Trail Creek Rd.;* ☎*303-567-0422),* a retired miner leads an underground tour.

▷ *Return to I-70 & continue 14mi west.*

Georgetown★★

I-70 Exit 228. △✕⑤🅿 ☎303-569-2555. www.georgetowncolorado.org.
The old town center of Georgetown is immaculately preserved. Now a museum, the **Hotel de Paris**★ *(409 6th St.;* ☎*303-569-2311, www.hoteldeparismuseum.org)* was built in 1875 by a French immigrant. The 1879 **Hamill House**★ *(305 Argentine St.;* ☎*303-569-2840)* reveals the luxury in which a silver baron lived. Tickets for a 1hr summer outing on the **Georgetown Loop Railroad**★★ *(1106 Rose St.;* ☎*888-456-6777, www.georgetownlooprr.com)* are available at the historic train depot. The 4.5mi of track between Georgetown and Silver Plume, another 19C mining town, feature a 360-degree loop on a bridge high over Clear Creek.

▷ *Continue 23mi west on I-70.*

The highway climbs steadily to the **Eisenhower Tunnel,** bored under the Continental Divide at 10,700ft. North America's highest road tunnel enables vehicles to avoid 11,992ft **Loveland Pass**★. Take Exit 216 and follow US-6 for views of mountains, valleys, lingering snowfields and (at 13,050ft) the **Arapahoe Basin Ski Area** *(*☎*970-468-0718),* which stays open later than any other Rocky Mountain resort—until July 4. The highway passes modern **Keystone Resort**★ *(*☎*970-496-2316),* en route back to its junction with I-70 at **Silverthorne**, noted for its outlet stores.

▷ *Continue 5mi west on I-70 to Exit 203. Turn south and take Rte. 9 for 9mi.*

On the left is **Dillon Reservoir,** cradled by mountains. Route 9 passes quaint **Frisco** and follows the Blue River. The Tenmile Range—mountains numbered (north to south) "Peak 1" through "Peak 10"—forms the western backdrop.

Breckenridge★★

Rte. 9, 87mi west of Denver. △✕&🅿 ☎*970-453-2913. www.gobreck.com.*

Now a resort town of 8,900, Breckenridge was founded in 1859 by gold miners. The **Country Boy Mine**★ 🆔 *(542 French Gulch Rd.; ☎970-453-4405, www.countryboymine.com)* offers tours and gold panning in French Creek.

Main Street is lined with restaurants and shops, most housed in Old West-style buildings. The **Summit Historical Society** *(☎970-453-9022)* offers walking tours and mining-district tours. Historic sites include the **Barney Ford House** *(Washington & Main Sts.),* owned by a freed slave who became a 19C business. **Father Dyer United Methodist Church** *(Wellington & Briar Rose Sts.)* is dedicated to a preacher who carried mail and God's word to remote mining camps.

A bike path along the Blue River becomes a cross-country skiing avenue in winter. Ski lifts serve downhill terrain that spreads across three mountains—Peaks 8, 9 and 10—with off-piste skiing available on Peak 7.

▶ *Return to I-70 and continue west 6mi to Exit 195. Take Rte. 91 south 24mi to Leadville.*

Exiting the interstate at the **Copper Mountain Resort**★ *(Rte. 91 at I-70 Exit 195; ☎970-968-2882),* Route 91 cuts across 11,318ft **Fremont Pass** and passes the open pit of the defunct American Climax Molybdenum Mine before descending into Leadville.

Leadville★★

US-24 & Rte. 91, 103mi west of Denver. △✕&🅿 ☎*719-486-3900. www.leadvilleusa.com.*

Situated at 10,152ft, Leadville was once Colorado's silver capital; in 1880, population soared to 24,000. Today the population is 2,700. But the main street is still flanked by fine Victorian commercial buildings.

Tickets for a multimedia show about the town's history are available at the **Leadville Visitor Center** *(809 Harrison Ave.; ☎719-486-3900).* The nearby **National Mining Hall of Fame and Museum**★★ *(120 W. 9th St.; ☎719-486-1229, www.mininghalloffame.org)* features a walk-through replica of a hard-rock mine. The **Tabor Opera House**★ *(308 Harrison Ave.)* was built in 1879. Remnants of millionaire Horace Tabor's **Matchless Mine** *(E. 7th St., 1mi east of downtown)* can also be visited.

About 5mi west of town is **Leadville National Fish Hatchery**★ *(Rte. 300),* built in 1889; tanks hold millions of trout for release into Colorado's streams. Behind the hatchery, hiking trails begin

Rocky Mountain goats graze on minerals on Mount Evans

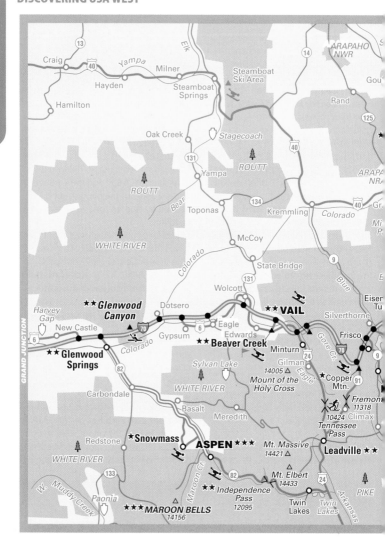

from the foot of 14,421ft **Mount Massive.** Immediately south is the state's highest crest, 14,433ft **Mount Elbert.** Beginning 13mi south of Leadville, Route 82 linking US-24 with I-70 at Glenwood Springs, crosses 12,095ft **Independence Pass**★★ and offers incredible views from numerous hairpin turns. Snow normally closes the 38mi stretch from **Twin Lakes** (*6mi west of US-24*) to Aspen from mid-October to Memorial Day.

▶ *From Leadville, take US-24 north 33mi to I-70.*

The site of **Camp Hale,** a World War II training base for the 10th Mountain Division, a ski-and-mountaineering contingent, lies near 10,424ft **Tennessee Pass.** Descending the pass, US-24 follows the Eagle River through a valley below 14,005ft **Mount of the Holy Cross,** so-named for its distinctive, intersecting, perpetually snow-packed gullies in the shape of a cross. US-24 meets I-70 near **Minturn,** a former rail town now becoming a Vail suburb.

▶ *Backtrack east 5mi on I-70 to Vail.*

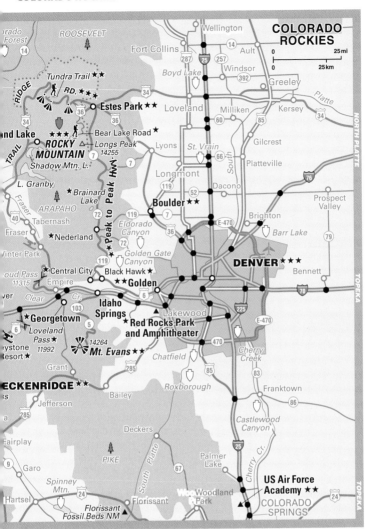

Vail★★

98mi west of Denver. △✕&P ☎*970-476-1000. www.visitvailvalley.com.*

One of North America's premier mountain resorts, Vail was founded in 1963 by veterans of the World War II 10th Mountain Division. Vail Village boasts pedestrian-only streets and chalet-style buildings with fashionable shops and restaurants. The **Colorado Ski Museum**★ *(231 S. Frontage Rd.; ☎970-476-1876, www.skimuseum.net)* documents the state's skiing and snowboarding heritage and commemorates the skiing

soldiers, who trained at Camp Hale. **Vail Nature Center**★ Kids *(831 Vail Valley Dr.; ☎970-479-2291, www.vailrec.com)* offers naturalist tours and guided hikes or ski trips year-round. The **Betty Ford Alpine Gardens**★★ *(173 Gore Creek Dr.; ☎970-476-0103, www.bettyfordalpinegardens.org),* established by the former First Lady, shows off 1,500 varieties of annuals and perennials.

The town of 5,000 sits at the foot of **Vail Mountain**★★★, the largest single-mountain ski area in the US—with a 3,360ft vertical drop. **Adventure**

Ridge★ **Kids** is the site of outdoor winter sports. In summer, the domed VistaBahn chairlift and Lionshead Gondola ascend for outstanding views.

▶ *Drive 10mi west from Vail on I-70.*

Beaver Creek★★
From I-70 Exit 167 at Avon, take Village Rd. 3mi south. ✕⟨⟩🅿 ☎*970-496-4500. www.beavercreek.com.*
This exclusive ski-and-golf resort community was created by the operators of the Vail resort in 1980. Ski terrain, which has hosted world-championship downhill races, connects two developments, Arrowhead and Bachelor Gulch. The **Vilar Center for the Arts**★ *(☎970-845-8497, www.vilarcenter.org)* hosts classical and popular performances.

▶ *Continue 50mi west on I-70.*

Glenwood Canyon★★
I-70 between Exits 133 & 116.
Colorado's geological history is written on the sedimentary walls of this spectacular 18mi gorge. The oldest rock was formed 570 million years ago in the Precambrian era. The youngest rock, up to 1,500ft above the river, is iron-rich sandstone. This portion of I-70, completed in 1992, was cantilevered from granite walls and routed through short tunnels to minimize damage to the landscape.

A paved biking and jogging trail runs the entire length of Glenwood Canyon. Exits access raft-launch areas and the **Hanging Lake Trail**★★, which ascends 1,000ft in 1mi to an exquisite lake.

Glenwood Springs★★
Rte. 82 at I-70 Exit 116, 158mi west of Denver. △✕⟨⟩🅿 ☎*970-945-6589. www. glenwoodchamber.com.*
This town of 8,500 is situated where the Roaring Fork meets the Colorado River below Glenwood Canyon. **Hot Springs Pool**★★ **Kids** *(401 N. River St.;* ☎*970-945-6571, www.hotspringspool.com)* claims to be the world's largest naturally spring-fed hot pool. Hourly tours visit lighted portions of the **Glenwood Caverns and Historic Fairy Caves**★★ **Kids** *(508 Pine St.;* ☎*970-945-4228, www.glenwood-caverns.com),* high above Glenwood Canyon.

▶ *Take Rte. 82 southeast 42mi to Aspen and conclusion of driving tour.*

Aspen★★★
200mi southwest of Denver. △✕⟨⟩🅿 ☎*970-925-1940. www.aspenchamber. com.*
Synonymous with glamour, Aspen boasts ski terrain that ranks among the finest in North America, as four separate resort mountains rise within 12mi of one another. High-season guests and part-

An Old Road, Aspen in Winter

© iStockphoto.com/Dustin Brunson

time residents include many celebrities. The Aspen Skiing Company and Aspen Institute for Humanistic Studies, both founded in the late 1940s, revived a rundown silver-mining town. Aspen's evolution into a world-class resort (and town of 6,000) became a model for other Rockies communities.

Known for chic boutiques and fashionable restaurants, historic downtown focuses on a pedestrian mall. Jerome B. Wheeler, president of Macy's department store in New York, came to Aspen during its boom years and in 1888 and 1889 built three enduring landmarks. The elaborate **Wheeler Opera House**★★ *(320 E. Hyman Ave.; ☎ 970-920-5770, www.wheeleroperahouse.com)* hosts films and live entertainment. The **Hotel Jerome**★ *(330 Main St.; ☎970-920-1000, hoteljerome.rockresorts.com)* has been luxuriously restored. The **Wheeler-Stallard House**★ *(620 W. Bleeker St.; ☎970-925-3721, www.aspenhistory.org)*, a Victorian showplace, is a museum of the Aspen Historical Society.

The **Aspen Art Museum**★ *(590 N. Mill St.; ☎ 970-925-8050, www.aspenart-museum.org)* offers exhibits of various works, many by local artists. The **Aspen Center for Environmental Studies** *(100 Puppy Smith St.; ☎970-925-5756, www.aspennature.org)* is set on Hallam Lake, maintained as a wildlife sanctuary. The **Aspen Music Festival and School**★★★ *(2 Music School Rd.; ☎970-925-9042, www.aspenmusicfestival.com)* presents summer concerts that often feature world-renowned musicians.

Aspen Mountain★★

✕🅿 ☎970-925-1220.
www.aspensnowmass.com.
Aspen's original ski mountain rises directly behind town, its slopes luring some of the world's best skiers. The **Silver Queen Gondola**★★ operates in summer for sightseeing; views from its 11,212ft summit take in wilderness areas. Northwest of town are two more resorts, **Aspen Highlands** *(Maroon Creek Rd. via Rte. 82)* and novice-oriented **Buttermilk Mountain** *(Rte. 82)*.

Snowmass★

Brush Creek Rd. via Rte. 82, 12mi northwest of Aspen. ✕🕭🅿 ☎970-925-1220. *www.aspensnowmass.com.*
Created in 1967, Snowmass has the most varied terrain of the four mountains. **Krabloonik Kennels**★★ 🄺🄸🄳🅂 *(Divide Rd. off Brush Creek Rd.; ☎970-923-3953, www.krabloonik.com)* operates dog-sled rides in winter. The **Anderson Ranch Art Center**★ *(5263 Owl Creek Rd.; ☎970-923-3181, www.andersonranch.org)* offers highly regarded workshops.

Maroon Bells★★★

13mi southwest of Aspen in the Maroon Bells-Snowmass Wilderness. △🕭🅿
The view of Colorado's most oft-photographed mountains is particularly inspiring across the still waters of **Maroon Lake**★★. Summers and weekends, private vehicles are prohibited from 10mi Maroon Creek Road, so shuttle buses make the trip from Rubey Park Transit Center *(Durant Ave. between S. Galena & S. Mill Sts.)*. In winter, **T-Lazy-7 Ranch** 🄺🄸🄳🅂 *(Maroon Creek Rd.; ☎970-925-4614, www.tlazy7.com)* operates snowmobile tours and sleigh rides.

Additional Sights

Steamboat Springs★★

US-40, 74mi north of I-70 Exit 157, 19mi west of Vail. △✕🅿 ☎970-879-0880. *www.steamboat-chamber.com.*
A true Western town (9,500) in the Yampa River Valley, Steamboat has preserved its ranch heritage. **F.M. Light & Sons**★ *(830 Lincoln Ave.; ☎970-879-1822, www.fmlight.com)* has sold Western clothing from the same location since 1905. The **Eleanor Bliss Center for the Arts** *(13th & Stockbridge Sts.; ☎970-879-9008)*, in a renovated 1908 rail depot, offers exhibits and performances. The **Tread of Pioneers Museum** *(800 Oak St.; ☎970-879-2214)* showcases artifacts in a 1908 Queen Anne-style home.

The paved **Yampa River Trail**★ is the core of a trail system bordering downtown. Shuttles take bathers up miles of backroads to **Strawberry Park Hot Springs** *(☎970-879-0342, www.strawberryhotsprings.com)*, where clothes are

Golden Aspen Trees backdropped by Crested Butte

optional after dark. Fabled for its ultra-light snowfall dubbed "champagne powder," **Steamboat Ski Area**★★ (*US-40, 3mi south of downtown; ☎970-879-6111; www.steamboat.com*) has 20 lifts and a 3,668ft vertical drop. The **Silver Bullet Gondola**★ runs in summer for sightseeing and **Howelsen Hill**★ (*River Rd.; ☎970-879-8499*) has a historic ski-jumping facility.

Crested Butte★★

Rte. 135, 28mi north of US-50 at Gunnison, 66mi west of Salida. ⚠ ✕ ♿ 🅿

☎*970-349-6438.*
www.crestedbuttechamber.com.
This entire former mining town of 1,600 is a National Historic District, its false-front Victorian buildings conveying an Old West flavor. Adjacent **Crested Butte Mountain Resort**★ (*Rte. 135, 2mi north of Crested Butte; ☎970-349-2222*) has off-piste terrain that is challenging enough to host extreme skiing competitions; in summer, these wildflower-cloaked slopes offer some of Colorado's best mountain-biking trails.

WESTERN SLOPE★

MICHELIN MAP 493 G 8, 9 AND MAP PP 144-145
MOUNTAIN STANDARD TIME

Rivers rolling west from the Rockies give life to this vast semi-desert land. The only major city is Grand Junction, whose 45,000 people live near the confluence of the Gunnison and Colorado Rivers. These two streams—and, to a lesser extent, the Yampa and White Rivers farther north—provide lifeblood for ranching and an agriculture industry that embraces peaches, apples, pears and wine grapes. Residents and visitors alike delight in the wares at numerous fruit stands July-October.

ℹ️ **Information:** ☎970-242-3214, www.coloradowest.org.
🧒 **Especially for Kids:** Cross Orchards Farm in Grand Junction.

Sights

Colorado National Monument★★

Off Rte. 340, via I-70 Exit 19 at Fruita, 12mi west of Grand Junction. ⚠ 🅿 ☎970-858-3617. www.nps.gov/colm.

This 32sq mi wilderness rises more than 2,000ft above the Colorado River. **Rim Rock Drive★★★ (23mi)** weaves past such red-rock formations as the Kissing Couple, Devils Kitchen and Window Rock.

Dinosaur National Monument★★

31mi north of US-40 at Dinosaur, 108mi north of Grand Junction. ⚠ 🅿 ☎970-374-3000. www.nps.gov/dino.

A scenic drive to **Harpers Corner** climaxes with a 1.5mi hike to a viewpoint over the confluence of the Yampa and Green Rivers at **Echo Park.** To see dinosaur skeletons, visitors must travel west 20mi on US-40 to Jensen, Utah, then north 7mi on Rte. 149 to the **Dinosaur Quarry**.

Black Canyon of the Gunnison National Park★★

Rte. 347, 5mi north of US-50, 8mi east of Montrose & 58mi west of Gunnison. ⚠ 🅿 ☎970-641-2337. www.nps.gov/blca.

This chasm combines both aspects for its dramatic appearance. The westward-flowing Gunnison River has scoured a virtually impenetrable 53mi-long, 2,700ft-deep, 1,000ft-wide path through Precambrian gneiss and schist. A 7mi road along the south rim offers 12 scenic overlooks.

Curecanti National Recreation Area★

US-50 between Montrose & Gunnison. ⚠ 🅿 ☎970-641-2337. www.nps.gov/cure.

Three consecutive reservoirs on the Gunnison River are the heart of this recreational heaven for water-sports lovers. Farthest upstream is **Blue Mesa Lake,** Colorado's biggest lake and the largest kokanee salmon fishery in the US. Below Blue Mesa are **Morrow Point Lake,** locked into the upper Black Canyon, and **Crystal Lake.**

SAN JUAN COUNTRY★★

MICHELIN MAP 493 F, G 9, 10
MOUNTAIN STANDARD TIME

Colorado's southwestern corner is a largely mountainous area dominated by the sharply angled slopes and precipices of the San Juan Mountains. The Rockies' youngest range includes more than 2 million acres of national forests, parks and designated wilderness areas laced with scenic rivers and lakes. Fourteen lofty peaks surpass 14,000ft; at lower elevations, ranching still holds sway.

🛈 **Information:** ☎800-933-4340 or www.swcolotravel.org.

A Bit of History

Historic 19C mining towns characterize human settlement in the high San Juans. But long before white settlement, Ancestral Puebloans were present. Between AD 600 and 1300, they built numerous cities amid the piñon-and-sage mesas feathering off the San Juans. Abandoned seven centuries ago, the foremost cliff-dwelling sites in the world are contained within Mesa Verde National Park.

Much later, pioneers seeking gold and silver discovered the San Juans. In 1880, a railroad—a portion of which survives today as the Durango & Silverton Narrow Gauge Railroad—was built to haul ore and supplies. The Million Dollar Highway was blasted through the mountains to link far-flung sites with service towns like Durango and Cortez; mine wealth built their Victorian main streets.

Driving Tour

2–3 days, 290mi

Durango★

US-160 & US-550. ☎970-247-0312. www. durango.org.
This Animas River town of 14,000 was founded in 1880 when the Denver and Rio Grande Railroad built a rail line to alpine mines near remote Silverton. The **Durango & Silverton Narrow Gauge Railroad**★★★ Kids *(479 Main Ave.; ☎970-259-2733, www.durangotrain.com)* still employs coal-fired steam locomotive engines to pull restored narrowgauge cars 45 slow miles through the wilderness. The train depot anchors the **Main Avenue National Historic District**★ *(Main Ave., 5th-12th Sts.)*, where the star attraction is the **Strater Hotel**★ *(699 Main Ave.; ☎970-247-4431, www. strater.com)*, a four-story brick Victorian that has the Diamond Belle Saloon, a bar with a honky-tonk pianist and garterclad waitresses.

▶ *Drive north 50mi from Durango on US-550.*

Silverton★

US-550 & Rte. 110. △✕⎙🅿 ☎800-752-4494. www.silvertoncolorado.com.
A boom town in the 1880s, Silverton relies largely on rail tourists on layover here, who have time to explore the 50-or-so Victorian buildings of the historic district (between 10th, 15th, Mineral & Snowden Sts.).
North of town, US-550 cores through country pocked by abandoned mines along the **Million Dollar Highway**★. Sheer drops plunge from the shoulders of this roadway to jagged rocks hundreds of feet below.

▶ *Continue north 25mi from Silverton on US-550.*

Ouray★

73mi north of Durango. △✕⎙🅿 ☎970-325-4746. www.ouraycolorado.com.
The seven-block **Main Street Historic District** of this "Switzerland of America," founded by miners in 1876, lies in a dramatic canyon. Visitors can see steam ris-

ing from the **Ouray Hot Springs Pool** *(US-550, north end of Ouray; ☎970-325-7072)*, its gallons of thermal water as hot as 104°F. South of town, in Uncompahgre Gorge, 285ft **Box Cañon Falls** *(Rte. 261, ☎970-325-4464)* becomes Ouray Ice Park *(www.ourayicepark.com)* in winter. In summer, Ouray is a center for Jeep excursions.

▶ *Drive north 10mi from Ouray on US-550; at Ridgway, turn west (left) on Rte. 162; after 23mi, turn east (left) on Rte. 145 and continue 17mi to Telluride.*

Telluride★★

125mi north of Durango. △✕⎙🅿 ☎888.605.2578. www.visittelluride. com.
The 1878 **National Historic District**, nestled in a steep-sided glacial box canyon, is linked with ultra-modern **Mountain Village** by a state-of-the-art gondola. Rich veins of silver and gold made Telluride a boisterous, Wild West town. Its affluence was not lost on Butch Cassidy, who in 1889 launched his outlaw career by robbing the Bank of Telluride. Nine years later, American politician William Jennings Bryan delivered his famous "Cross of Gold" speech (defending the falling gold standard) from the steps of **The New Sheridan Hotel** *(231 W. Colorado Ave.; ☎970-728-4351, www.newsheridan.com)*.
At the east end of Telluride's box canyon is Colorado's longest free-flowing waterfall, 365ft **Bridal Veil Falls**★.
Telluride Ski Resort★★ *(☎970-728-6900, www.tellurideskiresort.com)* is one of the Rockies' most acclaimed and challenging. Its 3,522ft vertical drop (climaxing at 12,266ft) is accessible from downtown or Mountain Village.

▶ *Drive south 65mi from Telluride on Rte. 145.*

Dolores

Rtes. 145 & 184, 45mi west of Durango. △✕⎙🅿 ☎970-882-4018. www.doloreschamber.com.
This small town has a historic train station and **Galloping Goose** *(Rte. 145; ☎970-728-5700)*, a hybrid train/bus con-

traption that once simultaneously carried passengers and removed snow from the railroad tracks. Three miles west is the **Anasazi Heritage Center**★★ *(Rte. 184;* ☎*970-882-5600, www.co.blm.gov/ ahc)*, a museum depicting Ancestral Puebloan culture throughout the Four Corners region. This is the visitor center for Canyons of the Ancients National Monument *(www.co.blm.gov/canm)*, *(County Rd. CC, 28mi northwest of Cortez)*.

▶ *Continue south 12mi from Dolores on Rte. 145.*

Cortez

US-160, US-666 & Rte. 145, 46mi west of Durango. ⚠🍴🅿☎*970-565-3414. www. swcolo.org.*
An agricultural town of 8,000, Cortez features a historic district that stretches along Main Street.
The **Ute Mountain Tribal Park**★★ *(12mi southwest via US-160;* ☎*970-749-1452; www.utemountainute.com; visit by guided tour only, Apr–Oct)* contains excavated cliff dwellings, petroglyphs and thousands of pottery shards. Tours depart from the tribe's **Visitor Center and Museum** *(US 160 and 491)*.

Less than an hour's drive is the **Four Corners Monument** *(US-160, 38mi southwest of Cortez)*, the only place where four US states intersect: Colorado, New Mexico, Arizona and Utah.

▶ *Take US-160 east 10mi from Cortez; turn south into Mesa Verde National Park.*

Mesa Verde National Park★★★

US-160, Mancos. ⚠🍴♿🅿☎*970-529-4465. www.nps.gov/meve.*
The first US national park to preserve the works of man (as opposed to nature), Mesa Verde was created in 1906. Today it attracts 650,000 annual visitors, mostly in summer, when they can walk through five major cliff dwellings and additional mesa-top structures displaying primitive construction methods used by Ancestral Puebloans between AD 750 and 1300.
The 21mi drive from the park entrance to the **Chapin Mesa Archaeological Museum**★ winds around the mesa, offering spectacular views of four states. Adjacent is **Spruce Tree House**★★★, a major cliff dwelling and the only one open year-round. Nearby, the 6mi **Mesa Top Loop Road** is also open year-round. Overlooks provide views of **Square Tower House**★★, the **Twin Trees**★ site and **Sun Temple**★. In warmer weather, guided tours are offered to spectacular sites built into overhanging cliffs at **Cliff Palace**★★ and **Balcony House**★★.

▶ *Continue east 36mi on US-160 to return to Durango.*

© Photo by Tom Stillo/CTO

Cliff Palace, Mesa Verde National Park

DALLAS–FORT WORTH AREA

The twin cities of Dallas and Fort Worth, together with their patchwork of suburbs, constitute the vast expanse of urbanized prairie termed the Metroplex, with a total population of 6 million. Though united by their physical proximity, the cities vary widely in history and character.

The gleaming towers of downtown Dallas are firmly anchored in trade and commerce. Although the city is widely thought of as an oil or cattle capital, Dallas is a major center for banking, transportation and retailing, and is headquarters for a host of US and international companies. Along with its corporate image, Dallas also enjoys cultural prestige. Institutions such as the Dallas Museum of Art and the Morton H.

Dallas-Fort Worth

TX

Meyerson Symphony Center have made ; the Dallas Arts District one of the largest and most significant in the US.

Dallas' darkest moment occurred in 1963 when US President John F. Kennedy was assassinated while touring the city in a motorcade. The tragic episode is remebered at Dealey Plaza and in The Sixth Floor Museum. The city has since made a point of emphasizing its cultural sophistication and diversity--Dallas' "competes" for pre-eminence not with Fort Worth, but Houston.

Fort Worth is proud of its "Cowtown" heritage, bringing its Old West history to life in the Stockyards National Historic District and the restored downtown, known as Sundance Square. Smaller and less hurried than its neighbor to the east, Fort Worth offers a surprisingly diverse array of attractions beyond its Wild West flavor, including a first-rate zoo and a cluster of renowned museums in the Cultural District.

Dallas Skyline

DALLAS★★

MAP P 157

CENTRAL STANDARD TIME

POPULATION 1,250,000

Dallas has a certain familiarity even for those who haven't previously been to "Big D." It's the city where President Kennedy was assassinated, venue of the Dallas television series and movie, home of the Dallas Cowboys football club, which fancies itself "America's team." Shoppers know the Dallas Market Center (2100 Stemmons Fwy.; ☎214-655-6100, www.dallasmarketcenter.com), **largest wholesale merchandise mart in the world, and the original Neiman-Marcus department store** (1618 Main St.; ☎214-741-6911, www.neimanmarcus.com), **a symbol of Texas wealth.**

- **Information:** ☎214-571-1000 www.dallascvb.com
- ▶ **Orient Yourself:** Many attractions are concentrated in three areas. Museums are clustered at Fair Park, site of the largest state fair in the US each October. The Dallas Arts District is the nation's largest urban arts district. The West End Historic District, occupying renovated warehouses, holds some of the city's best shopping and nightlife.
- **Don't Miss:** The Sixth Floor Museum
- **Organizing Your Time:** If you have kids, you'll want to allow a whole day for Arlington, home of Six Flags amusement park and the Ballpark at Arlington's excellent baseball museum.
- **Especially for Kids:** Six Flags Over Texas.

A Bit of History

Dallas began in 1841 as a trading post near a crossing on the Trinity River. By the time the US annexed Texas in 1845, the town's population had grown to 430, mostly farmers, traders and shopkeepers. It prospered as a supply station for settlers in the great westward expansion and as an agricultural center, particularly for the export of cotton. After suffering severe economic and social problems in the wake of the Civil War, during which it supported the Confederacy, Dallas rebounded as a trade center and a shipping point for the buffalo market. In the 1870s railway and telegraph lines further enhanced its position as a hub of commerce. The Federal Reserve Bank selected Dallas as the site for a regional bank in 1911, fostering the city's role as a financial center.

Dallas' strong ties with the aviation industry began with World War I, when Love Field was founded as an air-training facility. Today, although Love still operates as a commercial airport, it is overshadowed in suburban Grapevine by the enormous Dallas-Fort Worth International Airport, world headquarters of American Airlines.

Downtown Dallas★★

Downtown Dallas combines commerce and culture with shopping, dining and entertainment. The four-story **West End Marketplace** (Lamar St. north of Pacific Ave.; ☎214-741-7180; www.dallas-westend.org) is a renovated warehouse with more than 50 shops, restaurants, nightclubs and a cinema complex. A few blocks farther north is a state-of-the-art sports arena, **American Airlines Center** (2500 Victory Ave.; ☎214-665-4200, www.americanairlinescenter.com), home to pro basketball and ice hockey.

Deep Ellum (Elm St. east of Good-Latimer Expwy.; ☎214-748-4332, www.deepellumtx.com), a former industrial neighborhood east of downtown, now boasts a thriving nightclub scene ranging from jazz and blues to alternative music. In recent years, the scope of the avant-garde has spread beyond Elm

Address Book

For price ranges, see the Legend on the cover flap.

WHERE TO STAY

$$$$$ The Mansion on Turtle Creek – *2821 Turtle Creek Blvd., Dallas, TX.* ✕ ⚐ ⬚ ☎*214-559-2100. www.mansiononturtlecreek.com. 141 rooms.* Once a cotton magnate's home, The Mansion has marble rotundas, elaborate décor and impeccable service. The Mansion is the flagship of the Rosewood Hotels chain. A sister inn, **Hotel Crescent Court** (*400 Crescent Court, Dallas; ☎214-871-3200; $$$$$*), has a lavish spa.

$$$$$ Hotel Adolphus – *1321 Commerce St., Dallas, TX.* ✕ ⬚ ☎*214-742-8200 or 800-221-9083. www.hoteladolphus.com. 433 rooms.* This 80-year-old creation of unabashed Baroque flamboyance and period furniture, with lacquered chinoiserie, tapestries, and chandeliers, was built by a Dallas beer baron. The crown jewel is **The French Room** (*$$$*), serving creative cuisine under vaulted ceilings and gilded rococo arches.

$$$$ The Ashton Hotel – *610 Main St., Fort Worth, TX.* ✕ ⬚ ☎*817-332-0100 or 866-327-4866. www.theashtonhotel. com. 39 rooms.* This downtown brick-and-stone building was built in 1915 as a private club. The six-story Italianate landmark has been refurbished into a sleek nonsmoking hotel in which every room is different. The first-floor lobby and restaurant house a collection of mid-20C artists' works.

$$$ Etta's Place – *200 W. 3rd St., Fort Worth, TX.* ⬚ ☎*817-255-5760 or 866-355-5760. www.ettas-place.com. 10 rooms.* It's in a new building but this B&Binn echoes the 19C ambience of Sundance Square, right down to its name: Etta Place was the Sundance Kid's mistress. Each room is furnished with Western antiques. Breakfast is a hearty repast featuring handmade sausage and quiches.

$$$ Stockyards Hotel – *109 E. Exchange Ave., Fort, TX.* ⬚ ☎*817-625-6427 or 800-423-8471. www.stockyardshotel.com. 52 rooms.* Located in the historic cowtown district, this Old West hostelry recalls early Texas history: Some rooms are decorated with rawhide lamps and steer skulls. The Davy Crockett Suite even boasts a coonskin cap from the days when cattle barons and rustlers sat in the saddles at the bar.

$$$ The Stoneleigh Hotel – *2927 Maple Ave., Dallas, TX.* ✕ ⬚ ☎*214-871-7111 or 800-678-8946. www.stoneleighhotel.com. 158 rooms.* A Jazz Age landmark (1923), this hotel has spacious apartment-style rooms with walnut and mahogany furnishings, a fitness center, a Spanish-style restaurant and an attractive Uptown location.

$$-$$$ The Melrose Hotel – *3015 Oak Lawn Ave., Dallas, TX.* ✕ ⬚ ☎*214-521-5151 or 800-635-7673. www.melrosehotel.com 184 rooms.* Once a luxury apartment block, the historic (1924) Melrose boasts an understated exterior of simple brick with a carved frieze. The handsome porte-cochere leads to marble floors, tall columns and newly renovated rooms. **The Landmark** (*$$$*) serves fine regional cuisine.

WHERE TO EAT

$$$$ Star Canyon – *3102 Oak Lawn, The Centrum, Dallas.* ☎*214-520-7827. www.crww.com/starcanyon. Closed Sun.* **New Texas.** An open kitchen is the centerpiece of a room adorned with cowgirl murals and barbed-wire motifs. Offering salmon with black-bean banana mash, a foie-gras and corn-pudding tamale and rock-shrimp taquitos, it's top end for creativity.

$$$ Riscky's Steakhouse – *120 E. Exchange Ave., Fort Worth.* ☎*817-624-4800. www.risckys.com.* **American.** The interior of this local favorite resembles a street of old downtown Fort Worth, with a typical menu. Come for Texas T-bone or chicken-fried steaks; ask about batter-dipped "calf fries," cooked to a golden brown. Riscky's also has barbecue and Mexican cafes.

$$ The Lonesome Dove – *2406 N. Main St., Fort Worth.* ☎*817-740-8810. www.lonesomedovebistro.com.* 🕐 *Closed Sun.* **American.** Classically trained Chef

Tim Love has turned his attention to "cowboy cuisine" at this jovial Stockyards bistro. Love stuffs beef tenderloin with roasted garlic, turns buffalo into meatloaf, crusts venison with pistachio nuts and a cherry demi-glace.

$$ Joe T Garcia's – *2122 N. Commerce St., Fort Worth.* ☎817-626-4356. *www. joets.com.* **Mexican**. Joe T's is the epitome of Tex-Mex, where Mexican beer is freely consumed by cowboy-clad customers on a patio that regularly fills to its capacity of 300. Visiting celebrities gobble up renowned menudos and enchiladas, or buy a round of potent margaritas to enjoy in the mini-park.

$ Sonny Bryan's BBQ – *2202 Inwood Rd., Dallas.* ☎214-357-7120. *www.sonnybryans.com.* **Barbecue**. Sonny's opened in 1958 as a drive-in. The family recipes for slow-smoked brisket are a century old. Today, Texans slather Sonny's secret BBQ sauce onto spare ribs, chicken and pulled pork. The double-dipped onion rings are delectable.

Street (where speakeasies flourished during Prohibition) to nearby Main and Commerce streets.

Dallas Museum of Art★★

1717 N. Harwood St. ✕ & 🅿 ☎214-922-1344. *www.dm-art.org.*
In this vast, stair-stepped building (1984, Edward L. Barnes) a collection of global scope is presented: **Arts of the Americas★★★** is a broad survey of human cultural evolution in the Western Hemisphere. Beginning with amulets and jewelry of prehistoric civilizations, it follows creative man through the Spanish and British colonial periods, right up to 20C Texas. Highlights include paintings by Albert Bierstadt, Andrew Wyeth and Georgia O'Keeffe, as well as Frederic Church, Thomas Hart Benton and sculpture by James Earl Frasier.
European Painting & Sculpture★★ galleries showcase 19C canvases by Manet, Degas, Monet, Renoir, Van Gogh and Gauguin; and 20C works by Mondrian, Picasso, Braque and Modigliani. The **Contemporary Gallery★** presents works by Rothko, Pollock, Motherwell, Warhol and Diebenkorn.
The **Wendy & Emery Reves Collection★** features 19-20C European painting and diverse decorative arts. Its setting recalls a French Riviera villa, and it has a full room devoted to paintings and memorabilia of Sir Winston Churchill.
The **Arts of Africa and Arts of Asia and the Pacific** exhibits show a wide range of world cultures.

Crow Collection of Asian Art★

2010 Flora St. & ☎214-979-6430. *www. crowcollection.com.*
Real-estate magnate Trammell Crow and his wife, Margaret, built this elegant granite facility to house a renowned Asian collection of more than 500 pieces. Highlights include exquisite carved-jade pieces and a jewel-encrusted Indian marble gateway.

Nearby is the **Morton H. Meyerson Symphony Center★** (*2301 Flora St.;* ☎214-670-3600, *www.myersonsymphonycenter.com),* home of the Dallas Symphony Orchestra. The only such building designed by I.M. Pei (1989) incorporates the Eugene McDermott Concert Hall. Pei also designed the **Dallas City Hall** (*1500 Marilla St.;* ☎214-670-3011).

The Sixth Floor Museum at Dealey Plaza★★★

▥▥▥ *411 Elm St. at Houston St.* & 🅿 ☎214-747-6660. *www.jfk.org.*
On November 22, 1963, alleged assassin Lee Harvey Oswald fired shots at President John F. Kennedy from this level of the former Texas School Book Depository building. Today the entire 9,000sq-ft floor holds a moving tribute to Kennedy's life and career. The southeast corner window—from where Oswald allegedly shot the president—has been re-created to look as it did when investigators discovered it, with cardboard boxes stacked to create a hiding place. Newscaster Walter Cronkite's poignant announcement of the president's death is rebroadcast in

a TV clip. Nearby is a photo of Lyndon Johnson taking the presidential oath with Jacqueline Kennedy by his side. Display cases showcase international tributes.

The Sixth Floor Museum is within **Dealey Plaza National Historic Landmark** district, six square blocks that encompass sites important to the Kennedy assassination and its aftermath. East of Dealey Plaza, **John F. Kennedy Memorial Plaza** centers on a cenotaph, or open tomb, designed by Philip Johnson and dedicated in 1970.

Pioneer Plaza★★

🚸 *Young & Griffin Sts.*
The world's largest bronze monument occupies this 4.2-acre park area north of the Dallas Convention Center. *Cattle Drive* (1994, Robert Summers) features 40 longhorn steers being herded by a trio of mounted cowboys down a limestone ledge.

Fair Park★

Built to host the 1936 Texas Centennial Exhibition, these 277-acre grounds, a short distance east of downtown, host the largest state fair in the US *(Sept-Oct)*, which attracts the lion's share of 7 million annual visitors to Fair Park *(1300 Robert E. Cullum Blvd.; ☎214-670-8400, www.fairpark.org)*. Even during its "off-season," it bustles as a cultural center with its **Cotton Bowl** stadium *(☎214-939-2222)*; the **Music Hall at Fair Park** *(909 First Ave.; ☎214-565-1116)*; the **Smirnoff Music Center** *(1818 First Ave.; ☎214-421-1111, www.hob.com)* for open-air concerts. Also here are numerous museums, many of them—including the Hall of State, aquarium and natural-history museum—built in 1930s Art Deco style.

Hall of State

3939 Grand Ave. ♿ 🅿 ☎*214-421-4500. www.hallofstate.com.*
A showcase of Texas history, the limestone Hall of State is shaped like an inverted T. Larger-than-life bronze statues by Pompeo Coppini commemorate six Texas founding fathers,

including Stephen Austin, Sam Houston and Alamo defender William Travis. Ornate murals in the Great Hall depict historical events.

African American Museum★

3536 Grand Ave. ♿ 🅿 ☎*214-565-9026. aamdallas.org.*
This facility devoted to African-American history, art and culture occupies a two-story building (1993, Arthur Rogers) made of ivory stone with a 60ft dome in the shape of a 12C Ethiopian Orthodox cross. Its motifs symbolize pre-industrialized African cultures. Exhibits include selections from the **Billy R. Allen Folk Art Collection**, one of the best contemporary collections in the US.

Museum of Nature and Science

🚸 *3535 Grand Ave.* ♿ 🅿 ☎*214-428-5555. www.natureandscience.org.*
Dioramas of Texas wildlife and habitats combine with the first dinosaur discovered in this state and ecology exhibits.

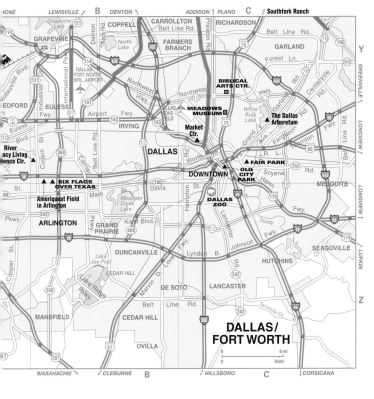

The entrance is marked by a bronze sculpture by Tom Tischler, based on a mammoth skeleton excavated in Dallas. More than 300 interactive displays explore scientific principles.

Less than a block away is **The Science Place Planetarium** (*First Ave. & Martin Luther King Blvd.*).

Dallas Aquarium at Fair Park★

Kids *1462 First Ave. & Martin Luther King Blvd.* ♿ 🅿 ☎214-670-8443. *www.dallas -zoo.org.*
Operated by the Dallas Zoo, the aquarium is home to about 5,000 aquatic animals of 400 species, many of them anomalous creatures such as fish with four eyes, fish that walk on land, and fish that are virtually invisible. Highlights include an Amazon River exhibit and native Texas species, including a 135-pound alligator snapping turtle.

Texas Discovery Gardens

3601 Martin Luther King Blvd. ♿ 🅿 ☎214-428-7476. *www.texasdiscovery gardens.org.*
An educational center for urban horticulture, this facility spans 7.5 acres of both decorative and native Texas plants. The **William Douglas Blanchly Conservatory is** a 6,800sq-ft glass facility that houses more than 250 species of African plants.

Age of Steam Railroad Museum

Kids *1105 Washington St.* ♿ ☎214-428-0101. *www.dallasrailwaymuseum.org.*
This collection of train engines and cars includes the largest diesel electric locomotive ever built. The Union Pacific "Big Boy" is a 100ft-long, 1.3 million-pound, 7,000-horsepower behemoth that could pull a mile-long train.

The Women's Museum★★

3800 Parry Ave. ♿ 🅿 ☎214-915-0861. *www.thewomensmuseum.org.*
This thoughtful facility highlights female achievements in commerce, politics, science and the arts. Though its mission is significant, the museum is also lots of fun: there are videos of famed comediennes such as Lucille Ball, for instance. Temporary exhibits tend toward serious topics such as domestic violence.

Additional Sights

Old City Park★

Kids *1717 Gano St.* ✕♿🅿 ☎214-421-5141. *www.oldcitypark.org.*
This 13-acre museum village, south of downtown, contains 37 restored buildings dated 1840-1910. Structures include a rail depot, hotel, bank, doctor's office and school. Costumed docents carry on chores in the garden, curing shed and livestock lot of the Living Farmstead.

Dallas Zoo★

Kids *650 S. R.L. Thornton Fwy., 3mi south of downtown at Marsalis Exit, I-35.* ✕♿🅿 ☎214-670-5656. *www.dallas-zoo.org.*
Founded in 1888, the zoo keeps 2,000 animals in two sections of 85 developed acres. The larger **ZooNorth** features new habitat areas such as a tiger exhibit. The Bird & Reptile Building contains a New Zealand lizard, considered the only surviving direct descendant of dinosaurs. **Wilds of Africa**★★, south of Cedar Creek, has six expansive habitats of different landscapes.

The Dallas Arboretum and Botanical Garden

8525 Garland Rd. ♿ 🅿 ☎214-515-6500. *www.dallasarboretum.org.*
Located on the shore of White Rock Lake, this 66-acre expanse is highlighted by the **Jonsson Color Garden**★, with 20,000 azalea bushes of some 2,000 varieties. Other features are the 1940 Spanish Colonial-style **DeGolyer House** (*tours daily*) and a half-dozen **storybook playhouses** Kids.

Meadows Museum★★

Bishop Blvd. at Binkley Ave., Southern Methodist University. ☎214-768-2516. *www.meadowsmuseum.org.*
Its interior fashioned after Madrid's famed Prado, this small university museum houses an outstanding collection of Spanish art. Oils, sculptures and works on paper span 1,000 years. Beginning with 10C Medieval and Renaissance paintings, it moves through Baroque Castilian (Velázquez) and Andalusian (Murillo) art to 18C dry-point etchings by Goya. There are 20C works by Miró and early Cubist still-lifes by Picasso.

Dallas Nature Center★

7171 Mountain Creek Pkwy., 2.5mi south of I-20. 🅿 ☎*972-296-1955. www.dallas naturecenter.org.*

This 633-acre park preserves the last remaining piece of native prairie in the Dallas metroplex. Nine hiking trails wind through juniper groves, mesquite prairies and wildflower meadows.

Excursions

Southfork Ranch

3700 Hogge Dr., Parker; 16mi north of downtown Dallas off US-75, Exit 30 East. ✕ 🅿 ☎ *972-442-7800. www.south forkranch.com.*

This sprawling mansion was used in exterior shots for the long-running *Dallas* TV series. Visitors board a tractor-drawn jitney to reach the Ewing Mansion for guided tours. TV clips, star interviews and "the gun that shot J.R." highlight the "Dallas Legends" exhibit.

Arlington

I-30, 16mi west of Dallas & 15mi east of Fort Worth. ☎ *800-342-4305. www.arlington.org.*

A city of 367,000, Arlington is best known for its theme parks and as the home of major league baseball's Texas Rangers.

The Ballpark in Arlington

▥ *1000 Ballpark Way.* ✕🅿 ☎*817-273-5222. www.texasrangers.com*

Built in 1994 (David M. Schwarz) in the style of early-20C ballparks, this $190 million stadium offers year-round tours. **Legends of the Game Museum and Learning Center★** Kids *(*☎*817-273-5600)* holds the largest collection of Baseball Hall of Fame memorabilia outside Cooperstown, NY; exhibits use baseball as a medium for teaching physics, history, and mathematics.

River Legacy Living Science Center

Kids *703 NW Green Oaks Blvd.* 🅿 ☎*817-860-6752. www.riverlegacy.org.*

Set on 1,000 acres of forest and floodplain beside the Trinity River, this facility explores North Texas flora and fauna. There are view rooms for bird-watching and interactive videos.

Six Flags Over Texas★

Kids ▥ *I-30 & Rte. 360.* ✕🅿 ☎*817-640-8900. www.sixflags.com.*

The state's tallest roller coaster, "Mr. Freeze," is in this 221-acre theme park, as is the Texas Giant, rated the world's No. 1 wooden roller coaster. The park is the base of the Six Flags chain. The seasonal **Six Flags Hurricane Harbor** *(1800 E. Lamar Blvd.;* ☎*817-640-8900, www.sixflags.com)* boasts water rides and more than 3 million gallons of water.

FORT WORTH★★

MAP P 157
CENTRAL STANDARD TIME
POPULATION 653,000

"The place where the West begins" wears its heritage like a medal. Established in 1849 as a US Army outpost on the Trinity River, Fort Worth was named for Mexican War hero William Jenkins Worth. In the 1860s the town became a shipping point for buffalo hunters on the Great Plains. No city nickname has endured like "Cowtown," a moniker adopted in the 1870s when beef cattle were driven up the Chisholm Trail from South Texas. Fort Worth was first a supply station and later, with the arrival of the railway, a major terminus itself.

- **Information:** ☎817-336-8791 www.fortworth.com
- ▶ **Orient Yourself:** From Fort Worth westward to the Rockies lie the sere plains once inhabited only by Comanches; thus the phrase "where the West begins."
- **Don't Miss:** The Kimbell and Amon Carter museums.
- Kids **Especially for Kids:** Pawnee Bill's Wild West Show; Fossil Rim.

A Bit of History

With the founding of the Stockyards in 1887, the town began earning a Wild West reputation. Saloons and brothels proliferated. The infamous Hell's Half Acre district served as headquarters for **Butch Cassidy** and his Wild Bunch. By 1904, more than 1 million head of cattle had passed through the Stockyards; cattle pens extended for nearly a mile. During the early 20C, Fort Worth expanded and diversified, especially in the aviation and oil industries; a huge natural gas field beneath the city has brought new 21C hydrocarbon wealth. Prosperity was the genesis of the world-class museums in its Cultural District.

At the heart of downtown Fort Worth is historic Sundance Square, a revitalized 20-block neighborhood named for notorious Western outlaw **Harry Longabaugh**, "The Sundance Kid."

Stockyards National Historic District★★

An Old West flair persists in old Cowtown (☎ 817-625-9715, www.fortworthstockyards.org). A steam train, year-round rodeos and top country-and-western nightlife couple with historic hotels, steakhouses and Western wear shops to give it a frontier flavor. The small **Stockyards Museum** (131 E. Exchange Ave.; ☎817-625-5087, www.stockyardsmuseum.org), in the 1902 Livestock Exchange Building, chronicles its history. At the century-old **White Elephant Saloon** (106 E. Exchange Ave.; ☎817-624-8273), patrons have left their Stetson hats nailed to the ceiling.

Cowtown Coliseum

Kids 121 E. Exchange Ave. ⅙ ☎817-625-1025. www.cowtowncoliseum.com.
Built in 1908, the coliseum presented the world's first indoor rodeo in 1918. Today, the Stockyards Championship Rodeo features bull riding, calf roping and barrel racing; and Pawnee Bill's Wild West Show is a revival of a Western show—with rope tricks and trick riding—that first played here in 1909.

Billy Bob's Texas★

▥ 2520 Rodeo Plaza. ✗⅙🄿 ☎817-624-7117. www.billybobstexas.com.
Billed as "the world's largest honky-tonk," this nightclub seats 6,000 and boasts dozens of bar stations, line-dancing lessons, two separate music stages and an indoor professional bull-riding arena.

Grapevine Vintage Railroad★

Kids 140 E. Exchange Ave. ☎817-410-3123. www.grapevinesteamrailroad.com.
With the oldest "puffer-belly" locomotive in the US (c.1896), the steam train pulls Victorian coaches and open-air cars on a 75min, 21mi ride between the Stockyards and suburban Grapevine. Passengers may watch craftspeople at the Grapevine Heritage Center or attend tastings by award-winning wineries on Grapevine's historic Main Street.

Sundance Square★

Not a square in the traditional sense, Sundance Square is the heart of downtown Fort Worth, a revitalized district of brick streets lined with shops and restaurants, hotels and museums. Anchoring the district is the 1895 Tarrant **County Courthouse**★ (100 W. Weatherford St.; b817-884-1111, www.tarrantcounty.com), patterned after the Texas State Capitol. Often featured in the now-syndicated Walker: Texas Ranger TV series, it boasts an unusual trompe l'oeil paint job that gives a building extension the same appearance as the original stone structure.

The $65 million **Nancy Lee and Perry R. Bass Performance Hall**★ (555 Commerce St.; ☎817-212-4325, www.basshall.com), designed by David M. Schwarz (1998), occupies a full city block. It is identified by its twin 48ft limestone sculptures—trumpet-heralding angels by Marton Varo. The Bass is home to the Fort Worth symphony, ballet and opera, and the Van Cliburn International Piano Competition.

©iStockphoto.com/Patrick Cassity

Fort Worth Architecture

Sid Richardson Collection of Western Art★

309 Main St. ♿ 🅿 ☎*817-332-6554. www. sidrichardsonmuseum.org.*
Five dozen paintings by Charles M. Russell and Frederic Remington are showcased in this Sundance Square museum, the personal collection of billionaire oilman Sid W. Richardson (1891-1959).

On the south side of downtown, famed architect Philip Johnson turned a vacant four-acre lot into the **Fort Worth Water Gardens**★ *(1502 Commerce St.),* a collection of brick-lined fountains, ponds, gardens and picnic alcoves.

Cultural District★★

Trinity Park is the focus of this district, which includes six major museums, Fort Worth's zoo and botanical garden.

Kimbell Art Museum★★★

⦚⦚⦚ *3333 Camp Bowie Blvd.* ✕♿🅿 ☎*817-332-8451. www.kimbellart.org.*
A showcase building (1972) and remarkable collection have made the Kimbell one of the finest small public art museums in the world. Architect Louis Kahn made innovative use of natural light, enabling curators to subtly rearrange generous space for special exhibitions.

Although space limits the museum from displaying more than a fraction of its permanent collection at any one time, visitors might see such masterworks as Rubens' *The Duke of Buckingham* (1625); Rembrandt's *Portrait of a Young Jew* (1663); and Cézanne's *Glass and Apples* (c.1879-82). Works by Titian, El Greco, Goya, Degas, Monet, Picasso and Miró are also in the collection. Rotating exhibits feature pre-Columbian, African and Asian art.

Amon Carter Museum★★★

3501 Camp Bowie Blvd. ☎*817-738-1933. www.cartermuseum.org.*
This small museum gained international stature with its three-fold 2001 expansion by Philip Johnson, who also designed the initial International-style building in 1961. The original first floor is devoted to late oilman-publisher Amon G. Carter's peerless collection of 391 works by famed Western artists Charles Russell (1864-1926) and Frederic Remington (1861-1909).
The new upper level is devoted to visiting exhibits and samplings from the rest of the Carter collection, ranging from Thomas Moran to Georgia O'Keeffe and Grant Wood. The photography collection's 230,000 images include works by Laura Gilpin, Eliot Porter, Richard Avedon and Robert Adams.

Modern Art Museum of Fort Worth★

University Dr. & Camp Bowie Blvd. ✕♿🅿
☎*817-738-9215. www.mamfw.org.* The oldest (1892) art museum in Texas now resides in a concrete-and-glass building with 53,000sq ft of gallery space, designed by Tadao Ando (2002); it uses skylights and clerestory windows to bring natural light inside. The collection offers a representative sampling of 20C artists, including Picasso, Rothko, Pollock, Warhol and Basquiat. A satellite museum, **The Modern at Sundance Square** *(410 Houston St.; ☎817-335-9215),* is located in downtown Fort Worth.

Fort Worth Museum of Science and History★

🚸 *1501 Montgomery St.* ✕♿🅿 ☎*817-255-9300. www.fwmuseum.org.* ⏰*Closed until late 2009.*
Computers to anthropology exhibits are featured at this family-oriented museum, which is being expanded, having incorporated the Cattle Raisers Museum.

National Cowgirl Museum & Hall of Fame★★

1720 Gendy St. ♿🅿 ☎*817-336-4475. www.cowgirl.net.*
A rarely acknowledged facet of Western history receives star treatment at this new (2002) facility in the Western Heritage Center. Women who once entered and won rodeo competitions alongside men are featured, along with such luminaries as artist Georgia O'Keeffe, singer Patsy Cline and actress Dale Evans. The collection includes archival photos, colorful clothing and cowgirl trophies.

Fort Worth Zoo★★

🚸 *1989 Colonial Pkwy.* ✕♿🅿 ☎*817-759-7555. www.fortworthzoo.com.*
Acclaimed both for its visitor accessibility and its animal-friendly habitats, this zoo is home to some 6,000 animals of Texas and exotic species. **Asian Falls** is the precinct of tigers and sun bears. **World of Primates** permit visitors to virtually enter the gorilla habitat. **Thundering Plains** showcases bison

and other animals of the Great Plains. Among indoor facilities is an enlightening **Insect City.Texas Wild**★ is a six-acre evocation of life and nature in the Lone Star State.

Fort Worth Botanic Garden★

3220 Botanic Garden Blvd. (off University Dr.). ♿🅿 ☎*817-871-7686. www.fwbg. com.*
Texas' oldest botanic garden began as a Depression-era relief program in 1933. The 109-acre gardens include more than 2,500 native and exotic species. An impressive begonia collection is in the Exhibition Greenhouse; tropical plants fill the lush, 10,000sq-ft Conservatory.

Excursions

Glen Rose

On US-67, 53mi southwest of Fort Worth. ☎*254-897-3081. www.glenrosetexas. net.*
Tucked amid oaks and cottonwoods along the Paluxy River, this erstwhile frontier town has been transformed into a weekend getaway center with galleries, cafes and small inns. Three miles southwest, **Fossil Rim Wildlife Center**★ *(2155 County Rd. 2008; ☎254-897-2960, www.fossilrim.org)* is a 2,700-acre safari park with herds of African antelope, giraffes, rhinoceros, ostriches and other species endangered in native ranges. Fossilized dinosaur tracks have been found in the limestone beds of **Dinosaur Valley State Park** *(Park Rd. 59, 4mi northwest of Glen Rose; ☎254-897-4588, www.tpwd.state.tx.us).*

Waco

On I-35, 87mi south of Fort Worth (via I-35W) and 90mi south of Dallas (via I-35E). ☎*254-750-5600. www.wacocvb.com.*
A cattle and cotton-farming center of 122,000 on the Brazos River, Waco is home to Baylor University. The **Taylor Museum of Waco History** *(701 Jefferson St.; ☎254-752-4774)* interprets the 1993 standoff between Branch Davidian cultists and the FBI.

Texas Ranger Hall of Fame and Museum★

Fort Fisher Park off University Parks Dr. (I-35 Exit 335B). ⚠ ♿ 🅿 ☎*254-750-8631. www.texasranger.org.*

The lawmen responsible for taming Texas are remembered in this museum. Displays include Billy the Kid's Winchester carbine, weapons packed by Bonnie and Clyde, and a gem-encrusted saddle. Dioramas recount the early days of the Rangers, beginning in the 1840s.

Dr Pepper Museum and Free Enterprise Institute

🄺🄸🄳🅂 *300 S. 5th St.* ♿ 🅿 ☎*254-757-1025. www.drpeppermuseum.com.*

The Dr Pepper soft drink was invented in 1885 by pharmacist Charles Alderton at Waco's Old Corner Drug Store. Today, in his 1906 bottling plant, a lifelike model of Alderton describes his concoction.

Armstrong Browning Library★★

700 Speight Ave., Baylor University. ♿ 🅿 ☎*254-710-3566. www.browninglibrary. org. Parking: Wiethorn Visitors Center, University Parks Dr.* ☎*254-710-2407.*

The library holds the world's largest collection of the works and belongings of British poets Robert Browning (1812-89) and Elizabeth Barrett Browning (1806-61). A.J. Armstrong, chairman of Baylor's English department for 40 years until his death in 1954, donated his personal collection to the university in 1918.

Cattle Drives

By the end of the Civil War, severe meat shortages in the East led Texas ranchers to employ new strategies to get beef to market. Most dramatic was the cattle drive: South Texas cowboys collected enormous herds of wild range cattle ("mavericks") and drove them north to railroads in Kansas. Although the heyday of the cattle drive lasted only a dozen years, its influence persists in popular myth.

Descendants of Spanish breeds brought to the New World, Texas Longhorns roamed freely over the grasslands of Texas and Mexico, numbering in the millions by the time of the first cattle drives in the late 1860s. The Chisholm Trail was the most famous of the cattle drive routes. In 1870 alone, 300,000 cattle were driven through San Antonio, Austin and north to Fort Worth, the last „civilized" stop before Indian territory.

By the late 1870s, the railroad was pushing south and west, eventually making the cattle drive obsolete.

©iStockphoto.com/Kriss Russell

Longhorn Cattle Drive

DENVER AREA

Nicknamed the "Mile High City" because its elevation is exactly 5,280ft above sea level, Denver is a growing metropolis of more than 2.4 million people. As the largest urban center within a 550mi radius—between Phoenix and Chicago, Dallas and Seattle—it is the capital of the Rocky Mountain region.

Denver is nestled near the foothills of the Rockies on a high plain that originally was Arapaho and Cheyenne Indian land. The alpine panorama to its west has become North America's greatest mountain playground, with many famous resorts (such as Vail and Breckenridge) and a remarkable concentration of peaks higher than 4,000m (13,124ft).

To the east are a few low hills, then flat land stretching across the Great Plains to the Mississippi River.

The main towns north and south of Denver cling to the Front Range, as the eastern edge of the Rockies is called. Little more than an hour's drive south is Colorado Springs, sprawling at the foot of immense Pikes Peak, its 14,110ft summit a landmark to westbound travelers since the early 1800s. The burgeoning city is home to the US Air Force Academy, the high-altitude US Olympic Training Center and numerous unique geological and architectural attractions. Two hours north of Denver is Cheyenne, the small Wyoming state capital that clings to its Wild West heritage. Cheyenne is quiet except during 10 days in late July and early August when it hosts Cheyenne Frontier Days, the world's largest outdoor rodeo.

© Photo by Brian Gadbery/CTO

The Taste of Colorado at Civic Center Park, Denver

DENVER★★★

MAPS PP 171 AND 144
MOUNTAIN STANDARD TIME
POPULATION 558,000

Denver today has become a services and high-tech based center, with telecommunications and computer industries contributing significantly to the economy. With thousands of state, local and federal employees, Denver has the country's second-highest percentage of government workers after Washington DC. The city is an important cultural center with museums, theaters and concert venues, and is one of only eight US cities with franchises in all four major-league sports: football, baseball, basketball and ice hockey. The annual National Western Stock Show & Rodeo *(www.nationalwestern.com)*, one of the largest events of its kind, ties Western tradition to modern times.

- **Information:** ☎303-892-1112 www.denver.org.
- ▶ **Orient Yourself:** Like most Western cities, the Denver area's streets are laid out in an east-west/north-south grid; streets run north-south, avenues east-west (except downtown). You can't lose track of compass directions—the Rockies are always in sight directly west.
- **Parking:** Parking near downtown can be scarce on weekdays, but there are ample reasonably priced lots near the Denver Art Museum, and west of Larimer Square toward the South Platte River.
- **Don't Miss:** The Denver Art Museum.
- **Organizing Your Time:** Plan to visit the Art Museum, state capitol and other Civic Center attractions in the morning; then hop the 16th Street Mall free bus to reach Larimer Square, Confluence Park, the aquarium and Elitch Gardens.
- **Especially for Kids:** The Downtown Aquarium; Elitch Gardens.

A Bit of History

Denver City was formed in 1860 by the merger of two gold-rush settlements. Despite a population laden with outlaws, prospectors and shysters, the frontier town survived the pioneer era as capital of the Colorado Territory.

Denver's prosperity was pegged to silver. Between the mid-1870s and mid-1890s, strikes in Leadville and Aspen turned miners into millionaires. Successful silver production required banks to underpin the enterprises, and trains to connect the mountain towns with Denver and the East.

By 1890 Denver was a fashionable city of 106,000 with fine hotels, stores and theaters. Electric lights were installed in 1883; the first streetcars in 1888

Today Denver remains a crossroads. Interstates 70 and 25 cross in Denver, and the 1995 opening of Denver International Airport, a key air hub, assured the city's importance.

Downtown Denver★

LoDo★★

Between Larimer & Wynkoop Sts., 20th St. & Speer Blvd. ☎303-628-5428. *www.lodo.org.*

Ardent preservationists fought for the renovation of 17 neglected c.1870-90 buildings. Their efforts culminated in 1973 in **Larimer Square**★★ *(1400 block of Larimer St.; ☎303-534-2367, www.larimersquare.com)*, a pedestrian-friendly block. The restoration movement boomed in the 1990s as 19C buildings and warehouses were revitalized into restaurants, clubs, galleries, shops, and upper-story apartments. The 1995 opening of **Coors Field** *(2001 Blake St.; ☎303-292-0200, www.coloradorockies.com)*, a major-league baseball stadium, climaxed the transformation.

Larimer Square anchors the southern end of the 26-block historic district. The 1895 **Union Station** *(1701 Wynkoop St.)*

Address Book Denver Area

🕭 *For price ranges, see the Legend on the cover flap.*

WHERE TO STAY

$$$$$ The Broadmoor – *1 Lake Ave., Colorado Springs, CO.* ✕ ♿ 🅿 🛌 Spa ☎719-577-5775 *or* 800-634-7711. *www. broadmoor.com. 700 rooms.* At first a casino, by 1918 it was a grand resort nestled against the Rocky Mountain foothills. Today it displays the same pink-stucco facade and curved marble staircase. Nine restaurants, a world-class spa, three golf courses and four swimming pools add to its charms.

$$$$ The Brown Palace Hotel – *321 17th St., Denver, CO.* ✕ ♿ 🅿 ☎303-297-3111 *or* 800-321-2599. *www.brownpalace.com. 230 rooms.* When entrepreneurs seeking silver and gold flocked west in 1892, they stayed at this distinguished inn. Presidents still shake hands in the grand atrium, its seven tiers of balconies lined in Mexican onyx and crowned by a stained-glass dome. Celebrities dine at the formal **Palace Arms ($$$)** among European battle flags.

$$$ Cheyenne Mountain Resort – *3225 Broadmoor Valley Rd.. Colorado Springs, CO.* ✕ ♿ 🅿 🛌 ☎719-538-4000 *or* 800-428-8886. *www.cheyennemountain.com. 316 rooms.* Denver families often escape for the weekend to this nouveau-rustic resort, on 217 acres at the foot of Cheyenne Mountain. There's golf, tennis, mountain biking, five swimming pools, a 35-acre lake for canoeing and fly fishing, and four restaurants and lounges.

$$$ The Cliff House @ Pikes Peak – *306 Cañon Ave. Manitou Springs, CO.* ✕ ♿ 🅿 ☎719-685-3000 *or* 888-212-7000. *www.thecliffhouse.com. 55 rooms.* Built in 1873 as a hot-springs resort, The Cliff House was abandoned for years until it reopened in 1999 after a $10 million renovation. The redesign retained the manse's Victorian ambience, from guest rooms to wide veranda and open gardens, but added 21C frills and a fine restaurant.

$$$ Hotel Boulderado – *2115 13th St., Boulder, CO.* ✕ ♿ 🅿 ☎303-442-4344 *or* 800-433-4344. *www.boulderado.com. 160 rooms.* A bright lobby, with a canopied ceiling of stained glass and mosaic tile, recalls an era of Victorian elegance intertwined with Boulder history for nearly a century. But **Q's Restaurant ($$$)** serves the most contemporary of award-winning cuisine.

$$$ Hotel Monaco – *1717 Champa St., Denver, CO.* ✕ ♿ 🅿 ☎303-296-1717 *or* 800-397-5380. *www.monaco-denver.com. 189 rooms.* In the heart of Denver, the Kimpton Group renovated two historic buildings, one of them a 1937 Art Moderne edifice, to create this boutique property. A 23ft hand-painted ceiling highlights the main lobby; guest rooms are furnished in whimsical luxury. The excellent **Panzano ($$$)** restaurant offers Italian cuisine.

$$$ The Oxford Hotel – *1600 17th St., Denver, CO.* ✕ ♿ 🅿 Spa ☎303-628-5400 *or* 800-228-5838. *www.theoxfordhotel.com. 80 rooms.* French and English antiques adorn rooms at Denver's oldest grand hotel. The red-brick exterior is classic; careful restorations have revealed false ceilings and silver chandeliers previously coated in paint. Built in 1891, it is on the National Register of Historic Places.

$$$ The Warwick – *1776 Grant St., Denver, CO.* ✕ ♿ 🅿 🛌 ☎303-861-2000 *or* 800-525-2888. *www.warwickdenver.com. 215 rooms.* This elegant midsize hotel has undergone extensive renovation, with data-ports and tasteful new furnishings. An atrium, fitness center, rooftop pool and restaurant add to the first-class image.

WHERE TO EAT

$$$ The Fort – *19192 Highway 8, Morrison, CO* ☎303-697-4771. *www.thefort.com. Dinner only.* **Regional.** Housed in an adobe replica of Southeast Colorado's Bent's Fort, this Denver institution is famed for its traditional High Plains repasts--elk, quail, the inimitable Rocky Mountain oysters, and a dozen dishes featuring buffalo. The outdoor patio has a smashing view of the Front Range.

$$$ Buckhorn Exchange – *1000 Osage St., Denver, CO ☎303-534-9505. www. buckhorn.com.* **Regional**. Like Theodore Roosevelt and his contemporaries, diners at Denver's oldest restaurant can try elk, pheasant and rattlesnake in the company of more than 500 animal trophies and 125 guns.

$$$ Craftwood Inn – *404 El Paso Blvd., Manitou Springs, CO. ☎719-685-9000. www.craftwood.com. Dinner only.* **Regional**. This Tudor-style restaurant of beamed ceilings and stained-glass windows, once a coppersmith shop, began serving food in 1940. Views of Pikes Peak are spectacular. The cuisine is robust Colorado: noisettes of caribou, loin of wild boar, grilled pheasant sausage and piñon trout.

$$$ John's Restaurant – *2328 Pearl St., Boulder, CO. ☎303-444-5232. www. johnsrestaurantboulder.com. Dinner only; ◷closed Sun–Mon.* **Continental**. Only 30 to 40 people a night are served in this quaint home, but they are rewar-

ded with chef-owner John Bizzarro's weekly choices, from Basque seafood stew to turkey breast with mole sauce. His caramel cheesecake has been a house favorite for 22 years.

$$$ Restaurant Kevin Taylor – *1106 14th St., Denver, CO. ☎303-820-2600. www.ktrg.net. Dinner only; ◷ closed Sun.* **American**. Showcase for the culinary talents of Denver's most acclaimed chef, this Hotel Teatro eatery offers fine dining amid contemporary decor. Chilled terrine of duck foie gras, venison loin over roasted pears, and warm banana parfait make a marvelous meal.

$$ Wynkoop Brewing Company – *1634 18th St., Denver, CO. ☎303-297-2700. www.wynkoop.com.* **American**. As the biggest brewpub in the US, the Wynkoop sells over 5,000 barrels a year. The LoDo warehouse has many whimsical annual "competitions," but normal days see the consumption of pub fare: hot artichoke dip, beer-braised pot roast and signature RailYard Ale.

remains a Beaux-Arts landmark on its northern fringe. Across the street from the depot is the **Wynkoop Brewing Company** *(1634 18th St.; ☎303-297-2700, www.wynkoop.com)*, Denver's original microbrewery and one of America's first in 1988; there now are a half-dozen small brewing companies in the area.

16th Street Mall★
16th St. between Market St. & Broadway. ✕&🅿

Extending southeast from the bus terminal to Civic Center Plaza, the tree-lined Mall is flanked by office towers, street-level cafes and shops, and 11 fountains. Horse-drawn carriages and free shuttle buses are the only vehicles. Highlights include the 1910 **D & F Tower**★ *(at Arapahoe St.)*, a 325ft replica of the campanile of St. Mark's Basilica in Venice; and the 1891 **Kittredge Building** *(at Glenarm Pl.)*, a Romanesque Revival structure. The **Historic Paramount Theatre** *(1631 Glenarm Pl.; ☎303-623-0106, www.paramountdenver.com)*, built in 1929, has one of two operating dual-console pipe organs in the US. The $100 million **Denver Pavilions** *(between*

Welton St. & Glenarm Pl.; ✕&🅿 *☎303-260-6000, www.denverpavilions.com)* is Denver's newest shopping-dining-entertainment complex.

Brown Palace Hotel★
321 17th St. at Tremont Pl. & Broadway. ✕&🅿 *☎303-297-3111. www.brown palace.com.*

Five US presidents and the Beatles have stayed at "The Brown," Denver's nine-story Italian Renaissance landmark (1892, Frank Edbrooke) made of red granite and sandstone. Stone medallions depicting Rocky Mountain animals are set between the seventh-story windows. Afternoon tea is served in the lobby.

Civic Center★★

Some of Denver's most important public buildings surround **Civic Center Plaza**★ *(between Broadway & Bannock St., W. Colfax & 14th Aves.)*, at the southeast edge of downtown. The grand space, sweeping westward from the capitol steps, was designed in 1904 by landscape architect

Frederick Law Olmsted Jr. and Chicago city planner E.H. Bennett. Dominating the west side is the neo-classical **City & County Building** (1932), Denver's city hall. The slim central tower houses the **Speer Memorial Chimes.**

Colorado State Capitol★★

200 E. Colfax Ave. (east side of Civic Center Plaza facing Lincoln St.) 🚹 ☎*303-866-2604. www.colorado.gov.*
The hilltop capitol (1886, Elijah Myers) is home to the General Assembly and offices of the governor. Constructed over 22 years in the shape of a Greek cross, the granite capitol is a smaller version of the US Capitol. Its gold-leaf dome is a gleaming 272ft-high landmark. From the third-floor rotunda, 93 steps climb into the dome for a commanding **view**★★ of the surrounding city. Two different steps leading to the building are marked as exactly a mile high.

Molly Brown House★

1340 Pennsylvania St., 3 blocks east of the capitol. ☎*303-832-4092. www.molly brown.org.*
Made famous by a Broadway musical and a 1964 movie, the "unsinkable" Molly Brown experienced new fame after the 1998 movie *Titanic*. Guided tours *(60min)* of the 7,700sq ft sandstone house (1889, William Lang) offer a glimpse into Denver's Gilded Age through the prism of this remarkable woman. In 1912, having raised two children and separated from her wealthy miner husband, Brown boarded the ill-fated Titanic. As the liner was sinking and later aboard the rescue ship, she tried to bring order to chaos. She subsequently ran for US Congress three times—twice before women gained the right to vote.

Colorado History Museum★

Kids *1300 Broadway.* 🚹 ☎*303-866-3682. www.coloradohistory.org.*
Galleries include exhibits on cowboys, pioneer lifestyle, and black and Hispanic cultures. Of note are artifacts from Mesa Verde, removed in the late 19C before the establishment of the national park; and a display of heavy mining machinery.

Denver Art Museum★★★

100 W. 14th Ave. Pkwy. ✕🚹🅿 ☎*303-640-4433. www.denverartmuseum.org.*
This exceptional museum spans two buildings. The twin-towered modern fortress looming over Civic Center Plaza (North Building, Gio Ponti, 1971), holds exhibits on seven vertically stacked, 10,000sq-ft gallery floors. The newer **Hamilton Building**★★ (Daniel Libeskind, 2006), designed to resemble a blossoming flower of titanium, granite and glass, reflects the architect's impression of lansdcape as he flew over Denver.
The museum's centerpiece is a superb 17,000-item **Native American Collection**★★★ *(2nd & 3rd floors)* that includes four house posts by famed carver Doung Cranmer; a Salish spirit figure and an Iroquois war club, both from the mid-1850s; Plains Indian horse trappings from the 19C; and a priceless California tribal feather blanket.
Maya, Aztec and Inca pieces contrast dramatically with European aesthetic in the **Pre-Columbian and Spanish Colonial**★★ collections *(4th floor)*, which culminate in a roomful of more modern Southwestern **santosa**. **European and American Art**a is organized thematically—landscapes in one area, portraits in another. **Western Art**★★ (Hamilton Building) includes a casting of *The Cheyenne* (1901) by Frederic Remington.

The Denver Public Library★★

10 W. 14th Ave. Pkwy. 🚹 ☎*303-640-6200. www.denver.lib.co.us.*
A striking Postmodern structure (1995, Michael Graves & Brian Klipp), this $64 million library boasts six public floors and 47 miles of shelves. Seventy panels by artist Edward Ruscha adorn its main hall and atriums. The acclaimed **Western History Collection** includes important early maps, documents and photographs; a $20 million art collection features work by Bierstadt and Moran.

US Mint★

Kids ⅠⅢⅠⅠ *W. Colfax Ave. & Cherokee St. (east of Civic Center Park).* ↖▪*Visit by guided tour only.* 🚹 ☎ *303-405-4761. www. usmint.gov.*

Practical Information

GETTING THERE

Denver International Airport (DEN) (☎303-342-2000; www.flydenver.com) is 23mi northeast of downtown. Rental car and shuttle service counters are in the main terminal. Ground transportation is on baggage-claim level. **RTD SkyRide and SuperShuttle** (☎303-370-1300; www.supershuttle.com) run buses and vans to downtown and surrounding areas. **Amtrak train:** Union Station (1701 Wynkoop St.; ☎800-872-7245; www.amtrak.com). **Greyhound and regional buses:** Main terminal (20th & Curtis Sts.; ☎303-293-6555 or 800-231-2222; www.greyhound.com).

GETTING AROUND

The Regional Transportation District (RTD) operates local and regional buses and a light rail line that runs through downtown (☎303-299-6000; www.rtd-denver.com). Coupons and tokens at Market Street and Civic Center stations and some grocery stores. The Free Zip Shuttle (free) runs around the Flatlron Shopping District. Taxi: American Cab(☎303-321-5555), Metro Taxi (☎303-333-3333), Yellow Cab(☎303-777-7777).

ACCOMMODATIONS

Contact the Denver Metro Convention & Visitors Bureau (below) for area lodging and reservations. Denver West Hotels (☎1-800-728-1492; www.denverwesthotels.com) represents lodgings on the west side of the metro area.

ENTERTAINMENT

Consult the Friday and Sunday editions or the online versions of the *Denver Post* (www.denverpost.com) and *Rocky Mountain News* (www.rockymountainnews.com), or the weekly *Westword* (www.westword.com), published Thursdays, for listings of current events, theaters and concert halls. Favorite **venues**: Denver Center for the Performing Arts (☎303-893-4100; www.denver-center.org), Historic Paramount Theatre (☎303-830-8497, www.paramountdenver.com), Coors Amphitheatre (☎303-220-7000; www.hob.com), Red Rocks Amphitheater (☎303-830-8497; www.redrocksonline.com).

VISITOR INFORMATION

The **Denver Metro Convention & Visitors Bureau (DMCVB)** (1555 California St., Suite 300, Denver CO 80202; ☎303-392-1112, www.denver.org) operates three visitor information centers: Denver International Airport main terminal, Tabor Center (entrance facing Larimer St.) and Cherry Creek Shopping Center. The free Official Visitors Guide contains detailed information on accommodations, area events and attractions, and dining (available online from the Denver CVB or in visitor centers and hotels).

One of four in the country, this mint strikes 10 billion coins a year and tends one-fourth of America's gold reserves—shipped from San Francisco in 1934 because Denver is not as vulnerable to earthquakes.

The five-story, granite-and-marble building (1906, James Knox Taylor) was modeled after the Medici Riccardi Palace in Florence, Italy. Displays of coins and currency, mint equipment and historic photos line visitors' galleries. Free weekday tours (20min, online reservations strongly suggested) offer views of the stamping and counting rooms.

West of Downtown

Neglected for decades, the area along the South Platte River, west of downtown, today shows off new attractions such as **The Pepsi Center** (www.pepsicenter.com) basketball and ice-hockey arena, built in 1999. Football stadium Invesco Field at Mile High (2001) (www.denverbroncos.com) incorporates the Colorado Sports Hall of Fame, which exalts such stars quarterback John Elway. **Confluence Park**★ (www.denvergov.org), where Cherry Creek and the South Platte River meet, is a place to cool off on hot days.

© Photo by Brian Gadbery/CTO

Examining one of the many works of art at the Denver Art Museum

Elitch Gardens★
Kids *2000 Elitch Cir. off Speer Blvd. (I-25 Exit 212A).* ✗ ♿ 🅿 ☎303-595-4386. www.elitchgardens.com. ◑Open May–Sept.
Established in 1890 in northwest Denver, Elitch Gardens moved to this riverside site in 1995. Thrill rides and a cartoon town are among its draws.

Downtown Aquarium★★
Kids ▥▥▥ *700 Water St. at 23rd Ave. (I-25 Exit 211).* ✗ ♿ 🅿 ☎303-561-4450. www.aquariumrestaurants.com.
This 1999 aquarium is distinguished by its focus on American river habitats. **Colorado River Journey** begins in the trout-rich streams of the Rockies and depicts a 1,500mi course through the arid Grand Canyon to the subtropical Sea of Cortez. Tropical seas and rainforest waters are also featured.

City Park★★

This grand space (1881) was modeled after the urban parks of Boston, New York, London and Paris. From the east end—which occupies 314 acres *(between Colorado Blvd and York St., 17th & 26th Aves.)*—visitors get a **view**★★ of the Denver skyline and the mountains.

Denver Museum of Nature and Science★★
Kids *2001 Colorado Blvd., City Park.* ✗ ♿ 🅿 ☎303-370-6357. www.dmns.org.

This three-story museum has grown to become one of the largest in the US, with more than 500,000 exhibits.
A section of the alpine Sweet Home Mine is re-created in the heralded gem display of **Coors Mineral Hall**★★★. A central room showcases the largest gold nugget (135oz) ever found in Colorado. **Prehistoric Journey**★★ is a 3.5-billion-year timeline that depicts the history of life on earth. **Dioramas**★ present flora and fauna of the Rocky Mountains, South America, Africa and the world. Other exhibits examine Native American and ancient Egyptian cultures.

Denver Zoo★
Kids *2300 Steele St., City Park.* ✗ ♿ 🅿 ☎303-376-4800. www.denverzoo.org.
Nearly 4,000 animals are at home in this 80-acre zoo, laid out around a 1.5mi loop. Summer visitors may tour the grounds aboard the Safari Shuttle, or the Pioneer Train, a scale model of an 1878 train. **Tropical Discovery**★★ is a rain-forest habitat under a glass pyramid. **Primate Panorama**★ features nocturnal lemurs, Asian orangutans and endangered African lowland gorillas.

Additional Sights

Denver Botanic Gardens★
909 York St. (4 blocks south of E. Colfax Ave.). ✗ ♿ 🅿 ☎303-865-3500. www.botanicgardens.org.
With 30 themed areas, these gardens are a tranquil oasis. **Boettcher Memorial Conservatory**★★ shelters tropical plants in a humid environment.

Cherry Creek Shopping District
1st Ave. between Steele St. & University Blvd. ✗ ♿ 🅿
This indoor mall *(3000 E. 1st Ave.;* ☎303-388-3900, www.shopcherrycreek.com) sits north of Cherry Creek Park. The adjacent streets of **Cherry Creek North** *(1st to 3rd Aves.;* ☎303-394-2903, www.cherrycreeknorth.com) are lined with boutiques, restaurants, galleries, salons and day spas. The **Tattered Cover**★ *(2955 E. Milwaukee St.;* ☎303-322-7727, www.tatteredcover.com) is one of the country's best bookstores.

Excursions

Golden★

15mi west of downtown Denver via I-70 (to Rte. 58) or US-6 (to 19th St.). ✕ & 🅿 ☎*303-279-3113. www.goldencochamber.org.*
Golden lost the state capital to Denver by one vote; population is near 20,000. Walking tours take in the **Astor House Museum** *(822 12th St.; ☎303-278-3557, www.astorhousemuseum.org),* built in 1867; the **Golden Pioneer Museum** *(923 10th St.; ☎ 303-278-7151, www.goldenpioneermuseum.com),* and the **Rocky Mountain Quilt Museum**★ *(1111 Washington Ave.; ☎303-277-0377, www.rmqm.org).*

Coors Brewing Company★

13th & Ford Sts. 🔎*Visit by guided tour only.* & 🅿 ☎*303-277-2337 or 303-277-2552 (foreign-language tours). www.coors.com.*

The world's largest brewing complex was founded in 1873 by immigrant brewer Adolph Coors. Tours follow the 16-week beer-making process through malting, brewing and packaging.

Colorado Railroad Museum★

🄺🄸🄳 *17155 W. 44th Ave.* 🅿 ☎*303-279-4591. www.crrm.org.*
The largest rail museum in the Rocky Mountains displays more than 70 examples of trains that brought development and settlement to the frontier West.

Buffalo Bill Grave & Museum

987-1/2 Lookout Mountain Rd. (I-70 Exit 256, 5mi west of Golden). ✕ & 🅿 ☎*303-526-0744. www.buffalobill.org.*
The inimitable "Buffalo Bill" Cody died while visiting his sister in Denver in 1917 and was buried atop Lookout Mountain. The gravesite, a simple stone plot near the museum, affords a **view**★ of the Front Range.

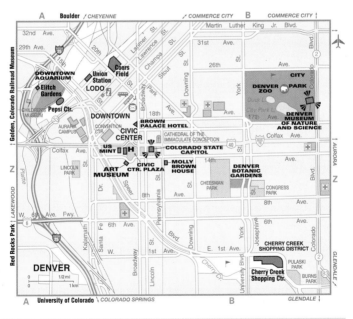

Lions at the Denver Zoo

Red Rocks Park and Amphitheater★

Hogback Rd., Morrison (via Rte. 26 off I-70 or Morrison Rd. off Rte. 470). ✕♿🅿 ☎720-865-2494. www.redrocksonline.com.
The 9,450-seat outdoor amphitheater is a natural bowl sculpted between two 300ft sandstone outcroppings. Major concert events are staged here. The 630-acre park has hiking and biking trails.

Mount Evans★

Highway 103 from Idaho Springs to Echo Lake; then Highway 5, 14 miles to summit. ☎303-567-3000. www.fs.fed.us/r2/arnf.
This scenic highway, managed by the Forest Service, tops out at 14,230 feet. On the way in, the **Dos Chappell Nature Center** focuses on the bristlecone pine forest outside. It's a short walk to the 14,264-foot summit, home to mountain goats and bighorn sheep—and 360-degree **views**★★ of the Front Range and Continental Divide.

Boulder★★

🧒 *29mi northwest of Denver via US-36.* △✕♿🅿 ☎303-442-2911. www.boulder coloradousa.com.
This city of 91,500 nestles against uplifted red-rock ridges called The Flatirons. Founded in 1859, Boulder boomed after Colorado founded its state university here in 1876. Modern Boulder is largely defined by limits on residential construction it adopted in 1977, and by the 84sq mi greenbelt that surrounds it.

University of Colorado's 25,000 students lend a youthful flavor.

Pearl Street Mall★ *(11th to 15th Sts.)* is a pedestrian zone of shops, galleries and sidewalk cafes; landmark buildings are the 1933 Art Deco **Boulder County Courthouse** *(13th & Pearl Sts.)* and the 1909 Italianate **Hotel Boulderado**★ *(2115 13th St. at Spruce St.; ☎303-442-4344, www.boulderado.com).* **Boulder Creek Path**★ 🧒 *(☎303-442-2911)* runs creekside for 16mi through the heart of the city. The glass architecture of the **Boulder Public Library**★ *(1000 Canyon Blvd.; ☎303-441-3100, www.boulder.lib. co.us)* straddles the creek near downtown. Facing a block of farmers' markets, the **Boulder Dushanbe Teahouse**★★ *(1770 13th St.; ☎303-442-4993, www. boulderteahouse.com),* is made of polychrome tiles, handcrafted by Tajikistani artisans in 1998 as a gift from Boulder's sister city of Dushanbe.

University of Colorado★

Broadway to 28th St. & University Ave. to Baseline Rd. ✕♿🅿 ☎303-492-1411. www.colorado.edu.
Two hundred buildings spread over this 786-acre campus. **Old Main** (1877), the university's first structure, is a turreted brick Victorian, but most buildings are pink sandstone with red-tile roofs—the legacy of Charles Klauder's 1917 plan inspired by the hill towns of Tuscany. Visitors are welcome at the **University of Colorado Museum of Natural History** *(Henderson Bldg., 15th St. & Broadway; ☎303-492-6892)* and **Fiske Planetarium & Observatory** *(Regent Dr. at Kittredge Loop Dr.; ☎303-492-5001).*

Chautauqua Park

Baseline Rd. & 9th St. Vehicle entrance at 6th St. ✕♿🅿 ☎303-442-3282. www. chatauqua.com.
In the late 19C, the nationwide Chautauqua movement encouraged retreats to nurture body, mind and spirit. This park opened in 1898 with tent lodgings and two buildings that still stand—the **Auditorium** (site of the Colorado Music Festival) and **Dining Room** (now a restaurant). Trails ascend from broad lawns into meadows beneath The Flatirons and the 33,000-acre **Boulder Moun-**

© Photo by Brian Gadbery/CTO

tain Parks★ (☎303-441-3440, www.bouldercolorado.gov). Those who don't hike **Flagstaff Mountain**★ can drive a twisting byway from Baseline Road to numerous scenic overlooks.

National Center for Atmospheric Research★

1850 Table Mesa Dr. ✕♿🅿 ☎303-497-1000. www.ncar.ucar.edu.

The stunning Mesa Laboratory (1966, I.M. Pei) is set against the Flatirons and inspired by ancient Southwest cliff dwellings. Guided 1hr tours include hands-on displays illustrating such topics as atmospheric phenomen, robotic meteorological instruments and aviation hazards.

COLORADO SPRINGS★★

MAP P 144
MOUNTAIN STANDARD TIME
POPULATION 360,890

Nestled at 6,035ft at the foot of soaring Pikes Peak, Colorado Springs enjoys one of the most beautiful settings of any North American city.

🛈 **Information:** ☎719-635-7506 www.experiencecoloradosprings.com
👁 **Don't Miss:** Pikes Peak; Garden of the Gods
Kids **Especially for Kids:** US Olympic Complex.

A Bit of History

Civil War Gen. William Jackson Palmer, builder of the Denver & Rio Grande Railroad, founded the city in 1871 on a rail link to the mining towns of Cripple Creek and Victor. He called it "Springs" to attract Easterners accustomed to fashionable health resorts. Spencer Penrose, who made a fortune in gold and copper, built the Pikes Peak Auto Highway and developed The Broadmoor as a world-class resort. During the Cold War, "The Springs" established itself as the hub of US military air defense. Many defense contractors are based in the city, which is also a home for numerous fundamentalist Christian organizations.

Downtown reflects the vision of its founders in broad avenues and fine old buildings. Early years are documented at the **Colorado Springs Pioneers Museum** (215 S. Tejon St.; ☎719-385-5990) in the 1903 courthouse. The **Colorado Springs Fine Arts Center**★ (30 W. Dale St.; ☎719-634-5581, www.csfineartscenter.org) features paintings by O'Keeffe, Russell and Audubon in an Art-Deco landmark (1936, John Gaw Meem).

Sights

Old Colorado City★

W. Colorado Ave. & cross streets from S. 24th to S. 27th Sts. ✕♿🅿 ☎719-577-4112. www.shopoldcoloradocity.com.
Before Colorado Springs there was El Dorado, settled in 1859 and soon renamed Colorado City. It became part of Colorado Springs in 1917. Housed in an 1890 church, the **Old Colorado City History Center** (1 S. 24th St.; ☎719-636-1225) exhibits historic photographs, documents and memorabilia. Colorado Avenue is lined with restaurants, artists' studios and Western collectibles galleries in restored buildings. **Van Briggle Art Pottery** (600 S. 21st St.; ☎719-633-7729) is a century-old facility whose works have been displayed at the Louvre and Metropolitan Museum of Art.

The Broadmoor★

1 Lake Circle; west end of Lake Ave. via I-25 Exit 138. ✕♿🅿 ☎719-577-5775. www.broadmoor.com.
Born in 1891 as a small casino at the foot of Cheyenne Mountain, The Broadmoor was reincarnated when Spencer Penrose bought the 40-acre site (and 400

adjoining acres) in 1916 and turned it into a world-class resort. European artisans created ornate frescoes and tile work, marble fixtures and other design elements in the pink-stucco, Italianate hotel. Today three golf courses, tennis courts, swimming pools, riding stables, nine restaurants and lounges, a conference center and spa make up the 700-room complex. Penrose's widow built the **Carriage House Museum** in 1947 for antique vehicles.

World Figure Skating Museum and Hall of Fame

Kids *20 1st St.;* ☎*719-635-5200, www. worldskatingmuseum.org.*
Situated one block north of The Broadmoor, this museum offers ice-skating memories from the 17C to the present.

Cheyenne Mountain Zoo★

Kids *4250 Cheyenne Mountain Zoo Rd. From The Broadmoor, take Lake Circle south to Mirada Rd. & west to Cheyenne Rd.* ✕&🅿 ☎*719-633-9925. www.cmzoo. org.*
Built in 1926 by Penrose on a forested hillside to house exotic animals he had received as gifts from around the world, the zoo was deeded to Colorado Springs in 1938. It is home to some 500 animals of 146 species. Many of its animal births have been endangered species, including a spectacled bear and a Sichuan takin. Other rare species include the snow leopard and black rhinoceros.

Will Rogers Shrine of the Sun★

☎*719-578-5367, www.cmzoo.org.*
To reach the shrine, motorists drive up a 1.5mi winding road to a plateau 2,000ft above Colorado Springs. The 100ft granite tower was built as a Penrose family tomb, but was rededicated to philosopher-humorist Rogers when he died in a 1935 plane crash. Tower landings are photo galleries of Rogers' life: a 94-step climb reveals a **view**★★ east.

Seven Falls★★

West end of Cheyenne Blvd.; off Mesa Dr. via Lake Ave. from The Broadmoor. ✕&🅿 ☎*719-632-0765. www.sevenfalls.com.*
A road threads through the Pillars of Hercules, a slot in South Cheyenne Can-

yon, and terminates at this 181ft series of waterfalls. Eagle's Nest, accessed by elevator or 185 steep steps, overlooks the falls. Another staircase (224 steps) ascends beside the falls to the start of the **Inspiration Point Trail** *(0.5mi).*

US Olympic Complex★★

Kids *1750 Boulder St. at Union Blvd.* &🅿 ☎*719-632-5551. www.usoc.org.*
One of three national training centers for amateur athletes, this complex was built in 1978 on the grounds of a former Air Force base. The visitor center *(1 Olympic Plaza)* houses the US Olympic Hall of Fame. Free tours *(60min)* take visitors down the Olympic Path to watch gymnasts and swimmers hone their skills; the International Center for Aquatic Research and a state-of-the-art sports-medicine clinic are of particular interest. More than 550 coaches and athletes, in two dozen sports, live here.

ProRodeo Hall of Fame and Museum of the American Cowboy★

Kids *101 ProRodeo Dr.; at Rockrimmon Blvd. off I-25 Exit 147.* &🅿 ☎*719-593-8840. www.prorodeohalloffame.com.*
Multimedia presentations trace the lifestyle of rodeo, from its 19C origins to the present. The hall of fame honors the most skilled cowboys, clowns, showmen and behind-the-scenes personnel with plaques or bronze statues. Other displays highlight cowboy gear and garb, saddles, ropes and personal souvenirs.

US Air Force Academy★★

Academy Dr. West off I-25 at Exit 156-B (North Gate Blvd.); 12mi north of downtown. △✕&🅿 ☎*719-333-1110. www. usafa.af.mil.*
This is the only US service academy in the West. A self-guided auto tour includes a B-52 display and scenic overlooks. The highlight is the **Cadet Chapel**★★★ (1963, Skidmore, Owings & Merrill), designed by Walter Netsch. Topped by 17 aluminum spires, each 150ft high, this soaring cathedral comprises individual Protestant, Catholic, Jewish and interfaith chapels. At 11:35am each weekday, the academy's 4,000 cadets march smartly to lunch across the square beside

the chapel. The nearby **Barry Goldwater Visitor Center**★ *(2346 Academy Dr.; ☎719-333-2025)* explains cadet life in interactive displays.

Garden of the Gods★★

Garden Dr. (north of US-24) or Gateway Rd. (west of 30th St.). ✖♿🅿 *☎719-634-6666. www.gardenofgods.com.*
Red-rock formations within this 1,400-acre geological wonder soar up to 300ft. Paved roads offer easy access to the best-known formations: Balanced Rock, Cathedral Spires, Kissing Camels, Three Graces and Tower of Babel. Most are better seen via foot, bicycle or horseback on trails of .5mi to 3mi in length. Guided walks on the east side of the park at a new **visitor center** *(1805 N. 30th St.)*, which offers a natural-history display and brief multimedia show. Just south at the **Rock Ledge Ranch Historic Site** *(Gateway Rd. & 30th St.; ☎719-578-6777)*, costumed docents portray life on an 1860s homestead, an 1880s ranch and an early-20C estate. The 1901 **Garden of the Gods Trading Post** *(324 Beckers Ln.; ☎719-685-9045)*, a Pueblo-style structure, is on the park's south side.

Pikes Peak★★★

✖♿🅿 *☎719-385-7325. www.pikespeak-colorado.com.*
At 14,110ft, Pikes Peak is not the highest mountain in the US, nor even Colorado. But it is arguably the most imposing high peak, probably the most famous, definitely the most accessible. Named in 1806 by Army Lieutenant Zebulon Pike, who declared the mountain "unconquerable," it has proven anything but. A railway mounted its flank in 1891. Spencer Penrose built a motor road in 1916 and bought the railway in 1925.
Visitors today ascend to the **Summit House** cafe and gift shop via railway, car or foot. The peak is often cold and windy, and snow may fall at any time. But when skies are clear, unrivaled **views**★★★ extend west into the snow-capped Rockies, east across the plains, north to Denver and south to the Sangre de Cristo range.
The **Pikes Peak Cog Railway**★★★ 🄺🄸🄳🄼 ⅢⅢ *(515 Ruxton Ave., Manitou Springs; ☎719-685-5401, www.cograilway.com)*

remains a great excursion. Small black coal-fired steam locomotives, tilted to keep the boilers level, originally pushed trains up the mountain's eastern side. Now diesel-electric models do so (🕑*late Apr–early Nov; 3hr round-trip includes 30min at summit)*. From its depot, the train climbs more than 6,500ft in a series of steep grades with constantly changing views. Marmots and bighorn sheep cavort among the rocks.
At the peak's broad summit, the cog railway meets the **Pikes Peak Highway**★★ *(☎719-385-7325)*, a meandering 19mi toll road. It begins at Cascade *(15mi west of Colorado Springs on US-24)*; after 7mi, at the **Crystal Reservoir and Visitor Center,** pavement is replaced by gravel. **Challenge Unlimited** *(☎719-633-6399)* offers a ride down the Barr Trail in a guided convoy of mountain bikes with good brakes.

Manitou Springs★

4mi west of Colorado Springs on US-24 bypass. △✖♿🅿 *☎719-685-5089. www.manitousprings.org.*
Indians and mountain men long knew of the restorative waters that bubbled from the ground northeast of Pikes Peak. A spa and hotels were established in the 1890s. Today galleries and inns occupy charming, if aging, structures, and open-air street trolleys make 1hr summer circuits of the downtown. **Miramont Castle**★ *(9 Capitol Hill Ave.; ☎719-685-1011)*, the 1895 sandstone mansion of a wealthy French priest, combines nine design styles in its 28 rooms.

Cave of the Winds★

🄺🄸🄳🄼 ⅢⅢ *US-24 Bypass, 2mi west of Manitou Springs.* ✖🅿 *☎719-685-5444. www.caveofthewinds.com.*
After two boys discovered a cavern entrance in 1880, Manitou resident George Snider broke through to a chamber—200ft long and 50ft high—that now is the centerpiece of a commercial cave still owned by the Snider family. Guides on the **Discovery Tour** *(45min)* explain limestone cave formation to visitors walking a well-lit concrete path. Participants in the **Lantern Tour** *(75min)* follow a guide in 1880s garb.

Storefronts in Manitou Springs

Manitou Cliff Dwellings Museum

[Kids] *US-24 Bypass, just above Manitou Springs.* ✕ 🅿 ☎*719-685-5242. www. cliffdwellingsmuseum.com.*

The 40 rooms and towers in Phantom Cliff Canyon were dismantled by archaeologists in the Four Corners area at the end of the 19C and reconstructed here as a re-creation of 12-13C Ancient Pueblo culture.

Excursions

Cripple Creek★★

45mi west of Colorado Springs via US-24 to Divide, then Rte. 67 south. △✕&🅿 ☎*719-689-3315. www.visitcripplecreek. com.*

When gold was discovered on the east flank of Pikes Peak in 1890, this town at 9,396ft elevation became the world's greatest gold camp. Within 10 years its population reached 25,000. Neighboring **Victor**, 6mi south, had 18,000 residents. Mining continued until 1961, by which time more than $800 million worth of ore had been taken.

Today a different kind of gold flows: limited-stakes gambling was legalized in 1991 and Cripple Creek (albeit with only 1,115 citizens today) has been revitalized. The **Cripple Creek & Victor Narrow Gauge Railroad**★ *(east end of Bennett Ave.;* ☎*719-689-2640, www. cripplecreekrailroad.com),* a 15-ton steam locomotive, pulls the train on a 4mi journey past abandoned mines to the ghost town of Anaconda (🕐*late May–early Oct).* The depot houses the **Cripple Creek District Museum** (☎*719-689-2634).* At the **Mollie Kathleen Gold Mine**★★ *(1mi north on Rte. 67;* ☎*719-689-2466, www.goldminetours.com),* visitors descend 1,000ft into a hard-rock mine, where veteran miners demonstrate the mining process.

Florissant Fossil Beds National Monument

35mi west of Colorado Springs via US-24. &🅿 ☎*719-748-3253. www.nps. gov/flfo.*

More than 50,000 fossils—one of the most extensive records of the Oligocene epoch, 35 million years ago—have been removed from the shale bed of ancient Lake Florissant. Among them are an 14,000 species of insects. Nature trails pass petrified sequoia stumps.

Royal Gorge Bridge and Park★★

[Kids] *Off US-50, 8mi west of Cañon City & 43mi southwest of Colorado Springs.* ✕&🅿 ☎*719-275-7507. www.royalgorgebridge.com.*

A suspension bridge claimed as the world's highest, 1,053ft above the Arkansas River and more than a quarter-mile long, opened in 1929. A funicular railway (1931) plunges from the rim; an aerial tramway (1969) spans the gorge. Rafting companies have run its whitewater for decades. In 1999, the **Royal Gorge Route**★★ began operating passenger trains on a 19C route through the river's gorge. Trains depart from **Cañon City's Santa Fe Depot** *(401 Water St.;* ☎*303-569-1041, www.royal gorgeroute.com).*

Great Sand Dunes National Park★★

ñ *Rte. 150, 164mi southwest of Colorado Springs via I-25 & US-160.* △&🅿 ☎*719-378-2312. www.nps.gov/grsa.*

North America's tallest sand dunes, nearly 750ft high, spread across 39sq mi beneath the Sangre de Cristo Mountains. Formed by winds over thousands of years, the dunes are bordered by a snowmelt mountain stream that creates for visiting families one of the world's biggest sandboxes.

CHEYENNE

MICHELIN MAP 493 H 7, 8
MOUNTAIN STANDARD TIME
POPULATION 56,000

Wyoming's capital and largest city was founded in 1867 as a construction camp for rail workers just 10mi north of the Colorado border. With the train came thousands of immigrants—some real-estate speculators and confidence men, but more honest merchants, tradesmen and cowboys, who worked the surrounding grasslands. Local citizens formed vigilante committees to rid the town of outlaws. Cheyenne then settled into frontier comfort with streets of handsome mansions and a thriving social scene. When Wyoming joined the Union in 1890, Cheyenne was chosen capital.

- **Information:** ☎307-778-3133 www.cheyenne.org
- **Don't Miss:** Cheyenne Frontier Days Old West Museum.
- **Especially for Kids:** Wyoming Territorial Park.

Visit

Cheyenne Frontier Days

☎307-778-7222, www.cfdrodeo.com
The world's largest outdoor rodeo, parade and carnival, this festival first held in 1897 consumes all of southeastern Wyoming in late July. At other times, even in winter when the legislature is in session, Cheyenne remains serene. Walking tours of the historic district begin at the 1886 **Union Pacific Depot** (121 W. 15th St.; ☎307-632-3905, www.cheyennedepotmuseum.org), now a museum devoted to the city's railroad history.

Sights

Wyoming State Capitol★

24th St. & Capitol Ave. ☎307-777-7021. www.wyoming.gov.
As statehouses go, this gray sandstone building (1890) is modest, but with such elegant fittings as a 24-carat gold-leaf dome and interior woodwork of maple and cherry. The stained-glass dome ceiling was imported from England. The third-floor Legislative Conference Room features a half-ton Tiffany chandelier and a 22ft mural by Mike Kopriva that depicts Wyoming history.

Wyoming State Museum

2301 Central Ave. ☎307-777-7022. wyomuseum.state.wy.us. Sharing two floors of the Barrett Building just southeast of the capitol, 10 galleries depict Wyoming's human and natural history. Exhibits focus on dinosaurs; Shoshone and Arapaho culture; gold, uranium and coal mining; jade prospecting; and cowboy traditions.

Warren ICBM & Heritage Museum

7405 Marne Loop, Francis. E. Warren Air Force Base. ☎307-773-2980. www.warrenmuseum.com
Warren was the most powerful US missile base in the Cold War and remains the Intercontinental Ballistic Missile (ICBM) command center. The museum focuses on the history of the ICBMs and the lives of missile crews.

Cheyenne Frontier Days Old West Museum★

4610 N. Carey Ave. Frontier Park. ☎307-778-1424. www.oldwestmuseum.org
Housed in the Cheyenne Frontier Days headquarters is this year-round tribute to the event's history. A 55min audiovisual presentation spotlights this big event on the professional rodeo circuit.

The World of Rodeo.

Throughout much of the rural West, rodeo is as popular as baseball or football. Like their 19C forebears who originated the sport, ranch hands vie to see who is the best rider, roper or wrestler. The best athletes, members of the Professional Rodeo Cowboys Association, can earn jackpots of many thousands of dollars. A typical rodeo has six events: bull riding, saddle- and bareback-bronc riding, steer wrestling, team and individual roping, plus women's barrel racing. Scoring is based on style and difficulty in the first three events; stronger, temperamental animals earn their riders more points. Skill and courage are critical, but the luck of the draw plays a part. In wrestling, roping and racing, speed is paramount.

©iStockphoto.com/Jerry Mayo

Excursions

Laramie

46mi west of Cheyenne via I-80 or Rte. 210. ☎307-745-7339. www.laramie.org.
Established, as Cheyenne was, as a railroad town, Laramie took a different path with the founding in 1886 of the University of Wyoming. Today at least half the town's 25,000 residents are students, faculty or staff.

University of Wyoming

Ivinson Ave. & 9th St. ✕ & ⓟ ☎307-766-1121. www.uwyo.edu.
Most buildings surrounding the campus quadrangle are limestone. A standout is the **Geological Museum** (*S.H. Knight Bldg.; b307-766-2646*), notable for a full-size copper tyrannosaur outside. Exhibits range from uranium to core samples from oil drilling. The **University of Wyoming Art Museum** (*2111 Willett Dr.; ☎307-766-6622*) focuses on Western art, including works by Catlin, Remington and Moran; it shares Antoine Predock's futuristic Centennial Complex with the **American Heritage Center,** an archival research facility.

Wyoming Territorial Park★

Kids *975 Snowy Range Rd. at I-80.* ✕ & ⓟ ☎*307-745-6161. www.wyoprisonpark.org.* ⓢ *Open May-Sept.*
Commemorating Old West heritage, this living-history park includes Wyoming's original Territorial Prison (1872-1901). Tours visit the cell that held Butch Cassidy, who served 18 months for horse-stealing. In Frontier Town, men and women in 19C garb perform crafts and trades in buildings moved from other parts of Wyoming. One structure holds the National US Marshals Museum.

Fort Laramie National Historic Site★★

113mi north of Cheyenne via I-25, US-26 & Rte. 160. & ⓟ ☎*307-837-2221. www. nps.gov/fola.*
Built by fur traders near the North Platte River in 1834, this key Oregon Trail fort was garrisoned by the Army in 1849. Major campaigns against hostile Indian tribes were launched from this bastion until it closed in 1890.
Half of its 22 buildings have been restored and furnished to their 19C appearance. The 1884 commissary holds a visitor center and museum with artifact displays, historic photos and other exhibits, including a scale model of the fort in its heyday.

EL PASO AREA

Separated from the Lone Star State's other population centers by more than 500mi of high desert, this bilingual city is the largest US-Mexico border city after metropolitan San Diego. Geographically and culturally, it is far nearer to Albuquerque and Tucson—and, indeed, to Ciudad Juárez, Mexico—than to Houston or Dallas. It's even in a different time zone than other Texas cities.

Fully three-quarters of its population is of Spanish heritage. Native American cultures of the Southwest, particularly the Pueblo tribe known as the Tigua, had a major impact on the region's development, as did white Americans, including railroad builders and soldiers.

The Rio Grande River rives New Mexico and sculpts the international boundary between Texas and Mexico. The most dramatic scenery is 300mi southeast of El Paso in the isolated canyons of Big Bend National Park. Much of this wilderness belongs to wild animals but nearby are human habitation sites considered among the oldest in North America.

Other national parks and monuments are within an easy day's drive east or north of El Paso, most of them in southern New Mexico. Best known is Carlsbad Caverns National Park, one of the world's largest underground labyrinths. Other attractions range from the ancient—like the centuries-old Puebloan cliff dwellings and pueblos—to the futuristic. The area claims the world's best-documented crash of a supposed UFO (unidentified flying object) as well as the wasteland that witnessed the world's first atomic bomb test.

Prickly Pear Cactus Bloom, Big Bend National Park

©iStockphoto.com/Eric Foltz

Address Book El Paso Area

For price ranges, see the Legend on the cover flap.

WHERE TO STAY

$$$ Hilton Camino Real – *101 S. El Paso St., El Paso, TX.* ☏915-534-3000 or 800-769-4300. *www.caminoreal.com/elpaso. 359 rooms.* At 17 stories, this historic landmark overlooks three states in two nations. Decked in brass, cherry and marble, the lobby is topped by a Tiffany glass dome of mosaic leaves and blue sky. The ambience of **The Dome** restaurant takes fine dining back to the turn of the 19C.

$$$ Gage Hotel – *102 US-90 West, Marathon, TX.* ☏432-386-4205 or 800-884-4243. *www.gagehotel.com. 37 rooms.* This adobe-style inn, built in 1927 and renovated in 1978, is an ideal place to pause en route to Big Bend. Some rooms have fireplaces; all boast historic artifacts. **Café Cenizo** (**$$**), entered off a rustic patio, features mesquite-smoked *codorniz* (quail stuffed with wild rice) and shrimp tossed with slivers of jalapeño.

$$$ The Lodge – *1 Corona Pl., Cloudcroft, NM.* ☏800-395-6343. *www.thelodgeresortcom. 61 rooms.* At 9,200ft elevation, The Lodge was built in 1899 as a retreat for overheated Texans. Paddle fans and gently clanging radiators remain. Guests perch on the copper-domed observatory for views that stretch 150mi, and eat creative Southwestern cuisine at **Rebecca's Restaurant ($$)**.

$ Gardner Hotel – *311 E. Franklin Ave., El Paso, TX.* ☏915-532-3661. *www.gardnerhotel.com. 40 rooms.* Well established when gangster John Dillinger slept here in the 1930s, this three-story brick hotel is neat, tidy and the region's best bargain. Rooms still have original antique furniture, with cable TV and new phones added. Located just a mile from the Mexican border, the Gardner includes the 10-dorm-room **El Paso International Hostel ($)**.

WHERE TO EAT

$$$ Double Eagle – *308 Calle de Guadalupe, Las Cruces, NM.* ☏575-523-6700. *www.double-eagle-mesilla.com.*
Southwestern-Continental. Built in the early 19C on Old Mesilla's historic Plaza, this National Historic Register building was a private residence until 1972. It remains a repository of fascinating antiques, from the cast-iron entry gates to imperial French crystal chandeliers. Menu highlights include tournedos Maximillian and grilled pecan trout.

$$$ La Lorraine – *2523 Sudderth Dr., Ruidoso, NM.* ☏575-257-2954. *Dinner only. Closed Sun.* **French.** Gallic owners have transformed this simple adobe, snuggled among shops on Ruidoso's main street, into a charming outpost of southern France. White-linen service features such dishes as châteaubriand, duck à l'orange, coquilles St. Jacques and crème rum brulée.

$$ Flying "J" Ranch – *Rte. 48, Alto, NM.* ☏575-336-4330. *www.flyingjranch.com.* **Barbecue.** A foot-stompin' night of gunfights, pony rides, gold panning and cowboy fixin's near Ruidoso, this chuck-wagon supper of beef, beans and biscuits recalls what cowboys once ate trailside. Guests explore an Old West village until the dinner bell rings, then are serenaded by a western band and its champion yodeler.

$$ Los Bandidos de Carlos and Mickey – *1310 Magruder St., El Paso, TX.* ☏915-778-3323. **Mexican.** With cathedral ceilings and terra-cotta tiles, this tribute to the Revolution is the city's prettiest Mexican restaurant. Hacienda walls have photos of everyone from Pancho Villa to Miss Texas to five-star generals. The menu features green chile stew and tacos in adobe sauce.

$$ Starlight Theatre – *Rte. 170, Terlingua, TX.* ☏432-371-2326. *www.starlighttheatre.com. Dinner only.* **American.** In the 1940s, the old Chisos Mining Company's Adobe Deco theater drew movie fans from far and wide. It's been given a new life as a dinner theater where live music and stage shows accompany satisfying meals. Diners might start with wild boar sausage on mixed field greens, then enjoy a chicken breast sautéed with mushrooms and spinach in a cream sauce.

EL PASO ★

MICHELIN MAP 492 G, H 12
MOUNTAIN STANDARD TIME
POPULATION 585,000

Located in Texas' westernmost corner, El Paso is linked to adjacent Ciudad Juá-rez, Mexico, just across the Rio Grande. International trade keeps the border busy in both directions. El Paso is a manufacturing center, especially active in the production of cotton clothing. The El Paso Museum of Art is the vanguard of downtown revitalization in the 14-block Union Plaza cultural and entertainment district.

Information: ☎915-534-0601, www.visitelpaso.com.
Don't Miss: El Paso Museum of Art.

A Bit of History

El Paso originally was home to Manso Suma Indians. The region was claimed for Spain in 1598 by Juan de Oñate, who named it El Paso del Rio del Norte. Six decades later, priests arrived to establish a series of missions on the Juárez side of the Rio Grande. In 1680, the Pueblo Indians in northern Mexico drove out Spanish settlers, who fled to the El Paso region with Christianized Indians known as Tiguas and Piros. They founded Ysleta and Socorro, and together with Franciscan padres built the first Texas missions.

In the mid-19C, the US Army constructed Fort Bliss for defense of the city and surrounding areas. El Paso was incorporated in 1873; it became a boomtown a decade later with the arrival of the railroad. Throughout the late 19C, the city had a Wild West reputation, with gunfights and a renegade atmosphere. The new (2007, Joe Gomez and Cesar Duran) **El Paso Museum of History** (510 Santa Fe St.; ☎915-351-3588, www.elpasotexas.gov/history) celebrates the area's distinctive, multicultural past.

Rising behind the city are the Franklin Mountains, southernmost tip of the Rockies. This warm, dry region is part of the Chihuahuan Desert; altitudes range from 3,800ft in the city to 7,200ft in the mountains.

Sights

El Paso Museum of Art ★★

1 Arts Festival Plaza at Santa Fe & Main Sts. ☎915-532-1707. www.elpasoartmuseum.org.
This spacious two-level museum includes a reference library, auditorium and the Arts Festival Plaza, which features a reflecting pool, waterfall and performance areas.
The **Works on Paper Collection** showcases drawings and prints from the 16-20C, including Cézanne, Degas, Picasso, Goya and Rivera. The **American Collection** (late 18C–mid-20C) has works by Frederic Remington and post-Depression Figurative painter Moses Soyer. The **Samuel Kress Collection** highlights 13-18C European paintings and sculpture, including pieces by Canaletto and Van Dyck. The **Spanish Viceroyal Collection** features 17-19C artists and includes Mexican folk retablos. Pieces created in the American Southwest and Mexico since 1945 are the emphasis of the **Contemporary Collection**.

El Paso Holocaust Museum and Study Center ★

401 Wallenberg Dr. ♿ 🅿 ☎915-351-0048. www.elpasoholocaustmuseum.org.
Memorializing the Holocaust's 6 million victims and its survivors, this museum's bone-chilling exhibits include a three-quarter-scale model of a railroad used to carry victims to concentration camps. The Garden of the Righteous commemo-

El Paso CVB

San Elizario Mission

rates non-Jews who risked their lives to assist Jews during the war.

Chamizal National Memorial★
800 S. San Marcial Dr. ♿ 🅿 ☎*915-532-7273. www.nps.gov/cham.*
Located near the Bridge of the Americas, this memorial to peaceful US-Mexico relations recalls the 1963 resolution of a century-old border dispute caused by the Rio Grande shifting course. A visitor center presents a 12min video on border history; **Los Paisanos Gallery** exhibits art from several countries. The park's 500-seat indoor theater offers evening performances by *ballet folklórico* troupes or modern dancers.

Mission Trail★
I-10 Zaragoza Exit, 4mi southeast of downtown. ♿ 🅿 ☎*915-534-0630.* South of El Paso along the Rio Grande are three 17C missions that once lured settlers as farming and ranching centers. Northernmost is **Mission Ysleta** *(Zaragoza Ave. at S. Old Pueblo Dr.;* ☎*915-859-9848, ysleta-mission.org),* built for Spanish and Tigua refugees from the Pueblo Revolt in 1680. Floods destroyed the original mission; this one dates from 1851. Descendants of those Tiguas still use the mission for religious services. Their **Tigua Indian Cultural Center**★ *(305 Ya Ya Lane;*

☎*915-859-7700)* has a museum, restaurant, gallery and weekend dances.
Mission Socorro★ *(Socorro Rd., 2.6mi south of Mission Ysleta;* ☎*915-859-7718, www.nps.gov/history)* also was built for refugees and rebuilt after a 19C flood. An example of Spanish Mission architecture, with roof beams hand-sculpted by Piro Indians, the mission is the oldest continuously active parish in the US.
Also still in use, the gilded **Presidio Chapel in San Elizario**★ *(Socorro Rd., 6mi south of Mission Socorro;* ☎*915-851-1682, www.nps.gov/history)* combines Southwestern attributes with European characteristics such as buttresses.

Franklin Mountains State Park★
1331 McKelligon Canyon Rd. (I-10 to Canutillo Exit, Loop 375 east 4mi to entrance). ⚠ ☎*915-566-6441. www.tpwd.state.tx.us.*
The largest urban wilderness park in the US spans 37sq mi of Chihuahuan Desert, from El Paso to the New Mexico state line. Along with desert plants such as sotol and ocotillo, the park is home to mule deer, birds and mountain lions.

Fort Bliss
Fred Wilson Rd. east of US-54. ☎*915-568-2121. www.bliss.army.mil.*
This fort was established in 1848 to protect the region from Indian attack. During the Civil War, it was headquarters for the Confederate forces of the Southwest, and later was a post for troops charged with capturing Apache chief **Geronimo**. At the Robert E. Lee entrance gate stands the **Buffalo Soldier Monument**. Feared and respected, the African-American Buffalo Soldiers patrolled the Western frontier during the late 19C. The **Fort Bliss Museum** *(Bldg. 5051;* ☎*915-568-4518),* in a replica of a c.1857 adobe fort, recalls the post's history.
Today Fort Bliss is a US Army Air Defense Center. The **US Army Air Defense Museum** *(Bldg. 5000;* ☎*915-568-5412)* has exhibits on the history of air defense including weapons and ammunition.

Excursions

Ciudad Juárez

Several international bridges cross the Rio Grande from downtown El Paso. For vehicles: Bridge of the Americas, Córdova Bridge, Zaragosa Bridge. For vehicles & pedestrians: Santa Fe Bridge, Stanton Bridge. ☎915-533-3644.

This city of more than 1 million was named for former Mexican president Benito Juárez. Business and family ties give Juárez a strong bond with El Paso that grew in the 1970s with the development of *maquiladoras*, or sister factories. Trolleys of the **El Paso-Juárez Trolley Company** (☎915-544-0061, www.borderjumper.com), depart for Juárez from the El Paso Convention and Performing Arts Center. Day-trippers cross the border to shop for handicrafts at the two-story **Mercado** (*Avenida 16 de Septiembre*). At night, Juárez has a lively nightlife that includes bullfights.

Parque Chamizal★

Directly south of Bridge of the Americas. This city park opposite Chamizal National Memorial includes an **anthropology museum** with displays on Mexican history. Exhibits include replicas of some of Mexico's most famous Aztec and Mayan sites, such as Uxmal and Chichén Itzá.

Misión de Nuestra Señora de Guadalupe★

Avenidas 10 y 16 de Septiembre, south of the Stanton Bridge.
Constructed in 1658-68, this adobe mission is noted for its carved ceiling and decorated log beams made from Spanish palms.

Guadalupe Mountains National Park★★

US-62/180, 110mi east of El Paso. ⚠ P ☎915-828-3251. www.nps.gov/gumo.
The highest mountains in Texas peak at 8,749ft at Guadalupe Peak. Part of the most extensive Permian limestone fossil reef in the world, this terrain ranges from lowland desert to high-country conifer forest. Mescalero Apaches hunted these mountains beginning in the early 16C. The Pine Springs' **Headquarters Visitor Center** focuses on the ecology and geology of the mountains. There are other exhibits at **Historic Frijole Ranch.** Of the 80mi of trails, the most popular are those to El Capitan limestone formation and to **McKittrick Canyon**, where maple, walnut, ash, oak and madrone trees show off their colors in fall.

BIG BEND AREA★★

MICHELIN MAP 492 H, I 13, 14
CENTRAL STANDARD TIME

Much of this rugged and sparsely populated region is preserved within sprawling Big Bend National Park, located where the Rio Grande takes a sharp turn from southeast to northeast. More than 100mi is edged by the Rio Grande's swirling waters, which have carved the Santa Elena, Mariscal and Boquillas Canyons. Cut deep into the Chisos Mountains, these limestone chasms at first appear barren. But closer inspection reveals them—and the surrounding Chihuahuan Desert—to be rich with animal, bird and plant life.

- **Information:** ☎432-837-3638, www.visitbigbend.com.
- ▶ **Orient Yourself:** Summer is not the best season to visit Big Bend because of the area's sometimes extreme heat.
- ☺ **Don't Miss:** Big Bend National Park.
- Kids **Especially for Kids:** McDonald Observatory.

A Bit of History

Man has lived in the Big Bend area at least 8,000 years. Ancient residents—who relied upon bison, and later agriculture, for sustenance—left pictographs and petroglyphs on canyon walls. By 1535, when the first Spanish arrived, the region was a seasonal home to the nomadic Chisos Indians. They were displaced by Mescalero Apaches and finally by Comanches, who moved through the area, making raids on Mexico, into the mid-19C.

After the Mexican War, US forts, including Fort Davis, gave security to modern settlement. Early 20C mining brought prospectors. In the 1930s, the state of Texas began to acquire and preserve land in the Big Bend area, consolidating it as Texas Canyons State Park. The state deeded the land to the US government in 1944 and the site became Big Bend National Park.

Driving Tour

4 days, 581mi one-way.

▸ *From El Paso, take I-10 east 157mi to Kent, then Rte. 118 south 37mi.*

McDonald Observatory★★
Kids *Rte. 118, 16mi northwest of Fort Davis.* P ☎432-426-3640. www.mcdonaldobservatory.org

Located far from city lights, this University of Texas facility is one of the world's best astronomy research centers. Visitors join tours of the 107in Harlan J. Smith Telescope and the Hobby-Eberly Telescope. Public viewings *(by reservation)* and family-oriented "star parties" are scheduled year-round.

▸ *Continue 16mi southeast on Rte. 118.*

Fort Davis National Historic Site★★
Main St. (Rtes. 17 & 118), Fort Davis. ♿ P ☎432-426-3224. www.nps.gov/foda.
Fort Davis is one of the best surviving examples of a frontier post. Built in 1854 to protect the El Paso-San Antonio road from Indian attack, it was abandoned during the Civil War; troops found mainly ruins when they returned to rebuild in 1867. Fort Davis' role as a bulwark for mail and wagon-train routes continued until 1891. Today costumed docents staff some of the buildings. Historical exhibits are at the fort museum, in a reconstructed barracks. The fort anchors the community of Fort Davis, home to about 1,200.

▸ *Follow Rte. 118 south 103mi through Alpine to Study Butte, at west entrance to Big Bend National Park.*

Balanced Rock, Big Bend National Park

Judge Roy Bean

From behind the bar of his saloon, Judge Roy Bean served up frontier justice with beer and whiskey, leaving a legacy of fact and fiction. A silver spike driven at Dead Man's Gulch, near Langtry, linked the final section of Southern Pacific track between New Orleans and San Francisco in 1882. With the railroad came an influx of rowdy construction crews and their attendant evils—stealing, gambling and prostitution. With no law enforcement office within 100mi, shopkeeper Roy Bean was named Justice of the Peace. Bean chose his jurors from among saloon customers. He presided over trials with a six-shooter at one hand and his single book of law at the other. His favorite punishment was to exile offenders into the desert without food, water, weapons or money. Bean died in 1903.

Big Bend National Park★★★

Rte. 118 south of Alpine or US-385 south of Marathon; Panther Junction is 320mi southeast of El Paso. △✕❖🅿 ☎432-477-2251. www.nps.gov/bibe.

Big Bend spans 1,252sq mi of spectacular canyons, lush bottomlands, sprawling desert and mountain woodlands on the north side of the Rio Grande. Ranging over 6,000ft of elevation, it boasts a wealth of animal and plant life, a remarkable geological history, and a long and fascinating chronology of human habitation.

The oldest rocks, nearly 300 million years old, were deposited as sediment on an ancient ocean floor. Marine fossils in Persimmon Gap predate dinosaurs, which wandered a swampy Cretaceous landscape 100 million to 65 million years ago. Among them was the largest flying creature ever known, a pterodactyl with a 51ft wingspread. Volcanism and tectonic buckling between 42 million and 26 million years ago created the Chisos Mountains, which top out at 7,835ft Emory Peak. The park's canyons were carved over the past 3 million years during the ice ages.

Ten thousand archaeological sites tell of hunters who ventured into the area 11,000 years ago pursuing giant bison and woolly mammoths. Artifacts found in caves and rock shelters indicate that these paleo-Indians had adopted a nomadic lifestyle by 6000 BC. Ruins of pueblo villages in the Rio Grande floodplain document a culture well established by AD 500. Later, Big Bend was a sanctuary for Apaches driven south by warlike Comanches in the 17C.

Survey parties explored Big Bend by riverboat and camel in the late 1850s. Ranching and mining achieved minor success. A small factory at **Glenn Spring** produced wax from the candelilla, a perennial desert plant, until Mexican bandits destroyed the community in 1916. The US Army then began an aerial border patrol in an attempt to capture the infamous Pancho Villa.

Big Bend has more species of migratory and resident birds—over 450—than any other national park. Bats, rodents and other small mammals are nocturnal; javelina and deer are often seen, mountain lions rarely. Reptiles thrive in the extreme climate. Torrential thunderstorms may follow droughts. Temperatures approach 120°F in summer but may drop below 10°F in winter.

Park headquarters and the main visitor center are at **Panther Junction** (*US-385 & Rio Grande Village Rd.*) in the heart of Big Bend. Other visitor centers—at **Persimmon Gap** (*US-385 at north entrance),* **Chisos Basin** (*Basin Rd.)* and **Rio Grande Village** (*Rio Grande Village Rd.)*—also provide information on archaeology and ecotourism activities. Campgrounds and rustic lodges are at various locations. Hikers can choose from 200mi of trails in the park, ranging from easy to strenuous. Naturalists guide walks year-round: several times daily between November and April. Outfitters based outside the park offer Rio Grande float trips through rugged canyons.

▸ *From Panther Junction, 25mi east of Study Butte, take US-385 north 69mi to Marathon. Turn east on US-90 for 115 mi to Langtry.*

Judge Roy Bean Visitor Center★

.5mi south of US-90 on Loop 25, Langtry.
♿ 🅿 ☎*432-291-3340.*
The story of the Wild West's most famous frontier judge is told in dioramas and exhibits. Adjacent stands **The Jersey Lilly,** the restored saloon and courtroom used by Judge Bean in the 1880s.

▶ *Continue east on US-90 for 18mi.*

Seminole Canyon State Park★★

US-90, 133mi east of Marathon. ⛺♿🅿
☎*432-292-4464. www.tpwd.state.tx.us.*
On the limestone walls of this park are pictographs drawn by ancient peoples 4,000 years ago. Symbols represent animals, hunters and supernatural shamans. Archaeologists believe the early residents of Seminole Canyon were hunter-gatherers, living on plants such as sotol, prickly pear and lechugilla. Ranger-led tours take visitors to the **Fate Bell Shelter**, an over-hang that displays the oldest rock art in North America.

▶ *Continue east on US-90 for 27mi.*

Amistad National Recreation Area★★

Kids *US-90 between Langtry and Del Rio, 160mi east of Marathon.* ⛺🅿☎*830-775-7491. www.nps.gov/amis.*
Surrounding Lake Amistad on the US-Mexico border, this recreation area is popular for water sports. The 85mi-long lake is formed by a dam built in 1969 below the confluence of the Pecos and Devils Rivers with the Rio Grande. Amistad, the Spanish word for "friendship," was a joint US-Mexico project. Much of the lake is lined with limestone canyons, some containing caves with prehistoric pictographs. There are more than 250 sites within 100sq mi.

▶ *Driving tour concludes in Del Rio, 41mi farther east.*

SOUTHERN NEW MEXICO★

MICHELIN MAP 493 G, H 11, 12
MOUNTAIN STANDARD TIME

Southern New Mexico is a cultural crossroads. Here the Hispanic culture of Mexico meshes with the Native American culture of the American Southwest, its glaze of "Anglo" society layered on top. Extending north of El Paso 150mi, from the Texas and Mexico borders through numerous fertile valleys and basins amid mountainous areas, this expansive region contains many natural and historical attractions.

🛈 **Information:** ☎575-827-7400, www.newmexico.org.
☺ **Don't Miss:** Carlsbad Caverns
Kids **Especially for Kids:** Museum of Space History.

A Bit of History

Millions of years ago, this was the floor of an inland sea. When the waters receded, a rich store of fossils was left. Carlsbad Caverns, one of the world's most complex cave systems, began forming within this fossil reef 250 million years ago. Relative newcomers, Ancient Puebloan and Mogollon Indians established a foothold only 8,000 years ago. Their legacy remains in the ruins of cliff dwellings and pueblo communities.

Ranching, farming and mining have supported the regional economy since the first Spanish missions were built in the 17C. In the late 19C, Las Cruces grew from a mining-supply center to become the largest city in the area.

On July 16, 1945, the first atomic bomb was exploded at the Trinity Site near White Sands. Two years later, some folks contend, an interplanetary spacecraft crash-landed near Roswell, its alien crew put under lock and key by the US Army. Meanwhile, the world's most powerful radio telescopes send signals toward unseen civilizations, and the Space Center in Alamogordo is a tribute to aerospace fact.

Driving Tour

5 days, 969mi round-trip

▸ *Tour begins and ends in El Paso. Take I-10 north 42mi to Las Cruces.*

Las Cruces
I-10, I-25 & US-70. ✕ ♿ 🅿 ☎*575-541-2444. www.lascrucescvb.org.*
This city of 86,000 sits in the fertile Mesilla Valley between the Rio Grande and the Organ Mountains. Juan de Oñate founded the village of La Mesilla in 1598 while searching for gold. Las Cruces was founded in 1849 on the east bank of the Rio Grande, US territory after the Mexican War; it was named for "the crosses" that marked primitive graves of travelers. In 1854, La Mesilla became part of the US when the Gadsden Purchase brought 45,000sq mi of Mexican territory to the US.
Built in 1851 and reconstructed in 1906, San Albino Church towers over **Old Mesilla Plaza★** *(Rte. 28, 4mi southwest of downtown Las Cruces).* Cafes, galleries and antique shops occupy its 19C buildings. In the Masonic cemetery is the grave of Sheriff Pat Garrett, who tracked and shot down Billy the Kid after the outlaw fled La Mesilla jail while awaiting execution.
The Mesilla Valley is a leading producer of chiles, pecans and cotton. Farm and factory tours can be arranged.

Fort Selden State Monument
Between I-25, exit 19, & Rte. 185, 15mi north of Las Cruces. ♿ 🅿 ☎*575-526-8911. www.nmmonuments.org.*
This adobe fort, built in 1865 and abandoned in 1891, was home to the Buffalo Soldiers, the famed African-American cavalry that shielded settlers from Indians. And it was the boyhood home of Gen. Douglas MacArthur, the World War II hero whose father was stationed here. A visitor center displays photos.

▸ *Take I-10 west 59mi to Deming, then US-180 north 53mi to Silver City.*

Silver City
Rte. 90 & US-180. ✕ ♿ 🅿 ☎*575-538-3785. www.silvercity.org.*
In the foothills of the Piños Altos Range, this town of 10,000 was founded as a mining community in the 1870s. Its downtown historic district features extensive brickwork in mansard-roofed Victorian homes, cast iron in commercial buildings. The 1881 H.B. Ailman House is home to the **Silver City Museum** *(312 W. Broadway;* ☎*505-538-5921).* Silver City is surrounded by the 3.3-million-acre Gila National Forest, whose Gila Wilderness Area was the first designated by the US Congress.

Gila Cliff Dwellings National Monument★
Rte. 15, 44mi north of Silver City. ♿ 🅿 ☎*575-536-9461. www.nps.gov/gicl.* The cliffside stone-and-masonry homes of a 13C Mogollon agricultural village are preserved within this park, a narrow, winding, 2hr drive from Silver City. In a side canyon above the West Fork of the Gila River, in a half-dozen shallow caves in a sandstone bluff, are 42 mostly intact rooms, believed to have housed as many as 50 people. A **loop trail** *(1mi)* climbs 175ft to the dwellings, giving visitors a rare glimpse of a prehistoric culture. The Mogollon were fine builders. Stones were anchored by clay mortar, roof beams cut with stone adzes and shaped by fire. The people hunted and tended fields of corn, squash and beans in the rich soil of the Gila floodplain.

▸ *Turn northwest on US-180 along the scenic Mogollon Rim for 93mi, then easterly on Rte. 12 for 74mi to Datil, at junction of US-60.*

Very Large Array★
VLA Access Rd. west of Rte. 52 & south of US-60, 9mi east of Datil and 50mi west of Socorro. 🅿 ☎*575-835-7302. www.vla. nrao.edu.*

The world's most powerful radio telescope, the structure is used by astronomers to research the nature of the universe. Composed of scores of dish-shaped metal mirrors, each 82ft in diameter, extending across the Plains of San Agustin in a trio of miles-long arms, the facility gathers radio signals from the Milky Way galaxy and beyond. At the **visitor center,** guests may view a slide show and displays on radio astronomy, then take a self-guided tour of one of the 230-ton antennae.

> *Continue east 61mi on US-60 to Socorro; then north 26mi on I-25 to Bernardo; then east 39mi on US-60 to Mountainair.*

Salinas Pueblo Missions National Monument★

Headquarters on US-60, one block west of Rte. 55, Mountainair. ♿ 🅿 ☎575-847-2585. www.nps.gov/sapu.

Stone ruins are all that remain of the pueblos of the Salinas Valley, inhabited by descendants of Ancient Puebloan and Mogollon peoples in the 13–17C. Conflicts with Apaches, as well as a severe drought and famine, led to their abandonment during the 1670s. The **visitor center** in Mountainair has exhibits. The **Abó Ruins** *(9mi west on US-60 & .5mi north on Rte. 513)* include an unexcavated pueblo and ruins of Misión de San Gregorio de Abó. The **Quarai Ruins**★ *(8mi north on Rte. 55, then 1mi west)* include walls of Misión de Nuestra Señora de la Purisima Concepción de Cuarac, most complete of the Salinas chapels. The **Gran Quivira Ruins**★ *(25mi south on Rte. 55)* have a small museum, excavations of the San Isidro Conventio and ruins of the Misión de San Buenaventura.

> *From Mountainair, drive east 12mi on US-60 to Willard; southeast 38mi on Rte. 42 to Corona; then south 47mi on US-54 to Carrizozo.*

Trinity Site

Range Rd. 7 in the White Sands Missile Range, 21mi south of US-380, 54mi west of Carrizozo.

At this location in the Jordana del Muerto desert, the world's first atomic bomb was exploded on July 16, 1945. 👁It is closed to the public, except on rare tour days.

> *Continue south 57mi on US-54 to Alamogordo.*

Alamogordo

US-54 & 70. ✕ ♿ 🅿 ☎575-437-6120. www.alamogordo.com.

The "Rocket City" was a mere desert oasis until World War II. Flanked on the north by lava fields, on the south by white sand dunes and on the east by the 1.1-million-acre Lincoln National Forest, this community has grown into a boomtown of 36,000 people. Holloman Air Force Base, home to the Stealth F-117A aircraft, and the White Sands Missile Range administer hundreds of square miles of uninhabited land to train bombing crews and to undertake rocket research.

New Mexico Museum of Space History★★

Kids *Rte. 2001 via Indian Wells Rd. & Scenic Dr., off US-54.* ♿ 🅿 ☎575-437-2840. www.nmspacemuseum.org.

A five-story, gold-colored cube at the foot of the Sacramento Mountains, this complex salutes man's exploration of space through exhibits on history, science and technology. Displays in the **Space Museum**★★ range from examples of Robert Goddard's early experiments in rocketry, to the capsule flown in 1961 by the first astrochimp, to futuristic models of space stations. The **International Space Hall of Fame** pays tribute to more than 150 space pioneers, including US and Soviet astronauts. **John P. Stapp Air and Space Park**★, named for the man who rode the Sonic Wind 1 rocket sled at 634mph, exhibits full-size spacecraft. The **Astronaut Memorial Garden**★ honors the seven men and women who lost their lives in the 1986 Challenger space-shuttle disaster.

White Sands National Monument★★

Kids *US-70, 15mi southwest of Alamogordo.* ♿ 🅿 ☎575-679-2599. www.nps.gov/whsa.

The world's greatest expanse of white gypsum sand dunes, this mountain-ringed northern edge of the Chihuahuan Desert is preserved as a delicate ecological system. Nearly half the sands are contained within this 240sq mi site in the Tularosa Basin, inhabited only by a few hardy plant species, a few small birds and other animals (some of which have evolved a white camouflage). The visitor center features displays on the ever-moving dunes, driven by a relentless southwesterly wind; they can be seen on an 8mi *(one-way)* drive through the park. The **Alkali Flat Trail** *(4.6mi)* is designed for backcountry hikers; the **Interdune Boardwalk** *(♿.25mi)* has interpretive exhibits on dune ecology.

▶ *From Alamogordo, return 3mi up US-54, then east 16mi on US-82.*

Cloudcroft

US-82. ✕♿🅿 ☎*575-682-2733. www.cloudcroft.net.*
Located at 8,663ft, about twice the elevation of Alamogordo, this mountain village of 750 offers hiking and mountain biking in summer, skiing in winter. **The Lodge at Cloudcroft** *(1 Corona Pl.; ☎800-395-6343, www.thelodgeresort.com)* is a Victorian gem built in 1898 for rail workers. The **National Solar Observatory** *(Rte. 6563, 17mi south of Cloudcroft; ☎575-434-7000, www.*

nso.edu) is located atop 9,255ft Sacramento Peak; tours begin at the **Sunspot Astronomy and Visitor Center** *(Sunspot Scenic Byway).*

▶ *Take Rte. 244 east and north 29mi to US-70 in the Mescalero Apache Indian Reservation, then east 12mi on US-70 to Ruidoso.*

Ruidoso

US-70 & Rte. 37. ⛺✕♿🅿 ☎*575-257-7395. www.ruidosonow.com*
A resort town of 7,698 on a Sacramento Mountain stream, Ruidoso (pronounced rue-uh-DOH-so) is famous for horse racing. On Labor Day, the All-American Futurity, with $2 million at stake, is run at **Ruidoso Downs** racetrack *(US-70, 4mi east of Ruidoso; ☎575-378-4431, www.ruidownsracing.com).* The Futurity is the final event of a 77-day season that begins in mid-May.
Ruidoso is on the northern edge of the 723sq mi Mescalero Apache Indian Reservation, highlighted by the luxurious Inn of the **Mountain Gods** resort *(Carrizo Canyon Rd.; ☎505-464-7777, www.innofthemountaingods.com).* The tribe also owns southern New Mexico's largest winter resort, **Ski Apache** *(Forest Rd. 532; ☎575-464-3600, www.skiapache.com),* with a gondola and eight chairlifts on a flank of 12,003ft Sierra Blanca.

White Sands National Monument

©iStockphoto.com/Steven Allan

Billy the Kid and Smokey Bear

Tributes to two American legends stand 12mi apart on US-380 north of Ruidoso. **Lincoln State Monument** *(36mi northeast of Ruidoso; ☎575-653-4372, www. nmmonuments.org)* preserves a 19C village that recalls the life of Billy the Kid. **Smokey Bear Historical Park** Kids *(118 Smokey Bear Blvd., Capitan, 24mi north of Ruidoso; ☎575-354-2748, www.smokeybearpark.com)* honors a national symbol.

Billy the Kid – Born of Irish immigrants, Henry McCarty (1859?-81), alias William Bonney, moved to New Mexico with his widowed mother after the Civil War. Orphaned in 1873, he worked as a cowboy in Arizona; he was pursued for thefts and one killing as he fled back to New Mexico in 1877. A range war in Lincoln County climaxed in 1878 with a 5-day gun battle in which Billy killed a sheriff and deputy. While awaiting execution, he overpowered a guard and as he escaped, killed two more deputies. Making his way to Fort Sumner, he found refuge in the abandoned fort now preserved as **Fort Sumner State Monument** *(Rte. 272, 7mi southeast of Fort Sumner off US-60/84; ☎575-355-2573, www.nmmonuments.org).* On the night of July 14, 1881, Sheriff Pat Garrett tracked down Bonney and shot him through the heart.

Smokey Bear – The real-life Smokey Bear emerged from the devastation of a Lincoln National Forest fire in 1950. Although badly burned, the rescued black-bear cub was nursed back to health and adopted by the US Forest Service. Smokey became the living symbol of a campaign, started during World War II, to prevent fires caused by careless humans. His cartoon image had captured American hearts via print media by the time the real cub was introduced. Smokey lived in the National Zoo in Washington DC until his death in 1976. He was returned to New Mexico and buried in Smokey Bear Historical Park. Smokey's message—"Only you can prevent forest fires"—has become part of American popular culture.

Hubbard Museum of the American West★★

Kids *841 US-70 West, Ruidoso Downs.* ♿🅿 ☎*575-378-4142. www.hubbardmuseum. org.*

More than 10,000 historical and cultural items chronicle the relationship between horse and man. Firearms, farm tools, wagons and carriages are on display, along with a fine art collection that includes works by Russell and Remington. At the entrance is one of the world's largest equine monuments, *Free Spirits at Noisy Water*, by Ruidoso sculptor Dave McGary. The bronze is more than 300ft long and stands over three stories high.

Spencer Theater for the Performing Arts★

Airport Rd. 220, Alto, 5mi north of Ruidoso. ♿🅿 ☎*575-336-4800. www.spencer-theater.com.*

Designed to echo the surrounding Capitan and Sacramento Mountains with white limestone and steep angles, this $20 million, 514-seat theater (1997, Antoine Predock) also showcases the glass art of Dale Chihuly. Dramatic, musical and dance performances are regularly scheduled.

▸ *Continue east 71mi on US-70 to Roswell.*

Roswell

US-70, 285 & 380. ✈♿🅿 ☎*575-623-5695. www.roswellnm.org.*

This city of 45,000 once was known merely for its ranching economy and esteemed military school. Then the "Roswell Incident" occurred. In 1947, a "flying saucer" or unidentified flying object (UFO) allegedly crashed in a field 20mi northwest. The incident was reported by local media but quickly hushed up by the US Army.

The **International UFO Museum & Research Center★** Kids *(114 N. Main St.; ☎505-625-9495, www.roswellufomuseum.com)* features exhibits both on the

Roswell Incident and cover-up, and on UFO sightings around the world.

At the **Roswell Museum and Art Center** *(11th & Main Sts.; ☎575-624-6744, www.roswellmuseum.org),* the highlights are the Robert H. Goddard Planetarium and the workshop of Goddard, father of modern rocketry. The art collection showcases works by Peter Hurd, Henriette Wyeth and Georgia O'Keeffe; the Rogers Aston Collection features Western history.

▶ *From Roswell, drive south 76mi on US-285 to Carlsbad. Turn southwest on US-62/180 for 16mi to Whites City, at entrance to Carlsbad Caverns National Park.*

Carlsbad Caverns National Park★★★

🛈 ⛰ *Off US-62, 23mi southwest of Carlsbad.* ✕ ♿ 🅿 ☎575-785-2232. *www. nps.gov/cave.*

One of the largest cave systems in the world, the labyrinth of Carlsbad Caverns takes in 88 known caves, including Lechuguilla Cave, at 1,567ft the deepest limestone cavern in the US.

The caverns were discovered in the early 1900s. Cowboy Jim White saw a cloud of dark smoke, rising on the horizon near dusk, that turned out to be thousands of Mexican free-tailed bats.(Bats still cling to the roof of the cave entrance \before beginning their nightly insect-hunting.) White descended on a rope ladder to the cave floor, where he was stunned by the

The Big Room, Carlsbad Caverns

formations: soda straws and ice-cream cones, strings of pearls and miniature castles. By 1923 the caves were part of the national park system.

Perpetually 56 degrees, the damp caves can be entered through their natural entrance or by elevator. Tour highlights include beautiful formations as the Temple of the Sun and the Frozen Waterfall.

▶ *Continue west on US-180, 35mi to Guadalupe Mountains National Park and another 110mi to El Paso.*

Courtesy of the New Mexico Tourism Department

GLACIER PARK REGION

One of North America's most awe-inspiring destinations is Waterton/Glacier International Peace Park, its jagged peaks, glacial lakes and U-shaped valleys straddling the US-Canada border. Far from major cities, relative isolation has enhanced its wilderness charms.

During the ice ages, glaciers plowed down Rocky Mountain river valleys, shaving mountains into horns and arêtes and gouging the valleys.

Some glaciers flowed far enough south to impound the Clark Fork River at the present site of Lake Pend Oreille, creating glacial Lake Missoula. Larger in volume than Lakes Ontario and Erie combined, the inland sea spread from the Flathead region to the Bitterroot Mountains. Whenever an ice dam broke, floods raged down the Columbia River drainage to the Pacific; each time, another glacier plugged the outlet and the lake refilled. Fertile sedimentary deposits are the lake's legacy in the Mission and Bitterroot Valleys.

Lewis' and Clark's 1804-06 odyssey took them across this ruggedly beautiful land: through the Bitterroot Valley, down the Columbia drainage. Even before the Corps of Discovery returned east, mountain men were headed west into these reaches. The pioneer influx led to conflict with Native Americans, whose free-roaming lifestyle disappeared into oppressive reservations.

Today, visitors can see bison and eagles, grizzly bears and mountain goats, they can meet real cowboys and Indians, stride across glaciers or into gold mines. America's Western heritage lives on through national and state parks, wildlife refuges, museums and historic preservation efforts.

Mount Gould and Grinnell Lake, Glacier National Park

GLACIER NATIONAL PARK★★★

MICHELIN MAP 493 D 3, 4
MOUNTAIN STANDARD TIME

Shaped by glaciers, the Glacier Park area is characterized by rugged mountains, lakes and valleys. About 75 million years ago, a geological phenomenon known as the Lewis Overthrust tilted and pushed a 3mi- to 4mi-thick slab of the earth's crust 50mi east, leaving older rock atop younger Cretaceous rock. These mountains now rise 3,000-7,000ft above valley floors, partially forming the Continental Divide. A wet coniferous ecosystem on the west side of the Divide is balanced by dry, sparsely vegetated terrain on the east side.

- **Information:** ☎406-888-7800 or www.nps.gov/glac
- **Don't Miss:** Going-to-the-Sun Road.
- **Also See:** Museum of the Plains Indian.

Sights

Glacier National Park★★★

Going-to-the-Sun Road off US-2, 35mi east of Kalispell. △✕♿🅿 *☎406-888-7800. www.nps.gov/glac.*

Known to native Blackfeet as the "Land of Shining Mountains," Glacier Park was homesteaded in the late 19C. Pressure to establish the park began in 1891 with the arrival of the Great Northern Railway; Congress gave its nod in 1910. The railroad built numerous delightful Swiss-style chalets and hotels, several of which still operate.

Glacier's rugged mountainscape takes its name not from living glaciers, but from ancient rivers of ice that carved the peaks, finger lakes and U-shaped valleys. The remoteness of the park's 1,584sq mi makes it an ideal home for grizzly bears and mountain goats, bighorn sheep and bugling elk.

Western Approaches

Coming from Kalispell, visitors pass through the village of Hungry Horse, named for two lost horses that nearly starved one long-ago winter. **Hungry Horse Dam** *(West Reservoir Rd., 4mi south of US-2; ☎406-387-5241),* which impounds a 34mi-long reservoir, offers grand views up the South Fork of the Flathead River, into the Bob Marshall Wilderness. Guided tours from a visitor center lead to the massive turbines and generators of the 564ft-high arched concrete dam.

Charming **West Glacier,** a park gateway town, is an outfitting center. Amtrak trains stop at a renovated depot that now houses the nonprofit Glacier Natural History Association. **Belton Chalet** *(12575 US-2 East; ☎406-888-5000, www.beltonchalet.com),* built by the Great Northern Railroad in 1910, is restored and listed on the National Register of Historic Places.

Going-to-the-Sun Road★★★

52mi from US-2 at West Glacier to US-89 at St. Mary. 🕐 *Closed mid Oct–late May due to snow.*

This National Historic Landmark may be America's most beautiful highway. Deemed an engineering marvel when completed in 1932, the narrow, serpentine roadway climbs 3,500ft to the Continental Divide at Logan Pass, moving from forested valleys to alpine meadows to native grassland as it bisects the park west to east. Passenger vehicles (size restrictions prohibit large RVs) share the route with Glacier's trademark red "jammer" buses, which have carried sightseers for more than 60 years.

Two miles from the road's beginning is **Apgar**, an assemblage of lodgings, cafes and shops at the foot of mountain-ringed **Lake McDonald★**. Like most park waters, this lake is fed by snowmelt and glacial runoff, and summer surface temperatures average a cool 55°F. The launch *DeSmet*, a classic wooden boat handcrafted in 1928, cruises from the rustic **Lake McDonald Lodge** *(Mile*

Address Book Glacier Park Region

For a legend of prices, see the cover flap.

WHERE TO STAY IN THE GLACIER PARK REGION

$$$$$ Averill's Flathead Lake Lodge – *Rte. 35, Bigfork, MT.* ✕🅿 ☎*406-837-4391. www.averills.com. 20 cabins. Open May–Sept.* This family-operated dude ranch, nestled in a bay on the east shore of Flathead Lake, offers a package experience of the new West. Log cottages surround a central lodge amid lush forestland. Visitors engage in horseback riding and fishing, or sailing and swimming at the private beach and marina.

$$$ The Coeur d'Alene – *115 S. 2nd St., Coeur d'Alene, ID.* ✕♿🅿🛉 Spa ☎*208-765-4000 or 800-688-5253. www.cdaresort.com. 336 rooms.* Consistently voted one of America's top resorts, this golf, sailing and tennis complex offers lodgings that range from economy to 18th-story tower penthouses. Housing four restaurants and saturated with amenities, it perches beside Lake Coeur d'Alene with a private beach and marina.

$$$ Glacier Park Lodge – *US-2 at Hwy. 49, East Glacier Park, MT.* ✕♿🅿 ☎*406-892-2525. www.glacierparkinc.com. 161 rooms.* The Great Northern Railway created the pitched roofline and rustic rooms in 1913 to attract wealthy travelers to the frontier. The vast lobby is a highlight of this grand building: 48ft timbers, with bark intact, create a rectangular basilica flanked by galleries and illuminated by skylights. Rooms are basic.

$$ The Copper King Mansion – *219 W. Granite St., Butte, MT.* ☎*406-782-7580. www.thecopperkingmansion.com. 5 rooms.* Built for a self-made copper millionaire in 1888, this opulent Victorian residence even offers a guided tour. It starts with the main hall's Staircase of Nations and moves to the ballroom, library and billiard room, all rich with stained-glass windows, gold-embossed leather ceilings, and inlaid woodwork.

$$ The Garden Wall Inn – *504 Spokane Ave., Whitefish, MT.* 🅿 ☎*406-862-3440 or 888-530-1700. www.gardenwallinn.*

com. 5 rooms. With clapboard siding and claw-footed tubs, this charming Colonial Revival bed-and-breakfast inn is named for the sheer cliffs that form the Continental Divide. The innkeepers, keen outdoors explorers, concoct gourmet breakfasts that might include huckleberry-pear crepes.

$$ The Sanders – *328 N. Ewing St., Helena, MT.* ☎*406-442-3309. www.sandersbb.com. 7 rooms.* Most of the original furnishings remain in this charming 1875 bed-and-breakfast Victorian, home for 30 years (until 1905) of frontier politician Wilbur Fisk Sanders and his suffragette wife, Harriet Fenn Sanders. Listed on the National Register of Historic Places, it has been lovingly maintained by Rock Ringling (scion of the circus family) and Bobbi Uecker.

WHERE TO EAT IN THE GLACIER PARK REGION

$$$ The Stonehouse – *120 Reeder's Alley, Helena, MT.* ☎*406-449-2552. Dinner only.* **American.** In the late 19C, fine dining meant white linen, even if atmosphere was rustic. This former miners' bunkhouse and four adjacent historic cabins perpetuate that theme. Specials include corn-fed steaks, stuffed catfish and wild game, and the Friday-night seafood buffet is always bustling.

$$ Belton Chalet – *US-2, West Glacier, MT.* ☎*406-888-5000. www.beltonchalet.com. Dinner only.* **Regional.** Built in 1910 as a Great Northern Railway hotel, this Swiss-style chalet was filled with Arts and Crafts furniture and blazing stone fireplaces. After a major historic preservation effort, it reopened in 2000 with a handful of guest rooms and a fine-dining restaurant. The Grill prepares entrees like rainbow trout, buffalo sausage and pheasant pot pie on an old boiler converted to an outdoor barbecue. A taproom is adjacent.

$$ The Bridge – *515 S. Higgins Ave., Missoula, MT.* ☎*406-542-0638.* **Italian & Seafood.** This neighborhood cafe occupies two floors of a century-old "dime-a-dance" hall, beside a small theater. A labor of love for its owners of 30 years, the bistro serves pasta, pizza, fresh seafood and vegetarian entrees.

11; ☎406-892-2525, www.lakemcdon-aldlodge.com), open summers. There's been a hotel here since 1895.

At **Trail of the Cedars**★ (Mile 16.5), a wheelchair-accessible boardwalk winds through old-growth cedar-hemlock forest and past a sculpted gorge. Able-bodied hikers can amble uphill another 2mi to Avalanche Lake, fed by waterfalls spilling from Sperry Glacier. Beyond, **Bird Woman Falls** cascades from Mt. Oberlin and the **Weeping Wall**★ gushes or trickles—depending on the season—from a roadside rock face.

At 6,680ft **Logan Pass**★★★ (Mile 33), visitors enjoy broad alpine meadows of wildflowers and keep their eyes open for mountain goats on the 1.5mi walk to **Hidden Lake Overlook**★★. White-flowered beargrass is beautiful in summer. Ripple-marked rocks more than 1 billion years old lie along the route to the observation post.

Descending Logan Pass, travelers may stop at the **Jackson Glacier Overlook** (Mile 37) or continue to **Sun Point**★ (Mile 41), where there is picnicking beside **St. Mary Lake** and a trailhead to **Baring Falls** (1mi). From **Rising Sun** (Mile 45), scenic 90min **lake cruises**★ aboard the 49-passenger Little Chief, built in 1925, are launched.

Eastern Valleys★★

A 21mi drive northwest from St. Mary leads to **Many Glacier**★★★ (12mi west of Babb off US-89). Three small glaciers

provide a memorable backdrop to the valley above Grinnell Lake. They may be reached by a 5mi hiking path (part of Glacier Park's stalwart 735mi trail network), or viewed from the landmark 1915 **Many Glacier Hotel**★ (b406-892-2525), or from a boat on sparkling Swiftcurrent and Josephine Lakes.

Two Medicine★ (13mi northwest of East Glacier Park off Rte. 49) is tucked into a carved glacial valley 38mi south of St. Mary via US-89 and has a general store and guided boat tours but no lodgings except a campground.

East Glacier Park

US-2 & Rte. 49.

This small town on the Blackfeet Indian Reservation is home to the 1913 **Glacier Park Lodge**★ (☎406-892-2525), whose lobby is columned with old-growth Douglas fir logs. The village boasts youth hostels, bicycle rentals, horseback outfitters and an Amtrak train depot.

Southern Boundary

Between East Glacier Park and West Glacier, a 57mi stretch of US-2 divides the park from the Great Bear Wilderness. From 5,220ft **Marias Pass** on the Continental Divide, there are superb views of the Lewis Overthrust. Tiny **Essex** (25mi east of West Glacier), on the Middle Fork of the Flathead River, is home to the **Izaak Walton Inn** (off US-2; ☎406-888-5700, www.izaakwaltoninn.com), built in 1939 for rail crews. Today the half-timbered inn is a mecca for railroad fans and cross-country skiers.

Blackfeet Indian Reservation

US-2 & US-89. ⚠✕🅿 ☎406-338-7521. www.blackfeetnation.com.

Bordered on the north by Canada, the Blackfeet Reservation stretches east from Glacier Park across 50mi of rolling hills and prairies notorious for hot, dry summers and wind-whipped winters. Today three Blackfeet confederacy tribes live in Montana and adjacent Alberta, earning livelihoods mainly in ranching and farming.

Rocky Mountain Big Horn Sheep

Excursion

Waterton Lakes National Park★★

Alberta Rte. 5 off Chief Mountain International Hwy. ⚠✕♿🅿 ☎*403-859-2224. www.pc.gc.ca/pn-np/ab.*
Yoked like oxen since 1932, Glacier Park and Canada's adjacent Waterton Lakes National Park share a similar topography and a history of cooperation. Together they form Waterton/Glacier International Peace Park.

The 195sq mi Waterton Lakes Park focuses around the distinctly Canadian townsite of **Waterton Park,** hugging the shoreline of Upper Waterton Lake. Visitors can walk to Cameron Falls *(.5mi)*, take a **lake excursion**★ aboard the launch *International*, and enjoy high tea at the gabled 1927 **Prince of Wales Hotel**★★ (☎*403-236-3400, www.princeofwaleswaterton.com),* whose stunning hilltop setting and commanding lake views befit its regal namesake.

FLATHEAD REGION★

MICHELIN MAP 493 E 3, 4
MOUNTAIN STANDARD TIME

Wherever the eye rests in the Flathead Valley, mountains loom. They follow the traveler like a shadow. Ice Age glaciers left behind these jagged peaks and a fertile river valley that now supports an agricultural economy. The Flathead Indian Reservation and Flathead Lake are both found in this striking land, where outdoor recreation is gradually supplanting logging as the major industry.

🔲 **Information:** ☎406-756-9091 or www.fcvb.org
🔘 **Don't Miss:** Kalispell.
🔘 **Also See:** The People's Center.

Sights

Kalispell

US-2 & US-93 west of Glacier Park. ⚠✕♿🅿 ☎*406-758-2800. www.kalispellchamber.com.*
Flathead County's commercial center, this town of 19,000 melds old and new Montana. The elegant **Conrad Mansion**★ *(313 6th Ave. E.; ☎406-755-2166, www.conradmansion.com),* a 26-room Norman-style home built in 1895, is Kalispell's crown jewel.

Whitefish★

US-93, 14mi north of Kalispell. ⚠✕♿🅿 ☎*406-862-3501. www.whitefishchamber.com.*
This small town of 6,000 gracefully balances its dual identity as a Western community and resort center. **Whitefish Lake**★ draws anglers and water skiers in summer; in winter, 7,000ft **Big Mountain**★ *(Big Mountain Rd., 8mi north of Whitefish; ☎406-862-2900, www.big-*

mtn.com) lures snow-sport enthusiasts. Summer visitors ride the gondola to the summit for wonderful **views**★★ into Glacier National Park and the Canadian Rockies.

Flathead Lake★★

Between US-93 & Rte. 35, 11 to 38mi south of Kalispell. ⚠
This 27mi-long lake, largest natural freshwater lake west of the Mississippi River, offers boating, sailing and fishing with gorgeous mountain **views**★.
With its Western-theme architecture and storybook lakeside setting, **Bigfork**★ *(Rte. 35, 17mi southeast of Kalispell;* ⚠✕♿🅿 ☎*406-837-5888, www.bigfork.org)* is a center for the arts and fine dining. Galleries and gift shops line its main street, and the **Bigfork Summer Playhouse** (☎*406-837-4886, www.bigforksummerplayhouse.com)* draws sellout crowds to productions of comedies and Broadway musicals.

Where the Buffalo Roam

Fifty million bison once migrated across North America from central Mexico to Canada. For thousands of years they sustained generations of Plains Indians. Hides provided clothing and lodging; bones became tools and weapons; flesh and organs fed families. The herds flourished until the late 19C, when hunters slaughtered them for tongues and hides, leaving carcasses to rot.

The **National Bison Range**★★ *(Rte. 212, Moiese, 31mi south of Polson;* ♿ 🅿 ☎ *406-644-2211, www.fws.gov/bisonrange)* was set aside in 1908 to preserve a small herd of buffalo, by then approaching extinction. About 370 buffalo now roam the range and provide breeding stock for private North American bison ranches, where as many as 200,000 of the great beasts are raised. Visitor center displays examine the behavior and history of these strong, temperamental animals. Drivers on the 19mi Red Sleep Mountain tour may view not only bison but also pronghorn, bighorn sheep, elk and mountain goats on more than 18,500 scenic acres.

© Comstock, Inc

Flathead Indian Reservation

US-93 between Kalispell & Missoula. ✕ ♿ 🅿 ☎ *406-675-2700. www.cskt. org/vi.*

Montana's Salish, Kootenai and Pend d'Oreille tribes reside on this reservation, established in 1855. Every July, traditional **celebrations**★ in the villages of Elmo and Arlee welcome visitors to see Native American dancing, music and games.

The reservation's commercial center is **Polson** *(US-93 & Rte. 35, 49mi south of Kalispell & 65mi north of Missoula;* ☎ *406-883-5969; www.polsonchamber.com)*, a boating and outfitting hub that hugs the foot of Flathead Lake.

Six miles south of Polson, **The People's Center**★ *(US-93, Pablo; b406-675-0160. www.peoplescenter.net)* relates the history of the Flathead tribes. Numerous prairie potholes, formed by glaciers 12,000 years ago, attract more than 180 bird species to **Ninepipe National Wildlife Refuge** *(US-93, 15mi south of Polson;* ☎ *406-644-2211, www.fws.gov)*, a 2,000-acre wetland. The 1891 **St. Ignatius Mission**★ *(US-93, 29mi south of Polson;* ☎ *406-745-2768)* is graced with handsome frescoes and murals and backdropped by the majestic Mission Mountains.

UPPER MISSOURI RIVER★

MICHELIN MAP 493 F 4
MOUNTAIN STANDARD TIME

The Missouri River played a key role in US westward expansion. Besides bringing the Lewis and Clark Expedition, fur traders, gold seekers and pioneer settlers into the region, it was part of a vast water-land route from St. Louis to the Pacific Ocean. Today, 149mi of the Missouri are a wild-and-scenic corridor rich in wildlife and pristine canyon scenes. Coursing through a land of buttes and prairies immortalized by cowboy artist Charles M. Russell, it's the last major free-flowing remnant of a historic waterway.

Information: ☎406-761-5036, www.russell.visitmt.com
Don't Miss: The C.M. Russell Museum.

Sights

Great Falls★★

US-87 & US-89 at I-15. ⚠🍴♿🅿 ☎406-761-4434. greatfallscvb.visitmt.com.
Great Falls drew national attention when explorers Lewis and Clark portaged five local waterfalls (now submerged or reduced by dams). With 57,000 residents, it is Montana's third-largest city, .
Lewis & Clark National Trail Interpretive Center★★ (4201 Giant Springs Rd.; ☎406-727-8733, www.fs.fed.us/r1/lewis-clark/lcic) honors the Corps of Discovery and the Plains Indians who assisted them. Following a **film**★ by director Ken Burns, visitors may explore interactive displays and exhibits that chronicle the voyageurs' odyssey. Outside, the 8mi **River's Edge Trail** entices bicyclists and walkers. Down the road at **Giant Springs Heritage State Park**★ (4600 Giant Springs Rd.; ☎406-454-5840, fwp. mt.gov) is one of the nation's largest freshwater springs and shortest rivers—the Roe, 201ft long.

Legendary artist Charlie Russell (1864-1926), who portrayed the vanishing American West in oils, watercolors and sculptures, made his home in Great Falls. The **C.M. Russell Museum**★★ (400 13th St. N.; ☎406-727-8787, www. cmrussell.org) features the world's largest collection of Russell masterpieces, plus the artist's home and log-cabin studio. Not far away, Romanesque 1896 **Paris Gibson Square** (1400 1st Ave. N.; ☎406-727-8255, www.the-square.org) has a contemporary art museum and a historical society.

Giant Springs State Park, Great Falls

© Donnie Sexton / Travel Montana

Fort Benton★
*Rte. 80 off US-87, 38mi northeast of Great
Falls.* △✕㐖🄿 ☎*406-622-3864. www.
fortbenton.com.*

The farthest point to which steamboats
could travel up the Missouri, Fort Benton developed as a river port. It was the
east end of the 642mi Mullan Road to
Walla Walla, Washington, linking the
Missouri and Columbia River drainages.
The **Museum of the Northern Great
Plains**★ *(1205 20th St. at Washington Sts.;
☎406-622-5316)* presents a vivid picture
of early settler life in the harsh conditions of the high plains.

Upper Missouri River Breaks
National Monument★
Access by river from Fort Benton. △
☎*406-622-4000. www.mt.blm.gov.*

Encompassing the 149 miles of the Upper
Missouri National Wild and Scenic River,
this remote region has changed little
since Lewis and Clark ventured through
in 1805. Designated a national monument in January 2001 and administered
by the Bureau of Land Management, it
is of historical, cultural, geological and
ecological importance.

Helena★★
US-12 at I-15. ✕㐖🄿 ☎*406-447-1530.
helenacvb. visitmt.com.*

Montana's capital, Helena perches
around Last Chance Gulch, one of America's richest gold strikes. A genteel town
of 28,000 with a rough-and-tumble heritage, Helena is full of old mansions and
mining legends. Prominent in town are
the twin-spired **St. Helena's Cathedral**★ *(Lawrence & Warren Sts.; ☎406-
442-5825, www.sthelenas.org)* and the
1888 Queen Anne-style **Original Governor's Mansion**★ *(304 N. Ewing St.;
☎406-444-4789).*

Situated on a hillside facing the Helena
Valley, the copper-domed **Montana
State Capitol**★★ *(1301 E. 6th Ave.;
☎ 406-444-4789, www.montanacapi-
tol.com)* is a grand structure with an
elegant French Renaissance rotunda.
Charles Russell's monumental *Lewis and
Clark Meeting Indians at Ross's Hole* (1912)
hangs here. Tours begin from the nearby
Montana Historical Society★ *(225 N.
Roberts St.; ☎406-444-2694, www.his.
state.mt.us),* which displays a fine collection of Russell canvases; its Montana
Homeland exhibit depicts the lifestyles
of native peoples.

At **Gates of the Mountains**★★ *(I-15 Exit
209, 18mi north of Helena; ☎406-458-
5241 www.gatesofthemountains.com),*
the Missouri River weaves through a
spectacular canyon formed from Precambrian sedimentary rock and Missis-
sippian limestone.

GOLD WEST COUNTRY★

MICHELIN MAP 493 E, F 4, 5
MOUNTAIN STANDARD TIME

About 75 million years ago, molten granite surged into the earth's crust to create
the mineral-laden Boulder Batholith—the genesis of southwestern Montana's
wealth and outlaw lore. Gold, silver and copper drew settlers to the area in the
mid- to late 19C. The charm of this historic region remains today.

🛈 **Information:** ☎800-879-1159 or goldwest.visitmt.com
🌀 **Don't Miss:** Pintler Scenic Highway.

Sights

Butte
I-15 & I-90. ✕㐖🄿 ☎*406-723-3177.
www.buttecvb.com.*

An erstwhile mining town of 32,000,
Butte called itself "The Richest Hill on
Earth." Tunnels beneath the town, if
unfurled, would stretch the length of
Montana— more than 500mi.

A **trolley tour** through historic Uptown includes the **Berkeley Pit**★ (*east end Mercury St. off Continental Dr.*), the largest truck-served open-pit copper mine in the US from 1955 to 1982.

Visitors roam a reconstructed mining camp at the **World Museum of Mining**★ (*west end Park St.; ☎406-723-7211, www.miningmuseum.org*), or tour Butte's last intact mine yard, the **Anselmo Mine**★ (*600 block of N. Excelsior St.*).

With its stained-glass windows and frescoed ceilings, the **Copper King Mansion**★ (*219 W. Granite St.; ☎406-782-7580, www.thecopperkingmansion.com*) recalls Butte's glory days.

Deer Lodge★

I-90, 41mi northwest of Butte. ⚠✕♿🅿

A traditional ranching town of 3,400, Deer Lodge captures the attention of Old West aficionados. At the 1,500-acre **Grant-Kohrs Ranch National Historic Site**★★ (*.75mi west of I-90 Exit 184; ☎406-846-2070; www.nps.gov/grko*), costumed Park Service rangers share the story of a ranch that once was headquarters of a four-state cattle empire.

Old Montana Prison★ (*1106 Main St.; ☎406-846-3111, www.pcmaf.org*), provides a glimpse of yesteryear's convicts. Among its six integral museums are the **Montana Auto Museum**★, which features antique roadsters and novelty cars, and (across Main Street) the **Frontier Museum**, showcasing guns and saloon paraphernalia.

Pintler Scenic Highway★★

Rte. 1 between I-90 Exits 208 & 153. ⚠✕♿🅿

This splendid 63mi road winds past ranches, over a mountain pass and along lakes. At one end is **Anaconda**★ (*Rte. 1, 24mi west of Butte via I-90; ☎406-563-2400, www.anacondamt.org*), known for its Art Deco theater and a landmark smelter stack. The highlight of quaint **Philipsburg**★★ (*Rte. 1, 55mi northwest of Butte; ☎406-859-3388, philipsburgmt.com*),is the **Granite County Museum**★ (*155 S. Sansome St.; ☎406-859-3020*), which holds the underground Granite Mountain mining exhibit and the Montana Ghost Town Hall of Fame. Within 60mi are 21 ghost towns, best preserved

of which is the 1890s gold camp of **Garnet**★★ (*39mi east of Missoula via Rte. 200 & Garnet Range Rd., or 57mi northwest of Philipsburg via I-90 & Bear Gulch Rd; ☎406-329-3914*).

Missoula★

US-12 & US-93 at I-90. ☎406-543-6623. www.missoulacvb.org.

A commercial and cultural center and home to the University of Montana, Missoula is a lively town of 64,000 residents. Built in 1877 for protection against Indians, **Fort Missoula** (*South Ave. west of Reserve St.; ☎406-728-3476*) served as a World War II internment center for Italians and Japanese Americans. The **US Forest Service Smokejumpers Training Center**★ (*5765 W. Broadway; ☎406-329-4900*) prepares an elite corps of men and women to fight wildfires.

Excursion

Bannack★★

South of Rte. 278, 26mi southwest of Dillon. ♿🅿 *☎406-834-3413. www.bannack.org.*

A booming 1860s mining camp near the Pioneer Mountains, Bannack was Montana's first territorial capital. Its 50-plus buildings stand as abandoned when the gold played out. Self-guided tours lead through a deserted main street that comes to life during July's **Bannack Days,** a full-dress 19C re-creation.

© Peg Owens/Idaho Tourism

Seaplane at Coeur d'Alene Lake

COEUR D'ALENE COUNTRY★

MICHELIN MAP 493 D, E 3, 4
PACIFIC STANDARD TIME

In the early 1800s, fur trappers began trading for pelts with the Indians of Idaho's Panhandle. The natives proved shrewd bargainers, inspiring the trappers to say they had hearts like awls—les coeurs d'alênes. When the Mullan Road was completed in 1862, linking the Missouri and Columbia River watersheds, mountainous northern Idaho opened for settlement. Miners came for gold but stayed for other riches in what became one of the world's foremost regions for the production of silver, lead and zinc.

- **Information:** www.visitnorthidaho.com
- ▶ **Orient Yourself:** Though it's in Idaho, the area's gateway is Spokane and its international airport.
- **Don't Miss:** Coeur d'Alene Lake
- **Also See:** The Silver Valley's mining history sites.

Sights

Coeur d'Alene★
I-90, 32mi east of Spokane, Washington.
△✕&🅿 ☎208-664-3194. www.coeurd-alene.org.
The former steamship port of 41,000 is now a summer playground for jet-skiers, parasailers, golfers and other recreation lovers. Beautiful **Coeur d'Alene Lake**★★ extends 23mi south.

Silver Valley★★
I-90, 20 to 60mi east of Coeur d'Alene.
△✕&🅿
More than a billion ounces of silver were extracted in the 20C at **Wallace**★★ (*I-90 Exit 62, 49mi east of Coeur d'Alene;* ☎208-753-7151, www.wallaceidahochamber.com), self-proclaimed "Silver Capital of the World." At the **Sierra Silver Mine**★★ (*420 5th St.;* ☎208-752-5151, www.silverminetour.org), retired miners demonstrate their equipment; tours include a narrated trolley ride through town. A handsomely restored train station (1901) houses railroad mementos at the château-style **Northern Pacific Depot Railroad Museum**★ (*219 6th St. at Pine St.;* ☎208-752-0111). The **Wallace District Mining Museum** (*509 Bank St.;* ☎208-556-1592) shows films explaining how Idaho's mining industry evolved.
Kellogg★ (*I-90 Exit 49, 36mi east of Coeur d'Alene;* △✕&🅿 ☎208-784-0821, www.silvervalleychamber.com),

Wallace's larger neighbor, has shifted haltingly from mining to tourism. Its unique **junk-art sculptures**★ (by David Dose) whimsically color the landscape. Summer weekends, a gondola and chairlifts at the **Silver Mountain** ski area (*610 Bunker Ave.;* ☎208-783-1111) carry visitors to the top of 6,300ft Kellogg Peak, where spectacular 360-degree **views**★★ encompass parts of Canada, Washington and Montana. The **Staff House Museum** (*820 W. McKinley Ave.;* ☎208-786-4141) features a mine model representing 135mi of tunnel.
All that remains of **Murray**★ (*Forest Rd. 9 via Forest Rd. 456, 18mi north of Wallace*), a gold-rush boomtown, are two saloons, a bank-turned-inn, and memories.
Old Mission State Park★★ (*I-90 Exit 40, Cataldo, 24mi east of Coeur d'Alene;* ☎208-682-3814, www.idahoparks.org) preserves Idaho's oldest structure, the 1850 Cataldo Mission. The restored church sits on a grassy knoll overlooking the Coeur d'Alene River valley.
Sandpoint★ (*US-2 & 95, 46mi north of Coeur d'Alene;* ☎208-263-0887, www.sandpointchamber.org), Lake Pend Oreille's largest town (with 8,000 people), has a small historical museum. Nearby **Schweitzer Mountain** (*Schweitzer Mountain Rd.;* ☎208-263-9555), a popular ski area, offers summer-weekend chairlift rides to its 6,400ft summit and memorable lake-to-mountain **views**★★.

GRAND CANYON REGION

Nearly 2 billion years in the making, 277mi long and averaging 10mi wide and 1mi deep, the Grand Canyon is superlative. Hundreds of side canyons, creeks and trails lie within the boundaries of Grand Canyon National Park. No other place has so much of the earth's geological history on display.

Most visitor services are centered on the canyon's South Rim. One may also explore the less commercialized North Rim and, beyond that, the largely undeveloped Arizona Strip just south of the Utah border. The drive from South Rim to North Rim takes a good four hours, and many visitors opt for a shorter hop to Williams (56mi south), terminus for the Grand Canyon Railway. Northwest of Williams via old Route 66—the historic, pre-interstate highway that linked Chicago with Los Angeles—lie the Native American reservation lands of the Havasupai and Hualapai tribes, with access to remote areas of the Grand Canyon far from the busy South Rim. Some 80mi southeast of the South Rim is cool, high-country Flagstaff, the region's biggest city. Nearby are the San Francisco Peaks, rising to 12,633ft at Humphreys Peak. The 30mi drive south from Flagstaff to Sedona, descending through the forests and famed red-rock scenery of Oak Creek Canyon, is brief but captivating. Sedona has lured artists and other creative types for a century. Northeast of Sedona, occupying nearly one-sixth of the state of Arizona, are the Navajo and Hopi Indian reservations. The Navajo is the largest US Indian reservation; within it are revered locales such as Canyon de Chelly and Monument Valley, plus numerous ancient Indian ruins. Immediately south of the reservation is Petrified Forest National Park and the Painted Desert, a subtly colorful wilderness.

Grand Canyon National Park

© iStockphoto.com/Ryan Morgan

GRAND CANYON NATIONAL PARK★★★

MAP PP 212-213
MOUNTAIN STANDARD TIME

If any single landscape feature symbolizes the United States in the minds of world travelers, it is Arizona's Grand Canyon.

- **Information:** ☎928-638-7888, www.nps.gov/grca.
- ▶ **Orient Yourself:** Though they are separated by just 10 miles as the crow flies, driving from South Rim to North Rim encompasses more than 200 miles and five hours.
- **Parking:** The lots at Grand Canyon Village on the South Rim fill up early on summer days.
- **Don't Miss:** It's worth the walk to one of the less-crowded viewpoints to quietly experience the sense of infinity the canyon engenders.
- **Organizing Your Time:** Perhaps the best way to visit the Grand Canyon is to drive to the South Rim early (arriving by 8 a.m.), then get on the road to the North Rim before noon for an overnight stay there.
- **Especially for Kids:** Grand Canyon Railway
- **Also See:** North Rim's Bright Angel Point

Geological Notes

Waters from seven western states—Arizona, Utah, New Mexico, Colorado and Wyoming, plus Nevada and California below the Grand Canyon—drain into the mighty Colorado River, 1,450mi long from its source in Colorado's Rocky Mountains to Mexico's Gulf of California.

This is not the world's deepest canyon. In North America alone, there are deeper chasms in Mexico (Copper Canyon), California (Kings Canyon) and the Pacific Northwest (Hells Canyon). Older rocks may be found in northern Canada and elsewhere. But the Grand Canyon of the Colorado River is known throughout the world for its spectacular landscape and its special, almost mystical characteristics.

At dawn and dusk, the low-angle sun highlights the vividly colored canyon walls. Bands of green, blue, purple, pink, red, orange, gold, yellow and white define a succession of exposed ancient rock layers. It is one of the most extreme cases of erosion anywhere, and a site where visitors feel humbled by the relentless sculpting power of nature.

A Bit of History

The Grand Canyon has been inhabited for at least 4,000 years, as evidenced by artifacts of the Desert Archaic culture, found in niches in the canyon walls. By AD 500, the Ancestral Puebloan culture was established. About 2,000 sites, including petroglyphs, have been found within park boundaries; most impressive is Tusayan Pueblo (c.1185) on the South Rim. These ancestors of the modern Hopi left the canyon by the late 13C, to be replaced by the forebears of the Hualapai and Havasupai, who today inhabit the western canyon.

The earliest European visit was by Francisco Vásquez de Coronado's gold-hungry 1540 expedition. In 1869 a one-armed Civil War veteran named John Wesley Powell led an expedition of nine men in small wooden boats down the canyon. Six men survived the journey through uncharted rapids, including Powell, who was at times lashed by ropes to his boat for safety. Two years later, the fearless Powell led a second expedition. Late-19C mining efforts in the canyon generally failed, but they opened the doors for a tourism industry. The first rim-top hotels were little more

Address Book

For price ranges, see the Legend on the cover flap.

WHERE TO STAY IN THE GRAND CANYON REGION

$$$$ L'Auberge de Sedona – *301 L'Auberge Ln., Sedona, AZ.* ☎928-282-1661 or 800-90-5745. *www. lauberge.com. 100 rooms and cottages.* The main lodge's huge rolling logs and stone columns blend into the chiseled buttes and spires of Sedona's geology. The 33 cottages, on the other hand, have a country-French feel. Eleven acres of botanical gardens are joined to the award-winning creekside **L'Auberge Restaurant ($$$)** by paths that wind past fruit trees and lilacs.

$$$-$$$$ Enchantment Resort – *520 Boynton Canyon Rd., Sedona, AZ.* ☎928-282-2900 or 800-826-4180. *www.enchantmentresort.com. 266 rooms.* Low-profile, adobe-style casitas, with beehive fireplaces and private balconies, are nestled in the red rocks of Boynton Canyon. The spa offers restorative Native American earth-clay wraps. Diners enjoy rack of lambwith a pistachio crust at the award-winning **Yavapai Restaurant ($$$)**, which has a 180-degree panoramic view.

$$$ Goulding's Lodge – *2mi west of US-163, Monument Valley, UT.* ☎435-727-3231. *www.gouldings.com. 62 rooms.* Set against ancient cliffs facing mystical Monument Valley, this outpost of civilization got its start in 1923 when Harry and Mike Goulding established a trading post. It grew to provide lodging, meals and tours as well as to serve Navajo tribespeople; the role it played in many Hollywood movies is recounted in a small museum.

$$$ El Tovar Hotel – *1 Main St., Grand Canyon, AZ.* ☎928-638-2631 or 888-297-2757. *www.grandcanyonlodges. com. 78 rooms.* Native stone and heavy pine logs create the atmosphere of an old European hunting lodge, and the views are out of this world: El Tovar has offered perspective on the Grand Canyon since 1905. Fresh Atlantic salmon, flown in daily, is a highlight of the Dining Room.

$$ La Posada – *303 E. 2nd St., Winslow, AZ.* ☎928-289-4366. *www .laposada. org. 21 rooms.* Fred Harvey used his Santa Fe Railroad to civilize the West with silverware and china, and La Posada was his last (1930) and most elegant hotel. Designed as a Spanish hacienda, with garden, ballroom and arcade, it was a favorite retreat for Hollywood stars and a popular stop on Route 66. Closed for 40 years; it reopened in 1997; restoration work is ongoing. Rooms don't have phones, but they do have baths and cable TV.

$$ Hotel Monte Vista – *100 N. San Francisco St., Flagstaff, AZ.* ☎928-779-6971 or 800-545-3068. *www. hotelmontevista.com. 50 rooms.* Guest rooms at this four-story remnant of the Roaring Twenties are named after some of the famous folks who once stayed here: Teddy Roosevelt, Humphrey Bogart, BobHope, Clark Gable, Carole Lombard, Jane Russell. Live bands still perform in its lounge, in the heart of Flagstaff's historic district.

WHERE TO EAT IN THE GRAND CANYON REGION

$$$ Cottage Place – *126 W. Cottage Ave., Flagstaff, AZ.* ☎928-774-8431. *www. cottageplace.com. Dinner only. Closed Mon.* **Continental**. Lodged in a beautiful 1909 bungalow home, this longtime restaurant (since 1980) brings a touch of Europe to Northern Arizona. Diners may start with brie en croute or escargots; then progress to Dijon-crusted salmon, pork schnitzel or a vegetarian asparagus risotto.

$$$ The Heartline Cafe – *1610 W. US-89A, Sedona, AZ.* ☎928-282-0785. *www.heartlinecafe.com.* **Regional.** Named for the Zuni bear fetish symbolizing health, long life and good luck, this eclectic but highly regarded restaurant has won regional acclaim. Menu items include tea-smoked duck salad, sautéed Cajun shrimp and pistachio-crusted chicken.

$$$ René at Tlaquepaque – *Rte. 179 at Oak Creek, Sedona, AZ.* ☎928-282-9225. *www.rene-sedona.com.* **Continental**. An institution in the Tlaquepaque Arts and Crafts Village, René is famed for its baked French onion soup and its sig-nature rack of lamb, carved tableside. Other favorites are Dover sole, sweet-potato ravioli, and flambéed cherries jubilee.

$ Junction Restaurant – *US-191 & Tribal Rd. 7, Chinle, AZ.* 🅿 ☎928-674-5874. www.bestwesternarizona.com. **Regional.** This otherwise nondescript restaurant in a Best Western motel focuses its menu on such traditional Navajo dishes as beef stew and Navajo tacos with homemade fry bread.

than mining camps. Guided mule trips took visitors to the canyon floor.

Not until 1919 was it set aside as a park. Much credit goes to the Fred Harvey Company, which built railroad hotels and restaurants throughout the South-west. Tourism began in earnest with the 1905 completion of the El Tovar Hotel, the most elegant in the West. Designer Mary Colter conceived many of the Harvey buildings, including the canyon-floor Phantom Ranch (1922), and the Bright Angel Lodge (1935). Most were staffed by "Harvey Girls," well-dressed and educated young women, usually from the East; the "Girls" are gone, but the lodges continue to serve visitors.

In its first year as a national park, 44,000 people visited the Grand Canyon. Today, about 5 million tourists enter the park each year. Their impact on the environ-ment has led the National Park Service to contemplate dramatic action to protect the Canyon for future generations, and to establish a model that likely will be adapted at other US national parks. Shuttle buses, operating along the South Rim and out West Rim Drive, attempt to ease traffic congestion.

Sights

South Rim★★★
Kids ⁞⁞⁞⁞

Most visitor activities in Grand Canyon National Park are focused along a 35mi strand of paved road that extends from the East Rim Entrance Station (29mi west of US-89 at Cameron) to Hermits Rest.

Grand Canyon Village
⚠✕♿🅿

Site of park headquarters, the main visi-tor center and the lion's share of historic hotels, restaurants and tourist facilities within the park, this community links

East Rim and West Rim drives with Wil-liams (56mi south via Rte. 64) and Flag-staff (80mi southeast via US-180).

The **Grand Canyon Village Historical District**★ comprises nine buildings, including the El Tovar Hotel, Hopi House, Bright Angel Lodge and Lookout Studio. Trains still arrive at the **Santa Fe Rail-way Station** (1909, Francis Wilson). Perched on the rim west of the Bright Angel Lodge is the **Kolb Brothers Studio** (1904). The two brothers pho-tographed tourists descending by mule into the canyon, processed the film at Indian Garden, 4.5mi (by trail) and 4,000ft below the rim, and one would run back uphill in time to sell the photos to returning visitors. The building is now a bookstore and art gallery.

A mile east of the visitor center, itself east of the historical district, the **Yava-pai Observation Station** acts as a sort of geology museum. Exhibits focus on the Grand Canyon's fossil record; guided geology walks depart several times daily. The **Rim Trail** *(9.4mi)* extends gently west from here to Hermits Rest, its first 2.7mi (to Maricopa Point) paved and highly accessible.

West Rim Drive (Hermit Road)★★
March 1 to November 30, only free shuttle buses ply this 8mi road west from Grand Canyon Village. The drive passes **viewpoints**★★★ at Maricopa Point, the John Wesley Powell Memo-rial, Hopi Point, Mohave Point and Pima Point before ending at **Hermits Rest**★, named for a 19C prospector, loner Louis Boucher.

East Rim Drive★★★
The 24mi road from Grand Canyon Vil-lage to the East Rim Entrance Station passes numerous dizzying viewpoints, including Yaki, Grandview, Moran and Lipan Points. A small pueblo ruin marks

the **Tusayan Ruin and Museum**★, 20mi east of the village. Displays trace the culture of pueblo-dwelling Ancestral Puebloans in the Grand Canyon region prior to the 13C.

The **Desert View Watchtower**★, 22mi from Grand Canyon Village, may be the most photographed structure in the park. Modeled after an ancient Pueblo lookout, the three-story building is dominated by a circular 70ft tower that commands expansive **views**★★★ of the convoluted canyon and Colorado River far below. The Painted Desert appears on the far eastern horizon.

Canyon Floor Trails★

From Grand Canyon Village, the depth of the Grand Canyon—South Rim to canyon floor—is about 5,000ft. The distance on foot, via any of several steep and narrow trails, is 7mi to 10mi. Most popular is the **Bright Angel Trail,** originating at Bright Angel Lodge in Grand Canyon Village. The trail descends 4,460ft in 9mi to the Colorado River at Phantom Ranch, which lodges adventurers in cabins or dormitories. The trail is recommended only for exceptionally fit individuals. Hikers are strongly advised not to try hiking to the river and back to the rim in a single day. An option for descending to the canyon floor is by commercial **trail ride** on the back of a mule: one day down, one day back *(reservations, booked well in advance:* ☎ *888-297-2757, www.grand-canyonlodges.com).*

More than a dozen different concessionaires offer guided rafting trips in a range of distances and vessel sizes. Bookings are essential months in advance. Trips can be as short as two days and as long as three weeks.

North Rim★★

Open May 15–Oct 16, weather permitting.
△✕&🅿

The drive from Grand Canyon Village (South Rim) to Grand Canyon Lodge on the North Rim *(Rte. 64 east to Cameron, US-89 north to Marble Canyon, US-89A west to Jacob Lake, then Rte. 67 south)* leads to a part of the park far less developed than the South Rim. It has the feel of a wilderness outpost cloaked in pine forest, rather than a crowded resort village. At 7,700-8,800ft above sea level, it is about 1,200ft higher than the South Rim; and it is several degrees cooler, with midsummer temperatures averaging in the high-70s (Fahrenheit) rather than mid-80s. To many visitors, the North Rim offers a connoisseur's experience of the Grand Canyon.

View From the West Rim Drive, Grand Canyon National Park

The North Rim visitor center, adjacent to the Grand Canyon Lodge complex, is a good place to get one's bearings. A paved .5mi trail leads from here to Bright Angel Point, with glorious **views**★★★ of the canyon. Also visible is the strenuous **North Kaibab Trail** *(14.2mi)*, which descends 5,840ft to Phantom Ranch. Day hikers should not venture beyond Roaring Springs (4.7mi each way), water source for the entire Grand Canyon National Park. Full- and half-day mule trips are available from the North Rim, but do not descend all the way to the river.

The **Cape Royal Road**★ extends 23mi from the Grand Canyon Lodge southeast across the Walhalla Plateau to Vista Encantadora and Cape Royal, with a spur route to Point Imperial, the highest point on the canyon rim at 8,803ft.

Grand Canyon Railway★

233 N. Grand Canyon Blvd., Williams, 65mi south of Grand Canyon Village. ✕&🅿️☎ *928-635-4253. www.thetrain.com.*
The Atchison-Topeka-Santa Fe Railroad operated between Williams and the canyon from 1901 to 1968; service was re-established in 1989. Today the restored Grand Canyon Railway runs daily trips from the 1908 Williams Depot. The one-way trip takes 2hrs 15min, and is enlivened by strolling musicians and the antics of Wild West characters on board. It is a worthy alternative to driving and parking at the crowded South Rim.

Havasupai Indian Reservation

From I-40 at Seligman, 44mi west of Williams, drive 34mi northwest on Rte. 66, then 65mi north on Tribal Road 18 to Hualapai Hilltop. Supai is another 8mi by foot or mule. ⛺✕☎ *928-448-2121.*
The village of **Supai**, site of the Havasupai tribal center, is at the bottom of the Canyon, where the Havasupai have lived at least since the 16C. Several hundred tribal members continue to farm the fertile bottomlands and provide tourism services. Accessible only by foot, mule or helicopter, Supai has a small tourist lodge, a restaurant, several shops, a campground and a post office. Visitors can see the farms and livestock areas kept along Havasu Creek by the Havasupai, and hike to nearby distinctive turquoise-colored **waterfalls** pouring out of steep cliffs.

Hualapai Indian Reservation

From I-40 at Seligman (44mi west of Williams), drive 41mi northwest on Rte. 66 to Peach Springs. ⛺✕☎ *928-769-2216.*

© National Park Service

How the Grand Canyon Was Formed

In the earth's infancy, the area now defined by the Grand Canyon was covered by shallow coastal waters and accented by active volcanoes. Over millions of years, layers of marine sediment and lava built to depths thousands of feet thick. About 1.7 billion years ago, heat and pressure from within the earth buckled the sedimentary layers into mountains 5-6mi high, changing their composition to a metamorphic rock called Vishnu schist. Molten intrusions in the mountains' core cooled and hardened into pink granite. Then erosion took over, reducing the mountains to mere vestiges over millions of years.

The process repeated itself, another shallow sea covering the land, more layers of sediment—12,000ft thick—being laid down. A new mountain range formed; erosion again assaulted the peaks so thoroughly that only ridges remained and, in many places, the ancient Vishnu schist was laid bare.

The horizontal layers above the schist, to 3,500ft below the modern canyon rim, were formed over 300 million years as oceans advanced across the Southwest, perhaps as many as seven times, and each time regressed. The environment was alternately marsh and desert, subject to rapid erosion. The era coincided with the age of dinosaurs and concluded about 65 million years ago with the end of the Cretaceous period. Then the Colorado River began to cut the canyon, gouging through rock and soil and carrying the debris away to sea. As erosion thinned the layer of rock above the earth's core, lava spewed to the surface. In fact, there have been several periods of recent volcanic activity in the Grand Canyon area, most recently in the 11C at Sunset Crater, southeast of the park.

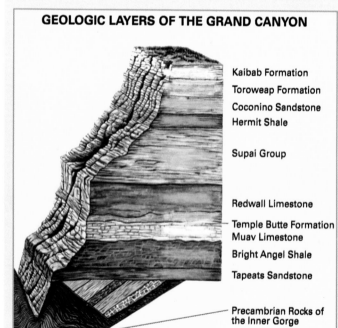

GEOLOGIC LAYERS OF THE GRAND CANYON

Kaibab Formation
Toroweap Formation
Coconino Sandstone
Hermit Shale

Supai Group

Redwall Limestone
Temple Butte Formation
Muav Limestone
Bright Angel Shale
Tapeats Sandstone

Precambrian Rocks of the Inner Gorge

Frank Sierra/National Park Service

The Hualapai control a 108mi-long portion of the South Rim, beginning about 50mi west of Grand Canyon Village. Here is the sensational **Grand Canyon Skywalk**★★ *(at Grand Canyon West; 877-716-9378, www.grandcanyonskywalk.com)*, a semicircular glass bridge that juts out over a side arm of the main canyon. Tribe members also operate bus tours and one- or two-day rafting trips on the Colorado River from Diamond Creek to Pearce Ferry. A permit, available in Peach Springs, is required for private car travel off Route 66.

FLAGSTAFF–SEDONA AREA★★

MAP PP 212-213
MOUNTAIN STANDARD TIME

Towering red-rock spires and buttes, and history-rich Native American sites, have long attracted visitors and new residents to these north-central Arizona towns. Flagstaff, established as a logging and livestock-ranching center, grew as a transportation hub—first for the railroad in 1882, later for auto travelers on historic Route 66. Today it is home to 58,000 people. Sedona, 28mi south, renowned for its wind- and water-sculpted scenery, is a magnet for artists, tourists and retirees. The cities are linked by spring-fed Oak Creek Canyon, a 1,200ft-deep gorge that descends 2,500ft down the southern escarpment of the vast Colorado Plateau.

- **Information:** ☎928-774-9541, www.flagstaffarizona.org; ☎928-282-7722, www.sedonachamber.com.
- **Don't Miss:** Oak Creek Canyon
- **Especially for Kids:** Slide Rock State Park.
- **Also See:** Montezuma Castle

A Bit of History

Redwall Limestone, the first stratum of sedimentary rock exposed in the red-rock formations, began to form 330 million years ago when seawater blanketed the area. The basaltic lava that caps the walls of Oak Creek Canyon was the result of volcanic activity 7 million years ago. Hunter-gatherer groups of Paleo-Indians probably occupied the region as early as 11,000 years ago. Over the centuries, various tribes, including the Hohokam and Sinagua, thrived here. In modern times, the Yavapai and Tonto Apaches made this area their home.

Flagstaff traces its history to 1876, when New England immigrants attached a US flag to the top of a tall, trimmed pine tree to honor their nation on Independence Day. That original flagstaff became a trail marker for westbound travelers. The opening in 1899 of Northern Arizona Normal School (now University) cemented the town's future. In the 1950s and '60s, Flagstaff was a key stop on historic Route 66, the "Mother Road" that ran 2,000mi from Chicago to Los Angeles in the days before the interstate highway system. A strip of neon motels, mom-and-pop cafes and "last-chance-for-gas" truck stops recalls that era.

Settlers trickled into Oak Creek Canyon after the first homesteader set up housekeeping in 1876, but by 1900 there were only about 20 families in the area. Sedona evolved after World War II into a destination that is part resort town, part artist colony and part retirement center. Today the town accommodates some 11,000 permanent residents and attracts about 2.5 million tourists each year.

Sights

Flagstaff★
I-40 & US-89. △✗⚐🅿
This city is the commercial hub for a huge and sparsely populated area. Within the boundaries of Coconino

County are Sedona, the Grand Canyon, Glen Canyon Dam, the western third of the Navajo Indian Reservation and three national monuments—Wupatki, Sunset Crater and Walnut Canyon.

From a visitor center in the 1926 Tudor Revival **railway station** (1 E. Rte. 66 at Leroux St.; ☎ 928-774-9541), walking tours depart for the downtown **historic district**, whose highlights include the 1889 Hotel Weatherford (23 N. Leroux St.). Seven sandstone structures on the **Northern Arizona University** campus (Kendrick St. & Ellery Ave., south of Butler Ave.; ☎ 928-523-9011, www.nau.edu), built between 1894 and 1935, are on the National Register of Historic Places. The 13,000sq ft **Riordan Mansion** (1300 Riordan Ranch St., east of Milton Rd.; visit by guided tour only, ☎ 928-779-4395, www.azparks.gov), 1904 home of two timber-baron brothers, features log siding, volcanic stone arches and Craftsman-style furniture.

Lowell Observatory★

Kids 1400 Mars Hill Rd. ♿ P ☎ 928-774-3358. www.lowell.edu.

Astronomer Percival Lowell established this facility in 1894, 1mi west of downtown Flagstaff. Here in 1930, Clyde Tombaugh discovered Pluto by photographing sections of the night sky at six-day intervals and looking for movements in the minuscule dots of light. Lowell's own 24in Clark refracting telescope is on display and in use during frequent nighttime sky-viewing sessions.

Museum of Northern Arizona★

Kids 3101 Fort Valley Rd. (US-180 North). ♿ P ☎ 928-774-5213. www.musnaz. org.

Well-considered exhibits provide an overview of southwestern Native American cultures, both ancient and modern, as well as an introduction to the geology, archaeology, anthropology and arts of northern Arizona.

Wupatki National Monument★

Sunset Crater-Wupatki Rd., east of US-89, 33mi northeast of Flagstaff. ♿ P ☎ 928-679-2365. www.nps.gov/wupa.

Hundreds of Pueblo-style masonry ruins are spread across this vast volcanic plain, remains of a Sinagua farming community that lived here 800 years ago. The highlight of the 55sq-mi preserve is the **Wupatki Ruins**, accessible from an overlook or a .5mi trail. The extraordinary site includes a 100-room pueblo, ball court and amphitheater.

Sunset Crater Volcano National Monument★

Sunset Crater-Wupatki Rd., east of US-89, 14mi northeast of Flagstaff. ♿ P ☎ 928-526-0502. www.nps.gov/sucr.

A 1,000ft-high cinder cone, which erupted in 1064, is surrounded by hundreds of acres of black lava flows and cinders, out of which sprouts an improbable pine forest. A 1mi trail skirts the base of the volcano. You cannot climb Sunset Crater itself, but trails access smaller, nearby cinder cones.

Walnut Canyon National Monument★

Walnut Canyon Rd., 3mi south of I-40, 7.5mi east of Flagstaff. ♿ P ☎ 928-526-3367. www.nps.gov/waca.

A set of Sinagua cliff dwellings, occupied from the early 12C to mid-13C, are built into the 350ft-high walls of Walnut Creek canyon. Most ruins are well below the canyon rim, nestled in alcoves in the overhanging rock. The **Island Trail** (.9mi) requires a degree of high-altitude fitness, but visitors who descend 185 ft (via 240 steps) are rewarded with the chance to crawl through two dozen ancient dwellings.

Meteor Crater★

Meteor Crater Rd., 8mi south of I-40, 38mi east of Flagstaff. ╳♿ P ☎ 928-289-2362. www.meteorcrater.com.

The best-preserved meteor impact site on earth was created 50,000 years ago. A relatively small meteorite, 150ft in diameter, left a hole 570ft deep and nearly 1mi across when it crashed into the earth; a .8mi trail (by guided tour only) now follows the crater rim. The **Museum of Astrogeology** has interactive displays on meteors and the threat of collisions with earth, and an **Astronaut Hall of Fame** honors space pioneers who once trained in the crater's virtual moonscape.

Oak Creek Canyon★★

Take US-89A south 14mi from Flagstaff to Oak Creek Vista to begin scenic drive. Note: The two-lane highway is often crowded with traffic. Drivers are cautioned to be patient; passing other vehicles may be difficult or dangerous.

Oak Creek began cutting its gorge into a fault line about 1 million years ago. Today a beautiful 14mi scenic drive plunges more than 2,000ft through a steep-walled, 1,200ft-deep canyon, about a mile wide. The main descent begins at **Oak Creek Vista★★** (elevation 6,400ft) with a dramatic 2mi series of switchbacks. Stunning views down the gorge encompass forests of ponderosa pine and fir trees crowning the Mogollon Rim.

The creek pours over tiers of smooth sandstone at **Slide Rock State Park★** Kids *(8mi north of Sedona; ☎ 520-282-3034, www.azparks.gov),* a hugely popular swimming hole on hot summer days. Just outside Sedona, the road skirts the banks of sparkling Oak Creek (elevation 4,300ft), where ash, cottonwood, sycamore, willow and walnut thrive.

Sedona★★

US-89A & Rte. 179. △✕⟊Ⓟ ☎ *928-282-7722. visitsedona.com*

This small city, its economy based upon tourism and the arts, owes its mystique to the variety of striking red buttes and spires that surround it. It is located in the heart of **Red Rock Country★★★**, bounded by Oak Creek and Sycamore Canyons, the Mogollon Rim and Verde Valley. The region takes its name from rust color exposed in three mid-level sandstone strata sculpted between 270 million and 300 million years ago.

Maps of the Sedona area identify such landmarks as Cathedral Rock, Bell Rock and Boynton Canyon. In the 1980s, some of these sites were identified as "vortices," where energy emanates from the earth. Sedona's red rocks have become a beacon for the New Age, attracting visitors seeking spiritual enlightenment. *(Vortex tours are offered by several local enterprises; contact the Sedona Metaphysical Spiritual Association, www. sedonaspiritual.com.)*

To experience Red Rock Country up close, you'll need sturdy hiking boots or a four-wheel-drive vehicle. Several companies provide off-road **Jeep tours** to vista points, vortices, wildflower meadows, Sinagua ruins and other sites. If you are driving yourself, the most convenient backcountry access is via **Schnebly Hill Road★** *(off Rte. 179, across the Oak Creek bridge from the US-89A "Y" junction).* This 12mi road—pavement gives way to rutted dirt after the first mile—rewards visitors with stunning **views★★★** of red-rock formations and a panorama that spans the valley below. Sedona's original commercial core is called not "downtown" but **Uptown.** Just north of the "Y" intersection on US-89A, a plethora of shops and galleries in Old West-style structures offer everything from Native American crafts to New Age items. Down the hill on Route 179 sits **Tlaquepaque Arts & Crafts Village** *(☎ 928-282-4838, www. tlaq.com),* a charming shopping complex modeled after the village of San Pedro de Tlaquepaque in Guadalajara, Mexico. Narrow passageways and tiled plazas are planted with profusions of bright flowers and shaded by venerable sycamore trees.

Chapel of the Holy Cross★

End of Chapel Rd. off Rte. 179, 7mi south of uptown Sedona. ⟊Ⓟ ☎ *928-282-4069. www.chapeloftheholycross.com.*

This awe-inspiring contemporary Catholic chapel was completed in 1956 (Anshen & Allen), the brainchild of local artist and rancher Marguerite Brunswig Staude. Characterized by its cruciform shape, the concrete aggregate-and-glass chapel rises 90ft from the base of a red-rock butte.

Tuzigoot National Monument★

Tuzigoot Rd. off Rte. 279, Clarkdale; 23mi southwest of Sedona via US-89A to Cottonwood. ⟊Ⓟ ☎ *928-634-5564. www. nps.gov/tuzi.*

Occupied from 1000 to 1400, this ancient Sinagua pueblo tops a ridge 120ft above the Verde River. At its height in the late 1300s, Tuzigoot (Apache for "crooked water") was home to about 225 people, who lived in 86 ground-floor rooms and perhaps 15 second-story rooms, and farmed the fertile valley. Limestone and sandstone boulders, bound together with mud mortar, formed the pueblo's walls. Modern visitors, following a gently sloping .25mi trail, may enter several rooms to glimpse how the Sinaguans lived. Artifacts in the visitor center help interpret cultural practices.

Jerome★

US-89A, 29mi southwest of Sedona. ✕♿🅿 ☎ *928-634-2900. www.jerome-chamber.com.* Clinging precariously to the slope of Cleopatra Hill, 2,000ft above the adjacent plain, Jerome began as a rough-and-tumble mining camp in 1876. One of the world's richest veins of copper ore—more than $4 billion worth was extracted—had the community flourishing by the early 20C. In the late 1920s, population stood at 15,000, but then Jerome went into a steady decline until the last mine closed in 1953.

Today the town has 470 residents, 300 historic structures and a handful of artisans' galleries along its winding streets. Booklets for self-guided tours are available at the visitor information trolley on Hull Avenue.

Exhibits at **Jerome State Historic Park★** *(Douglas Rd.;* ☎ *928-634-5381, www.azparks.gov),* in a 1916 adobe mansion built for mine owner "Rawhide Jimmy" Douglas, explore town history.

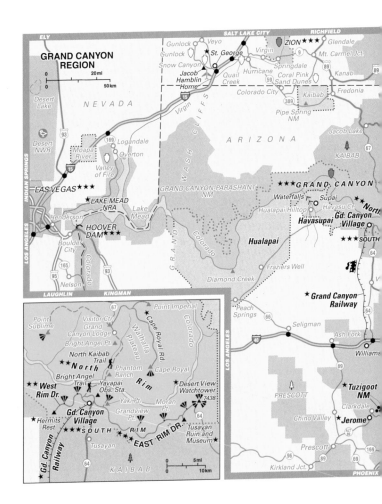

Montezuma Castle National Monument★

Montezuma Rd., Camp Verde, 1mi east of I-17 Exit 289. ♿ 🅿 ☎ *928-567-3322. www. nps.gov/moca.*

Impossibly tucked into a natural limestone alcove 50-100ft above the floor of Beaver Creek, Montezuma Castle was part of a larger early-12C Sinaguan community. The five-story, 20-room "castle" was misnamed by Europeans, who presumed it had been constructed for 16C Aztec emperor Montezuma.

Not intended as a fortress, the dwelling's location protected its occupants from the elements and supplied natural insulation against heat and cold. Nor did it take up valuable farmland.

©National Park Service

Montezuma Castle T-shaped Entrance

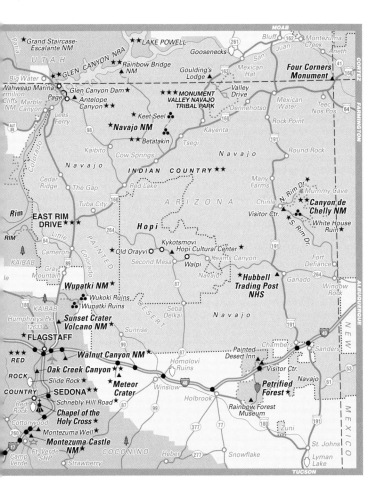

INDIAN COUNTRY★★

MAP PP 212-213
MOUNTAIN STANDARD TIME

The largest of all Native American enclaves, the Navajo Indian Reservation covers more than 27,000sq mi of mountains, forests, buttes, mesas and other wide-open desert spaces whose imagery is so often associated with the Southwest. The reservation mainly cloaks northeastern Arizona, though small portions extend into southeastern Utah and northwestern New Mexico.

- **Information:** ☎623-412-0297, www.explorenavajo.com
- ▶ **Orient Yourself:** Both the Hopi and Navajo nations are sovereign entities with their own laws and customs--please be sure to observe these, such as the alcohol ban on reservation lands.
- **Don't Miss:** Monument Valley.
- **Also See:** Canyon de Chelly.

Most tribal land is open range. The Navajo—descended from nomadic hunter-gatherers, who migrated around 1600 to the Four Corners area after the disappearance of the earlier Ancient Puebloan and Sinagua cultures—have raised sheep on isolated homesteads for centuries. The wool produces the distinctive Navajo rug and blanket weavings renowned around the world.

After the Mexican War gave the US control of the Southwest, Navajo raids induced the Army to invade tribal lands. In 1863-64, troops razed the earth, destroying homes and crops, killing people and livestock. The 8,500 survivors were marched nearly 300mi to a reserve in eastern New Mexico, a tragic ordeal etched firmly in Navajo memory as the "Long Walk." But the Army's plan to turn nomadic herdsmen into sedentary farmers failed, and in 1868, the Navajo were allowed to return to their own land with enough sheep to start anew.

About 100,000 Navajo live on their reservation today; a similar number have left to seek work in towns and cities. Many who remain continue to ranch tribal lands and speak the Navajo language, a complicated tongue used during World War II as an unbreakable code against the Japanese.

It is common on the reservation to see contemporary homes with satellite dishes and new cars. Alongside these often stands at least one hogan, a traditional round log-and-adobe structure. Hogans always face east to greet the sunrise.

Surrounded by the Navajo Reservation is the 2,400sq mi **Hopi Indian Reservation,** home to about 10,000 descendants of the Ancient Puebloan peoples. Arizona's only Pueblo tribe (most are in New Mexico), the Hopi live in 12 villages, most on a trio of 6,000ft mesas. Masters of dryland farming, the Hopi have lived here since the 11C; they remain perhaps the most traditional of any Native American tribe. Their devotion to the spiritual world is reflected in their carvings of colorful kachinas, benevolent cloud dwellers supplicated for rain, good crops and a harmonious life. (Hopi means "people of peace.")

Both the Navajo and the Hopi are sovereign entities within Arizona and the United States. Tourists are welcome on reservations; however, *alcohol is strictly prohibited--do not bring any on tribal land*. Because there is no private land ownership, and nearly all reservation land is part of someone's traditional use area, off-road travel requires special permission.

Sights

Navajo National Monument★
Rte. 564, 10mi north of US-160, 21mi west of Kayenta. △ P ☎ *928-672-2700. www.nps.gov/nava.*

Two of the finest Ancient Puebloan ruins are located here at 7,300ft in little-visited Tsegi Canyon. The 135 rooms of **Betatakin**★★ ("ledge house"), late-13C home of a community of 100, nestle into a huge, south-facing alcove in a sandstone cliff. **Keet Seel**★ ("remains of square houses"), occupied about AD 950 to 1300, was larger (160 rooms) and probably was home to 150.

From a visitor center and museum, a steep trail *(.5mi)* leads to a spectacular overlook of Betatakin, across a narrow canyon. The only way to visit the ruins up close is on a ranger-led hike *(5mi round-trip)*, offered daily *(May–Sept)* to 20-25 visitors on a first-come, first-served basis. Keet Seel, an overnight trek, is an arduous 8.5mi each way *(60-day advance reservations recommended)*.

Monument Valley Navajo Tribal Park★★★

Tribal Rd. 42, 4mi east of US-163, 24mi north of Kayenta. ⚠🏕🚻♿🅿 ☎ *435-727-3353. www.navajonationparks.org.*

To many, Monument Valley represents the essence of the American Southwest conveyed in movies, commercials and print ads. The distinctive landscape—Tse' Bii' Ndzisgaii to the Navajo—covers 150sq mi on both sides of the Arizona-Utah border. Massive sandstone monoliths rise up to 1,000ft from a relatively flat desert floor. In early morning or late afternoon, the low sun highlights the red color of the rock.

The unpaved, 17mi **Valley Drive**, for high-clearance or four-wheel-drive vehicles only, loops through the park and past many of its most prominent features, including The Mittens, Elephant Butte, Camel Butte, The Thumb and the Totem Pole. Other monoliths like Sentinel Mesa, Castle Butte and The King on His Throne are easily viewed from the visitor center. Guided Jeep and horseback tours reach parts of Monument Valley that are off-limits to private vehicles, including several Navajo homesteads and isolated petroglyphs.

Hollywood director John Ford set many of his Western movies here, beginning with *Stagecoach* in 1938. Ford cast John Wayne as his star in such movies as *Fort Apache* (1948) and *She Wore a Yellow Rib-* *bon* (1949). Visiting production crews are often seen today. At **Goulding's Lodge** *(Goulding's Rd., 2mi west of US-163 in Utah;* ☎ *435-727-3231, www.gouldings. com),* where Ford's crews were based, a small museum surveys the film history of the area.

Four Corners Monument

1mi north of US-160, 11.5mi northeast of Teec Nos Pos. 🅿

The point at which Arizona, New Mexico, Colorado and Utah converge is covered by a cement slab bearing each state seal.

Canyon de Chelly National Monument★★

Tribal Rds. 7 & 64, 3mi east of US-191 at Chinle. ⚠🏕🚻♿🅿 ☎ *928-674-5500. www. nps.gov/cach.*

This 130sq mi park holds two scenic canyon networks framed by sheer cliff walls. In the fertile canyon bottoms lie at least nine major ruins dating from AD 350 to 1300.

The reddish cliffs rise just 30ft above the Chinle Wash at the meeting of the canyons—26mi-long Canyon de Chelly *(SHAY)* to the south, 25mi-long Canyon del Muerto to the north. Miles upstream, they climb as high as 1,000ft above canyon floors that are often covered in water. Modern Navajo farmers plow fields and graze cattle and sheep alongside the ancient ruins.

Perhaps better than any other site, Canyon de Chelly reveals the historical range of Southwest Indian culture. Archaeologists have unearthed evidence of the earliest Archaic Indians and ensuing Basketmakers. After the Ancient Puebloans (11-13C) disappeared around 1350, their Hopi descendants moved in during the 14-15C. Navajo have been farming here since the 17C.

From the **visitor center** *(Tribal Rds. 7 & 64),* which offers a small museum and a 22min video presentation, two self-guided drives trace the canyon rims. The 16mi **South Rim Drive**★ *(Tribal Rd. 7)* is more traveled. From its White House Overlook, a trail *(1.3mi)* descends 600ft to the multistory **White House Ruin**★, an Ancient Puebloan site and the only ruin that may be visited without an official guide. The 15mi **North Rim Drive**★ *(Tribal Rd. 64)* overlooks such sites as Antelope House, named for late-7C paintings found near a Basketmaker pit house, and Mummy Cave, continuously occupied by various cultures for 1,000 years. Each drive takes about 2hrs to complete.

Tours by Jeep, horseback or foot, guided by Navajo locals, provide a more in-depth understanding of the canyons' cultural and natural history, as well as the opportunity to visit more ruins and to meet Navajos farming the canyon.

Hubbell Trading Post National Historic Site★

Rte. 264, 1mi west of Ganado. ♿ 🅿 ☎ *928-755-3254. www.nps.gov/hutr.*

The oldest continuously operating trading post on the Navajo Reservation was established in 1878 by John Lorenzo Hubbell. He provided his Navajo clientele with items they couldn't make, such as sugar and coffee, and matches, nails and shovels, in exchange for rugs and blankets, silverwork and turquoise jewelry.

Visitors today still can buy a good shovel or a cold drink, as well as rugs and saddles, jewelry and carved wooden kachina dolls. Navajo weavers demonstrate traditional techniques on looms in a visitor center.

Hopi Indian Reservation

Rte. 264 between Tuba City & Ganado. ⛺ 🍴 ♿ 🅿 ☎ *928-734-2441. www.hopibiz.com.*

The reservation's 12 principal villages are strung like desert pearls along Route 264 as it climbs over and around three sheer-walled mesas collectively known as Tuuwanasavi, "the center of the earth" in Hopi culture. **Old Orayvi**★, on the more westerly Third Mesa *(50mi east of Tuba City)*, was first occupied about 1100 and is presumed to be the oldest continuously inhabited village in the US. **Walpi**, on First Mesa *(19mi east of Old Orayvi)*, dates from about 1700. Both villages appear today as weathered dwellings of adobe and hand-hewn stone, though pickup trucks and TV antennae are signs of modern influence.

A good place for visitors to get their bearings is the modern **Hopi Cultural Center**★ *(Rte. 264, Second Mesa;* ☎ *520-734-2401, www.hopiculturalcenter.com).* The museum (attached to a 33-room inn) has excellent exhibits on Hopi history and lifestyle, and tribal artisans market their distinctive silver jewelry and wood carvings, including *kachinas.*

Highly traditional, the Hopi welcome visitors, but no photography, tape recording or even sketching may be done in the villages. Ceremonial dances, always of spiritual significance, may be open to visitors *(inquire locally);* they are announced only a week in advance, in accordance with ritual practices.

Excursion

Petrified Forest National Park★

I-40 Exit 311, 26mi east of Holbrook. 🍴 ♿ ☎ *928-524-6228. www.nps.gov/pefo.*

An immense and colorful concentration of petrified wood and fossils, more than 225 million years old, is spread over the striated, pastel-hued badlands of the Painted Desert.

The main park road runs 28mi between I-40 and US-180, making it an easy detour from the interstate. At its north end, the **Painted Desert Visitor Center** offers a 20min film and exhibits. Two miles up the road is the **Painted Desert Inn**, a national historical landmark, built in 1924. The structure was originally a trading post, then an inn for travelers; it's now a museum and gift shop.

Overlooks on the southbound road pass 13C Ancient Puebloan ruins and a landscape strewn with colorful petrified logs. The terrain is like a moonscape, with pastel bands of pink, yellow and golden sands, blue-and-gray badlands and bleak hills in stark streaks of black and white. Several short hikes access off-road areas. Removal of petrified wood or rock specimens is prohibited.

HAWAII

The very word "Hawaii" evokes romantic and magical images. The chain of 132 volcanic islands, many no more than rocky bird sanctuaries, stretches 1,600mi across the Pacific Ocean some 2,500mi southwest of Los Angeles, at a similar latitude to Mexico City. The eight principal islands are clustered at the south-eastern end of the archipelago, across a little more than 500mi.

Seven of the eight islands—with a total land area of 6,422sq mi—are inhabited. The largest and geologically youngest is Hawai'i, aka "The Big Island." O'ahu, home of Pearl Harbor and the state capital of Honolulu, is by far the most populated island, with more than 875,000 of the state's 1.28 million people.

Native Polynesians, the first of whom migrated to Hawai'i from the Marquesas Islands sometime after AD 400, simply called their world 'aina, the land, as opposed to kai, the sea. British Captain James Cook, the first European to sight the islands in 1778, named the archipelago the Sandwich Islands—after his sponsor, the Earl of Sandwich.

Hawaii

The Island of Hawaii was the home of King Kamehameha I (c.1758-1819), who united the other islands under his conquering rule. The monarchy lasted less than a century before pressure from Protestant missionaries, traders, whalers and sugar planters led to change. Briefly a republic (1893-98), Hawaii was annexed as a US territory in 1898 during the Spanish-American War.

The most dramatic 20C event was the 1941 Japanese bombing of Pearl Harbor, propelling the US directly into World War II. When the war ended, tourism on Waikiki Beach exploded; later other islands joined the boom. Hawaii became the 50th US state in 1959. Today, the amiable spirit of aloha—a term that can mean hello, goodbye, love or welcome—persists in the general good will of the people.

Orchids Grown in Hawaii for Making Leis

©iStockphoto.com/Scott Leigh

HONOLULU ★★

MAP P 223
HAWAIIAN STANDARD TIME
POPULATION 378,000

Honolulu sprawls across the southeast quadrant of the island of O'ahu. The world's largest Polynesian city is a bustling modern metropolis of skyscrapers and traffic, extending from Waikiki's surf-washed beaches to the 3,000ft crest of the jungle-swathed Ko'olau Range. Here the first missionaries gathered their Hawaiian congregations, the only royal palace in the US was erected, and eight decades of sun-worshipers have spread their beach towels.

- 🛈 **Information:** ☎808-524-0722, www.visit-oahu.com
- ▸ **Orient Yourself:** Small as Oahu is, its climate varies widely: the farther west you go from downtown Honolulu, the less rain.
- 😊 **Don't Miss:** The Bishop Museum.
- 🧒 **Especially for Kids:** Sea Life Park; Children's Discovery Center.

A Bit of History

Officially, all of O'ahu *(oh-AH-hoo)* is the City and County of Honolulu *(hoh-no-LOO-loo)*. But the 608sq-mi island is not entirely urbanized. There are fertile farms, mountain rain forests, and green vistas of pineapple and sugar fields. One-quarter of O'ahu's land is occupied by military bases representing more than 44,000 Army, Navy, Air Force and Marine personnel. Many are based at Pearl Harbor, a deep slot in the south-central coast of the island.

Across the Ko'olaus from Honolulu extends the lush Windward Coast of the island, with its suburban communities of Kailua and Kaneohe. West of Pearl Harbor is the drier Waianae Coast and the big-wave beaches of Makaha. A route through the agricultural center of O'ahu leads to the North Shore, fabled for its country living and renowned surfing venues like Sunset Beach and Waimea Bay.

Sights

Downtown Honolulu ★★
Honolulu Harbor to Vineyard Blvd. between Ward Ave. & River St.
While Waikiki, with its beach, hotels, restaurants and nightclubs, may be the traditional center of Hawaii's tourism industry, downtown Honolulu is the hub of history.

Mission Houses Museum ★★
553 S. King St. at Kawaiahao St. ☎808-531-0481. www.missionhouses.org.
The modest wood-frame house, oldest Western-style structure in Hawaii, was brought in pieces by ship around Cape Horn and assembled in 1821 by the first American Calvinist missionaries, with Hawaiian assistance.

Kawaiahao Church ★★
957 Punchbowl St. ♿ 🅿 ☎808-522-1333. *kawaiahao.org*
Designed by its first minister in 1837, this church was constructed of coral blocks cut and carried from a reef off Honolulu Harbor. The setting for 19C royal coronations, weddings and funerals is revered by isle residents. Visitors are welcome at the Sunday sermon, still given partly in the Hawaiian language.

Iolani Palace ★★
S. King & Richards Sts. ♿ 🅿 ☎808-522-0832. *www.iolanipalace.org.*
This rococo structure is the only royal palace in the US. King David Kalakaua, back from travels in Europe, erected it in 1882; its last royal occupant was Queen Liliuokalani, whose government was overthrown in 1893. Across King Street is a statue of **Kamehameha the Great** (Kamehameha I). A modern statue of

Address Book Hawaii

For price ranges, see the Legend on the cover flap.

WHERE TO STAY IN HAWAII

$$$$$ Four Seasons Hualalai – *100 Kaupulehu Dr.; Ka'upulehu-Kona, HI 96740 (Big Island).* ✕🔥📶🏊 Spa 📞 *808-325-8000 or 888-236-3026. www. fourseasons.com/hualalai. 243 rooms.* An intimate bungalow-style resort, this lush retreat melts easily into the natural environment. Guests swim in a saltwater pond to cool off after a round of golf or a full spa treatment. The Pacific-fusion specialty restaurant, **Pahui'a** (**$$$$**), focuses around an aquarium.

$$$$$ Grand Wailea Resort – *3850 Wailea Alanui, Wailea, HI 96753 (Maui).* ✕🔥📶🏊 Spa 📞 *808-875-1234 or 800-888-6100. www.grandwailea.com. 780 rooms.* A $30-million art collection greets visitors to this spectacular hotel on 40 beachfront acres. An elaborate spa, a poolside water playground, seven distinct tropical gardens and four nearby golf courses compete for visitor attention. The best of six restaurants is **Kincha ($$$$)**, serving Japanese food.

$$$$$ Halekulani – *2199 Kalia Rd., Honolulu, HI 96815 (O'ahu).* ✕🔥📶🏊 📞 *808-923-2311 or 800-367-2343. www. halekulani.com. 456 rooms.* One of the top hotels in the world, the graceful Halekulani presides over the shores of Waikiki Beach like an aging grande dame. Spacious rooms overlook the Pacific Ocean from towers as lofty as the clientele. The service is top-drawer. For dining, both **La Mer ($$$$)** and **Orchid's ($$$$)** are worth a visit.

$$$$$ (with meals) Kona Village Resort – *Queen Ka'ahumanu Hwy., Kailua-Kona, HI 96745 (Big Island).* ✕📶🏊 📞 *808-325-5555 or 800-367-5290. www.konavillage.com. 125 rooms.* Hammocks sway beneath coconut palms beside thatched-roof beachfront cottages. This Polynesian-style resort is a world unto itself, and there are no phones or TVs to disturb the reverie. Kids and parents kayak and windsurf by day and enjoy luaus in the oceanview restaurant by night.

$$$$$ Princeville Resort – *5520 Ka Haku Rd., Princeville, HI 96722 (Kaua'i).* ✕🔥📶🏊 📞 *808-826-9644 or 866-716-8110. www.princevillehotelhawaii.com. 252 rooms.* This huge resort commands a dramatic view over the rugged cliffs of Hanalei Bay on Kauai's north side. Every activity under the sun is offered, including visits to the legendary Na Pali coast. Dining is world-class.

$$$$$ The Royal Hawaiian – *2259 Kalakaua Ave., Honolulu, HI 96815 (O'ahu).* ✕🔥📶🏊 Spa 📞 *808-923-7311 or 866-716-8109. www.royal-hawaiian.com. 527 rooms.* The storied Pink Palace of the Pacific was a Hollywood playground when built in Spanish-Moorish style in 1927; today it retains its chic Art Deco-era sensibility. Luaus with Polynesian dances are staged weekly. The mai-tai is said to have been first created in the eponymous bar.

$$$$ Hilton Hawaiian Village Beach Resort & Spa – *2005 Kalia Rd., Honolulu, HI 96815 (O'ahu).* ✕🔥📶🏊 Spa 📞 *808-949-4321. www.hawaiian-village.hilton.com. 2,998 rooms.* The world's largest oceanfront hotel has five separate towers and myriad fine shops, restaurants and lounges. The immaculate grounds wrap around a lagoon, above which fireworks burst Friday evening. **Bali-by-the-Sea ($$$$)** and the **Golden Dragon ($$$)** offer fine dining, and the acclaimed Bishop Museum has a branch in the new Kalia Tower.

$$$$ Outrigger Waikiki on the Beach – *2335 Kalakaua Ave., Honolulu, HI 96815 (O'ahu).* ✕🔥📶🏊 Spa 📞 *808-923-0711 or 800-688-7444. www. outrigger.com. 530 rooms.* Flagship of a Pacific regional hotel group, this hotel offers such unexpected frills as classes in Hawaiian history, music and healing, and nightly showroom concerts by The Society of Seven. **Duke's Canoe Club ($$$)**, honoring early-20C sportsman Duke Kanahamoku, is the top restaurant/lounge.

$$$ Hana Hale Inn – *Uakea Rd. (P.O. Box 374), Hana, HI 96713 (Maui).* 🔥📶 📞 *808-248-7461. www.hanahaleinn.com. 6 rooms.* The units that make up this "House of Light" stretch along Hana Bay in a village-like setting, near an ancient

Hawaiian fish pond. Each of the charming units has a full kitchen and modern amenities in the heart of a Polynesian jungle.

$$$ Lahaina Inn – *127 Lahainaluna Rd., Lahaina, HI 96761 (Maui).* ✕ ☎ *808-661-0577 or 800-669-3444. www.lahainainn. com. 12 rooms.* Once a whaling town, Lahaina offers a charming counterpoint to the luxury hotels on much of Maui. This fine old inn, built as a mercantile in 1938, is the jewel of Lahaina, stuffed with antique wooden furniture and more than a couple of tall tales.

$$$ Waimea Plantation Cottages – *9400 Kaumualii Hwy., Waimea, HI 96796 (Kaua'i).* ✕ 🅿 🛏 Spa ☎ *808-338-1625 or 877-997-6667. www.waimea-plantation. com. 44 cottages.* Charming early-20C sugar workers' bungalows stretch among 27 acres of coconut groves along a black-sand beach on Kauai's west side. Units with full kitchens and televisions are perfect for families.

$$$ The Manoa Valley Inn – *2001 Vancouver Dr., Honolulu, HI 96822 (Oahu).* 🅿 ☎ *808-947-6019. www.manoavalleyinn. com. 7 rooms.* A 1919 post-Victorian in a lush neighborhood near the University of Hawaii, this charming bed-and-breakfast was restored in the late 1970s and filled with period antiques. All rooms feature four-poster beds; some share bathroom facilities.

$$$ Volcano House – *Crater Rim Drive, Hawaii Volcanoes National Park, Volcano, HI 96785 (Big Island).* ✕🅿 ☎ *808-967-7321. www.volcanohousehotel. com. 42 rooms.* This rustic lodge is the world's only hotel perched at the edge of an active volcano. Choose a crater-view room in the original building, rather than one in the newer extension. Ten camper cabins (⊜) are budget-priced.

WHERE TO EAT IN HAWAII

$$$$ Chef Mavro – *1969 S. King St., Honolulu (O'ahu).* ☎ *808-944-4714. www.chefmavro.com. Dinner only.* ◷ *Closed Mon.* **French-Hawaiian.** Owner-chef George Mavrothalassitis, a native of France's Provence region, has won acclaim for creative tasting menus that pair each item with wine. Diners enjoy prawn salad with hummus and cumin, sesame-crusted uku (snapper) with lotus root and enoki mushrooms, filet mignon Marseillaise, and unusual island sweets.

$$$ Indigo – *1121 Nu'uanu Ave., Honolulu (O'ahu).* ☎ *808-521-2900. www. indigo-hawaii.com.* ◷ *Closed Sun-Mon.* **Asian.** Owner-chef Glenn Chu, raised in a Taoist family in Manoa Valley, has designed an eclectic menu with entrées like Emperor Po's ginger ham shanks and grilled shrimp with Thai macadamia-nut pesto. A gong announces the chocolate volcano dessert. The restaurant and its popular Green Room lounge are near downtown Honolulu and old Chinatown.

$$$ Merriman's – *Opelo Plaza, 67-1227 Opelo Rd., Kamuela (Big Island).* ☎ *808-885-6822. www.merrimanshawaii. com.* **Hawaiian.** The home of modern Hawaiian cuisine, Merriman's boasts baby vegetables from the slopes of Waimea and mahimahi from the sea. Wok-charred ahi tuna is the signature dish of chef Peter Merriman, who draws on the varied cultural palette of Hawaiian people.

$$$ PacificO's – *505 Front St., Lahaina (Maui).* ☎ *808-667-4341. www.pacificomaui.com.* **Pacific Rim.** Delectable cuisine that ranges from tandoori-spiced seafood to peppered beef is served outdoors, under umbrellas, beside the crashing surf. Chef James McDonald's selections are tantalizing and artfully prepared—including a homemade ravioli with saffron coconut sauce.

$$$ Roy's Restaurant – *6600 Kalanianaole Hwy. Honolulu (O'ahu).* ☎ *808-396-7697. www.roys-restaurants.com.* **Hawaiian fusion.** Chef Roy Yamaguchi fires up dishes like opakapaka smothered in macadamia nut sauce to roasted duck with passion fruit. The first of Roy's 15 restaurants around the world, this two-level dining room overlooks the Pacific from the Hawaii-Kai area of Honolulu.

$$ Brennecke's Beach Broiler – *Poipu Beach (Kaua'i).* ☎ *808-742-7588. www. brenneckes.com.* **Seafood and Steak.** This casual, upbeat restaurant facing Poipu Beach Park, by a well-known surfing break, is noted for its fresh fish charbroiled over charcoal of native kiawe wood, similar to mesquite … and for its excellent salad bar. An integral surfing activity center offers a beachside deli. **$$ Keo's in Waikiki** – *2028 Kuhio Ave., Honolulu (O'ahu).* ☏ *808-951-9355. www.keosthaicuisine.com.* **Asian.** As Hawaii's preeminent Thai chef, Keo Sananikone helped launch the revolu-

tion in North American Thai restaurants in 1977. Of his five local restaurants, this is nearest to major hotels. The original, **Mekong I** *(1295 S. Beretania St.,* ☏ *808-591-8841, $$),* still holds its own.

Liliuokalani stands on the other side of the palace facing the capitol.

Queen Emma's Summer Palace★
2913 Pali Hwy. &♿P ☏*808-595-3167.*
Emma, wife of King Kamehameha IV, was of Hawaiian-British heritage and thus was an early symbol of cosmopolitanism in the isles. Royal Hawaiian and personal artifacts are displayed in her Victorian-era Nuuanu Valley retreat.

Hawaii State Capitol★
S. Beretania St. between Richards & Punchbowl Sts. ♿P ☏*808-586-0146. www.capitol.hawaii.gov.*
Designed and built in 1969, the capitol has pillars that resemble palm trees. The sloping exteriors of the House and Senate chambers project from a pool, reminiscent of volcanoes rising from the sea.

Honolulu Academy of Arts★
900 S. Beretania St. at Ward Ave. ✕♿P ☏ *808-532-8700. www.honolulua cademy.org.*
A few blocks east of the capitol, this airy building has open courtyards and an excellent collection of Asian art, including Japanese woodblocks presented by late author James Michener.

Aloha Tower★
1 Aloha Tower Dr. ✕♿P ☏*808-528-5700. www.alohatower.com.*
Once Hawaii's tallest building, this 10-story spire has greeted four generations of cruise-ship passengers since 1921. Permanently berthed at the nearby **Hawaii Maritime Center★** *(Pier 7, Honolulu Harbor;* ☏*808-523-6151, www. holoholo.org/maritime/)* is the 19C sailing ship *Falls of Clyde,* a 266ft-long, four-masted square-rigger. Pier 7 is home berth to the *Hokule'a,* a 60ft replica of

Hawaiian Coastline with Volcanic Outcroppings

© PhotoDisc, Inc

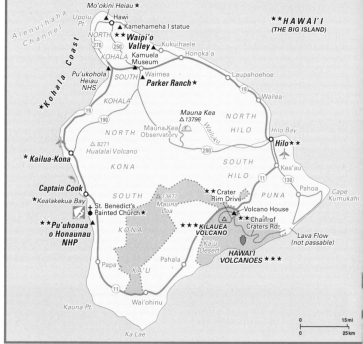

an ancient Polynesian canoe that has made numerous voyages to and from Tahiti since it was built in 1976.

Between the harbor and Waikiki, just off Ala Moana Boulevard, the **Hawaii Children's Discovery Center** (Kids 111 Ohe St; ☎808-524-5437, www.discovery centerhawaii.com) focuses on the islands' wide ethnic diversity. Interactive exhibits allow kids to explore their own bodies and learn what being an adult entails.

Waikiki★★

Ala Wai Canal to Diamond Head, east of the Ala Wai Yacht Harbor.

Once a lounging place for Hawaiian royalty, the 2mi-long suburb of Waikiki (literally, "spouting water") is recognized by the forest of towers created by its hotels. **Waikiki Beach★★★** remains one of the best places in the world to learn surfing, a sport invented here hundreds of years ago. At Waikiki Beach Center stands a statue of **Duke Kahanamoku** *(Kalakaua Ave. near Kaiulani Ave.),* Hawaii's three-time Olympic

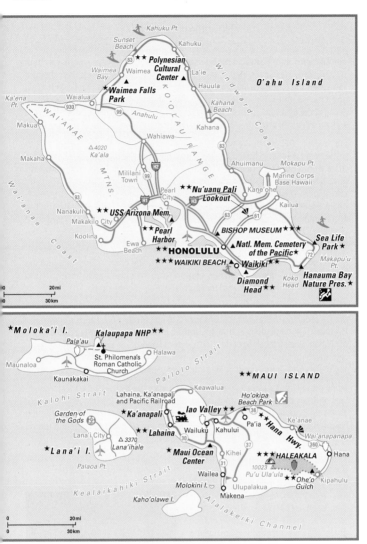

swimming champion (1912-20), who introduced surfing to California and Australia. Non-surfers may ride the waves in an outrigger canoe or take a cruise on a sailboat that casts off right from the shoreline. Opposite the beach, visitors browse through small shops and stands in the **International Market Place** ★ (2330 Kalakaua Ave.; ☎808-971-2080), under and around the same giant banyan tree for half a century.

The **Moana Hotel** ★ (2365 Kalakaua Ave.; ☎ 808-922-3111, www.moana-surfrider.com), now enshrouded in the Sheraton Moana-Surfrider, has been restored to 1901 Victorian elegance. The **Royal Hawaiian** ★ (2259 Kalakaua Ave.; ☎808-931-7194, www.royal-hawaiian. com), Waikiki's "Pink Palace," is a Moorish building constructed in 1925, when most visitors came to Hawaii on ocean liners to stay for a month or longer.

At the east end of Waikiki is 140-acre **Kapiolani Park.** The park encompasses the **Honolulu Zoo** (151 Kapahulu Ave.; ☎ 808-971-7171, www.honoluluzoo. org) and **Waikiki Shell**, venue for open-air concerts and the late-morn-

Hawaiian Culture

About 9 percent of Hawaii's population call themselves Hawaiian, although the number with pure Hawaiian blood may be less than 1 percent—perhaps about 10,000. Many Hawaiians died in the 19C from introduced diseases. Over the past 150 years, they intermarried easily, especially with Caucasians (*haoles* in Hawaii) and Chinese. But their influence on the islands goes far beyond their numbers. Some of the best-known aspects of Hawaiian culture—music, dance, food and the welcoming *aloha* attitude—have been absorbed by all.

For at least 1,000 years, the Polynesian Hawaiians lived alone in the islands. They came in great double-hulled canoes—first from the Marquesas Islands between AD 400 and 750, later from Tahiti about 1100—and built houses of thatched grass. Their lives revolved around fishing, cultivating taro and yams, gathering fruit and raising pigs. They had a sophisticated knowledge of astronomy and an appreciation for the effect of the seasons on farming and harvesting. They imbued birds, fish and inanimate objects with supernatural powers. Things that were sacred were labeled as *kapu*, or forbidden.

As the centuries passed, the Hawaiians ceased to build large ocean-going vessels. Stories of their former lands became mere songs and chants. They retained the basic spoken Polynesian language, adapting it to their own needs; ancestors and ancient gods were remembered through recitation of genealogy.

After 1820, American missionaries transliterated Hawaiian to make it a written language, reducing the number of consonants to just seven—*h, k, l, m, n, p* and *w*. The Hawaiian language today is regularly spoken in daily life only on the private island of Ni'ihau. Hawaii locals speak either standard English or a type of pidgin composed mainly of English words, but with unusual inflection and numerous Chinese, Japanese and Filipino words stirred into conversation.

Many other cultural aspects were developed after contact with the West. Hawaiians embraced the diatonic musical scale and harmonies introduced by missionaries for singing hymns. From Spanish-speaking cowboys (*paniolo*) on the Big Island, Hawaiians learned guitar; they loosened the strings to change the tuning and invented the lovely "slack-key" style of playing.

When Portuguese immigrants arrived in the late 19C, Hawaiians learned to play the four-stringed *braga* and renamed it the ukulele. Along with a drum, it was played to accompany the hula. Performed with fierce rhythms—and only by men in ancient Hawaii, where it was a religious ritual—hula evolved into a graceful dance for women. (Grass skirts were a 20C import from Micronesia; dancers were traditionally clad in ti leaves.)

© PhotoDisc, Inc

Traditional tunes are likely to be performed at a luau. This outdoor feast—complete with a *kalua* pig roasted in an *imu* (underground oven)—may be the best way to sample typical Island foods. Expect to be served *poi* (taro-root paste, offered fresh or fermented), *laulau* (steamed meat, fish and taro leaves wrapped in ti leaves), *lomi-lomi* (salted salmon mixed with tomatoes and onions) and *haupia* (coconut pudding).

ing Kodak Hula Show *(2805 Monsarrat Ave.; ☎808-527-5400)*. Denizens of the deep are observed at the compact but well-designed **Waikiki Aquarium**★ *(2777 Kalakaua Ave.; ☎808-923-9741, www.waquarium.org)*. The third-oldest aquarium in the US features more than 350 species of Pacific marine life, including the melodically named *humuhumunukunukuapua'a*. Nearby, Cirque Hawaii *(325 Seaside Ave.; 808-922-0017, www.cirquehawaii.com)* is this wildly popular theater-acrobatic troupe's Honolulu show.

Diamond Head★★

Diamond Head Rd., .5mi east of Waikiki.

The famous backdrop in pictures of Waikiki Beach is this extinct volcanic crater. The 760ft summit is easily climbed by a **trail** *(.7mi)* that begins on the crater floor. Part of the route tunnels through old World War II fortifications, so a flashlight is advised.

National Memorial Cemetery of the Pacific★

Ward Ave. & Prospect Dr. ☎808-532-3720. www.cem.va.gov.

Occupying an extinct crater known simply as Punchbowl, this "Arlington of the Pacific" is the final resting place for more than 40,000 US military personnel. Many visit the graves of World War II correspondent Ernie Pyle and Hawaii astronaut Ellison Onizuka, who died in the *Challenger* space-shuttle disaster of 1986.

Bishop Museum and Planetarium★★★

1525 Bernice St. ☎808-847-3511. www.bishopmuseum.org.

The premier treasury of the past in Hawaii—and, indeed, in the Pacific—is somewhat off the beaten path in the Kalihi district. Most archaeological and anthropological work done in Polynesia today is based here, and the Bishop Museum's collection of Hawaiiana is unequaled.

A dozen structures make up the museum. The original turreted stone building, the imposing Victorian known as **Hawaiian Hall**★, was built in 1898-1903. Stairways and corridors lead to collections of regalia from the 19C Hawaiian monarchy, including crowns and feathered capes. Icons of gods carved from native koa wood are exhibited with woven pandanus mats and shark-tooth drums. Other items represent the bygone whaling era and Asian cultures. The fine natural-history collection is particularly strong on bird and marine life.

Native arts and crafts—including hula dancing, lei making and quilting—are demonstrated daily.

A branch of the Bishop Museum has been established in the Hilton Hawaiian Village *(2005 Kalia Rd., Waikiki; b808-949-4321)* at Waikiki. Exhibits describe traditional Hawaiian life in pre-European Waikiki.

Nuuanu Pali Lookout★★

Nuuanu Pali State Park, Pali Hwy. (Rte. 61).

Oahu's premier viewpoint offers a wonderful (if windy) vista over the Ko'olau Range and the windward side of the island; it also has great historical significance. Kamehameha I drove the army of O'ahu up to this point in 1795. When opposing warriors began falling by the hundreds over the 1,000ft-high cliff (*pali*, in Hawaiian), the battle and the island were won.

Hanauma Bay Nature Preserve★

Koko Head, Kalanianaole Hwy. (Rte. 72), 12mi east of Waikiki. ✂ P *☎808-396-4229. www.honolulu.gov/parks.*

An extinct volcanic crater with its seaward side recaptured by surf, this turquoise-hued cove is the single favorite destination in Hawaii for snorkelers to view colorful reef fish and other marine life. Film buffs remember it in *Blue Hawaii* with Elvis Presley (1962).

Kids Sea Life Park Hawaii★

Makapuu Point, Kalanianaole Hwy. (Rte. 72), 15mi east of Waikiki. ✂ ♿ P *☎808-259-7933. www.sealifeparkhawaii.com.*

A 300,000gal **Hawaiian Reef Tank**★★ features a spiral ramp that circles a giant aquarium inhabited by over 2,000 marine creatures, including stingrays and sharks. Other exhibits feature penguins, monk seals, sea lions, dolphins, whales, and the world's only

Practical Information

Area code: 808

GETTING THERE

Hawaii's main airports (*www.hawaii. gov/dot/airports*) are accessed from the US mainland by numerous major airlines and by **Hawaiian Airlines** (☎838-1555 or 800-367-5320; *www. hawaiianairlines.com*) and **Aloha Airlines** (☎484-1111 or 800-367-5250; *www.alohaairlines.com*).

O'ahu: Honolulu International Airport ☎836-6413, www.honoluluairport. com. **Kaua'i:** Lihue Airport ☎246-1448. **Maui:** Kahului Airport ☎872-3893. **Big Island:** Hilo International Airport ☎934-5840; Kona International Airport ☎329-3423. **Shuttle services** connect airports, hotels and tourist attractions.

GETTING AROUND

Inter-island flight times average 30min. Aloha and Hawaiian Airlines (above), along with **Island Air** (☎484-2222 or 800-652-6541; *www.islandair. com*), provide extensive inter-island coverage. **Pacific Wings** (☎873-0877, *www.pacificwings.com*) has scenic tours and charters.

TheBus, Oahu's **mass transit system** (*$1.50/ride*), covers the full island (☎848-5555; *www.TheBus.org*). Waikiki Trolley (*www.waikikitrolley.com*) has foue lines linking Waikiki and downtown Honolulu with other attractions.

ACCOMMODATIONS

Lodging options range from world-class resorts to small hotels and bed-and-breakfasts. Package deals may couple hotels with car rentals and airlines. Consult a travel agent to find the best overall value.

Reservation services: Affordable Paradise Bed & Breakfast (☎261-1693; *www.affordable-paradise.com*); All Islands Bed & Breakfast (☎263-2342; *www.all-islands.com*); Bed & Breakfast Honolulu (☎595-7533; *www.hawaiibnb. com*); Hawaii's Best Bed & Breakfasts (☎885-4550; *www.bestbnb.com*); Go Condo Hawaii (☎818-879-5665; *www. gocondohawaii.com*); Hawaii Connection (☎818-879-5665; *www.hawaii-connection.com*). **Hostels:** Hostelling International Honolulu (☎946-0591); InterclubWaikiki Hotel & Hostel (☎924-2636); Pineapple Park Hostels, Big Island (☎968-8170; *pineapple-park. com*). Additional information on hostels can be found online: www.hostels.com or www.hiayh.org. **Camping:** Most counties require camping permits. For more information, contact the regional visitors bureaus (*below*).

VISITOR INFORMATION

Hawaii Convention and Visitors Bureau ☎923-1811 or 800-464-2924, www.gohawaii.com. Individual islands: **O'ahu Visitors Bureau** ☎524-0722, www.visit-oahu.com; **Kaua'i Visitors Bureau** ☎245-3971, www.kauaidis-covery.com, **Maui Visitors Bureau** ☎244-3530, www.visitmaui.com; **Big Island Visitors Bureau** ☎961-5797, www.bigisland.org.

known **wholphin**—a dolphin-whale cross-breed.

Pearl Harbor★★

6mi west of downtown via H-1 Freeway & Kamehameha Hwy. (Rte. 90).
Here on December 7, 1941, more than 2,300 servicemen were killed in a surprise early-morning Japanese air attack on the US naval fleet. Eighteen ships, including six battleships and three destroyers, sank in the greatest US military disaster. President Franklin Roosevelt declared it "a date which will live in infamy" as he plunged the nation into World War II.

USS Arizona Memorial★★

1 Arizona Memorial Dr. ♿ 🅿 ☎808-422-0561. www.nps.gov/usar.
Floating over the hulk of a sunken battleship, the concave, 184ft white-concrete bridge marks the permanent tombof 1,177 sailors killed in the Pearl Harbor attack. Each victim's name is inscribed in white marble on one wall. The macabre outline of the ship's hull is visible below. Launches depart on

a first-come, first-served basis from a shoreline **visitor center**.

USS Bowfin Submarine Museum & Park★

11 Arizona Memorial Dr. ♿ 🅿 ☎*808-423-1341. www.bowfin.org.*

A walk through the *Bowfin*, credited with sinking 44 Japanese ships, helps define the tight quarters of submissions. Tickets are sold for visits to the nearby **USS Missouri**★ *(*☎*808-423-2263, www.ussmissouri.org)*, on which the Japanese surrender was signed in Tokyo Bay on September 2, 1945. The **Pacific Aviation Museum** *(Hangar 37, Ford Island, 319 Lexington Blvd.;* ☎*808-441-1000, www.pacificaviationmuseum.org)* honors the role aircraft played in World War II.

Excursions

Polynesian Cultural Center★★

55-370 Kamehameha Hwy. (Rte. 83), Laie, 27mi north of Honolulu. ✖♿🅿 ☎*808-293-3333. www.polynesia.com.*

The Church of Jesus Christ of Latter-day Saints (the Mormons) has had a strong presence in Hawaii since 1919. In 1955, the church established a college, now a campus of Utah's Brigham Young University. Students from all over Oceania attend classes, earning tuition by working or performing at the Cultural Center. Visitors can spend an entire day wandering through the "villages" of Hawai'i, Samoa, Tonga, Tahiti, the Marquesas, Fiji and Aotearoa (Maori New Zealand), capping the evening with a spectacular 90min show of Pacific song and dance. The young staff, in nativdress, exhibit and teach skills such as making tapa cloth, weaving pandanus leaves, opening coconuts and learning to play ukulele.

Waimea Valley Audubon Center★★

Kamehameha Hwy. (Rte. 83), 7mi east of Haleiwa & 31mi north of Honolulu. ☎*808-638-9199. waimea.audubon.org.*

Once a money-losing "adventure park," this beautiful valley on Oahu's windward (wet) side has been transformed into a conservation park devoted to preserving the valley's lush ecosystem. Visitors can stroll serene paths, admire native plants and birds, and marvel at the 45-foot waterfall and pool that are the park's centerpiece.

KAUA'I★★

MAP P 222
HAWAIIAN STANDARD TIME

Known to locals as "The Garden Island," lush and tropical Kaua'i (kow-WHY) has a less developed atmosphere than the other three main islands.

- **Information:** ☎808-245-3971, www.kauaidiscovery.com
- ▶ **Orient Yourself:** As on all the islands, the northeast shore is the windward (wet) side, and the southwest shore is dry.
- **Don't Miss:** Kokee State Park
- **Organizing Your Time:** It takes about six hours to circumnavigate the entire island, from Kee Beach to Kokee State Park.
- **Also See:** Waimea Canyon

Geological Notes

Centered on a single extinct volcano, **Mt. Waialeale** (5,148ft)—often the wettest spot on earth with average annual rainfall of 460in—Kaua'i is geologically the oldest inhabited Hawaiian island. It has been eroded to the point it has several rivers, the only island so blessed. It also is more separated physically from

© PhotoDisc, Inc

Kaua'l Landscape

the other main islands: O'ahu, Kaua'i's nearest significant neighbor, is out of sight about 90mi over the horizon. Kaua'i was the only island not won in violent conflict by Kamehameha I: It was ceded almost amicably by King Kaumuali'i in 1810. The isle is said to be the home of the *menehune*, a leprechaun-like people who once served the taller Polynesians.

Most visitors arrive at Lihue, seat of Kaua'i's county government and its largest town. Two routes circle most of the island. The **Kaumualii Highway** *(Rte. 50)* heads in a westerly direction, with spur roads to Poipu Beach and Waimea Canyon. The **Kuhio Highway** *(Rte. 56)* rounds the island to the north from Lihue, winding past the community of Hanalei. Despite the torrents that deluge the peak of the island, many of the beaches get as little as 10in annual rainfall.

Sights

Lihue

The urban hub of Kaua'i is this small town of 5,900. Its **Kaua'i Museum** *(4428 Rice St.;* ☎*808-245-6931, www.kauaimuseum. org)*, which traces early island history, has excellent collections of traditional quilts and gourd calabashes. **Kilohana** *(Kaumuali'i Hwy.;* ☎*808-245-5608, www. kilohanakauai.com)* preserves a 1935 sugar plantation and mansion within an artsy shopping complex.

Poipu★

Poipu Rd. (Rte. 530); 12mi southwest of Lihue. ☎*808-742-7444. www.poipubeach.org.*

A natural tunnel of swamp mahogany trees leads drivers down Maluhia Road (Rte. 520) into the 1835 plantation village of Koloa and on to **Poipu Beach**★ on the south coast. A public park adjoins a string of resort hotels. Down the shoreline to the west is a natural feature called **Spouting Horn**★ *(Lawai Beach Rd.).* Ocean waves push through the remains of an ancient lava tube and a spout of water shoots skyward.

National Tropical Botanical Garden★

Lawai Beach Rd. opposite Spouting Horn. ♿ 🅿 ☎*808-742-2623. www.ntbg.org.*

The 252-acre **McBryde Garden** has the world's largest collection of native Hawaiian flora, plus other rare Pacific species. Adjacent **Allerton Garden** has more than 80 additional landscaped acres. The National Garden also has a research library and herbarium here. Affiliated gardens are on Kaua'i's north shore (Limahuli Garden and Preserve, near Haena) and on Maui (Kahanu Garden, in black volcanic soil near Hana).

Waimea Canyon State Park★★
Koke'e Rd. (Rte. 550) via Waimea Canyon Dr.

Called the "Grand Canyon of the Pacific," Waimea Canyon's size and depth are startling for a small tropical island. From the principal lookout, about 13mi uphill from Waimea, vivid pinks, greens and browns accent the contours of three tributary canyons. A distant waterfall tumbles 800ft over a cliff; the ribbon-like Waimea River, draining rainy Waialeale, weaves a course 3,000ft below. Access to the canyon is only by trail.

Koke'e State Park★★
Koke'e Rd. (Rte. 550); 19mi north of Waimea. www.hawaii.gov/dlnr/dsp.

A cool mountain oasis, this lovely forested park boasts a small natural-history museum (b808-335-9975, www.kokee. org) and access to 45mi of hiking trails, one of which visits the unique ecosystem of the **Alaka'i Swamp**. At the end of the road, at 4,000ft elevation, a dramatic overlook of the **Kalalau Valley** *(below)* makes it clear why no road will ever completely encircle Kaua'i: The steep mountains and deep valleys of the **Na Pali Coast**★★★ are too rugged to be tamed.

Fern Grotto★
174 Wailua Rd., Kapaa; off Kuhio Hwy. (Rte. 56) 6mi north of Lihue. www.fern-grottokauai.com.

Live ferns hang naturally from the roof of a cave, reached by boat tours that begin near the mouth of the broad Wailua River. Singing, guitar-playing boatmen favor passengers with renditions of the "Hawaiian Wedding Song" and other melodies.

Hanalei★★
Kuhio Hwy. (Rte. 56); 33mi northwest of Lihue.

The road to the north shore passes the expansive **Princeville Resort Kauai**★ *(5520 Ka Haku Rd., ☎808-826-9644, www.princeville.com)*. Large trucks and tour buses can't get much farther than this, restricted by the load limit on a narrow, rickety old bridge. That suits the residents of sleepy Hanalei just fine. Fishing, swimming and other water sports at **Hanalei Bay**★ seem to be the extent of high-energy activity. Those who enjoy local history can visit the **Waioli Mission House**★ *(Kuhio Hwy.; ☎808-245-3202, www.hawaiimuseums. org)*, built in 1836 by missionaries and now furnished with period pieces.

A little west of Hanalei is **Lumahai Beach**★, the golden strand where Mitzi Gaynor tried to "Wash That Man Right Out of My Hair" in the 1958 movie South Pacific. The end of the road is **Ke'e Beach,** which offers swimming inside its reef.

Though cars can go no farther, this is the beginning of a remarkable 11mi trail along the rugged cliffs of the Na Pali Coast (above) into the **Kalalau Valley**★★. For healthy hikers carrying proper gear, this is a memorable trek.

Excursion

Ni'ihau
From various points along the road to Waimea Canyon and Koke'e State Park *(above)*, one can see, 17mi offshore, the outline of the 72sq mi "Forbidden Isle" of Ni'ihau *(NEE-ee-how)*. The owners of the island are fiercely protective of the 200-or-so native Hawaiians who still live there without electricity or other conveniences, speaking their ancient language.

Ni'ihau may only be visited on the private helicopter tour *(Niihau Helicopters; ☎877-441-3500, www.niihau.us)* or hunting safaris run by the Robinson family, which has owned the island and its sheep ranch since 1864.

MAUI★★

MAP P 223
HAWAIIAN STANDARD TIME

The demigod Maui, whose exploits have been celebrated throughout Polynesia for a millennium or longer, is the source of this popular island's name. On "his" island, Hawaiians say he once inaugurated a Stone Age daylight savings time, ascending the dormant volcano Haleakala (literally, "house of the sun") to capture the sun itself as it rose from the crater. According to legend, the sun promised Maui that henceforth it would move more slowly across the sky so that Maui's sister could thoroughly dry her tapa cloth in its rays.

- **Information:** ☎808-244-3530, www.visitmaui.com
- **Don't Miss:** Haleakala National Park
- **Organizing Your Time:** Traffic in Kahului can be congested, so count on extra time getting to and from the airport.
- **Also See:** Lahaina

Two mountain masses dominate Maui, Hawaii's second-largest island (729sq mi). Haleakala caps east Maui, while the highly eroded West Maui Mountains form the center of the other section. In ancient geological time they were two separate islands. Eventually, when the sea level dropped, an isthmus formed between them. Today much of this fertile central flat area is taken up with fields of sugar cane.

Sights

Central Maui★

The twin towns of **Wailuku** and **Kahului**—the latter the site of Maui's main airport—occupy the north-central coast. (Together, their population is about 35,000.) At the 1842 **Bailey House** (2375-A Main St., Wailuku; ☎808-244-3326, www.mauimuseum.org), the Maui Historical Society has a museum of artifacts. The **Alexander & Baldwin Sugar Museum** (3957 Hansen Rd., Puunene; ☎808-871-8058, www.sugarmuseum.com), in a late-19C sugar-mill superintendent's residence, details the history and future of sugar production in Hawaii. For a broad agricultural perspective, the 120-acre **Maui Tropical Plantation**★ (Honoapiilani Hwy., Waikapu; ☎808-244-7643, www.mauitropicalplantation.com) offers walking and tram tours of crops of sugar, pineapple, mac-

adamia nuts, coconuts, guavas, bananas, passion fruit, Maui onions, Kona coffee and more.

The major resort areas of central Maui, **Wailea** and **Makena**, encompass a group of charming beaches with fine hotels, golf courses and championship tennis courts.

Iao Valley State Park★★

Iao Valley Rd. (Rte. 320), 5mi west of Wailuku. ♿ 🅿 *www.hawaii.gov/dlnr/dsp.*

Iao is the reason Maui was nicknamed the "Valley Island." The bright green cliffs and burbling stream at the eroded core of an age-old volcano have made it a popular picnic and hiking venue. Its highlight is **Iao Needle**★★, a basaltic spire that rises 1,200ft above the 2,250ft valley floor. A 1.5mi trail meanders beneath cliffs that spout spectacular waterfalls after heavy rains.

Maui Ocean Center★

192 Ma'alaea Rd., Ma'alaea. 🍴♿🅿 *☎808-270-7000. www.mauioceancenter.com.*

Exhibits in this new aquarium take visitors from Hawaii's sandy shores to deep ocean trenches, pausing en route to study colorful reef life. Special exhibits include a touch pool, a whale discovery center and an acrylic tunnel demonstrating life in the open ocean.

Lahaina★★

Honoapiilani Hwy. (Rte. 30). ☎808-667-9175. www.visitlahaina.com.

For nearly two centuries, this quaint community of 10,000 has been the center of activity in west Maui. The town figured prominently in *Hawaii*, author James Michener's novelized history. Along its waterfront, Lahaina exudes an atmosphere reminiscent of the 19C when pious missionaries and rollicking whalers vied for the loyalty of the native Hawaiian population.

Whales are still an attraction from November to June. In the 9mi-wide channel between Lahaina and **Lana'i** *(p xxx)*, the great creatures play, mate and give birth before migrating to northern waters for the summer.

Lahaina walking tours begin under a giant **banyan tree★** planted April 24, 1873. It spreads over an entire town square, about two-thirds of an acre. The 1901 **Pioneer Inn** *(658 Wharf St.; ☎808-661-3636)* is one of the oldest hotels still operating in the islands. Across Front Street, the former home of Lahaina's medical missionary is the **Baldwin House★** *(120 Dickenson St.; ☎808-661-3262)*. Dr. Dwight Baldwin is credited with saving much of the local population in the 1850s when he vaccinated hundreds against a smallpox epidemic.

Kaanapali★

Honoapiilani Hwy. (Rte. 30), 3.5mi north of Lahaina. ☎808-661-3271. www.kaanapaliresort.com.

Hawaii's first planned resort community features a shopping area called **Whalers Village** *(2435 Kaanapali Pkwy.; ☎808-661-4567, www.whalersvillage.com)*, with a museum based on old-time whaling. The **Lahaina, Kaanapali and Pacific Railroad** *(975 Limahana Pl., Lahaina; ☎808-667-6851, www.sugarcanetrain.com)*, riding on a late-19C right-of-way, makes the 6mi run between Kaanapali and Lahaina, complete with a singing conductor.

Haleakala National Park★★★

Haleakala Hwy. (Rte. 377), 36mi southeast of Kahului. ✕⚫🅿 ☎808-572-4400. www.nps.gov/hale.

The dormant volcano Haleakala *(ha-lay-AH-ka-la)* completely dominates east Maui. The spectacular desolation of its enormous crater valley—7.5mi long, 2.5mi wide and 3,000ft deep—has been compared to the mountains of the moon. Pastel hues of red, yellow and orange, as well as gray, purple, brown, black and pink, accent cliff sides and cinder cones. Here and there sprouts a silversword, an agave-like relative of the sunflower that extends a 6ft stalk of small red flowers once a human generation, then promptly dies. Among the lava flows walks Hawaii's state bird, the *nene*, the world's rarest goose. Thirty miles of trails crisscross the crater floor.

The experience of watching the sun rise above the rim can be worth a dark, cold, early-morning drive from a beachside resort to the peak's 10,023ft summit. On the often-chilly mountaintop, the **Haleakala Observatory** comprises several scientific and military technical installations.

Hana Highway★★

⚠ *Rte. 360.*

Motorized adventurers need an early start to reach the east end of Maui via this narrow, winding, 53mi road. Three miles past **Paia**—an old sugar-plantation town, 7mi east of Kahului—it passes **Ho'okipa Beach Park,** a famed windsurfing venue. A good picnic stop is **Puohokamoa Falls,** 22mi before **Hana,** a somnolent little village on an attractive bay.

Dedicated explorers may continue to **Oheo Gulch★★** *(Pulaui Hwy., 10mi south of Hana; ☎808-248-7375, www.nps.gov/hale)* in the Kipahulu District of Haleakala National Park. A series of small waterfalls tumble from the southeast flank of Haleakala, feeding from one pool to another. These are often referred to as the Seven Sacred Pools—although there are two dozen pools and the ancient Hawaiians, apparently, never regarded them as sacred. The simple marble grave of famed aviator **Charles Lindbergh** (1902-74) rests on a promontory in the churchyard of the 1850 Palapala Hoomau Hawaiian Church, 1.2mi past Oheo Gulch.

Excursions

Lana'i★

www.lanai-resorts.com.

Lana'i *(lah-NAH-ee)* was once known as the "Pineapple Isle." From 1922 until the early 1990s the Dole Company made the 141sq mi island the single largest pineapple plantation in the world. Today the fruit has become more profitable to raise in foreign lands. Two resort hotels now anchor the economy for the 3,164 isle residents. Few paved roads cross Lana'i, so visitors must rent a four-wheel-drive vehicle to explore out-of-the-way places. Among them are **Lanaihale** *(Munro Trail east of Lanai City),* the 3,370ft island summit; and **Garden of the Gods** *(Polihua Rd. northwest of Lanai City),* dominated by strange volcanic rock formations.

Moloka'i★

☎808-553-5221. *www.molokai-hawaii.com.*

Moloka'i *(MOLE-oak-eye)* also once supported itself with pineapple. Though heavy unemployment now plagues the 6,000-or-so residents, Moloka'i continues to be known as the "Friendly Isle." Its hub is the quiet port village of **Kaunakakai**, whose clapboard main street is reminiscent of a 19C Old West town.

Kalaupapa National Historical Park★★

Kalaupapa. ☎808-567-6802, *www.nps.gov/kala.*

This unique site encompasses a 13.6sq-mi peninsula separated from the rest of Moloka'i by a 1,600ft cliff. To create an isolation colony for victims of Hansen's Disease (leprosy), Molokaians were relocated from the beautiful windswept promontory in 1865, to be replaced the following year by banished lepers. In 1873, Father Damien de Veuster, a saintly Belgian priest, arrived to live and work (and die, in 1889) among the infected. His original **St. Philomena's Roman Catholic Church** stands above the ruins of the village of Kalawao. Several dozen elderly leprosy patients, who pose no health threat to adult visitors, continue to live at Kalaupapa.

Access is by small plane or private boat—or for the adventurous, by foot or **mule** (☎808-567-6088, *www.muleride.com).* A 3.2mi trail with 26 switchbacks begins at **Pala'au State Park** *(Rte. 470, 10mi north of Kaunakakai).* There is no road access between Kalaupapa and the rest of Moloka'i.

HAWAII (THE BIG ISLAND)★★

MAP P 222

HAWAIIAN STANDARD TIME

The Big Island is aptly named. It measures 4,038sq mi—nearly twice as large as the rest of the major islands combined. Because volcanic eruptions regularly add more lava to the shoreline, it is actually increasing in size. For all its bulk, however, it is sparsely populated, with 165,000 residents.

- **Information:** ☎808-886-1655 (Waikoloa) or ☎808-961-5797 (Hilo); www.bigisland.org
- ▶ **Orient Yourself:** It's easy to keep track of where you are, as the island's twin summits, Mauna Loa and Mauna Kea, are always in sight.
- ☺ **Don't Miss:** Hawaii Volcanoes National Park.
- ◷ **Organizing Your Time:** The "Big" island is aptly named--it takes many hours to drive from Kona to Hilo. Plan adequate time for journeys around the island.
- ✎ **Also See:** Parker Ranch

Two volcanic mountains dominate the landscape. In the north, Mauna Kea (13,796ft), long dormant, is home to several astronomical observatories. In the south, Mauna Loa (13,677ft) is considered live but is usually sleeping. The active Kilauea Volcano, however, spews lava from the lower slopes of Mauna Loa.

As the birthplace of Kamehameha I, and the site of Captain Cook's ill-fated final visit, the Big Island is rich in traditional Hawaiian history.

The separate coasts of the Island of Hawai'i are readily distinguished by their climates: The drier Kona side is on the west; the much wetter Hilo side is east of the volcanoes. Most major resorts are on the Kona and adjoining Kohala coasts.

Sights

Kailua-Kona★

The center of commercial activity in Kona is the sometimes-frenetic town of Kailua, called Kailua-Kona to differentiate it from Kailua, Oahu. Offshore waters provide some of the best deep-sea fishing in the world.

Kailua was the first capital of the Hawaiian Islands: Kamehameha I made his home here. A scaled-down representation of Ahuena Heiau at **Kamakahonu**,

the king's final residence *(75-5660 Palani Rd.; ☎808-323-3222)*, is on hotel grounds beside the pier. The ruler died there in 1819. The 1838 **Hulihe'e Palace**★ *(Ali'i Dr.; ☎ 808-329-1877, www.daughter-sofhawaii.org)* was a retreat for later monarchs.

Opposite is **Mokuaikaua Church**★, Hawaii's first Christian church, built by missionaries in 1837.

Captain Cook

Mamalahoa Hwy. (Rte. 11),
14mi south of Kailua.

This village is named for the British explorer who introduced the world to Hawaii. The **Kona Coffee Living History Farm** *(Mamalahoa Highway; ☎808-323-2006, www.konahistorical.org)* depicts the lifestyle of early Japanese coffee plantation workers. A short road leads downhill to **Kealakekua Bay**★, site of Cook's visit and death in 1779. The road ends near **Hikiau Heiau** *(Napo'opo'o; ☎ 808-323-2005)*. A *heiau* is a sacred site used by ancient Hawaiians, a sort of open-air temple. The bay is now a marine reserve, popular for snorkeling.

Pu'uhonua o Honaunau National Historical Park★★

Rte. 160, Honaunau Bay, 22mi S of Kailua. 👤 🅿 ☎*808-328-2288. www.nps.gov/puho.*

Captain James Cook

No name is more synonymous with exploration in the Pacific Ocean than that of Captain James Cook. He made three voyages between 1767 and 1779, and is credited with discovering nearly all there was to be found in the vast Pacific.

Born in Yorkshire, England, in 1728, Cook escaped a humdrum life by joining the British navy. He gained acclaim as a navigator and cartographer, and at 40, was commissioned to lead an expedition to Tahiti to observe the transit of Venus across the sun. This voyage extended from 1767 to 1771; Cook discovered several islands and mapped the New Zealand and Australian coasts.

On his second voyage (1772-75), Cook circumnavigated the earth while searching vainly for the fabled "great southern continent," a theory popular in Europe. He did discover Tonga, New Caledonia and Easter Island.

Cook failed in his third voyage (1776-79) to find a northern passage from the Pacific to the Atlantic, though he traced the west coast of North America from Oregon to the Arctic Ocean. When he discovered Hawaii, natives initially welcomed him warmly, perhaps mistaking him for the peripatetic god Lono. But Cook and several of his men were killed in a skirmish over a stolen boat at Kealakekua Bay. A white obelisk marks the spot where the navigator is believed to have fallen.

Until the early 19C, this walled site was a sanctuary for Hawaiians who violated the kapus of society. If they could gain entry to the *pu'uhonua* (place of refuge), they were safe from capital punishment, as a *kahuna* (priest) would absolve them of their sin. Pacifists and defeated warriors also found refuge here. Today a **trail** *(.5mi)* leads from a visitor center past several archaeological sites, including a reconstructed temple and thatched huts where traditional crafts are demonstrated.

Uphill about 2.5mi from the historical park, a side road leads to **St. Benedict's Painted Church**★ *(follow signs from Rte. 160),* decorated long ago by its Belgian priest. An amateur *trompe l'oeil*, the wall behind the altar was painted to give his remote congregation an idea of how a grand European cathedral looked.

Kohala Coast★

Queen Ka'ahumanu Hwy. (Rte. 19, South Kohala) & Akoni Pule Hwy. (Rte. 270, North Kohala). ☎808-886-4915. www.kohala-coastresorts.com.
North of Kailua, along the edge of a lava desert, is a series of eight impressive resorts. The **Hilton Waikoloa Village** *(425 Waikoloa Beach Dr., Waikoloa; ☎808-886-1234)* has a colony of dolphins that swim and play with guests chosen by lottery for the experience. The Ka'upulehu Cultural Center of **The Four Seasons Hualalai** *(100 Ka'upulehu Dr., Ka'upulehu-Kona; ☎808-325-8000)* has interactive history programs. **Mauna Kea Beach Hotel** *(62-100 Mauna Kea Beach Dr., Kohala Coast; ☎808-882-7222)* was the first resort here, built by Laurence S. Rockefeller in 1966.
Ancient archaeological sites mark the windswept coastline of North Kohala. **Pu'ukohola Heiau National Historic Site** *(.2mi north of intersection of Rtes. 19 & 270, Kawaihae; ☎808-882-7218, www.nps.gov/puhe)* was built as a temple around 1550 and reconstructed in 1791 by Kamehameha I, who murdered his last Big Island rival here to make himself supreme chief.
The **Mo'okini Heiau**★ *(1.5mi on dirt road at Upolu Airport turnoff from Rte. 270),* dating from AD 480, overlooks

the Alenuihaha Channel 19mi north of Kawaihae. Nearby is the **King Kamehameha I Birth Site** *(.3mi farther on same road).* The islands' conqueror may have entered the world on the birthing stones at one end of the compound in 1758, the year of Halley's Comet, as legend tells of a great light in the night sky at his birth.
The old plantation village of **Hawi** is sprucing up with galleries, boutiques and cafes. Outside Kapa'au Courthouse stands a nine-ton, bronze **Kamehameha I statue** *(Rte. 270);* crafted in Italy in 1879, it sank in a shipwreck off the Falkland Islands but was later recovered.

Parker Ranch★★

Kawaihae Rd. (Rte. 19) & Mamalahoa Hwy. (Rte. 190), Waimea/Kamuela. ✕&🅿 ☎808-885-7655. www.parkerranch.com.
With about 350sq mi and more than 55,000 head of cattle, these pasturelands make up one of the largest ranches in the US. The Parker family's original 1840s ranch house, **Mana Hale** *(☎808-885-5433),* is open for tours; the home of past-owner Richard Smart, **Puopelu**, is now a museum of French Impressionism and Chinese art. Exhibits and a short film at the **Parker Ranch Visitor Center and John Palmer Parker Museum** *(Rte. 19, Waimea)* tell the history of the ranch, which began as a land grant from Kamehameha I to Parker, a sailor from Massachusetts who married a Hawaiian princess and stayed. The nearby **Kamuela Museum** *(Rtes. 19 & 250; ☎808-885-4724)* is less polished but offers an eclectic collection of artifacts.

Waipio Valley★★

Overlook at end of Rte. 240, 8mi north of Honokaa off Mamalahoa Hwy. (Rte. 19).
This spectacular wedge-shaped valley—6mi long, 1mi wide, flanked by 2,000ft cliffs that funnel ribbon-like waterfalls into streams emerging on a sandy ocean beach—is accessible only by foot or four-wheel-drive vehicle. Most travelers view it from a dramatic overlook near the small village of **Kukuihaele**. Inhabited for 1,000 years,

© PhotoDisc, Inc

Volcanic Crater

the lush valley was once home to 4,000 or more Hawaiians.

Hilo★★

www.gohilo.com.
The island's seat of government is this east-shore city of 42,000. Rebuilt after disastrous tsunamis (tidal waves) in 1946 and 1960, the community has a hodgepodge look. New homes and businesses have been constructed on higher ground, farther from the water. Early-20C commercial buildings, seemingly frozen in an age of hand-cranked cash registers and creaking wooden floors, mark the original downtown. Here is the **Lyman Mission House and Museum** *(276 Haili St.; ☎808-935-5021, www.lymanmuseum.org)*, an 1839 missionary's home restored as a period museum.

With 136in annual rainfall, Hilo is a floral center, especially for anthuriums and orchids. Many hotels are near the rocky shoreline of Hilo Bay, along tree-lined Banyan Drive and **Liliuokalani Gardens**, named for the last queen. Some have nice views of **Mauna Kea** to the northwest, often crowned by snow.

Hawaii Volcanoes National Park★★★

Mamalahoa Hwy. (Rte. 11), Volcano, 28mi southwest of Hilo. ☎808-985-6000. www.nps.gov/havo.

Not many places offer the chance to visit a live volcano. At the **Kilauea Visitor Center★★**, tourists may inspect exhibits and learn from rangers how to view the craters safely. **Volcano House** *(☎808-967-7321)*, a rambling wooden hotel first built in 1877, sits on the brink of Kilauea Caldera, at 4,000ft elevation. Steam rises from the caldera's deep **Halemaumau Crater★★**, which erupted most recently in 1982 and likely will again.

The 11mi **Crater Rim Drive★★** circles the great pit and offers a chance to see (and smell) steam and sulfur fumes emanating from the ground. The drive crosses the moonlike Ka'u Desert, where the **Thomas A. Jaggar Museum★** *(3mi west of Volcano House)* presents geological exhibits, and continues through a fern forest, where the 450ft-long **Thurston Lava Tube★** *(2mi east of Volcano House)* beckons visitors.

Although **Kilauea Volcano★★★** has been in continual eruption since January 3, 1983, it is generally unseen. Magma moves through 7mi of lava tubes under the surface, and only where it breaks out above the island's southern shore is it visible. The 2,000°F molten rock pours into the water, creating a boiling sea and sending steam high into the sky—a plume seen from the end of the 20mi **Chain of Craters Road★★**, extending off Crater Rim Drive 4mi southeast of Volcano House. Park rangers advise which path, if any, is cool enough to approach the lava.

HOUSTON AREA

The largest city in Texas (fourth largest in the US) sits just inland from the Gulf of Mexico in flat bayou country. The Houston Ship Channel has made the city the largest foreign-trade port in the United States, and it is the hub of a metropolitan area of more than 5 million people.

Houston is best known for its petrochemical industry. Oil was discovered in 1901, and within five years the city was headquarters for 30 oil companies and seven banks. "Black gold" anchored the economy for most of the 20C; it remains a major player today, along with the medical and aerospace industries.

Houston's wealth has given the city a rich cultural life. One of the few US cities with permanent ballet, opera, symphony and theater companies, Houston is second only to New York in number of theater seats. More than 30 museums are funded by oil fortunes. Professional baseball, football and basketball franchises anchor the sports scene. The Houston Astros baseball team played from 1965 to 1999 in the world's first domed stadium, the **AstroDome** *(8400 Kirby Dr. at I-610 Loop South; ☎713-799-9544)*, before moving to a new downtown stadium in 2000.

Galveston, in sharp contrast to Houston, is primarily a resort destination. The barrier island fills on weekends and summer days with Houstonians getting away from the city. Connected to the mainland by bridge, Galveston Island lies 50mi from Houston via Interstate 45. Much of its activity takes place along the Seawall, constructed to protect the island from storms. The city itself is home to numerous small museums, art galleries, historic homes and The Grand 1894 Opera House.

Houston
TX

Houston Skyline

HOUSTON★★

MICHELIN MAP 492 L 14

CENTRAL STANDARD TIME

POPULATION 2,150,000

Houston embodies much of Texas' mystique, the myth that bigger is better. The city sprawls across more than 617sq mi of bayou country; the metropolitan area takes in nearly 9,000sq mi and is bound by one of the most intricate highway systems in the nation. As the fourth-largest US city (after New York, Los Angeles and Chicago), Houston is a giant in international shipping, petrochemicals, aerospace and finance. Its varied economy has attracted an equally diverse population; dozens of languages are heard in the metropolitan area.

- 🛈 **Information:** ☎713-437-5200, www.visithoustontexas.com.
- ▶ **Orient Yourself:** Houston's 8-mile light rail system, the MetroRail tram, connects downtown with the Museum District.
- 🅿 **Parking:** Ample pay lots in the Museum District serve visitors; bargain hunters can scout for spots several blocks away in nearby residential neighborhoods.
- 🤲 **Don't Miss:** The Menil Collection.
- 🕐 **Organizing Your Time:** Plan to devote at least two days to the Museum District. A half-hour drive through River Oaks, gawking at mansions, is a fine diversion on the way to the Galleria.
- Kids **Especially for Kids:** Johnson Space Center; Museum of Natural Science.
- 👶 **Also See:** Bayou Bend; River Oaks.

A Bit of History

In August 1836, two New York land speculators, brothers Augustus and John Allen, navigated Buffalo Bayou from Galveston Bay. They founded a settlement and named it in honor of Gen. Sam Houston, who had vanquished the Mexican army at San Jacinto four months earlier. The new community was capital of the Republic of Texas from 1837 to 1839.

Initially beset by yellow fever and mud, Houston grew as a cotton-shipping center. After the 50mi Ship Channel was dredged in 1914, it became a major port for all types of trade. The discovery of oil in 1901 triggered modern prosperity, boosted by the location of the Lyndon B. Johnson Space Center southeast of Houston in 1961. The collapse of Enron in 2001, largest US bankruptcy ever, had only a modest dampening effect on the city's economy.

Sights

Three sectors of Houston are of interest to visitors. Downtown is the hub of commerce and performing arts. Easy to spot on the downtown Houston skyline is the 75-story **Chase Tower** (600 Travis St.). The 700-acre **Texas Medical Center** (1155 Holcombe St.), just south of downtown, is the largest health-care complex in the world, and draws patients from across the globe.

The Museum District is the location of most major museums, plus Hermann Park, the city's largest; immediately south is the huge Texas Medical Center. Uptown Houston, on the west side of the city, is the main shopping district, including the huge Galleria complex.

Downtown Houston★

✕👶🅿 Framed by I-45 & US-59 south of Buffalo Bayou.

Buffalo Bayou, the original corridor of settlement, runs along the north side of downtown. Sam Houston Park (below) recalls this first community; above it rises a web of freeways. The commer-

Address Book Houston Area

For price ranges, see the Legend on the cover flap.

WHERE TO STAY IN THE HOUSTON AREA

$$$$ The Lancaster – *701 Texas Ave., Houston, TX.* ✕&♿ P 🅿 ☎713-228-9500 or 800-231-0336. www.thelancaster.com. *84 rooms.* More English country manor than hotel, the Lancaster is a place of oil paintings and overstuffed chairs. Bistro Lancaster is like a London men's club with a Louisiana flair: A mahogany bar and lanterns shaped like hunting horns mix with Gulf Coast specialties like jumbo lump crabcakes in smoked corn and truffle sauce.

$$$$ Hotel Zaza – *5701 Main St., Houston, TX.* ✕&♿ P 🅿 ☎713-526-1991. www.hotelzaza.com/houston. *308 rooms.* Rebranded the Zaza after extensive renovations, what was formerly The Warwick opened in 1925, favored by oil barons who traveled by train to Houston for urban escapades. Located in the heart of the Museum District, the 12-story brick structure's rooms are spacious and elegant.

$$$ Hotel Galvez – *2024 Seawall Blvd., Galveston, TX.* ✕&♿ P 🅿 ☎409-765-7721 or 888-939-8680. www.galveston.com/galvez. *231 rooms.* Built in 1911, the "Queen of the Gulf" has endured hurricanes and is listed on the National Register of Historic Places. Restoration uncovered grand archways and original stencilwork, and yielded rooms in rich gold and sepia.

$$$ Sara's B&B – *941 Heights Blvd., Houston, TX.* 🅿 ☎713-868-1130 or 800-593-1130. www.saras.com. *12 rooms.* Rock in a wicker chair on the wrap-around porch of Sara's romantic clapboard Queen Anne inn. Many of the whimsically themed rooms have iron beds covered in lace and ruffles. The Fort Worth Room has a pine bed, stagecoach lamps and barbed-wire decorations.

$$$ The Tremont House – *2300 Ship's Mechanic Row, Galveston, TX.* ✕&♿ P ☎409-763-0300. www.galveston.com/thetremonthouse. *117 rooms.* This B&B-style inn is hardly modest. Guests on the second and third floors have 15ft ceilings and 13ft windows. From a four-story glass-topped atrium lobby, a piano player sends music filtering to the balconies every night.

WHERE TO EAT IN THE HOUSTON AREA

$$$ Américas – *1800 Post Oak Blvd., Houston.* ☎713-961-1492. www.cordua.com. ⏰ *Closed Sun.* **Latin American.** With trees and flowers, this skylit spot is like an Amazon rain forest. Pargo Américas is the house version of Gulf snapper, crusted with fresh corn ; grilled tenderloin is finished with a chimichurri sauce, and sweet soufflé-style rice pudding provides a perfect ending.

$$$ Brennan's – *3300 Smith St., Houston.* ☎713-522-9711. www.brennanshouston.com. **Creole**. White tablecloths, hardwood paneling and windows overlooking a lanterned courtyard make for an evening of Creole classics and seasonal dishes. Seafood lovers are delighted by shrimp creole, potato-crusted crabcakes and Gulf Coast gumbo.

$$$ Café Annie – *1728 Post Oak Blvd., Houston.* ☎713-840-1111. www.cafeannie.com. ⏰ *Closed Sun.* **Contemporary Southwest.** Chef Robert Del Grande melds border cuisine with Gulf Coast ingredients at this high-energy, San Francisco-style eatery. The signature dish is a delectable layered tostada with crabmeat, and the cocoa-roasted chicken also has earned acclaim.

$$$ Gaido's – *3700 Seawall Blvd., Galveston.* ☎409-762-9625. www.gaidosofgalveston.com. **Seafood**. S.J. Gaido's great-grandchildren still peel shrimp and filet fish the old-fashioned way. The catch of the day is prepared 10 ways: Locals enjoy the Texas catfish Sapporito style (crusted in crushed crackers and garlic) or Castilla style (blackened, topped with asiago cream sauce).

$$ Benno's on the Beach – *1200 Seawall Blvd., Galveston.* ☎409-762-4621. www.bennosofgalveston.com. **Seafood**. Most people enter Benno's straight from the sand, in bathing suits and sandals, then eat alfresco on the bustling terrace. Benno's is famed for deep-fried

Cajun seafood, its crabs and crawfish spiced with Louisiana heat.

$$ Vietopia – *5176 Buffalo Speedway, Houston.* ☎713-664-7303. *www.4anyorder.com/Vietopia*. **Vietnamese**. Dark wood trim and swirling bamboo ceiling fans set the tone at this upscale showcase for cuisine brought to Texas by its many Viet immigrants. Best are dishes that rely on Gulf seafood, such as shrimp sauteed with ginger and scallions, or crispy fish topped with peanuts and onions.

cial district runs east 14 blocks to the George R. Brown Convention Center. The Theater District *(below)* extends north and east of Sam Houston Park. Several 19C buildings have been preserved at **Old Market Square** *(Preston, Travis, Congress & Milam Sts.)*; the original **Allen's Landing** *(Commerce & Main Sts.)* is three blocks beyond. More than 50 blocks (about 6mi) of downtown are interconnected by the growing **Houston Underground,** a tunnel system that shelters the population from summer humidity and winter rain, not to mention year-round street traffic.

Sam Houston Park★

1100 Bagby St. ♿ 🅿 ☎713-655-1912. *www.heritagesociety.org.*
Seven restored 19C–early-20C homes, and an 1891 German Lutheran church, have been relocated to this 19-acre park. Oldest is an 1823 pioneer home; most elaborate, a 17-room house built by oil pioneer Henry T. Staiti in 1905. **The Heritage Society Museum** has exhibits on five centuries of history.

Theater District★

Preston Blvd. to Capitol St., both sides of Louisiana St.
Both the Houston Grand Opera and Houston Ballet perform at the **Wortham Theater Center** *(510 Preston Blvd.;* ☎713-237-1439, *www.worthamcenter. org)*, noted for its six-story grand foyer. The Houston Symphony Orchestra is home in the block-sized J**ones Hall for the Performing Arts** *(615 Louisiana St.;* ☎713-227-3974, *www.joneshall.org)*, identified by its facade of travertine marble. **The Alley Theatre** *(615 Texas Ave.;* ☎713-220-5700, *www.alleytheatre.org)*, whose balcony offers a view of the city skyline, hosts one of the oldest and most highly regarded professional theater companies in the US.

Museum District★★

Houston's main cultural neighborhood is 2mi southwest of downtown via Main Street. A half-dozen important art museums, various science and history museums and Houston's children's museum are found here close to Hermann Park.

Menil Collection★★★

1515 Sul Ross St. ♿ 🅿 ☎713-525-9400. *www.menil.org.*
One of the world's foremost collections of 20C art, with an emphasis on Surrealism, is presented here. Established in 1987 for the collection of John and Dominique de Menil, the museum exhibits only a small part of more than 15,000 paintings, sculptures, photographs and books. Italian architect Renzo Piano's design has been acclaimed for its use of natural light.

The **Surrealist collection★★★** features more works by René Magritte and Max Ernst than any other museum in the world. Also represented are paintings by Cézanne, Klee and Matisse; early Cubist work by Braque, Léger and Picasso; Abstract Expressionism by Pollock and Rothko; and late-20C works by Johns, Rauschenberg, Stella and Warhol. Other galleries hold Paleolithic carvings from the eastern Mediterranean; Byzantine and medieval works; and tribal arts of Africa, Oceania and the Pacific Northwest coast. The adjacent **Cy Twombly Gallery** *(1501 Branard St.)* houses 35 works by the noted Expressionist.

One block east, maintained by the Menil, **The Rothko Chapel**★ *(3900 Yupon St.;* ☎713-524-9839, *www.rothkochapel.org)* is an ecumenical center. The octagonal Chapel (1971, Philip Johnson), holds 14 paintings (1965-66)—variations on a theme of black—by Mark Rothko. Outside in a reflecting pool stands *Broken Obelisk*, a sculpture (1967) honoring Martin Luther King Jr. by Barnett Newman.

The Menil's **Byzantine Fresco Chapel Museum**★ (4011 Yupon St.; ☎713-521-3990, www.menil.org)) holds the only intact Byzantine frescoes in the Western Hemisphere, rescued from thieves attempting to smuggle the 13C artwork out of Turkish-controlled Cyprus.

Contemporary Arts Museum★
5216 Montrose Blvd. ✕ ♿ 🅿 ☎713-284-8250. www.camh.org.
Occupying a distinctive metal parallelogram (1972, Gunnar Birkerts), this cutting-edge museum offers frequently changing exhibits of modern art in spacious upstairs and downstairs galleries.

The Museum of Fine Arts, Houston★★
1001 Bissonnet St. ✕ ♿ 🅿 ☎713-639-7300. www.mfah.org.
Founded in 1900 as the first municipal art museum in Texas, this 300,000-square-foot facility is the sixth-largest art museum in the US. A wide-ranging permanent collection of more than 56,000 works is the inventory for exhibits in the new **Audrey Jones Beck Building** (José Rafael Moneo, 2000), an austere Postmodern white-granite edifice. Highlights include the **Beck Collection**★ of Impressionist and Post-Impressionist art, with works by Manet, Van Gogh, Renoir, Gauguin, Toulouse-Lautrec, Degas, Matisse and Cassatt; and the **Glassell Collection**★★ of African gold. Here also are Egyptian, Greek and Roman antiquities; Renaissance and 18C art; and stunning American folk-art quilts. A fine collection of Remington works and Southwest Indian art are featured in the **Western art** collection.
The original light-filled, Neoclassical **Caroline Wiess Law Building** (1924) across Main Street is given over largely to temporary and traveling exhibitions. A tunnel connects the two buildings and a popular basement café. Between the Law Building and the museum-operated **Glassell School of Art** (5101 Montrose Blvd.) is the **Cullen Sculpture Garden**★ (1986, Isamu Noguchi).

The museum displays American decorative arts at Bayou Bend Collection and Gardens, and European decorative arts at **Rienzi** (1406 Kirby Dr.; ☎713-639-7800), including a fine collection of 18C Worcester porcelain.

Houston Zoo
🅺 1513 N. MacGregor Way. ✕ ♿ 🅿 ☎713-533-6500. www.houstonzoo.org.
Spanning 55 acres at Hermann Park, the zoo is home to 5,000 animals of 700 species.

Houston Museum of Natural Science★★★
🅺 1 Hermann Circle Dr. ✕ ♿ 🅿 ☎713-639-4629. www.hmns.org.
This outstanding four-floor museum requires two days to see properly. The **Paleontology Hall** exhibits over 450 fossil specimens chronicled by time and location. Adjacent to the Welch Chemistry Hall is a 63ft-tall Foucault pendulum. The **Wiess Energy Hall**★★ features one of the world's most comprehensive exhibits on oil and natural gas. Unique high-tech displays, using virtual reality and video holography, trace petrochemical production from discovery to delivery.
The **Cockrell Butterfly Center**★, a 25,000sq ft glass pyramid, houses 2,000 free-flying butterflies. The Brown Hall of Entomology showcases the insect world. The **Cullen Hall of Gems and Minerals**★★★ is a world-class collection of priceless specimens, dramatically illuminated. A sister exhibit, the Smith Gem Vaulta, opened in 2006. Lifelike dioramas present wildlife of Texas and Africa's Serengeti Plain; the Strake Hall of Malacology showcases 2,500 rare seashells, mainly from the Gulf of Mexico. The **John P. McGovern Hall of the Americas** focuses on native cultures from the Arctic to the Andes.
Lower-level exhibits are geared to schoolchildren. The **Arnold Hall of Space Science** incorporates the Challenger Learning Center, where students in a Mission Control mock-up may communicate with others in a remote flight simulator.

John P. McGovern Museum of Health & Medical Science★

1515 Hermann Dr. ♿ 🅿 ☎713-521-1515. *www.mhms.org.*

As home to the world's largest medical center, Houston makes a natural location for this educational center. In the Amazing Body Pavilion, visitors take a walking tour of the human body, including a 10ft brain, a giant eyeball, a 22ft backbone.

The Children's Museum of Houston★

Kids *1500 Binz St.* ✗♿🅿 ☎713-522-1138. *www.cmhouston.org.*

Hands-on exhibits in the Technikids Gallery show everyday applications of science through experimentation. The Investigations Gallery teaches where food comes from, beginning with a farm exhibit and continuing through nutrition, shopping and money management.

Holocaust Museum Houston★★

5401 Caroline St. ♿🅿 ☎713-942-8000. *www.hmh.org.*

This compact but memorable museum (1996, Ralph Appelbaum and Mark Mucasey) is unmistakable for the broad, dark, brick cylinder—reminiscent of a Nazi death-camp smokestack—that rises above it. The exhibit traces Jewish history and the roots of anti-Semitism to the World War II-era Holocaust, followed by the Liberation. **The Memorial Room**★, with walls of remembrance, tears and hope, provides a quiet place of reflection.

Additional Sights

Bayou Bend Collection and Gardens★★

1 Westcott St. ♿🅿 ☎713-639-7750. *www.mfah.org.*

Part of The Museum of Fine Arts, this spectacular collection showcases 17-19C American decorative arts with 5,000 objects of furniture, ceramics, silver, paper, glass, textiles and paintings. It is located in Bayou Bend (1927, John F. Staub), the Neo-Palladian-style former estate of governor's daughter Ima Hogg (1882-1975). On display are a silver sugar bowl crafted by Paul Revere, colonial portraits by John Singleton Copley and Charles Willson Peale, and furniture by

---

The Republic of Texas

Texans are proud that their state was once the independent Republic of Texas.

Following the victory over Gen. Santa Anna at the Battle of San Jacinto on April 21, 1836, a new government was formed. Sam Houston, hero of San Jacinto, was elected the republic's first president in September 1836. Among his first concerns were the continued threats of attack by Indians and renewed attempts by Mexico to extend its borders across the Rio Grande into Texas.

Houston's initial efforts at establishing diplomatic relations with other countries, including the United States, failed. A breakthrough came when a trade treaty was signed with the United Kingdom. Fearing an alliance between Texas and Britain, the US recognized Texas as sovereign in 1837. Soon France, Belgium, The Netherlands and Germany also recognized the young republic.

In 1839, a permanent capital was established at the frontier village of Waterloo, renamed Austin. A national flag was adopted, featuring a single five-pointed star on a field of blue, flanked by horizontal red-and-white stripes; today, Texas continues to be known as the Lone Star State.

Texas President Houston was reelected to a second term in 1841. Much of his subsequent effort was directed toward achieving statehood within the US for reasons of defense and economy. On October 13, 1845, the people of Texas voted 4,245 to 257 in favor of annexation. US President John Polk signed Texas' admission to the union in December of that year. On February 19, 1846, the flag of the Republic of Texas flew over Austin for the final time.

John Townsend. Surrounding the home are 14 acres of woodlands and eight formal gardens.

The Galleria

5075 Westheimer St. at Post Oak Blvd. ✕ ♿ ℙ ☎*713-622-0663. www.simon. com.*

Department stores, two large hotels and an ice rink (beneath an arched glass ceiling) anchor Houston's largest shopping complex. Patterned after a plaza in Milan, Italy, the center dominates the Uptown Houston district, west of Loop 610 and north of the Southwest Freeway.

Space Center Houston★★★

Kids *1601 NASA Road 1, Clear Lake, 25mi south of downtown Houston off I-45.* ✕ ♿ ℙ ☎*281-244-2100. www.space centerhouston.org.*

Official visitor center of the National Aeronautics and Space Administration (NASA) Houston complex, this $70 million facility adjacent to the Johnson Space Center—the mission control, training and research facility for the US space program—offers live shows, presentations and interactive exhibits.

Guided tram tours take visitors for a behind-the-scenes look at the Johnson Space Center to view Mission Control and astronaut training facilities. Live satellite links provide up-to-date information on current space flights. Exhibits include spacecraft from early *Mercury*, *Gemini* and *Apollo* missions; visitors may try on space helmets, touch moon rocks, use a simulator to land a shuttle or take a space walk. At Kids Space Place, 40 interactive areas invite exploration as children ride across the moon's surface in a Lunar Rover or command a space shuttle.

San Jacinto Battleground State Historic Site★

Kids *3523 Battleground Rd. (Rte. 134), La Porte, 21mi east of downtown Houston via Rte. 225.* ♿ ℙ ☎*281-479-2431. www. tpwd.state.tx.us.*

Though the Alamo is far more famous, this spot is actually more crucial to Texas history. A 570ft obelisk, covered with fossilized shellstone, (1939) recalls the 1836 victory here by Texas troops, establishing their freedom from Mexican colonial rule. An elevator takes visitors to the top of the monument for a grand view. On the ground floor is the **San Jacinto Museum of History**, documenting Texas' formative years.

Opposite the battleground site, the **Battleship Texas**★ (☎*281-479-2431*) recalls far more recent battles. Commissioned in 1914, the 573ft battleship served in both world wars before it was decommissioned in 1948. Rescued from demolition, the ship is now open for self-guided tours of both its main deck and lower levels.

NASA Booster Rocket at the Space Center Houston

©iStockphoto.com/Dave Huss

Huntsville★

Location via I-45, 69mi north of Houston. ♿ 🅿 ☎ 936-295-8113. *www.huntsville texas.com.*

Set in rolling, pine-clad hills, Huntsville greets travelers with a 67ft statue of its most famous citizen, Sam Houston (1793-1863). Sculptor David Adickes donated the statue to the city in 1994.

Sam Houston Memorial Museum★ *(1836 Sam Houston Ave.; ☎936-294-1832, www.samhouston.org)* preserves two of Houston's homes and details his colorful career. The only man to be governor of two states, Tennessee and Texas, Houston led the fight for Texas independence and its admission into the United States, but refused to support the Confederacy. His grave is in Oakwood Cemetery *(Avenue I & 9th St.).*

Huntsville also is the home of the massive Texas State Prison complex. The **Texas Prison Museum** *(1113 12th St.; ☎936-295-2155)* contains, among other things, items that belonged to notorious outlaws Bonnie Parker and Clyde Barrow, killed nearby in 1936.

Brazos Bend State Park★

Kids *21901 Farm-Market Rd. 762, Needville, 40mi southwest of downtown Houston via US-59 (Southwest Freeway).* ♿ 🅿 ☎979-553-5101. *www.tpwd.state.tx.us.*

One of the largest expanses of public land in the Houston area is also the best place to see once-rare, now-common Gulf Coast native alligators. An extensive network of hiking trails leads visitors around the huge marsh complex shared by waterfowl and gators, and along the Brazos River in undisturbed sycamore-pecan woodlands.

GALVESTON★

MICHELIN MAP 492 L 9
CENTRAL STANDARD TIME
POPULATION 57,000

Located 50mi south of Houston, Galveston Island is both a summer getaway and a year-round historic destination. The compact barrier island—32mi long but just 2mi wide—is especially known for its beaches, miles of which were included in Texas' first beach replenishment program. In-city beaches are hectic strips where being "seen" may be the most popular sport. The broad, peaceful expanse of Galveston Island State Park (b409-737-1222) begins 13mi southwest of town and extends for several miles. The city, at the eastern end of the island, focuses around a 36-block historic district.

🛈 **Information:** ☎888-425-4753, www.galveston.com

▶ **Orient Yourself:** The farther west and south you go along the island, the less developed it becomes, culminating in a fairly wild stretch of barrier island illustrative of the pre-settlement Gulf Coast.

☺ **Don't Miss:** Galveston's opulent historic mansions.

🕐 **Organizing Your Time:** Figure at least two hours drive time to Galveston from Houston.

Kids **Especially for Kids:** Moody Gardens

A Bit of History

Home to the Akokisa Indians in the 16C, Galveston Island remained unsettled by Europeans until the early 19C, when pirate Jean Lafitte established the village of Campeche as his base. When he was forced out by the US Navy, the village was renamed, and Galveston slowly developed as a port city. Galveston became the richest city in Texas and home to many state "firsts": post office, hospital, naval base, telephone, private bank, gas and electric lights, and more. At the turn of the 19C, thousands of immigrants made their way through the port, second only to New York's Ellis Island as a US entry point. But Galveston suffered a catastrophic blow on September 8, 1900, when it was struck by one of the worst hurricanes in US history. Known as The Great Storm, it killed more than 6,000 residents and destroyed one-third of the city. When it rebuilt, Galveston constructed a 10mi seawall and raised the level of the island.

Sights

The Strand National Historic Landmark District★

The Strand, 20th-25th St.; visitor center, 2016 The Strand. ✕&⟨P⟩ ☎*409-763-7080. www.galvestonhistory.org.*

In the late 19C, The Strand was the city's business district. Bankers and traders filled the buildings of The Strand, which became known as the Wall Street of the Southwest. Today trolleys clang along the historic streets, transporting visitors through a district filled with specialty shops and restaurants, housed in one of the nation's largest areas of Victorian commercial architecture.

The Grand 1894 Opera House *(2020 Post Office St.; ☎ 409-765-1894)* has been restored to its appearance when it hosted such performers as Sara Bernhardt and John Philip Sousa. The **Galveston County Historical Museum** *(2219 Market St.; ☎409-766-2340)* recounts the island's fascinating history.

Hard by The Strand, Galveston's **Waterfront District★** embraces a still-active port; several attractions reflect its seafaring character. The **Great Storm multimedia presentations** *(Pier 21; ☎409-763-8808)* draws on contemporary accounts to offer an entertaining and level-headed recounting of the catastrophic hurricane. The **Texas Seaport Museum** *(Pier 21; ☎409-763-1877)* has a restored 1877 three-masted sailing vessel, the *Elissa*, plus a database with the names of more than 133,000 immigrants who entered the US here. **The Ocean Star** *(Pier 19; ☎409-766-7827)* is a retired offshore drilling platform now converted to a museum; it explains how oil is found and produced from deep-sea beds.

Historic Homes

Numerous 19C homes, many along Broadway south of The Strand, are open for tours. **The Bishop's Palace** *(1402 Broadway; ☎ 409-762-2475)*, a castle-like 1886 Victorian, was built for a railroad founder and later belonged to a diocesan bishop. Constructed of Texas granite, white limestone and red sandstone, it features elaborate woodwork, mantels and fireplaces. The 1895 Romanesque-style **Moody Mansion** *(2618 Broadway; ☎409-762-7668)* features a French rococo reception room and a Classical Revival library.

Three homes are operated by the Galveston Historical Foundation *(☎409-765-7834, www.galvestonhistory.org)*. The 1859 **Ashton Villa** *(2328 Broadway)* is a stately Italianate mansion. The 1838 **Menard Home** *(1605 33rd St.)*, an antebellum estate of Greek Revival style, is furnished with Federal and American Empire antiques. The 1839 **Williams Home** *(3601 Avenue P)* is both a Creole plantation house and a sea captain's home.

Moody Gardens★★

⟨Kids⟩ *1 Hope Blvd.; take 81st St. to Jones Rd.* ✕&⟨P⟩ *b800-582-4673. www.moodygardens.com.*

Beginning in 1986 as a therapy center for patients with head injuries, Moody Gardens has expanded into a leading attraction. The glass **Rainforest Pyramid★★** is home to more than 1,700 tropical plants, fish, birds and insects. The **Discovery Pyramid** showcases the world of space through exhibits and interactive displays. The **Aquarium Pyramid★** contains 1.5 million gallons of water for marine life from the North and South Pacific Oceans, South Atlantic Ocean and Caribbean Sea.

KANSAS CITY AREA

The mid-American prairie's rich, fertile soil generates an unlimited bounty of wheat and feed grains, supporting vast herds of cattle. Few objects obstruct the sun as it rises and sets on wide, sweeping plains that stretch endlessly to the horizons. The land's pristine beauty inspires artists, nature lovers and outdoorsmen.

Originally inhabited by Kansa (Siouan) Indians and herds of bison as broad as the state of Rhode Island, this region's modern history began with the Lewis and Clark Expedition of 1803-06. The explorers identified a site where the Kansas River met the Missouri River as a good place to build a fort; in 1821, fur traders took their advice. By the 1830s, Westport Landing (renamed Kansas in 1850 and Kansas City in 1889) was outfitting westbound travelers with provisions, and many wagon trains began their journeys on the Oregon, California and Santa Fe Trails from here. Thousands more hopeful settlers headed up the wide Missouri on steamboats and promises.

In the pre-Civil War years, territorial Kansas was caught in controversy over slave-versus-free state status. Violent confrontations between partisans on both sides flared for years, even after "Bleeding Kansas" was admitted to the Union as a free state in 1861.

Kansas City subsequently developed as a rail center. Today, the city has grown into the 21C as a graceful metropolis with beauty, culture and a healthy economy. Omaha, a 3hr drive north and the largest city in the adjoining state of Nebraska, also grew around the railroad. Today it is a grain- and livestock-shipping center well known for its fine museums and zoo, and for blues, jazz and barbecue.

"The Scout" overlooks downtown Kansas City from Penn Valley Park

Courtesy of the Kansas City Convention & Visitors Association

KANSAS CITY★★

MICHELIN MAP 492 L, 9
CENTRAL STANDARD TIME
POPULATION 447,000 (MISSOURI), 143,000 (KANSAS)

Located in the geographical center of the lower 48 states, Kansas City is a bustling metropolis of 2 million that spans two states, icnludes two separate identically named cities, and serves as a hubfor excursions into the heartland. Wide, tree-lined boulevards, more than 200 fountains and myriad parks belie the larger city's reputation as dull; it certainly isn't drab, with as many days of sunshine as Miami or San Diego.

- **Information:** ☎816-221-5242, www.visitkc.com
- ▶ **Orient Yourself:** The two separate Kansas City's are nicknamed "KCMo" and "KCK."
- **Don't Miss:** The Jazz Museum and Negro Leagues Baseball Museum.
- **Especially for Kids:** Science City at Union Station.
- **Also See:** The Harry S. Truman Museum in Independence.

A Bit of History

US President **Harry S Truman** (1884-1972), painter **Thomas Hart Benton** (1889-1975) and animator **Walt Disney** (1901-66) all considered Kansas City home.

Most of Kansas City isn't even in Kansas. Professional sports, jazz clubs, art museums and barbecue restaurants—to name a few of the things for which it's renowned—are all found in the larger Missouri city.

Sights

Arabia Steamboat Museum★

400 Grand Ave. ✕&P ☎816-471-1856. *www.1856.com.*

On September 5, 1856, a sidewheeler carrying 130 passengers and 200 tons of cargo sank upriver from Kansas City. Not until 1988 did treasure hunters lift the vessel (one of 289 swallowed by the Missouri River) from 45ft of mud and water. The cargo—Wedgwood china, brandied cherries, tobacco, cognac, doorknobs, pickles, boots, guns, clothing and other pioneer needs—is now on display as a living time capsule.

The *Arabia* anchors one side of **City Market** *(5th St. between Wyandotte & Grand Aves.),* a historic district at Kansas City's 19C riverport.

Crown Center

2450 Grand Ave. ✕&P ☎816-274-8444. *www.crowncenter.com.*

Surrounding the world headquarters of Hallmark Cards, this complex has 60 shops, hotels, restaurants and theaters. In the **Hallmark Visitors Center** (Kids ☎816-274-5672; *www.hallmark.com),* guests discover the history of the world's largest greeting-card company. At the south end of downtown, the **Crossroads Arts District★** (www.kccrossroads.org) is one of the most active such areas in the US, with dozens of galleries devoted to regional and national artists, plus cafes, nightclubs and shops.

Kansas City Union Station★★

Kids *30 W. Pershing Rd. at Main St.* ✕&P ☎816-460-2020. *www.sciencecity.com.*

This grand Beaux-Arts train station (1914, Jarvis Hunt), with 850,000sq ft of floor space, is second in size in the US only to New York's Grand Central Station. Beautifully renovated in 1999, exhibits and guided tours recall the building's history. Casual and upscale restaurants offer dining options for visitors to the shows and attractions in the Theater District.

Science City at Union Station★

Kids Interactive exhibits cover two floors, beginning with Festival Plaza, a welcome center with a TV-newspaper laboratory.

Address Book Kansas City Area

For price ranges see the legend on the cover flap.

WHERE TO STAY IN THE KANSAS CITY AREA

$$$ Circle S Ranch & Country Inn – *3325 Circle S Lane, Lawrence, KS. Take 35th St. east off County Rd. 1045, north from US-24/59,* ✕&🅿 ☎785-843-4124 *or 800-625-2839. www.circlesranch. com. 12 rooms.* Prairie heritage reigns at the Circle S, domain since 1868 of five generations of innkeeper Mary Stevenson's family. A barn-like lodge contains a spacious homestead; visitors explore 1,200 acres of tallgrass, encountering bison and longhorn cattle, then sit for elegant *prix-fixe* dinners, 14mi north of Lawrence.

$$$ Hotel at Old Town – *830 E. 1st St., Wichita, KS.* &🅿 ☎316-267-4800 *or 877-265-3869. www.hotelatoldtown.com. 115 rooms.* Occupying a massive 1906 former warehouse building, this charmingly restored all-suite hotel provides historic ambience (complete with old-style piano bar) but state-of-the-art amenities including full kitchens and compact-disc players.

$$$ The Raphael Hotel – *325 Ward Pkwy., Kansas City, MO.* ✕&🅿 ☎816-756-3800 *or 800-821-5343. www. raphaelkc.com. 123 rooms.* Iron lanterns arch over the driveway and a glass foyer covers the entrance of this brick charmer facing Country ClubPlaza. As the city's most elegant small hotel, the nine-story Raphael, built in 1927, offers an old-world touch of marble tiles and wooden ceilings in the lobby, and modern amenities in all rooms. The **Raphael Restaurant** (🕐 *closed Sun; $$$*) is one of the city's finest.

$$$ Southmoreland on the Plaza – *116 E. 46th St., Kansas City, MO 64112.* &🅿 ☎816-531-7979. *www.southmoreland.com. 13 rooms.* Two blocks from Country ClubPlaza, this c.1913 urban inn feels like a New England B&B. From its cozy Mary Atkins Room to the Clara and Russell Stover Suite, with a deck and cannonball bed dedicated to the chocolatier, guests are guaranteed quaint, vintage Americana and gourmet breakfasts.

$$ Magnolia Hotel Omaha – *1615 Howard St., Omaha, NE.* ✕&🅿 ☎402-342-2222 *or 888-915-1110. www. magnoliahotelomaha.com. 145 rooms.* This stately and historic hotel, between downtown and the bustling Old Market, is anything but cookie-cutter. Built in 1923, renovated in 1996, the inn wraps around a central courtyard and reflecting pools; Oriental rugs, tapestries and oil paintings cloak its walls, and guest rooms are furnished in mahogany. The **Aquila Bistro ($$)** serves three meals daily.

WHERE TO EAT IN THE KANSAS CITY AREA

$$$ Savoy Grill – *219 W. 9th St., Kansas City, MO.* ☎816-842-3890. *www.savoy-grill.net.* **American**. When bandleader Benny Goodman was "Stompin' at the Savoy" in the early 20C, he was on stage here. Kansas City's oldest extant restaurant opened in 1903 in the Savoy Hotel, an erstwhile luxury inn 15 years older. Six US presidents—Taft, Teddy Roosevelt, Harding, Truman, Ford and Reagan—have dined at the Savoy. Stained-glass windows, Italian tile floors and a carved oak bar remain from past eras. The fare is traditional steak and seafood.

$$-$$$ M's Pub – *422 S. 11th St., Omaha, NE.* ☎402-342-2550. *www.mspubomaha. com.* **American and Continental.** You still can get a kosher hot dog at M's, as you could 30 years ago. But this Old Market standby has evolved. The intimate crowd favorite boasts a 200-bottle wine list and such nightly gourmet specials as "duck-duck-goose," duck-leg confit and sliced breast in foie gras demi-glace.

$$ The Golden Ox – *1600 Genessee St., Kansas City, MO.* ☎816-842-2866. *www.goldenox.com.* **American**. Hand-cut steaks at this Stockyards classic are charbroiled over hardwood in the middle of the dining room. Old photographs hang on dark wood-paneled walls, and the carpet boasts the branding iron marks of great cattlemen. The Stockyards have closed but the Ox remains a popular local gathering place.

Young visitors are encouraged to walk inside a human body, design a car, train for the decathlon, track a tornado, dig up prehistoric fossils, visit a farm, even travel to outer space.

18th & Vine Historic District★

During Prohibition (1919-33), Kansas City officials turned a blind eye to all-night speakeasies, thus attracting jazz musicians such as native son **Charlie "Bird" Parker** and **Count Basie**, who formed his band here. Some 120 night-clubs prospered, thanks in part to Tom Pendergast—a political boss who later helped launch Harry Truman's career. Liquor flowed freely; gambling, drugs and prostitution thrived. Famed musicians like Dizzy Gillespie and Big Joe Turner migrated to Kansas City to work. When the clubs closed for the evening, they retired to the **Mutual Musicians' Foundation** (1828 Highland St., 816-471-5212, www.thefoundationjamson.org), a hot-pink bungalow that served as a rehearsal hall; today it remains a second home to jazz musicians. The best time to pack into this tiny room is after midnight Friday or Saturday, when local artists gather to jam, sometimes until dawn.

The Museums at 18th and Vine★★
🧒 1616 E. 18th St. ♿ 🅿 ☎816-474-8463.

The heritage of Kansas City's African-American community is celebrated at the **Horace M. Peterson III Visitor Center**. Exhibits and a 15min film set the scene for visits to its two component museums. Across 18th Street, the renovated 500-seat **Gem Theater** (1912) hosts musical and theatrical productions.

Music memorabilia, interactive exhibits and a jukebox of jazz classics are features of **The American Jazz Museum**★ (☎816-474-8463, www.americanjazzmuseum.com). Special displays honor Louis Armstrong, Duke Ellington, Ella Fitzgerald and Charlie Parker. The Kansas City Institute for Jazz Performance & History teaches the nuances of swing and bebop, while **The Blue Room** (☎816-474-2929) offers live performances four nights a week.

The history of African-American baseball—from post-Civil War origins to Jackie Robinson's entry to the major leagues in 1947—is recounted in the **Negro Leagues Baseball Museum**★★ (☎816-221-1920; www.nlbm.com). Designed around a baseball diamond with real-game sound effects, it features bronzes of such famous players as Satchel Paige, Josh Gibson, "Cool Papa" Bell and Buck O'Neil, longtime museum leader.

Westport Historic District

40th to 43rd Sts. at Main St. & Westport Rd. ✕♿🅿 ☎816-756-2789. www.westporthistorical.org.

18th & Vine Museums: the American Jazz Museum and Negro Leagues Baseball Museum

Courtesy of the Kansas City Convention & Visitors Association

Kansas City Barbecue

Kansas City is renowned for its barbecued beef, pork and chicken. The Yellow Pages alone list more than 60 BBQ joints. That doesn't begin to include the little roadside stands without phones; non-traditional restaurants that serve "other" dishes beside ribs; and hundreds of thousands of backyard grills.

The first documented barbecuer in Kansas City was Henry Perry, who served ribs from an old streetcar barn in 1916. During Prohibition, traveling musicians working the speakeasies spread the word about barbecue. Night or day, ribs, briskets and other cheap cuts of meat were smoked, doused with sauce and served in leftover newspapers. Many of the rib joints didn't even open until midnight. Today, many don't close till well past midnight. Popular local spots include Arthur Bryant's, Gates, Hayward's and K.C. Masterpiece.

In 1836, when westbound wagon trains were outfitted here, Westport Landing's small population included John Sutter (central to the 1849 California Gold Rush) and scouts Kit Carson and Jim Bridger. Today, the historic brick buildings are a hip crossroads with specialty shops, boutiques, galleries, restaurants and nightlife venues.

The Nelson-Atkins Museum of Art★★★

4525 Oak St., east of Country ClubPlaza at Rockhill Rd. ✕&🅿 ☎816-751-1278. *www.nelson-atkins.org.*

With more than 33,000 works in 60 galleries and nine period rooms, this recently expanded (2006) museum near Country ClubPlaza is one of the finest general art museums in the US. It is renowned for Chinese antiquities, paintings by European masters, and a collection of 20C sculpture.

European paintings (14C-19C), sculpture and decorative arts (11C-18C) include noted works by Rembrandt, Pissarro, Gauguin, Monet and others. American works, including Thomas Hart Benton's 10-panel *The American Historical Epic* (1919-24), shares space with other 20C masters such as Miró, O'Keeffe, Picasso and Rothko. A museum highlight is an alcove devoted to seven works by famed Japanese-American sculptor Isamu Noguchi.

Highlighting the Asian collection are a Chinese temple room with a 15C carved wooden ceiling, 13C BC furnishings and porcelain, and an array of T'ang Dynasty tombfigures. The adjacent 22-acre

Kansas City Sculpture Park★★, one of the finest such facilities in North America, presents the largest US collection of bronzes (more than 50) by Henry Moore, and the museum's trademark *Shuttlecocks* by Claes Oldenburg and Coosje van Bruggen.

Kemper Museum of Contemporary Art★

4420 Warwick Blvd.; one block east of 45th & Main Sts. ✕&🅿 ☎816-753-5784. *www.kemperart.org.*

An art museum for people who think they don't like art, this facility (1994, Gunnar Birkerts) entertains and challenges. Its collection features Chihuly, Diebenkorn, Hockney, Johns, Motherwell, Stella and Thiebaud, and photographers Mapplethorpe and Wegman..

Country Club Plaza

450 Ward Pkwy.; between Main, Summit, Brush & W. 46th Sts. at J.C. Nichols Pkwy. ✕&🅿 ☎816-753-0100. *www.countryclubplaza.com.*

Built in 1922 as the first planned shopping center in the US, this unique 14 sq-block district features Spanish Moorish architecture of red-tiled roofs, elegant domes, ornate ironwork, romantic courtyards, statues and fountains.

Toy and Miniature Museum of Kansas City★

🄺🄸🄳🅂 *5235 Oak St.* &🅿 ☎816-333-9328. *www.umkc.edu/tmm.*

More than 100 dollhouses, miniatures and antique toys (including model trains) are displayed in this 24-room,

1911 mansion on the edge of the University of Missouri-Kansas City campus. Special collections feature Russian lacquer boxes and 19C folk art. The Raggedy Ann and Andy dolls in Room 15 evoke many childhood memories.

Kansas City Zoo★★

Kids *6700 Zoo Dr., east end of Swope Park, between 63rd St. & Gregory Blvd. west of I-435.* ✕ & P ☎816-513-5700. *www.kansascityzoo.org.*

This 200-acre zoo is realistic not only for more than 800 animals, but for visitors who can seek out lions and giraffes on the plains of Kenya, gorillas and leopards in the Congolese rain forest, kangaroos and emus in the Australian outback. The Okavango Elephant Sanctuary lures its pachyderms to a muddy waterhole. Children ride ponies and camels, paddleboats and trains, or watch live animal shows. On summer weekends, visitors can camp out, join a nocturnal safari and enjoy breakfast with the animals.

Thomas Hart Benton Home and Studio

3616 Belleview St.; two blocks west of Southwest Trafficway. ☎816-931-5722. *www.mostateparks.com/benton.htm.*

This Victorian stone mansion (1903) in the graceful Roanoke district is where Benton and his wife, Rita, lived for 36 years. The famous painter died in his studio in 1975 when he was 85, getting ready to sign a 6ft-by-10ft acrylic he had just finished for the Country Music Hall of Fame.

Excursions

Harry S Truman Presidential Museum and Library★★

500 W. US-24 at Delaware St., Independence. & P ☎816-268-8200. *www.trumanlibrary.org.*

A 20min drive from downtown Kansas City, the Truman Museum—reopened in 2001 after a $22.5 million renovation—tells the story of the plain-speaking haberdasher whose terms in office (1945-53) were a bridge between World War II and the Korean War. A 45min documentary film introduces the man. Documents and artifacts chronicle Truman's life, and an interactive theater allows visitors their input in the most important decisions of the Truman Presidency, including dropping atomic bombs on Japan in 1945, recognizing Israel in 1948 and committing US combat forces to South Korea in 1950. In the courtyard are the graves of Harry (1884-1972) and his wife, Bess (1885-1982).

The house in which the Trumans lived from 1919 onward is preserved as the **Truman Home**★ *(219 N. Delaware St.).* Tickets must be purchased at the **Harry S Truman National Historic Site visitor center** *(223 N. Main St.; ☎816-254-9929; www.nps.gov/hstr).*

National Frontier Trails Center★

318 W. Pacific Ave. at Osage St., Independence. & P ☎816-325-7575. *www.frontiertrailscenter.com.*

Located in a 19C brick mill five blocks south of the Independence Square staging ground for travelers on the Oregon, California and Santa Fe Trails, this museum offers an excellent primer on the westward migration. An 18min film details the specifics of crossing the continent. Exhibits bring to life the trials and tribulations of pioneers, as recalled in their letters and diaries. Across the street is the 1855 **Bingham-Waggoner Estate** *(313 W. Pacific Ave.; ☎816-461-3491),* home of frontier artist-politician George CalebBingham.

Atchison

US-59 & 73, 50mi northwest of Kansas City. ☎913-367-2427. *www.atchisonkansas.net.*

Home of the famed Atchison, Topeka & Santa Fe Railroad of song fame, this charming town has converted its old train depot into the intriguing **Atchison Rail Museum and County Historical Society Museum** *(200 S. 10th St.; ☎913-367-6238, www.atchisonhistory.org).* More visitors come to see the **Amelia Earhart Birthplace** *(223 N. Terrace St.; ☎913-367-4217, www.earhartmuseum.org),* the home where the famed aviatrix spent her childhood.

St. Joseph★★

I-29 & US-36, 60mi north of Kansas City. ☎816-233-6688. www.stjomo.com. Tourism in this friendly city of about 74,000 thrives on its fame as launch pad for the Pony Express. For 18 months in 1860-61, riders departed from the westernmost US rail station to deliver mail to Sacramento, California. The riders—among them 15-year-old William "Buffalo Bill" Cody and a young James "Wild Bill" Hickok—made the 1,966mi run in only 10 days. The original stables today harbor the excellent **Pony Express Museum**★ *(914 Penn St.; ☎816-279-5059, www.ponyexpress.org).*

Three blocks away, the **Patee House Museum**★ *(12th & Penn Sts.; ☎816-232-8206)* has eclectic exhibits in what was,

in 1858, one of the finest hotels in the West. On its grounds is the **Jesse James Home**. At 34, James, a notorious outlaw, had abandoned his life of crime and lived quietly with his wife and two children in this shuttered clapboard house. But on April 3, 1882, 22 years to the day after the first Pony Express ride, he was shot in cold blood—in this house—by a member of his own gang seeking a $10,000 reward.

An unsung highlight of St. Joseph is **The Albrecht-Kemper Museum of Art**★ *(2818 Frederick Ave.; ☎816-233-7003; www.albrecht-kemper.org).* The collection includes fine American works by Thomas Hart Benton, Mary Cassatt, William Merritt Chase, Frederic Remington, Wayne Thiebaud, the Wyeth family and others.

KANSAS PRAIRIE

MICHELIN MAP 493 K, L 9, 10
CENTRAL STANDARD TIME

The producers of The Wizard of Oz had it all wrong when they depicted Kansas in black and white. The Sunflower State state may not have towering mountains or rushing ocean waves, but it has a quiet, primal beauty that captivates one's senses.

- 🛈 **Information:** ☎786-296-2009, www.travelks.com
- ▶ **Orient Yourself:** The easternmost section of Kansas is actually rolling hills; the flat plains most people envision as Kansas constitute the western two-thirds of the state.
- ☺ **Don't Miss:** Tallgrass Prairie Preserve.
- 🄺🄸🄳 **Especially for Kids:** Cosmosphere.

A Bit of History

Until the invention of the steel plow, this state, like others of the Great Plains, was covered with tall-grass prairie. It was a daunting sight—a quarter-billion acres of dancing grasses, many taller than a mounted horse. Settlers eventually conquered the prairie, turning it into Kansas City, Lawrence, Wichita and rich farmland where much of America's wheat and corn is grown. But even today, it's not hard to see why Dorothy left Oz convinced there was "no place like home" in Kansas.

Sights

Lawrence★★

I-70 & US-59, 31mi west of Kansas City. ☎785-865-4499. www.visitlawrence.com. This college town of just over 88,000 is a slice of mid-America. A restored 1889 Union Pacific station houses the **Lawrence Visitor Center** *(N. 2nd & Locust Sts.).* After viewing a 25min film on local history, visitors wander the nearby downtown **historic district** *(Massachusetts St. & adjacent streets from 6th to 11th Sts.).* The **Watkins Community Museum of History** *(1047 Massachusetts St.; ☎785-841-4109)* has exhibits recalling the dark day in 1863 when a renegade Confederate officer named William Quantrill led a force of 400 men in the burning of Lawrence and the murder of 200 men and boys.

Three fine museums share the 1,000-acre University of Kansas campus, founded in 1866. **The Natural History Museum**★ (Kids *Dyche Hall, 14th St. & Jayhawk Blvd.;* ☎785-864-4450 *; www. nhm.ku.edu)* has dioramas of more than 250 mounted mammals. Four floors of exhibits feature fossils, including the imposing Kansas mosasaur; life on the Great Plains; and an exhibit on Indians of the plains. The **Spencer Museum of Art**★ (*1301 Mississippi St.;* ☎*785-864-4710; www.spencerart.ku.edu)* offers a general overview of 4,000 years of world art history, including 18C-20C European and American works, from Monet to O'Keeffe, and centuries of Chinese and Japanese paintings.

Topeka

I-70 & US-75, 56mi west of Kansas City. ☎ *785-234-1030. www.visittopeka. travel.*

This quiet city of 122,000 centers on the limestone **Kansas State Capitol** *(300 W. 10th St. at Jackson St;* ☎*785-296-3966, www.kshs.org),* built between 1866 and 1903 in French Renaissance style. Gage Park contains the **Topeka Zoological Park** (Kids *635 SW Gage Blvd.;* ☎*785-272-5821; www.topeka.org/zoo),* one of the country's finest community zoos; Historic **Ward-Meade Park** (Kids *124 NW Fillmore St.;* ☎*785-368-3888)* holds a late-19C town square and other historical buildings. Spacious, well-presented exhibits in the **Kansas Museum of History**★ (Kids *6425 SW 6th St.;* ☎*785-272-8681; www.kshs.org)* trace state heritage, from its native cultural origins into the 1950s.

Eisenhower Center★★

200 SE 4th St. at Buckeye St., Abilene, 147mi west of Kansas City. ☎*785-263-4751. www.dwightdeisenhower.com.*

After viewing a 30min orientation film on Gen. Dwight D. Eisenhower (1890-1969), World War II hero and US president, guests may tour Eisenhower's boyhood home. The **Eisenhower Museum**★ displays a lifetime of memorabilia, including original oils by DDE himself, an accomplished hobby painter. The Presidential Library houses documents and historical materials from DDE's terms of office (1953-61). The Eisenhower family is entombed at the Place of Meditation.

The little town of Abilene itself has a remarkable history. Founded in the 1860s, it was the original Kansas cowtown at the end of the Chisholm Trail. Many of its 19C and early-20C homes and commercial buildings are on the National Register of Historic Places; some are open for tours.

Rolling Hills Refuge★

Kids *625 N. Hedville Rd., Salina, 180mi west of Kansas City via I-70 Exit 244.* ☎*785-827-9488. www.rhrwildlife.com.*

A prairie oasis for world wildlife, this 95-acre conservation center is an unlikely home for threatened and endangered species. Indian and white rhinos, Amur leopards, orangutans and many other creatures thrive here. Visitors may walk refuge paths or opt for a tram ride.

Tallgrass Prairie National Preserve★★

Rte. 177, 2mi north of US-50 near Strong City, 127mi southwest of Kansas City. P ☎*620-273-8494. www.nps.gov/tapr.*

Established in 1997, this is the only unit of the National Park System preserving the virgin tall-grass ecosystem that once cloaked the Great Plains. The 10,894-acre national preserve has a hiking trail; in summer there's a 7mi interpretive bus tour and tours of a 19C limestone ranch home, a barn and a one-room schoolhouse.

Cosmosphere★★

Kids *1100 N. Plum St., Hutchinson, 210mi southwest of Kansas City.* ☎*316-662-2305. www.cosmo.org.*

An 83ft-tall Mercury rocket greets visitors to this Smithsonian affiliate, one of the premier space museums in the US. The highlight exhibit traces the history of rocketry, beginning with the landmark Nazi V-2 rocket, on carrying through the US-Soviet "space race" of the Cold War era, to current times. Numerous Russian artifacts are on display, along with the command module from the troubled *Apollo 13* mission: Cosmosphere's Spaceworks made 80 percent of the props for the Hollywood movie.

Wichita★

I-35 & I-135 at US-400, 183mi southwest of Kansas City. ☎316-265-2800. www.visitwichita.com.

Wichita in the 1860s and 70s was a cattle-drive hub on the Chisholm Trail. Now the largest city in Kansas with more than 358,000 citizens, it is "hip" enough that entertainer Elton John custom-orders headwear from a haberdasher (Hatman Jack's) in suburban Delano. Today's cultural hub is a broad parkland at the confluence of the Little Arkansas and Arkansas Rivers. Among the "Museums on the River" are **Exploration Place**★ (Kids *300 N. McLean Blvd.; ☎316-263-3373; www.exploration.org),* an impressive new, interactive science museum with a CyberDome Theater and motion simulator; the **Old Cowtown Museum** (Kids *1871 Sim Park Dr.; ☎316-660-1871; www.oldcowtown.org),* which

preserves 47 structures from the 1870s; the **Mid-America All-Indian Center** (Kids *650 N. Seneca St.; ☎316-262-5221; www.theindiancenter.org),* whose Indian Center Museum recreates a traditional 19C village; and the Wichita Art Museum (*619 Stackman Dr.; b316-268-4921; www.wichitaartmuseum.org),* housing many American masterpieces. Also on the river is **Botanica: The Wichita Gardens** (*701 N. Amidon St.; ☎316-264-0448; www.botanica.org),* with 4,000 plant species spread across 9.5 acres of former golf course.

Sculptures by Rodin, Miró and Moore surround the **Edwin A. Ulrich Museum of Art** at The Wichita State University *(School of Art and Design, 1845 N. Fairmount St.; ☎316-978-3664; www.wichita.edu/ulrich).* The **Sedgwick County Zoo**★ (Kids *5555 Zoo Blvd.; ☎316-660-9453; www.scz.org),* with 473 species on 247 acres, is especially noted for its snake-breeding program, its orangutan and chimpanzee habitat, and its habitats for rare North American animals.

Tallgrass Prairie National Preserve

Kansas Department of Commerce/Richard Smalley

OMAHA

MICHELIN MAP 491 K, L 8
CENTRAL STANDARD TIME
POPULATION 428,000

Named for a Siouan tribe whose appellation means "people upstream," Omaha sits on rolling bluffs overlooking the Missouri River not quite 200mi north of Kansas City. The city was founded in 1854; in 1863, it was chosen as the eastern terminus of the transcontinental railroad. Cobblestone lanes and 1880s warehouses survive from an era when tons of cargo were loaded onto westbound trains from Missouri River steamboats; this district, the Old Market *(Farnam to Jackson, 10th to 13th Sts.; ☎402-341-1877, www.oldmarket.com)*, later became Omaha's wholesale produce district before its Victorian buildings were restored as galleries, boutiques and cafes. Horse-drawn carriages still ply the streets, giving a taste of past glory.

- **Information:** ☎402-444-4660 , www.visitomaha.com
- **Don't Miss:** Joslyn Art Museum.
- **Especially for Kids:** Henry Doorly Zoo.
- **Also See:** Old Market District.

A Bit of History

Among Omaha's finest estates is **Joslyn Castle** *(3902 Davenport St.; ☎402-595-2199)*, the 1902 Scottish baronial-style home of businessman George Joslyn and his wife, Sarah, who endowed the Joslyn Art Museum *(below)*. The neighborhood hub remains **St. Cecilia's Cathedral** *(701 N. 40th St.)*, a twin-spired, Spanish Mission-style house of worship.
In the first half of the 20C, President Gerald Ford (né Leslie King, Jr.) and African American leader Malcolm X (né Malcolm Little) were born in Omaha, as were the Reuben sandwich, Raisin Bran and the TV dinner (by Swansons). Today Omaha is a food-processing, transportation and telecommunications hub.

Sights

Joslyn Art Museum★★
2200 Dodge St. ✕ & 🅿 ☎402-342-3300. www.joslyn.org.
This pink-marble fortress is an outstanding example of Art Deco architecture, built by Sarah Joslyn in 1931 as a memorial to her husband. The collection includes works from the ancient world to the present, emphasizing 19-20C European (Degas, Matisse, Monet, Renoir) and American (Cassatt, Homer, Remington, Benton, Wood, Pollock) art. More than 400 **Karl Bodmer watercolors★★**—of landscapes and native culture—document the Swiss artist's 1832-34 journey up the Missouri River with Prince Maximilian of Germany.

Durham Western Heritage Museum★
801 S. 10th St. & 🅿 ☎402-444-5071. www.dwhm.org.
In its heyday, 64 trains and 10,000 people a day passed through this Art Deco-style Union Pacific Railroad station (1931, Gilbert Stanley Underwood). Now restored, it features a waiting room with gold- and silver-leaf trim, 13ft chandeliers and a classic working soda fountain.

Omaha's Henry Doorly Zoo★★★
3701 S. 10th St. ✕ & 🅿 ☎402-733-8401. www.omahazoo.com.
Among the unique features of this 110-acre, world-class zoo is the Lied Jungle★★, a 1.5-acre indoor rain-forest exhibit that pulsates with life from Asia, Africa and South America. Monkeys howl and macaws screech as visitors duck under vines and waterfalls, walk through caves and swing across rope bridges. The **Cat Complex★**, featuring 85 felines—including lions, tigers and

leopards—is North America's largest. Scott Aquarium displays 20,000 species of fish, 8ft-long sharks and a colony of penguins.

The **Desert Dome**, a geodesic dome 13 stories high and 230ft in diameter, depicts Africa's Namib Desert, Australia's Great Sandy Desert and North America's Sonoran Desert.

In 1998, the zoo opened its **Lee G. Simmons Conservation Park & Wildlife Safari** Kids *(16406 N. 292nd St., Ashland, off I-80 Exit 426; ☎402-733-8401)*, 26mi southwest of Omaha.

Girls and Boys Town★

Kids *137th St. & W. Dodge Rd., 10mi west of downtown Omaha. ☎402-498-1140. www.girlsandboystown.org.*

In 1917, Father Edward Joseph Flanagan borrowed $90 to rent a downtown Omaha boardinghouse as a home for the city's abused, abandoned and disabled boys. The first Christmas, they had nothing but a barrel of sauerkraut to eat. But in 1921, with many success stories under his belt, Father Flanagan purchased Overlook Farm, the 900 acres that make up today's Girls and Boys Town.

Exhibits in the **Hall of History** include photos, artifacts, even the Oscar that actor Spencer Tracy won for playing Flanagan in the 1938 movie Boys Town. The village is a national historic landmark where 550 youths live today.

Strategic Air and Space Museum★

Kids *28210 West Park Hwy., Ashland, off I-80 Exit 426, 26mi southwest of downtown Omaha. ☎402-944-3100. www.sacmuseum.org.*

This imposing, modern (1998) glass-and-steel structure, the size of six football fields, holds examples of all 33 warplanes and each of six missiles used by the former Strategic Air Command worldwide including the SR-71 Blackbird (world's fastest plane).

Western Historic Trails Center

Kids *3434 Richard Downing Ave., Council Bluffs IA, just east of Omaha off I-80 Exit 1B. ☎712-366-4900.*

The 19C Lewis and Clark, Mormon, California and Oregon Trails are commemorated here in film, photograph, artifact and interactive map. Visitors walk the Path of Names, emigrant names carved in granite with the Indian nations they displaced.

Excursions

Lincoln★

I-80 & US-77, 53mi southwest of Omaha. ☎402-434-5335. www.lincoln.org.

Nebraska's capital since 1867, Lincoln has grown into a thriving city of 221,000. Its historic center is the **Haymarket** *(7th to 9th & O to R Sts., www.historichaymarket.info)*, a c.1900 warehouse district revitalized by the National Trust for Historic Preservation. **Lincoln Station** *(201 N. 7th St.; ☎402-434-5348)* is an active rail depot with a visitor information center.

The **State Capitol** *(15th & K Sts.; b402-471-0448, www.capitol.org)*, built in 1922-32 (Bertram Goodhue), features a mosaic dome beneath a 400ft Art Deco-style skyscraper with a 14th-floor observation deck. Outside lies a famous sculpture of Abraham Lincoln, the capital's namesake, by Daniel Chester French. The Capitol is home to the only unicameral state legislature in the US.

The **University of Nebraska State Museum**★ *(Morrill Hall, 14th & Vine Sts.; ☎402-472-2642; www.museum.unl.edu)* has a superb collection of fossil mammoths and modern elephants, plus gem, natural-history and Native American artifact displays. Also on campus, the **Sheldon Memorial Art Gallery** *(12th & R Sts.; ☎402-472-2461; www.sheldonartgallery.org)* focuses on 20C American art, including works by Eakins, Sargent, O'Keeffe and Rothko.

LAS VEGAS AREA

Las Vegas is the largest and most distinctive resort destination in the world, a late-20C boomtown based on gambling, entertainment and recreation. Boosted by a mild winter climate and an advantageous setting along busy Interstate 15 between the Los Angeles area and Salt Lake City, the once-small railroad town staked its future upon the 1931 legalization of gambling by the state of Nevada. It has developed with unprecedented extravagance. Las Vegas now ranks among the prime tourist and convention destinations in the US, and boasts one of the fastest growing residential populations of any US city.

Such prosperity is an anomaly in North America's hottest, driest desert, the Mojave (mo-HAH-vee). Remarkable for its lofty mountains, its high plateaus and the lowest elevations in the Western Hemisphere, the Mojave reaches from

western Arizona to the Sierra Nevada, fading north to the Great Basin and south into the Colorado and Sonoran Deserts. Here Ancestral Puebloan clans established isolated farms before AD 1000, followed in the mid-19C by Mormon emigrants.

The construction of Hoover Dam on the Colorado River in the 1930s revolutionized settlement patterns in the desert by providing cheap hydroelectricity and abundant reservoir water, enabling new communities to sprout and existing towns to prosper. As it has for more than a century, water continues to fuel conflict, as Las Vegas attempts to extract new water supplies from northern Nevada and Utah.

Las Vegas by Night

LAS VEGAS ★★★

MICHELIN MAP 493 C, D 9, 10
MOUNTAIN STANDARD TIME
POPULATION 530,000

Globally famed for its spectacular casinos, lavish resort hotels, world-class entertainment, lax social ethos and garish character, Las Vegas is without peer on the planet. More than 35 million visitors spent $31.6 billion in 2001, and exponential growth continues, with hotel rooms expected to exceed 130,000 by the end of 2003. Dubbed "Lost Wages" by visitors who regularly invest their paychecks at the gaming tables, Las Vegas made a brief stab at being a family destination, but has since revived its no-holds-barred persona.

- **Information:** ☎702-892-7575, www.visitlasvegas.com
- ▶ **Orient Yourself:** There's little need for a car in Vegas--once ensconced in one of the myriad hotels on or near "the strip," most attractions are within walking distance.
- **Don't Miss:** There's nothing on earth like The Strip.
- **Especially for Kids:** Numerous hotel outdoor shows are still family-oriented--and the rides atop the Stratosphere are guaranteed to challenge the most fearless.
- **Also See:** Red Rock Canyon

A Bit of History

Meadows (vegas) at which travelers on the Old Spanish Trail made watering stops distinguished the city's humble beginnings. In 1855, Mormon pioneers established the **Mormon Fort** (*908 Las Vegas Blvd. N.; ☎702-486-3511, parks. nv.gov*) but abandoned it three years later to ranchers. The San Pedro, Los Angeles & Salt Lake Railroad, later the Union Pacific, planned its route through here in the early 20C, building a train yard at what became Fremont Street and auctioning off 1,200 lots in a single day in May 1905. The town became a rail-transfer point during construction of Hoover Dam, but its prosperity and future character owed far more to the legalization of gambling in 1931, and the later collapse of Havana as a nightclubmecca.

Gambling clubs grew up along Fremont Street, which acquired the sobriquet "Glitter Gulch" by virtue of the casinos' brilliant signs. Taking advantage of cheaper land and fewer restrictions beyond the city limits, investors in the 1940s began to build new casinos along the main highway to Los Angeles, a thoroughfare soon dubbed "The Strip." Although the booming gambling business initially attracted organized crime, alarmed state authorities imposed stiff regulations on the industry, driving many shadier interests to sell out to corporate buyers. Among the most acquisitive was reclusive millionaire Howard Hughes, who started his Las Vegas empire by buying the Desert Inn in 1966.

Las Vegas casinos grew and prospered through the 1970s, attracting a strictly adult clientele. Part of their appeal was sophisticated entertainment by such acts as Elvis Presley, Nat King Cole, Liberace, Frank Sinatra, Sammy Davis Jr., and Dean Martin. By the 1980s, however, pressure to compete with new gaming venues in Atlantic City, New Jersey, and other places prompted a trend toward remarkable resorts that offer shows and gambling, but also amusement parks, simulation rides and gourmet dining.

Sights

Fremont Street Experience ★★

Fremont St. between Main St. & Las Vegas Blvd. ☎702-678-5777. www.vegasexper ence.com.

Suspended 90ft over downtown, a barrel-arched canopy jolts to life several

Address Book Las Vegas Area

For price ranges see the Legend on the cover flap.

WHERE TO STAY IN THE LAS VEGAS AREA

$$$$ Four Seasons Hotel Las Vegas – *3960 Las Vegas Blvd. S., Las Vegas, NV.* ✕&P⚊~ ☎702-632-5000 or 877-632-5000. www.fourseasons.com/lasvegas. *424 rooms.* Occupying the 35th to 39th floors of the Mandalay Bay Resort's 43-story glass tower is this quiet, elegant retreat from glitter. The non-gaming hotel combines spacious rooms with top-end shops and an intimate spa. Every element is sublime, from poolside misting devices to filet mignon with tiger prawns in the **Charlie Palmer Steak ($$$)** restaurant.

$$$$ Hyatt Regency Lake Las Vegas Resort Spa & Casino – *101 Montelago Blvd., Henderson, NV.* ✕&P⚊Spa ☎702-567-1234 or 800-633-7313. www.lakelasvegas.hyatt.com. *496 rooms.* This Arabesque oasis spreads along the shore of a 320-acre manmade lake, 17mi east of The Strip. Flanked by two golf courses, the new resort has such design flairs as Moorish arches and ironwork. Despite its Moroccan theme, **Japengo ($$$)** features Pacific Rim cuisine.

$$$$ Bellagio – *3600 Las Vegas Blvd. S., Las Vegas, NV.* ✕&P⚊Spa ☎702-693-7111 or 888-987-6667. www.bellagio.com. *3,005 rooms.* Arguably Vegas' most sophisticated casino-hotel, this Strip property offers Northern Italian sensibility in its décor and ambience. Fountains dance amid light and music on an eight-acre lake. Chihuly glass sculpture in the lobby, a fine-art museum and botanical conservatory, several of the city's finest restaurants, and a strict no-unaccompanied-minors policy all add to its adult appeal.

Furnace Creek Inn & Ranch Resort – *Rte. 190, Death Valley, CA.* ✕&P⚊ ☎760-786-2345 or 800-236-7916. www.furnacecreekresort.com. *Inn has 66 rooms ($$$$; ranch has 224 units ($$)).* One resort with two hotels, Furnace Creek includes a 1927 Mission-style luxury inn, set in an oasis-like palm grove, and a rambling late-19C Western ranch resort of cabins and motel-style rooms.

In the complex are four restaurants, two bars, and a golf course 214ft below sea level.

$$$ The Venetian – *3355 Las Vegas Blvd. S., Las Vegas, NV..* ✕&P⚊Spa ☎702-733-5000 or 877-283-6423. www.venetian.com. *3,036 rooms.* The Strip's first all-suite hotel boasts huge standard rooms (700sq ft), a spa run by the renowned Canyon Ranch, and the Guggenheim Hermitage Museum with masterworks from two of the world's great art collections. Replicas of the architectural highlights of Venice, Italy, including a Grand Canal lined with shops and fine restaurants, transport guests to another world.

$$ Boulder Dam Hotel – *1305 Arizona St., Boulder City, NV.* ✕&P ☎702-293-3510. www.boulderdamhotel.com. *22 rooms.* Built in 1933 to house supervisors on the Hoover Dam project, this National Historic Trust property—an air-conditioned rarity at the time—soon was welcoming European royalty and Hollywood celebrities. The Dutch Colonial-style inn was refurbished in the 1990s and reopened as a bed-and-breakfast in 2000.

WHERE TO EAT IN LAS VEGAS

In addition to the suggestions below, nearly every major hotel has a casino buffet catering to visitors with big appetites and slender wallets.

$$$$ Aureole – *3950 Las Vegas Blvd. S. at the Mandalay Bay.* ☎702-632-7401. www.aureolerestaurant.com. *Dinner only.* **American**. Chef Charlie Palmer's high-tech restaurant boasts a four-story, glass-enclosed wine tower crawling with human "wine angels" who retrieve diners' selections from among 10,000 bottles. The top-shelf menu includes citrus-braised lobsters and fruit-wood-grilled salmon with sage ratatouille and fennel.

$$$$ Le Cirque – *3600 Las Vegas Blvd. S. at Bellagio.* ☎702-693-7223. www.bellagio.com. *Dinner only.* **French**. The colorful circus décor doesn't detract from the serious food at this top-end Strip hotel. Chef David Werly's signature dish is honey-glazed duck; beef tenderloin comes with sauteed foie gras.

$$$$ Picasso – *3600 Las Vegas Blvd. S. at Bellagio.* ☎*702-693-7223. www.bellagio.com. Dinner only.* 🕐 *Closed Wed.* **Continental**. Original Picasso works hang on the walls of this eclectic yet sophisticated restaurant. Chef Julian Serrano, first Las Vegas-resident chef to win the James Beard Award as best in the Southwest, prepares outstanding French and Spanish-inspired cuisine.

$$$ Delmonico Steak House – *3355 Las Vegas Blvd. S. at The Venetian.* ☎*702-414-3737. www.emerils.com.* **Creole-American**. Not a typical steakhouse, this spacious restaurant—with vaulted ceiling and 12ft oak doors—is an updated take on Chef Emeril Lagasse's New Orleans eatery. Diners may relax in the piano bar after chateaubriand for two, a double-cut pork chop or blackened

snapper. Lagasse has a seafood café in the **MGM Grand** (☎*702-891-7374,* **$$$**).

$$$ Piero's Restaurant – *355 Convention Center Dr.* ☎*702-369-2305. www.pieroscuisine.com. Dinner only.* **Italian**. Locals love this celebrity magnet, an old-time Vegas place with tiger-print carpeting and a lively bar crowd. Stone-crabclaws and mixed-grill items are served at booths lining the walls.

$$ Billy Bob's Steak House and Saloon – *5111 Boulder Hwy. at Sam's Town.* ☎*702-456-7777. Dinner only.* **Steaks**. Famous for its generous portions of steak, ribs and barbecued chicken, this rustic, ranch-style restaurant is located 7mi east of Las Vegas on the Boulder Strip.

---

times nightly. The illuminated extravaganza of flashing, rolling images is generated by more than 2 million fiber-optic lights and synchronized to music from a 540,000-watt sound system. Created by a consortium of 11 casinos, the attraction was designed to rejuvenate tourism along five blocks that were the first focus of Vegas' gaming industry. Patrons were enticed to clubs and casinos like the Lady Luck, the Golden Nugget and Benny Binion's **Horseshoe Club.** Illuminated marquees and neon signs were so colossal and flashy that the street was universally known as Glitter Gulch. A 60ft-tall talking cowboy, **Vegas Vic**★★, has been an icon since 1951.

The Strip★★★

2000-4000 blocks of Las Vegas Blvd. S.
This 4.5mi stretch of urban highway—extending from the Stratosphere in the north to Mandalay Bay Resort in the south—embraces Las Vegas' greatest concentration of resorts and casinos, and its most sensational architecture and street-side displays.

When casinos first boomed on Fremont Street, The Strip was a stretch of vacant highway. In 1941, seeking to avoid taxes and restrictions on buildings within city limits, Thomas Hull chose a lonely site to build El Rancho Vegas. Later that year, Guy McAfee—who coined the reference

to "The Strip"—opened The Last Frontier. In 1946, Benjamin "Bugsy" Siegel's Flamingo Hotel became only the third Strip resort, but its upscale tone set it apart from downtown casinos. By the 1960s, scores of flashy new casinos and resorts were displacing the downtown venues as visitor favorites. That trend has accelerated. The Strip today is undisputedly a prime locus of world tourism.

Most of the largest US hotels occupy sites along the Strip and its intersecting blocks. The enormous scale of these properties has been ameliorated with a growing network of elevated walkways and between selected casinos.

A public conveyance, **The Strip Trolley** (☎*702-382-1404, www.striptrolley.com*), makes stops at major casinos and a detour to the Las Vegas Convention Center. The $650 million Las Vegas Monorail *(702-699-8299, www.lvmonorail.com)* runs down the east side of The Strip (behind hotels) from the MGM Grand to the Sahara Hotel, and will one day extend to both Fremont Street and McCarran International Airport.

Guggenheim Hermitage Museum★★

3355 Las Vegas Blvd. S. at The Venetian. ♿🅿 ☎*702-414-2440. www.guggenheimlasvegas.org.*

A unique alliance between two of the world's great art museums—in New York City and St. Petersburg, Russia—this venue exhibits works from the collections of both. Dutch architect Rem Koolhaas designed the main museum (2001), a 210ft-by-160ft gallery with a retractable skylight just off The Venetian's main lobby; its steel façade contrasts dramatically with the derivative-faux architecture of Strip casinos. Exhibitions presents masterworks of Western art. American Frank O. Gehry created the Guggenheim-Las Vegas, a separate gallery whose exhibits focus on more contemporary topics. Gehry's design features curved polished stainless-steel walls, glass floors and towering chain-link curtains.

Liberace Museum

1775 E. Tropicana Ave. ♿ 🅿 ☎*702-798-5595. www.liberace.org.*
Filled with flamboyant costumes, ostentatious automobiles and ornate pianos once owned by pianist Wladziu Valentino Liberace (1919-87), this museum is a monument to the quintessential Las Vegas showman.

Nevada State Museum★

700 Twin Lakes Dr. ♿ 🅿 ☎ *702-486-5205.*
Devoted to the history, flora and fauna of the Las Vegas area, this museum is a fine starting point for exploring nearby deserts and mountains.

Excursions

The Springs Preserve★★

333 S. Valley View Blvd. between US 95 and Alta Drive. ⚠♿🅿 ☎*702-822-7700. www.springspreserve.org.*
Opened in 2007 as the city's first nod to its desert history, this 180-acre park occupies the site of the original springs that were the birthplace of Las Vegas. The **Origen Experience** is a three-gallery museum that depicts the human history of the area. The **Desert Living Center**★★ promotes respect for the region's sensitive environment; outside, four trails (1.8mi) lead through gardens that display native Mojave vegetation and ways residents can wisely landscape their yards. The springs themselves stopped flowing in 1962.

Red Rock Canyon★★

W. Charleston Blvd. (Rte. 159), 17mi west of Las Vegas. ⚠♿🅿 ☎*702-363-1921. www.nv.blm.gov/redrockcanyon.*
A stunning escarpment of banded white, red and gray rock, 20mi long and 3,000ft high, represents the western extent of the Navajo Sandstone Formation prevalent in the Colorado Plateau. It was formed 180 million years

Red Rock Canyon

©iStockphoto.com/Jaap Hart

Casinos on the Strip

These casino-hotels, presented from north to south, are listed as attractions only. Ratings reflect degree of tourism interest, not lodging recommendation.

Stratosphere★ – *2000 Las Vegas Blvd. S.* ✕👤Ⓟ ☎*702-380-7777. www.stratospherehotel.com.* This 1,149ft tower is a pedestal capped by a 12-story "pod." Four double-deck elevators climbfrom ground-floor casino to **observation deck** in 30 seconds; **views**★★ are tremendous. The **High Roller** (coaster) loops giddily around the outside of the pod, while riders of the **Big Shot** ascend 160ft up the building's needle-like mast before free-falling with a force four times gravity.

Sahara Hotel & Casino – *2535 Las Vegas Blvd. S.* ✕👤Ⓟ ☎*702-737-2111. www.saharahotel.com.* Built in 1952, The Moorish-motif Sahara hosted many well-known entertainers of the 1950s to 70s, including The Beatles in their first Vegas appearance. Now more history than mystery, it reaches to a young audience with a high-speed roller coaster and virtual speedway.

Circus Circus★ – *2880 Las Vegas Blvd. S.* ✕👤Ⓟ ☎*702-734-0410. www.circuscircus.com.* Famed for the live trapeze artists and tightrope walkers beneath the "Big Top" of its main casino, this circus-themed casino entertains younger guests with roller coasters, water rides, a bungee-cord trampoline and laser tag in the five-acre **Adventuredome**, America's largest indoor theme park.

Treasure Island at the Mirage★★ – *3300 Las Vegas Blvd. S.* ✕👤Ⓟ ☎*702-894-7111. www.treasureisland.com.* In keeping with a buccaneer theme, a well-orchestrated **battle show**★★ between a pirate ship, Hispàniola, and a British man-o'-war, H.M.S. Britannia—with pyrotechnics and swashbuckling sailors—blasts away periodically in a "Caribbean lagoon" outside the entrance. **Mystèrea** (☎*702-894-7722)*, a Cirque de Soleil fantasy, plays twice nightly within.

The Mirage★★ – *3400 Las Vegas Blvd. S.* ✕👤Ⓟ ☎*702-791-7111. www.themirage.com.* South Seas flair is bolstered by a tropical "island" embellished by lagoons, waterfalls and a **volcano**★ that spews fire, smoke and burning coconut-scented oil. Behind the hotel are dolphin pools and a zoo enclosure. The **Secret Garden of Siegfried & Roy**★ houses white tigers and other exotic animals appearing in a nightly magic show (☎*702-792-7777)*.

The Venetian★★★ – *3355 Las Vegas Blvd. S.* ✕👤Ⓟ ☎*702-414-1000. www.venetian.com.* An engaging imitation of Venice, Italy, the resort features architectural replicas of the **Doge's Palace, St. Mark's Square,** the **Campanile** and **Rialto Bridge.** Singing gondoliers pole vessels along the replicated **Grand Canal**★★, lined by a faux-15C street of shops and restaurants. The acclaimed Guggenheim Hermitage Museum (see listing) is just off the lobby; **Madame Tussaud's**★ portrays in wax more than 100 celebrities from sports, film and entertainment.

Imperial Palace Hotel & Casino – *3535 Las Vegas Blvd. S.* ✕👤Ⓟ ☎*702-731-3311. www.imperialpalace.com.* The **Antique & Classic Auto Collection**★ displays 200 of a collection of 750 cars, motorcycles and trucks—among them Jack Benny's 1910 Maxwell, Marilyn Monroe's 1955 Lincoln Capri, Elvis Presley's 1976 Cadillac Eldorado, and several Model J Duesenbergs.

Caesar's Palace★★ – *3570 Las Vegas Blvd. S.* ✕👤Ⓟ ☎*702-731-7110. www.caesars.com/palace/win.* Imperial Rome sets the theme for this vast complex, adorned with majestic fountains and marble statues including a copy of Michelangelo's *David*. The **Forum Shops**★★, a sumptuous mall in the form of a splendid Roman street, have a sky-like ceiling illuminated to simulate passing days and nights.

Bellagio★★★ – *3600 Las Vegas Blvd. S.* ✕👤Ⓟ ☎*702-693-7111. www.bellagio.com.* A lake with twice-hourly **light and fountain shows**★★ graces the foreground of this opulent complex, designed to recall a village on Italy's Lake Como. From the **Conservatory and Botanical Gardens**★, a popular wedding venue, visitors enter the **Bellagio Gallery of Fine Art**★★, whose rotating exhibits may feature Fabergé eggs, Calder mobiles, or works by Rembrandt, Van Gogh and Picasso. Famed for its restaurants, the resort will not admit minors who are not hotel guests.

Paris Las Vegas★★ – *3655 Las Vegas Blvd. S.* ✕&P ☎*702-946-7000. www .paris-lv.com*. Towering over scaled-down likenesses of the **Arc de Triomphe**, the Champs-Elysées and a Parisian marketplace is a 50-story replica of the **Eiffel Tower**★★, sporting an observation deck reached by glass elevators. The casino is set amid old Paris streets complete with cobblestones and street lamps.

Monte Carlo Resort & Casino★ – *3770 Las Vegas Blvd. S.* ✕&P ☎*702-730-7777. www.monte-carlo.com*. Patterned after Monaco's Palais du Casino, this elegant hotel sports its own microbrewery and cultivates adult patronage. Magician Lance Burton performs in a theater designed for his illusions.

New York-New York★★ – *3790 Las Vegas Blvd. S.* ✕&P ☎*702-740-6969. www. nynyhotelcasino.com*. This building simulates the Manhattan skyline with 12 skyscrapers, including a 47-story version of the **Empire State Building**. The street-level facade is a tableaux of other structures, including a 300ft-long **Brooklyn Bridge**★ and a 150ft-tall **Statue of Liberty**★★. Fire boats spray over New York Harbor; inside, the casino is in a pastiche of Central Park. The **Manhattan Express** roller coaster dips through the roof in a 144ft plunge at 67mph.

MGM Grand★ – *3799 Las Vegas Blvd. S.* ✕&P ☎*702-891-1111. www.mgmgrand. com*. With 5,044 guest rooms, the world's largest hotel reflects a Hollywood theme in its shops and decor. **CBS Television City**★ features a studio walk with screening rooms for TV pilots. **Lion Habitat**★, where visitors may get close to a half-dozen live cats, extends the theme of the 45ft bronze lion (on a 25ft pedestal) at the hotel entrance.

Tropicana Resort & Casino – *3801 Las Vegas Blvd. S.* ✕&P ☎*702-739-2222. www.tropicanalv.com*. Noted for the 4,000sq-ft **stained-glass ceiling** that curves over the main casino floor, the Tropicana is home to the classic Parisian revue, the **Folies-Bergère**★. Also here is the Casino Legends Hall of Fame, whose exhibits date back to the earliest days of Vegas gaming.

Excalibur★ – *3850 Las Vegas Blvd. S.* ✕&P ☎*702-597-7700. www .excaliburcasino.com*. This complex suggests a castle bristling with ramparts, battlements and bailey towers, from which an automated Merlin periodically emerges to wage magical battle against a mechanical dragon. Keeping with the Camelot theme, the hotel shopping mall is a Medieval village with wandering minstrels. Shows in **King Arthur's Arena** include knights, acrobats and fireworks.

Showgirls

Luxor★★ – *3900 Las Vegas Blvd. S.* ✕&P ☎*702-262-4000. www.luxor. com*. A 10-story sphinx stands before this stunning 36-story pyramid, clad in 13 acres of bronze-tinted glass. By night a 315,000-watt laser—the **Xenon Light**★★—shoots from the pyramid's apex into the sky, visible up to 250mi. On an atrium terrace is the **Tomband Museum of King Tutankhamen**★, a copy of the original Egyptian tomband its artifacts. Hotel rooms are reached by unique elevators—"inclinators"—that ride through a shaft angled at 39 degrees.

Mandalay Bay Resort & Casino★ – *3950 Las Vegas Blvd. S.* ✗♿🖥 ☎*702-632-7777. www.mandalaybay.com.* A tropical water theme lends elegance to a resort noted not only for its restaurants, theater and events center, but for an artificial wave pool and beach at its 11-acre **Lagoon** complex. In **Shark Reef★★** aquarium, 100 sharks, crocodiles, moray eels and venomous lionfish glide through a replicated sunken temple.

ago of sand dunes cemented and tinted by water acting on iron oxide and calcium carbonate.

With more than 30mi of trails, a **visitor center★** and many boulders and sheer walls popular among rock climbers, the 300sq-mi Red Rock **Canyon National Conservation Area★★** preserves the northern end of the formation. Among highlights along a 13mi loop road are the old **Sandstone Quarry★★**, where blocks of red-and-white rock were mined from 1905 to 1912, and the adjacent Calico Hillsa. Hikers explore ancient petroglyphs at **Willow Spring** or escape desert heat via the **Ice Box Canyon Trail★** *(2.5mi round-trip)* into a steep, narrow canyon.

The more recent history of the canyon is preserved at the 528-acre **Spring Mountain Ranch State Park★** *(Rte. 159, Blue Diamond; b702-875-4141, parks.nv.gov)*, dating from 1876. The ranch was once owned by German actress Vera Krupp and purchased in 1967 by reclusive financier Howard Hughes. A re-created ghost town called **Old Nevada★** *(Rte. 159, Bonnie Springs; b702-875-4191, www. bonniesprings.com)* has transformed another pioneer ranch. A saloon, restaurant, wax museum, church and other buildings along the dusty main street serve as backdrops for mock shootouts and melodramas.

Spring Mountains National Recreation Area★

Rtes. 156, 157 & 158, 35mi northwest of Las Vegas. ⛺♿🖥 ☎*775-331-6444. www.fs.fed.us/htnf.*

A biologically unique oasis surrounded by the Mojave Desert, Mount Charleston (11,918ft) and other peaks of this 494sq-mi Toiyabe National Forest preserve are home to 23 species found nowhere else, including Palmer's chipmunks. The Spring Mountains are a haven for deer, elk, mountain lions, wild horses and bighorn sheep. Skiers throng to **Las Vegas Ski and Snowboard Resort** *(Rte. 156)* each winter, while mild summer temperatures draw motorists to enjoy 11 campgrounds and the **Mount Charleston Hotel** *(☎702-872-5500, www. mtcharlestonhotel.com)*.

Linking the Kyle and Lee Canyons, the 9mi Deer Creek Road *(Rte. 158)* offers access to **Desert View Trail** *(.1mi)* where views north into the Nevada Test Site range once attracted crowds to witness atomic-bombtests in 1952-62.

Desert National Wildlife Range★

Mormon Well Rd., 31mi north of Las Vegas off US-95. ⛺ ☎*702-515-5450. www.fws. gov/ desertcomplex.*

The largest US wildlife sanctuary outside of Alaska protects 2,200sq mi of mountainous habitat favored by desert bighorn sheep, Nevada's state mammal. Travel is restricted to designated roads, and no all-terrain vehicles are permitted. Information and maps are available from the **Corn Creek Field Station,** a historic oasis that has been Indian camp, stagecoach stop and ranch.

LAKE MEAD AREA★

MICHELIN MAP 493 D 9, 10
MOUNTAIN STANDARD TIME
TOURIST INFORMATION ☎702-293-8907 OR WWW.NPS.GOV/LAME

North America's largest, deepest reservoir is a deep-blue desert lake along the Nevada-Arizona border. Created in 1936 on the Colorado River with construction of the Hoover Dam, highest dam in the Western Hemisphere, Lake Mead has become a recreational showpiece, bringing boating, water skiing, fishing and other water sports to an arid land.

- 🛈 **Information:** ☎702-293-8907, www.nps.gov/lame
- 🚫 **Don't Miss:** Hoover Dam.
- **Especially for Kids:** Lake Mead.
- **Also See:** London Bridge in Lake Havasu City.

A Bit of History

The region's history goes back far before the 20C. Colonies of Ancestral Puebloans farmed the fertile valley of the Muddy River, near Overton, as early as AD 800. Their Paiute successors were working the bottomlands when Mormon settlers arrived in the mid-19C.

Sights

Clark County Museum★
1830 S. Boulder Hwy., Henderson, 15mi southeast of Las Vegas. ♿ 🅿 ☎702-455-7955. co.clark.nv.us.
This large, pueblo-style exhibit hall highlights southern Nevada history with dioramas of Pleistocene animals, an ancient pueblo, Colorado River steamboating, mining and gambling. Outside, on **Heritage Street**★★, are such relocated buildings as a c.1900 desert mining settlement and the 1931 Boulder City rail depot.

Boulder City★
US-93, 25mi southeast of Las Vegas. ☎702-293-2034. www.boulder-city-chamber.com.
Tidy and green, Boulder City is the only gambling-free community in Nevada. Constructed in 1931 for 8,000 dam workers, it was the first US city built according to Community Planning Movement principles, integrating social planning into physical design. Saco Reink DeBoer

designed greenbelts, schools, parks and separate zones for residential, business, government and industrial uses. The city now has 15,000 residents; its national historic district encourages pedestrian use with shady arcades and Southwest-Art Deco architecture, although the prominent 1933 **Boulder Dam Hotel**★ *(1305 Arizona St.; ☎702-293-3510, www.boulderdamhotel.com)* strays from the plan with its Colonial Revival facade. The two-story hotel also houses the **Hoover Dam Museum**★ *(☎702-294-1988, www.bcmha.org),* where exhibits and a film provide background on the physical hardships and social conditions prevailing during the Depression-era construction project.

Hoover Dam★★★
〰 *US-93, 31mi southeast of Las Vegas.* ♿ 🅿 ☎702-494-2517. www.usbr.gov/lc/hooverdam.
Stretched like a gargantuan wall across the 800ft-deep Black Canyon of the Colorado River, Hoover Dam is a intensely dramatic monument to civil engineering. Designed, built and operated by the federal Bureau of Reclamation for flood control and to provide water for irrigation, municipal use, electricity and recreation, it was the world's largest hydroelectric dam from its completion in 1936 until 1949. Rising 726.4ft from a 660ft-thick base to a 45ft-wide crest, capable of producing nearly 50 million kilowatts from 17 massive generators, Hoover Dam was the primary catalyst

behind the population and economic boom of Arizona and Nevada.

Conceived to control devastating floods on the lower Colorado, the dam was first planned for Boulder Canyon, upstream from the present site. Four tunnels were bored through canyon walls to divert the river; after two cofferdams were built, the construction area was pumped dry and excavated to bedrock. The first concrete was poured in June 1933, the last in 1935, two years ahead of schedule. The dam began operation in October 1936. The project (including Boulder City) was under budget at a cost of $165 million, but 96 construction workers died on the job.

A multi-story parking garage on the Nevada side of the dam (RVs must park on the Arizona side) also holds a **Visitor Center**★, from which there are sensational **views**★★ down the front of the dam and Black Canyon. Multimedia presentations focus on the construction; an upstairs gallery includes a dynamic desert **flash-flood demonstration**★. Visitors may choose between two guided tours of the dam, a shorter sightseeing tour and the more comprehensive **Hard-Hat Tour**★★★.

Lake Mead National Recreation Area★

US-93 & Rte. 166, beginning 27mi east of Las Vegas. △✕⚴🅿 ☎702-293-8990. *www.nps.gov/lame.*

Embracing two vast reservoirs on the Colorado River, this 2,350sq-mi desert preserve was created in 1936. Although 67mi-long **Lake Mohave**, impounded by Davis Dam in 1950, subsequently became an integral part of the park, the centerpiece remains **Lake Mead.**

With six large, full-service marinas on Lake Mead, and two on Lake Mohave, the recreation area offers superlative opportunities for boating, fishing, water skiing and houseboating. Miles of remote inlets and coves provide privacy. **Sightseeing cruises** of short duration depart from Lake Mead Marina near Boulder Beach, on the lake's western shore. **River-rafting** day trips from below Hoover Dam to Willow Beach are also popular.

The information source is the **Alan Bible Visitor Center**★★ (*Lakeshore Scenic Dr. at Rte. 93, 2mi west of Hoover Dam;* ☎702-293-8990), with many interactive exhibits on geology and natural history. The **Northshore Scenic Drive** (*Rte. 167*) offers the most impressive desert views on the Nevada shore, including ruddy-colored sandstone formations around the Redstone Picnic Area, where the gentle **Redstone Trail**★ (*.5mi loop*) explores the petrified sand dunes.

Valley of Fire State Park★★

Rte. 169, 55mi northeast of Las Vegas. ☎702-397-2088. *parks.nv.gov.*

Nevada's oldest state park preserves 35,000 acres of desert scenery, including a half-mile-thick layer of Aztec Sandstone Formation, dyed reddish or leached white by chemical erosion and shaped by wind into arches, fins, knobs, domes, ridges and other odd shapes. From the **visitor center**★★, a 7mi spur road leads to the **White Domes Area**★★, a landscape of multihued monuments and smooth, wind-carved sandstone. The intriguing **Petroglyph Canyon Trail**★★ (*.8mi round-trip*) traverses a narrow canyon to **Mouse's Tank**★★, a natural, water-filled basin where a renegade Paiute hid out in 1897. On the west end of the park, a steep metal stairway climbs up to **Atlatl Rock**★, named for

©iStockphoto.com/Craig Shanklin

Aerial View of Hoover Dam and Lake Mead

a rare petroglyph of an atlatl, a weapon that predates the bow and arrow.

Lost City Museum of Archaeology★

1721 S. Rte. 169, south of Overton, 63mi northeast of Las Vegas. ♿🅿 ☎702-397-2193. This flat-roofed adobe was built in 1935 to preserve archaeological discoveries. On its hilltop site is a reconstructed Ancestral Puebloan house atop a genuine **pueblo foundation★**.

Laughlin

Rte. 163, 21mi east of US-95, 96mi south of Las Vegas. ☎702-298-2214. www.laughlinchamber.com. Contrary to Las Vegas, where casinos are loath to divert gamblers' attention from the tables, casinos here often sport big picture windows on the river.

Excursion

Lake Havasu City

Rte. 95, 19mi south of I-40, 154mi south of Las Vegas. ☎928-855-4115. www.havasuchamber.com.

Spreading over the Arizona bank of Lake Havasu, a reservoir created by the Parker Dam in 1938, this resort and retirement town of 45,000 is celebrated as the site of the rebuilt **London Bridge★**.

DEATH VALLEY NATIONAL PARK★★★

MICHELIN MAP 493 C 9, 10
MOUNTAIN STANDARD TIME

At nearly 5,300sq mi, this sun-blasted expanse of mountain, canyon and playa is the largest national park in the contiguous US. Confronting visitors with vast, silent, stark landscapes unobscured by vegetation or human intrusion, Death Valley is a veritable textbook on geology. The enormous basin—130mi long, 5mi to 25mi wide—formed progressively as a block of the earth's crust sagged and sank between parallel mountain ranges, creating an astounding difference in elevations. Altitudes range from 11,049ft at Telescope Peak to 282ft below sea level near Badwater. The mountains are flanked by alluvial fans, delta-like deposits built up as debris washes out of numerous canyons during flash floods.

🛈 **Information:**☎760-786-3200, www.nps.gov/deva
▶ **Orient Yourself:** From the bottom of Death Valley to the top of Telescope Peak, a view common in the valley, is more than twice the depth of Grand Canyon.
👁 **Don't Miss:** Zabriskie Point and Dante's View.
🕐 **Organizing Your Time:** An overnight stay in Death Valley, either at one of its famous lodges or in a campground, is a lifetime memory--in the cool season. It's best to visit between late autumn and early spring, as the relentless summer sun heats the valley to some of the highest temperatures on earth. The 134°F recorded at Furnace Creek has been exceeded only in the Sahara Desert.
👣 **Also See:** Badwater

A Bit of History

For centuries, the Panamint Shoshone made seasonal hunting and gathering forays into the valley during cooler months. Death Valley proved a formidable obstacle to 19C western migration, acquiring its name after an emigrant party was stranded for weeks searching for a way out in 1849. Prospectors combed surrounding mountains in the late 19C and early 20C, striking isolated pockets of gold and other metals, sparking short-lived mining booms and leaving a heritage of abandoned settlements. Commercial exploitation of borax

© PhotoDisc, Inc

Zabriskie Point

brought the famed 20-mule-team wagons required to haul the white mineral to a distant railhead. Organized tourism followed after railroad magnates built the Furnace Creek Inn in 1927.

Sights

Park services and lodgings are concentrated at Furnace Creek, Stovepipe Wells and Panamint Springs. Visitors gather information at the **Death Valley Visitor Center** *(Rte. 190; ☎760-786-2392).*

Furnace Creek
Rtes. 190 & 178, 121mi northwest of Las Vegas.
Death Valley's main concentration of lodging and other facilities clusters around an oasis of date palms, planted in 1924 and still producing fruit. **Furnace Creek Ranch** *(☎760-786-2345, www.furnacecreekresort.com)* occupies the site of the 1874 Greenland Ranch. On a hill .5mi east of the ranch, the elegantly appointed **Furnace Creek Inn** *(☎760-786-2345),* built in 1927, remains the premier hotel in the park.

Badwater Road★
Rte. 178 south of Furnace Creek.
Following Death Valley's barely perceptible descent to the lowest point in the Americas, the paved road to Badwater *(36mi round-trip)* traverses a spectacularly bleak, sunken salt pan that sprawls westward to the escarpment of the 11,200ft Panamint Range.
From a small parking area west of the road *(2.5mi from Furnace Creek)*, a gently climbing trail *(2mi round-trip)* winds through the badlands of **Golden Canyon**★★, cut by flash floods through tilted deposits of an ancient alluvial fan. **Artist's Drive**★ *(10mi from Furnace Creek)* winds through the steep foothills of the Amargosa Range, where brilliant hues of red, pink, yellow, green and purple climax at the highly mineralized **Artist's Palette**★★. A picture of exquisite desolation, the **Devil's Golf Course** surrounds its viewing area *(12mi from Furnace Creek, then 1.3mi west)* with a jagged chaos of low salt pinnacles. Reached by a short hike *(.8mi round-trip)* through a narrow, high-walled canyon in the Amargosas *(accessible by a 1.8mi dirt road, 13.5mi from Furnace Creek)*, the **Natural Bridge**★ forms a massive, 35ft arch of rock above the canyon floor. A shallow pool of alkali water at 279.8ft below sea level, **Badwater**★ is virtually the nadir of the Western Hemisphere.

Zabriskie Point★★
Rte. 190, 4.5mi east of Furnace Creek.

267

Overlooking Golden Canyon on the east, this renowned vista point commands splendid views over a bizarre landscape of multicolored badlands, uplifted and tilted by tectonic movements and eroded by wind and rain. Another 1.2mi east, a 2.9mi scenic drive detours through **20-Mule-Team Canyon**, where deposits of high-grade borax were once mined.

Dante's View★★★
Dante's View Rd., 24mi southeast of Furnace Creek via Rte. 190.
From a 5,475ft perch atop the Amargosa Range on Death Valley's eastern wall, this point presents a stunning **view**★★★ of the continent's most extreme elevation contrast.

Stovepipe Wells Sand Dunes★★
Rte. 190, 6mi east of Stovepipe Wells.
The park's most accessible sand dunes pile up in billowing hills, reached either by foot from the highway *(park on the shoulder within sight of the dunes)* or via a turnoff 1mi west of the junction of Route 190 and Scotty's Castle Road.

Titus Canyon Road★★
98mi round-trip from Furnace Creek. Take Rte. 190 north to Beatty Cutoff, then to Daylight Pass and Nevada Rte. 374. Road ends at Rte. 190, 34mi north of Furnace Creek.
Among the most memorable drives in the park, this one-lane dirt road traverses a landscape of layered cliffs, peaks of tilted and twisted sediments, and remnants of great volcanic eruptions. From a high point of 5,250ft in the Grapevine Mountains, it winds and squeezes into Death Valley past the ghost town of **Leadfield** and through the **narrows**★★ of Titus Canyon.

Scotty's Castle★
Rte. 267, 53mi north of Furnace Creek.
☎760-786-2392.
Begun in 1924, this eclectic, Spanish-Moorish complex of house and grounds was commissioned by Albert Johnson, a Chicago insurance magnate and financial backer of Walter Scott, a charlatan who solicited investments for suspect mining operations.

Excursion

Mojave National Preserve★
South of I-15 & Rte. 164, 53mi south of Las Vegas; Baker is at Rte. 127 & I-15, 113mi south of Furnace Creek. ☎760-252-6100. *www.nps.gov/moja.*
This pie-shaped area of some 2,500sq mi embraces a stark landscape of precipitous mountain ranges, dry lake beds, lava mesas, sand dunes, limestone caverns, lava tubes and the nation's largest forest of Joshua trees. It is home to some 700 species of plants and nearly 300 species of animals.
In Barstow is the **California Desert Information Center** *(831 Barstow Rd.; ☎760-255-8760).* There are two **Mojave Desert Information Centers** *(72157 Baker Blvd., Baker, b760-733-4040; also 707 W. Broadway, Needles, ☎760-326-6322).*

Kelso Dunes★
Access on foot from a dirt road that turns off Kelbaker Rd., 7.4mi south of Kelso Station.
Billowing up to 600ft above the floor of the Devils Playground, these 45 acres of sand dunes are among the highest in the Mojave.

Hole-in-the-Wall★★
26mi from I-40 via the paved Essex & Black Canyon Rds. ☎760-928-2572.
A jumble of volcanic cliffs profusely pocked with clefts and cavities, Hole-in-the-Wall is one of the more bizarre geologic features of Black Canyon. From the visitor center, a footpath *(2mi round-trip)* leads down narrow, twisting **Banshee Canyon**★★ by means of iron hoops bolted to the steepest sections of rock.

Mitchell Caverns★
22mi north of I-40 via paved Essex Rd. ☎760-928-2586.
Concealed within the Providence Mountains, six limestone caverns were formed by percolating groundwater millions of years ago.

LOS ANGELES AREA

Filling a vast coastal plain framed by towering mountains, this sprawling, sun-drenched megalopolis is the second-largest metropolitan area in the US, a collection of once-distinct cities and towns that have grown together. Its enviable climate, its role as an international entertainment center and its remarkable ethnic and cultural diversity contribute to a heady mix of sights and experiences with an ambience so casual that locals refer to their home merely by initials: "L.A.," or the nickname "the Southland."

Greater Los Angeles spills beyond the Los Angeles Basin, a mostly flat plain that runs inland from the Pacific Ocean to the uplands. Skirting the basin to the northwest are the Santa Monica Mountains, which rise from the sea at Oxnard, 70mi northwest of downtown L.A., and create the higher elevations of Beverly Hills, Hollywood and Griffith Park. These mountains are reminders of geological stress frequently manifested in **earthquakes**, and form a natural barrier for **smog**—smoke, automotive exhaust and industrial pollutants transformed by sunlight into airborne sludge. Though strict laws have improved air quality in recent years, smog remains oppressive on hot summer days. Today the city of Los Angeles covers more than 467sq mi. Almost 10 times that area is embraced by L.A. County. About 80 incorporated cities are within the county, many completely surrounded by the city of L.A. Population of the city exceeds 3.8 million, county 9.9 million, metropolitan area 14 million to 17 million, depending on which definition you use. *See Michelin Green Guide California.*

Los Angeles Memorial Coliseum

LACVB/Michele & Tom Grimm

Address Book Los Angeles Area

For prices, see the Legend on the cover flap.

WHERE TO STAY IN THE LOS ANGELES AREA

$$$$$ Casa del Mar – *1910 Ocean Front Walk, Santa Monica, CA.* ✕ 🚶 🅿 ⚓ Spa ☎*310-581-5533 or 800-446-8500. www. hotelcasadelmar.com. 129 rooms.* An opulent beach club for well-to-do Angelenos in the Twenties, the Casa was neglected after its use as a military hotel in World War II. A $60 million restoration in the 1990s returned the elegant seven-story inn to its former stature. The **Catch ($$$$)** restaurant looks out on Santa Monica Bay.

$$$$$ Hotel Bel-Air – *701 Stone Canyon Rd., Los Angeles, CA.* ✕ 🚶 🅿 ⚓ ☎*310-472-1211 or 800-648-4097. www. hotelbelair.com. 92 rooms.* Ranked among the world's finest hotels, the Bel-Air is secluded among 12 acres of lush gardens and waterfalls not far from Westwood. Pink, Mission-style, tile-floored bungalows harbor individually decorated lodgings. The Restaurant **($$$$)** serves California-French cuisine on a bougainvillea-covered terrace.

$$$$$ The Ritz-Carlton Laguna Niguel – *1 Ritz-Carlton Dr., Dana Point, CA.* ✕ 🚶 🅿 ⚓ ☎*949-240-2000 or 800-542-8680. www. ritzcarlton.com. 393 rooms.* South of the artists' enclave of Laguna Beach, this grand hotel perches on a hilltop above a lovely beach for walking. Luxury abounds in its crystal chandeliers and rich tapestry fabrics; oceanfront rooms enjoy Pacific views. **Restaurant 162** offers California-style seafood from a perch overlooking the ocean **($$$$)**.

$$$$ Shutters – *1 Pico Blvd., Santa Monica, CA.* ✕ 🚶 🅿 ⚓ ☎*310-458-0030. www.shuttersonthebeach.com. 198 rooms.* A beachside-cottage feel belies the stylish service and dining behind the white shuttered windows. Cozy provincial furnishings line the lobby's piano bar. Guests relax by the pool, in the spa, and over dinner at the **One Pico ($$$)** restaurant.

$$$$ Disney's Grand Californian Hotel – *1600 S. Disneyland Dr., Anaheim, CA.* ✕ 🚶 🅿 ⚓ ☎*714-956-6425 or 800-225-2024. www.disneyland.com. 750 rooms.* Built in early-20C Craftsman style, reminiscent of great national-park lodges, this is one of three Disneyland Resort hotels. Together with the refurbished **Disneyland Hotel ($$$$)** and **Disney's Paradise Pier Hotel ($$$$)**, the resort has 2,242 rooms. **Napa Rose ($$$)** offers fine dining.

$$$$ Hotel Oceana Santa Barbara – *202 W. Cabrillo Blvd., Santa Barbara, CA.* 🚶 ⚓ ☎*805-965-4577 or 800-965-9776. www.hoteloceana.com. 122 rooms.* This modern boutique hotel offers the ambience of a European inn on the Pacific: It's labeled "beach-house chic." Guest rooms wrap around garden courts. Hotel Oceana also has a luxury 63-suite Santa Monica property.

$$$$ Millennium Biltmore Hotel Los Angeles – *506 S. Grand Ave., Los Angeles, CA.* ✕ 🚶 🅿 ⚓ ☎*213-624-1011 or 866-610-9330. www.regalbiltmore. com. 683 rooms.* Home of the first (1927) Oscars ceremony and once a magnet to presidents, kings and Hollywood celebs, the Renaissance-style Biltmore has maintained its prestige through the decades. It remains a presence on Pershing Square in the heart of downtown.

$$$$ The Willows Historic Palm Springs Inn – *412 W. Tahquitz Canyon Way, Palm Springs, CA.* ✕ 🚶 🅿 ⚓ ☎*760-320-0771 or 800-966-9597. www. thewillowspalmsprings.com. 8 rooms.* A striking Mediterranean villa in Old Palm Springs, The Willows has frescoed ceilings, balconies and its own waterfall. Rooms have claw-foot tubs, slate floors and garden patios.

$$$ Artists' Inn Bed and Breakfast – *1038 Magnolia St., South Pasadena, CA.* 🅿 ☎*626-799-5668 or 888-799-5668. www.artistsinns.com. 10 rooms.* Each guest room in this Victorian home reflects a different artist or period: The Gauguin suite takes guests to Tahiti with a bamboo bed, while bright colors in the Expressionist suite recall Matisse. Full gourmet breakfasts with homemade muffins are served on the large front porch overlooking 100 rose bushes.

$$$ Mosaic Beverly Hills – *125 S. Spalding Dr., Beverly Hills, CA.* ✕&🅿🛗 ☎*310-278-0303 or 800-463-4466. www. mosaichotel.com. 46 rooms.* A mid-priced treasure in a neighborhood not known for moderation, this charming boutique property offers a serene palm-shaded swimming pool, a cozy restaurant and a 24hr fitness center.

$$$ Hotel Queen Mary – *1126 Queen's Hwy., Long Beach, CA.* ✕&🅿 ☎*310-435-3511 or 800-437-2934. www.queenmary. com. 365 rooms.* Once the oceans' greatest luxury liner, this Art-Deco masterpiece is permanently docked at the south end of the I-710 freeway. Its three decks of wood-paneled staterooms are quaint but romantic and memory-inducing. Its best restaurants are **Sir Winston's ($$$$)**, for Continental cuisine, and **The Chelsea ($$$)**, for seafood.

$$ Hotel Figueroa – *939 S. Figueroa St., Los Angeles, CA.* ✕&🅿🛗 ☎*213-627-8971 or 800-421-9092. www.figueroahotel.com. 285 rooms.* This exotic downtown hotel, dating from 1926, feels like an enclave of Morocco. The arched terra-cotta entrance leads to a lobby decked in cacti and Spanish tiles; the pool is surrounded by a lavish garden. Some rooms feature wrought-iron bed frames and reflect a desert palette.

$$ The Venice Beach House – *15 30th Ave., Los Angeles, CA.* 🅿 ☎*310-823-1966. www.venicebeachhouse. com 9 rooms.* Framed by a picket fence and charming garden, this bed-and-breakfast inn recalls the early-20C days of its beach community's founding as a Venetian-style artists' community. Some rooms have private entrances; others have cathedral ceilings or rocking chairs.

WHERE TO EAT IN THE LOS ANGELES AREA

$$$$ JiRaffe – *502 Santa Monica Blvd., Santa Monica, CA.* ☎*310-917-6671. www. jirafferestaurant.com. No weekend lunch.* 🕐 *Closed Mon.* **California-French.** From the airy storefront of this chic restaurant, rising star Rafael Lunetta prepares such hearty bistro-style dishes as duck breast with couscous and Black Mission figs, and pancetta- and potato-crusted monkfish.

$$$$ Patina – *141 S. Grand, in Disney Concert Hall., Los Angeles.* ☎*213-972-3331. www.patinagroup.com. Dinner only (lunch Fri).* **California-French.** Founding Chef Joachim Splichal's glitzy new location is ultra-high profile, but the food continues to earn acclaim. Five types of caviar lead the way to hearty, French-inflected roast fish and meat dishes, or top-price prix fixe menus of seafood or squaband veal.

$$$$ The Sky Room – *40 S. Locust Ave. at The Breakers, Long Beach.* ☎*562-983-2703. www.theskyroom.com. Closed Sun.* **American.** A cornerstone of Conrad Hilton's hotel empire in the 1930s and 40s, the imposing Baroque-style Breakers is now a senior residence. But its penthouse Sky Room is as lively as ever. Where Liz Taylor and others frolicked, live bands play in Art-Deco elegance. Classic cuisine includes tableside Caesar salad, rack of lamband a plethora of fresh seafood.

$$$$ Water Grill – *544 S. Grand Ave., Los Angeles.* ☎*213-891-0900. www. watergrill.com. No weekend lunch.* **Seafood.** In downtown's vintage Pacific Mutual Building is this fine seafood restaurant. Preparations are simple and elegant. Dishes include marinated squid with mint and green tomatoes, Atlantic cod with steamed mussels, and John Dory sautéed with eggplant purée.

$$$ Anaheim White House – *887 S. Anaheim Blvd., Anaheim, CA.* ☎*714-772-1381. www.anaheimwhitehouse.com.* **Northern Italian.** A 1909 Craftsman home once surrounded by orange groves, the White House became a restaurant befitting a president in 1981. Veronese owner-chef Bruno Serato features fresh seafood and game dishes, including lobster ravioli and braised Sonoma rabbit on orzo.

$$$ Fresco at the Beach – *901 E. Cabrillo Blvd. in the Santa Barbara inn, Santa Barbara, CA. b805.966.9856. www. santabarbarainn.com.* **California-French.** With beachfront views and a bright, airy interior, this new cafe in the Santa Barbara Inn offers "European comfort food." Italian seafood stew, grilled filet mignon and chicken cacciatore lead the menu; live entertainment is presented most evenings.

$$$ Shiro – *1505 Mission St., South Pasadena, CA.* ☎626-799-4774. *Dinner only.* ⏰ *Closed Mon.* **Japanese.** Sizzling whole catfish, stuffed with ginger, lightly fried and served in ponzu sauce, is but one reason why Shiro captures a devoted clientele. All of the sauces and seafood dishes are marvelous at this friendly, off-the-beaten-track restaurant.

$$$ Spago Beverly Hills – *176 N. Cañon Dr, Beverly Hills, CA.* ☎310-385-0880. *www.wolfgangpuck.com.* **Continental.** Celebrity chef Wolfgang Puck draws Hollywood glitterati to feast on "designer pizzas," risottos, fish and duck, or Austrian classics such as Wiener Schnitzel. This super-chic restaurant is painted in amethyst, green and amber and decorated with Italian marble and jewel-toned art glass. Puck's exhibition kitchen started the trend of food as entertainment.

$$$ Twin Palms – *101 W. Green St., Pasadena, CA.* ☎626-577-2567. *www.twin-palms.com.* **California-French.** Two Canary Island date-palm trees rise above a central, tent-draped courtyard that is one of Old Town Pasadena's most popular gathering places. Rotisserie chicken, Moroccan lambsirloin and calamari with rock shrimp are standouts on an eclectic menu. Live jazz bands perform nightly.

$$ The Original Pantry – *877 S. Figueroa St., Los Angeles, CA.* ☎213-972-9279. *www.pantrycafe.com.* **American.** Since opening in 1924, this downtown institution declares itself "never closed, never without a customer." White-jacketed waiters—some here for 40 years—serve such tried-and-true dishes as pot roast, baked chicken and apple pie at the cash-only eatery. Former Mayor Richard Riordan is a co-owner.

LOS ANGELES★★★

MAP PP 278-279
PACIFIC STANDARD TIME
POPULATION 3,850,000

Los Angeles has the benefits and challenges of a major metropolis, though both the pros and cons are magnified by its enormous size and near-mythic reputation. The city's ethnic diversity endows it with rich cultural resources and can make a drive across town seem like a dizzying world tour. In 2006 more than half the population of L.A. County spoke a language other than English--mostly Spanish, but also Korean, Russian, Thai, Vietnamese and many others.

- **Information:** ☎213-624-7300 www.greaterlosangeles.com.
- **Parking:** Parking at the Getty Center has proved a major problem--be sure to call ahead to reserve a spot.
- **Don't Miss:** The Getty Center; Pasadena.
- **Organizing Your Time:** It's impossible to condense a comprehensive LA experience into any reasonable length of time, so focus on your personal interests: Hollywood, art, live entertainment, cultural diversity and so on.
- **Especially for Kids:** Universal Studios.

A Bit of History

Anthropologists estimate that 5,000 Gabrieleño Indians lived in this area before the first Spanish colonizing expedition in 1769. The mission town (1781) was named El Pueblo de Nuestra Señora la Reina de Los Angeles de Porciúncula, "The Town of Our Lady the Queen of the Angels by the Porciúncula (River)." By the time the dusty town was designated capital of Mexican California in 1845, it had become the commercial and social center for a region of vast cattle ranches and vineyards.

After the city passed into American hands, the advent of the railroad promoted a population boom. Images of a sun-kissed good life helped create communities like Hollywood, and by 1900 Los Angeles was home to more than 100,000. L.A.'s reputation was further enhanced by the **citrus industry**, as vast orange groves were planted to meet rising nationwide demand for the fruit. Growth, however, was severely limited by a lack of water. To meet this need, the $24.5 million **Los Angeles Aqueduct** opened in 1913, its Sierra Nevada waters coursing through 142 separate mountain tunnels. Although the controversial project ruined the livelihoods of many farmers, it enabled unprecedented growth for L.A.

The early 20C brought the fledgling motion-picture industry from New York and Chicago to Southern California, whose varied locations and consistently gentle climate encouraged outdoor filming. The studios settled in and around Hollywood. By 1920, 80 percent of the world's feature films were being produced in California, and by the mid-20C, Hollywood's film industry employed more than 20,000 people. Movie stars bought homes in the hills of Hollywood and nearby Beverly Hills.

After World War II, the halcyon days of the Eisenhower era encouraged still more Americans to head west. Orange groves gave way to housing tracts. The city is still healing from devastating racial riots in 1965 and 1992, yet the efforts of individuals and local and federal organizations are bearing fruit. Groups such as the **Los Angeles Conservancy** dedicate themselves to preserving historic architecture, from the Art Deco masterpieces of Wilshire Boulevard to residences by such architects as Frank Lloyd Wright. The city hosted the **Summer Olympic Games** in 1932 and 1984, and its unquenchable dynamism continues unabated.

Downtown Los Angeles★

El Pueblo de Los Angeles Historic Monument★

Roughly bounded by Arcadia, N. Spring, Macy & N. Alameda Sts. ✕ ♿ ☎*213-628-1274. www.cityofla.org/elp/.*

The city's historic heart is a 44-acre cluster of early-19C buildings. The village was restored as a Mexican marketplace between 1926 and 1930. Shops and wooden stalls along brick-paved **Olvera Street**★, a pedestrian way, sell an assortment of crafts, clothing and food. A zigzag pattern in the pavement marks the path of the city's first water system (1781). The oldest house in Los Angeles, the one-story **Avila Adobe**★ *(E-11 Olvera St.),* was built in 1818. The nearby **Sepulveda House** *(W-12 Olvera St.),* a two-story Victorian (1887), blends Mexican and Anglo influences.

The Plaza *(Olvera St. between Main & Los Angeles Sts.)* has occupied its site since 1825; on its west side is **Our Lady Queen of the Angels Catholic Church** *(535 N. Main St.),* built in 1822 and popularly known as Old Plaza Church.

Union Station

800 N. Alameda St. opposite El Pueblo. ☎*213-683-6875.*

A $13 million combined venture of the Southern Pacific, Union Pacific and Santa Fe Railroads (1939, Parkinson & Parkinson), this building gracefully blends Mission Revival, Spanish Colonial, Moorish and Art Deco styles.

Chinatown

Roughly bounded by Sunset Blvd. and Alameda, Bernard & Yale Sts.

This small (15 sq-block) district serves as one of two main centers for the city's residents of Chinese descent. A pagoda-style gateway *(900 block of N. Broadway)* marks the entrance to **Gin Ling Way**; chinoiserie-embellished buildings line this original pedestrian precinct. Herbalists, curio shops, restaurants and discount stores attract shoppers.

Little Tokyo

Roughly bounded by E. 1st, E. 3rd, Los Angeles & Alameda Sts.

Japanese immigrants in late-19C Los Angeles congregated in the area preserved as the **Little Tokyo Historic District** *(1st St. between San Pedro St. & Central Ave.).* Today, the **Japanese American Cultural and Community Center** *(244 S. San Pedro St.; ☎213-628-2725, www. jaccc.org)* and Japan America Theatre host community events. Adjacent is the **James Irvine Garden**★, an 8,500sq-ft garden designed in traditional style by Takeo Uesugi. Overlooking the garden is a brick sculpture plaza designed by L.A. native and internationally acclaimed artist **Isamu Noguchi** (1904-88).

Japanese American National Museum★

369 E. 1st St. ✕ ♿ ☎213-625-0414. www. janm.org.

America's first museum dedicated to Japanese-American history occupies the former Nishi Hongwanji Buddhist Temple (1925) and a new Pavilion (1998), linked by a plaza with a stone-and-water garden.

Civic Center Area

Roughly bounded by W. 1st, Hope, Temple & Los Angeles Sts.

The largest center for municipal administration in the US, this group of buildings and open plazas, planned and erected between the 1920s and the

Los Angeles City Hall

LACVB/Michele & Tom Grimm

1960s, occupies 13 blocks. The random array of structures ranges in style from the monumental **Hall of Justice Building** (1925), with its Neoclassical details *(northeast corner of S. Broadway & W. Temple St.),* to the contemporary structures of the Music Center.

Los Angeles City Hall★★

200 N. Spring St. ☎213-485-2891. www. cityofla.org.

City Hall's 28-story, pyramid-topped 454ft tower (1928) remains one of downtown L.A.'s most distinctive features and most widely recognized symbols. The 135ft-wide **rotunda**★ reveals French limestone walls and a floor composed of 4,156 inlays cut from 46 varieties of marble. The **observation deck** Kids in the tower (27th floor) affords sweeping **panoramas**★★ of the Los Angeles Basin.

Music Center

North of 1st St. between Hope & Grand Aves. ☎213-972-7211. www.musiccenter. org.

Los Angeles' elegant hilltop mecca for the performing arts (1964, Welton Becket) includes three white marble structures occupying a seven-acre plaza. Largest and most opulent building in the complex is the 3,197-seat **Dorothy Chandler Pavilion**★ (1964); this imposing composition of towering windows and columns hosts music, opera and dance productions. Innovative dramatic works are presented at the 752-seat **Mark Taper Forum** (1967), a low, cylindrical structure framed by a reflecting pool and a detached colonnade. The rectilinear 2,071-seat **Ahmanson Theatre** (1967) hosts plays, musicals, dance concerts and individual performing artists. The $170 million, Frank Gehry-designed **Walt Disney Concert Hall** opened in 2004, a fancifully shaped metal structure acclaimed for its acoustics.

The Cathedral of Our Lady of the Angels★

Bounded by N. Hill St. & N. Grand Ave., W. Temple St. & the Hollywood Fwy. (US-101). ☎213-637-7000. http:// cathedral. la-archdiocese.org.

L.A.'s $163-million cathedral, opened in 2002, fills a 5.6-acre site between the Music Center and Hall of Justice. Spanish architect José Rafael Muneo's striking design allows natural light to floor the congregational space through alabaster glass, beneath a copper roof. A 150ft campanile rises beside the cathedral.

Business District★★

Roughly bounded by Figueroa, 2nd, Spring & 9th Sts.

Anchored by Broadway and Spring Street, Los Angeles' historic business center reveals Beaux-Arts and Art Deco buildings dating primarily from 1890-1930; today it presents a lively Latino street scene. Queen of the district is the **Bradbury Building**★★ *(304 S. Broadway; ☎213-626-1893),* a modest brick building (1893, George H. Wyman) whose marvelous five-story **atrium** was inspired by a futuristic novel of the time, Edward Bellamy's *Looking Backward.* Skylit from the rooftop by diffuse natural light, the atrium has lacey wrought-iron railings and open-cage elevators, red-oak trim and stair treads of Belgian marble. It is opposite the **Grand Central Market**★ *(315 S. Broadway; ☎213-624-2378, www.grandcentralsquare.com),* built in 1897 and converted to a public market in 1917.

The gleaming commercial skyscrapers of Los Angeles' new downtown community are focused around 5th and Grand Streets. They are climaxed by **Library Tower**★ *(633 W. 5th St.),* among the tallest office buildings in the US west of Chicago. Soaring 1,017ft, the 73-story Italian-granite building (1992, I.M. Pei) is topped by an illuminated crown. It stands opposite the **Los Angeles Central Library**★ *(630 W. 5th St.; ☎323-228-7000, www.lapl.org/central),* a striking building (1926, Bertram Goodhue) conceived as an allegory on "The Light of Learning," expressed through sculptures, murals and tilework.

Around the corner is the **Millennium Biltmore Hotel**★★ *(506 S. Grand Ave.; ☎213-624-1011).* The 11-story, 700-room inn (1923, Schultze & Weaver), which was once the largest hotel in the West, displays opulent 16C Italian-style brickwork and terra-cotta, and high, hand-painted ceilings, in its Rendezvous Court. Another downtown landmark is **The Westin Bonaventure**★ *(404 S. Figueroa St.; ☎213-624-1000),* a 35-story hotel (1976, John Portman) composed of five cylindrical towers of mirrored glass.

Museum of Contemporary Art (MOCA)★★

250 S. Grand Ave. ✕ ♿ 🅿 ☎*213-626-6222. www.moca.org.*

An assemblage of geometric forms clad in red sandstone and green aluminum, this museum showcases late-20C visual art. Arata Isozaki (1986) designed an intimate, low-lying **complex**★ of cubes, a cylinder and 11 pyramidal skylights above underground galleries. Changing selections from the permanent collection include pieces by Borofsky, Johns, Nevelson, Oldenburg, Pollock, Rauschenberg, Rothko and Stella. Temporary shows are held here and at **The Geffen Contemporary at MOCA**★ *(152 N. Central Ave.; ☎213-626-6222).*

Exposition Park Area★★

This park *(bounded by Exposition Blvd., Figueroa St., Martin Luther King Blvd. & Vermont Ave.)* occupies the site of the original (1872) city fairgrounds, 3mi southwest of downtown adjacent to the **University of Southern California** campus. A 1913 civic campaign made it the setting for public museums and exhibit halls, athletic facilities and gardens, laid out in grand Beaux-Arts tradition by landscape architect Wilber D. Cook Jr. A $350 million facelift has added greenery, promenades and new facilities.

Los Angeles Memorial Coliseum★★

3911 S. Figueroa St. ✕ ♿ 🅿 ☎*213-748-6136. www.lacoliseum.com.*

This 92,000-seat oval (1923, Parkinson & Parkinson) is Los Angeles' preeminent sports stadium, hosting football, soccer, rock concerts and other outdoor events. Once the world's largest arena, the Coliseum gained renown as the principal venue of the 1932 and 1984 Olympic Summer Games.

Natural History Museum of Los Angeles County★★

Kids *900 Exposition Blvd.* ✕ ♿ 🅿 ☎*213-763-3466. www.nhm.org.*

The third-largest natural-history museum in the US holds more than 33 million specimens and artifacts. The dignified Beaux-Arts structure (1913) contrasts with the skeletons of a tyrannosaur and a triceratops poised for battle that greet visitors in the main foyer. The **Halls of African and North American Mammals** display animals in natural habitats. The **Hall of Gems and Minerals**★ houses more than 2,000 specimens. Two history halls depict ancient Latin American cultures and California's peoples from 1540-1940. The **Discovery Center** offers fossils and bones to touch, live creatures to pet. The **Insect Zoo** includes terrariums crawling with live specimens. Native American cultures are represented by a large collection of Zuni fetishes. The **Hall of Birds**★ is filled with interactive displays, including three walk-through habitats.

California ScienCenter★

Kids *700 State Dr.* ✕ ♿ 🅿 ☎*323-724-3623. www.californiasciencecenter.org.*

The largest and oldest (1951) institution of its kind in the western US, this reconstructed complex includes an IMAX theater and numerous interactive galleries. Exhibits in **World of Life** and **Creative World** explore the relationship between science and technology, from human cells to solar cars.

Nearby, the ScienCenter's Frank Gehry-designed **Air and Space Gallery** (1984) holds a three-story open space with stairs, landings and walkways that provide close-up looks at a century of replica aircraft, ranging from a pre-Wright Brothers glider to an A-12 Blackbird.

California African American Museum★

600 State Dr. ✕ ♿ 🅿 ☎*213-744-7432. www.caamuseum.org.*

This facility focuses on the heritage of California's large African-American popluation, particularly the role of black people in settling the West. Exhibits range from ancient West African art to modern music and art.

Griffith Park★★

Enter from Los Feliz Blvd., Ventura Fwy. (Rte. 134) or Golden State Fwy. (I-5). Open daily 6am - 10pm. ☎*323-913-4688.*

One of the largest urban parks in the US, Griffith Park straddles 4,103 acres (6.4sq mi) of the Santa Monica Mountains northwest of downtown Los Angeles. Wealthy miner Col. Griffith J. Griffith donated the land in 1882, along with money for a park observatory and the **Greek Theatre**, an open-air concert venue. A zoo, two museums and recreational facilities complement those attractions, but Griffith Park remains

Natural History Museum of Los Angeles County

LACVB/Michele & Tom Grimm

Practical Information

GETTING THERE

Fice large airports handle commercial traffic. Largest is **Los Angeles International Airport (LAX)** (*☎310-646-5252; www.lawa.org*), 10mi southwest of downtown. Also: **Burbank-Glendale-Pasadena Airport (BUR)** (*☎818-840-8840; www.burbankairport.com*), 16mi north of downtown; **Long Beach Airport (LGB)** (*☎562-270-5200; www.lgb.org*), 22mi south of downtown; **Orange County/John Wayne Airport (SNA)** (*☎949-252-5200; www.ocair.com*), 35mi southeast of downtown; **Ontario International Airport (ONT)** (*☎909-937-2700; www.lawa.org*), 35mi east of downtown. **Rental-car** agency branches are at all airports; call for ground transportation information.

Amtrak train: Union Station (*800 N. Alameda St.; ☎800-872-7245; www.amtrak.com*). Greyhound bus: Downtown depot (E. 7th & Alameda Sts.; *b800-231-2222; www.greyhound.com*).

Richard Carroll and LA INC/LACVB

GETTING AROUND

Express-bus and Metro rail service provided by Los Angeles County Metropolitan Transit Authority (MTA) (*☎213-922-6000 or 800-266-6883; www.mta.net*). Fares vary from $2.00 depending on distance and time. Purchase tickets at stations. The DASH (Downtown Area Short Hop) shuttle system (*☎213-808-2273; www.ladottransit.com*) runs frequently through downtown L.A. (*25 cents*) and in other neighborhoods. Taxi: Checker CabCo. (*☎310-300-5007*), Yellow Cab (*☎877-733-3305*).

ACCOMMODATIONS

Hotels.com (*☎800-246-8357; www.hotels.com*) and Hotel Reservaton Network (*☎800-715-7666; www.hoteldiscount.com*) provide free reservation services. The *Essential L.A. vacation guide (below)* contains a lodging directory.

Accommodations range from deluxe hotels *(over $350/day)* to budget motels *(as little as $40/day)*. Most bed-and-breakfast inns are found in residential sections of the city *($80–$200/day)*.

Entertainment – Consult the "Calendar" section of The Los Angeles Times (www.latimes.com) or the LA Weekly (www.laweekly.com) for a schedule of cultural events and addresses of principal theaters and concert halls. Tickets may be obtained from: **Ticketmaster** (*☎213-480-3232, www.ticketmaster.com*) or **Musical Chairs** (*☎310-207-7070; www.musicalchairstickets.com*).

VISITOR INFORMATION

Call the **Los Angeles Visitor Information Hotline** (*☎800-228-2452; www.lacvb.com*) to obtain Essential L.A., a free vacation-planning guide. **Los Angeles Convention & Visitors Bureau** information centers: Downtown, 685 Figueroa St. (*☎213-689-8822*).

---

largely a natural oasis inhabited by deer, opossums, quail and raptors. Miles of hiking and bridle trails weave through the park.

Griffith Observatory★★★

Kids *2800 E. Observatory Rd. > Visit by shuttle only; reservations necessary.* ✕ 🅿 *☎213-473-0800. www.griffithobs.org.* On the south slope of 1,625ft Mount Hollywood, this Art Deco observa-

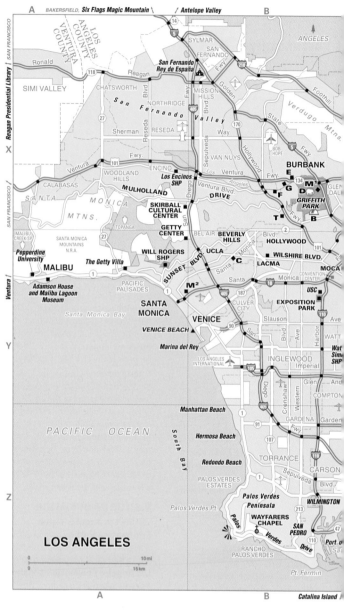

LOS ANGELES					
		Hollywood Freeway	BX	Santa Ana Freeway	CZ
		Huntington Drive	CDX	Santa Monica Boulevard	BY
		Imperial Highway	BDY	Santa Monica Freeway	BCY
Arrow Highway	DX	Katella Avenue	CDZ	Sepulveda Boulevard	BX, BZ
Artesia Freeway	CZ	Lincoln Avenue	CDZ	Sherman Way	ABX
Azusa Avenue	DXY	Long Beach Boulevard	CYZ	Simi Valley-San Fernando	
Carson Street	CZ	Long Beach Freeway	CYZ	Freeway	ABX
Colima Road	CDY	Main Street	DZ	Slauson Avenue	BY
Colorado Boulevard	CX	Mulholland Drive	ABX	Sunset Boulevard	ABY
Crenshaw Boulevard	BYZ	Orange Freeway	DYZ	Ventura Boulevard	BX
Foothill Boulevard	DX	Palos Verdes Drive	BZ	Ventura Freeway	ABX
Foothill Freeway	BDX	Pomona Freeway	CDY	Warner Avenue	DZ
Garden Grove Freeway	CDZ	Reseda Boulevard	AX	Western Avenue	BYZ
Gardena Freeway	BCZ	Riverside Freeway	DZ	Westminster Avenue	CZ
Golden State Freeway	BX	San Bernardino Freeway	CDY	Wilshire Boulevard	BY
Harbor Boulevard	DZ	San Diego Freeway	ADXZ	Willow Street	CZ
Harbor Freeway	BY	San Gabriel River Freeway	CY	Yorba Linda Boulevard	DZ

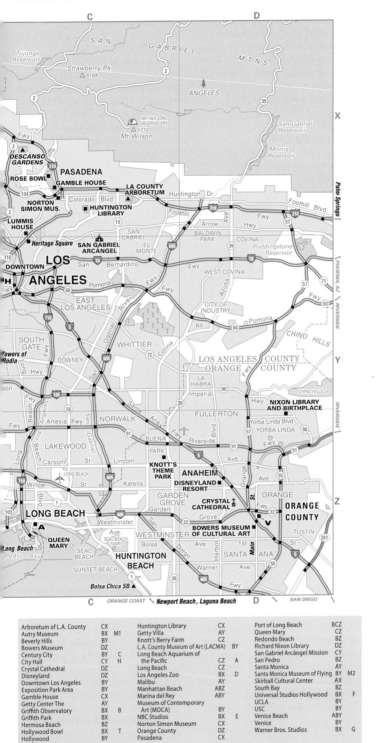

tory (1935) is a local landmark. A 240-pound brass Foucault pendulum in the **rotunda** demonstrates the earth's rotation. Beneath an 84ft copper dome is a **planetarium**. **Views**★★★ sweep to downtown L.A., the coast and the nearby Hollywood Sign (p 281).

Museum of the American West★★

Kids 4700 Zoo Dr. ✕ & 🅿 ☎323-667-2000. www.autrynationalcenter.org.
Established in 1988 by Western singer-film star Gene Autry (1907-98), this collection is presented in spacious galleries. The various exhibits range from a large collection of Colt firearms to western movie memorabilia and art. Several galleries explain the romance and lure of the West that drew settlers from the region's diverse ethnic groups.

Los Angeles Zoo★★

Kids 5333 Zoo Dr. ✕ & 🅿 ☎323-644-4200. www.lazoo.org.
Begun in the late 1890s by silent-film producer William Selig to provide animals for motion pictures, the zoo was donated to the city in the early 1920s. In 1966 it moved to 80 acres in northeastern Griffith Park; today it has more than 1,200 creatures of 400 species, including some 70 endangered species. A walkway leads to a three-acre children's zoo, then extends to trails that follow hilly terrain to visit aquatic animals, birds, and denizens of Australia, North America, Africa, Eurasia and South America. A documentary display is devoted to the California condor, and the zoo's successful part in breeding this rare species and reintroducing it to the wild.

Wilshire Boulevard★

Wilshire Boulevard is the city's grandest thoroughfare, extending west 16mi from downtown through central Los Angeles, Beverly Hills and Westwood to Santa Monica. The so-called **Miracle Mile** (La Brea to Fairfax Aves.) shows off some remarkable Art Deco buildings.

La Brea Tar Pits★

North side of Wilshire Blvd., west of Curson Ave.
Some 38,000 years ago, saber-tooth tigers, mammoths and giant sloths that came here to drink from pools were trapped in a thick, tar-like asphalt (*brea* in Spanish) at the surface. Since 1905, excavations have unearthed more than 100 tons of specimens—the world's largest cache of Ice Age fossils. Asphalt still bubbles through the water.

Page Museum at the La Brea Tar Pits★★

Kids 5801 Wilshire Blvd. & 🅿 ☎323-934-7243. www.tarpits.org.
Cast-fiberglass friezes of Ice Age animals top this square-sided museum. Skeletons are reconstructed from more than 4.5 million bones of 390 species found at the pits. Displays create the illusion of skeletons—of a **saber-tooth cat** and 9,000-year-old La Brea Woman—transforming into flesh and blood. In a glass-windowed **paleontology laboratory**, scientists clean and examine bones.

Los Angeles County Museum of Art (LACMA)★★★

5905 Wilshire Blvd. ✕ & 🅿 ☎323-857-6000. www.lacma.org. LACMA remains open during construction; however some galleries are closed for reinstallation of the collections by early 2008. Contact the Registrar in advance to determine if a particular work of art is on view: ☎323-857-6000.
This sprawling complex is the nation's largest art museum west of Chicago. LACMA's holdings comprise more than 100,000 works that range from Egyptian and Asian art to contemporary works. Its **Rifkind Center for German Expressionist Studies** is the largest and most comprehensive collection of its kind in the world. Other strengths include Old Masters paintings, West Mexican sculpture and Islamic works of art. In 2005 LACMA began Phase I of a master design that will include a new entrance pavilion and the new Broad Contemporary Art museum next to LACMA West.
In the **Ahmanson Building** are most of the permanent collections: modern art from Picasso to Hans Hoffman (*plaza*

level); ancient Egyptian, Mesopotamian, Iranian, Greek and Roman art as well as Middle Ages to 19C works *(second level)*; and Islamic, South and Southeast Asian, Indian, Tibetan and Nepalese art *(third level)*.

The **Hammer Building** displays **Impressionist** and post-Impressionist works by such artists as Cézanne and Degas. By fall 2008, it will contain **Chinese and Korean** art on the second level.

The **Modern and Contemporary Building** *(which will be renamed)* will house **American Decorative Arts** and **American Painting and Sculpture** *(second level)*. The third-level Art of the Ancient Americas and Latin American Art (colonial contemporary) will not be on view during Phase I. The plaza level will be devoted to special exhibits.

Open-air **sculpture gardens**, one with Rodin bronzes, the second with contemporary works by Alexander Calder and Henry Moore, flank the building.

The **Pavilion for Japanese Art** (1988, Bruce Goff and Bart Prince), a curvilinear structure surrounded by Japanese gardens, highlights the Price Collection of **Shin-enkan**: some 300 scroll paintings and screens created during the Edo period (1615-1868). Also exhibited are textiles, ceramics and lacquerware.

One block away, a 1939 Streamline Moderne edifice became **LACMA West** *(Wilshire Blvd. & Fairfax Ave.)* in 1998. The building has permanent exhibits on **Latin American** art and an interactive children's gallery.

Petersen Automotive Museum★★

[Kids] *6060 Wilshire Blvd.* ♿ 🅿 ☎323-930-2277. *www.petersen.org.*

Imaginative dioramas, photographs and computer stations show how automotive evolution influenced the growth of Los Angeles, the quintessential "car town." More than 200 rare cars, trucks and motorcycles are displayed. The **Streetscape** exhibit sets classic vehicles into dioramas illustrating Los Angeles at various points in history. Exhibits detail civic decisions to build broad boulevards, and eventually freeways, in place of trolley and streetcar lines.

Farmers' Market★

6333 W. Third St. at S. Fairfax Ave. ✗ 🅿 ☎323-933-9211. *www.farmersmarketla. com.*

This open-air market retains a rustic charm with more than 100 permanent businesses. Greengrocers and butchers serve locals; international food and souvenir stands cater to visitors.

Hollywood★★

As much a state of mind as a geographic entity, Hollywood is the symbolic and real heart of the movie industry. Part of the city of Los Angeles, it is located 6mi west of downtown and 12mi east of the Pacific coast, sweeping south from the Hollywood Hills (an extension of the Santa Monica Mountains). Prohibitionist H.H. Wilcox founded the suburb in 1883, and by the turn of the 20C the quiet community of 5,000 was most notable for a lack of saloons. It was incorporated in 1903, and seven years later was annexed by L.A. in anticipation of water from the Los Angeles Aqueduct *(p 273)* and the growth that would ensue.

In 1911, filmmaker David Horsely opened Hollywood's first movie studio in an abandoned roadhouse. By 1912, five large East Coast film companies and many smaller producers had relocated here. Investors in 1923 developed "Hollywoodland," a tract of elegant Mediterranean homes in the hills of Beachwood Canyon. To publicize the venture, the financiers erected what now is known as the **Hollywood Sign**★, of white sheet-metal letters 30ft wide and 50ft tall. *Located in Griffith Park, the sign is best viewed from the Griffith Observatory.*

Through the 1940s, Hollywood remained the center of the film industry and community, although many studios relocated to other nearby areas such as Burbank. Some landmark buildings subsequently deteriorated, but since the 1980s, energetic efforts have restored several landmarks along Hollywood and Sunset Boulevards. The Hollywood Chamber of Commerce *(7018 Hollywood Blvd.;* ☎323-469-8311, *www.hollywood-chamber.net)* has more information.

Hollywood Boulevard★★

Hollywood's main thoroughfare is 4.5mi long. The 1mi stretch between Gower Street and Sycamore Avenue is easily undertaken by foot. Grand movie palaces—including the **Pantages Theater**★ *(6233 Hollywood Blvd.)*, **Egyptian Theater**★ *(6712 Hollywood Blvd.)* **El Capitan Theater**★★ *(6838 Hollywood Blvd.)*—rub shoulders with souvenir stands and theme museums.

Embedded in the sidewalks of the **Walk of Fame**★ *(Hollywood Blvd. between Gower St. & La Brea Ave., and Vine St. between Sunset Blvd. & Yucca St.; ☎323-469-8311)* are more than 2,500 bronze-trimmed coral-terrazzo stars, conceived in 1958 by the Hollywood Chamber of Commerce as a tribute to entertainment personalities.

The intersection of **Hollywood and Vine** was immortalized as the hub of Hollywood in the 1930s and '40s. Its landmark is the **Capitol Records Tower**★ *(1750 Vine St.)*, a 150ft-tall complex of offices and studios (1954, Welton Becket) that resembles a stack of records surmounted by a phonograph needle.

Hollywood & Highland★

Hollywood Blvd. & Highland Ave. ✕ ✆ 🅿
The new hub of Hollywood is this $615 million development (2001, Ehrenkrantz, Eckstut & Kuhn) which is anchored by David Rockwell's 3,650-seat **Kodak Theatre** *(323-308-6300, www.kodaktheatre. com)*, new home of the Academy Award ceremonies (late March). The **Awards Walk**, a staircase from Hollywood Boulevard, cites every "best picture" honoree since the first Oscars were doled out in 1927. Retail shops surround Babylon Court, with 33ft-high elephant statues flanking a courtyard that echoes a 1916 D.W. Griffith movie set; winding into it is a granite path of anonymous "How I Got to Hollywood" quotes.

Grauman's Chinese Theatre★★

6925 Hollywood Blvd. ☎323-464-8111. *www.manntheatres.com/chinese.*
An ornate fantasy of chinoiserie, this theater (1926, Meyer & Holler) was com-missioned by showman **Sid Grauman.** Opened in 1927 for the gala premier of Cecil B. deMille's *King of Kings*, "The Chinese" is an eclectic, mansard-roofed pagoda, topped by stylized flames and flanked by white-marble dogs. The U-shaped cement forecourt features footprints and signatures of more than 180 Hollywood stars, with new ones added each year.

The Hollywood Museum★

7021 Hollywood Blvd. ♿🅿 ☎323-465-7900. *www.hollywoodmuseum.com.*
This museum preserves the Hollywood mystique. Displays on makeup, costumes and technological innovation dot the rotunda, supplemented with film clips and celebrity sound bites. It now offers exhibits that provide a living time-line of film-industry history.

Sunset Boulevard★

Stretching 20mi from El Pueblo to the Pacific Ocean, this thoroughfare runs past the Latino neighborhoods of Elysian Park; the studios and street life of Hollywood; the mansions of Beverly Hills; and the upscale neighborhoods of Westwood, Bel Air, Brentwood and Pacific Palisades. Its most famous stretch is the 1.5mi **Sunset Strip**★★ *(Crescent Heights Blvd. to Doheny Dr.)*. Hugging the Santa Monica Mountains, the street transits a once-unincorporated strip (hence its nickname) between Los Angeles and Beverly Hills. It is now part of the city of **West Hollywood**, whose identity as one of L.A.'s largest gay enclaves is more evident on Santa Monica Boulevard.

Melrose Avenue★

Although it stretches 7mi from Hollywood to Beverly Hills, Melrose distills its creativity and craziness into 16 blocks between La Brea and Fairfax Avenues. Boutiques, restaurants and shops specializing in bizarre collectibles and gifts draw a swath of humanity that ranges from Versace-clad businesspeople, to pierced-and-tattooed Generation Xers, to the flamboyantly gay, to camera-toting tourists from Tokyo.

Paramount Studios★

5555 Melrose Ave. ✕ ☎*323-956-1777.*
www.paramountstudios.com.
This complex is the only major studio left
in Hollywood; daily guided tours require
reservations. The wrought-iron Spanish
Renaissance-style gates, surmounted by
"Paramount Pictures" in script, endure
as a well-known symbol just north of
Melrose at Marathon Street.

Hollywood Forever

6000 Santa Monica Blvd., adjoining Para-
mount Studios lot. ☎*323-469-1181. www.*
hollywoodforever.com.
The 65-acre cemetery (formerly Hollywood Memorial Park) shelters the graves
of such Hollywood legends as Rudolph
Valentino, Douglas Fairbanks, Tyrone
Power and Cecil B. DeMille.

Hollywood Bowl★★

2301 N. Highland Ave. ✕👤📶 ☎*323-850-*
2000. www.hollywoodbowl.org.
Occupying a hollow surrounded by acres
of greenery, this natural amphitheater
is a popular concert site and summer
home to the Los Angeles Philharmonic
Orchestra, a Hollywood icon since 1919.
A series of band shells designed by Lloyd
Wright (son of Frank Lloyd Wright)
replaced the original concrete stage in
1927; a 100ft white quarter-sphere was
finalized in 1929. The shell was acousti-
cally modified by Frank Gehry in 1970
and 1980. Frank Sinatra, the Beatles, Igor
Stravinsky and Luciano Pavarotti have all
performed here.

Universal Studios Hollywood★★★

👶 *100 Universal Plaza, Universal City,*
3mi northwest of Hollywood Blvd. via
US-101. ✕👤📶 ☎*818-622-3801. www.*
universalstudios.com.
Part film and TV studio, part live-entertainment complex and amusement park,
420-acre Universal Studios sprawls over
a hillside above the San Fernando Valley. Silent-film producer Carl Laemmle
established a studio here in 1915. In 1964
Universal began to offer tram rides to
boost lunchtime revenues at its commissary; visitors were shown makeup
techniques, costumes, a push-button
monster and a stunt demonstration.
Today, Universal Studios Hollywood is
among the largest man-made tourist
attractions in the US, annually welcoming 5 million visitors. Adjoining are the
Universal Amphitheatre, a live concert
venue; and **Universal CityWalk**, a shopping, dining and entertainment complex
designed to appear as a compressed version of Los Angeles.
Live-performance stages in the upper
section of the park—the **Entertainment Center**—present regular shows

LACVB

Hollywood Bowl

Television Tapings

To attend the taping of a TV show as a member of the studio audience, visit the network's web site and click on the show you are interested in-- for example, the Letterman show at CBS. Or, you can sign up for limited same-day tickets at the individual studio. At Grauman's Chinese Theater (p 282) and Universal Studios (p 283), representatives circulate offering same-day tickets. **Audiences Unlimited** (all major networks); ☎ 818-753-3470; www.tvtickets.com. **ABC Tickets,** abc.go.com. **CBS,** www.cbs.com. N**BC Audience Services,** www.nbc. com. Fox, www.fox.com. **Paramount**, www.paramount.com.

inspired by popular films and TV programs. The **Animal Actors Stage** presents stunts performed by more than 60 trained animals. The **Universal Starway**, a .25mi covered escalator, descends to the **Studio Center**, situated in and around actual sound stages and backlots. A comprehensive look at the art and illusion of filmmaking is offered. The **Special Effects Stages** offer lessons in moviemaking magic: sound, makeup and computer effects. Among film-related rides are **Jurassic Park** (an escape from dinosaurs), **Terminator 2: 3-D** (with a live-action story line), **Backdraft** (chemicals burst into flames) and Shrek (join the cartoon character's world).

On the **Studio Tour★★** (45min), trams wind through movie sets portraying the Wild West, small-town America, New York City, Mexico, Europe and other locales. En route, they pass the Bates house built for Alfred Hitchcock's Psycho (1960); are attacked by the shark from Steven Spielberg's Jaws (1975); and encounter a rampaging 6.5-ton, 30ft King Kong. Trams also endure a collapsing bridge, a flash flood, the parting of the Red Sea, and an earthquake measuring 8.3 on the Richter scale.

Beverly Hills★★

Surrounded by Los Angeles and West Hollywood, Beverly Hills (www.beverlyhillsbehere.com) is an independent 6sq mi municipality of 35,000 citizens, founded in 1907. The city's name is synonymous with wealth and elegance, qualities seen in village-like shopping streets lined with international boutiques, fashionable restaurants and luxurious mansions lining gracious, tree-shaded drives. Architect Wilbur Cook laid out the grid; landscape architects John and Frederick Law Olmsted plotted sinuous drives through the foothills. The 1912 Beverly Hills Hotel (9641 Sunset Blvd.) began to attract stars to the area; Mary Pickford and Douglas Fairbanks built the first mansion, **Pickfair** (1143 Summit Dr.), high on a hill in 1920.

Rodeo Drive★★

This renowned street is a three-block stretch of mostly two- and three-story buildings north of Wilshire Boulevard. Boutiques and clothiers, jewelers, antique dealers and art galleries cater to expensive tastes. On the northeast corner of Wilshire and Rodeo Drive, the four-story **Via Rodeo** shopping complex (1990) whimsically resembles the street of an Italian hillside town. **Anderton Court** (328 N. Rodeo Dr.), an angular complex with an open ramp that winds around a spire, was built in 1954 from a Frank Lloyd Wright design.

Westside

University of California, Los Angeles (UCLA)★

Roughly bounded by Le Conte, Hilgard & Veteran Aves. and Sunset Blvd. ✕ ♿ 🅿 ☎310-825-4321. www.ucla.edu.

Lodged on a 420-acre foothills campus between Westwood Village and Bel Air, UCLA is the largest member of the University of California's nine-campus system, with more than 35,000 students. Brick-and-stone buildings of the Lombard Romanesque style encircle **Royce Quadrangle★**. **Royce Hall** (1929) houses an 1,850-seat theater. The entrance to **Powell Library** (1928) was modeled after the Church of San Zeno in Verona.

Fowler Museum at UCLA★ (☎310-825-4361, www.fowler.ucla.edu), an anthropology museum, is noted for its **silver collection** from England, Europe and America. The **Franklin D. Murphy Sculpture Garden**★★ (northeast corner of campus; ☎310-443-7000, www.hammer.ucla.edu) showcases more than 70 works by such leading artists as Rodin, Matisse, Miró and Moore.

UCLA Hammer Museum ★

10899 Wilshire Blvd., Westwood Village. 🅰 🅿 ☎310-443-7000. www.hammer. ucla.edu.

The **Armand Hammer Collection**, begun by the wealthy industrialist in the 1920s, features paintings and drawings by Old Masters (Tintoretto, Titian, Rubens), Impressionists and Postimpressionists (Degas, Manet, Cézanne, Gauguin, Toulouse-Lautrec).

The **UCLA Grunwald Center for the Graphic Arts** is one of the top three US collections of works on the paper.

The Getty Center★★★

1200 Getty Center Dr., just off I-405. ✕🅰🅿 ☎310-440-7300. www.getty.edu.

Oil millionaire **Jean Paul Getty** (1892-1976) began collecting paintings in 1931. After World War II, he resided in Europe, developing his worldwide oil business while expanding his art holdings and commissioning a Malibu museum, to display them. The collections quickly outgrew the Malibu space, and the Getty Center opened in 1997.

Architect Richard Meier designed the facility, a travertine-clad complex melding six buildings on a 110-acre campus with courtyards, walkways, fountains, gardens and stunning views. The **Central Garden** was conceived by artist Robert Irwin. The various branches of the J. Paul Getty Trust, including research and conservation organizations, occupy several of the structures; the **J. Paul Getty Museum**★★★ takes the remainder of the complex.

The museum showcases its founder's superior assemblages of French decorative arts; 17-20C European paintings, including such well-known works as

Rembrandt's *St. Bartholomew* (1661) and Van Gogh's *Irises* (1889); and works on paper, encompassing drawings, illuminated manuscripts and photographs. It occupies five pavilions arranged around an open courtyard and bridged by walkways on two levels, allowing visitors to create their own routes through the collections. Paintings are on the upper floors, displayed in natural light augmented as needed by artificial illumination.

Highlights include **illuminated manuscripts**★★, monumental French tapestries from the period of Louis XIV, and Impressionist canvases, including works by Renoir, Pissarro, Monet, Manet, Van Gogh, Munch and Cézanne.

Skirball Cultural Center★★

2701 N. Sepulveda Blvd., just off I-405. ✕🅰🅿 ☎310-440-4500. www.skirball.org. The West Coast's preeminent Jewish cultural center describes and interprets Judaism, and chronicles the tumultuous history of the faith from its origin to the present. **Visions and Values: Jewish Life from Antiquity to America** tells of cultural influences affecting the Jews and spread by them during migrations. The importance of the flow of time is illustrated in religious holidays; "Sacred Space" explains artistry and symbolism in temples. 🄺🄸🄳🄂 Noah's Ark is a new (2006) interactive exhibit which interprets the Biblical tale for young visitors.

Excursions

Santa Monica★

14mi west of downtown Los Angeles. ☎310-319-6263. www.santamonica.com.

This seaside city of 88,000 is a center of entertainment and arts, replete with galleries, theaters, fashionable cafes and boutiques. Both visitors and residents throng the **Third Street Promenade**★, a pedestrian mall (3rd St. between Wilshire Blvd. & Broadway), and **Santa Monica Place** (Broadway between 2nd & 4th Sts.), a shopping center designed by Frank Gehry (1979).

Jutting 1,000ft over the ocean, the wooden **Santa Monica Pier**★★ 🄺🄸🄳🅂 (*end of Colorado Ave.*) has been a landmark and gathering place since the early 20C. Its 9.5-acre expanse features an antique **carousel**★, fishing docks and an amusement park evoking the carnival spirit of a festive past. The present structure consists of the Municipal Pier (1909) and Pleasure Pier (1916), the latter designed by Coney Island creator Charles I.D. Looff. Both were restored during the 1980s.

Santa Monica Museum of Flying★★

🄺🄸🄳🅂 *Santa Monica Airport.* ✕&🄿 ☎310-392-8822. www.museumofflying.com.
Housed in a hangar at the first site of Donald Douglas Aircraft Co., this museum has 45 vintage aircraft, many restored to flight condition. Displays, films and models illuminate airplane construction and aviation history.

Malibu★

Pacific Coast Hwy. (Rte. 1), bordering Santa Monica to the northwest.
Malibu enjoys the loveliest setting of any Los Angeles-area beachside community. An exclusive residential enclave, the **Malibu Colony**, was established here in 1928, the beachside homesites drawing many celebrities. Stars still occupy multimillion-dollar homes in the security-gated colony, while others live in luxury aeries clinging to the mountainsides. In fall 2007 several homes and businesses were destroyed in a sweeping fire.

The Getty Villa★★★

17985 Pacific Coast Hwy., between Sunset & Topanga Canyon Blvds. Admission free, but timed reservation ticket required. 310-440-7300. www.getty.edu.
Sequestered in a lushly landscaped 65-acre canyon, this re-creation of a 1C BC Roman villa overlooks the Pacific. A replica of a villa in Herculaneum buried during the eruption of Mount Vesuvius in AD 79, the building was erected in 1974 and now is a showcase for Greek, Roman and Etruscan antiquities.

Venice and South Bay★

Venice Beach★★ is renowned not only for its sand but for its colorful street life—particularly along **Ocean Front Walk,** a beachside pedestrian way lined with cafes, boutiques and souvenir stalls, plus folksingers and rappers, comedic jugglers and swimsuit-clad skaters and muscle-bound weightlifters. South along the coast is **Marina del Rey,** the world's largest artificial harbor for 10,000 private yachts and sailboats.

Pasadena★★

9mi northeast of downtown Angeles. ☎ 626-795-9311. www.pasadenacal.com.
A city of 146,000, Pasadena boasts architectural and cultural attractions worthy of a larger community. A winter resort in the 1880s (many lavish mansions survive today), its early prosperity is reflected in the Spanish Baroque and Renaissance buildings of the **Civic Center**, erected in the 1920s.
In 1889 Pasadena's elite Valley Hunt Clubmarked New Year's Day with a parade of flower-decked coaches. Over the years the carriages evolved into elaborate floats covered with flowers, and in 1916 the parade was coupled with a championship college football game. Today the **Rose Parade**★★ and the **Rose Bowl Game** are televised across North America.

Norton Simon Museum★★★

411 W. Colorado Blvd. jō b626-449-6840. www.nortonsimon.org.
Elegantly displayed in a spare contemporary building are 1,000 works from a private art collection spanning seven centuries of European painting and sculpture and 2,000 years of Asian sculpture. Entrepreneur Norton Simon (1907-93) began collecting paintings in 1954, beginning with canvases by Gauguin, Bonnard and Pissarro. Before he died, Simon had amassed more than 11,000 pieces, with particular strengths in 14-18C European art, French Impressionist paintings, the works of Edgar Degas, and Indian and Southeast Asian sculpture. Immediately recognizable are Renoir, Monet and Van Gogh, as well as Degas' famous sculpture, *The Little Fourteen-Year-Old Dancer* (1878-81). Also presented are Picasso (*Woman with a*

Book, 1932), Daumier, Manet, Toulouse-Lautrec, Cézanne, Matisse, Modigliani, Braque, Klee and Kandinsky.

Gamble House★★

4 Westmoreland Pl., paralleling 300 block of N. Orange Grove Blvd. Visit by guided tour only. ☎626-793-3334. www.gamble-house.org.

A masterpiece of the Arts and Crafts movement (1907-09, Charles and Henry Greene), this house was the winter residence of David Gamble, heir of the Procter & Gamble soap company. Covered in redwood shingles, the sprawling, two-story gabled "bungalow" and its contents show a dedication to craftsmanship and integrated design. Decorative masterworks include furnishings and intricate woodwork.

Huntington Library, Art Collections and Botanical Gardens★★★

1151 Oxford Rd., San Marino, off E. California Blvd. 2.3mi southeast of downtown Pasadena ✕&🅿 ☎626-405-2100. www.huntington.org.

The Huntington comprises one of the world's finest research libraries of rare books and manuscripts; a world-class collection of 18-19C British art, French and American works; and renowned botanical gardens. Secluded in the upscale Pasadena suburb of San Marino,

it occupies the ranch of rail tycoon Henry E. Huntington (1850-1927).

The stately **Library**★★ houses 3.5 million manuscripts and 357,000 rare books, with emphasis on British and American history, literature and art from the 11C to the present. Displays include the **Ellesmere Chaucer**, an exquisitely illustrated manuscript (c.1410) of *The Canterbury Tales*, and a **Gutenberg Bible** (c.1450), one of few vellum copies in the US. Other highlights are a **First Folio** of William Shakespeare's plays and large edition of Audubon's Birds of America.

The **Huntington Art Gallery**★★ is housed in the Beaux-Arts-style former residence. Its collection of **British art**★★★ is considered outstanding, particularly for its 20 full-length portraits. Among them are Gainsborough's *Jonathan Buttall: "The Blue Boy"* (c.1770) and Lawrence's *Sarah Barrett Moulton: "Pinkie"* (1794). The **Virginia Steele Scott Galleries** feature works of American art ranging from the 18C to the early 20C.

Covering 150 acres, the **Botanical Gardens**★★ include 14,000 species. The 12-acre desert garden presents more than 5,000 types of mature cacti and succulents. The terraced **Japanese garden**★ encompasses a koi pond, moon bridge, Zen rock garden and bonsai. Rose and camellia gardens have more than 1,400

Santa Monica Pier

LACVB/Richard Carroll

cultivars. Others display herbs, palms, Australian plants and tropical species.

San Gabriel Arcángel Mission★

537 S. Mission Dr., San Gabriel, 7mi southeast of Pasadena via I-210, Sierra Madre Blvd. & Junipero Serra Dr. 🚿♿🅿 ☎626-457-3035. www.sangabrielmission.org. The mission was established in 1771 and moved here in 1775. The impressive **church** (1779-1805), still active, was inspired by the Moorish cathedral in Cordova, Spain. A cemetery dates from 1778. On the grounds are remnants of a water cistern, an aqueduct, soap and tallow vats, a kitchen and a winery.

Los Angeles County Arboretum and Botanical Garden★★

301 N. Baldwin Ave. at I-210, Arcadia, 5mi east of Pasadena. ✕♿🅿 ☎626-821-3222. www.arboretum.org. These 127-acre grounds showcase 30,000 plants of more than 7,000 species, including 150 species of eucalyptus and 2,299 species of orchids. A spring-fed lake was once a location for Hollywood films. South of the lake are historic buildings furnished in period style: reconstructed Gabrieleño wickiups; the rustic, three-room **Hugo Reid Adobe** (1840); and the ornately decorated **Lucky Baldwin Cottage** (1885).

Warner Bros. Studios★

4000 Warner Blvd., Burbank, off Rte. 134 (Ventura Fwy.) at Hollywood Way, 14mi west of Pasadena. Visit by guided tour (3hrs) only; reservations required. ♿🅿 ☎818-954-8687. www.studio-tour.com. This 108-acre complex has been Warner Bros. headquarters since 1928. Today its 33 sound stages are in constant use for movies, TV programs, commercials and sound recordings. Visitors are transported via golf cart to the backlot for a no-frills walk through sets, prop rooms, and construction shops.

NBC Studios

Kids *3000 W. Alameda Ave, Burbank, off Rte. 134 (Ventura Fwy.), 14mi west of Pasadena. Visit by guided tour (1hr) only.* ♿ ☎818-840-3537. Housing the largest color television studio in the US, this complex offers a look

at simple static and videotaped displays. Tours begin with a history of NBC, visit studios like The Tonight Show with Jay Leno, and demonstrate special effects, sound, makeup, costumes and sports broadcasting.

Long Beach★

25mi south of Los Angeles. ☎562-436-3645. www.visitlongbeach.com. Long Beach's growth began in earnest with the 1921 discovery of oil at Signal Hill. World War II brought a naval port and shipbuilding facilities; today the 2,807-acre **Port of Long Beach** ranks first in foreign-trade value and total liner-cargo tonnage among all US ports. Together with the adjacent Worldport L.A., it is the largest, busiest waterborne shipping center in the US. The sprawling city now has a population of 475,000.

Queen Mary★★★

Kids *1126 Queens Hwy.* ✕ ☎562-435-3511. www.queenmary.com. Dominating Long Beach Harbor, this renowned passenger ship was permanently docked after 31 years in England's Cunard White Star line. The 81,237-ton vessel is 1,019ft long. Built in Scotland in 1930-34, the *Queen Mary* made her maiden voyage in May 1936. Converted for military use during World War II, she carried more than 750,000 troops over 550,000mi, earning the nickname "Gray Ghost" for her camouflage paint and zig-zag routes. The ship returned to civilian use in July 1947 and became a favorite of such celebrities and socialites. By the mid-20C, air travel had eclipsed the era of the great passenger ships, and the *Queen Mary* completed the last of her 1,001 transatlantic voyages in 1967. Visitors may explore the bridge, officers' quarters and other operational centers; passenger suites and dining rooms; and the engine room, with its massive propeller box. Guided tours penetrate luxuriously furnished staterooms. A hotel occupies three of the 12 decks.

Scorpion Submarine★

Kids *1126 Queens Hwy.* ☎562-4352-0424. www.russiansublongbeach.com. The 3,000-ton *Scorpion*—more officially, the Soviet Foxtrot-class submarine Povodnaya Lodka B-427—is moored next to the *Queen Mary*. Nearly all of this 1972 diesel-electric sub(decommissioned in 1994) is open for tours.

Long Beach Aquarium of the Pacific★★

Kids *100 Aquarium Way (off Shoreline Dr. south of Ocean Blvd.).* ✕&🅿 ☎562-590-3100. www.aquariumofpacific.org.

The flowing wave shapes of this $117 million shoreside aquarium (1998) contain a fine marine exhibition. Its canvas is the Pacific Ocean, represented by more than 10,000 creatures—from the icy arctic waters off Russia and northern Japan, the temperate waters of the California and Mexico coasts, and the tropical islands and lagoons of the Palau archipelago in Micronesia. These three marine ecozones are divided into 17 major habitats and 30 smaller exhibits with more than 550 species of fish, birds, marine mammals, turtles and other denizens of the Pacific.

Catalina Island★

By passenger ferry from Long Beach, San Pedro or Newport Beach (45min-2hrs one way). ☎310-510-1520. www.catalinachamber.com.

Catalina's only town (of 3,200), **Avalon** is packed with pastel-colored houses and bungalows, hotels and restaurants. Autos are restricted. The stately **Wrigley Mansion** (1921), now a country inn, overlooks the town from 350ft above crescent-shaped Avalon Bay—not far from the adobe **Zane Grey Hotel** (1929), former home of the Western novelist. From the **Pleasure Pier**, glass-bottomed boats depart to view undersea life.

The old **Casino Building**★★ (*1 Casino Way;* ☎ *310-510-2000*), a 140ft-tall, circular Art Deco building (1928-29) with Spanish and Moorish flourishes, dominates Avalon Bay's north end. In the 1930s and 40s, big-band legends as Benny Goodman and Kay Kyser performed in its **Avalon Ballroom**. Murals adorn the box-office loggia and 1,184-seat Avalon Theatre.

The 38-acre **Wrigley Memorial and Botanical Garden** (*1400 Avalon Canyon Rd., 1.3mi inland from Avalon Bay;* ☎*310-510-2595*) highlights Catalina's native plants. Exhibits at the nearby **Santa Catalina Island Interpretive Center** (*Avalon Canyon Rd.;* ☎*310-510-2514, parks.co.la.ca.us*) examine isle flora and fauna, marine ecology, geology and native history.

San Pedro

Rtes. 47 & 110, 6mi west of Long Beach & 22mi south of downtown Los Angeles.

Linked to Long Beach by the **Vincent Thomas Bridge**, San Pedro's vast Worldport L.A. is one of the nation's busiest ports and the West Coast's leading passenger terminal. Harbor history is told at the **Los Angeles Maritime Museum** Kids (*Berth 84, foot of 6th St.;* ☎*310-548-7618, www.lamaritimemuseum.org*). Housed in an innovative gray structure (1981, Frank Gehry) designed to evoke maritime images, the **Cabrillo Marine Aquarium**★ Kids (*3720 Stephen White Dr. off Pacific Ave.;* ☎*310-548-7562, www.cabrilloaq.org*) offers an introduction to California marine life

ORANGE COUNTY★★

MICHELIN MAP 493 B10, 11 AND MAP P 279
PACIFIC STANDARD TIME
POPULATION 3,002,000

Sprawling east and south of Los Angeles, Orange County's broad plain, formerly cloaked with the orange groves for which the county is named, is an exurban metropolis that extends 22mi from the 5,687ft crest of the Santa Ana Mountains to Pacific beaches. Population has more than doubled since the 1960s, especially in and around Anaheim and Santa Ana, capitals of suburban housing and shopping malls.

- **Information:** ☎714-765-8888 or www.anaheimoc.org
- **Don't Miss:** Disneyland Park
- **Organizing Your Time:** Allow 3 days. Disneyland is much bigger than California Adventure--plan to devote twice as much time to the bigger park.

Disneyland® Resort★★★

Kids ⅢⅢ *Between Katella Ave., West St., Ball Rd. & Harbor Blvd., Anaheim.* ☎*714-781-4565. www.disneyland.com.*
For 46 years after it opened in 1955 as America's ultimate fantasy land, Disneyland was without peer. In 2001, after a $1.4 billion expansion, Disneyland evolved into Disneyland Resort. The original 90-acre park was joined by the 55-acre Disney's California Adventure. Linking the two is Downtown Disney. .
Walter Elias Disney (1901-66) began working in animation before he headed for Hollywood at age 22. He and his brother, Roy, established a studio and scored their first big success with the 1928 debut of *Steamboat Willie*, starring a character named **Mickey Mouse** and combining animation with sound. In the early 1950s, Disney purchased a 180-acre tract of orange groves for an amusement park. The park opened in July 1955 to national fanfare.

Disneyland Park★★★

Roughly elliptical in shape, Disneyland has eight distinct sections radiating from a Central Plaza.
Tidy Victorian storefronts, horse-drawn trolleys and a double-decker omnibus accent **Main Street, USA,** an idyllic re-creation of early-20C, small-town America. Evenings bring **"Remember... Dreams Come True"** fireworks show, featuring a Tinker Bell fly-by. **"The Walt Disney Story"** traces the construction of Disneyland and the Disney empire. At the Main Street Cinema, animated black-and-white classics, including *Steamboat Willie*, are continuously screened. Passengers board the **Disneyland Railroad** here to circle the park.
Tomorrowland represents a look at an imagined future. **"Space Mountain"** is a roller coaster enclosed in a futuristic mountain. **"Star Tours,"** conceived by *Star Wars* creator George Lucas, takes travelers to the Moon of Endor by means of special effects. The **"Astro Orbiter"** is both a 64ft-high kinetic sculpture and a spinning ride. **"Honey, I Shrunk the Audience"** is a 3-D film presentation (viewers wear special glasses) based on the hit film *Honey, I Shrunk the Kids*. **"Innoventions"** showcases emerging technologies in electronics and computer applications.
Fantasyland was Walt Disney's personal favorite. The main entrance is through **"Sleeping Beauty Castle,"** a renowned icon with gold-leafed turrets and a moat. At the **"King Arthur Carrousel,"** Disney movie tunes are pumped from a calliope as antique horses take their riders in continual circles. **"It's a Small World"** boats float visitors past 500 Audio-Animatronics® children and animals representing nearly 100 nations, all singing a theme song promoting cultural understanding. Carnival-style rides include the **"Mad Tea Party,"** a tilt-a-whirl of colorful cups and saucers.

For the very young, **"Dumbo the Flying Elephant"** soars up and down in gentle circles; **"Storybook Land Canal Boats"** glide past a series of scale-model miniatures. Bigger kids prefer the **"Matterhorn Bobsleds,"** which speed downhill through ice caves.

Mickey's Toontown is an exclusive residential address for Disney characters. At **"Mickey's House,"** the celebrity mouse may pose for a photo. His loyal sweetheart invites friends to check on what's cooking at **"Minnie's House."** Donald Duck's boat, the **"Miss Daisy,"** offers a bird's-eye view of Toontown from its bridge, adjacent to **"Goofy's Bounce House,"** an inflatable dwelling for the younger set. A spiral staircase invites exploration of **"Chip 'n Dale's Tree House."**

Frontierland offers a return to the Old West. The **"Golden Horseshoe Stage"** features musical revues. **"Big Thunder Mountain Railroad,"** a runaway mine train, scales the crags and caves of a reddish mountain. Plying the **"Rivers of America"** are the **"Mark Twain Steamboat,"** a Mississippi River paddle wheeler, and the **"Sailing Ship Columbia,"** a three-masted windjammer. Coonskin-capped guides paddle voyageurs in **"Davy Crockett's Explorer Canoes."** At night, visitors crowd the riverbank to see **"Fantasmic!,"** a fiber-optic show (22min) with Disney animation at its pyrotechnic best.

Riders float through the swamps and bayous within **"Splash Mountain,"** at the top of which awaits a 52ft flume that hurtles down a 47° slope to a drenching splash.

New Orleans Square is a re-created French Quarter. In the **"Pirates of the Caribbean,"** which spurred the namesake movies, visitors float through a swamp and enter a village of buccaneers. Ghosts spook the **"Haunted Mansion";** doom buggies travel eerily among holographic specters.

Adventureland's **"Enchanted Tiki Room"** stars fantastical tropical birds and flowers with enough charisma to inspire the audience to sing along. **"Jungle Cruise"** safari boats travel through a forest populated by mechanized crocodiles, hippos, elephants and tigers. In the **"Indiana Jones Adventure®,"** transport vehicles make a harrowing journey through an archaeological site.

Disney's California Adventure★★

This new park, which visitors enter beneath a replica of San Francisco's Golden Gate Bridge, celebrates its home state in three "lands." Golden State pays homage to the state's historical, agricultural and recreational treasures; Hollywood Pictures Backlot recalls the golden days of Hollywood; Paradise Pier is a beachfront amusement zone.

Golden State visitors may head for Condor Flats, designed as a 1940s high-desert airfield, to go **"Soarin' Over California."** This simulated ride surrounds guests in a giant projection dome and takes them on a flight around the state. There's hiking and whitewater rafting on **"Grizzly Peak"**; the 3-D It's Tough to Be a Bug at **"Bountiful Valley Farm"**; wines in the Napa Valley, and seafood with sourdough on Monterey's Cannery Row.

Hollywood Pictures Backlot, a two-block version of Hollywood Boulevard, includes an animation studio and live-entertainment theater. **"Jim Henson's Muppet Vision 3D"** showcases the lovable puppet creatures, while **"Twilight Zone Tower of Terror"** simulates a horrifying 13-storey elevator ride.

Paradise Pier is not for the faint of heart. Among the thrill rides, **"California Screamin'"** is a roller coaster that accelerates from 0 to 55mph in less than 5sec. **"Maliboomer"** is a 180ft free fall; **"Jumpin' Jellyfish"** is an underwater parachute ride. **"Sun Wheel"** is a giant Ferris wheel.

Downtown Disney★

Linking the two theme parks with the hotels along a long avenue, this arcade includes everything from a 12-theater cinema complex to dining-and-performance venues for jazz, Latin, rock and blues music.

Additional Sights

Knott's Theme Park

Kids ||||| *8039 Beach Blvd., Buena Park, off I-5.* ✕ & 🅿 ☎714-220-5200. *www. knotts.com.*

In the 1920s, Walter Knott established a berry farm and roadside stand here. During the Great Depression, his wife, Cordelia, began selling chicken dinners. In 1940 Knott constructed an Old West town to amuse hungry patrons waiting to get in. Today Knott's features many relocated or replicated historic structures along with 165 rides and shows. Among the most popular is the Silver Bullet rollercoaster.

Bowers Museum of Cultural Art★★

2002 N. Main St., Santa Ana; off I-5. ✕ & 🅿 ☎714-567-3600. *www. bowers.org.*

Dedicated to indigenous fine art of the Americas, Africa and the Pacific Rim, this collection comprises 85,000 artifacts dating from 1500 BC to the mid-20C. Highlights include the **African collection**, **pre-Columbian collection** and **Native American art**. Artifacts from California's mission and rancho periods have a gallery.

The Richard Nixon Library & Birthplace★

18001 Yorba Linda Blvd., Yorba Linda, 3.5mi east of Rte. 57 (Orange Fwy.). & 🅿 ☎714-993-5075. *www.nixon foundation.org.*

Letters, papers, memorabilia and interactive exhibits illustrate and commemorate the life of Richard Nixon (1913-94), 37th US president (1969-74).

Newport Beach★

Pacific Coast Hwy. (Rte. 1) & Newport Blvd. (Rte. 55). ☎949-719-6100. *www.visitnewportbeach.com.*

The maritime roots of this resort and residential community of 75,000 are evident on the **Balboa Peninsula**, a large pleasure-craft anchorage. The **Balboa Pavilion**★ *(400 Main St.)* was a popular dance hall in the 1940s. Extending east is the **Fun Zone** **Kids** of arcades and carnival rides. Private companies operate **harbor cruises.**

The respected **Orange County Museum of Art**★ *(850 San Clemente Dr., Fashion Island, off Jamboree Rd.;* ☎949-759-1122, *www.ocma.net)* focuses on modern and contemporary work, especially 20C California art.

Laguna Beach★

Pacific Coast Hwy. (Rte. 1) & Laguna Canyon Rd. (Rte. 133). ☎949-497-9229. *www. lagunabeachinfo.org.*

A magnificent sea-cliff setting★ has attracted artists since 1903. More than 90 studios and galleries share the community of 23,727. The **Laguna Art Museum**★ *(307 Cliff Dr.;* ☎949-494-8971,

Silver Bullet at the Knott's Theme Park

www.lagunaartmuseum.org) is a center for modern California art.

San Juan Capistrano Mission★★
Ortega Hwy. (Rte. 74) & Camino Capistrano, San Juan Capistrano, off I-5. ☎949-234-1300. www.missionsjc.org.
The seventh California mission was founded in 1776 by Padre Junípero Serra. In its **Great Stone Church** (1806) three rooms in the west wing display items from Native American, mission and rancho periods. In the east wing is the original mission chapel (1777).
Both San Juan Capistrano and the mission are famous for the swallows that return each year from winter nesting grounds in Argentina; their arrival is celebrated with a popular festival.

PALM SPRINGS★★

MICHELIN MAP 493 C 11
PACIFIC STANDARD TIME
POPULATION 42,807

Palm Springs is the most celebrated of a string of resort and retirement towns in the Coachella Valley east of Los Angeles. The area annually welcomes 3 million visitors and part-time residents, among them celebrities who come to play golf (close to 100 courses dot the valley) and browse the upscale galleries and boutiques.

- **Information:** ☎760-770-9000, www.palmspringsusa.com
- ▶ **Orient Yourself:** The divide between coastal LA and inland desert, San Gorgonio Pass is one of the windiest places in the US, and holds one of the nation's biggest wind-power farms.
- **Don't Miss:** The aerial tramway.
- **Especially for Kids:** Living Desert Wildlife Park.

Sights

Palm Springs Aerial Tramway★★★
Kids *Tramway Rd. west off Rte. 111, 2mi north of downtown Palm Springs.* ✕&🅿 *☎760-325-1391. www.pstramway.com.*
Revolving, 80-passenger gondolas ascend the face of Mount San Jacinto (ha-SIN-toe) on cables suspended from towers anchored in the rocky slope. The 5,900ft climb *(14min)* to the 8,516ft summit crosses five biotic zones, from desert to alpine forest with winter snow.

Palm Springs Art Museum★★
101 Museum Dr., 2 blocks west of N. Palm Canyon Dr. and Tahquitz Wy. ✕& *☎760-325-0189. www.psmuseum.org.*
The museum offers a survey of the natural history, anthropology and art of California's deserts. Exhibits in the **Central Gallery** include Native American basketry, Asian art (collected by actor William Holden), and furniture and bronze sculptures by actor George Montgomery. The **Natural Science wing** introduces geology, flora and fauna. On the upper level is a 15ft glass sculpture by Dale Chihuly.

Indian Canyons★
S. Palm Canyon Dr., 4mi south of downtown Palm Springs, off Rte. 111. 🅿 *☎760-325-3400. www.aguacaliente.org.*
The Agua Caliente Band of Cahuilla Indians retains ownership of three canyons in the San Jacinto Mountains with groves of **fan palms**, California's only native species of palm: **Palm Canyon**★★ **Andreas Canyon**★ *(.8mi)* and more remote **Murray Canyon** *(1mi)*. From the **Tahquitz Canyon Visitors Center**★ *(500 W. Mesquite Dr.; ☎760-416-7044, www.tahquitzcanyon.com)* ranger-led tour depart for another canyon with rock art and a 60ft waterfall.

Living Desert Zoo and Gardens★★

Kids *Portola Ave., 1.3mi south of Rte. 111, Palm Desert, 15mi east of Palm Springs.* ✕ ♿ 🅿 ☎ *760-346-5694. www.livingdesert.org.*

This 1,200-acre botanical garden and zoo offer a survey of 1,500 plants and animals from arid lands. A path connects gardens representing each main subdivision of North American deserts, including the Upper Colorado Desert, the Yuman Desert and the arid Baja Peninsula.

Excursions

Joshua Tree National Park

North entrance at Twentynine Palms (Rte. 62), 52mi northeast of Palm Springs & 140mi east of Los Angeles via I-10. ♿ ☎760-367-5500. www.nps.gov/jotr.

This 1,240sq-mi park contains two very distinct deserts—the high (Mojave) and low (Colorado). The transition can be experienced in a short drive.

The **Joshua tree** (*Yucca brevifolia*) is common in the cool Mojave Desert (above 3,000ft) and can grow as tall as 40ft.

Rim of the World Drive★★

Rte. 18 from San Bernardino to Big Bear City (40mi), 85mi northwest of Palm Springs via I-10.

The rugged San Bernardino Mountains dominate the landscape north of their namesake city. Rising to 11,499ft at San Gorgonio Mountain, the range harbors **Big Bear Lake**★, 6mi long. The drive links Big Bear with **Lake Arrowhead**, a summer-home colony.

CENTRAL COAST★

MICHELIN MAP 493 A, B10
PACIFIC STANDARD TIME

The Central Coast region balances a vital agricultural economy with a robust tourist industry. Natural beauty, historic Spanish roots, and a blend of cultural sophistication with casual friendliness contribute to its popularity.

🛈 **Information:**☎805-966-9222 www.santabarbaraca.com
Kids **Especially for Kids:** Sea Center.

Sights

Ventura

Pacific Coast Hwy., US-101 & Rte. 126, 62mi west of Los Angeles. ☎805-648-2075. www.ventura-usa.com.

This low-key coastal city of 110,000 grew up around San Buenaventura Mission..

San Buenaventura Mission

225 E. Main St. ☎805-643-4318. www.sanbuenaventuramission.org.

Padre Serra set his ninth mission halfway between San Diego and Carmel. Inside the structure (1809) that serves as parish church, the reredos was made in Mexico City. A **museum** displays religious relics.

Channel Islands National Park★

Headquarters, 1901 Spinnaker Dr., Ventura. ⚠ ☎805-658-5730. www.nps.gov/chis. This park encompasses the northern five of eight islands along the coast south of Santa Barbara:

Anacapa Island, 14mi west of Ventura; **Santa Cruz Island**, where sea lions inhabit **Painted Cave**★; **Santa Rosa Island**; **San Miguel Island** , which harbors a caliche forest, the calcium-carbonate castings of ancient trees; tiny **Santa Barbara Island** is a breeding ground for elephant seals.

The **visitor center** is at park headquarters. Boats depart from Ventura with **Island Packers** (☎805-642-1393), from Santa Barbara with **Truth Aquatics** (☎805-962-1127).

Santa Barbara★★

US-101, 94mi west of Los Angeles. ☎805-966-9222. www.santabarbaraca.com.
Red-tile roofs, stucco buildings and palm-fringed beaches create a Mediterranean ambience in this coastal city of 90,000. The showpiece is the 1929 **Santa Barbara County Courthouse**★★ *(1100 block of Anacapa St.; ☎805-962-6464, www.sbcourts.org)*, a Moorish castle around a sunken garden.

The city's **waterfront**★ extends from the **Santa Barbara Yacht Harbor** *(W. Cabrillo Blvd.)* to **Stearns Wharf**★ *(foot of State St.)*. The **Nature Conservancy Visitor Center** *(☎805-962-9111, www.tnc.org)* has displays on the Channel Islands; the **Sea Center** Kids *(☎805-962-2526, www.sbnature.org)* is an aquarium; and **Shoreline Park** provides a vantage point to watch whales during the migrating season *(Nov–Apr)*.

Santa Barbara Museum of Art★

1130 State St. ✕👤 ☎805-963-4364. www.sbmuseart.org.
Galleries showcase Asian, European and American art. **Greek and Roman antiquities** include the Lansdowne Hermes (AD 2C). **French and British art, American art** and a gallery of 20C art round out the exhibits.

Santa Bárbara Mission★★★

2201 Laguna St. 👤 ☎805-682-4713. www.sbmission.org.
California's 10th mission dominates the city. Dedicated in 1786, the first church was replaced three times by larger structures. The present church (1820) serves as a parish church, research library and archive for the entire chain.

The **padres' quarters** contain mission artifacts from the late 18C to early 19C. The **interior** of the church is adorned with bright motifs; the painted canvas reredos (1806) formed the basis for the detailed design scheme.

Santa Barbara Museum of Natural History★

2559 Puesta del Sol. From the mission turn right on Los Olivos St. 👤👤 ☎805-682-4711. www.sbnature.org.

Santa Barbara Mission, Front Façade

Santa Barbara Conference & Visitors Bureau And Film Commission

Exhibits in this complex display flora, fauna, geology and ethnography of the West Coast. The **Chumash Indian Hall** contains artifacts from this tribe.

Solvang

Rte. 246 east of US-101, 34mi northwest of Santa Barbara.
Founded as a Danish farm colony in 1911, Solvang retains Danish provincial architectue at **Elverhøj Museum** *(1624 Elverhoy Way; ☎805-686-1211)*, which resembles an 18C Jutland farmhouse.

Santa Inés Mission★

1760 Mission Dr., Solvang. 👤👤 ☎805-688-4815. www.missionsantaines.org.
Founded in 1804, Santa Inés was the final link in the chain between San Francisco and San Diego. In the museum **vestments**★ date back to the 16C.

La Purísima Mission★★

2295 Purisima Rd., via Mission Gate Rd., 1.8mi off Rte. 246 near Lompoc, 53mi northwest of Santa Barbara via US-101 and Hwy. 1. 👤 ☎805-733-3713. www.lapurisimamission.org.
The long, narrow **church** (1818) was built to provide access to travelers on El Camino Réal. The **residence building**★ housed padres' quarters, a library, office, wine cellar, guest quarters and chapel. Plants raised for food and medicine are cultivated in the **mission garden**★.

OKLAHOMA

It's fitting that Oklahoma means "red people" in the Choctaw language. The human history of this state revolves around its native population, largest in the US. Long before Coronado traipsed through in 1541, Osage, Kiowa, Comanche and Apache tribes had outposts in the short-grass plains. Wichitas and other sedentary tribes built mound homes in the green mountains of the east.

After the Louisiana Purchase of 1803, the growing population of the eastern US eyed the plains as a "remedy" for what they perceived as "the Indian problem." Despite treaties with the US, Native Americans were forcibly evacuated from their homelands: most tragic was the "Trail of Tears" march to Oklahoma in 1838-39 (👉 see sidebar). For a

time, Cherokees, Choctaws, Seminoles, Chickasaws and Creeks lived peacefully in their new home, setting up tribal governments, schools and farms. But after the Civil War, the US government took their Oklahoma lands as "punishment" for siding with the Confederacy. In 1889, 50,000 people raced to stake their plots. Cheaters staking early claims led to the state's nickname: the Sooner State.

Oklahoma City became the largest stockyard in the US. Oil was discovered in the state as early as 1901, and In 1907, Oklahoma was the 47th state admitted to the Union.

Today, Indian festivals and museums are treasured fixtures, and oil money has given Oklahoma City and Tulsa world-class cultural facilities. Reflecting Rodgers and Hammerstein's musical *Oklahoma!*, a cowboy ambience pervades the state in art, music and wardrobe.

Oklahoma City Skyline

Address Book Oklahoma

For price ranges, see the Legend on the cover flap.

WHERE TO STAY

$$$ Hotel Ambassador – *1324 S. Main St., Tulsa.* ✕ ♿ 🅿 ☎*918-587-8200 or 888-408-8282. www.hotelambassador-tulsa.com. 55 rooms.* This 10-story boutique hotel boasts a Mediterranean terra-cotta façade. Built in 1929, it was fully restored and reopened in the late 1990s. In the basement, **The Chalkboard** (**$$$**) brasserie offers sophisticated contemporary dinner cuisine.

$$$ McBirney Mansion – *1414 S. Galveston St. at Riverside Dr., Tulsa.* ♿ 🅿 ☎*918-585-3234. www.McBirneyMansion. com. 9 rooms.* Overlooking the Arkansas River, this elegant three-story landmark is on the National Register of Historic Places. Stone pathways wind through gardens and ponds. Wine and appetizers are served each evening in the grand library; breakfast comes to rooms in baskets with fresh flowers.

$$$ The Waterford Marriott – *6300 Waterford Blvd., Oklahoma City.* ✕ ♿ 🅿 ⛲ ☎*405-848-4782 or 800-992-2009. www.marriott.com. 197 rooms.* Rooms at this luxury hotel, in an upscale midtown residential neighborhood, are equipped with the latest amenities. Live music is served with gourmet regional specialties in the **Garden Terrace** (**$$**).

$$$ The Grandison at Maney Park – *1200 N. Shartel St., Oklahoma City.* 🅿 ☎*405-232-8778 or 888-799-4667. www. bbonline.com/ok/grandison. 9 rooms.* A charming 1904 Victorian within walking distance of downtown Oklahoma City, this three-story inn boasts an eclectic variety of rooms behind its mahogany woodwork and original stained glass. Rooms vary from Florentian and Turkish themes to even a treehouse.

WHERE TO EAT

$$$$ The Coach House – *6437 Avondale Dr., Oklahoma City.* ☎*405-842-1000. www.restaurant-row.org/coach.* **Contemporary.** Once a coach house, this restaurant recalls a European country inn. Delicate pâtés, delectable lamb and duck dishes, and a to-die-for Grand Marnier soufflé are served on linen with fine crystal and china.

$$$ The Haunted House – *7101 N. Miramar Blvd. (off I-44 Frontage Rd. east of Martin Luther King Ave.). Oklahoma City.* ☎*405-478-1417. Dinner only. Closed Sun.* **Steak and Seafood.** This spooky, hard-to-find estate home, shrouded in woodland, was the scene of a trio of unsolved murders in 1963-64. Fine steaks highlight a brief menu.

$$$ Mickey Mantle's Steakhouse – *7 Mickey Mantle Dr., Oklahoma City.* ☎*405-272-0777. www.mickeymantlesteakhouse.com.* **Steak and Seafood.** Honoring the New York Yankee slugger and Oklahoma native, this casually elegant restaurant, opposite the Bricktown Ballpark, is flush with baseball photos, trophies and memorabilia.

$$ Bourbon Street Cafe – *1542 E. 15th St., Tulsa.* ☎*918-583-5555. www. bourbonstreetcafe.com.* **Cajun-Creole.** Fried alligator tail, crawfish etouffée, jambalaya and bourbon pecan pie are a few of the offerings at this lively New Orleans-style restaurant, first of three in Oklahoma. (Another is on Bricktown Canal in Oklahoma City.) Diners enjoy live jazz and Delta-toned libations.

$$ Cattlemen's Steakhouse – *1309 S. Agnew St., Oklahoma City.* ☎*405-236-0416. www.cattlemensrestaurant.com.* **American.** In the heart of Stockyards City, guests can enjoy hand-cut steaks cooked over hot coals—just as cowboys have done since 1910, when they stopped in after round-ups. The name changed in 1945 when the restaurant changed hands in a craps game.

$ Ann's Chicken Fry House – *4106 NW 39th St., Oklahoma City.* ☎*405-943-8915. Closed Sun.* **American.** OKC's surviving Route 66 diner remains a local landmark with the high tail fins of a pink '50s car still parked streetside. Oklahomans visit for the chicken-fried steaks, of course.

$ Metro Diner – *3001 E. 11th St., Tulsa.* ☎*918-592-2616.* **American.** Waitresses in poodle skirts swirl past the tables of this classic Route 66 diner. Order a 50s-style burger, a chocolate malt and a slice of apple pie, as the jukebox pumps out "Rock Around the Clock."

OKLAHOMA CITY★★

MICHELIN MAP 492 K 11
CENTRAL STANDARD TIME
POPULATION 537,000

Oklahoma City has grown from a land-grab tent city of 10,000 to a bustling urban hub with more than a million residents in its metropolitan area. It stretches across three counties and 650sq mi on the banks of the North Canadian River, ranking it as one of the largest cities, geographically, in the US.

- **Information:** ☎405-297-8912, www.visitokc.com
- **Don't Miss:** National Cowboy & Western Heritage Museum
- **Organizing Your Time:** Allow two days to see Oklahoma City and Norman, but allot another day for Eastern Oklahoma's countryside.
- **Especially for Kids:** Omniplex.

A Bit of History

Oil was discovered here in 1928; oil wells still can be found all over the city, seven on the grounds of the state capitol. Western heritage is apparent in everything from museums and restaurants to the locals' favorite garb: cowboy boots and shirts.

In 1993, residents voted more than $300 million for urban revitalization. Two years later, the shocking terrorist bombing of the city's federal building took 168 lives; the Oklahoma City National Memorial helped the recovery process.

Sights

Oklahoma City National Memorial★★

620 N. Harvey Ave. at NW 5th St. ☎405-235-3313. www.oklahomacitynationalmemorial.org.

With its two massive gates, reflecting pool and 168 empty glass-and-granite chairs, this memorial, designed by Hans Butzer, Torrey Butzer and Sven Berg, stands as a solemn reminder of the April 19, 1995, terrorist bombing of the Alfred P. Murrah Federal Building that killed 168 men, women and children. Housed in the adjacent Journal Record Building (damaged in the incident) is Memorial Center, where poignant exhibits trace the tragedy—the largest terrorist attack on US soil prior to the Sept.

11, 2001, attack on New York's World Trade Center.

Oklahoma City Museum of Art★★

415 Couch Dr. between Walker & Hudson Aves. ☎405-236-3100. www.okcmoa.com.

Its new $18.5 million arts center has helped Oklahoma's oldest museum find a place on the world art stage. Architect Allen Brown's three-story limestone building incorporates Art Deco elements of the former Centre Theatre (lobby, staircase); a 10-ton, 45ft glass sculpture by Dale Chihuly dominates its atrium. Founded in 1910, the museum's contemporary history dates from 1968, when it purchased the collection of the Washington Gallery of Modern Art upon its merger with the Corcoran Gallery of Art. Now the cornerstone of a 3,100-piece collection, these 153 pieces highlight such artists as Claes Oldenburg, Helen Frankenthaler and Richard Diebenkorn.

Myriad Botanical Gardens★

Reno & Robinson Sts. ☎405-297-3995. www.myriadgardens.com.

Conceived by architect I.M. Pei, this 17-acre garden, modeled after Copenhagen's Tivoli Gardens, features rolling hills, a lake and a suspended, translucent bridge, seven stories high and 224ft long. Inside are exotic plants, a skyway and a 35ft waterfall.

Bricktown★★

Main St. & Sheridan Ave. between E.K. Gaylord & Stiles Sts. ✕ ♿ 🅿 ☎*405-236-8666. www.bricktownokc.com.*

Water taxis on the 1mi **Bricktown Canal** pass lively cafes, fountains and waterfalls at this restored warehouse district recalling San Antonio's River Walk. A statue of Mickey Mantle (1931-98) stands in front of the **Southwestern Bell Bricktown Ballpark** *(Mickey Mantle Dr. & Sheridan Ave.)*, a minor-league stadium.

Stockyards City★★

Agnew & Exchange Sts., just south of I-40. ✕ ♿ 🅿 ☎*405-235-7267. www.stockyardscity.org.*

This historic cattle market has been restored to early-20C glory. See a live cattle auction *(Mon-Wed)* at the **Oklahoma National Stock Yards Company** *(2501 Exchange Ave.; ☎405-235-8675)*, or watch craftsmen make saddles, boots and other Western wear: Langston's *(2224 Exchange Ave.; ☎405-235-9536)* has the state's best selection.

Oklahoma State Capitol★

NE 23rd St. & Lincoln Blvd. ✕ ♿ 🅿 ☎*405-521-3356.*

On the capitol grounds are working oil wells that have generated some $8 million in revenue since first drilled. With 650 rooms, the Greco-Roman building of limestone, granite and marble features history murals and portraits of famous Oklahomans. Built in 1914-17, the capitol was not crowned with the dome of its original design; work to correct that "oversight" concluded in 2002.

Oklahoma Historical Society & State Museum of History★

2100 N. Lincoln Blvd. ♿ ☎*405-522-0765. www.ok-history.mus.ok.us.*

Among this museum's galleries is the American Indian Gallery, which differentiates the 68 tribes forced to migrate to Oklahoma in the late 19C. Exhibits include a bison-hide tepee and a wagon used in two land runs.

A few blocks west is the **Harn Homestead & 1889er Museum**★ *(313 NE 16th St.; ☎405-235-4058, www.harnhomestead.com)*—a pioneer farm with a homestead, barn, schoolhouse.

National Cowboy & Western Heritage Museum★★★

Kids *1700 NE 63rd St.* ✕ ♿ 🅿 ☎*405-478-2250. www.nationalcowboymuseum.org.*

The entrance opens onto *The End of the Trail* (1915), James Earle Fraser's famous 18ft sculpture of an Indian rider on a weary horse. To the right a hallway leads past Prosperity Junction, a re-creation of a late-19C cattle town. Gallery highlights include: **Art of the American West** featuring works by Charles Russell, Frederic Remington and leading contemporary artists; the **American Cowboy Gallery** focuses on the working cowboy; the **Joe Grandee Museum of the Frontier West** limns the legacy of the West's traders, soldiers, conservationists and other; the arena-like **American Rodeo Gallery** pays tribute to this colorful sport.

Omniplex★★

Kids *2100 NE 52nd St.* ✕ ♿ 🅿 ☎*405-602-6664. www.omniplex.org.*

This 10-acre complex contains three museums, the OmniDome theater, a planetarium, botanical gardens, art galleries and science exhibits. Highlights include vintage aircraft and NASA artifacts in the **Kirkpatrick Science and Air Space Museum**★ *(☎405-602-6664)*; Native American cradle boards of the **Red Earth Indian Center**★ *(☎405-427-5228, www.redearth.org)*; and a "laserscape" photo-mural of the Grand Canyon in the **International Photography Hall of Fame and Museum**★★ *(☎405-424-4055, www.iphf.org)*.

Oklahoma City Zoo and Botanical Garden★

Kids *2101 NE 50th St.* ✕ ♿ 🅿 b*405-424-3344. www.okczoo.com.*

This 110-acre park features more than 2,100 animals. Dolphin and sea-lion shows and the primate habitat are popular attractions, along with a butterfly garden, "endangered species carousel" and safari tram that circles the zoo.

Norman

I-35, US-77 & Rte. 9 on south boundary of Oklahoma City. ✕ ♿ 🅿 ☎*405-321-7260. www.normanok.org.*

This city of 103,000 people has several museums on or near its University of Oklahoma campus: the **Jacobson House Native American Cultural Center** (609 Chautauqua St.; ☎405-366-1667, www.jacobsonhouse.com); the **Fred Jones Jr. Museum of Art**★ (410 W. Boyd St.; ☎405-325-3272, www.ou.edu/fjjma); and the **Sam Noble Museum of Natural History**★ [Kids] (2401 Chautauqua St.; ☎405-325-4712, www.snomnh.ou.edu). in 1999, Sam Noble paleontologists discovered the world's tallest dinosaur—in southeastern Oklahoma.

Excursions

Guthrie★★

US-77 & Rte. 33, 32mi north of Oklahoma City via I-35. ✕ & P ☎405-282-1947. www.guthrieok.com.
Founded in 1889, Guthrie hosted territorial and state government meetings until June 1910, when the governor—in a feud with the local newspaper editor—had the state seal stolen and moved to Oklahoma City. Now with 11,000 citizens, Guthrie boasts a 400-block National Historic Landmark District.

First Capital Trolley (2nd & Harrison Sts.; ☎405-282-6000) offers hourly tours of the city's Victorian architecture. Other highlights include the **Oklahoma Territorial Museum** (406 E. Oklahoma St.; ☎405-282-1889, www.oklahomaterritorialmuseum.org) and the **Scottish Rite Temple** (900 E. Oklahoma St.; ☎405-282-1281), completed in 1929 with Greek, Roman, Egyptian and Assyrian architectural influences.

Anadarko

US-62 & Rte. 9, 60mi southwest of Oklahoma City. ✕ & P ☎405-247-6651. www.anadarko.org.
Here the **National Hall of Fame for Famous American Indians**★ (US-62; ☎405-274-5555) displays bronze busts of Chief Joseph, Sitting Bull and other famous Native Americans. The **Southern Plains Indian Museum** (US-62; ☎405-247-6221) holds the **Oklahoma Indian Arts and Crafts Cooperative**★. Tourist-oriented **Indian City USA** (Rte. 8, 2.5mi south; b405-247-5661, www.indiancityusa.com) has replica tribal villages.

Wichita Mountains National Wildlife Refuge★

Rtes. 49 & 115, 90mi southwest of Oklahoma City via I-44. ⚠ & P ☎580-429-8587. wichitamountains.fws.gov.
Its rocky tors rising above prairie lakes, this reserve has a winding road to the top of 2,464ft **Mount Scott**★. The eastern part features **Holy City of the Wichitas** (☎580-429-3361), an Easter Passion Play set hand-crafted of rock.

Fort Sill Military Reservation★

I-44 Exit 41 (Key Gate), Lawton, 87mi southwest of Oklahoma City. ✕ & P ☎580-442-8111. http://sill-www .army.mil.
This frontier post of the Indian Wars contains original stone buildings built by the Buffalo Soldiers of the 10th Cavalry. Among them are the guardhouse where Geronimo was prisoner, and post headquarters, now the **Fort Sill Museum** (437 Quanah Rd.; ☎580-442-5123).

Chickasaw National Recreation Area★

Rte. 7, Sulphur, 84mi south of Oklahoma City via I-35. ⚠ & P ☎580-622-3165. www.nps.gov/chic.
Ancient Indians called this area of mineral springs, streams and lakes "the peaceful valley of rippling waters." Today's visitors fish, swim, camp or hike 20mi of trails. The **Travertine Nature Center** has exhibits on history, geology and fauna.

TULSA★

MICHELIN MAP 492 L 10
CENTRAL STANDARD TIME
POPULATION 382,000

A fixture on fabled Route 66 in its 1930s–1960s heyday, Tulsa has gorgeous Art Deco architecture, nationally acclaimed art museums and notable opera, ballet and symphony companies. *Fortune* magazine has ranked it as one of the nation's top 15 cities in quality of life.

Information: ☎918-560-0263, www.visittulsa.com.

Don't Miss: The Gilcrease Museum.

Especially for Kids: Discoveryland.

A Bit of History

Tulsa dates its history from a Creek Indian conclave in 1836. The city grew as a cattle-ranching center in the 1870s but wasn't incorporated until 1898. After oil was discovered in nearby Red Fork in 1901, Tulsa boomed. Another big strike in 1905—the Glenn Pool, at that time the world's largest—made this city on the banks of the Arkansas River a center of oil exploration. Between 1907 and 1920, Tulsa's population increased tenfold to 72,000. Today it has some 1,000 petroleum-related businesses, ranging from drilling contractors to wildcatters to refining operators.

Sights

Downtown Art Deco District★

Between 1st & 8th Sts., Cheyenne & Detroit Sts. ✕♿🅿 ☎918-583-2617. www.tulsa-downtown.org.
The legacy of the early oil barons and a $1 million-a-month construction boom in the 1920s can be seen on a walking tour of the historic central business district. Only New York and Miami Beach claim more Art Deco buildings.
The 1927 **Philtower Building** (*511 S. Boston St.*), with its green-and-red tiled roof, monogrammed door knobs, brass elevator doors and 25ft vaulted ceilings, was once the tallest building in Oklahoma. It is linked by an underground tunnel to the 1930 **Philcade Building** (*5th & Boston Sts.*), whose flamboyant Zigzag Style conceals carved-stone

birds, reptiles and mammals in the terra-cotta foliage above its ground-floor windows. The Deco style employed by the Public Works Administration in the Depression Era represented a transition from Zigzag to Streamline. Perhaps Tulsa's finest example is the 1931 **Tulsa Union Depot** (*3 S. Boston St.*), now an office complex.

Gilcrease Museum★★★

1400 Gilcrease Museum Rd., off US-64 west of downtown. ✕♿🅿 ☎918-596-2700. www.gilcrease.org.
The world's largest collection of art of the American West, the Gilcrease exhibits paintings, drawings, prints and sculptures by more than 400 artists—with significant holdings of works by Frederic Remington, Charles Russell, Albert Bierstadt, George Catlin, Nicolai Fechin, William R. Leigh, Thomas Moran and Olaf Seltzer. It features outstanding Native American art and artifacts, including one gallery devoted to Okla-

Art deco tile detail from 1920s filling station in Tulsa

homa Indians; an interactive exhibit on Mexican art, history and culture; and myriad historical manuscripts, documents and maps.

Local oilman Thomas Gilcrease (1890-1962) began collecting in 1922 when few others were interested in Western art. In 1949, he built this museum on his estate. The 460-acre grounds contain theme gardens, outdoor sculpture, natural meadows and woodlands.

Philbrook Museum of Art★★

2727 S. Rockford Rd. ✖ ♿ 🅿 ☎*918-749-7941. www.philbrook.org.*
Set in 23 acres of English-style gardens that invite exploration, this castle-like Italianate villa (1927, Edward Buehler Delk) was the home of oilman Waite Phillips. Donated to the City of Tulsa in 1938, it is today a renowned museum of fine and decorative arts of the Americas and Europe, Asia and Africa. The collection ranges from classical antiquities to 20C pieces, and includes Italian Renaissance oils and sculptures. Bouguereau's *The Shepherdess* (1890s) highlights the 19C French Salon.

Native American Dancer

Fred W. Marvel/OKLAHOMA TOURISM

Tulsa Zoo and Living Museum★

Kids *6421 E. 36th St. N., between US-75 and US-169.* ✖ ♿ 🅿 ☎*918-669-6600. www.tulsazoo.org.*
The highlight of this zoo is the Robert J. LaFortune North American Living Museum complex of four primary ecosystems—Arctic tundra, Southwest desert, Eastern forest and Southern lowlands—with animals, plants and cultural displays. The Tropical American Rainforest has jaguars and howler monkeys; at the Elephant Encounter, guests watch large pachyderms at work and play. Researcher Jane Goodall has acclaimed the Chimpanzee Connection. A zoo train circles the park's 70 acres, providing access to its 1,500 animals.

Oral Roberts University★

7777 S. Lewis Ave. ✖ ♿ 🅿 ☎*918-495-6161. www.oru.edu.*
Banners from 60 nations and the 60ft, 30-ton Praying Hands (1981, Leonard McMurry), among the largest bronze sculptures on earth, greet visitors to this 500-acre Christian campus. .

DiscoveryLand!★

Kids *5mi west of Rte. 97 on W. 41st St. S.* ✖ ♿ 🅿 ☎*918-245-6552. www.discovery-landusa.com.* 🕐 *Open June-Aug.*
Although most visitors go only for the delightful 3hr production of Rodgers and Hammerstein's *Oklahoma!* (staged outdoors in a 2,000-seat amphitheater), DiscoveryLand! also offers a Western musical revue, a barbecue and lots of kids' activities. Native dancers perform in a recreated Plains Indian village. *Oklahoma!* features a cast of 50 with horses and a real surrey with a fringe on top.

Excursions

J.M. Davis Arms & Historical Museum★

333 Lynn Riggs Blvd. (Rte. 66), Claremore, 29mi northeast of Tulsa. ♿ 🅿 ☎*918-341-5707. www.state.ok.us.*
Hotelier John Monroe Davis began to amass guns when he was 7 years old. When his collection of 20,000 guns, 1,200 steins, 70 saddles and 600 World

War I posters began to consume the old Mason Hotel, the state took it over.

Will Rogers Memorial★★

Rte. 88, Claremore, 25mi northeast of Tulsa via Rte. 66. 🏕 🅿 ☎918-341-0719. *www.willrogers.com.*

Overlooking Tiawah Valley, this limestone memorial, with nine galleries and a children's museum, tells the story of Will Rogers' homespun life. The "Cowboy Philosopher" was a trick roper, movie star, radio commentator and newspaper columnist. Rogers (1879-1935) originally bought the 20-acre spread to build his retirement home prior to his death in an air crash. The museum that frames the family tombhas statues, paintings, celebrity photos, saddles, dioramas, video kiosks and six theaters showing films in which Rogers starred. **Will Rogers Birthplace**, a log-walled, two-story house at Dog Iron Ranch on Lake Oologah *(EW 38 Rd., Oologah, 12mi north of Claremore)*, has an airstrip, an oak barn and friendly farm animals for petting.

Five Civilized Tribes Museum★

Agency Hill, Honor Heights Dr., Muskogee. 🚽 🅿 ☎918-683-1701. *www.fivetribes. org.*

Housed in the former Union Indian Agency Building, built of native stone in 1875, this museum tells of the five tribes—Cherokee, Chickasaw, Choctaw, Creek and Seminole—who were forcibly moved to Indian Territory (now Oklahoma) in the 19C. The museum has an art collection of more than 800 items of Native American art and sponsors four major art competitions annually.

The Cherokee Heritage Center★

Willis Rd., Park Hill; 2mi south of Tahlequah east of US-62. 🚽 🅿 ☎918-456-6007. *www.cherokeeheritage.org.*

Tahlequah was the end of the "Trail of Tears" for the Cherokees. The Heritage Center, established in 1963, is on 44 wooded acres south of town. Modern Cherokees lead interpretive tours of a replica pre-European settlement where craftspeople reenact the activities of their ancestors, demonstrating practices such as flint-knapping, basketry and pottery. Adams Corner Rural Village represents a typical 1880s Cherokee community. The Cherokee National Museum features a poignant exhibit recalling tribal history.

Woolaroc Ranch★★

Rte. 123, 12mi southwest of Bartlesville via US-60. 🍴 🚽 🅿 ☎918-336-0307. *www.woolaroc.org.*

Established in 1925 as the country estate of Frank Phillips, founder of Phillips Petroleum, this 3,600-acre ranch and wildlife preserve has a museum with a world-class collection of Western art; a spectacular lodge (Phillips' former home), and a Native American Heritage Center. There is also an Oklahoma oil history area and a "traders camp" where frontier rendezvous are reenacted. More than 700 animals, including buffalo, elk, deer and longhorn cattle, graze freely in the Osage Hills.

The Trail of Tears

Despite the US treaty of 1791 which recognized the Cherokee Nation's right to ancestral lands in the Southeast, Congress in 1830 passed the **Indian Removal Act**. The US militia rounded up 15,000 Cherokees, along with Chickasaws, Choctaws, Creeks and Seminoles, and in 1838 moved them to a camp in Tennessee, many in shackles. In the treaty, the Cherokees had agreed to give up hunting; but they had built homes, farms and other businesses and even published a newspaper. Yet now they are forced to abandon their ancient burial grounds. From Tennessee, in severe winter weather, they were marched at gunpoint 800mi to Indian Territory, now the state of Oklahoma. It took six months and cost more than 4,000 lives. Those who resisted were either forcibly removed or shot on sight. Over 25 percent of the Cherokee population perished. Designated in 1987 as Trail of Tears National Historic Trail (☎505-988-6888, *www.nps.gov/trte*), the route now stands as a symbol of the tragedies suffered at the hands of the US government.

PHOENIX-TUCSON AREA

To some, southern Arizona's Sonoran Desert is brutal. Its average annual rainfall is less than 10in and temperatures often exceed 100°F. Forty-foot saguaro skeletons mark this land as an alien climate for most visitors.

But others find heaven here. A brief, sudden thunderstorm can cause the desert to erupt in color—the ocotillo's flaming orange, the palo verde's yellow, the prickly pear's peach, the saguaro's ivory. And Phoenix, fifth-largest city in the US, has more major golf and spa resorts than anywhere else between Florida and Southern California.

Thousands of years ago, this land of stark beauty was home to Tohono O'odham and Hohokam Indians, who built an elaborate canal system for irrigating fields of squash, beans and corn. In the 16C, Spaniards tramped through the mountains searching for gold, and though they found no riches, the conquistadors paved the way for priests and soldiers who established missions and walled forts called presidios.

Most of this rugged country didn't become US territory until 1853 Gadsden Purchase.

Soon after, folks came to mine or ranch. The most prosperous early communities in the Arizona Territory were in the far southeast. The copper town of Bisbee had opera, money and Victorian architecture. Tombstone's silver mine was prolific, its citizens wealthy, its restaurants "the best between New Orleans and San Francisco." Today the sunshine and heat of the Sonoran Desert are the chief draws in one of the fastest-growing regions in the US.

View of Lake Pleasant

PHOENIX ★

MAP PP 314-315
MOUNTAIN STANDARD TIME
POPULATION 1,461,575

Located in the heart of the Sonoran Desert, greater Phoenix is known as the Valley of the Sun. This desert oasis stretches across more than 2,000sq mi and takes in Scottsdale, Tempe, Mesa and other communities surrounding the relatively young urban center of Phoenix. Main streets are laid parallel in 1mi-by-1mi grids, making orientation and navigation simple.

- **Information:** ☎602-254-6500. www.phoenixcvb.com.
- **Orient Yourself:** Although Interstate 10 is an east-west highway, it heads almost straight south out of central Phoenix to Tucson. Expressways encircle the metro area, but the broad boulevards are still often the best way to cover ground.
- **Parking:** There is adequate parking at virtually all Phoenix-area attractions; the transit system is inadequate. From May through October, walking great distances is not a good idea in the hot sun.
- **Don't Miss:** The Heard Museum is one of the best facilities devoted to native peoples of North America.
- **Organizing Your Time:** Allow 2 days to visit Phoenix. Plan your outdoor activities for before 1 pm, except November through March.
- **Especially for Kids:** Arizona Science Center; the Phoenix Zoo.
- **Also See:** Scottsdale's galleries hold superb Western arts and crafts.

A Bit of History

A mid-1860s hay camp built atop a Hohokam site was dubbed "Phoenix," intimating that a new city might rise from ancient ruins just as the mythical bird rose from its ashes. A town site was laid out in 1870. By the end of that decade the village was a supply center for central Arizona mines and ranches; by 1900 it was territorial capital. Its transition from frontier town was assured in 1911, one year before Arizona became the 48th US state, when the Salado (Salt) River was dammed 60mi east of Phoenix. Roosevelt Dam and Theodore Roosevelt Lake fostered growth.

The Southern Pacific arrived in 1926. Chewing-gum magnate William Wrigley Jr., industrialist Cornelius Vanderbilt Jr. and architect Frank Lloyd Wright established second homes in the area, beginning a boom that continues today.

Downtown

The city hub is Patriots Square, flanked by Washington and Jefferson Streets, and on its east by Central Avenue. A $1 billion revitalization has made **Civic Plaza** a major cultural center, with **Phoenix Symphony Hall** (225 E. Adams St.; ☎602-495-1999, www.phoenixsymphony.org) and the **Herberger Theater** (222 E. Monroe St.; ☎602-254-7399, www.herbergertheater.org). **Heritage and Science Park** (between N. 5th, N. 7th, E. Washington & E. Monroe Sts.) contains the Arizona Science Center and the Phoenix Museum of History.

Arizona Center (E. Van Buren St. between N. 3rd & N. 5th Sts.; ☎602-271-4000, www.arizonacenter.com), a shopping complex with fountains and sunken gardens, is just north. A few blocks west is the **Orpheum Theatre** (203 W. Adams St.; ☎602-234-5600, www.phoenix.gov), built in Spanish Colonial Revival style in 1929 and recently restored. The **Dodge Theatre** (between N. 4th, N. 5th, Adams & Washington Sts.; ☎602-379-2888, www.dodgetheatre.com) is a new, $35-million performing-arts facility.

Address Book Phoenix-Tucson Area

For prices, see the Legend on the cover flap.

WHERE TO STAY IN THE PHOENIX-TUCSON AREA

$$$$$ The Boulders – *34631 N. Tom Darlington Dr. (off Rte. 74), Carefree.* ☎602-488-9009 or 866-397-6520. www.theboulders.com. *208 rooms.* The red boulders in front of this world-class resort are just part of the allure of this resort, a mecca for spa, golf and tennis lovers just northeast of Phoenix. Finest of four restaurants is **The Latilla ($$$$)**, acclaimed for Southwest regional cuisine.

$$$$$ Hyatt Regency Scottsdale at Gainey Ranch – *7500 E. Doubletree Ranch Rd., Scottsdale.* ☎480-444-1234 or 800-233-1234. www.scottsdale.hyatt.com. *493 rooms.* A "water playground," with swimming pools and a sand beach, is at the heart of this desert resort. Extending into a lagoon is **Ristorante Sandolo ($$$$)**, where singing waitstaff bring gourmet Italian food, then send diners on Venetian gondola rides. The Hopi Learning Center, staffed by tribal artisans and educators, lends a Southwest note.

$$$$$ Royal Palms Hotel and Casitas – *5200 E. Camelback Rd., Phoenix.* ☎602-840-3610 or 800-672-6011. www.royalpalmshotel.com. *116 rooms.* An intimate and secluded resort at the foot of Camelback Mountain, Royal Palms was built in Spanish Colonial style in 1929 as the gracious summer estate of a cruise-line executive. Guests now approach along a driveway lined with regal palm trees. The original mansion houses highly regarded **T. Cook's ($$$$)**, serving Mediterranean-style cuisine.

$$$$$ Tanque Verde Ranch – *14301 E. Speedway Blvd., Tucson.* ☎520-296-6275 or 800-234-3833. www.tanqueverderanch.com. *73 rooms.* Stays at this plush ranch retreat beside Saguaro National Park include unlimited riding, cowboy barbecues and Mexican fiestas. Cacti and pink-stucco casitas surround the main house, where guests linger over rustic communal tables. Founded in 1868, the ranch covers 640 acres.

$$$$$ Canyon Ranch – *8600 E. Rockcliff Rd., Tucson.* ☎520-749-9000 or 800-742-9000. www.canyonranch.com. *110 rooms.* This high-profile spa opened in 1979 to help inaugurate the notion of long, European-style restorative retreats. Offerings range from chi qong to Ayurvedic wraps in separate facilities for men and women. The 150-acre site is in the Santa Catalina foothills, with deluxe stucco casitas scattered amid desert landscaping.

$$$$ Westward Look Resort – *245 E. Ina Rd., Tucson.* ☎ 520-297-1151 or 800-722-2500. www.westwardlook.com. *244 rooms.* An artful cross between a guest ranch and a leisure resort, the comfy casitas here line a ridge beneath the Santa Catalina Mountains. A lavish exercise center complements a pool, extensive trail system and lovely landscaped grounds.

$$$$ Arizona Inn – *2200 E. Elm St., Tucson.* ☎520-325-1541 or 800-933-1093. www.arizonainn.com. *86 rooms.* Little has changed since Franklin Roosevelt came to "rough it" in the 1930s at this hacienda-style hotel. Velvet lawns surround pink casitas with sunny patios, and the pool is enclosed by rose-covered walkways. The handsome **Dining Room ($$$)** features creative American cuisine.

$$$$ Hermosa Inn – *5532 N. Palo Cristi Rd., Paradise Valley.* ☎602-955-8614 or 800-241-1210. www.hermosainn.com. *35 rooms.* Cowboy artist Lon Megargee built this 1930s hacienda as a home and studio. Casitas spread over six acres of prickly pear and barrel cactus. Aged chaps on walls, create a ranch feel. The original house is now **Lon's at the Hermosa ($$$)**, a fine-dining restaurant.

$$$$ Rancho de la Osa – *Sasabe.* ☎520-823-4257 or 800-872-6240. www.ranchodelaosa.com. *21 rooms.* Nestled near the Boboquivari Mountains, this historic Spanish hacienda includes a 1725 cantina believed to be the oldest building in Arizona in continuous use. The modern adobe casitas are furnished with Mexican antiques and most have a wood-burning fireplace. Aside from horseback riding, hiking and swimming, guests venture out to watch for the 300 species of birds that are regular visitors to the area.

$$ Copper Queen Hotel – *11 Howell Ave., Bisbee.* ✕ 🅿 ⌚ ☎*520-432-2216. www.copperqueen.com. 45 rooms.* Built in 1902 as the hub of a copper-mining metropolis of (then) 20,000, this landmark property still rivets the attention of visitors. Completely renovated, all rooms have modern amenities amid authentic period furnishings.

$$ Hotel San Carlos – *202 N. Central Ave., Phoenix.* ✕ 🅿 ⌚ ☎*602-253-4121 or 866-253-4121. www.hotelsancarlos.com. 133 rooms.* A yellow-brick downtown classic since 1928, the San Carlos is a historic anomaly in a region of spa resorts and golf haciendas. The lobby's chandeliers and period wallpaper give an Old World ambience; the rooftop pool is a modern amenity. **Seamus McCaffrey's Irish Pub ($$)** offers traditional pub fare.

WHERE TO EAT IN THE PHOENIX-TUCSON AREA

$$$$ Janos – *3770 E. Sunrise Dr. at Westin La Paloma Resort, Tucson.* ☎*520-615-6100. janos.com.* **Southwestern.** Award-winning chef Janos Wilder's menu may feature wild-mushroom and smoked-poblano flan, pecan-breaded catfish with chile butter, or grilled rabbit with roasted pepper purée. The adjacent **J Bar ($$)** serves more casual (and more economical) but equally notable meals.

$$$$ Mary Elaine's – *6000 E. Camelback Rd. at The Phoenician, Scottsdale.* ☎*480-423-2530. www.thephoenician. com.* **French.** European elegance pervades this restaurant—from its hand-painted 24-karat-gold ceiling and fine-art collection, to the exquisite service and romantic backdrop of city lights from the dining patio. Dishes include pan-seared foie gras, chilled cucumber consommé, and filet of turbot with black truffles and hearts of palm.

$$$ The Arizona Kitchen – *300 Wigwam Blvd. at The Wigwam Resort,* *Litchfield Park.* ☎*623-535-2598. www. wigwamresort.com. Dinner only. Closed Sun-Mon.* **Southwestern.** Native American accents apply to cuisine and décor at this west Phoenix favorite. Blue-corn duck burritos, mesquite-smoked corn chowder, quail with pomegranate molasses glaze, and buffalo sirloin with a vanilla-bean chili sauce are highlights.

$$$ Fuego! – *6958 E. Tanque Verde Rd., Tucson.* ☎*520-886-1745. www.fuegores taurant.com. Dinner only.* **Southwestern.** Fuego (Spanish for "fire") is the fashion here. Dishes may be finished off with a flame of tequila, either on the patio or inside the earth-toned dining room. The namesake appetizer contains chef Alan Zeman's own chorizo; trademark dishes are prickly-pear pork and ostrich or emu specials.

$$$ La Hacienda – *7575 E. Princess Dr. at The Fairmont Scottsdale Princess, Scottsdale.* ☎*480-585-4848. www. fairmont.com/scottsdale/. Dinner only. Closed Wed.* **Mexican.** Housed in a territorial ranch house, La Hacienda takes a gourmet approach to traditional Mexican cookery. Tamales come with adobo cream sauce; the caldo (stew) melds shrimp with poblanos and tomatillos. The signature dish is slow-roasted whole pig.

$$$ Old Town Tortilla Factory – *6910 E. Main St., Scottsdale.* ☎*602-945-4567. www.oldtowntortillafactory.com. Dinner only.* **Southwestern.** Fresh tortillas, made daily in two dozen flavors, are the basis for a creative gourmet menu. In rich wood decor beneath cathedral ceilings, servers present pork chops crusted with red chilies and raspberries, filet mignon stuffed with roasted poblano, and wild-mushroom tacos.

$$ Café Poca Cosa – *110 E. Pennington, Tucson.* ☎*520-622-6400. Closed Sun and Mon.* **Mexican.** Housed in a sleek new setting that features polished metal and pomegranate walls, Tucson's premier Mexican restaurant is more popular as ever. Guaymas, Sonora native Suzana Davila's menu has imaginative food from all regions of Mexico, including 26 varieties of mole and her own plum salsa. Décor focuses on Mexican art and Mayan masks.

Kachina Dolls

A Hopi kachina (*kat-SEE-na*) made by a well-known carver can fetch $10,000, although the average price ranges from $500 up. Originally carved by Hopi men and given to their female children to ensure fertility, these dolls (*tihu* to the Hopi) represent the spirits who intercede with the gods in the growing season. Children are given kachinas not as toys but to inspire spiritual values. Hopi religion forbids certain dolls to be produced for any-one outside the tribe. But many other figures, such as Mud Head Clown and Morning Kachina, are found in muse-ums and shops around the state. No kachina is considered authentic unless it is carved from the root of a cotton-wood tree, is anatomically correct and bears the artist's signature.

A Kachina Doll

Heritage Square

Between E. Monroe & E. Adams, N. 5th & N. 7th Sts. ✗ ♿ 🅿 ☎ *602-262-5071. www.phoenix.gov/parks*
Of the homes from the Phoenix town-site, built 1895–1902, the 1895 **Rosson House** (*113 N. 6th St.; ☎602-262-5029,www.rossonhousemuseum.org*) is the oldest. Devonshire teas are served at the **Teeter House** (*622 E. Adams St.; ☎602-252-4682*). A toy museum is in the **Stevens House** (*602 E. Adams St.*).

Arizona Science Center★

Kids *600 E. Washington St., Heritage and Science Park.* ✗ ♿ 🅿 ☎ *602-716-2000. www.azscience.org.*
This concrete monolith (1997, Antoine Predock) has 350 hands-on exhibits, a five-story theater and cutting-edge planetarium. **The World Around You** focuses on geology, hydrology and space sciences; **Networks** compares a ham radio operation with the internet.

Phoenix Museum of History★

105 N. 5th St., Heritage and Science Park. ♿ 🅿 ☎ *602-253-2734. www.pmoh.org.*
Displays in this sleek, modern building give a history of Phoenix's evolution from dusty desert town to metropolis.

Chase Field★

401 E. Jefferson St. ✗ ♿ 🅿 ☎ *602-462-6500. www.arizonadiamondbacks.com.*
This natural-grass baseball stadium has a retractable roof and a centerfield swimming pool where home runs make a big splash. "The Bob," as locals know it, is home to the Arizona Diamondbacks. A museum, **Cox Clubhouse★** Kids, has Hall of Fame memorabilia.

Arizona Capitol Museum

W. Washington St. & 17th Ave. ♿ ☎ *602-926-3620. www.lib.az.us/museum.*
The Territorial Capitol when it was built in 1900, this tuff-and-granite structure became state capitol in 1912. Displays include artifacts from the USS Arizona, sunk at Pearl Harbor in 1941.

The Heard Museum★★★

2301 N. Central Ave. ♿ 🅿 ☎ *602-252-8848. www.heard.org.*
Devoted to Native American culture and art, this museum contains almost 40,000 works of art. Arches, colonnades and courtyards are hallmarks of Spanish Colonial architecture. Its 1929 founding is told in the **Sandra Day O'Connor Gallery. Home: Native People in the Southwest** displays some 2,000 treas-ures from the collections. The **Katsina Doll Gallery★★** holds nearly 500 hand-

carved Hopi kachinas. **Remembering Our Indian School Days**★★ depicts the boarding schools American Indian children were forced to attend.

Phoenix Art Museum★★

1625 N. Central Ave. ✕♿P ☎*602-257-1222. www.phxart.org.*

An **orientation theater** introduces the 14,000-work collection, which includes a reproduction of Gilbert Stuart's 1796 portrait, *George Washington*, pictured on the $1 bill. Featured are American art of the 19C-20C, Western Americana and European art. Latin American art is represented by Rivera, Tamayo, Orozco and Kahlo.

Papago Salado

Southeast Phoenix, between Scottsdale and Tempe north of the Salt (Salado) River, is dominated by 1,200-acre **Papago Park**. 16C Spanish explorers, who at Pueblo Grande found remains of a Hohokam civilization, labeled these vanished desert farmers *papago*, or "bean eaters." They left a complex system of aqueducts among the buttes.

Desert Botanical Garden★★

1201 N. Galvin Pkwy., Papago Park. ✕♿P ☎*602-941-1225. www.dbg.org.*

With more than 20,000 desert plants, this arid-lands arboretum has won awards for environmental education. Trails snake past cacti and succulents, regional plants and animals. Displays include Indian and Hispanic residents' use of native plants.

Phoenix Zoo★

Kids *455 N. Galvin Pkwy., Papago Park.* ✕♿P ☎*602-273-1341. www.phoenix-zoo.org.*

A motorized **Safari Train** runs through the four habitat where 1,300 animals reside. The **Forest of Uco** simulates a Colombian rain-forest. The **Arizona Trail** visits a desert home for coyotes, Mexican wolves and other Southwest wildlife. White rhinos, Sumatran tigers, South American spectacled bears and a breeding colony of Arabian oryxes are among 150 endangered animals.

Hall of Flame Museum of Firefighting

Kids *6101 E. Van Buren St., Papago Park.* ♿P ☎*602-275-3473. www.hallofflame.org.*

Retired firefighters share tales of their profession as visitors operate alarms and see fully restored fire engines dating back to 1725.

Pueblo Grande Museum and Archaeological Park

4619 E. Washington St. ♿P ☎*602-495-0901. www.pueblogrande.com.*

In the 14C, 1,000 people lived at this Hohokam site beside the head gate of the canal system. Storage rooms, cemeteries and ball courts are discernible. at this National Historic Landmark.

Scottsdale

Founded as a farm village in 1888, Scottsdale *(☎480-421-1004; www.scottsdalecvb.com)* is full of resorts, golf courses and shopping districts. In this city of 240,000 are are more art galleries per capita than any other US city.

Downtown Scottsdale

Camelback Rd. south to 2nd St., 68th Ave. east to Civic Center Blvd. ✕♿P ☎*480-947-6423. www.downtownscottsdale.com.*

In this arts district *(Main St., Marshall Way and Fifth Ave)* for 20-plus years, galleries have scheduled new exhibits and artist appearances to coincide with **Scottsdale ArtWalk** *(Thu nights; free trolley shuttles).* Among the city's famed **shopping centers**★★ are glitzy **Scottsdale Fashion Square** *(Camelback & Scottsdale Rds.; ☎480-941-2140, www.fashionsquare.com);* **The Borgata** *(61661 N. Scottsdale Rd.; ☎480-953-6311, www.borgata.com);* and **El Pedregal Festival Marketplace** *(Scottsdale Rd. & Carefree Hwy.; ☎480-488-1072, www.elpedregal.com),* home to the **Heard Museum North** *(34505 N. Scottsdale Rd.; ☎480-488-9817).*

Old Town Scottsdale★

Scottsdale Rd. north and south of First Ave. ✕🚻🅿

A faux strip of the 19C West, Old Town has wooden sidewalks, hitching rails, and rustic storefronts. Its pink ice-cream parlor, the **Sugar Bowl** *(4005 N. Scottsdale Rd.; ☎480-946-0051),* has been an institution since 1958.

Neighboring **Scottsdale Mall** includes the **Scottsdale Museum of Contemporary Art**★ *(7374 E. 2nd St.; ☎480-994-2787, www.smoca.org),* the **Scottsdale Center for the Arts** *(7380 E. 2nd St.; ☎480-994-2787, www.scottsdalearts.org)* and the **Scottsdale Historical Museum** *(7333 Scottsdale Mall; ☎480-945-4499, www.scottsdalemuseum.com).*

Other area attractions perpetuate the Old West theme. The quirky **Buffalo Museum of America** 🄺🄸🄳🅂 *(10261 N. Scottsdale Rd.; ☎480-951-1022)* has eclectic bison memorabilia. **Rawhide Western Town** 🄺🄸🄳🅂 *(5700 West North Loop Rd., Chandler; ☎480-502-5600, www.rawhide.com)* re-creates an 1880s community with stagecoach rides, mock gunfights and burro rides for kids.

Cosanti

6433 Doubletree Ranch Rd., Paradise Valley 🅿 ☎*480-948-6145. www.cosanti. org.*

Italian architect Paolo Soleri showcases "arcology," which he defines as the integration of architecture and ecology in new urban habitats. A prototype is under construction an hour's drive north: **Arcosanti** *(off I-17 Exit 262, Cordes Junction; ☎520-632-7135, www.arcosanti.org)* will combine compact structure with large solar greenhouses to house 6,000 people on 25 acres.

Taliesin West★★

12621 Frank Lloyd Wright Blvd., via Taliesin Dr. off Cactus Rd. ☛*Visit by guided tour (1-3hrs) only.* 🅿 ☎ *480-860-2700. www.franklloydwright.org.*

Frank Lloyd Wright built this complex of low-lying buildings by gathering desert stone and sand from washes. Taliesin West served as his winter home, from 1937 until his death in 1959.

Additional Sights

South Mountain Park Preserve★

10919 S. Central Ave. 🅿 ☎*602-495-0222. www.phoenix.gov/parks.*

This municipal park offers city views from **Dobbins Lookout** and trails for hiking, biking and riding. At its foot is **Mystery Castle** 🄺🄸🄳🅂 *(800 E. Mineral Rd., end of S. 7th St.; ☎602-268-1581),* an 8,000sq-ft manse hand-built in 1930-45 of everything from desert rocks to Bing Crosby's golf club *(☛tours available).*

Taliesin West

Tempe

US-60 & Loop 202, 9mi east of Phoenix.
☎*480-894-8158. www.tempecvb.com.*
✕&🅿

Founded in 1871on the Salt River, this city of 180,000 is home to Arizona State University. The Tempe (tem-PEE) historical district extends along Mill Avenue. On the fringe of Papago Park, the **Arizona Historical Society Museum** *(1300 N. College Ave.; ☎480-929-0292, www.arizonahistoricalsociety.org)* focuses on water's role in the Valley of the Sun.

Arizona State University

South bank of Salt River east of Mill Ave.
✕&🅿 ☎*480-965-9011. www.asu.edu.*
Highlight of the 44,000-student strong campus is circular **Grady Gammage Auditorium**★ *(Apache Blvd. & Mill Ave.; ☎480-965-3434, www.asugammage. com)*, Frank Lloyd Wright's last major nonresidential design (1959). Antoine Predock's 1989 **J. Russell and Bonita Nelson Fine Arts Center**★ *(10th St. & Mill Ave.)* is a collision of boxes, triangles and terraces that resembles a Hopi pueblo and a desert mountain range.

Guadalupe

Avenida del Yaqui, south off Baseline Rd. at I-10 Exit 155.
This settlement looks like a small village in Mexico but has a **farmers' market** *(9210 W. Avenida del Yaqui; ☎480-494-0706, guadalupefarmersmarket.com)* a Mexican bakery and a mercado.

Mesa

US-60 & Rte. 87, 15mi east of Phoenix.
✕&🅿 ☎*480-827-4700. www.mesacvb. com.*
Fast-growing Mesa was founded by Mormon pioneers in 1878. The faith's **Arizona Temple** *(525 E. Main St.; ☎480-833-1211)* remains a landmark. The **Mesa Southwest Museum** *(53 N. Macdonald St.; ☎480-644-2230, www.cityofmesa.org/ swmuseum)* features Hohokam and pioneer history. At Falcon Field *(Greenfield & McKellips Rds.)*, the **Champlin Fighter Aircraft Museum** *(4636 Fighter Aces Dr.; ☎480-830-4540)* and the **Commemorative Air Force Museum–Arizona Wing** *(2017 N. Greenfield Rd.; ☎480-924-1940)* showcase vintage aircraft.

Excursions

Apache Trail★★

Rte. 88 & US-60. ⚠✕&🅿
This 164mi loop includes a 78mi stretch of Route 88 between Apache Junction and Globe that crosses over the **Superstition Mountains,** skirts **Weaver's Needle Lookout** and passes three major lakes—Canyon, Apache and Roosevelt—created by **Roosevelt Dam**. The 25mi from **Tortilla Flat**, a ghost town of six residents, to Roosevelt is a narrow, winding gravel road.

Tonto National Monument★

Rte. 88, 4mi east of Roosevelt Dam. 🅿
☎*928-467-2241. www.nps.gov/tont.*
This preserve holds the remains of 13C Salado Indian cliff dwellings. A .5mi trail climbs to the 20-room Lower Dwelling where the Salado slept, cooked and stored crops. Tours of the Upper Dwellings require reservations *(Nov-Apr)*.

Boyce Thompson Arboretum★

37615 Rte. 60, Superior. &🅿 ☎*520-689-2811. arboretum.ag.arizona.edu.*
Mining magnate William Boyce Thompson turned this site beneath Picketpost Mountain into a 300-acre public park in the 1920s. The 1.5mi main trail provides an overview; other trails take in a variety of vegetation that attracts a year-round colony of colorful birds. A hidden canyon, desert lake and interpretive center with two greenhouses are on site.

Casa Grande Ruins National Monument★

1100 Ruins Dr., Rte. 87, Coolidge. 52mi southeast of Phoenix; take Rte. 387 at I-10 Exit 185 and follow signs. &🅿 ☎*520-723-3172. www.nps.gov/cagr.*
Along the Gila River, this four-story, 60ft-long structure was among the last constructions of the 12C Hohokam. Built of sand, clay and limestone mud, it became the first US archaeological preserve in 1892. South along the interstate is **Picacho Peak State Park** *(I-10 Exit 219)*, a solitary 1,500ft-high landmark.

TUCSON★★

MAP PP 314-315
MOUNTAIN STANDARD TIME
POPULATION 535,000

Unlike Phoenix, which has conquered the desert with massive irrigation projects, Tucson embraces dry land. With little or no agriculture, the city has come to consider green lawns a waste of time and water. Most residents focus on enjoying the sunshine (350 days a year) and high Sonoran Desert. Five mountain ranges surround this city that sprawls across 500sq mi and includes the University of Arizona.

- **Information:** ☎520-624-1817, www.visittucson.org
- ▶ **Orient Yourself:** The Santa Catalina Mountains compose the northern boundary of the Tucson metro area. Streets run north-south or east-west, except in the historic district downtown.
- **Don't Miss:** Tucson's Arizona-Sonora Desert Museum.
- **Organizing Your Time:** Allow 1 day.Tucson's mild months are November-March; the rest of the year, plan to visit outdoor desert sights before 1pm, and mountain or indoor attractions in the afternoon.
- **Especially for Kids:** The hummingbird exhibit at the Desert Museum and Pima Air & Space Museum.

A Bit of History

Tucson's night skies have inspired astronomers, professional and amateur, to set up telescopes. City regulations restrict outdoor lighting at night to preserve the starscape.The first stargazers, the Hohokam, left petroglyphs, ball courts and pit houses that may be seen in parks, canyons and excavations around the city. Pima and Tohono O'odham tribes later took up residence. The name "Tucson" was not applied until 1694, when Spanish missionaries had trouble pronouncing *stjukshon*, an Indian word that means "spring at the foot of a black mountain." The city was founded in 1775 by Irishman Hugh O'Connor, an explorer for the Spanish crown. The walled **Presidio San Agustín del Tucson** was built under his direction; a reconstruction can be found in the El Presidio Historic District.

Tucson became part of newly independent Mexico in 1821, then was transferred to the US with the Gadsden Purchase in 1853. It became capital of the Arizona Territory in 1867. The seat of government later moved north to Phoenix, but Tucson is well established as a cultural center.

Downtown Area

Tucson's downtown core is condensed within a few square blocks east of Interstate 10. Some old adobes and Spanish Colonial edifices remain. A walking tour takes in the 1896 **St. Augustine Cathedral** (192 S. Stone Ave.; ☎520-623-6351, www.staugustinecathedral.com). At the original presidio site, Tucson's government complex includes the **Pima County Court House** (Church Ave. between Alameda & Pennington Sts.) with its tiled Spanish-style dome. El Presidio Historic District preserves 19C and early-20C homes and shops, including **La Casa Cordova** (Meyer & Telles Sts.), perhaps Tucson's oldest (c.1850) surviving building. A new (2007) reconstruction of the **1775 Presidio**★ (Church & Washington Sts.; 520-884-4214; www.tucsonpresidio trust.org) recalls life in the fort.

Tucson Museum of Art & Historic Block★

140 N. Main Ave. ✕&🅿 ☎520-624-2333. www.tucsonarts.com.

This contemporary museum showcases avant-garde art and photography in a series of descending galleries, plus fine 19-20C American works (Thomas Moran,

Arthur Dove, Anton Refreigier, Marsden Hartley). The museum boasts a sculpture garden and a gallery of Western art.

Old Town Artisans

201 N. Court Ave. ✕♿🅿 ☎*520-623-6024.*
www.oldtownartisans.com
This restored 1850s adobe in El Presidio holds shops selling Latin American folk art and Native American tribal art.

University of Arizona★

Between Euclid & Campbell Aves., 6th & Elm Sts. ✕♿🅿 ☎*520-621-2211. www.arizona.edu.*
More than 36,000 students attend this 352-acre top research institution 1mi northeast of downtown.
West of campus, **Fourth Avenue**'s (*University Blvd. to 9th St.*) eccentric shops, unusual restaurants and colorful murals are joined by a **trolley-car barn** *(4th Ave. & 8th St.; www.oldpueblotrolley.org);* on weekends, the Old Pueblo Trolley runs to the UA Main Gate and back.

Arizona State Museum★

1013 E. University Blvd. at Park Ave. ♿🅿 ☎*520-621-6302. www.statemuseum.arizona.edu.*
This anthropology museum specializes in cultures of the Southwest and Mexico. In the north building, the **Paths of Life**★★ exhibit interprets origins, history and modern lifestyles of 10 desert cultures. A **Mexican mask** exhibit in the south building contains more than 350 colorful folk-art masks.

UA Museum of Art★

1031 N. Olive St.; E. 2nd St. & Speedway Blvd. ♿🅿 ☎*520-621-7567. www.art-museum.arizona.edu.*
Paintings by Rembrandt, Picasso and O'Keeffe, and Jacques Lipchitz sculptures, highlight a collection dating from the 15C to contemporary.

Center for Creative Photography★★

Olive St. between E. 2nd St. & Speedway Blvd. ♿ ☎*520-621-7968. www.creative-photography.org.*
Founded in 1975 by Ansel Adams, the center celebrates 20C photography as an art form. Changing exhibits draw also from the work of other photographers.

Flandrau Science Center and Planetarium★

🧒 *Cherry Ave. & University Blvd. mall, east side of campus.* ♿ ☎*520-621-4515. www.gotuasciencecenter.org.*
Interactive exhibits deal with mirrors, vacuums, holograms, kinetics and other basic physics. An observatory offers star-gazing through a 16in telescope.

Arizona Historical Society Museum Tucson★

949 E. 2nd St., across Park Ave. from UA campus. ♿🅿 ☎*520-628-5774. www.arizonahistoricalsociety.org.*
Exhibits include re-created O'odham, Mexican and Anglo-American homes of the 1870s. The Arizona Mining Hall features an underground copper mine that illustrates mining, smelting and production processes.

North Side

Tucson Botanical Gardens

2150 N. Alvernon Way, south of Grant Rd. ♿🅿 ☎*520-326-9686. www.tucson botanical.org.*
This 5.5-acre urban oasis holds gardens with cacti, wildflowers and Native American crops. A xeriscape demonstrates landscaping in an arid climate.

Center for Desert Archaeology★

3975 N. Tucson Blvd. ⛰🅿 ☎*520-885-6283. www.centerfordesertarchaeology.org.*
Archaeologists lead half-day tours to such prehistoric sites as Catalina State Park, where the center has uncovered Hohokam petroglyphs and a 1,500-year-old village.

Sabino Canyon★★

5900 N. Sabino Canyon Rd. at Sunrise Dr. ♿🅿 ☎*520-749-2861. www.sabinocan yon.com.*
A shuttle bus takes visitors into this canyon in the Santa Catalina Mountains. Once visited by mammoths and soldiers, who rode from Fort Lowell to swim, the canyon was "civilized" in the 1930s . Flash floods here in 2005 demonstrated the power of summer thunderstorms.

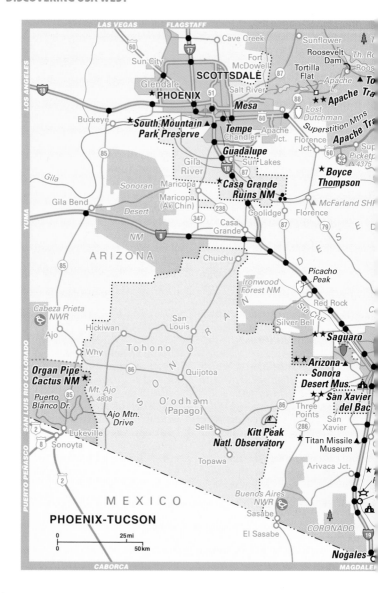

PHOENIX-TUCSON

0   25mi

0   50km

West Side

Overlooking downtown is "**A" Mountain** (*Sentinel Peak Rd., off Congress St.*), so nicknamed for a big "A" whitewashed on the side of Sentinel Peak in 1915 by fans of the university football team. **Views★★** are excellent from atop the peak. Much of west Tucson is embraced within **Tucson Mountain Park** (*Gates*

Pass & Kinney Rds.), 27sq mi of mountain and mesa lands.

Old Tucson Studios★

Kids *201 S. Kinney Rd.* ✕ & 🅿 ☎520-883-0100. www.oldtucson.com.
Hollywood in the desert, this 1880s Western town has been the location for more than 350 movies and TV shows since it was built in 1939 by Columbia Pictures as the set for *Arizona*, starring

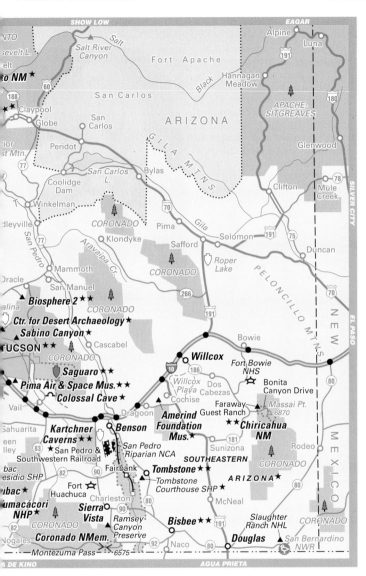

William Holden. John Wayne (*Rio Lobo*, 1966; *McClintock*, 1962) did several films here; Clint Eastwood (*The Outlaw Josey Wales*, 1976) and Paul Newman (*Hombre*, 1966) were among other stars.

The dusty frontier town was turned into an entertainment park in 1959, but has continued to operate as a film set. Visitors can saunter by jails, saloons and dance halls. **Town Hall** is a museum of film history; there are stunt shows, stagecoach rides, gunfights, theaters, and a thrilling **Iron Door Mine Ride.**

Arizona-Sonora Desert Museum★★★

Kids *2021 N. Kinney Rd.* ☎*520-883-2702. www.desertmuseum.org.*

A combination zoo and botanical park with natural-history exhibits, this is also one of the world's leading institutions devoted to the study and appreciation

The Giant Saguaro

The giant saguaro is found only in the highly specialized Sonoran Desert climate. The largest species of cactus in the US grows slowly: after three years, a young saguaro is barely half an inch high. It will be 50 before it flowers and 75 before it sprouts its first arm. An individual saguaro produces some 40 million seeds, but generally only one develops into a mature plant. For germination, heavy summer rains must fall; of those that sprout, only 1 percent survive. It's illegal to damage saguaros or remove them from the desert, living or dead, without a permit. But poaching has long been a problem. Investigators for the Arizona Department of Agriculture, sometimes called "Cactus Cops," patrol the desert in search of violators. The ultimate revenge was exacted years ago on a Phoenix man who began blasting a saguaro with a 16-gauge shotgun. A spiny 4ft arm fell off the cactus, crushing the vandal.

Photo courtesy Scottsdale Convention & Visitors Bureau

Saguaro Cactus Blooms

of deserts. The "museum" is best seen by walking 2mi of trails through 21 acres of desert. More than 300 animal and 1,300 plant species, all indigenous to the Sonoran Desert, include ocelots and jaguarundi in a red-rock canyon, mountain lions and black bears in a mountain woodland, bighorn sheep climbing rock ledges, javelina rooting among prickly pears. Visitors come nose to snout or Tucson's night skies have inspired astronomers, both professional and amateur, to set up telescopes of all sizes and shapes. Tucson has a greater concentration of observatories within a 50mi radius than anywhere else on earth. City regulations restrict outdoor lighting at night to preserve the starscape beak with Gila monsters, prairie dogs and red-tailed hawks.

A limestone cave with stalagmites and stalactites contains an **Earth Sciences★** display. In the **Hummingbird Aviary★★**, native hummingbirds buzz by. Nocturnal desert dwellers are active by day in **Life Underground.**

Saguaro National Park★★

⚠️♿🅿️ ☎520-733-5100. www.nps.gov/sagu.

The giant saguaro, iconic symbol of the Southwest, grows only in the Sonoran Desert of Arizona and northern Mexico. This park protects thriving communities of the cacti, which can grow to 50ft in height, 8 tons in weight and 200 years in age. Saguaros anchor diverse communities of animals and smaller plants.

The park has two units. In the 37sq mi **Tucson Mountain District** (2700 N. Kinney Rd.; ☎520-733-5158), saguaros are thicker and younger. Beginning from the Red Hills Visitor Center, 1mi north of the Desert Museum, trails and the **Bajada Loop Drive** (9mi) offer fine views of cacti climbing mountain slopes.

The 103sq-mi eastern unit of the national park, the **Rincon Mountain District** (3693 S. Old Spanish Trail; ☎520-733-5153), is on the east side of Tucson, 15mi from downtown. The **Cactus Forest Drive** (8mi) loops from the visitor center through a saguaro forest; 128mi of hiking and horse trails climb over 7,000ft ridges into a woodland shared by scrub oak and ponderosa pine.

South Side

Mission San Xavier del Bac★★

1950 W. San Xavier Rd. ♿ 🅿 ☏*520-294-2624. www.sanxaviermission.org.* The oldest US Catholic church still in use, San Xavier del Bac was founded in 1692 by Father Eusebio Kino, the mission wasn't finished until 1797. With bricks, stone and limestone mortar, Tohono O'odham Indians created an exquisite white-domed building of Mexican Renaissance, Moorish and Byzantine styles. The walls and ceilings of the sanctuary, entered through mesquite-wood doors, are beautifully painted in historical frescoes. Throughout are statues and carvings. Small handmade objects with ribbons, *milagros*, are left by people seeking a miracle or giving thanks for one already granted.

Pima Air and Space Museum★★

Kids *6000 E. Valencia Rd. at I-10 Exit 267.* ✗ ♿ 🅿 ☏ *520-574-0462. www.pimaair.org.*
This museum boasts a full replica of the Wright Brothers' 1903 Flyer and the SR-71 Blackbird, capable of speeds over 2,000mph. Visitors see 200 military, private and commercial planes, including the Air Force One used by President Kennedy. Tours visit the **Aerospace Maintenance and Regeneration Center** (AMARC) on Davis-Monthan Air Force Base, where retired aircraft are stored. The **Challenger Learning Center** enrolls kids in space "missions." Pima operates the **Titan Missile Museuma** (*1580 W. Duval Mine Rd., Sahuarita, at I-19 Exit 69, 25mi south of Tucson;* ☏*520-625-7736)*, a chilling reminder of the Cold War. For two decades, the US kept 54 nuclear-warhead missiles ready to be launched at a moment's notice from various sites. All except this one were dismantled in the mid-1980s. .

Excursions

Colossal Cave Mountain Park★

Kids *Old Spanish Trail, 6mi north of I-10 Exit 279, Vail, 25mi southeast of Tucson.* ☏ *520-647-7275. www.colossalcave.com.*

Biosphere 2

Tours of this large dry cave follow a .5mi route planned by the Civilian Conservation Corps in the mid-1930s. .

Biosphere 2

32540 S. Biosphere Rd., near Oracle, 40mi north of Tucson. ☏*520-838-6200. www.b2science.org.*
The spaceship-like facility in which eight researchers lived for two years is now managed by the University of Arizona. 🎧Guided tours lead visitors through parts of the self-sustaining laboratory that gained world attention in 1991-93; the majority of the facility is still devoted to environmental research.

Kids Kitt Peak National Observatory★

Rte. 86, Tohono O'odham Reservation, 46mi west of Tucson. ♿ 🅿 ☏ *520-318-8726. www.noao.edu/kpno.* Atop 6,875ft This is the world's largest collection of optical telescopes, funded by the National Science Foundation and managed by a consortium of universities. 🎧Tours (*1hr)* canvass an array of observatories up to 18 stories tall.

Organ Pipe Cactus National Monument★

Rte. 85, 140mi west of Tucson via Rte. 86. ⛺ ♿ 🅿 ☏*520-387-6849. www.nps.gov/orpi.*
This 516sq mi preserve on the Mexican border is the only place in the US to see wild organ pipe cacti, cousins of the saguaro. In spring and summer, their lavender-white, night-blooming flowers open. Dirt-surfaced **Ajo Mountain Drive** (*21mi)* winds along the foothills of the 4,800ft Ajo Range. **Puerto Blanco Drive** (*53mi)* circles past Quitobaquito Spring, a historic waterhole that attracts more than 260 species of birds.

SOUTHEASTERN ARIZONA ★

MAP PP 314-315

MOUNTAIN STANDARD TIME

Southeast Arizona is a landscape rife with Old West history. Here the Apache Indians—led by Cochise and his successor, Geronimo—battled the US Cavalry to a standstill. Here Wyatt Earp and Doc Holliday got into a disagreement with the Clanton Gang at the O.K. Corral. Today, with rugged mountains, desert vistas and superb bird-watching, this former frontier land bordering Mexico offsets its colorful past with some of the most impressive scenery in the Southwest.

- **Information:** ☎520-432-9215. www.explorecochise.com, www.visittucson.org.
- ▶ **Orient Yourself:** This area south of Tucson is at a relatively higher elevation and somewhat cooler.
- **Don't Miss:** Kartchner Caverns.

Sights

Tubac

I-19 Exit 34, 45mi south of Tucson. ✕ 🅿
☎520-398-2704. www.tubacaz.com.
Tubac was the first European settlement in Arizona. **Tubac Presidio State Historic Park**★ *(Presidio Dr. & Burreul St.; ☎520-398-2252, www.azparks. gov)* recounts the 250-year history of the fortress.
Tubac's economy centers on 80 **artists' studios** and galleries that line the half-dozen streets of the historic village.

Tumacácori National Historical Park ★

I-19 Exit 29, 50mi south of Tucson. ♿ 🅿
☎520-398-2341. www.nps.gov/tuma.
Construction of Tumacácori's Franciscan mission began in 1800. Tours take in the sanctuary, cemetery, granary, convent.

Tombstone ★★

US-80 between Benson & Bisbee, 67mi southeast of Tucson via I-10 Exit 303. ✕ ♿ 🅿 ☎520-457-3929. www.tombstone.org.
"The Town Too Tough to Die" still harks back to 1881, when Marshal Wyatt Earp, his brothers and Doc Holliday vanquished the cattle-rustling Clanton Gang in the legendary "Gunfight at the O.K. Corral." Buildings still stand from the halcyon mining years of 1877-85. Wooden sidewalks line **Allen Street**★★. Horse-drawn stagecoaches offer tours, shops sell Western souvenirs and saloons like Big Nose Kate's are open for business. Gunslingers, gamblers and dance-hall hostesses wander the town of 1,504. Gunfights are reenacted daily at the original **O.K. Corral** *(Allen St. between 3rd & 4th Sts.; ☎520-457-3456, www.ok-corral.com)*. Other sights to see are the 1881 **Bird Cage Theatre** *(6th & Allen Sts.; ☎520-457-3421)*; the **Rose Tree Inn** *(4th & Toughnut Sts.; ☎520-457-3326)*; and **Tombstone Courthouse State Historic Park**★ *(219 E. Toughnut St.; ☎520-457-3311, www.azparks.gov)*.

Bisbee ★★

US-80 & Rte. 92, 96mi southeast of Tucson. ⛺ ✕ ♿ 🅿 ☎520-432-4321. www.bisbeearizona.com.
This historic mining town, its buildings swaggering up the sides of Mule Mountain, was the largest settlement between St. Louis and San Francisco when ore was discovered in 1880. The Copper Queen Mine closed in 1975—after $2 billion in copper, gold, lead, silver and zinc had been taken. Today a number of Bisbee's 6,200 people operate galleries, shops and coffeehouses within the late-19C and early-20C buildings of Italianate Victorian architecture. The **Bisbee Mining and Historical Museum** *(5 Copper Queen Plaza; ☎520-432-7071, www.bisbeemuseum.org)* once served as the mining company's office. The **Copper Queen Hotel** *(11 Howell St.; ☎520-432-2216, www.copperqueen.com)* has dominated the town since 1902.

Queen Mine Tours★★ *(118 Arizona St.; ☎520-432-2071, www.queenminetour. com)* are guided by retired miners. A 13mi bus tour visits the **Lavender Pit**, a massive open-pit mine.

Douglas

US-80 & US-191, 119 miles southeast of Tucson. ✕&🅿 *☎520-364-7501. www. discoverdouglas.com.*

This old copper town of 15,000, bordering Agua Prieta, Mexico, has 335 buildings on the National Historic Register. The 1907 **Gadsden Hotel** *(1046 G Ave.; ☎520-364-4481, www.hotelgadsden. com)* has a neo-Renaissance lobby with a marble staircase and a 42ft stained-glass mural. The **Slaughter Ranch** is a National Historic Landmarka *(Geronimo Trail; ☎520-558-2474, www.slaughter-ranch.com),* 15mi east, that recalls turn-of-the-20C cattle ranching. The 300-acre site has an adobe ranch house, ice house, wash house, granary and commissary.

Benson

I-10 Exits 302-306, 45mi east of Tucson. △✕&🅿 *☎520-586-4293. www.benson visitorcenter.com.*

Founded in 1880 on the Southern Pacific line, Benson grew as a copper-smelting center. The **Benson Railroad Historic District** *(E. 3rd St.)* preserves late-19C buildings.

Kartchner Caverns State Park★★

ò Rte. 90, 8.7mi south of Benson. &🅿 *☎520-586-2283. www.azparks.gov. Guided tours (75min) only, reservations strongly recommended (☎520-586-2283).*

This huge "wet" limestone cave in the Whetstone Mountains was discovered in 1974 but kept secret until 1988. Unveiled to the public in late 1999, the stunning cave, home to 2,000 bats, is actively dripping stalactites and growing stalagmites. Visitors enter via the **Discovery Center**, with exhibits and videos on cave geology; natural history and spelunk-ing. Two separate tours are available, one includes one of the largest known (21ft-by-.25in) soda straws, and a 58ft column called Kubla Khan. The entire cave may rival New Mexico's Carlsbad Caverns in size.

Amerind Foundation Museum★

1mi east of I-10 Exit 318, Dragoon, 16mi east of Benson. 🅿 *☎520-586-3666. www. amerind.org.*

A nonprofit archaeology institute, Amerind is devoted to studying native cultures from Alaska to Patagonia. Exhibits include beadwork, costumes, pottery, basketry, ritual masks, weapons, children's toys and clothing, and cover everything from Cree snowshoe-making tools to the finest 19C Navajo weavings. Its Spanish Colonial Revival buildings (1931-59, H.M. Starkweather) blend dramatically with the boulders of Texas Canyon.

Chiricahua National Monument★★

Rte. 186, 37mi southeast of Willcox. △🅿 *☎520-824-3560. www.nps.gov/chir.*

Chiricahua Apaches called this the "Land of the Standing-up Rocks," a name befitting the fantastic wilderness of sculptured columns, spires, grottoes and balanced rocks that climaxes this preserve. The region became a national monument in 1924 after promotion by the Swedish-immigrant owners of the **Faraway Guest Ranch** ("so god-awful far away from everything"), now a historic property open for guided tours.

From the entrance station, beautiful **Bonita Canyon Drive** rises 8mi, past a small visitor center, to spectacular Massai Point at 6,870ft atop the Chiricahua Range. More than 20mi of hiking trails extend to such unusual rock formations as Duck on a Rock and Totem Pole. Believed to have been formed 27 million years ago in the wake of a nearby volcanic eruption, the Chiricahuas harbor numerous rare birds.

PORTLAND AREA

The commercial and cultural capital of the state of Oregon, Portland commands a prominent position straddling the Willamette River where it meets the Columbia. Well over 2 million people inhabit the metropolitan area, spreading their homes across a verdant landscape of fields, rolling hills and forested ridges about 100mi upriver from the Pacific Ocean. A friendly city of unpretentious charm, Portland boasts a handsome downtown core, some 200 parks and gardens, a superb light rail system, and lively neighborhoods on both sides of the Willamette.

The greater state of Oregon *(OAR-a-gun)*—bordered by California on the south and Washington state on the north—embodies the West of sweeping ranchlands, sky-thrusting mountains and a cherished independence. The snow-topped spine of the Cascade

Range divides the wet maritime region of an awesome 362mi Pacific coastline and the lush Willamette *(will-AM-it)* Valley from the deserts of the east.

The Lewis and Clark Expedition passed through in 1805-06. Fur traders followed. By 1846 a treaty with Britain established America's right to the land south of the 49th parallel; the state of Oregon was carved from the southwestern part of this new territory.

For much of the 20C to the present, Oregon has been at the forefront of social reform, struggling with the clash between environmental protection and resource exploitation. In the western part of the state, timber and fishing have given way to high-tech industries, metal processing and tourism.

Portland Skyline, with Mount Hood in the Background

© Portland Oregon Visitors Association

PORTLAND ★★

MICHELIN MAP 493 B 4
PACIFIC STANDARD TIME
POPULATION 537,081

The Willamette River, spanned by a dozen distinctive bridges, acts as a natural dividing line between the city's hilly, forested west side and flatter eastern neighborhoods. Less internationally conspicuous than Seattle (three hours' drive north), Portland prides itself on a progressive, relaxed atmosphere, and is particularly noted for its jazz and blues clubs.

- **Information:** ☎503-275-9750, www.travelportland.com.
- ▶ **Orient Yourself:** Most attractions lie downtown and in Washington Park, both served by the city's exceptional light rail system. Mount Hood, directly east of downtown, is an omnipresent landmark for direction—if it's visible.
- **Parking:** Parking on the east side of the Willamette (in the OMSI lot, for instance) is cheaper than in downtown, which can be reached via a five-minute stroll across one of the city's many bridges.
- **Don't Miss:** Powell's City of Books; the International Rose Test Garden in Washington Park.
- **Organizing Your Time:** Visitors strapped for time can devote one busy day to downtown (the Chinese Garden, Art Museum, Powell's Books) and the next day to Washington Park's zoo, rose garden and Japanese garden.
- **Especially for Kids:** OMSI is superb for kids of all ages.

A Bit of History

Before the 1842 opening of the Oregon Trail, American Indians, then trappers and homesteaders settled at the confluence of the Willamette and Columbia rivers. Portland burgeoned with the arrival of the railroads in the 1880s. Its river-junction location made it a shipping center; trade extended to China. The war years created demand for shipyard workers, swelling Portland's population.

Portland's progressive urban identity dates from its 1972 Downtown Plan, which laid out guidelines for development. Today the downtown is pedestrian-friendly, and Pearl District to the north (www.explorethepearl.com)—once run-down warehouses—has been rejuvenated with shops, cafes and residential complexes. Both are linked by the Portland Streetcar (www.portland-streetcar.org).

Originally based on timber and shipping, the city's economy has been bolstered by high-tech companies, especially semiconductor firms located in the suburbs.

Sights

Oregon History Center★

1200 SW Park Ave. ♿ ☎ 503-222-1741. www.ohs.org.

Eight-story *trompe l'oeil* murals of Lewis and Clark and the Oregon Trail rise beside the entrance plaza of this archival museum. Filled with interactive displays, the **Portland!**★ exhibit traces city history, beginning with the 1840s and 1850s to the rise of the car culture of the 1950s.

Portland Art Museum★

1219 SW Park Ave. ✕♿🅿 ☎ 503-226-2811. www.pam.org.

The oldest (1892) art museum in the Pacific Northwest occupies a low brick building with travertine trim (1932, Pietro Belluschi, remodeled in 2000), and a new wing, housed in a former Masonic temple. Highlights include the **European Galleries** and **East Asian Galleries**. The museum's new Center for Northwest Art brings regional artists to the fore; the **Center for Native American Art** boasts prehistoric, historic and contemporary crafts by North American

Address Book Portland Area

🕭 *For price ranges, see the Legend on the cover flap.*

WHERE TO STAY

$$$$ The Benson Hotel – *309 SW Broadway, Portland.* ✕ 👤 🅿 📧 *503-228-2000 or 800-426-0670. www. bensonhotel.com. 286 rooms.* Lumber baron Simon Benson completed this grand hotel in 1912, and its opulence has endured. Elaborate Austrian crystal chandeliers illuminate the marble floors and walnut walls of the lobby, and the rooms have an equally lavish ambience. **The London Grill ($$$)** has been a fixture for more than 50 years.

$$$$ Skamania Lodge – *1131 Skamania Lodge Way, Stevenson, WA.* ✕ 👤 🅿 🛳 📧 *509-427-7700 or 888-993-6523. www.dolce.com/skamania/. 254 rooms.* Built within the Columbia River Gorge National Scenic Area, this grand lodge boasts a three-story lobby with windows framing the gorge itself. Throughout are works of Northwest regional art. All rooms have views of either river or forested mountains; **The Dining Room ($$$)** serves salmon from its wood-burning oven.

$$$ Stephanie Inn – *2740 S. Pacific Hwy., Cannon Beach.* ✕ 👤 🅿 📧 *503-436-2221 or 800-633-3466. www.stephanie-inn.com. 50 rooms.* The Stephanie's wood beams and local stone settle it comfortably into its beachside site. Every window looks out to sea or mountain, and guests step off a porch onto the beach. The restaurant is famed for its Oregon coastal cuisine.

$$$ The Governor Hotel – *611 SW 10th Ave., Portland.* ✕ 👤 🅿 🛳 📧 *503-224-3400 or 800-554-3456. www.govhotel. com. 100 rooms.* Murals recall the early-19C expedition of Lewis and Clark; the original stained-glass dome and tiled floor remain from 1909 construction. This classic hotel combines mahogany detailing with large and contemporary rooms, all within a grand shell. **Jake's Grill ($$)** retains the atmosphere of a century-old restaurant.

$$$ Peerless Hotel – *243 Fourth Street, Ashland. 541-488-1082*

or *800-460-8758. www.peerlessrestaurant.com. 6 rooms.* Fashioned from a historic brick boardinghouse, the Peerless's rooms are unreservedly lavish with satin brocade, brass fixtures and Victorian wallpaper. One expecially comfy suite has not one, but two, large clawfoot tubs.

$$$ Sunriver Resort – *1 Center Drive, Sunriver. 541-593-1000 or 800-801-8765. www.sunriver-resort.com.* This classy resort development has a large (209 rooms) deluxe hotel, numerous rental condominiums and homes, two golf courses, 35 miles of paved bike trails, and a lovely site along the Deschutes River beneath Mount Bachelor and Paulina Peak. It's a perfect base from which to explore Central Oregon's innumerable natural attractions--or just relax in the pine-scented sunshine of the High Desert.

$$ Hotel Vintage Plaza – *422 SW Broadway, Portland.* ✕ 👤 🅿 📧 *503-228-1212 or 800-243-0555. www.vintage-plaza.com. 107 rooms.* A wine theme pervades this charming European-style boutique hotel, built in 1894 and renovated in 2000. Every room of this Kimpton hotel is named for an Oregon vineyard or winery, and evenings bring wine tasting in the fireside lobby. An Italian restaurant, **Pazzo ($$$)**, serves three meals daily.

WHERE TO EAT

$$$ Chateaulin – *50 E Main St., Ashland.* 📧 *541-482-2264. www.chateaulin. com. Dinner only.* **French**. Tucked inconspicuously into a historic building near Ashland's town plaza, Southern Oregon's oldest fine dining establishment has held its quality for three decades. The menu's strength is lamb, beef and duck dishes done in simple country style; advance reservations are a must in summer.

$$$ Bluehour – *250 NW 13th Ave., Portland.* 📧 *503-226-3394. www.bluehouronline.com.* **Creative Continental**. This swank Pearl District establishment is a popular spot for after-theater desserts and espresso drinks. Earlier diners can choose among such dishes as oysters poached in dry Vermouth, seared scallops with puréed celery root, New York steak with Bordelaise sauce and grilled chicken with fried sage and shiitake caps.

$$$ Caprial's Bistro – *7015 SE Milwaukie Ave., Portland.* ☎ *503-236-6457. www.caprialandjohnskitchen.com/bistro. Closed Sun-Mon.* **Northwest Regional.** Celebrity chef Caprial Pence and her husband, John, operate this casual eatery (with a cooking school) in the Westmoreland district. The open kitchen offers up wonderful lunches, from an heirloom tomato tart to "hot-as-hell" chicken on Chinese noodles. Dinner features include seafood stew in a tomato-and-orange broth and braised duck with a blackberry-and-tamarind sauce.

$$$ Excelsior Inn – *754 E. 13th St., Eugene.* ☎ *541-342-6963. www.excelsiorinn.com.* **Creative Italian.** An elegant Victorian steps from the University of Oregon is home to this restaurant, bistro and bed-and-breakfast inn. Hungry diners may start with a butter-lettuce pear salad with hazelnuts and Gorgonzola, then proceed with alce alla Piemontese (grilled elk medallions with a fig molasses demi-glace) or grilled prawns atop a roasted-pepper risotto. The **Excelsior Bistro ($$)** offers a more casual menu of pastas and sandwiches.

$$$ Wildwood – *1221 NW 21st Ave., Portland.* ☎ *503-248-9663. www.wildwoodrestaurant.com.* **Northwest Regional.** Noted chef Cory Schreiber's open kitchen adds activity to this warm, bright space with its floors of Douglas

fir. The menu changes daily, but there are always fresh dishes such as salmon with sugar-pea vinaigrette or portobello mushroom-and-potato lasagna, all with Northwest hints.

$$ Brasserie Montmartre – *626 SW Park Ave., Portland.* ☎ *503-224-5552. www.brasseriemontmartre.com.* **Continental**. Like a supper club out of Moulin Rouge, this Bohemian restaurant could be in Paris' Montmartre quarter, with live jazz nightly and excellent food values. The artsy clientele enjoy ménage à trois (a trio of house-made pâtés), French onion soup, Boudin blanc sausage and seafood bisque or crèpes.

$$ Jake's Famous Crawfish Restaurant – *401 SW 12th Ave., Portland.* ☎ *503-226-1419. www.mccormickand-schmicks.com.* **Seafood**. Jake Freiman cooked up his first crawfish in 1892, and his place has offered an orgy of seafood ever since. Alaskan Copper River salmon, Hawaiian striped marlin and Quilcene oysters are just a few of the myriad marine delicacies. They may be roasted on cedar planks, grilled with papaya salsa, or battered in beer.

$$ Pine Tavern – *967 NW Brooks St., Bend.* ☎*541-382-5581. www.pinetavern.com* **American**. At 66, the Tavern is central Oregon's oldest and best-known restaurant, built around a 200ft-tall ponderosa pine that extends through the roof. Known for beef purchased from local ranchers, the food fits this former timber town: Pan-fried trout, meatloaf and barbecue ribs are still served today as they were by the original owners.

groups. An outdoor sculpture mall features works by Henry Moore, Barbara Hepworth and Pierre-Auguste Renoir.

Chinese Classical Garden★★
NW 3rd & Everett Sts.; ☎*503-228-8131. www.portlandchinesegarden.org.* One of just two such gardens in North America (the other is in Vancouver, British Columbia), this 2000 addition to Portland's small international district is a highly stylized retreat whose high-walled courtyards, pools, walkways and meditation rooms are designed

to mute the urban bustle outside its walls. Encompassing a city block (40,000 square feet), the garden's highlights include a 7,000-square-foot "lake," and Tai Hu limestone rocks, 500 tons of which were shipped here from China.

Powell's City of Books★★
1005 W. Burnside; ☎ *503-228-4651. www.powells.com.* One of the most popular attractions in Oregon is this pioneering bookseller, now grown to a monolith that encompasses an entire block and holds more

Portland Aerial Tram and Mount Hood

than 1 million titles. First in the US to mix used and new books on its shelves, Powell's today is so large visitors need store maps to navigate the 22 sections.

Governor Tom McCall Waterfront Park★

Bordering SW Naito Pkwy. & the Willamette River between Marquam Bridge & Steel Bridge.

This grassy 23-acre park stretching along the Willamette was named for a governor who was a proponent of land-use planning. Among eight bridges that may be seen are the dark-green **Hawthorne Bridge** (1910), oldest operating vertical-lift bridge in the world, and the **Steel Bridge** (1912, the world's only telescoping double-deck vertical-lift bridge. **Portland Spirit River Cruises**★ (☎503-224-3900, www.portlandspirit.com) offer year-round departures (from Salmon Street Springs) that pass Ross Island, home to nesting eagles and ospreys. The new (2006) **Portland Aerial Tram**★ (www.portlandtram.org) offers visitors a view of the city and surrounding volcanic peaks during a 3min passage from the riverbank to Oregon Health Sciences University on the bluffs above.

Oregon Museum of Science and Industry★★

Kids *1945 SE Water St.* ✕ ♿ 🅿 ☎ *503-797-4000. www.omsi.edu.*

This brick-and-glass building (1992, Zimmer Gunsul Frasca) on the Willamette incorporates an old power plant, and harbors two floors of hands-on exhibits, an Omnimax theater, a planetarium and a submarine. In the Earth Science Hall, the **Earthquake Room**★ offers the jolting experience of a major quake.

Washington Park★★

Entrances south of W. Burnside Rd. & west of SW Vista Ave. ☎503-823-7529. *www.portlandonline.com/parks.*

Within the boundaries of this urban oasis are a handful of notable attractions. The **International Rose Test Garden**★★ *(400 SW Kingston Ave.;* ☎503-823-3636, *www.rosegardenstore.org)* displays 9,000 roses of 550 species. Just uphill, the 5.5-acre **Japanese Garden**★★ *(611 SW Kingston Ave.;* ☎ *503-223-1321, www.japanesegarden.com)* includes a moon bridge, ceremonial teahouse and Zen-inspired sand-and-stone garden.

In the 173-acre **Hoyt Arboretum** *(4033 SW Fairview Blvd.;* ☎503-865-8733, *www.hoytarboretum.org)* are 900 species of trees and trails winding through stands of magnolia, oaks and maples. At the **World Forestry Center**★ Kids *(4033 SW Canyon Rd.;* ☎ *503-228-1367, www.world-forestry.org)* a multilingual talking tree greets visitors and explains how a tree grows. The **Oregon Zoo**★ Kids *(4001 SW Canyon Rd.;* ☎503-226-1561, *www.oregonzoo.org)* keeps more than 1,300 animals, including **Asian elephants**★.

Pittock Mansion★★

3229 NW Pittock Dr., off NW Barnes Rd. ✕ 🅿 ☎ *503-823-3623. www.pittockmansion.com.*

The most opulent home in Portland perches on a 940ft crest in Imperial Heights. Built in 1914 (Edward T. Foulkes) for Henry Pittock, publisher of *The Oregonian* newspaper, the manse is a French Renaissance Revival-style château with exterior sandstone walls. Tours take in magnificent marble and woodwork and luxurious early-20C furnishings.

Elk Rock Gardens at the Bishop's Close★★

SW Military Lane, 6mi south of downtown Portland via SW Macadam Ave. b 503-636-5613. www.diocese-oregon.org/theclose.

Estate owner Peter Kerr, a prosperous grain merchant, made his blufftop 1916 Scottish manor home the focal point for an English landscape garden designed by John Olmsted. Kerr supplemented it with plants he collected during world travels. Both house and gardens now belong to the Episcopal church.

Excursions

Mount Hood★★

US-26, 50mi east of Portland. ☎ 503-622-3017. www.mthood.org.

The snow-cloaked cone of Oregon's highest peak pierces the sky at 11,239ft. In 1805, explorers Lewis and Clark were the first white Americans to set eyes on the volcanic peak, previously named by British sailors. It became a beacon to Oregon Trail travelers in the mid-19C. Their wagon ruts remain visible just west of **Barlow Pass** *(Rte. 35 east of US-26).*

Nearby **Timberline Lodge**★ *(off US-26, 6mi north of Government Camp; ☎ 503-622-7979, www.timberlinelodge.com),* built by the Works Progress Adminis-

tration in 1936-37, is a fine example of American craftsmanship. From here, hikers can essay the spectacular 40mi **Timberline Trail**★★.

Columbia River Gorge★★

I-84 from Troutdale to The Dalles, 17 to 84mi east of Portland. ☎541-308-1700. www.fs.fed.us/r6/columbia.

Extending from suburban Portland to the mouth of the Deschutes River, the 455sq-mi Columbia River Gorge National Scenic Area includes waterfalls, state parks and 700ft-high cliff-edge vistas. The second-largest river in the US (after the Mississippi) slices volcanic basalt along the Oregon-Washington border. Providing a scenic alternative to the interstate is the **Historic Columbia River Highway**★★ *(US-30).* Completed in 1915, it now may be driven only in two distinct sections linked by I-84: 22mi from Troutdale *(Exit 17)* to Ainsworth State Park *(Exit 40)* and 16mi from Mosier *(Exit 69)* to The Dalles *(Exit 84).* The best views are from **Portland Women's Forum State Park** *(Mile 10)* and the **Vista House at Crown Point**★ *(Mile 11;* ☎ *503-695-2230, www.vistahouse.com).* Don't miss **Multnomah Falls**★★ *(I-84 Exit 31;* ☎ *541-308-1700),* a mesmerizing 620ft plunge of water.

US Army Corps of Engineers visitor centers at **Bonneville Locks and Dam**★★

Windsurfing the Gorge

©iStockphoto.com/ Ben Blankenburg

Sailboarders have found a paradise at the Columbia River Gorge town of **Hood River** *(I-84 Exit 63, www.hoodriver.org).* Here at a natural break in the Cascade Mountains, steady currents from the east meet strong winds from the west, so that summer winds average 20-25mph. Windsurfing enthusiasts discovered the gorge in the mid-1980s, and Hood River, a cozy hillside town of about 5,000 people, witnessed an adrenaline shot to its economy. The US Windsurfing Association has chosen Hood River as its home base, as have more than three dozen sailboard retailers, distributors, and custom-board and accessory manufacturers.

(I-84 Exit 40; ☎ 541-374-8820, www.nwp. usace.army.mil/op) and **The Dalles Lock and Dam**★ (I-84 Exit 87; ☎ 541-296-9778, www.nwp.usace.army.mil/op) show how the river has been harnessed. At the **Columbia Gorge Discovery Center**★★ (5000 Discovery Dr., The Dalles; ☎ 541-296-8600, www.gorgediscovery.org), where visitors can toy with a windsurfing simulator.

Oregon City★

12mi south of Portland on Rte. 99E at I-205. ☎ 503-655-5511. www.mthood territory.com.
Established in 1844 at the end of the 2,000mi Oregon Trail, this town of 25,754 is the oldest settlement in the Willamette Valley. It was the first capital of the Oregon Territory.

End of the Oregon Trail Interpretive Center★

1726 Washington St. ♿ 🅿 ☎ 503-657-9336. www.endoftheoregontrail.org.
Located on Abernathy Green, the main arrival area for Oregon Trail travelers, the center is housed in three 50ft-high buildings shaped like covered wagons. Tour guides in pioneer costume recount the hardships of the overland journey.

Vancouver National Historic Reserve★

750 Anderson St. off Mill Plain Blvd., Vancouver, WA, 8mi north of Portland. ♿ 🅿 ☎ 360-992-1800. www.vnhrt.org.
The Hudson's Bay Company had its headquarters here in 1825-46 and the first US military post in the Pacific Northwest was founded here in 1849. Visits usually begin in the 1878 **Victorian O.O. Howard House Visitor Center**★. Just north is **Officers Row**★, which includes the 1886 **Marshall House**★ (☎ 360-693-3103), home to General George C. Marshall, who commanded the Vancouver Barracks from 1936-38. **Fort Vancouver National Historic Site**★ 🅺🅸🅳🆂 (♿ 🅿 ☎ 360-816-6230, www.nps.gov/fova) offers 🐾guided tours of the reconstructed Hudson's Bay Company stockade.

WILLAMETTE VALLEY AND SOUTHERN OREGON★★

MICHELIN MAP 493 A, B 4, 5, 6
PACIFIC STANDARD TIME

Broad, fertile Willamette Valley is Oregon's heart. Running 110mi south from Portland to Eugene and 30mi between the Cascades and the Coast Range, this destination of Oregon Trail travelers began attracting pioneers in the 1840s. Today, despite being the state's most populated area outside metropolitan Portland, most of the valley retains a rural feel: a landscape of farmland, tulip fields, hazelnut orchards and covered bridges.

- **Information:** Willamette Valley: ☎866-548-5018, www.oregonwinecountry. org; Southern Oregon, ☎541-779-4691, www.sova.org.
- ▶ **Orient Yourself:** The drive from Portland to Ashland, the southernmost Oregon city on I-5 (which runs north-south) takes about 5hrs. Medford and Eugene have major regional airports. The area's best-known attractions today are Crater Lake, and Ashland's Shakespeare festival.
- ⏱ **Organizing Your Time:** If you want to see a play during Ashland's Oregon Shakespeare Festival, May, September and October offer fine weather and fewer crowds. Crater Lake can be seen best in July in a half-day visit.

Sights

Oregon Wine Country★

Via Rte. 99 West off I-5, 20–40mi SW of Portland. b866-548-5018, www.oregon winecountry.org.

Situated on the same latitude as France's Burgundy region, the northern Willamette Valley has developed into one of the finest viticultural regions in the world. Established in the 1960s, the industry remained relatively unknown until a Pinot Noir from Eyrie Vineyards did the unimaginable in a French-sponsored tasting in 1979: It outperformed several esteemed French wines. Many family-run operations are open for tours and tastings.

t orchards and roadside stands. At the heart of the wine country is the pleasant Linfield College town of **McMinnville**, whose biggest attraction has nothing to do with wine. The **Evergreen Aviation Museum**★ *(500 NE Captain Michael King Smith Way; 503-434-4180, www.sprucegoose.org)* holds the **Spruce Goose**★★ built and flown just once in 1947 by billionaire aviator Howard Hughes. Despite its nickname, it is made mostly of birch.

Salem★

I-5 & Rte. 99 East, 44mi south of Portland. b800-874-7012. www.travelsalem.com.

The capital of Oregon and the state's third-largest city with about 143,000 residents, Salem traces its founding to 1840, when Jason Lee moved the headquarters of his Methodist mission to this mid-Willamette Valley location.

Lee's home and several other early buildings still stand at the **Mission Mill Museum**★★ *(1313 Mill St.; ✕ & ▣ ☎ 503-585-7012, www.missionmill.org)*, a five-acre historical park that includes the 1889 Thomas Kay Woolen Mill.

Downtown, the domed **Oregon State Capitol**★ *(900 Court St. NE; ✕ & ▣ ☎ 503-986-1388),* built in 1938 (Francis Keally) in the Greek Revival style, is topped by a bronze-and-gold-leaf statue of a pioneer.

A half-hour's drive East of Salem is **Silver Falls State Park**★★ *(Rte. 214, Sublimity ☎ 503-873-8681);* Oregon's largest state park at 8,700 acres. Its highlight, in addition to a historic lodge and a variety of recreational facilities, is the **Trail of Ten Falls**, a 7mi loop along Silver creek that takes hikers through deep forests to ten cascading falls, ranging in height from 27 ft to 178 ft.

Eugene★

Rtes. 99 & 126 just west of I-5, 108mi south of Portland. ☎ 541-484-5307. www.visit lanecounty.org.

Oregon's second-largest urban area (146,000) still has ties to its agricultural and timber-industry roots. But the **University of Oregon**★ *(18th Ave. to Franklin Blvd., Agate to Alder Sts.; ☎ 541-346-3201, www.uoregon.edu)* is today the pacesetter. Founded in 1876 and now

Crater Lake

© National Park Service

enrolling more than 18,000 students, this university is largely accountable for Eugene's thriving counterculture, evident in its casual dress, health-food stores and environmental organizations. The UO **Jordan Schnitzer Museum of Art**★★ *(Memorial Quadrangle near Kincaid St.; ☎ 541-346-3027, uoma.uoregon. edu)* is a fantasy of intricate brickwork. The **Museum of Natural History**★ *(1680 E. 15th Ave.; ♿ 🅿 ☎ 541-346-3024, naturalhistory.uoregon.edu)* is devoted mainly to indigenous peoples, including the local Kalapuya culture.

Crater Lake National Park★★★

Rtes. 62 & 138 west of US-97, 145mi southeast of Eugene. ☎ 541-594-3000. www. nps.gov/crla.

The deepest lake in the US at 1,932ft rests in the crater of a collapsed volcano. Ringed by mountains tinged with snow most of the year, this crystal-clear sapphire lake, 6mi in diameter, attracts hikers, geologists and those compelled by the mysterious eye-like blue caldera. A cataclysmic eruption 7,700 years ago hurled more than 18 cubic miles of pumice and ash into the air and surrounding valleys. The collapsed mountain created a bowl-shaped caldera that filled with pure rainwater and snowmelt.

A 33mi Rim Drive circles the lake and offers spectacular **views**★★. Among the best are those from **Sinnott Memorial Overlook** *(Rim Village, south side of lake)* and **Cloudcap**, highest point on the Rim Drive (7,865ft). Better yet is the perspective from atop 8,929ft **Mount Scott**★★, requiring a strenuous 5mi round-trip hike to the park's highest summit. A 7mi spur road off Rim Drive leads to **The Pinnacles**★★, 80ft tall hollow fossilized fumaroles.

Ashland★★

Rte. 99 at I-5 Exit 14, 180mi south of Eugene. b541-482-3486. www.ashland chamber.com

This town of 21,000 on the northern flank of the Siskiyou Mountains has turned itself into a premier cultural center. After failing to turn its lithium-rich springs into a world-class spa, the town capitalized on the dreams of a drama professor and converted an old bandshell into an outdoor amphitheater. There, in 1935, the city kicked off the first **Oregon Shakespeare Festival**★★★ *(15 S. Pioneer St.; ☎ 541-482-4331, www. osfashland.org)*. February to October, the festival stages about a dozen plays a year in its three theaters, featuring works by Shakespeare and other playwrights. On **backstage tours**★★, visitors watch the production staff creating costumes and sets.

Jacksonville★★

Rte. 238, 14mi northwest of Ashland. ☎ 541-899-8118. www.jacksonvilleoregon. org.

Enveloped by rolling hills clad in pear and apple orchards, Jacksonville, once an1850s gold-rush town, is a National Historic District. A visitor center at the old railway depot *(Oregon & C Sts.)* has walking-tour maps. The summer-long **Britt Festivals**★★ fill the hills with classical, blues, jazz and rock music.

Oregon Caves National Monument★★

Rte. 46, 20mi east of Cave Junction & 92mi west of Ashland via I-5 & US-199. 🍴 🅿 ☎ 541-592-2100. www.nps.gov/ orca.

Folded into the southwestern corner of Oregon, this web of marble and limestone chambers is bejeweled with stalactites, stalagmites and other wondrous calcite formations in 3mi of known passageways. On 75min tours, visitors climb 500 stairs, duck through low-ceilinged tunnels and enter chambers like Watson's Grotto and the Ghost Room.

OREGON COAST★★

MICHELIN MAP 493 A, B, 4 A 5, 6
PACIFIC STANDARD TIME

The 362mi Oregon coastline is a scenic blend of wave-swept rocks and sandy beaches. Even the few places where homes and businesses border the shore are nature's province: A 1967 state law made all Oregon beaches public. Though much of the forest just inland has been heavily logged, a tall border of spruce and cedar presses up to the shore, forming a key part of the coastal ecosystem.

- **Information:** ☎541-574-2679. www.visittheoregoncoast.com
- ▶ **Orient Yourself:** U.S. 101, the main highway traversing the coast, skirts the shore several miles from the water. Visitors reach beaches and headlands through state parks on the west side of the highway.
- **Don't Miss:** Heceta Head.
- **Organizing Your Time:** July and August can be foggy months on the Oregon Coast.
- **Especially for Kids:** The Oregon Coast Aquarium.

Sights

Astoria★
US-26, 30 & 101, 96mi northwest of Portland. b 503-325-6311. www.oldoregon.com
Founded as a fur-trading post in 1811, Astoria was the first US settlement west of the Rocky Mountains. By the 1850s it was a thriving port at the mouth of the Columbia River. The town of 10,000 remains a busy port. Exhibits at the **Columbia River Maritime Museum**★ *(1792 Marine Dr.; ☎ 503-325-2323, www.crmm.org)* tell the seafaring heritage.

Fort Clatsop National Memorial★★ *(6mi southwest off US-101; ☎ 503-861-2471, www.nps.gov/lewi)* preserves the site where Lewis and Clark spent the winter of 1805-06, in a re-created fort redolent of smoked meat, dried skins and wet wood.

Cannon Beach★
US-101, 22mi south of Astoria & 80mi west of Portland. ☎ 503-436-2623.
This hamlet of 2,000 caters to artist-residents and well-heeled travelers.

Oregon Dunes

© iStockphoto.com/Neta Degany

HaystackRock rises 235ft at water's edge. **Ecola State Park**★★ *(2mi north of Cannon Beach;* ☎ *503-436-2844, www.nps.gov/lewi)* embraces 9mi of old-growth forest and coastline.

Three Capes Scenic Drive★★

40mi from Tillamook to Pacific City, west of US-101; 63mi south of Astoria. From Tillamook, take Third St. west & follow signs. ☎ *503-842-7525. www.tillamook chamber.org*

This delightful spin takes in dairy farms, bays of diving pelicans, coastal forest, seaside hamlets, dunes and vistas of the open Pacific from state parks at Capes Meares, Lookout and Kiwanda. Drive out to **Cape Meares**, where an 1890 lighthouse perches on a high cliff.

Newport★

US-101, 136mi south of Astoria & 88mi west of Salem. ☎ *541-265-8801. www. newportchamber.org*

This town of 10,000 has a tradition of agriculture, fishing and logging along with tourism.

Across the Yaquina Bay bridge stands the **Oregon Coast Aquarium**★★ 🖼 *(SE Ferry Slip Rd., .25mi east of US-101;* ☎ *541-867-3474, www.aquarium.org),* which displays 200 marine species, most of them native to Oregon waters. About .25mi north, the **Hatfield Marine Science Center**★ 🖼 *(2030 S. Marine Science Dr.;* ☎ *541-867-0100, hmsc.ore-gonstate.edu),* headquarters for Oregon State University's marine-research program, offers oceanography exhibits.

Four miles up the coast, the **Yaquina Head Outstanding Natural Area**★★ *(NW Lighthouse Dr., .5mi west of US-101;* ☎ *541-574-3100, www.blm.gov/or)* occupies an ancient finger of lava that protrudes into the Pacific. The adjacent **Yaquina Head Lighthouse** (1873) is, at 93ft, the tallest lighthouse in the state.

Yachats★

US-101, 159mi south of Astoria & 88mi west of Eugene. ☎ *541-547-3530. www. yachats.org.*

The village of Yachats *(YA-hots)* is the gateway to **Cape Perpetua Scenic Area**★★ *(US-101, 3mi south;* ☎ *541-547-3289),* which combines coastal forest and rocky shoreline in its 2,700 acres.

Oregon Dunes National Recreation Area★★

West side of US-101 for 48mi from Florence (186mi south of Astoria & 61mi west of Eugene) to Coos Bay. ⚠ ♿ 🅿 ☎ *541-271-3611. www.fs.fed.us/r6/siuslaw.*

This strand of coastal dunes, some as high as 200ft, offers an ecosystem of sand, tree islands, wetlands, estuaries and beaches via trails and roads. From the **Oregon Dunes Visitor Center** *(US-101, north end of Reedsport),* rangers will direct travelers to trails and overlooks. The **Siltcoos Recreation Area**★ *(Siltcoos Beach Rd. off US-101, 7mi south of Florence)* has a 1mi boardwalk that loops along a lagoon. Hikers on the **Umpqua Scenic Dunes Trail**★★ *(US-101, 11mi south of Reedsport)* top off a .5mi forest walk by ascending the highest dunes in the area for panoramas.

Coos Bay★

US-101, 234mi south of Astoria & 109mi southwest of Eugene. ☎ *541-269-0215. www.oregonsbayareachamber.com*

The largest natural harbor between Puget Sound and San Francisco Bay is a major shipping center for forest products. A waterfront boardwalk, shops and galleries attract tourists. From 150ft bluffs at **Cape Arago State Park**★ *(Cape Arago Hwy., 14.5mi southwest of Coos Bay;* ☎ *541-888-3778, www.oregon-stateparks.org),* one may sight whales, seals and sea lions.

CENTRAL AND EASTERN OREGON★

MICHELIN MAP 493 B, C, D 4, 5, 6
PACIFIC STANDARD TIME

Oregon divides dramatically along the spine of the Cascades. West is a green land of farms, orchards and lush forest. East is higher, drier land, more open and less populated. Uplifted by tectonic forces, piled higher with deposits of lava and ash, the region was born of volcanic cataclysm and shaped by erosion.

- **Information:** Central Oregon, ☎541-389-8799, www.visitcentraloregon.com. Eastern, ☎541-523-9200, www.eova.com.
- ▶ **Orient Yourself:** Bend is the commercial and visitor capital for eastern Oregon; most of the sights below can be visited using Bend as a base.
- ◷ **Organizing Your Time:** It's worth the long day trip to Hart Mountain National Antelope Refuge.

A Bit of History

Long an Indian home, central and eastern Oregon were passed up by early white pioneers en route to the fertile Willamette Valley. Later arrivals found this country excellent for ranching and mining. Natural resources still provide an economic foundation, but the region remained sparsely populated until tourism took root in outdoor recreation in the 1960s and 70s. With the growth in popularity of snow skiing, mountain biking, golf and white-water rafting, the area has attracted more permanent residents seeking a laid-back lifestyle.

Sights

Bend★
US 20 & 97, 163mi southeast of Portland. ☎ 541-382-3221. www.bendchamber. org.
This city of 72,000 hugs the banks of the Deschutes River. The Three Sisters mountains and other snow-capped peaks provide a stirring backdrop to the west. Early-20C buildings downtown hold restaurants and shops. The **High Desert Museum**★★(Kids US-97, 3.5mi south of Bend; ☎ 541-382-4754. www.highdesert.org) is a small zoo and regional museum. It features life-size dioramas and a "Desertarium." River

otters frolic in a stream near a center for birds of prey.

Newberry National Volcanic Monument★★
Lava Lands Visitor Center, US-97 13mi south of Bend. ☎541-593-2421. www. fs.fed.us/r6/centraloregon.
Extending from the Deschutes River 24mi southeast to 7,987ft Paulina Peak, this 55,000-acre site embraces lava caves, ancient archaeological sites and two crater lakes. The Newberry volcano last erupted 1,300 years ago; hot springs still bubble beneath lake surfaces.
At the **Lava Cast Forest**★ (Forest Rd. 9720, 12mi southeast of visitor center), a 1mi trail loops through molds made 6,000 years ago. The 18sq mi **Newberry Caldera**★★ (Rte. 21, 25mi southeast of visitor center) is a huge crater that contains spring-fed Paulina and East Lakes. The only break in the steep 700–1,700ft walls of the caldera is at **Paulina Falls**, which drop dramatically 80ft off the outer face. Paiute Indians quarried black obsidian from the crater for tools.

Cascade Lakes Highway★★
West on Rte. 372, south on Forest Rd. 46, east on Forest Rd. 42. ☎ 541-388-5664. www.fs.fed.us/r6/centraloregon
This 91mi drive passes tree-fringed lakes, rustic fishing camps and mountain trailheads. Alpine **views**★★★ are stunning from atop 9,065ft **Mount Bachelor**★

(☎541-382-2442, www.mtbachelor.com), considered the Northwest's best ski resort. A chairlift operates to the summit year-round.

Hart Mountain National Antelope Refuge★★

Hart Mountain Road, 240mi southeast of Bend, 60mi northeast of Lakeview. ☎541-947-2731. www.fws.gov/sheldon hartmtn.

This remote conservation area is one of the best places to see free-roaming wild animals—deer, bighorn sheep, coyotes and pronghorn antelope, for whom the refuge was established in 1936. At nearby **Steens Mountain**★ *(541-573-4400, www.blm.gov/or/districts/burns),* the 52-mile Steens Mountain Backcountry Byway affords access to the mountain's 9,700-ft summit, and the home of a herd of wild horses.

Warm Springs Indian Reservation

US-26, 108mi southeast of Portland & 55mi north of Bend.

The largest of eight native reservations in Oregon was created in 1855 from 10 million acres of Wasco and Sahapto tribal land. In addition to a resort, its highlight is the **Museum at Warm Springs**★★ Kids *(US-26, Warm Springs; ☎541-553-3331, www.warmsprings.biz/museum),* which contains tribal heirlooms and a village of various domicile types.

Smith Rock State Park★★

NE Crooked River Dr., Terrebonne, 23mi north of Bend. ⚠ P ☎ *541-548-7501. www.oregonstateparks.org*

Renowned for its rock climbing, these multicolored cliffs frame the Crooked River Canyon. Outcroppings of solidified magma tower 550ft above the river.

John Day Fossil Beds National Monument★★

Sheep Rock Unit, Rte. 19, 2mi north of US-26, 115mi northeast of Bend. Painted Hills Unit, Burnt Ranch Rd., 7mi north of US-26, 88mi northeast of Bend. Clarno Unit, Rte. 218, 101mi northeast of Bend. ☎ *514-987-2333. www.nps.gov/joda.*

Preserving a small portion of the 10,000sq mi of fossil beds covering north-central Oregon, the monument holds fossilized plants and animals that lived here 50 million to 10 million years ago. The **Sheep Rock Visitor Center**★ displays fossils of saber-tooth cats, rhinoceroses and entelodonts (bison-sized pigs). A few miles north, interpretive trails lead to **Blue Basin**★, a natural amphitheater loaded with fossils.

National Historic Oregon Trail Interpretive Center★★

Rte. 86, 5mi east of I-84 at Baker City. ♿ P ☎ *541-523-1843. www.or.blm.gov/oregontrail.*

Perched atop Flagstaff Hill, the museum overlooks ruts made by covered wagons on the Oregon Trail. Hands-on

© National Park Service

John Day Fossil Beds National Monument

exhibits and full-scale dioramas render indelible images of the travails of early pioneers.

Hells Canyon National Recreation Area★★

Extending about 80mi on either side of the Oregon-Idaho border, 350mi east of Portland. Headquarters: Rte. 82, Enterprise. ☎541-426-5546. www.fs.fed.us/hellscanyon.

The Snake River carves the boundary between Oregon and Idaho through the deepest canyon in North America. The canyon is a vertical landscape whose dark cliffs and grassy foothills tumble 6,000–8,000ft, from the Wallowa Range and Seven Devils Mountains to the north-flowing river at its heart.

The **canyon floor**★★ may be reached below Hells Canyon Dam *(via Rte. 86, 91mi east of Baker City)*. From here, the only way to proceed is by boat or on foot. With modern inflatable rafts and jet boats, running the river has become almost routine, if still challenging. The best canyon overlooks are from Oregon's 208mi **Wallowa Mountains Loop**★★ *(from LaGrande, on I-84, drive northeast on Rte. 82 through Enterprise and Joseph to Rte. 350, south on Rte. 39, then west on Rte. 86 through Halfway to Baker City; ☎541-426-5546)*.

Nez Percé National Historical Park★

The park comprises 38 sites in four states, including the 1877 battlefields and locations important to tribal legend. The tribe's story is documented at the main visitor center and museum *(US-95, Spalding, Idaho, 14mi east of Lewiston; ☎ 208-843-7001; www.nps.gov/nepe)*, along with the Spalding-Allen Collection★★ of artifacts and hide clothing dating from 1836.

Pendleton

US-395 & Rte. 11 at I-84, 209mi east of Portland. ☎ 541-276-7411. www.pendletonchamber.com.

Tucked beneath high bluffs along the Umatilla River, this city of 16,500 is renowned for its wool blankets; guided tours of the **Pendleton Woolen Mills**★ *(1307 SE Court Pl.; ☎541-276-6911)* offer a look at the production process.

The **Pendleton Round-up**, held every September since 1910, is one of the world's biggest rodeos. The **Round-Up Hall of Fame**★ *(Round-up Grounds, I-84 Exit 207; ☎ 541-276-2553, www,pendletonroundup.com)* commemorates the event and its participants.

Tamastslikt Cultural Center★

Rte. 331, Mission, 7mi east of Pendleton. △✕⑤🅿 ☎ 541-966-9748. www.tamastslikt.com.

Located on the Umatilla Indian Reservation, this excellent new museum tells the story of the area's indigenous people—Cayuse, Umatilla and Walla Wallas.

SALT LAKE CITY AREA

Set between the Wasatch Mountains and the saline expanse of the Great Salt Lake and Desert, Salt Lake City was founded in the 1840s by persecuted religious refugees from the east. It grew as the world capital of the Church of Jesus Christ of Latter-day Saints (Mormons), a distinction that still dominates social, cultural and political life in the region. Salt Lake City is a thriving modern city, firmly rooted in its heritage and a leading center of the high-technology and biomedical industries.

The Great Salt Lake itself, less than 15mi west of the city, spreads across 2,500sq mi when filled to capacity, but nowhere is it deeper than 42ft. Twice as salty as any ocean, it draws water and dissolved minerals from mountain streams, yet it has no outlet and little aquatic life.

More than 1 million people live today in Salt Lake County. Many more live a short drive south in Provo and north in Ogden, for a metropolitan population of nearly 1.8 million. Within an hour's drive of these three urban hubs are 10 downhill and six cross-country ski resorts—an unparalleled concentration that helped earn Salt Lake the honor of hosting the 2002 Winter Olympic Games. Many of the competitions were held around Park City, a mining town high in the Wasatch Range 30mi east of Salt Lake City. Not only is this sophisticated resort center surrounded by three world-class ski areas, it is home to the renowned annual Sundance Film Festival.

Historic Temple Square and Salt Lake Temple

 The Salt Lake Convention & Visitors Bureau

Address Book Salt Lake City Area

For prices, see the Legend on the cover flap.

WHERE TO STAY IN THE SALT LAKE AREA

$$$$$ (winter) **Stein Eriksen Lodge** – *7700 Stein Way, Deer Valley Resort, Park City, UT.* ✖&🅿️ 🄴 Spa ☎435-649-3700 or 800-453-1302. www.steinlodge.com. 127 rooms. Skiers pay top dollar to experience the alpine décor, prime service and ski-in, ski-out privileges of "The Stein"—named for Norway's 1952 Olympic champion, still a frequent guest. Summer guests get a massive stone fireplace and courtyard waterfall at 8,200ft elevation. **The Glitretind** **($$$)** restaurant serves contemporary cuisine year-round.

$$$$ **The Grand America Hotel** – *555 S. Main St., Salt Lake City.* ✖&🅿️🄴 Spa ☎801-258-6000 or 800-621-4505. www.grandamerica.com. 775 rooms. Earl Holding, whose hotel and resort empire extends to Idaho's Sun Valley Resort, spared no expense in creating his crown jewel before the 2002 Winter Olympics. A 24-story, white-granite hotel with central gardens and a boutique sensibility, the Grand America has French cherry-wood furniture, English wool carpets, Italian glass chandeliers and marble that carries into guest rooms.

$$$ Alta Lodge – *Rte. 210, Alta.* ✖ ☎801-742-3500 or 800-707-2582. www.altalodge.com. 57 rooms. Beds are narrow, and there are no TVs, but that's part of the charm. Opened in the late 1930s by the Denver & Rio Grande Railroad, and owned by Alta Mayor Bill Levitt since 1956, the Lodge is an institution for the skier's skier. Unpretentious regulars come for family-style dining and floor-to-ceiling windows looking out to the Wasatch Mountain peaks.

$$$ Homestead Resort – *700 N. Homestead Dr., Midway.* ✖&🅿️🄴 ☎435-654-1102 or 888-327-7220. www.homesteadresort.com. 152 rooms. A Swiss farmer discovered mineral "hot pots" over a century ago in the Heber Valley, 20mi southeast of Park City; buggy-loads of visitors convinced him to create a resort. Lodgings now range from cottages and condos to The Virginia House, a Victorian B&B; decor is Southwestern or New England. Guests may snorkel year-round or ride in a horse-drawn sleigh.

$$$ Hotel Monaco – *15 W. 200 South, Salt Lake City.* ✖&🅿️ ☎801-595-0000 or 800-805-1801. www.monaco-saltlakecitycom. 225 rooms. Salt Lake's preeminent boutique hotel, the Monaco occupies a restored 15-story Deco-era bank building. Eclectic décor extends from the lobby to guest rooms, where pets are welcomed. Chef Robert Barker presides over the kitchen at **Bambara ($$$)**, one of the city's best restaurants; try the buffalo carpaccio or tea-cured duck.

$$$ Peery Hotel – *110 W. 300 South, Salt Lake City.* ✖&🅿️ ☎801-521-4300 or 800-331-0073. www.peeryhotel.com. 73 rooms. A classic grand staircase is the centerpiece of the newly renovated and smoke-free Peery, built in 1910 in Prairie Style with classical Revival motifs. European ambience extends from the expansive lobby to **Christopher's ($$$)**, a steak-and-seafood restaurant.

$$ The Inn at Temple Square – *71 W. South Temple St., Salt Lake City.* ✖&🅿️ ☎801-531-1000 or 800-843-4668. www.theinn.com. 90 rooms. Erected in 1930, this stately, restored brick hotel has a prime spot opposite the Mormon temple. The rooms have four-poster beds; wallpaper and fabric bloom with floral patterns. Rates include a breakfast buffet and airport shuttle.

WHERE TO EAT IN THE SALT LAKE AREA

$$$$ The Metropolitan – *173 W. Broadway, Salt Lake City.* ☎801-364-3472. www.themetropolitan.com. Dinner only. Closed Sun. **American.** An old warehouse, converted with such daring strokes as a curved-slat fir ceiling and steel trusses, now houses Salt Lake's best restaurant. The inventive menu, prepared in the open kitchen, features dishes like seared foie gras in sourcherry sauce, oyster soup with French truffles, and roasted Alaskan caribou loin.

$$$ Chimayo – *368 Main St., Park City.* ☎435-649-6222. www.chimayorestaurant.com. Dinner only. **Southwestern**. In a handsome Spanish Colonial-style room with heavy-oak decor, Chef Bill White blends regional elements with a French approach. Examples are roasted poblano-and-corn masa soup with toasted walnuts, and buffalo meatloaf with a juniper berry-infused demi-glâce.

$$$ Log Haven Restaurant – *Millcreek Avenue (3800 South), 4mi east of S. Wasatch Blvd., Salt Lake City.* ☎801-272-8255. www.log-haven.com. Dinner & Sun brunch only. **American.** Built in 1920 of Oregon logs hauled up Millcreek Canyon by horse-drawn wagon, this forest cabin nestles at the base of the Wasatch Range. Walls glow with rustic warmth, and the food is gourmet: flatiron-seared buffalo and coriander-rubbed ahi tuna with lemon-guava sauce are house favorites.

$$$ Market Street Grill – *48 W. Market St., Salt Lake City.* ☎801-322-4668. www.marketstreetgrill.com. **Seafood.** More fresh shellfish (300 pounds daily) are shucked at the Grill and adjoining Oyster Bar than anywhere else in Utah. The noisy restaurant seats as many as 250 diners under mock palm trees in the 1906 New York Building. Fresh fish is flown in daily: mahimahi from Hawaii, orange roughy from New Zealand, lobster tails from Canada.

$$$ Snake Creek Grill – *650 W. 100 South, Heber City.* ☎435-654-2133. www.snakecreekgrill.com. Dinner only. Closed Mon-Tue. **Eclectic**. Park City locals say the town's best restaurant is miles away in Heber Old Town, an abandoned railroad village. Chef-owner Barbara Hill prepares such gourmet comfort food as ten-spice salmon with Japanese noodles and zucchini-tomato risotto. Antiques and funky collectibles on a wood-plank floor help create a homey roadhouse ambience.

$$$ 350 Main – *350 Main St., Park City.* ☎435-649-3140. www.350main.com. **Contemporary** Chef Michael LeClerc drew upon four continents of culinary experience in developing his eclectic menu. Signature dishes include a sashimi-style ahi-and-hamachi tower with tobiko caviar, and pepper-crusted venison with cranberry-orange marmalade. A central fireplace area is at the heart of this restaurant, which occupies an old saloon in the 1910 Golden Rule Building.

$ Rio Grande Café – *270 S. Rio Grande St. (244 West), Salt Lake City.* ☎801-364-3302. **Mexican**. Old timers at this diner in the old rail depot claim the establishment is haunted by an eerie but harmless ghost, the "Purple Lady." The menu features tacos, burritos, blue-corn enchiladas and chile-verde tamales.

SALT LAKE CITY★★

MICHELIN MAP 493 E, F 7, 8
MOUNTAIN STANDARD TIME
POPULATION 182,000

Historic Temple Square, with its concentration of buildings tied to Mormon religion and history, is the central attraction of Salt Lake City, certainly worthy of several hours' exploration by anyone with a desire to understand this important modern world religion. Other sights include museums and especially, scenic attractions.

- **Information:** ☎801-534-4900 or www.visitsaltlake.com. The **Visitor Information Center** is in the Convention Center *(90 S. West Temple St.; ☎801-521-2822)*.
- ▶ **Orient Yourself:** *Because of the strong influence of the Mormon church, few sights (except natural ones) are open Sundays. Call ahead to check.* The distinctive Mormon **city-grid plan** persists in Salt Lake City. Long blocks of broad streets radiate in 10-acre squares from Temple Square. Addresses and street names, confusing to visitors, reveal their direction from the hub. Thus 201 E. 300 South

Street is two blocks east and three blocks south of Temple Square; 201 S. 300 East Street is two blocks south and three east of the square.

P **Parking:** There's no parking at Temple Square, and the two hours available from metered spots on nearby streets aren't adequate. Use parking garages.

Don't Miss: Temple Square.

Especially for Kids: Tracy Aviary.

A Bit of History

Salt Lake City was founded in 1847 by Mormon pioneers led by **Brigham Young.** A late frost, a drought and a plague of crickets nearly destroyed their harvest until seagulls descended upon the insects and enabled the settlers to survive that winter.

Ownership of the Salt Lake Valley transferred from Mexico to the US in 1848, and in 1850 the Utah Territory was formed, with Brigham Young as its first governor. To the Mormons, their home was the State of Deseret. A deseret honeybee is acknowledged in *The Book of Mormon* for its industriousness; bee-like hard work and a sense of community, coupled with extensive irrigation, enabled the Mormons to succeed.

Utah's isolation ended in 1869 with the completion of the first transcontinental railroad. Through World War I, copper, silver, gold and lead mines opened in Utah canyons. Mine owners built luxurious manors in the city, in stark contrast to modest Mormon homes.

Largely because of early Mormon adherence to polygamy, Congress was slow to grant statehood to Utah. Only after the church withdrew its sanction of multiple-spouse marriages was Utah admitted to the union (in 1896, as the 45th state).

Sights

Historic Temple Square★★★
50 W. South Temple St. (between North, South & West Temple Sts. & Main St.). 801-240-4872. www.lds.org.
This landscaped 10-acre plot is the hub of downtown and the heart of the Mormon faith. Here are the six-spired temple, the silver-domed tabernacle, the Assembly Hall and several statues and monuments. Young Latter-day Saint missionaries from the world over conduct **free tours★★** and discuss their faith in 30 languages. Although only baptized Mormons may enter the **Salt Lake Temple★** (or any other temple), audiovisual presentations in the **North and South Visitors Centers** show its highlights. The red-sandstone foundation was laid in 1853-55. The structure has granite walls 9ft thick at ground level, 6ft thick at top, and a statue of the angel Moroni, cast in copper (by sculptor Cyrus E. Dallin) trumpeting from a 210ft spire.

The **Salt Lake Tabernacle★** took just three years to construct; it opened in 1867. Seating 6,000 people, it contains an 11,623-pipe, 32ft-tall **organ★★** that accompanies the world-famous **Mormon Tabernacle Choir.** Weekly broadcast choir performances *(9:15am Sun)* or rehearsals *(8pm Thu)* are free. Daily organ recitals are also offered.

The semi-Gothic **Assembly Hall★** (1880) is a miniature cathedral that now hosts free concerts and lectures. The **Miracle of the Gulls Monument** (1913, Mahonri Young), honor the seagulls that saved the first pioneers' crop. The **Nauvoo Temple Bell**, a 782-pound bronze bell rings hourly on the square. Outside the southeast corner of Temple Square is the **Brigham Young Monument** (1897). Opposite Temple Square to the west are the following two important facilities.

Museum of Church History and Art★★
45 N. West Temple St. 801-240-3310. www.lds.org/churchhistory.
This well-presented museum is an essential stop for visitors seeking to understand The Church of Jesus Christ of Latter-day Saints. Interpretive exhibits tell the history of the religion. There are galleries of 19-20C Mormon and American Indian art and portraits of historic church leaders.

Utah State Capitol building, Salt Lake City

Family History Library★

35 N. West Temple St. ♿ ☎*801-240-2331.*
www.familysearch.org.
The world's largest collection of genealogical materials offers free public access for research. Church staff are available to assist. Established in 1894, this is the hub of more than 3,400 Family History Centers in 65 countries and territories. An introduction is offered at the Family Search Center *(below)*.

Church Office Building

50 E. North Temple St. ☎*801-240-1000.*
This 26-story building holds the administrative offices of the church. From the top-floor observation deck, there are **views★★** of the greater Salt Lake area.

Joseph Smith Memorial Building★

15 E. South Temple St. ✗♿🅿 ☎*801-240-3130. www.jsmb.com.*
The former Hotel Utah (1911), restored in 1987, reopened as a community center. **"Legacy"** *(*☎*801-240-4383)*, a 53min film telling the saga of the pioneers, is shown in a theater. The **Family Search Center** *(*☎*801-240-4085, www.lds.org/placestovisit)* introduces visitors to genealogical research by means of computers access.

The Beehive House★

67 E. South Temple St. ✗♿ ☎*801-240-2681. www.lds.org/placestovisit.*

The official home of Brigham Young and his large family from 1854 to 1877, this restored National Historic Landmark is filled with period furnishings. Guided tours take in family rooms, several bedrooms, the kitchen and office.
Young's gravesite is a block east of here in the tiny **Mormon Pioneer Memorial Cemetery** *(140 E. First Ave.)*.

Salt Palace Convention Center

100 S. West Temple St. ♿🅿 ☎*801-534-4777. www.saltpalace.com.*
This large building includes The **Visitor Information Center** *(90 S. West Temple St.;* ☎*801-521-2822)*. Across from Temple Square is the 1993 **Maurice Abravanel Concert Hall** *(123 W. South Temple St.;* ☎*801-355-2787. www.arttix.org)*, home of the Utah Symphony Orchestra. The **Delta Center** *(301 W. South Temple St.;* ☎*801-325-2500)* is home to professional basketball.
The Gateway *(400 W. South Temple St.;* ☎*801-456-0000)* is an elegant new shopping complex. Near the city center, **Galivan Plaza** *(239 S. Main St.;* ☎*801-535-6110)* has a seasonal ice-skating rink and summer concerts. Farther east, **Trolley Square** *(600 South & 700 East Sts.;* ☎*801-521-9877)* is a shopping center on the National Register of Historic Places.

Utah State Capitol★★

North end of State St. ♿ 🅿 ☎*801-538-3000. www.utahstatecapitol.utah.gov.*
Completed in 1915 (Richard Kletting), this Renaissance Revival-style building was patterned after the US Capitol. The interior of the dome, 165ft above the foyer, is adorned with seagulls and historic murals. 👁Guided tours are offered half-hourly on weekdays.

Pioneer Memorial Museum

300 N. Main St. ♿ 🅿 ☎*801-538-1050. www.dupinternational.org.*
Located opposite the State Capitol to the west, this collection of pioneer artifacts—on four floors and in an adjacent carriage house—includes sacred and sectarian items, especially from 1847-69.

University of Utah★

Presidents Circle & University St., 2mi east of downtown via 200 South. ✕♿🅿 ☎*801-581-6515. www.utah.edu.*
Founded in 1850 as the University of Deseret, this 1,494-acre campus is Utah's oldest. Opening and closing ceremonies of the 2002 Olympic Winter Games were held at its Rice-Eccles Stadium. Paleontology exhibits in the **Utah Museum of Natural History**★ Kids *(1390 E. Presidents Circle;* ☎*801-581-6927, www.umnh. utah.edu)* include dinosaur skeletons; the Geology Hall emphasizes Utah's mining industry.

Utah Museum of Fine Arts★

410 S. Campus Center Dr. (1725 East). ✕♿🅿 ☎*801-581-7332. www.utah. edu/umfa.*
A new five-story building is home to a permanent collection of 17,000 objects that features paintings and decorative arts from all over the world.

Red Butte Garden★

300 Wakara Way off Foothill Dr. ♿🅿 ☎*801-581-4747. www.redbuttegarden. org.*
Spread across a semi-arid hillside above the university, these gardens preserve wildflowers, shrubs and trees (1,500 species), and cultivated gardens.

This Is the Place Heritage Park★

Kids *2601 Sunnyside Ave. east of Foothill Dr.* ♿🅿 ☎*801-582-1847. www.thisistheplace.org.*
It is said that as Brigham Young and his party crested the Wasatch Range in 1847, Young gazed upon the Salt Lake Valley and said, "This is the place." On the centennial of that occasion, **This Is The Place Monument** was erected to honor the passage from Illinois on the 1,300mi Mormon Pioneer National Historic Trail. Mormon pioneer lifestyle (c.1847-69) is re-enacted in **Old Deseret Village**★★ in summer. In three dozen reconstructed buildings villagers demonstrate domestic crafts and skills.

Utah's Hogle Zoo

Kids *2600 Sunnyside Ave. east of Foothill Dr.* ✕♿🅿 ☎*801-582-1631. www.hogle zoo.org.*
More than 1,000 animals, both exotic and regional, are displayed at this community zoo. Children are delighted by a working scale-model railroad.

Tracy Aviary

Kids *Liberty Park, 589 E. 1300 South St.* ♿🅿 ☎*801-596-8500. www.tracy aviary.org.*
Established in 1938, this is one of the oldest public bird parks in the US. Some 500 birds of 150 species, including exotics and 21 threatened or endangered species, live here.

Excursions

Big Cottonwood Canyon★

Rte. 190, extending 15mi east from I-215 Exit 6. △✕♿🅿
Old mining claims and impressive scenery mark this canyon that extends into the Wasatch Range from southeast Salt Lake City. Two popular ski areas, both rising above 10,000ft, nestle at its end. Powder-rich **Solitude** *(28mi from downtown;* ☎*801-534-1400)* is just two miles from family-oriented **Brighton** *(30mi from downtown;* ☎*801-532-4731).*

Little Cottonwood Canyon★

Rte. 210, extending 14mi south & east from I-215 Exit 6. △✕♿🅿

Salt Lake Convention & Visitors Bureau/Eric Schramm

Spiral Jetty by Robert Smithson (1970), North End of the Great Salt Lake

The primary lures of this gorge, shorter and narrower than Big Cottonwood, are its two vaunted resorts. Nearest to Salt Lake City is **Snowbird**★ *(25mi from downtown; ☎801-933-2222)*, whose 11,000ft summit and 3,240ft vertical surpass all other Wasatch resorts. A 125-passenger aerial tramway climbs from base to summit in 8min and provides a contemporary European-style ambience. **Alta**★★ *(27mi from downtown; ☎801-359-1078)* opened in 1938 as the second (after Idaho's Sun Valley) destination ski resort in the western US. Famed for relaxed, old-fashioned atmosphere and deep powder snow (over 500in per year), Alta steadfastly refuses to install high-capacity or high-speed lifts or to permit snowboarding, and daily lift rates are lower than other top resorts. In the village library, the **Alta Historical Society** *(☎801-742-3522)* maintains a permanent exhibit on Alta's silver-mining boom days of 1864-78.

Kennecott's Bingham Canyon Mine★★

4.5mi southwest of the intersection of Rtes. 48 & 111 near Copperton, and 29mi from downtown Salt Lake City via Rte. 48, west off I-15 Exit 301. ♿ P *☎801-252-3234. www.kennecott.com.*

The largest open-pit mine on earth is more than 2.5mi in diameter and nearly 4,000ft deep—more than twice the height of the world's tallest buildings. Since mining operations began in 1906, 6 billion tons of earth have been removed from what was once a mountain. The Bingham Canyon Mine has yielded more wealth than the California, Comstock and Klondike rushes combined: 15 million tons (30 billion pounds) of copper ore, 700 million pounds of molybdenum, 175 million ounces of silver and 20 million ounces of gold. Exhibits in the Kennecott Utah Copper Corporation **visitor center**★, on the east side of the pit, tell the history of the company and mine, and describe the process of concentrating, smelting and refining to produce copper from ore. The best panoramas of the mine are from an outside observation area.

Great Salt Lake State Park★★

Kids *I-80 Exit 104, 17mi west of Salt Lake City. ☎801-250-1898. stateparks.utah.gov.*

A marina and beach provide access to the largest US lake west of the Mississippi River. Only the Dead Sea has a higher salt content. Brine shrimp harvested in the Great Salt Lake are sold in Asia as food for tropical fish. Waterbirds of all varieties thrive here—more than 257 species inhabit the shores and island.

NORTHERN UTAH★

MICHELIN MAP 493 E, F 8
MOUNTAIN STANDARD TIME

A startling backdrop to the Salt Lake area, the Wasatch Mountains rise like a 7,000ft wall east of the metropolis, 150mi from Logan south to Nephi, climbing over 11,000ft elevation. Once an obstacle to exploration, they were pierced by silver miners in the late 19C. Today the range is a leading source of white gold—the downy powder into which winter-sports lovers cast skis and snowboards. Utah's vehicle license plates even declare: "The Greatest Snow on Earth." Park City, largest of the resort communities and a mere 35mi east of Salt Lake City, was the hub of most mountain activities during the 2002 Olympic Winter Games. For overall information, visit www.skiutah.com.

- **Information:**☎800-200-1160, www.utah.com
- **Don't Miss:** Park City's Main Street
- **Kids Especially for Kids:** Utah Olympic Park.

Sights

Park City★★
Rte. 224, 5mi south of I-80 Exit 145. △✕&P ☎435-649-6100. www.park-cityinfo.com.
A rich mining district in the late 19C, producing more than $400 million in silver, Park City was founded in 1872. In its heyday, nearly 10,000 residents supported theaters, dance halls, saloons and brothels. An 1898 fire destroyed three-quarters of the city; the surviving 19C structures now are part of the **Main Street National Historic District**★★, which entices visitors with galleries, boutiques and restaurants. Walking tours begin from the **Park City Museum** *(528 Main St.;* ☎435-645-5135), in the territorial jailhouse.
Park City established itself as a year-round resort in the 1960s. Modern growth has it approaching its halcyon size. Three major ski areas are a short shuttle-bus run from Main Street; one, family-oriented **Park City Mountain Resort**★ *(Lowell Ave.;* ☎435-649-8111), is mere steps away. Elegant, celebrity-conscious **Deer Valley Resort**★ *(Deer Valley Dr.;* ☎435-649-1000) bars snowboarders. Flush with new development is **The Canyons**★ *(The Canyons Dr.;* ☎435-649-5400), 3mi north off Route 224. Between them, the three similarly sized resorts offer 9,290ft of vertical (at least 3,000ft each) served by 44 lifts.

Near The Canyons is the **Utah Olympic Park**★ (**Kids** *Bear Hollow Dr. off Rte. 224;* ☎435-658-4200, www.olyparks.com). A training facility for US national teams, it has four jumping hills of 18m–120m, four ramps for freestyle aerial jumps and a 1,335m (4,331ft) bobsled/luge track. The public may watch athletes perform, take a bobsled ride or invest in a 2hr ski-jumping lesson.
The arts calendar is highlighted by the **Sundance Film Festival**★★ *(*☎801-328-3456 or 435-645-0110, www.sundance. org/festival)* in January. The world's best independent filmmakers premiere new works at this Robert Redford-produced event, held in Park City (not at Redford's boutique eponymous ski area) since 1986.

Heber Valley Historic Railroad★
ñ 450 S. 600 West St., Heber City, 18mi southeast of Park City. P ☎435-654-5601. www.hebervalleyrr.org.
Restored vintage coaches and a 1907 steam locomotive take passengers on an excursion around Deer Creek Reservoir, to Vivian Park in Provo Canyon.

Sundance Resort
Rte. 92, Sundance, 15mi north of Provo via US-189. ✕&P ☎801-225-4107. www. sundanceresort.com.
 Purchased in 1969 by actor-director Robert Redford and named for the Utah-born character he played in *Butch Cas-*

sidy and the Sundance Kid, this enclave is devoted to recreation and environment. In winter a modest ski area serves a flank of 11,750ft Mount Timpanogos. In summer, Sundance is a hiking and riding center with outdoor musical theater.

Timpanogos Cave National Monument★

⫼ *Rte. 92, American Fork, 9mi east of I-15 Exit 287.* ✕ 🅿 ☎*801-756-5238. www. nps.gov/tica.*

Advance ticket purchase recommended weekends. Three limestone caverns, linked by man-made tunnels, are located on the northern slope of Mount Timpanogos. Reached by a steep 1.5mi, 1,065ft uphill hike from the canyon-floor visitor center, its impressive features are still in formation: dripstone, helictites, stalagmites and stalactites.

North American Museum of Ancient Life

🄺 *Thanksgiving Point Resort, 3003 N. Thanksgiving Way, Lehi (I-15 Exit 287).* ✕🅕 ☎*801-768-2300. www.thanks-givingpoint.com.*

Sixty full dinosaur skeletons, interactive displays and a giant-screen theater are integral to this educational facility. The museum is part of a new theme village and residential community with botanical gardens, a children's farm, shopping, performing-arts venues and a golf course.

Provo

US-89 & US-189 at I-15 Exit 268. △✕🅕🅿 ☎*801-379-2555. thechamber.org.*

The third-largest city in Utah, with 115,000 people, Provo nestles midway down the eastern shore of large freshwater Utah Lake. Besides Brigham Young University, the city boasts the gold-spired **Provo Mormon Temple** *(N. Temple Dr. off N. 900 East)*, on a hill above the university, and the **Utah County Courthouse** *(Center St. & University Ave.)*, built in the 1920s of limestone.

Brigham Young University★

Campus Dr. off E. 1230 North. ✕🅕🅿 ☎*801-422-4636. www.byu.edu.*

The educational center of Mormonism was established in 1877 by Brigham

Young. One of the largest private universities in the US, the 634-acre campus has several museums. The **Museum of Art** *(☎801-378-8287)* features 19C American and European works and a collection of musical instruments. The **Earth Science Museum★** *(☎801-378-3680)* boasts an outstanding research collection of Jurassic dinosaurs. The **Monte L. Bean Life Science Museum** *(☎801-422-5051)* explores natural history. The **Museum of Peoples and Cultures** *(☎801-422-0020)* focuses on Southwest Indian, Mexican and Mayan artifacts.

Springville Museum of Art★

126 E. 400 South, Springville, 6mi south of Provo. 🅿 ☎*801-489-2727. sma.nebo. edu.*

Perhaps the best collection of Utah art and artists, this small museum has 11 exhibition galleries presenting works by painters, sculptors and printmakers since 1862.

Antelope Island State Park★

🄺 *Rte. 127; 7.5mi west of I-15 Exit 335 via Rte. 108; 40mi northwest of Salt Lake City.* △✕🅕🅿 ☎*801-652-2043. stateparks. utah.gov.*

A long causeway crosses the shallow flats of the Great Salt Lake to this 28,000-acre wildlife refuge, largest island in the lake. From a new visitor center (4528 W. 1700 South, Syracuse), guests can hike, bike or ride horses on 40mi of trails. Besides antelope, the island is home to mule deer, bighorn sheep, coyotes, bobcats, upland game birds, waterfowl, and 500 bison descended from a late-19C herd.

Hill Aerospace Museum

🄺 *7961 Wardleigh Rd., Hill Air Force Base.* 🅕🅿 ☎*801-777-6818. www.hill. af.mil.*

One of the largest collections of vintage aircraft and ordnance in the US includes more than 50 bombers, cargo planes, helicopters, engines, missiles, bombs and other weapons.

Ogden

US-89 east of I-15 Exit 344. ✕🅕🅿 ☎*866-867-8824. www.ogdencvb.org.*

Salt Lake Convention & Visitors Bureau/Lee Cohen

Downhill skiing

This scenic 62mi route follows Ogden River Canyon upriver past Pineview Reservoir and across the crest of the Wasatch Range. Leaving Ogden, it skirts the **George S. Eccles Dinosaur Park** Kids *(1544 E. Park Blvd.; ☎801-393-3466, www.dinosaurpark.org),* whose 98 replicas of tyrannosaurs, pterodactyls and their ilk are depicted in a realistic outdoor setting. A southbound turnoff from the reservoir, 17mi east of Ogden, climbs to **Snowbasin Resort** *(Rte. 226, Huntsville; ☎ 801-620-1000),* which hosted downhill and super-G ski racing during the Winter Olympics.

Excursion

Golden Spike National Historic Site★

32mi west of I-15 Exit 368, Brigham City, via Rtes. 13 & 83. ☎435-471-2209. www.nps.gov/gosp.

This site recalls the completion of the transcontinental railroad with the driving of a symbolic "golden spike"$ connecting Central Pacific and Union Pacific lines on May 10, 1869. Although trains have long used a different route across the Great Salt Lake Desert, working replicas of the two **steam locomotives** that first met here are on display May to October. Costumed reenactments of the original ceremony are often staged.

Established as a railroad town, Ogden—now with 78,000 residents—echoes its past in restored buildings along its historic **25th Street.** In the former depot, the **Utah State Railroad Museum** *(2501 Wall Ave.; ☎801-393-9886, www.theunionstation.org)* has historic exhibits and a model-railroad room. Also here are car and firearms museums, mineral exhibits, and Ogden's Visitor Information Center.

Ogden River Scenic Byway★
Rte. 39 east from Ogden to Huntsville. ⚠

GREEN RIVER COUNTRY

MICHELIN MAP 493 F 7
MOUNTAIN STANDARD TIME

Largely isolated from population centers and major highways, northeastern Utah has developed in relative seclusion on either side of the lofty Uinta Mountains and along the Green River and its tributaries. Its principal interest to tourists today revolves around water sports, especially river rafting, and its deposits of dinosaur bones, among the richest on earth. Backpackers and mountain climbers strive for the summits of 13,528ft Kings Peak, Utah's highest, and a raft of other 12,000ft-plus pinnacles. Sprawling through the heart of the region is the Uinta and Ouray Indian Reservation (Fort Duchesne; ☎435-722-5141), home to 1,600 members of four related tribes.

🛈 **Information:** ☎800-200-1160, www.utah.com
▶ **Orient Yourself:** The Uinta Mountain range runs east-west.
Kids **Especially for Kids:** College of Eastern Utah Prehistoric Museum.

Sights

Price

US-6 & 191 and Rte. 10, 118mi southeast of Salt Lake City. △✕ ☎*435-637-3009. www.castlecountry.com.*

This late-19C coal town still produces large quantities of coal and other minerals. The **College of Eastern Utah Prehistoric Museum** 🄺🄸🄳🅂 *(155 E. Main St.; ☎435-637-5060, museum.ceu.edu)* displays several full-size dinosaur skeletons and 12C Fremont Indian figurines of unbaked clay. Curators provide self-guiding tour information to the **Cleveland-Lloyd Dinosaur Quarry**★ *(BLM 216 Rd., 11mi east of Cleveland & 30mi southeast of Price via Rtes. 10 & 155),* where the bones of at least 70 species of prehistoric animals have been unearthed. **Nine Mile Canyon Road**★ *(60mi from Wellington, US-6/191, to Myton, US-40/191),* a backcountry route beginning 7mi east of Price, leads to ancient Indian petroglyphs.

Vernal

US-40 & 191, 176mi east of Salt Lake City. ☎*435-789-6932. www.dinoland.com.*

Western gateway to **Dinosaur National Monument**★★ and southern gateway to Flaming Gorge National Recreation Area *(below),* Vernal is in an area of extreme geological interest. Its Utah Field House of **Natural History State Park** 🄺🄸🄳🅂 *(235 E. Main St.; ☎435-789-3799)* re-creates prehistoric ecosystems and populates them with 18 life-size dinosaur figures. An adjacent museum displays fossils, gems and Indian artifacts.

Flaming Gorge National Recreation Area★

US-191 & Rte. 44, 43mi north of Vernal. ☎*435-789-1181. www.fs.fed.us/r4.*

Straddling the Utah-Wyoming border, this recreation area surrounds a 91mi-long reservoir that backs up through canyons carved through the Uinta Mountains by the Green River. The **Red Canyon Visitor Center and Overlook**★★ *(Rte. 44; ☎435-889-3713)* offers a bird's-eye view of the reservoir, in summer, from 1,400ft above Red Canyon. Guided tours of a 502ft concrete-arch dam are provided at the **Flaming Gorge Dam Visitor Center** *(US-191, Dutch John; ☎435-885-3135).*

SAN ANTONIO AREA

Any attempt at understanding Texans must begin in the San Antonio area, for here is the heart of Texas history and culture. Originally inhabited by Indians of the warlike Comanche tribe, the region was settled by Spanish missionaries at the end of the 17C. In 1836 one mission, converted to military use and known as The Alamo, became a stronghold for 189 Texas patriots who gave their lives defending the bastion against the vast forces of Mexico's General Antonio López de Santa Anna. Their sacrifice became a rallying cry—"Remember The Alamo!"—for other rebels who soon defeated Santa Anna and won Texas independence.

The Hispanic presence remains strong in central and south Texas, an area that claims San Antonio as its cultural, spiritual and economic hub. Spanish is heard as often as English. Gondolas ply the waters of the Rio San Antonio, passing strollers on the cypress-shaded River Walk, which meanders past row after brightly lit row of atmospheric restaurants. From atop one of the city's newer buildings, the 750ft Tower of the Americas, you can gaze down upon some of its oldest, the quartet of 18C missions that make up San Antonio Missions National Historical Park.

An hour's drive northeast is Austin, the lively state capital. The University of Texas, the political ambience and an influx of high-tech industry have engendered a spirit of intellectual and cultural excitement. Scores of nightclubs have led Austin to become known as the "Live Music Capital of the World."

The Alamo

© SACVB/Berne Broudy/Donohue Photography 2006

Address Book San Antonio Area

🐌 *For prices, see the Legend on the cover flap.*

WHERE TO STAY IN THE SAN ANTONIO AREA

$$$$ The Fairmount Hotel – *410 S. Alamo St., San Antonio, TX.* ✕&🅿 ☎*210-224-8800. www.thefairmounthotel-sanantonio.com. 37 rooms.* A small jewel of dark-red brick, carved limestone and elaborate pediments, this ornate Italianate railway hotel was built in 1906 and moved six blocks and across a bridge in 1985. All the marble finishes and soft guest-room colors survived. The deluxe **Sage ($$$)** restaurant serves Italian cuisine.

$$$ Driskill Hotel – *604 Brazos St., Austin, TX.* ✕&🅿 ☎*512-474-5911 or 800-252-9367. www.driskillhotel.com. 205 rooms.* Double balconies, arched windows and a hand-laid marble lobby floor made Austin's grandest and most historic hotel into a frontier palace. Col. J.L. Driskill's 1886 Victorian vision lives on with period furnishings, original artwork and a custom-made stained-glass dome. Lobster-and-corn enchiladas are a menu feature at famous **The Driskill Grill ($$$)**.

$$$ Havana Riverwalk Inn – *1015 Navarro St., San Antonio, TX.* ✕&🅿 ☎*210-222-2008 or 888-224-2008. www.havanariverwalkinn.com. 27 rooms.* Individual room decor is unique at this 1914 Mediterranean Revival-style inn. Room 300 boasts an armoire from a palace in India and a bed with posts from a French estate. Room 104 has an iron-haloed convent bed. Throughout are exposed brick walls and hardwood floors. All rooms are non-smoking.

$$$ The Menger Hotel – *204 Alamo Plaza, San Antonio, TX.* ✕&🅿🏊 Spa ☎*210-223-4361 or 800-345-9285. www.historicmenger.com. 318 rooms.* A glazed iron canopy and intricate railings form the facade of the elegant Menger, built in 1859, barely a generation after the fall of The Alamo. Leaded skylights in a grand three-story lobby guide guests to opulent rooms of dark wood trim. Wildgame dishes have been on the **Colonial Room ($$$)** menu for a century.

$$ AbButler's Dogtrot at Triple Creek – *801 Triple Creek Rd., Fredericksburg, TX 78624.* 🅿 ☎*830-997-8279 or 877-262-4366. www.abbutler.net. 2 rooms.* Within this rustic log cabin, built in 1800, are such elegant touches as a fireplace and whirlpool bath. Situated 4mi from Fredericksburg, the Dogtrot is one of several inns marketed by **Fredericksburg Traditional Bed and Breakfast Inns** *(www.fredericksburgtrad.com).*

$$ Dixie Dude Ranch – *Ranch Rd. 1077 (P.O. Box 548), Bandera, TX.* ✕🅿🏊 ☎*830-796-7771 or 800-375-9255. www.dixieduderanch.com. 20 rooms.* Spend a few nights (three minimum) at this working 1901 Hill Country ranch and you might slow down to real cowboy life. Lodgings are rustic but modern, and prices include three meals and two horseback rides a day.

WHERE TO EAT IN THE SAN ANTONIO AREA

$$$ Biga on the Banks – *203 S. St. Mary's St., San Antonio.* ☎*210-225-0722. www.biga.com. Dinner & Sun brunch only.* **Creative American.** Natural light flows through a wall of windows on River Walk into Biga's modern hacienda-like interior. Design elements honor the city's cultural heritage. Chef-owner Bruce Auden always has soft-shell crab on the menu in summer; other dishes include a Hunan-style veal chop and a sage-and-onion-stuffed portobello mushroom.

$$$ Boudro's – *421 E. Commerce St., San Antonio.* ☎*210-224-8484. www.boudros.com.* **Southwestern & Cajun.** This fine River Walk restaurant offers a bistro blend of France and Louisiana with regional cuisine. Diners may choose blackened prime rib with fine wine at a cozy inside table or prickly-pear margaritas on the riverside patio. River-barge dining cruises feature pecan-grilled steaks, smoked-shrimp enchiladas and guacamole made tableside.

$$ Altdorf Biergarten – *301 W. Main St., Fredericksburg.* ☎*830-997-7865.* **German.** In a town of German heritage, this may be the single best place to absorb Deutsch culture. Up to 150 people sit outside with steins of beer listening to oom-pah bands. Bavarian specialties include bratwurst, knockwurst, wiener and jaeger schnitzel, all served with sweet-and-sour potatoes, red cabbage or sauerkraut.

$ La Margarita – *120 Produce Row, San Antonio.* ☎*210-227-7140.* **Mexican**. Strolling mariachi bands and sizzling fajitas create a fiesta-like atmosphere at this Market Square restaurant, fueled by margaritas that sell by the liter. Very popular is the Queso Flameado, a flaming combination of cheese and sausage; the usual Mexican fare also features burritos, tacos and enchiladas.

$$ Liberty Bar – *328 Josephine St., San Antonio.* ☎*210-227-1187.* **Southern**. Not only has the Liberty been in continuous operation since 1890—it's in the same Hobart family. What's more, since a flood in the 1920s, the Liberty and its floor have had a decidedly westward lean. But that hasn't slowed Texans' affections for pickled serrano chiles, lambsausage, Fanny's pot roast or famous buttermilk pie.

$$ Guero's Taco Bar – *1412 S. Congress Ave., Austin.* ☎*512-447-7688. www.guerostacobar.com.* **Mexican**. This Tex-Mex spot, occupying a late-19C feed store, is a big part of the hip Austin scene. The kitchen serves shrimp fajitas, huachinango (garlic-jalapeño red snapper), and chicken three ways: chipotle (smoky jalapeño), tampiqueño (salsa and jack cheese) or guanajuato (guacamole).

$ Stubb's Bar-B-Q – *801 Red River St., Austin TX.* ☎*512-480-8341. www.stubbsaustin.com.* **Barbecue**. C.B. Stubblefield once promised diners "Cold Beer and Live Music." His legacy lives on with nightly soul food and rhythm-and-blues. Diners may start with Texas fries or onion rings, then devour Stubb's Major BBQ plate of smoked beef brisket, sausage and ribs, ladled with C.B.'s original sauce.

SAN ANTONIO★★★

MAP P 351

CENTRAL STANDARD TIME

POPULATION 1,300,000

San Antonio's historic sites and world-class museums, semitropical climate, multicultural ambience and manageable size combine to make it a shining star of tourism.

- **Information:** ☎210-207-6700, www.SanAntonioCVB.com.
- ▸ **Orient Yourself:** Most attractions (Riverwalk, Alamo, Market Square, La Villita) are within easy walking distance of major downtown lodgings.
- **Parking:** Parking is very difficult to find around the Alamo. Best to take a taxi or walk from your hotel.
- **Don't Miss:** The Paseo del Rio--Riverwalk.
- **Organizing Your Time:** Allow 2 days for San Antonio. The Riverwalk is most magical in the evening, when it's gaily lit. Plan to cruise the river and have dinner at one of the innumerable waterside restaurants.

A Bit of History

Before Franciscan priests founded missions in the 1690s, Coahuiltecan Indians dominated the region. Two decades later, San Antonio de Bejar became a military garrison for the Viceroy of Spain; it was a fulcrum of the Texas Revolution when The Alamo fell to Santa Anna in 1836. Following the Civil War, San Antonio became a cattle center and population boomed. After a devastating flood in 1921 led the city to consider covering its river and turning it into a storm sewer, the San Antonio Conservation Society raised funds to redesign the eyesore into a tourist attraction. Robert H. H. Hugman's park-like first phase was constructed in 1939-41. When the city spruced up for its HemisFair 1968 world's fair, Hugman's dream of a festive shopping and dining promenade was realized.

Sights

The Alamo★★★

300 Alamo Plaza at Crockett St. ♿ ☎*210-225-1391. www.TheAlamo.org.*
The "Cradle of Texas Liberty" fronts a busy plaza in the heart of downtown. Mission San Antonio de Valero—known as The Alamo (Spanish for "cottonwood")—is an enduring symbol of Texas and one of the most photographed buildings in the US. It was built in 1718, secularized in 1793 and occupied as a Spanish, then Mexican military garrison in the early 1800s. In December 1835, rebellious Texans drove oppressive Mexican troops from San Antonio and consolidated their defenses within The Alamo. But Gen. Santa Anna, the Mexican president, led thousands of troops in an assault on the former mission two months later. The 13-day siege (February 23-March 6, 1836) was not over until every last one of The Alamo's 189 defenders—including commander William B. Travis, renowned knife fighter Jim Bowie and the legendary Davy Crockett, who left Congress to explore Texas' new frontier—had perished. "Remember The Alamo!" became the battle cry of the war of Texas independence, which climaxed less than two months later when Gen. Sam Houston defeated Santa Anna at San Jacinto, near Houston.

Although surrounded by hustle, bustle and numerous tourist traps, the site commands quiet respect. The Alamo is an apt memorial to the courage of the men who fought for Texas in the face of insurmountable odds. Its centerpiece is **The Shrine**★★★, the former mission church, where exhibits canonize the men who died here. Further exhibits in

Cradle of Con Carne

Market Square was the birthplace of chili con carne, the spicy stew that today is generally considered the state dish of Texas. Young girls known as "chili queens" first sold the concoction from small stands in the San Antonio market.

the **Long Barrack Museum**★★ describe historic events leading to the siege and its aftermath.

River Walk★★★

▦ *Bridge entrances at Losoya and Commerce Sts.* ✕♿ ☎*210-227-4262. www.thesanantonioriverwalk.com.*
Also called Paseo del Rio, this verdant promenade meanders below street level through 2.5mi of downtown, weaving along both banks of a horseshoe-shaped bend in the slow-flowing San Antonio River. Sidewalk cafes, small shops and nightclubs are wedged between the arched bridges of this cypress-shaded walkway. Strollers snake like a conga line through busy areas; other stretches have a quiet, park-like atmosphere.

Work Projects Administration crews built the cobblestone and flagstone path in 1939-41 under the direction of architect Robert Hugman and engineer Edwin Arneson. The plan included the **Arneson River Theatre**, an open-air amphitheater with a stage on one

River Walk

side of the stream, terraced seating on the other.

The best way to view River Walk without joining the pedestrian crowds is aboard Rio San Antonio Cruises **Kids** IIIII (☎210-244-5700, www.riosanantonio.com). The 60min open-air cruises feature lighthearted historical narratives by informative guides; the same company operates river taxis that ply the waters.

La Villita★

418 Villita St., between S. Alamo & S. Presa Sts. ✕ ♿ ☎210-207-8610. www.lavillita.com. At the time The Alamo was a military outpost, "The Little Village" developed as a temporary community of people without land title. The Mexican surrender climaxing the Texas Revolution was signed here. Today this is a National Historic District. Early 19C structures house artisans in 26 studio shops, restaurants and a museum exhibit.

Market Square★★

Kids *514 W. Commerce St. at Santa Rosa St.* ✕ ♿ 🅿 ☎210-207-8600. www.marketsquaresa.com.
This traditional Mexican marketplace, extending across several blocks, began as an early-19C farmers' market. Later, pharmaceutical items were sold at **Botica Guadalupana**, oldest continuously operated drugstore in central and south Texas. Today a Latin flavor persists in the shops and restaurants, including **El Mercado**, largest Mexican mall in the US. At two long-standing restaurants, **La Margarita** and **Mi Tierra**, troupes of mariachi musicians serenade diners.

Spanish Governor's Palace★

105 Plaza de Armas. ☎210-224-0601.
This National Historic Landmark near Market Square is Texas' sole surviving example of a colonial aristocrat's home. It was completed in 1749 (as the date on its massive door indicates) and restored in 1931. Self-guided tours wind through an enclosed fountain courtyard and chambers furnished with 18C antiques.

Casa Navarro State Historic Park★

228 S. Laredo St. ☎210-226-4801. www.tpwd.state.tx.us.
The three refurbished buildings on this site—an adobe-and-limestone house, kitchen and office—come to life on curator-led tours. Home builder José Antonio Navarro (1795-1871) was a lifelong San Antonio rancher and statesman.

Tower of the Americas★

Kids *600 HemisFair Park.* ✕ ♿ 🅿 ☎210-207-8615. www.toweroftheamericas.com.
The city's finest **views**★★★ are from this 750ft tower overlooking the grounds of HemisFair 1968. Visitors are whisked day and night to the 500ft level on a 1min ride in a glass-enclosed elevator. This is one of the tallest free-standing structures in the Western Hemisphere—67ft higher than the Washington Monument.

Institute of Texas Cultures★

Kids *801 S. Bowie St.* ♿ 🅿 ☎210-458-2300, www.texancultures.utsa.edu.
Twenty-seven distinct ethnic and cultural groups are profiled at this Hemis-Fair Park heritage museum. An outdoor interpretive area replicates a 19C pioneer village.

San Antonio Missions National Historical Park★★

2202 Roosevelt Ave. ♿ 🅿 ☎210-534-8833. www.nps.gov/saan.
The Alamo was not the only mission in the valley of the Rio San Antonio. Four others were erected in 1720-31 near the river, which supplied water for drinking and crop irrigation by means of an *acequia* (aqueduct). The park comprises these Franciscan missions, which portray the size and scope of traditional compounds—including a church and chapel, convent, Coahuiltecan living quarters, farmland, a granary and a blacksmith. All four still support active parishes.

The chain begins at **Mission Concepción**★ (*807 Mission Rd. at Felisa St., 2.3mi south of The Alamo via S. St. Mary's St.;* ☎210-534-8833). Of special note are traces of geometric designs painted by

Coahuiltecans on the interior walls of the magnificent mission church (c.1731) and convent.

Mission San José y San Miguel de Aguayo★★ (*6701 San Jose Dr, 2.2mi south of Mission Concepción; ☎210-534-8833*) was once "Queen of the Texas Missions." At its peak, San José was a major social and cultural center and home to 300 people; it remains an impressive fortress today. A bilingual Sunday-morning Mariachi Mass, featuring religious music by mariachi musicians in its 1720 chapel, highlights a visit. The national historical park's primary **visitor center** is nearby.

Structures within the agricultural compound of **Mission San Juan Capistrano** (*9101 Graf Rd., 2.5mi south of Mission San José; ☎210-534-8833*) have been extensively restored, including the 1772 chapel, rectory and Indian quarters. Priests rescued precious icons from the 1740 church at Mission San Francisco de la Espada (*10040 Espada Rd., 1.5mi south of Mission San Juan; ☎210-627-2021*) during a 1997 fire.

San Antonio Museum of Art★★★

200 W. Jones Ave. ✕🅰🅿 *b210-978-8100. www.samuseum.org.*

This large, bright, thoroughly remodeled museum, housed in the 1904 Lone Star Brewery Company building, has impressive collections of Egyptian, Greek and Roman antiquities in its west wing; Asian works include ancient Chinese tombfigures. Among 17-18C European masters exhibited in the Great Hall are Steen, Hals and Bosch; 18-20C American works include oils by Copley, Stuart, Sargent and Homer.

The $11 million **Nelson A. Rockefeller Center for Latin American Art**★★ opened as a three-story east wing in 1998. It traces 4,000 years of Indian and Hispanic culture—pre-Columbian, Spanish Colonial, folk and modern art. An interactive education center introduces cultural history of Mexico, Central and South America. Exhibits feature Mesoamerican culture from Olmec, Mayan, Aztec, Toltec and other periods, as well as Andean ceramics and gold work. Spanish Colonial works are primarily religious in nature, encompassing more than 100 paintings and objects. Folk art includes utilitarian and ceremonial pieces plus decorative items in wood, metal, ceramics, paper and textiles. Modern art features such 20C masters as Rivera, Tamaya, Torres-Garcia and Siqueiros.

Brackenridge Park

Kids *3500 N. St. Mary's St.* ✕🅰🅿 ☎210-207-7275.

A popular picnic destination, the 343-riverside-acre park is home to the **San Antonio Zoo and Aquarium** (*3903 N. St. Mary's St.; ☎210-734-7184*), lodged in a former rock quarry. Nearby, the **Japanese Tea Gardens** (*3800 N. St. Mary's St.*) offer lush flowers, climbing vines and tall palms alongside koi-filled pools.

Witte Museum★

Kids *3801 Broadway.* 🅰🅿 ☎210-357-1900. www.wittemuseum.org.

The Witte showcases human and natural history and culture, from anthropology to fashions and decorative arts. Exhibits in the main building (1926, Robert M. Ayres) include **Texas Wild**★, which depicts the state's ecological zones. **Ancient Texans**★★ focuses on the Lower Pecos culture of the Rio Grande Valley. A half-dozen relocated pioneer homes share grounds behind

San Antonio Museum of Art

Courtesy San Antonio Museum of Art

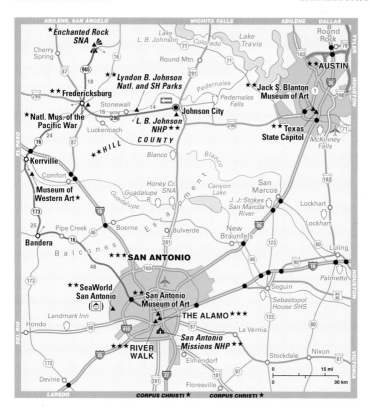

the museum. The **H-E-B Science Tree-house**★ (1997, Lake/Flato) has four levels of science exhibits, perched over the San Antonio River on concrete oak trees created by sculptor Carlos Cortes.

San Antonio Botanical Gardens and Halsell Conservatory★

555 Funston Pl. ✕ ⚓ 🅿 ☎*210-207-3250. www.sabot.org.*
Within these 33-acre gardens the centerpiece is the **Lucile Halsell Conservatory**★★, a 90,000sq-ft cluster of individual glass houses tucked into the earth around a courtyard sunk 16ft underground to escape the hot Texas summers.

Marion Koogler McNay Art Museum★★

6000 N. New Braunfels Ave. ⚓ 🅿 ☎*210-824-5368. www.mcnayart.org.*
A world-class collection of 19C and 20C European and American art occupies this 24-room Spanish Mediterranean-style manor (1926, Atlee B. & Robert M. Ayres), former home of oil heiress and art collector Marion McNay. Galleries surround a landscaped garden patio or overlook the courtyard from balconies. The collection is strong in Post-Impressionist French art. Five decades of Picasso's works are in three rooms; 20C paintings by Braque, Matisse, Modigliani and Chagall also are presented. American Modernist works include O'Keeffe, Dove, Pollock, Hockney and Motherwell.

Excursions

Fiesta Texas★

🄺🄸🄳🅂 ⅻ *17000 I-10 West.* ✕⚓🅿 ☎*210-697-5050. www.sixflags.com.*
This popular theme park showcases the music of Texas, from 50s rock 'n' roll to tejano to German polka. Shows are interspersed with thrill rides and water rides, especially popular in summer.

AUSTIN★★

MAP P 351
CENTRAL STANDARD TIME
POPULATION 680,000

The Texas capital, located between the rolling Hill Country and fertile farmland, has a vibrant cultural life and a young population that includes 50,000 University of Texas students. Founded in 1835 as Waterloo, it became the seat of government upon independence, changing its name to honor statesman Stephen F. Austin. Austin experienced steady growth that included construction of a new state capitol, dedicated in 1888. The city was plagued by flooding along the Colorado River until a series of flood-control dams were constructed in 1938, forming the chain of Highland Lakes that includes Town Lake and Lake Austin.

🛈 **Information:** ☎800-926-2282 or www.austintexas.org
♿ **Don't Miss:** Jack Blanton Museum of Art.
Kids **Especially for Kids:** Barton Springs Pool.

The City Today

Austin balances its serious role as seat of state government with the youthful exuberance of the university and its vibrant cultural life. The **Sixth Street Entertainment District**, extending seven blocks from I-35 to Congress Avenue, is home to dozens of clubs that have built Austin's reputation as a mecca for musicians in all genres, including blues, country, rock and jazz.

The nation's largest urban **colony of bats** nestles beneath downtown Austin's Congress Avenue bridge from March to October between migrations to Mexico. The nearby **Barton Springs Pool** (Kids *2101 Barton Springs Road, in Zilker Park; 512-476-9044, www.ci.austin.tx.us/parks),* fed by huge underground springs, is one of the most popular places in Texas to cool off on hot days.

Sights

Texas State Capitol★★

Congress Ave. at 11th St. ✕ ♿ 🅿 ☎512-463-5495. www.tspb.state.tx.us.
Dominating Austin's skyline, the Renaissance Revival-style capitol was built in 1888 (Elijah E. Myers) of red granite and limestone. Over 302ft in height, it is 14ft taller than the US Capitol. 📷Guided tours, departing from the south foyer every 15min, visit the chambers of the state legislature, which meets in odd-numbered years from January through May. In the foyer, statues by 19C sculptor Elisabet Ney memorialize founding fathers Stephen Austin and Sam Houston; paintings by W. H. Huddle portray Davy Crockett at The Alamo and the surrender of Santa Anna at San Jacinto. A terrazzo floor—depicting the Lone Star of the Republic of Texas surrounded by the coats of arms of other nations whose flags have flown here—is the centerpiece of the rotunda. The **Capitol Complex Visitors Center** *(112 E. 11th St.; ☎512-305-8400)* is at the southeast corner of the exquisite, 22-acre grounds. The center is housed in the former General Land Office Building (1857), oldest surviving state building in Texas. Inside, a theater shows *A Lone Star Legacy: The Texas Capitol Complex,* a 23min film narrated by famed Texas newsman Walter Cronkite.

Lyndon Baines Johnson Presidential Library and Museum★★

2313 Red River St. ♿ 🅿 ☎512-916-5136. www.lbjlib.utexas.edu.
Located on the UT campus, this monumental facility honors the Hill Country's most famous native son. Lyndon Johnson (1908-73) served as US president following John F. Kennedy's assassination; his turbulent term (1963-69) was marked by the Vietnam War and

civil-rights movement. The eight-story library (1971, Skidmore, Owings and Merrill), constructed of travertine marble, is the repository for all presidential documents produced during the LBJ administration—more than 36 million pieces of paper.

Three floors—the first, second and eighth—are open to the public. Tours begin with a 23min film on LBJ's childhood in the Hill Country, his political life in the House and Senate, and finally his White House years. Accompanying exhibits place his life in the context of US history. Display cases showcase handmade gifts from US citizens and bejeweled keepsakes from foreign heads of state. On the eighth floor, Johnson's Oval Office at the White House is replicated in seven-eighths scale.

Texas State Capitol Rotunda, Interior

© Austin Convention and Visitors Bureau

Bob Bullock Texas State History Museum★

1800 N. Congress Ave. ✕♿🅿 ☎512-936-8746. www.thestoryoftexas.com.
Named after an illustrious Texas lieutenant governor, this sunset-red expanse of granite, framed by a 35ft-tall bronze star and the six flags of Texas, has three floors of exhibits on the state's geographical and cultural regions, its human history, and juxtaposes the Texas cowboy myth against the realities of ranching and oil-exploration.

Jack S. Blanton Museum of Art★★

Harry Ransom Center, University of Texas, 21st & Guadalupe Sts. ♿🅿 ☎512-471-7324. www.blantonmuseum.org.
The Blanton's permanent collection of more than 13,000 works ranges from ancient to contemporary art. The ground floor features the **Mari & James Michener Collection** of 20C American art; donated by the late novelist and his wife, it offers hundreds of modern masterworks, from Cubist to Abstract Expressionist. The **C.R. Smith Collection** of 19C American art includes Henry Farny's 1899 portrait of Sitting Bull and works by Bierstadt, Moran and Russell. The **Suida-Manning Collection** on the second floor has important Renaissance and Baroque art, including works by Rubens and Veronese. The **Latin Ameri-**can Art gallery presents contemporary work from artists in Central and South America. An original 15C Gutenberg Bible, one of the few copies in the US, is displayed on the ground floor of the Ransom Center.

Also in the city are the **Austin Museum of Art at Laguna Gloria** (*3809 W. 35th St.;* ☎512-458-8191), with a collection of 20C American art; the **Elisabet Ney Museum** (*304 E. 44th St.;* ☎512-458-2255), 19C studio of Texas' first sculptor; and the **Umlauf Sculpture Garden and Museum** (*605 Robert E. Lee Rd.;* ☎512-445-5582), showcasing the work of 20C sculptor Charles Umlauf.

Lady Bird Johnson Wildflower Research Center★★

4801 La Crosse Ave. ✕♿🅿 ☎512-292-4100. www.wildflower.org.
Created by the former First Lady in 1982--her legacy is beautifully visible along Texas highways during April's wildflower extravaganza--this facility is dedicated to conserving and promoting the use of indigenous plants, including 400 species native to Texas. The 42-acre site includes 23 separate research, display and botanical theme gardens—ablaze with color particularly in April and May—as well as natural grasslands and woodlands, an observation tower, stone cisterns, aqueducts, courtyards and nature trails.

HILL COUNTRY★★

MAP P 351

CENTRAL STANDARD TIME

The scenic Hill Country northwest of San Antonio was shaped 30 million years ago when the earth buckled and kicked up strata of limestone and granite into rugged hills and steep cliffs. Rivers, lakes, limestone caves and other natural attractions mark the region's 25,000sq mi.

- 🛈 **Information:** www.hillcountryinfo.com
- ▶ **Orient Yourself:** The Balcones Fault, the uplift that is the boundary of the Hill Country, runs just west of Interstate 35 from San Antonio most of the way to Fort Worth.
- ☺ **Don't Miss:** Fredericksburg; wildflower season in April.
- 🕐 **Organizing Your Time:** Though this drive can be done in two days, in spring it's a wonderful place to linger at the many small inns in the region. The best times to visit are spring, when the region is painted with fields of bluebonnets, coreopsis and paintbrush, and autumn, when Spanish oak and sumac infuse the plateau with color. Summer days are hot and humid, winter often chilly and overcast.

A Bit of History

The Hill Country was originally home to several Indian tribes, including Apache, Tonkawa and Comanche. Republican (1836-45) and early statehood periods were marked by immigration from the eastern US, France, Denmark, Sweden, Czechoslovakia and especially the German Rhine states. Today the Hill Country's character is largely the legacy of a German small-landholder tradition.

Driving Tour

2 days, 226mi

- ▶ *Take US-281 from San Antonio 63mi north, or US-290 from Austin 48mi west, to Johnson City.*

Johnson City

Though named for Sam Ealy Johnson, grandfather of former US President Lyndon Baines Johnson, attractions in this small community of 1,200 people today focus on "LBJ," its most famous son.

Lyndon B. Johnson National Historical Park★★

Ave. G & Ladybird Lane. ♿ 🅿 ☎830-868-7128. www.nps.gov/lyjo.

The life and family heritage of LBJ (1908-73) is portrayed in exhibits at the **Visitor Center.** The **LBJ Boyhood Home** *(Elm St. & Ave. G; guided tour only)* has been restored to its 1920 appearance and furnished with family heirlooms. The **Johnson Settlement** *(west end of Ladybird Lane)* preserves the tiny log home and outbuildings of cattle rancher Sam Johnson and his brother, Tom, in the 1860s.

- ▶ *Continue 14mi west on US-290.*

Lyndon B. Johnson National and State Historical Parks★★

US-290, Stonewall. ♿ 🅿 ☎830-644-2252. www.tpwd.state.tx.us.

LBJ's "Texas White House"—the president's sprawling ranch beside the Pedernales River—is the featured attraction at these combined parks, which span 1,200 acres. Buses depart from the State Park Visitor Center; those awaiting a **tour** ⫼ can view a film and displays on Johnson's life. The 90min National Park Service tour travels to the **LBJ Ranch,** stopping at the one-room Junction School where Johnson began his education. The bus slows for photos of the Texas White House, then continues past an airstrip and cattle barns to LBJ's reconstructed birthplace home and the family cemetery where he is buried. Private vehicles are permitted on the ranch only between 5pm and sunset.

Within the state-park boundary is the 1918 **Sauer-Beckmann Living History Farm**, furnished in period style and manned by costumed interpreters who perform the daily chores of a c.1900 Texas-German farm family.

▶ *Continue another 16mi west on US-290 to Fredericksburg.*

Fredericksburg★★

This community of 10,000 was settled in 1846 by 120 German pioneers who ventured to Texas in response to a land-grant program. Their heritage persists along wide streets lined with picturesque homes of native limestone, *Fachwerk* and Victorian gingerbread. Signs on guest houses, restaurants and gift shops invariably declare, *"Wir sprechen Deutsch."* Such annual festivals as Oktoberfest pack the lanes with revelers, and oom-pah music carries the day.

Historical artifacts are displayed in the **Vereins Kirche Museum** (Marktplatz; ☎ 830-997-2835) and the **Pioneer Museum Complex** (309 W. Main St.; ☎830-997-2835). Eighty-three buildings are designated sites in Fredericksburg's 30-block historic district; many have been converted to charming bed-and-breakfast inns.

National Museum of the Pacific War★

340 E. Main St. ♿ 🅿 ☎*830-997-4379. www.nimitz-museum.org.*

Honoring Admiral Chester Nimitz, a World War II hero and Fredericksburg native, this site comprises a museum—housed in a curiously shiplike 1852 hotel—and nine acres of adjacent grounds. Nimitz became Commander-in-Chief of US Pacific forces on December 25, 1941, and directed 2.5 million troops until the Japanese surrender in August 1945. Behind the museum lies the Garden of Peace, a classic Oriental garden presented in respect of Nimitz by the people of Japan.

▶ *Drive 18mi north on Ranch Rd. 965.*

Enchanted Rock State Natural Area★

🏞 *16710 Ranch Rd. 965.* ⛺ 🅿 ☎*325-247-3903. www.tpwd.state.tx.us.*

This state park features one of the largest stone formations in the West, a 640-acre granite outcropping. The ascent takes about an hour, and hikers are rewarded with a magnificent **view**★★ of the Hill Country. In warm weather *(Apr–Oct),* it's wise to begin the hike early in the morning, as a visitor limit may close the park to crowds until 5pm on weekend days.

▶ *Return to Fredericksburg and take Rte. 16 for 24mi south.*

Cowboy Artists of America Museum★

1550 Bandera Hwy. (Rte. 173) Kerrville. ♿ 🅿 ☎*210-896-2553. www.caamuseum.com.*

This hilltop museum features work by 26 contemporary Western artists—including Gordon Snidow of New Mexico and Robert Scriver of Montana—whose paintings and sculptures capture the spirit and traditional lifestyle of the plains. The building (1982, O'Neill Ford), constructed in Mexican style of 18 brick domes, surrounds an open sculpture garden. Visitors may take in special programs on the folklore, music and history of the Old West.

▶ *Continue on Rte. 173 for 25mi south.*

Bandera

Bandera claims to be "The Cowboy Capital of the World." Rodeos are scheduled weekly from late May to early September. Local dance halls—such as the sawdust-floored Arkey Blue's Silver Dollar—are filled with two-steppers, clad in jeans and cowboy hats, dancing to country-and-western music most nights. The country surrounding Bandera is dotted with family-oriented guest or "dude" ranches where rates typically include all meals and horseback-riding programs.

▶ *Return to San Antonio on Rte. 16, about 48mi.*

CORPUS CHRISTI★

MICHELIN MAP 492 K 15
CENTRAL STANDARD TIME
POPULATION 285,000

Where the South Texas plains meet the Gulf of Mexico, the thriving harbor city of Corpus Christi nestles beside broad Corpus Christi Bay. Its calm waters, shielded from the wind-whipped gulf by the sandy, reef-like barrier of Mustang and Padre Islands, have made "Corpus" one of the busiest ports in the US and the home of one of its largest naval air bases.

🄸 **Information:** ☎361-561-2000 or www.corpuschristicvb.com.
🄳 **Don't Miss:** USS Lexington
🄺🄸🄳🅂 **Especially for Kids:** Texas State Aquarium.

Sights

Museum of Science and History★

🄺🄸🄳🅂 *1900 N. Chaparral St.* ♿🅿 ☎361-826-4650. www.ccmuseum.com. Highlights of the **Museum** are a 17ft scale model of an offshore oil rig. Outside stand the **Ships of Columbus**★, life-size replicas of the *Pinta* and *Santa María* constructed by the Spanish government to commemorate the explorer's 1492 voyage.

Texas State Aquarium★

🄺🄸🄳🅂 *2710 N. Shoreline Dr.* ♿🅿 ☎361-881-1200. www.texasstateaquarium.org. Gulf of Mexico marine life are at "home" in ecosystem exhibits that include marsh and shoreline, pier and estuary. Islands of Steel replicates an offshore oil platform surrounded by nurse sharks and amberjack. Outdoors are touch tanks of small sharks and stingrays, as well as river otters, sea turtles and a rare white alligator.

USS Lexington Museum on the Bay★★

🄺🄸🄳🅂 *2914 N. Shoreline Blvd.* ♿🅿 ☎361-888-4873. www.usslexington.com. This mammoth World War II aircraft carrier, berthed near the aquarium across the Harbor Bridge from downtown, was the most decorated carrier in US Navy history. Today "The Lex," its main deck larger than three football fields, offers self-guided tours.

Padre Island National Seashore★★

⚠♿🅿 ☎361-949-8068; www.nps.gov/pais. This 70mi of undeveloped beach stretchs south from Corpus Christi to Port Mansfield, the southern 55mi of it off-limits to all but four-wheel-drive vehicles. Park Road 22—an extension of South Padre Island Drive (Rte. 358), which crosses the JFK Bridge and Causeway 25mi east of Corpus Christi—ends just past **Malaquite Beach Visitor Center** *(20420 Park Rd.)*. Even for visitors driving standard vehicles, these northern 10mi of national seashore offer a taste of the vast sand-and-shell beaches, dunes and grasslands beyond.

Excursion

King Ranch★

King Ave., Kingsville; take US-77 to Rte. 141, turn right (west) onto King Ave., proceed 3mi to blinking light; follow signs from ranch gate (on left) to visitor center. 🅿 ☎361-592-8055. www.kingranch.com. One of the largest US cattle ranches, King Ranch sprawls across 1,300sq mi 39mi south of Corpus Christi. It was founded in 1853 by steamboat pilot Richard King, whose sixth-generation descendants still own the ranch.
Highlights of a 90min bus tour include the grave of horse-racing's 1946 Triple Crown winner, Assault, and a weaver's cottage where dozens of Texas ranch brands—including King's own distinctive "running W"—are on display.

SAN DIEGO AREA

This sun-kissed area of Southern California mixes relaxed residential communities with glistening beaches, scenic mountains and the beginnings of a vast desert. Just north of San Diego is La Jolla, an upscale enclave of boutiques and coastal scenery. Beyond the urban area, San Diego County's 4,255sq mi encompass towns, beaches and rural climes. An inland jumble of mountains and valleys climaxes at Anza-Borrego Desert State Park.

California began in San Diego. Hunter-gatherer Indians of the Kumeyaay tribe probably watched a trio of Spanish ships under Juan Rodríguez Cabrillo enter San Diego Bay in 1542 before sailing north. The next flotilla visited in 1601, but it was another century before Europeans came to stay. Jolted by English land claims from Point Reyes to Canada, Spain launched its own colonists, led by Capt. Gaspar de Portolá and Padre Junípero Serra. The pair established California's first mission and Spanish garrison at San Diego on July 16, 1769. The mission was eventually moved 6mi to the San Diego River; both church and state prospered in the remote outpost, albeit slowly. Following Mexican independence in 1821, a town, or *pueblo*, now called Old Town San Diego, grew below the garrison. The pueblo became a center for *Californios*, ranchers of Spanish and Mexican descent who owned parcels of California land. An American corvette captured San Diego during the Mexican American War in 1846. Mexican Governor Pío Pico surrendered near San Diego a year later, completing the US conquest of California.

San Diego enjoys a mild coastal climate, but east of the hills that block the daily sea breeze, temperatures may soar into triple digits in summer.

Horton Plaza, San Diego

©Joanne DiBona/San Diego CVB

Address Book San Diego Area

⌕For prices, see the Legend on the cover flap.

WHERE TO STAY IN THE SAN DIEGO AREA

$$$$$ La Costa Resort and Spa – *Costa del Mar Rd., Carlsbad, CA.* ✕👤🅿🏊 🆂🅿🅰 ☎*760-438-9111 or 800-854-5000. www.lacosta.com. 479 rooms.* Sprawled across 450 hilltop acres along the coast north of San Diego, this utopian escape boasts two golf courses, 21 tennis courts and five heated pools, as well as spirulina wraps and shiatsu massage. La Costa is a true splurge for recharging body and mind. Special spa cuisine is a menu option at each of five restaurants, including the **Bluefire Grill ($$$$)**.

$$$$$ La Valencia – *1132 Prospect St., La Jolla, CA.* ✕👤🅿🏊 🆂🅿🅰 ☎*858-454-0771 or 800-451-0772. www.lavalencia. com. 117 rooms.* On a bluff overlooking the Pacific, this landmark pastel-pink stucco palace is a statement of opulent American beachside style. Surrounded by palms, topped by Spanish tile and a domed tower, La Valencia has witnessed more than 75 years of California sunsets. Accommodations include 15 new Ocean Villas. Of three restaurants, the **Sky Room ($$$$)** is most intimate, its tables overlooking La Jolla Cove.

$$$$ Hotel del Coronado – *1500 Orange Ave., Coronado, CA.* ✕👤🅿🏊 🆂🅿🅰 ☎*619-435-6611 or 800-468-3533. www.hoteldel.com. 692 rooms.* This seaside gingerbread castle is a massive white Victorian of whimsical turrets and red-shingled roofs. "The Del" has hosted 14 presidents and countless celebrities since 1888. Guests stroll the resort's 26 oceanfront acres and indulge in a massive Sunday brunch in the **Crown Coronet Room ($$$)**, with its 33ft-high, rib-vaulted ceiling.

$$$$ Hotel Parisi – *1111 Prospect St., La Jolla, CA.* ✕👤🅿 ☎*858-454-1511. www.hotelparisi.com. 20 rooms.* New Age devotees have their indulgences, and this boutique hotel in the heart of La Jolla is a fine example. The all-suite property was designed using feng shui guidelines "to induce positive energy flow." A psychologist and acupuncturist are among specialists on call; rooms have 10ft ceilings and ocean views.

$$$$ Horton Grand Hotel – *311 Island Ave., San Diego, CA.* ✕👤🅿 ☎*619-544-1886 or 800-542-1886. www. hortongrand.com. 132 rooms.* This historic Victorian-era hotel has been restored to its 1886 glory, when it shone above the brothels, saloons and opium dens of young San Diego's red-light district, now the Gaslamp area. Period decor—including an Austrian grand staircase—recaptures 19C charm.

$$ Crystal Pier Hotel – *4500 Ocean Blvd., San Diego, CA.* 👤🅿 ☎*858-483-6983 or 800-748-5894. www.crystalpier. com. 29 rooms.* On a dock that juts into the ocean at Pacific Beach, a series of blue-and-white cottages provide unique over-the-water lodging. The 1927 bungalows have kitchenettes and wicker-chair furnishings, patios with umbrellas and deck furniture. Guests rent rods and fish from the pier, or close their shutters and fall asleep to the sound of rumbling surf.

WHERE TO EAT IN THE SAN DIEGO AREA

$$$ Café Pacifica – *2414 San Diego Ave., San Diego.* ☎*619-291-6666. www. cafepacifica.com.* **Seafood**. An Old Town favorite, Café Pacifica serves up fine seafood in its sun-dappled dining room. Monthly menus may include bluenose sea bass braised in sake over jicama and Granny Smith apple salad; a sure bet is the variety of fresh fish simply grilled with your choice of sauces and salsas.

$$$ Croce's – *802 5th Ave., San Diego.* ☎*619-233-4355. www.croces.com.* **American**. This shrine to folk-rock singer Jim Croce was opened by his wife, Ingrid, after Jim died in a 1973 plane crash. Its bars offer live music every night—often from A.J. Croce, a child when his father passed on. The walls are decorated with photos, original lyrics and guitars. Seafood specialties (grilled swordfish in a carrot-ginger glaze) and rack of lambare fine dining choices.

$$$ George's at the Cove – *1250 Prospect St., La Jolla.* ☎*858-454-4244. www.georgesatthecove.com.* **Sea-**

food. All three stories of this seaside showplace have views of La Jolla Cove, whether inside the formal modern dining room or out on the terrace, under canvas umbrellas. George's is famous for fish—including sautéed Arctic char, dusted in anise seeds, and applewood-smoked salmon—and for its signature soup of smoked chicken, broccoli and black beans.

$ Goldfish Point Cafe – *1255 Coast Blvd., La Jolla. b858-459-7407.* **American**. Perched atop the bluff overlooking La Jolla cove, this hugely popular breakfast-and-lunch eatery draws an equal mix of locals, tourists and stu-

dents. Coffee, pastries and fresh-made sandwiches are good, but the prime draw is the stunning view--the tables are oriented to face the cove◒

$ Corvette Diner – *3946 Fifth Ave., San Diego.* ☎*619-542-1476. www. cohnrestaurants.com.* **American**. A disc jockey plays requests at this classic 1950s diner, as pink-and-black poodle-skirted waitresses carry burgers, fries and shakes to crowded tables. Photos of Elvis and Sinatra adorn the walls, alongside neon signs and 50s kitsch. Soda jerks mix cherry Cokes at the fountain as cooks sling hash behind the counter.

SAN DIEGO★★★

MICHELIN MAP 493 B11
PACIFIC STANDARD TIME
POPULATION 1,257,000

Cosmopolitan San Diego is California's second-largest city and the sixth-largest in the US. Balboa Park's cultural institutions share the mesas and canyons north of downtown with Spanish-style mansions. San Diego Bay was Pacific Fleet headquarters during both world wars and remains an important naval center. World-class tourist attractions, proximity to beaches and a mild climate have earned San Diego a reputation as one of the most livable cities in the nation.

- 🛈 **Information:** ☎619-232-1212 or www.sandiego.org.
- 🅿 **Parking:** Parking is free at Balboa Park, but spaces fill up after 11am; use the park's free trams to get around. Take an Old Town Trolley tour to get around.
- 😊 **Don't Miss:** Balboa Park, Old Town and San Diego Zoo & Wild Animal Park.
- 🕐 **Organizing Your Time:** Take a trolley to Downtown, Old Town, Balboa Park (free trams within the park) and Seaport Village; allow 4 hours for each.

Old San Diego★★★

Sights preserving and commemorating the birth of San Diego and the beginning of the European presence in Alta California lie in the vicinity of Interstate 8 as it stretches east to west, roughly following the course of the San Diego River.

Old Town San Diego
State Historic Park★★

2645 San Diego Ave.; exit I-5 at Old Town Ave. ✕♿🅿 ☎*619-220-5422. www.parks. ca.gov.*
A broad plaza surrounded by restored adobe and wooden structures lies at the

foot of Presidio Hill. Colorful shops and eateries re-create Mexican and early American periods. The 1853 **Robinson-Rose House**, at the plaza's west end, has a diorama of Old San Diego in its visitor center. **La Casa de Machado y Silvas**★ (1830-43), restored as a period restaurant, once was a boardinghouse, a brothel and a church. **La Casa de Machado y Stewart**★ (1833) is an outstanding example of adobe restoration. **La Casa de Estudillo**★★ (1829), largest and most impressive of the original adobes, has 13 rooms connected by a veranda; it offers a glimpse of upper-class lifestyle. The first floor of **La Casa de Bandini**★, a popular Mexican restaurant, was built by Peruvian Juan Bandini in 1829; in 1869, a second floor was added and it became a hotel.

Presidio Park★

Presidio Dr.; from Old Town, take Mason St. north to Jackson St.; turn left and follow signs.

Highlight of this beautifully landscaped park is the **Junípero Serra Museum** (☎619-297-3258, www.sandiegohistory. org), a stately white Mission Revival building (1929, William Templeton Johnson). Its five galleries of early San Diego history include a remarkable collection of Spanish Renaissance furniture and an exhibit interpreting the effect of colonization on local Indians.

Mission Basilica San Diego de Alcalá★★

10818 San Diego Mission Rd.; from Old Town, take I-8 east 7mi to Mission Gorge Rd. and follow signs. ☐ ☎619-281-8449. www.missionsandiego.com.

California's first mission occupies a secluded site on the north slope of Mission Valley. Padre Junípero Serra's 1769 Presidio Hill mission was relocated here by Padre Luis Jayme in 1774. The mission was restored between 1895 and 1931 and designated a Minor Basilica by Pope Paul VI in 1976.

An original white-stucco, buttressed facade and five-bell campanario herald the entrance to the complex. The sparsely furnished **Casa del Padre Serra,** where the friar resided during frequent visits, is all that remains of the original monastery. The narrow 139ft-by-34ft church **interior** is restored to its 1813 appearance; early hand-carved wooden statues are in the sanctuary.

Balboa Park★★★

San Diego's cultural focal point is a 1,200-acre park immediately north of downtown, holding one of the most extensive collections of cultural attractions on the continent. Lawns, gardens and century-old shade trees harbor the world-renowned San Diego Zoo, as well as theaters and museum buildings created for two world's fairs. The 1915 Pan-

ama-California Exposition was a city of stylized pavilions surrounding two central plazas—Plaza de Balboa and Plaza de Panama—linked by El Prado, a broad pedestrian thoroughfare. Architecture was Spanish Colonial Revival, a rich hybrid of Moorish, Baroque and rococo ornamentation contrasting with colorful tiles and unadorned walls. The 1935 California Pacific International Exposition added new pavilions surrounding Pan-American Plaza in Art Deco, Mayan-Aztec and Southwestern styles.

The **Visitors Center** in the House of Hospitality *(1549 El Prado;* ✕ ♿ ☐ ☎619-239-0512; www.balboapark.com) offers books, maps and general information. Parking is free, as are trams between attractions.

San Diego Zoo★★★

Kids ||||| *2920 Zoo Dr.; Open year-round daily 9am–4pm (until 9pm in summer and 6pm during school vacations). $19.50; children (3-11) $11.75.* ✕ ♿ ☐ ☎619-234-3153, www.sandiegozoo.org.

One of the largest and most celebrated zoological parks in the world, the San Diego Zoo occupies 100 acres of hillsides and ravines at the northern end of Balboa Park, lushly landscaped with some 6,500 botanical species. Habitats disguise moats and fences used to separate, protect and display 4,000 animals of 800 species, divided into 10 bioclimatic zones.

Guided bus tours *(30–40min)* orient visitors to the undulating terrain. Moving sidewalks climb steep hills to assist those who wander the network of pathways by foot. Kangaroo Bus Tours allow hop-on, hop-off access to major points of interest. The Skyfari aerial tram carries visitors to the **Polar Bear Plunge**, with an underwater viewing area on a 14ft-deep moat. Animal shows *(25min)* are staged in Wegeforth Bowl and Hunte Amphitheater.

Ituri Forest is the zoo's newest theme area: The Central African rain forest displays hippopotamuses, okapi, forest buffalo, spot-necked otters, monkeys and birds. Residents of **Gorilla Tropics** include troops of western lowland gorillas and pygmy chimpanzees. Three separate aviaries hold hundreds of species of rare birds; a fourth has hummingbirds. A winding trail descends **Tiger River** into a misty rain forest, passing crocodiles, Chinese water dragons, fishing cats, tapirs, pythons and mouse deer, ending at a Sumatran tiger habitat. In **Bear Canyon** is the Giant Panda Research Station, housing a pair of pandas on loan from China.

San Diego Natural History Museum★

Kids *1788 El Prado.* ✕♿ P ☎*619-232-3821. www.sdnhm.org.*

A major 2001 expansion more than doubled the size of this museum, preserving the original 1933 building facade but creating a new north-facing entrance set in a four-story wall of glass. A new permanent exhibit recreates a walk across Baja California and San Diego County, from deep ocean through high mountains to low desert; live animals, state-of-the-art dioramas and computer stations add to its interactive nature. Other displays highlight geology and paleontology.

Reuben H. Fleet Science Center

Kids *1875 El Prado.* ✕♿ P ☎*619-238-1233. www.rhfleet.org.*

Five galleries, a dome-screen Space Theater for planetarium shows and IMAX films, and a 23-rider SciTours motion simulator for "space voyages" share this Spanish Colonial-style building.

Casa de Balboa★

1649 El Prado. ✕♿ P.

This richly ornamented structure (1914) is based on the Federal Government Palace in Queretaro, Mexico. The **Museum of San Diego History** (☎*619-232-6203, www.sandiegohistory.org)* looks at the city's development since 1850. The **Museum of Photographic Arts** (☎*619-238-7559, www.mopa.org),* presents rotating exhibits of historic and contemporary photography, including video and film.

Timken Museum of Art★★

1500 El Prado. ♿ P ☎*619-239-5548. www.timkenmuseum.org.*

© Joanne DiBona/San Diego CVB

Balboa Park Tower

Clad in Italian travertine marble, the museum (1965) displays a collection of 50 European and American paintings and tapestries, and 17 remarkable **Russian icons★★** of the 14-19C. Works by Hals, Rubens, Rembrandt, Bierstadt and Copley are among those on exhibit.

San Diego Museum of Art★

1450 El Prado. ✕♿ P ☎*619-232-7931. www.sdmart.com.*

The ornate Plateresque facade of this building (1926) was inspired by Spain's University of Salamanca. Depicted are Spanish Baroque masters; replicas of Donatello's *Saint George* and Michelangelo's *David*; and heraldry of Spain, America, California and San Diego.

Highlights of the wide-ranging collection include such Medieval European art as Luca Signorelli's *Coronation of the Virgin* (1508) and El Greco's T*he Penitent Saint Peter* (c.1600). Impressionism is represented in works by Monet, Degas, Matisse and Pissarro. Acclaimed 20C works include Modigliani's *Le Garçon aux Yeux Bleux (The Boy With Blue Eyes)* and Georgia O'Keeffe's *White Trumpet Flower* (1932). An extensive collection of contemporary art features Deborah Butterfield, Bruce Conner, David Hockney and Wayne Thiebaud.

Mingei International Museum★★

1439 El Prado. ♿ 🅿 ☎ *619-239-0003. www.mingei.org.*

This museum's expansive collection holds 17,500 objects from 141 countries, with special concentrations in Asian, Mexican, African and US "art of the people." Highlights include Navajo weavings and Mexican retablos.

San Diego Museum of Man★★

Kids *1350 El Prado.* 🅿 ☎ *619-239-2001. www.museumofman.org.*

Exhibits on human evolution (including a cast of "Lucy," among the oldest protohuman skeletons yet found), anthropology and ethnology are drawn from a collection of more than 70,000 artifacts. Emphasis is placed on the cultures of Egypt and pre-Columbian Mayas and Incas. The museum occupies the **California Building**, a Spanish Colonial structure (1915) with a massive Moorish-tile dome and three-belfry, 180ft campanile that rings on the quarter-hour.

San Diego Aerospace Museum★★

Kids ⫿⫿⫿ *2001 Pan American Plaza.* ♿ 🅿 ☎ *619-234-8291. www.aerospacemuseum.org.*

The white and blue, ring-shaped, Art Moderne structure (1935) displays six dozen vintage aircraft from biplanes to space capsules, 14,000 scale models, and 10,000 aviation-related items. Next door is the **San Diego Automotive Museum**★ Kids *(2030 Pan American Plaza;* ♿ 🅿 ☎ *619-231-2886, www.sdautomuseum.org)*, with classic automobiles and motorcycles.

Downtown San Diego

Civic leaders and developers restored the Gaslamp Quarter's Victorian treasures in the 1970s and 80s, spurring further revitalization along Broadway. A waterfront redevelopment soon followed, including Seaport Village, the San Diego Convention Center and numerous luxury hotels. Across Harbor Drive from the convention center, **PETCO Park**, the new $474 million, 42,445-seat Padres baseball stadium, was completed in 2004 (📷 *tours available:* ☎ *619-795-5000; www.sandiego.padres.mlb.com).*

Gaslamp Quarter★

4th & 5th Aves. between Broadway & Harbor Dr. ☎ *619-233-5227. www.gaslamp.org.*

Sixteen blocks of restored late-19C and early-20C Victorian buildings have become San Diego's trendiest restaurant and nightlife district. Walking tours begin from a neighborhood visi-

San Diego Skyline

tor center in the 1850 saltbox **William Heath Davis House** *(410 Island Ave.).*

Broadway★

Shopping and office complexes of cutting-edge architectural distinction reign here. **Horton Plaza**★ *(bordered by Broadway & G St., 1st & 4th Aves.; ☎619-239-8180)* is a mall (1985, Jon Jerde) with twisting post-Modern passageways and a 50-color crazy-quilt of design styles. The **U.S. Grant Hotel**a *(326 Broadway; b619-232-3121)* is a stately, 11-story Italian Renaissance Revival inn (1910); its interior boasts 107 chandeliers and 150 tons of marble. **Emerald Plaza**★ *(402 W. Broadway)* is perhaps the most memorable building (1990, C.W. Kim) on the skyline, a 30-story cluster of eight hexagonal glass office towers lit at night with emerald-green neon. The newly expanded Museum of Contemporary Art San Diego Downtown *(1100 & 1001 Kettner Blvd., between Broadway and BStreet,*
858-454-3541) includes commissions by Richard Serra and RIchard Wright.

Waterfront★

One of the city's first modern harborside projects was **Seaport Village**★ *(West Harbor Dr. at Kettner Blvd.; ☎619-235-4014),* a 14-acre shopping-and-dining complex of New England- and Mediterranean-style buildings linked by cob-blestone pathways and a boardwalk. Its centerpiece is an 1890 carousel. Not far away is the huge **San Diego Convention Center** *(111 W. Harbor Dr.; ☎619-525-5000),* its open-air rooftop plaza surmounted by a giant white tent that resembles a futuristic sailing vessel.

San Diego Maritime Museum ★

Kids *1306 N. Harbor Dr. ☎619-234-9153. www.sdmaritime.com.*
Historic ships are the centerpieces of this floating museum. The **Star of India**★★, oldest iron merchant ship afloat (launched from Britain's Isle of Man in 1863), circumnavigated the globe 21 times in the late 19C. The **Berkeley** (1898), second propeller-driven ferry on the Pacific coast, was built in San Francisco. Moored alongside is the **Medea** (1904), a 140ft iron-hulled luxury steam yacht that once plied the lochs of Scotland. Also on hand are a Soviet submarine and a replica of a British Navy frigate that was used in the move Master and Commander.

Additional Sights

Coronado★

Take I-5 south to Rte. 75; cross westbound toll bridge.
This affluent enclave of residences, hotels, restaurants and boutiques is serenely sheltered on a peninsula .5mi across the bay from downtown San Diego. Its landmark structure is the **Hotel del Coronado**★★ *(1500 Orange Ave.; ☎619-435-6611, www.hoteldel. com),* California's sole surviving Victorian seaside resort (1888). Its white wood and red shingles, sweeping balconies and graceful spires rising beside Coronado's southern shore are immortalized in books and film.

Cabrillo National Monument★★

1800 Cabrillo Memorial Dr., Pt. Loma; from downtown San Diego, drive 7mi north on Harbor Dr., then left on Rosecrans St., right on Canon St. & left on Catalina Blvd. ♿P
☎619-557-5450. www.nps.gov/cabr.
Located on the crest of a sandstone ridge 400ft above the sea, this park commemorates the Spanish discovery

©Joanne DiBona/San Diego CVB

Catching a Wave

Although Malibu's Surfrider Beach claims to be the birthplace of surfing in California, every beach with predictable waves, from La Jolla north to Santa Barbara and beyond, has a loyal band of surfers. Most sit patiently just beyond the surf line, waiting for the next perfect wave, then paddle madly to catch the crest and ride to shore. The artistry and grace on display—as surfer after surfer skims the face of a breaking wave—is breathtaking.

There may be as many surf shops as fast-food outlets along San Diego County beaches, which have bigger waves in winter but bigger crowds in summer. Most surfers wear wet suits all year to ward off the chill. Watching surfers is even more popular than surfing itself; bring a light jacket in winter, plenty of drinking water in summer, and sunblock all year. Binoculars bring the action closer.

Favorite surfing beaches include Swami's, in Encinitas, named for a meditation center on the cliffs above the beach; and the entire beachfront of Oceanside. The latter town also has one of the nation's finest surfing museums: the **California Surf Museum** (223 North Coast Hwy.; ☎ 760-721-6876, www.surfmuseum.org).

of the California coast in 1542. From the foot of a **statue** of explorer Juan Rodríguez Cabrillo, visitors may watch the passage of Navy ships, planes and submarines. A short uphill walk from the **visitor center** is the **Old Point Loma Lighthouse** (1855), one of the oldest on the coast.

SeaWorld San Diego★★

Kids ⅲⅲⅲ 500 SeaWorld Dr.; take I-5 to SeaWorld Dr. Exit. ✕ & 🅿 ☎619-226-3901. www.seaworld.com.
The first (1964) of three US SeaWorlds, this Mission Bay marine park mixes education and entertainment in five live shows and 25 exhibits and aquariums. Highlight of the animal shows (25min) is the **Shamu Adventure**★, featuring a family of trained orcas (killer whales). Other shows feature dolphins, sea lions, walruses and birds. **Rocky Point Preserve**★ invites visitors to touch and feed bottle-nosed dolphins. **Wild Arctic**★ mimics an arctic research station with polar bears, walruses, seals and beluga whales. **Penguin Encounter** re-creates icy Antarctica. **Shark Encounter** offers a close-up look at these marine predators. **Manatee Rescue** is the only non-Florida venue with the endangered sea cows. The revolving **SkyTower** provides bird's-eye views of the park and San Diego skyline from a 265ft observation point. **Guided tours** (90min), offer a behind-

the-scenes look at SeaWorld's animal-rescue, training and medical facilities.

Excursions

La Jolla★★

12mi northwest of downtown San Diego via I-5 and Ardath Road. ☎619-236-1212. www.lajollabythesea.com.
An upscale, sun-kissed suburb, La Jolla (la-HOY-ya) hugs a breathtakingly beautiful shoreline. The community is noted for posh shopping; important national research enclaves lie at its fringes. Rugged coastal beauty beckons swimmers and snorkelers to cliff-fringed **La Jolla Cove**★★, downslope from Prospect Street.

Museum of Contemporary Art, San Diego★★

700 Prospect St. ✕ & ☎858-454-3541. www.mcasd.org.
San Diego's premier venue for contemporary art occupies the remodeled home of publishing baroness Ellen Browning Scripps (1916, Irving Gill). Exhibits rotate from a permanent collection of 3,000 Minimalist and Conceptual paintings, photographs, video and mixed-media pieces. A sculpture garden with native plants overlooks the Pacific.

Birch Aquarium at Scripps★★

Kids *2300 Expedition Way, off Torrey Pines Rd. south of La Jolla Village Dr.* ✕ & 🅿 ☎*858-534-3474. www.aquarium.ucsd.edu.*

The contemporary Mission-style complex, atop a bluff above the Scripps Institution of Oceanography, encompasses a modern aquarium and the largest US museum of oceanography. Marine life from the Pacific Northwest, Southern California, Mexico and tropical seas is displayed in 33 tanks housing some 3,500 fish of 280 species. Exhibits in the Hall of Oceanography cover the history and future of marine science, the physics of seawater, and the ocean's effect on climate and weather.

Salk Institute★

10010 N. Torrey Pines Rd. & 🅿 ☎*858-453-4100. www.salk.edu.*

This striking Louis Kahn structure (1960) features two identical six-story buildings of reinforced concrete, teak and steel, facing each other across a travertine courtyard bisected by a narrow channel of water. Some 400 scientists conduct research here.

Torrey Pines State Reserve★

N. Torrey Pines Rd., 2mi north of Genesee Ave., 1mi south of Carmel Valley Rd. 🅿 ☎*858-755-2063. www.torreypine.org.*

This 1,750-acre blufftop preserve was established in 1921 to preserve one of the world's rarest evergreens. Fewer than 4,000 Torrey pines (Pinus torreyana) remain from an ancient forest; they grow naturally only here and on Santa Rosa in the Channel Islands.

San Diego County Coast

North of La Jolla, scenic beaches and beach towns are strung like pearls along Route S21, the commercial artery that parallels Interstate 5. It passes through **Del Mar,** home of the renowned Del Mar Racetrack, and **Encinitas**, world-famous for its poinsettias, before reaching Carlsbad, a spa town which now is mostly visited for its big outlet center.

LEGOLAND California★

Kids *(1 LEGO Dr., off Cannon Rd. east of I-5;* ✕ & 🅿 ☎*760-918-5379, www.legoland.com).*

The first US theme park for the Danish-designed children's building blocks uses 30 million signature LEGO bricks in 5,000 models of animals, buildings and famous sights. Childhood stories are rendered along Fairy Tale Brook; life-size African beasts lurk on Safari Trek; an Adventurers ClubWalk penetrates the Pyramids, an Amazon rain forest and an arctic icescape.

San Diego Wild Animal Park★★★

Kids ⋔⋔ *15500 San Pasqual Valley Rd., Escondido, 30mi northeast of San Diego; take I-15 to Via Rancho Parkway Exit and follow signs north and east.* ✕ & 🅿 ☎*760-747-8702. www.sandiegozoo.org.*

Exotic and endangered animals find safe haven in this 2,200-acre park of rolling grasslands and botanical gardens operated by the San Diego Zoo, created as a breeding facility to ensure the survival of species.

Visitors enter through **Nairobi Village**, a replica Congo fishing village with exotic-bird aviaries. Animal shows demonstrate natural behaviors and abilities of birds of prey, North American animals and Asian elephants. There are six principal

San Diego Wild Animal Park

© Joanne DiBona/San Diego CVB

biogeographical areas: East and South African savanna, North African desert, Asian plains and waterholes, and Mongolian steppe. Roaming freely are herds of giraffes, wildebeests, gazelles, oryxes and the largest collection of southern white rhinoceroses in the US. Walking exploration is encouraged in **Heart of Africa.** Warthogs, duikers, bonteboks, elands, giraffes, cheetahs and vultures are among free-roaming denizens. Several smaller habitats feature success stories from zoo breeding programs, including Sumatran tigers, Przewalski's wild horses, okapi and pygmy chimpanzees.

The highlight of **Condor Ridge**★★ is the park's most celebrated captive breeding success, rare California condors.

San Luis Rey de Francia Mission★★

4050 Mission Ave., San Luis Rey, 40mi north of San Diego via I-5 & Rte. 76. ♿🅿 ☎*760-757-3651. www.sanluisrey.org.*

The "King of the Missions" was founded in 1798 and named for 13C crusader King Louis IX of France. It became one of the most successful outposts of Catholicism in California, with 2,800 neophytes in residence. The mission housed a Franciscan monastery in the late 19C and now serves an active parish.

A domed bell tower crowns the right front corner of the large cruciform mission church. Only 12 arches remain of the 32 that formerly graced a two-story cloister. Within the mission is a rare collection of old Spanish **vestments**.

ANZA-BORREGO DESERT★★

MICHELIN MAP 493 C, D 11
PACIFIC STANDARD TIME
TOURIST INFORMATION B760-767-4205

Inland San Diego County is a jumble of mountains and valleys that climax at Anza-Borrego Desert State Park, the largest state park in the western US. West of the mountains are the charming hamlet of Julian and the Palomar Observatory atop 6,126ft Palomar Mountain. East of the state park is the agriculturally rich Imperial Valley, with the Salton Sea at its north end.

- ▌ **Information:** ☎619-445-4180, www.visitsandiegoeast.com
- ▶ **Orient Yourself:** This part of San Diego County holds the cool mountain heights around Julian, and the Mojave Desert fringes on the east side of the mountains.

Sights

Anza-Borrego Desert State Park★★

80mi northeast of San Diego via Rte. 78. △♿ ☎*760-767-5311. www.park. ca.gov.*

Named for Juan Bautista de Anza, the Spanish military explorer who traversed the region in 1774, and for endemic *borregos*, or bighorn sheep, this 939sq-mi preserve contains mountains, badlands, hidden palm groves and pioneer trails. Check at the **visitor center** (200 Palm Canyon Dr., Borrego Springs; ♿🅿 ☎760-767-4205) for road conditions in areas

accessible only by four-wheel-drive vehicle. A Wildflower Hotline (☎760-767-4684) estimates bloom dates.

The **Erosion Road Auto Tour**, running east along Route S22 from Borrego Springs, traverses rolling plains below the Santa Rosa Mountains. Markers describe geologic forces that shaped the landscape. At Mile 29.3, a sandy side road leads 4mi to Font's Point and **views**★★ over the Borrego Badlands. Popular hiking trails include the 3mi **Borrego Palm Canyon Trail** (trailhead at campground 2mi north of visitor center), a moderately difficult canyon trail that ascends an alluvial fan to a hidden fan-

© DesertUSA.com

Wildflowers, Anza-Borrego Desert State Park

palm oasis; and the .5mi **Narrows Earth Loop Trail** *(trailhead 12.2mi south of Borrego Springs on Rte. S3, then 4.7mi east on Rte. 78)*, which offers an extended look at canyon geology.

Excursions

Julian★
57mi northeast of San Diego via I-8 & Rte. 79. 760-765-1857. www.julianca.com.
At 4,200ft, this village is a popular weekend getaway spot known for apples, peaches, pears and 19C-style storefronts along Main Street. Eight miles northwest is the **Santa Ysabel Asistencia Mission** *(Rtes. 79 & 78; b760-765-0810)*, established in 1818 as an outpost of the San Diego de Alcalá Mission.

Palomar Observatory
Kids P *Rte. S6, 55mi northeast of San Diego via I-15 & Rte. 76. ☎760-742-2111. www.astro.caltech.edu/palomar.*
Located near the peak of 6,126ft Palomar Mountain, this California Institute of Technology observatory boasts the celebrated **Hale Telescope**★, with its 200in Pyrex lens, has a range surpassing 1 billion light years.

Imperial Valley★
117mi east of San Diego via I-8, Rte. 111 (north) & Rte. 78 (east).
Fields of lettuce, melons, tomatoes, and other vegetables cluster around El Centro, main town of this sub-sea-level valley. Its east side is part of the **Imperial Sand Dunes Recreation Area** *(Rte. 78; ☎760-344-3919)*, whose dunes crest up to 300ft. Eighty percent of these hills, once known as the Algodones Dunes, are open to off-road vehicles (ORVs), but the Imperial Sand Dunes National Natural Landmark remains a protected area. Osborne Overlook, 3mi east of Gecko Rd. off Rte. 78, offers the best viewpoint.

Salton Sea
168mi east of San Diego via I-8 & Rte. 86.
This sea was formed when Colorado River irrigation canals went haywire and flooded an ancient lake bed in 1905, creating an inland sea 35mi long by 15mi wide but just 20ft deep. The **Salton Sea National Wildlife Refuge** *(Rte. 86; ☎760-348-5278)* protects migratory bird habitat on the marshy southern shore. The **Salton Sea State Recreation Area** *(Rte. 111)* and other north-shore areas offer swimming beaches.

SAN FRANCISCO AREA

From the redwood forests to the towering cliffs of Big Sur, Northern California possesses machless natural beauty. The cosmopolitan city of San Francisco and its surrounding Bay Area form the hub of a region that embraces the Wine Country of the Napa and Sonoma Valleys, the charming and historic Monterey Peninsula, the remote coves and beaches of the rocky Pacific coast, historical mission settlements and the deep forest solitude of the Redwood Empire. *For in-depth coverage, see the Michelin Green Guide San Francisco.*

The rugged mountains that run the length of California's northern coast once formed part of the Pacific Ocean floor. Some 25 million years ago, the tectonic collision of the Pacific and North American plates formed the Coast Ranges. The San Andreas Fault, running parallel to this continental collision zone, is the largest of many earthquake faults that periodically shake the region.

Northern California's natural resources supported a dense native population. Spanish soldiers, building mission settlements in the 18C, decimated it trying to colonize the land. The mission society ended with Mexican secularization of the missions in 1834. After the US seized California in 1846, and especially with the gold rush of 1849, immigrants flooded into the state, shifting economic and political power from the Spanish capital of Monterey to the San Francisco Bay Area. Development of the North Coast accelerated as redwood forests were harvested for timber to build San Francisco.

Golden Gate Bridge

Rick Dole/©MICHELIN

SAN FRANCISCO★★★

MAP PP 372-373
PACIFIC STANDARD TIME
POPULATION 740,000

Founded as Mission Dolores (by priests) and the Presidio (by soldiers) in 1776, San Francisco grew from the pueblo of Yerba Buena. In 1835, English sailor William Richardson, married to the daughter of the Presidio comandante, set up a tent where Grant Avenue now runs. Yerba Buena grew modestly on trade, changing its name to San Francisco after the US claimed California in 1846.

- **Information:** ☎415-391-2000, www.onlyinsanfrancisco.com.
- ▶ **Orient Yourself:** The farther west you go toward the Pacific, the more likely you'll encounter the city's famous fog.
- **Don't Miss:** Golden Gate Bridge; SF Museum of Modern Art.
- **Organizing Your Time:** Allow a week to see the sights of the city. Visit Golden Gate Bridge in the afternoon, when it is less likely to be fogged in, and Chinatown in the early evening, when it is at its most dynamic.
- **Especially for Kids:** Exploratorium; Cable Car Museum

A Bit of History

The discovery of Sierra gold in 1848 put San Francisco in the fast lane toward the future. The village exploded into a boomtown serving 90,000 transients. New buildings rose daily (and burned with alarming frequency). Another burst of fortune came with the discovery in 1859 of a vein of Nevada silver known as the Comstock Lode. Its investors' profits flooded San Francisco with fabulous wealth. Ostentatious and high-living new millionaires funded a wide range of civic improvements and construction—factories, offices, theaters, wharves, hotels, ferries and the famous cable cars. The city's famous liberal openness derives from those early days of progressivism.

With a population of nearly 400,000 at the turn of the 19C, San Francisco was the largest American city west of the Mississippi River. An earthquake and fire in 1906 destroyed the city center, leaving 250,000 people homeless and 674 dead or missing. The plucky city reconstructed with phenomenal speed, riding its progressive momentum through the first half of the 20C with epic civil-engineering projects that included two of the largest bridges in the world.

San Francisco—called simply "the City" by almost everyone in Northern Califor-nia—now vies with Los Angeles as the premier banking and cultural center of the West Coast. By the 1970s, tourism had become the city's biggest business, as it remains today.

Sights

Union Square
Roughly bounded by Sutter, Taylor, Kearny & O'Farrell Sts.

San Francisco's prestigious urban shopping district faces 2.6-acre **Union Square Park**★ with Saks Fifth Avenue, Macy's and Nordstrom. **Neiman-Marcus** has a **rotunda**★ topped by an art-glass dome. The **Westin St. Francis Hotel**★★ *(335 Powell St.; ☎415-397-7000),* west of the square, is a Renaissance and Baroque Revival landmark finished in 1904 and rebuilt after 1906. An active theater district fans out to the west, embracing the **Geary Theater**★ *(415 Geary St.; ☎415-749-2228, act-sf.org),* home of the American Conservatory Theater, and the **Curran Theatre**★ *(445 Geary St.; ☎415-551-2000, www.shnsf.com).*

Financial District★★
Bounded by Market, Kearny & Jackson Sts. and The Embarcadero.

The city's banking, commodities-trading and corporate-business center is

Address Book San Francisco Area

♿*For price ranges, see the Legend on the cover flap.*

WHERE TO STAY IN THE SAN FRANCISCO AREA

$$$$$ Campton Place Hotel – *340 Stockton St., San Francisco, CA.* ✕♿ ☎415-781-5555 or 866-969-1825. *www. camptonplace.com. 110 rooms.* An intimate hotel once popular with the white-gloved "carriage trade" set, the Campton Place is the epitome of fine service. Asian-inspired decor squares off with the French-style **Campton Place Restaurant** ($$$$) to provide a rarefied experience in a discreet location just off Union Square.

$$$$$ Meadowood – *900 Meadowood Ln., St. Helena, CA.* ✕♿🅿️🛝 🆂🅿🅰 ☎707-963-3646 or 800-458-8080. *www. meadowood.com. 99 rooms.* Words don't do justice to this world-class resort just off Napa's Silverado Trail. The Meadowood offers exquisite grounds and rustic cottages that dot a cool wooded grove. Service is top-flight. The resort offers golf, tennis, croquet and the **Restaurant at Meadowood** ($$$$), offering regional cuisine.

$$$$$ Post Ranch Inn – *Hwy 1, Big Sur, CA.* ✕♿🅿️🛝 🆂🅿🅰 ☎831-667-2200 or 800-527-2200. *www.postranchinn.com. 30 rooms.* Views of the Pacific Ocean at Pfeiffer Point extend from the inn's steel-roofed redwood cottages. Guests may recline under skylights on the denim bedspreads in their minimalist rooms, or walk the 98-acre ranch through oak and madrone forest. At night, there are stargazing classes or dips in the warm-water basking pool.

$$$$ The Claremont – *41 Tunnel Rd., Berkeley, CA.* ✕♿🅿️🛝 🆂🅿🅰 ☎510-843-3000 or 800-551-7266. *www.claremontresort.com. 279 rooms.* Sprawling across the Berkeley-Oakland hills a mere 30min drive from downtown San Francisco, the blazing white, castle-like Claremont offers activities for all. There's a newly expanded spa and fitness center, tennis club, pools and kids' camp. Room décor, especially in the new wing, reflects a casual West Coast elegance.

$$$$ The Fairmont San Francisco – *950 Mason St., San Francisco, CA.* ✕♿🅿️ 🆂🅿🅰 ☎415-772-5000 or 800-257-7544. *www.fairmont.com. 591 rooms.* This famous hotel atop NobHill survived the 1906 earthquake and saw the 1945 creation of the United Nations. Handsomely appointed rooms are in the original building and a 1961 tower with extensive views across the city. An $85 million renovation was completed in 2001. The hotel has four restaurants.

$$$$ Inn Above Tide – *30 El Portal, Sausalito, CA.* ♿🅿️ ☎415-332-9535 or 800-893-8433. *www.innabovetide.com. 30 rooms.* Guest rooms at this inn, built upon the water, boast picture windows that frame spectacular views (binoculars provided). Decorated in a seaside palette of soft blues and greens, rooms feature waterside decks; many have fireplaces. Rates include room-service continental breakfast and sunset wine-and-cheese reception.

$$$$ Westin St. Francis – *335 Powell St., San Francisco, CA.* ✕♿🅿️🛝 ☎415-397-7000 or 800-937-8461. *www.westin. com. 1,195 rooms.* The most visible hotel in the city from its location facing Union Square, Westin's flagship hostelry is a Renaissance- and Baroque-revival structure built in 1904. A historic charm pervades rooms in this main building; more contemporary rooms with city views occupy a 32-story tower built in 1972. High tea is served daily in **The Compass Rose**.

$$$ Hotel Monaco – *501 Geary St., San Francisco, CA.* ✕♿🅿️ ☎415-292-0100 or 866-622-5284. *www.monaco-sf.com. 201 rooms.* This Theater District boutique hotel, a 1910 Beaux-Arts classic, offers the warmth and comfort of home. Baroque-plaster fireplaces and sumptuous striped armchairs invite lobby conversation; Provençal fabrics drape over the beds in guest rooms. Downstairs, the stunning **Grand Café** ($$$) offers a French bistro-style lunch and dinner.

WHERE TO EAT IN THE SAN FRANCISCO AREA

$$$$ Chez Panisse – *1517 Shattuck Ave., Berkeley.* ☎510-548-5525. *www.chezpanisse.com. Closed Sun.*

California. California cuisine was born here under the watchful eye of culinary doyenne Alice Waters. Organic greens and heirloom vegetables pair with free-range poultry and carefully selected meats to create memorable prix-fixe meals that change nightly. Make reservations a month in advance.

$$$$ Gary Danko – *800 North Point St., San Francisco.* ☎*415-749-2060.* *www. garydanko.com.* **Continental.** Elegant but understated décor allows chef-owner Danko's culinary creations to take center stage at his restaurant near Fisherman's Wharf. Diners choose from among five-course tasting menus; one such offered Dungeness crabcake with bell-pepper and wasabi sauces, seared filet of beef with Stilton cheese and potato gratin, and a passion fruit-and-mango Napoleon.

$$$$ Jardinière – *300 Grove St., San Francisco.* b*415-861-5555.* *www. jardiniere.com. Dinner only.* **California French.** Bubbles sparkle on the domed ceiling of the Champagne Rotunda in this elegant two-story restaurant, favored for pre- or post-theater dining. Chef-owner Traci Des Jardins may start diners with duck confit salad or a chanterelle-and-asparagus tart, then present herb-crusted loin of lambwith potato gnocchi, followed by blueberry cake with lemon sabayon.

$$$ Lark Creek Inn – *234 Magnolia Ave., Larkspur.* ☎*415-924-7766.* *www. larkcreek.com.* **American.** This Marin County restaurant occupies a spacious Victorian house surrounded by towering redwoods. Deft use of seasonal fresh produce yields elegant simplicity in traditional dishes like Caesar salad and Yankee pot roast, as well as seared skate wing and chestnut ravioli. Sunday brunch may be served on the patio.

$$$ Mustard's Grill – *7399 St. Helena Hwy., Yountville.* ☎*707-944-2424.* *www. mustardsgrill.com.* **American.** A long-standing Napa Valley favorite, this casual ranch-style restaurant draws winemakers and industry VIPs for its fresh cuisine and top-notch wine list. The menu ranges across American regional dishes with nods to Continental and Asian, from seared ahi tuna to barbecued baby back ribs. Some come just for the sublimely thin and crispy onion rings served with house-made ketchup.

$$$ Nepenthe – *Hwy. 1, Big Sur.* ☎*831-667-2345.* *www.nepenthebigsur. com.* **American.** Greek mythology describes nepenthe as a potion used to obliterate pain and sorrow. And indeed, the spectacular views from Nepenthe's terraces, 800ft above the Pacific and 31mi south of Carmel, inspire pure joy. Built of redwood and adobe in 1949, the restaurant offers a basic menu of chicken, steaks and seafood. Regulars love the Ambrosiaburger, ground steak on a French roll.

$$ Café de la Presse – *352 Grant Ave., San Francisco.* ☎*415-398-2680.* *www. cafedelapresse.com.* **French.** Casual brasserie meals are served at this café and international newsstand near Chinatown. Menus du jour may feature French onion soup, crab-and-mushroom cassoulet and tournedos au grill. The espresso bar, with its selection of pastries, is popular among the locals.

$$ Fior d'Italia – *601 Union St., San Francisco.* ☎*415-986-1886.* *www.fior. com.* **Northern Italian.** America's oldest Italian restaurant, this institution opened in 1886 and has faced upon Washington Square since 1954. Historical photos line the walls; the Tony Bennett Room honors San Francisco's favorite crooner. Cuisine remains tradition-bound: calamari, gnocchi, osso buco and Caesar salad win raves.

$$ The Slanted Door – *584 Valencia St., San Francisco.* ☎*415-861-8032.* *www. slanteddoor.com* **Asian.** This nondescript but trendy Mission District cafe offers Vietnamese-inspired food in a bustling atmosphere. Crispy imperial rolls, green papaya salad with grapefruit jicama and grilled Muscovy duck with plum sauce are among the stars.

$ Dottie's True Blue Café – *522 Jones St., San Francisco.* ☎*415-885-2767. Breakfast and lunch only. Closed Tue.* **American.** A kitschy nook, Dottie's is an edge-of-the-Tenderloin oasis. Its menu offers whole-wheat and raspberry-cornmeal pancakes, eggs with black-bean cakes and smoked chicken-apple sausage.

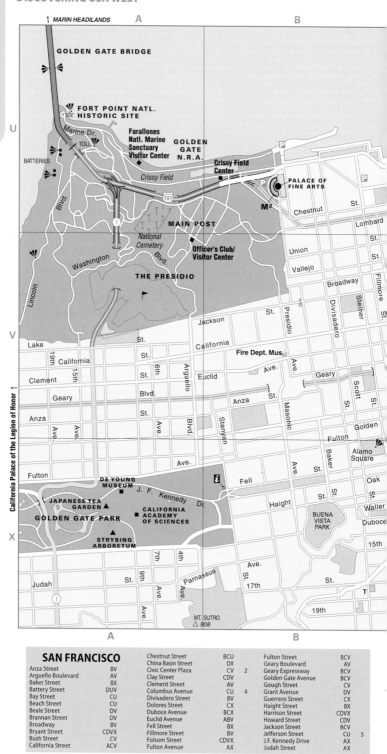

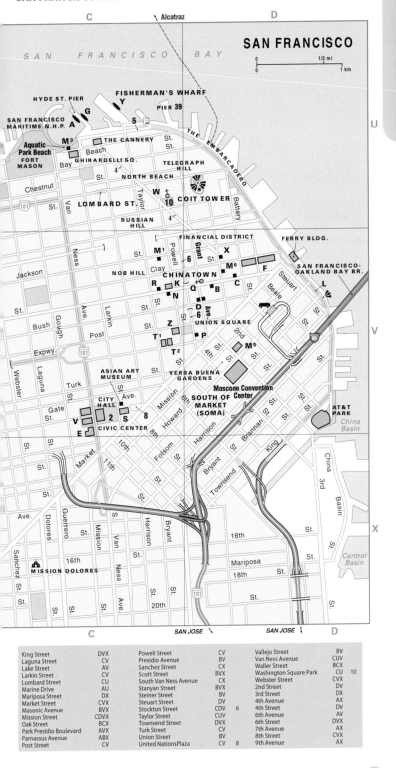

SAN FRANCISCO								
Alcatraz	CU		Eureka	CU	G	Nob Hill	CV	
Aquatic Park Beach	CU		Exploratorium	BU	M2	North Beach	CU	
Asian Art Museum	CV		Fairmont Hotel	CV	K	Old St. Mary's Cathedral	DV	Q
Balclutha	CU	A	Ferry Building	DV		Pacific-Union Club	CV	R
Bank of California	DV	C	Financial District	DV		Palace of Fine Arts	BU	
Bay Bridge	DV		Fisherman's Wharf	CDU		Performing Arts Center	CV	V
Cable Car Museum	CV	M1	Fort Point	AU		Pier 39	CU	
Cal. Academy of Sciences	AX		Geary Theater	CV	T2	Presidio The	AV	
555 California Street	DV	B	Ghirardelli Square	CU		Presidio Museum	BU	M4
Cannery The	CU		Golden Gate Bridge	AU		Russian Hill	CU	
Chinatown	CDV		Golden Gate Park	AX		San Francisco Public Library	CV	S
Chinatown Gate	DV	D	Herb Caen Way	DV	L	SS Peter and Paul Church	CU	W
City Hall	CV		Hyde Street Pier	CU		Strybing Arboretum	AX	
Civic Center	CV		Japanese Tea Garden	AX		Telegraph Hill	CDU	
Coit Tower	DU		Legion of Honor	AV		Transamerica Pyramid	DV	X
Curran Theater	CV	T1	Main Post	ABU		Union Square	CDV	
Davies Symphony Hall	CV	E	Mission Dolores	CX		USS Pampanito	CU	Y
De Young Museum	AX		Moscone Convention Center	DV		Visitor Center	AU	
Embarcadero The	DU		National Maritime Museum	CU	M3	Wells Fargo History Museum	DV	M6
Embarcadero Center	DV	F	Museum of Modern Art	DV	M5	Westin St. Francis Hotel	CV	Z
			Neiman-Marcus	DV	P	Yerba Buena Garden	DV	

concentrated in a triangular district around California and Montgomery Streets. The building at **555 California St.** is the former headquarters of Bank of America, which financed much of the development of San Francisco; a grand **view**★★★ extends from its 52nd-floor Carnelian Room restaurant (☎415-433-7500). Wells Fargo Bank recalls its Old West roots at the **Wells Fargo History Museum**★ Kids (420 Montgomery St.; ☎415-396-2619, www.wellsfargohistory. com). The city's grandest bank edifice is the Neoclassical **Bank of California**★★ (400 California St.).

San Francisco's tallest building, the 48-story **Transamerica Pyramid**★★ (600 Montgomery St., www.thepyramidcenter. com), rises 853ft from street level to the tip of its 212ft hollow lantern; built in 1972, the slender pyramid is a symbol of the city. **Embarcadero Center**★ (bounded by Sacramento, Battery & Clay Sts. & the Embarcadero, www.embarca derocenter.com), a series of four slablike office towers (1967-72), incorporates a three-level, open-air shopping center. Its **SkyDeck**★★ (One Embarcadero Center; ☎415-772-0555) offers views of the city and bay from the 41st floor.

Chinatown★★★

Bounded by Montgomery, California & Powell Sts. and Broadway. www.san franciscochinatown.com.

A teeming fusion of Cantonese market town and Main Street USA, Chinatown spreads along the lower slope of NobHill. With 30,000 residents in its 24-block core, it is one of the most densely populated neighborhoods in North America. The main thoroughfare,

Grant Avenue★★, starts with a flourish at **Chinatown Gate** on Bush Street and runs eight blocks north to Broadway. Exotic ambience is provided by distinctive architectural chinoiserie: painted balconies, curved-tile rooflines, and red, green and yellow color schemes. Shops selling souvenirs, jewelry, artwork, furniture, cameras and electronics share the street with tourist restaurants, hardware stores, banks, poultry and fish markets, herbalists' shops, tea stores and cafes that cater to local residents.

Old St. Mary's Cathedral★ (660 California St. at Grant Ave.; ☎415-288-3800, www.oldsaintmarys.org), dedicated in 1854, was built of brick and iron shipped from New England, laid upon a foundation of granite quarried in China.

Portsmouth Square★ (between Clay & Washington Sts., one-half block below Grant Ave.), the original plaza of Yerba Buena, is now a social gathering point for Chinatown residents.

A less commercialized neighborhood of markets surrounds **Stockton Street**★, a block uphill from Grant, and a maze of narrow alleys between. **Waverly Place**★ is noted for its temples and brilliantly decorated balconies. The 1852 **Tin How Temple** (125 Waverly Pl., 4th floor; b415-421-3628) is Chinatown's oldest.

The story of the Chinese experience in the American West is depicted at the new museum of the **Chinese Historical Society of America Museum** (965 Clay St.; ☎415-391-1188, www.chsa.org). Located in a former YWCA building with pagoda-like towers, designed by Julia Morgan (1932), it has six galleries and a learning center.

North Beach★★

Columbus Ave. and adjacent streets from Pacific Ave. to Bay St. sfnorthbeach.org.

The erstwhile heart of the Italian community, North Beach inspires dawdling at coffeehouses by day and restaurants by night. The Beat Generation—"beatniks"—flocked here in the 1950s seeking relaxed Mediterranean attitude along with the cheap food and drink of family-run trattorias, bars and cafes. A traditional Latin flavor persists at **Washington Square Park★**, backed by the twin spires of **SS Peter and Paul Church★** *(666 Filbert St.; ☎415-421-0809)*, known as the Italian Cathedral.

On the east side of North Beach, 274ft **Telegraph Hill★** is capped by fluted-concrete **Coit Tower★★★** 𝗞𝗶𝗱𝘀 *(☎415-362-0808)*, which rises an additional 212ft to an observation deck offering fine city **views★★**. Built in 1934 during the Great Depression, the tower has a lobby decorated with **murals★★** painted by 26 local artists as part of the Public Works of Art Project. Bluntly critical of social and political conditions, the murals sparked heated controversy.

Russian Hill★

Roughly bounded by Columbus Ave., Bay & Polk Sts., Broadway & Mason St.

From Hyde Street, visitors gaze north to extensive **views★★★** down Hyde Street Hill. Turning east, **Lombard Street★★★** undulates through flower gardens to Leavenworth Street; the one-block stretch is nicknamed "The Crookedest Street in the World." The eight switchbacks were built in 1922, taming the hillside's gradient of 27 percent to a manageable 16 percent.

NobHill★★

Roughly bounded by Broadway and Stockton, Bush & Polk Sts.

NobHill achieved its reputation as an abode of the rich in the late 1860s. Construction of a cable-car line in 1873 made the hilltop more accessible, and by the 1880s the residents included railroad potentates and silver barons. With the exception of James Flood's mansion, now the exclusive **Pacific-Union Club★** *(1000 California St.)*, all original mansions were destroyed in the 1906 fire.

The opulent **Fairmont Hotel★★** *(950 California St.; ☎ 415-772-5000, www.fairmont.com)* is famed for **views★★★** from its Crown Room restaurant. The **InterContinental Mark Hopkins** *(999 California St.; ☎415-392-3434, www.intercontinental.com)* offers **views★★★** from its swank bar, the **Top of the Mark**.

The most dynamic site on NobHill is the **Cable Car Museum★★** 𝗞𝗶𝗱𝘀 *(1201 Mason St.; ☎415-474-1887, www.cablecarmuseum.org)*, which doubles as the powerhouse for the clanging cars of San Francisco's steep hills, gripping a moving cable that loops continuously through a slot in the city streets. From the balcony of the museum, visitors may gaze upon the humming engines and whirling sheaves that drive the cable.

Civic Center★

Bounded by Market St., Van Ness & Golden Gate Aves.

San Francisco's governmental center comprises one of the nation's finest groupings of Beaux-Arts-style buildings. The design was inspired by the 1905 Burnham Plan, prepared by Chicago architect Daniel Burnham at the behest of city leaders who subscribed to the City Beautiful Movement. Buildings are arranged along a central axis running three blocks west from Market and Leavenworth Streets to City Hall. At

Chinatown Temples

Brigitta L. House/MICHELIN

the eastern head of this pedestrian mall, **United Nations Plaza**★ commemorates the founding of the UN at Civic Center in 1945. After passing the **San Francisco Public Library**★ *(100 Larkin St.; ☎415-557-4400, sfpl.lib.ca.us)*, the axis opens up to the formal gardens and reflecting pool of **Civic Center Plaza**, foreground for the imposing dome of **City Hall**★★ *(facing Polk St.).* Rising to 307ft above a massive, four-story colonnaded building, the black and gold dome is 13ft taller than that of the US Capitol building in Washington DC. Inside, a grand staircase ascends to a 181ft open rotunda.

On the west side of City Hall, the **San Francisco War Memorial and Performing Arts Center**★★ *(Van Ness Ave. between McAllister & Grove Sts.; ☎415-552-8338, sfwmpac.org)* comprises the War Memorial Opera House and the Veterans Building, site of a theater and art gallery. Immediately south is **Davies Symphony Hall** *(Grove St. & Van Ness Ave., www.sfsymphony.org)*, home of the renowned San Francisco Symphony.East of city hall, San Francisco's new **Asian Art Museum**★★★ *(200 Larkin St.; ☎415-581-3500, www.asianart.org)* opened in early 2003. French architect Gae Aulenti converted the former Main Library, a 1917 Beaux-Arts building. The museum features the finest collection of Asian art in the US: The collection includes Chinese ceramics and bronzes, Japanese screens and scroll paintings, Korean stoneware and Indian sacred sculptures and spans 6,000 years of history.

Mission Dolores★

16th & Dolores Sts. ☎415-621-8203. www.missiondolores.org.

Officially named Mission San Francisco de Asis, the city's oldest extant structure dates from 1791. The 4ft-thick adobe walls of the sturdy **chapel**★★ are covered with stucco and roofed by a beamed ceiling painted with Ohlone Indian designs. The marked graves of Catholic pioneers adorn the chapel and **cemetery**★, where thousands of Ohlone neophytes lie in unmarked plots.

Yerba Buena Gardens★★

Bounded by Mission, Howard, 3rd & 4th Sts.

Uniting an outdoor garden with cinemas, galleries, playgrounds, museums and the **Moscone Convention Center,** Yerba Buena Gardens is the city's most ambitious recent entertainment and cultural complex. At the 5.5-acre **Esplanade**, visitors relax on grassy terraces and visit a memorial to Dr. Martin Luther King Jr., curtained by an exhilarating waterfall. Adjacent are the theaters, gallery and forum of the **Yerba Buena Center for the Arts**★ *(3rd & Mission Sts.; ☎415-978-2787, www.ybca.org)*, and the new **Rooftop at Yerba Buena Gardens**★★ 🄺🄸🄳🅂 *(750 Folsom St.; ☎415-777-3727, www.yerbabuenagardens.com)*, a children's complex with a high-tech studio-theater and year-round ice-skating rink. The four-story **Metréon** 🄺🄸🄳🅂 *(4th & Mission Sts.; ☎415-369-6000)* houses 15 cinemas and a 600-seat IMAX theater.

San Francisco Museum of Modern Art★★

151 3rd St. ☎415-357-4000. www.sfmoma.org.

This premier showcase for contemporary art occupies an innovative building (1995, Mario Botta) opposite Yerba Buena Gardens. The **atrium**★★ resembles an urban piazza, sheathed in bright woods and polished granite. A grand staircase rises through the building's heart, culminating in a narrow steel **catwalk**★ five stories above the rotunda floor. Permanent holdings include 1,200 paintings, 500 sculptures, 9,000 photographs and 3,000 works on paper, representing major artists and schools of Europe and the Americas.

The Embarcadero★

Along San Francisco Bay from China Basin to Fisherman's Wharf.

The warehouse of the waterfront have either been torn down or converted into offices, shops and restaurants.

Lumbering across the bay are the towers, two-tiered roadway and twin suspension spans of the western part of **San Francisco-Oakland Bay Bridge**★★. Joining the eastern cantilever section at Yerba Buena Island, the 5.2mi bridge is one of the world's longest high-level steel bridges. When opened in 1936, it ended the bay ferries and their terminus, the 1898 **Ferry Building**★★ *(foot of Market St.).* The 253ft clock tower was the city's only high-rise undamaged by the 1906 quake; it has been converted to a shopping, dining and office complex.

Fisherman's Wharf★★★

[Kids] *North of Bay St. between The Embarcadero & Van Ness Ave. www.fishermanswharf.org.*
The Wharf draws throngs to its colorful docks, carnival amusements and multitudinous seafood eateries. Although fishermen still bring in their catch during early-morning hours, tourism now dominates. Most popular of the diversions is **Pier 39**★ [Kids], a marketplace of shops, restaurants, aquarium and theater; it is famed for the pod of California sea lions that slumber off its west side.
Pier 45 visitors may tour the World War II submarine **USS Pampanito**★★ [Kids] *(*☎*415-447-5000),* one of several ships at the **San Francisco Maritime National Historic Park** *(Beach St. at Polk St.;* ☎*415-447-5000, www.nps.gov/safr).* Other ships moored at the **Hyde Street Pier**★★ [Kids], include the three-masted, steel-hulled square-rigger, **Balclutha**★★, and the 1890 passenger and car ferry, **Eureka**★.
Terminus for **bay cruises**★ *(Pier 39, b415-705-5555, www.blueandgoldfleet.com)* and ferry excursions to Marin County *(Pier 39 1/2),* Alcatraz and Angel Island, Fisherman's Wharf lures shoppers in search of souvenirs. T-shirts and knick-knacks dominate the shops of **Jefferson Street,** while a more eclectic array fills the refurbished warehouses at **The Cannery at Del Monte Square**★★ *(2801 Leavenworth St.)* and the old chocolate factory of **Ghirardelli Square**★ [Kids] *(Larkin, Beach, Polk & North Point Sts.).*

Alcatraz★★★

[Kids] |||| *Ferry departs from Pier 33.* ☎*415-705-5555. www.blueandgoldfleet.com.*
Known as "The Rock," this barren 12-acre island began as an army fortress and prison in 1850. It became famous as a maximum-security penitentiary for "desperate and irredeemable criminals" after being transferred to the US Department of Justice in 1933. Among its notorious inmates were Al Capone, George "Machine Gun" Kelly and Robert Stroud, the "Birdman of Alcatraz." Worsening conditions, and the possible success of a 1962 escape attempt, prompted the government to close the prison. Today the island is open to tourists who watch an **orientation video** and take a self-guided audio tour of the bleak **cellhouse**★★, the recreation yard, the cafeteria and control center.

Palace of Fine Arts★★

Baker & Beach Sts.
The sole remaining structure from the celebrated Panama-Pacific International Exposition of 1915, the Palace was designed by Bernard Maybeck as a fanciful Roman ruin. The wood-and-plaster building was spared demolition by admiring citizens. Rebuilt in concrete,

©John Anderson/MICHELIN

Fisherman's Wharf

the Palace now houses the **Exploratorium**★★ [Kids] *(3601 Lyon St.; b415-397-5673, www.exploratorium.edu),* science museum with exhibits in physics, electricity, life sciences, thermodynamics, weather and other subjects.

The Presidio★★

West of Lyon St. & south of the Golden Gate Bridge. ☎415-561-4323. www.nps.gov/prsf.

This 1,480-acre former military reservation is now part of the Golden Gate National Recreation Area. Established in 1776, it remained an army base through most of the US eras, though an angry shot was never fired. A brick barracks on the historic **Main Post**★★ has been converted to a **Visitor Center** *(Montgomery St.).* A bastion built in 1861 to guard the Golden Gate from Confederate attack during the Civil War, **Fort Point National Historic Site**★ *(end of Marine Dr.; ☎ 415-556-1693, www.nps.gov/fopo)* sits beneath the Golden Gate Bridge, work on which keeps the fort closed Monday-Thursday.

Golden Gate Bridge★★★

[Kids] *US-101 north of the Presidio. ☎415-921-5858. www.goldengatebridge.org.*

As much a symbol of the US to the Pacific Rim as the Statue of Liberty is across the Atlantic, this graceful Art Deco suspension bridge spans the channel via twin 746ft towers and an intricate tracery of cables that support a 1.6mi roadway. Despite treacherous tidal surges, strong winds, bone-chilling fogs and the deaths of 10 workers in a scaffolding collapse the bridge opened in 1937 to great fanfare. Some 130,000 vehicles cross it daily. Astounding **views**★★ of the city, the Marin Headlands and the vertiginous 220ft drop to the surface of San Francisco Bay are reserved for pedestrians and bicyclists.

Legion of Honor★★

Legion of Honor Dr. & El Camino del Mar, Lincoln Park. ☎ 415-750-3600. www.thinker.org.

Perched on a hillside overlooking the west side of the Golden Gate, this stately edifice (1924) is a replica of Paris' Palais de la Légion d'Honneur. A glass pyramid was added to the outdoor Court of Honor in the 1990s, serving as a skylight for underground galleries while paying homage to I.M. Pei's larger pyramid at the Louvre in Paris. The Legion's permanent holdings include Medieval stained glass, carvings, panels and tapestries, Rodin sculptures, and paintings from the early Italian Renaissance through the French Impressionist period.

Golden Gate Park★★★

Stanyan St. to Ocean Beach, between Fulton St. & Lincoln Way. ☎415-831-2700. www.sfgov.org.

Spreading across 1,017 acres of meadows and gardens, the largest cultivated urban park in the US stretches 3mi from Haight-Ashbury to the Pacific. One-half-mile wide, it is large enough to accommodate 27mi of footpaths and 7.5mi of horse trails—linking the Pacific with an enchantingly natural, yet entirely artificial, scenery of lakes and woods.

Strybing Arboretum★★ *(Martin Luther King Jr. Dr.;☎415-661-1316, www.sfbotanicalgarden.org)* covers 70 acres of rolling terrain with 6,000 species of plants from all over the world, arranged according to region of origin. The **Japanese Tea Garden**★★ [Kids] *(west of Music Concourse; ☎415-752-4227)* harbors a delightful maze of winding paths, ornamental ponds swarming with koi, bonsai, stone lanterns, a pagoda and a Zen rock garden. Near the center of the garden is a 10.5ft-tall Buddha image; cast in Japan in 1790, it is the largest bronze statue of the spiritual figure outside Asia.

De Young Museum★★

Music Concourse. ☎415-750-3600. www.thinker.org/deyoung.

Herzog & de Meuron, Swiss architects whose designs include London's new Tate Gallery, designed this new (2005) three-story structure of recycled redwood, eucalyptus and copper. The De Young is noted for its **American Collection**, including works by Bierstadt, Eakins, Sargent, Homer, Diebenkorn, O'Keeffe, Hopper and Wood. Other collections include African and Oceanic art, and pre-Columbian American art.

Practical Information

GETTING THERE

The Bay Area has three major airports: **San Francisco International Airport (SFO)** (☎650-821-8211; www.flysfo.com), 11mi south of downtown; Oakland International Airport (OAK) (☎510-577-4000; www.oaklandairport.com), 22mi southeast of downtown San Francisco; and **San Jose International Airport** (SJC) (408-501-7600; www.sjc.org), 42mi south of San Francisco. From SFO and Oakland, taxi to downtown about $45.

Amtrak train: 5885 Land Regan St. (☎800-872-7245; www.amtrak.com). **Greyhound bus:** 101 7th St. (☎800-231-2222; www.greyhound.com).

GETTING AROUND

Route and fare information on all Bay Area transportation systems by calling Bay Area Traveler Information (☎415-817-1717; transit.511.org). Most public transportation in San Francisco is operated by the San Francisco Muncipal Railway **(Muni).** Lines operate daily 5:30am–12:30am; a limited number of routes operate 24hrs/day. Fare for buses and streetcars is $1.10; transfers are free, exact fare required. **Cable cars** operate daily 6am–12:30am; fare $2. Purchase tickets on-board or at the Visitor Information Center (below). Muni Passports are good for one ($6), three ($10) or seven ($15) days. **BART** (Bay Area Rapid Transit), the region's expansive light-rail system, is convenient for trips to Berkeley and Oakland (☎415-989-2278; www.bart.gov) and to the San Francisco and Oakland airports. **Taxi:** National (☎415-333-3333), Yellow Cab(☎415-333-3333).

ACCOMMODATIONS

San Francisco Lodging Guide (www.onlyinsanfrancisco.org) from the San Francisco Convention & Visitors Bureau *(below)*. Reservation services: San Francisco Reservations (☎800-677-1500; www.hotelres.com); Quikbook (☎800-789-9887; www.quikbook.com). Bed & Breakfast San Francisco (☎800-452-8249; www.bbsf.com).

ENTERTAINMENT

Consult the arts and entertainment sections of local newspapers like the daily *Chronicle (www.sfgate.com)* or the *San Francisco Weekly (www.sfweekly.com)* for listings of current events, theaters and concert halls, or call the Cultural Events Hotline (☎415-391-2000; www.onlyinsanfrancisco.org). Obtain event tickets from Tickets.com (☎510-762-2277; www.tickets.com) or Tix Bay Area, a Ticketmaster outlet, which offers full and half-price tickets for selected events on the day of the show (☎415-430-1140; www.theatrebayarea.org).

VISITOR INFORMATION

City information center at Hallidie Plaza *(900 Market St.;* ☎415-391-2000, www.onlyinsanfrancisco.org). City Pass offers discounted admission to several attractions, as well as a 7-day MUNI pass. *(www.citypass.com).*

Cable Car

© PhotoDisc., Inc.

EAST BAY★

Directly across the bay from San Francisco, Oakland and Berkeley nestle on the flanks of steeply wooded hills. The San Francisco-Oakland Bay Bridge (1936) ushered in a new era for the Oakland. Berkeley is famous for its University of California branch.

- **Information:** ☎ 510-839-9000, www.oaklandcvb.com; ☎ 510-549-7040, www.visitberkeley.com.
- **Kids Especially for Kids:** USS Hornet.

Sights

Oakland Museum of California★★

Kids *1000 Oak St., Oakland.* ☎*510-238-2200. www.museumca.org.*

The **Hall of California Ecology**★ *(1st level)* simulates a walk eastward across California. The **Cowell Hall of California History**★ *(2nd level)* displays 6,000 artifacts, from native basketry to the lifestyles of Websurfers. The **Gallery of California Art**★★ *(3rd level)* features the works of California Impressionists, the Oakland-based Society of Six landscapists, and the Bay Area Figurative movement.

USS Hornet★★

Kids *Pier 3, Alameda.* ☎*510-521-8448. www.uss-hornet.org.*

This Essex-class aircraft carrier, 894ft-long, served in the Pacific, destroying enemy craft without once sustaining a hit. In 1969, the Hornet retrieved the crew of *Apollo 11* after splashdown from the first manned lunar landing. Exhibits on the **Hangar Deck** highlight this mission.

University of California★★

Roughly bounded by Bancroft Way, Oxford St. & Hearst Ave., Berkeley. ☎*510-549-7040. www.berkeley.edu.*

John Galen Howard designed the 178-acre "Cal" campus (now 30,000 students-strong) with Neoclassical buildings of white granite walls and red-tile roofs. **Sproul Plaza**★ *(Bancroft Way & Telegraph Ave.)* remains a lively gathering place. At the plaza's north end, **Sather Gate** has marked the ceremonial entrance to campus since 1910.

Designed to recall a Roman temple, **Doe Library**★ oversees 8 million bound volumes. Adjacent **Bancroft Library** (☎*510-642-3781, bancroft.berkeley.edu*) stores rare books and the largest collection of Mark Twain's manuscripts and papers. 307ft Sather Tower, known as **The Campanile**★★ Kids *(*☎*510-642-5215),* supports four clock faces and a carillon ; the eighth floor offers **views**★★ of the surrounding campus.

Excursions

Blackhawk Auto Museum★★

3750 Blackwawk Plaza, Danville. ☎*925-736-2277. www.blackhawkmuseum.org.* The collection includes rare Duesenbergs and European custom coaches.

Eugene O'Neill National Historic Site★★

Shuttles from Railroad Ave. & Church St., Danville. ☎*925-838-0249. www.nps.gov/euon. Visit by reservation only.*

Modest **Tao House** was home for more than six years to playwright Eugene O'Neill (1888-1953), who wrote four of his greatest plays here.

John Muir National Historic Site★

Rte. 4, Martinez. ☎*925-228-8860. www.nps.gov/jomu.*

This Italianate frame residence was home to conservationist John Muir (1838-1914) from 1890 until his death. He wrote many books in second-floor his "scribble den" .

MARIN COUNTY ★★

MAP P 382

PACIFIC STANDARD TIME

Roughly divided by a mountainous spine into an eastern corridor of upscale suburbs and bayside towns, and a far larger western portion of dairy farms, rural villages and extensive parklands, Marin County is conveniently situated for day trips at the north end of the Golden Gate Bridge.

- **Information:** ☎415-925-2060 or www.visitmarin.org.
- **Don't Miss:** Muir Woods
- **Organizing Your Time:** Plan to cross the Golden Gate Bridge northbound well before noon, and return late afternoon or late evening.

Sights

Marin Headlands★★

Alexander Ave. exit from northbound US-101; turn left, then right onto Barry Rd. ☎*415-331-1540. www.nps.gov/goga.* These windswept coastal cliffs and hills anchor the northern end of the Golden Gate. Of strategic importance, the area was long owned by the US Army and thus was spared commercial development. Today part of Golden Gate National Recreation Area, the headlands are reached by **Conzelman Road,** which offers **views**★★★ of San Francisco and the Golden Gate. The road passes abandoned military installations and ends near **Point Bonita Lighthouse**★. The **Marin Headlands Visitor Center**★ mounts exhibits on the natural and human history of the headlands.

Sausalito★

4mi north of San Francisco via US-101. ☎*415-332-0505. www.sausalito.org.* Developed as a resort in the 1870s, Sausalito has winding streets, attractive hillside neighborhoods and fine views. Visitors arrive on sunny days and weekends to window-shop and relax in boutiques and restaurants along **Bridgeway Boulevard**★, the waterfront commercial district. The docklands of **Marinship** *(1mi north on Bridgeway)*, a shipbuilding center during World War II, now shelter a houseboat community. The **Bay Model Visitor Center**★ *(2100 Bridgeway Blvd.;* ☎*415-332-3871, www.spn.usace.army.*

Marin Headlands

MICHELIN

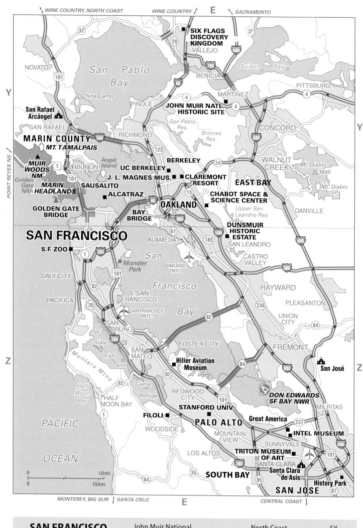

mil/bmvc) holds a two-acre hydraulic scale model of the San Francisco Bay and Delta. The US Army Corps of Engineers uses it to study the effects of dredging, shoreline development and other ecological projects.

Muir Woods National Monument★★★

Kids *Muir Woods Rd., 19mi north of San Francisco.* ☎415-388-2595. *www.nps. gov/muwo.*

Named for conservationist John Muir, this 560-acre plot of virgin forest is the largest grove of coast redwoods near San Francisco. Saved from the ax by its rugged canyon, the park contains 6mi of trails that wind along Redwood and Fern Creeks, and up the slopes of Mount Tamalpais. The level, paved **Main Trail** *(1mi)* loops from the visitor center through giants more than 1,000 years old in **Bohemian Grove.**

Mount Tamalpais State Park★★

Panoramic Hwy., 20mi north of San Francisco. ☎415-388-2070. www.parks. ca.gov.

The serpentine ascent of the 2,572ft east peak of Mount Tamalpais *(tam-ul-PIE-us)*, locally known as "Mount Tam," is rewarded with sweeping **views**★★ embracing San Francisco, its bay and the Pacific Ocean. Hundreds of miles of trails lace the mountain's flanks, leading to reservoirs, remote cascades and the Pacific shore.

Point Reyes National Seashore★★

[Kids] *Bear Valley Rd. off Hwy. 1 at Olema, 40mi north of San Francisco. ☎415-464-5100. www.nps.gov/pore.*

This 102sq-mi park embraces white sand beaches, rocky headlands, windswept moors, salt marshes, lush forests and abundant wildlife. The cape is located where the Pacific Plate meets the North American Plate along an active San Andreas rift zone clearly marked by Bolinas Bay, Olema Valley and Tomales Bay. The **Bear Valley Visitor Center**★ *(west of Hwy. 1 intersection)* contains exhibits on local ecology and history. Hikers on the adjacent **Earthquake Trail**★ *(.6mi)* can see a fence line that was shifted 16ft by the 1906 earthquake. A 22mi drive from the visitor center is **Point Reyes Lighthouse**★★, clinging to a rocky shelf on a 600ft precipice. Equipped with a Fresnel lens imported from France in 1870, the lighthouse offers sweeping **views**★★ of the Farallon Islands and of magnificent winter whale migrations.

WINE COUNTRY★★

MICHELIN MAP 493 A 8

PACIFIC STANDARD TIME

Within a two-hour drive north from San Francisco, Napa and Sonoma Counties thrive on the abundant sunshine, occasional fogs and fertile soil that produce grapes for some of North America's finest wines. A Hungarian immigrant, Agoston Haraszthy (1812-69), planted the first commercial vineyards and founded the Buena Vista Winery★★ *(18000 Old Winery Rd., Sonoma; ☎707-938-1266, buenavista-carneros.com)* in 1857. Other vintners followed Haraszthy's lead, expanding the acreage under cultivation, experimenting with new varietals and production methods. The industry recovered from a plague of phylloxera that devastated vineyards in the late 19C, but a heavier blow fell when Prohibition (1919-33) curtailed production of alcoholic beverages. Not until the early 1970s did the wine industry recover completely.

- ☐ **Information:** ☎707-522-5800, www.sonomacounty.com; ☎707-226-7459, www.napavalley.org.
- ☺ **Don't Miss:** St. Helena; Calistoga.
- ◔ **Organizing Your Time:** Driving Napa Valley's main road, Hwy 29, often entails sitting in long lines of traffic May-November. The Silverado Trail, the road on the east side of the valley, may be less crowded.
- [Kids] **Especially for Kids:** Charles M. Schulz Museum.

Harvesting Grapes in the Napa Valley

Sights

Napa

Rtes. 29 & 121. ☏707-226-7459.
A charming city of 75,000 on the banks of the Napa River, Napa boasts scores of elegant Victorian residences from the late 19C, when riverboat captains and bankers helped turn the town into a regional center.

COPIA: The American Center for Wine, Food and the Arts★★

500 First St. ✕ ♿ 🅿 ☏707-259-1600. www.copia.org.
This $70-million cultural and educational center occupies 12 river-bend acres just east of downtown. Professional chefs, winemakers and artists share their passions in cooking and wine-tasting classes, tours and lectures. A core exhibit, "Forks in the Road," interprets the distinctiveness of American culture and lifestyle through food and drink. Lush kitchen gardens surround the center.

di Rosa Preserve★★

5200 Carneros Hwy. (Rte. 121). 🅿 ☏707-226-5991. www.dirosapreserve.org.
René di Rosa's personal store of late-20C Bay Area art comprises one of the largest collections of regional art in the US. Nearly 2,000 works by some 750 artists are presented on his 250-acre estate. Many are displayed on the walls of a c.1870 stone winery, surrounded by vineyards and 150yr-old olive trees; others are sculptures that line a lakeshore.

St. Helena★

Rte. 29. ☏707-963-4456. www.sthelena. com.
A base for exploring Napa Valley, this town of 6,000 boasts fine restaurants along a picturesque main street. The **Robert Louis Stevenson Silverado Museum**★ *(1490 Library Ln.; ☏707-963-3757, www.silveradomuseum.org)* is devoted to the life and works of the Scottish author whose Napa Valley honeymoon in 1880 is described in *The Silverado Squatters*. The **Culinary Institute of America at Greystone** *(2555 Main St.; ☏707-963-7115, www.ciachef. edu),* West Coast branch of the premier culinary institution in the US, occupies a massive stone building (1889).

Calistoga★

Rtes. 29 & 128. ☏707-942-6333. www. calistogafun.com.
Founded in 1859, this resort town of 5,000 is famed for hot-spring spas. Tourists "take the waters," enjoy mud baths or ride hot-air balloons. Privately owned **Old Faithful Geyser**★ *(Tubbs Ln.; ☏707-942-6463, www.oldfaithfulgeyser.com)* spews superheated water 60ft in the air about every 40min.

Sonoma★★

Rte. 12. ☏707-996-1090. www.sonoma valley.com.

The Wine Country's most historically significant town, now with 10,000 residents, Sonoma is built around the largest Mexican-era plaza in California. On June 14, 1846, the eight-acre public square was the scene of the **Bear Flag Revolt,** when American settlers raised a flag emblazoned with a bear, proclaiming California an independent republic; it became a US possession a month later. Around the plaza stand a venerable array of buildings under the auspices of **Sonoma State Historic Park**★★ (☎707-938-9560, www.parks.ca.gov). They include **San Francisco Solano Mission**★ (1823), California's northernmost and final mission; **Sonoma Barracks**★, (1841), built for Mexican troops; the **Toscano Hotel,** a general store in the 1850s; and the 1840 **Blue Wing Inn**, a two-story adobe saloon and hotel. Also managed by the park is **Lachryma Montis**★ *(north end of 3rd St. W.;* ☎707-938-9559)*, retirement home of Mariano Vallejo (1807-90), founder of the pueblo of Sonoma.

Jack London State Historic Park★★

2400 London Ranch Rd., Glen Ellen. ☎707-938-5216. www.parks.ca.gov.

Sprawling among peaceful hills, 80-acre Beauty Ranch was the Sonoma Valley home of writer Jack London (1876-1916) in his later life. London planned Wolf House, a four-story mansion of hewn red boulders and redwood logs; it burned just a few days before he and his wife, Charmian, were to move in. Charmian later resided at the **House of Happy Walls**★, now a museum furnished with memorabilia and furniture custom-made for Wolf House. A wooded trail leads to the Londons' hilltop graves and the impressive ruins of **Wolf House**★.

Santa Rosa

US-101 & Rte. 12. ☎707-577-8674. www.visitsantarosa.com.

This city of 155,000 is the seat of Sonoma County. Its historic district dates from 1870. Horticulturalist Luther Burbank (1849-1926) lived most of his adult life in Santa Rosa; **Burbank Home & Gardens**★ *(Sonoma & Santa Rosa Aves.;* ☎707-524-5445, ci.santa-rosa.ca.us) preserves his residence and workshop.

Charles M. Schulz Museum and Research Center★

Kids *1 Snoopy Lane, off Steele & Hardies Lanes.* ♿ 🅿 ☎707-579-4452. www.charlesmschulzmuseum.org.

For nearly 50 years, until his death in early 2000, Santa Rosa resident Charles Schulz illustrated the world's most popular comic strip, *Peanuts*. This museum celebrates his cartoon characters.

NORTH COAST★★

MICHELIN MAP 493 A 6, 7, 8
PACIFIC STANDARD TIME

The first Europeans to colonize this coast were Russians—at Fort Ross, in 1812. The fort was abandoned in the 1830s. Gold was discovered on the Klamath and Smith Rivers in 1848; after the mid-19C, logging dominated the economy. Sawmills and port facilities sprang up in the coastal towns of Mendocino, Arcata, Eureka and Crescent City. Since 1918, acres of old-growth redwoods have been preserved in state and federal parks.

- **Information:** ☎415-292-5527, www.redwoodempire.com.
- **Orient Yourself:** From the Golden Gate, **Highway 1**★★ follows the coast north for 205mi, mostly via well-paved, two-lane road. In Humboldt County, it meets US-101, known as the **Redwood Highway.**
- **Don't Miss:** Humboldt Redwoods State Park.
- **Organizing Your Time:** Distances are vast in Northern California—it takes 7hrs to drive straight through to Eureka from San Francisco.
- **Kids** **Especially for Kids:** The drive-through tree along US 101.

Sights

Fort Ross State Historic Park★★

Hwy. 1, 97mi north of San Francisco. ☎707-847-3286. www.parks.ca.gov.
Built high on a grassy promontory above a sheltered cove, Fort Ross reigned as Russia's easternmost outpost for nearly three decades after its founding in 1812. Russian and Aleut colonists hunted sea otters for their pelts and farmed to support Alaskan colonies. The stockaded fort was abandoned after the sea-otter population collapsed in the mid-1830s. Deeded to the State of California in 1906, it has been partially restored with an Orthodox **chapel, officials' quarters** and two **blockhouses**.

Mendocino★★

Hwy. 1, 72mi north of Fort Ross. ☎707-961-6300. www.mendocinocoast.com.
Seated on a foggy headland where the Big River meets the Pacific, this picturesque Victorian village appears little changed from its heyday as a lumber town in the late-19C. Favoring New England-style architecture, it has a "skyline" of clapboard houses with steep gabled roofs, wooden water towers, a Gothic Revival-style **Presbyterian church** (1868) and the false-fronted **Mendocino Hotel** (1878). Mendocino's prosperity declined in the 1920s; in the 1960s artists discovered the tranquil atmosphere and idyllic setting. Hollywood directors

have shot numerous films here. Enveloping the town, **Mendocino Headlands State Park**★★ *(☎707-937-5804, www.parks.ca.gov)* preserves marvelous **views**★★ of fissure-riddled rocks and sea caves.

Humboldt Redwoods State Park★★

South entrance on US-101, 6mi north of Garberville. ☎707-946-2263. www.parks.ca.gov.
Established along the Eel River in 1921, this 80sq-mi park contains a spectacular reserve of coast redwoods easily seen along the **Avenue of the Giants**★★★, which runs 29mi through its heart, paralleling US-101 and the Eel River. A nature trail through **Founder's Grove**★★ begins at the Founder's Tree, once considered the world's tallest (364ft before the top 17ft broke off). The world's largest remaining virgin stand of redwoods is the **Rockefeller Forest**★★★, encompassing 16sq mi of the Bull Creek watershed west of the Eel River. Hiking trails probe the sublime depths of these venerable groves.

Eureka★

US-101. ☎707-443-5097. redwoods.info.
The largest Pacific coastal community in the US north of San Francisco, this town of 25,000 grew as a shipping hub for minerals and lumber in the mid- to late 19C. Buildings in its 10-block waterfront

Fort Ross State Historic Park

© John Anderson/MICHELIN

historic district *(2nd & 3rd Sts. between E & M Sts.)* include the ornate Victorian **Carson Mansion**★★ *(2nd & M Sts.)*, a three-story redwood mansion built in 1886 for a lumber magnate.

Redwood National and State Parks★★

Mainly along US-101 between Orick & Crescent City. ☎707-464-6101. www.nps.gov/redw.

With majestic redwood groves and 33mi of beaches, this 165sq-mi expanse joins three venerable state parks—**Prairie Creek Redwoods** *(☎707-465-7347)*, **Del Norte Coast Redwoods** *(☎707-465-2146)* and **Jedediah Smith Redwoods** *(☎707-458-3018)*—within the jurisdiction of Redwood National Park. The parks are cooperatively managed and casually linked by a network of highways and roads, few of them designed for sightseeing. There are two visitor centers: the **Redwood Information Center** *(US-101, 1mi south of Orick; ☎707-464-6101)* and **Park Headquarters** *(1111 2nd St., Crescent City; ☎707-464-6101)*. Highlights include the **Lady Bird Johnson Grove**★★ and **Tall Trees Grove**★, both in the Redwood Creek watershed. The latter contains a 367.8ft-high **tree**★, discovered by a National Geographic Society scientist in 1963 and believed to be the world's tallest. The Newton B. Drury Scenic Parkway passes through **Prairie Creek Meadows** with its herds of grazing Roosevelt elk and **Fern Canyon**★, a narrow ravine walled with lush ferns.

SOUTH BAY★

MAP P 382
PACIFIC STANDARD TIME

California's third-largest city, center of the US high-tech industry, San Jose sprawls around the southern end of San Francisco Bay. Founded as a farming pueblo in 1777, the city was state capital for several months in 1849. Electronics factories began to replace orchards in the mid-20C. By the late 1960s, San Jose began to define itself as the "capital of Silicon Valley." Such computer giants as IBM, Apple and Hewlett Packard developed facilities in the city and its environs.

🛈 **Information:** ☎408-295-9600, www.sanjose.org.
☺ **Don't Miss:** Filoli
🧒 **Especially for Kids:** Tech Museum of Innovation.

Sights

Filoli★★

Cañada Rd., Woodside, 13mi north of Palo Alto. ☎650-364-8300. www.filoli.org.
This 700-acre estate was built in 1916 for Empire Mine owner William Bourne (1857-1936). The modified Georgian Revival **mansion**★★, designed by Willis Polk, is furnished with 17-18C Irish and English furniture. Bruce Porter and Isabella Wood designed the 16-acre **gardens**★★★ in Italian and French style.

Stanford University★★

Main Quadrangle on Serra St., Palo Alto. ☎650-723-2560. www.stanford.edu.
Railroad magnate Leland Stanford (1824-93) and his wife, Jane, established this private institution in memory of their late son. Now it is a leading academic and research center (17,000 students). The campus—a creation of architect Charles Allerton Coolidge and landscape architect Frederick Law Olmsted—is noted for Romanesque buildings shaded by eucalyptus, bay and palm trees.

The historic heart of campus is the **Main Quadrangle**★, a cloistered courtyard bordered by colonnaded buildings. Its **Memorial Church**★★, built in 1903 by Jane Stanford, is famed for its Byzantine-style mosaics, stained glass and 7,777-pipe organ. **Hoover Tower**★ *(☎650-723-2053)*, a 285ft landmark campanile with a 35-bell carillon, offers views over campus from its observation deck.

Iris & B. Gerald Cantor Center for Visual Arts★ *(Lomita Dr. & Museum Way; ☎650-723-4177, museum.stanford. edu)* houses 20,000 pieces of ancient to contemporary sculpture, paintings and crafts from six continents. The adjacent **Rodin Sculpture Garden**★ contains 20 large-scale bronze casts by famed French sculptor Auguste Rodin.

Intel Museum★★

2200 Mission College Blvd., Santa Clara. ☎408-765-0503. www.intel.com/ museum.

As the world's largest semiconductor company, the Intel Corporation invented (in 1968) the technology that put computer memory on tiny silicon chips. Exhibits here in the company headquarters walk visitors through the principles of transistor technology.

The Tech Museum of Innovation★★

Kids *201 S. Market St., San Jose. ☎408-294-8324. www.thetech.org.*

This interactive exhibition of cutting-edge technology is housed in a domed, mango-colored building. The Tech entertains all ages, but mainly courts young people with playful exhibits in such fields as space exploration, microelectronics and robotics.

San Jose Museum of Art★

110 S. Market St., San Jose. ☎408-271-6840. www.sjmusart.org.

This facility concentrates on art of the 20C and 21C, drawing on its collection to display works by artists such as Ed Ruscha, Joan Brown and Tino Rodriguez. Highlights include three unusual chandeliers by Dale Chihuly.

Rosicrucian Egyptian Museum★

1342 Naglee Ave., San Jose. ☎408-947-3636. www.egyptianmuseum.org.

Set amid a complex of Egyptian and Moorish-style buildings in Rosicrucian Park, this treasury is modeled after the Temple of Amon at Karnak. Among the 5,000 pieces are pottery, jewelry, glass, mummies, sarcophagi, painted coffins and a full-scale reproduction of a **Middle Kingdom Rock Tomb**★.

Winchester Mystery House

Kids *525 S. Winchester Blvd., San Jose. ☎408-247-2101. www.winchester mysteryhouse.com.*

This rambling, 160-room mansion is the legacy of Sarah Winchester, heir to the Winchester arms fortune. In superstitious hope of prolonging her life by appeasing ghosts of people killed with Winchester rifles, she compulsively expanded the house from 1884 to her death in 1922, creating a hodgepodge of rooms and hallways, secret passages, and doors and stairways that go nowhere.

MONTEREY AND BIG SUR★★★

MICHELIN MAP 493 A 9
PACIFIC STANDARD TIME

Sebastián Vizcaíno sailed into Monterey Bay in 1602, his enthusiastic response to the harbor enhanced by the lack of anchorages along the Big Sur coastline. Not until 1770 did Spain found the presidio, chapel and pueblo that became its California capital. Padre Junípero Serra subsequently moved his mission a few miles south to Carmel, away from the influence of Monterey.

🛈 **Information:** ☎831-649-1770, montereyinfo.org.
😍 **Don't Miss:** Hearst Castle.
🕐 **Organizing Your Time:** Be sure to reserve tickets for Hearst Castle weeks in advance, *before* you make the drive south. Monterey itself is worth a full day; driving the Coast Highway to San Luis Obispo takes three to four hours.
Kids **Especially for Kids:** Monterey Bay Aquarium.
🕯 **Also See:** The Steinbeck National Museum.

A Bit of History

On July 7, 1846, a few weeks after the Bear Flag Revolt in Sonoma, the US officially seized California at Monterey. But after Sierra gold was discovered in 1848, Monterey's political and economic preeminence gave way to San Francisco. In the 1880s, Chinese and Italian fishermen discovered the wealth of Monterey Bay and built a port and cannery town of national significance, until harvests were depleted in the 1950s. In its heyday, industry was focused at Cannery Row, a raucous industrial strip described by author John Steinbeck as "a poem, a stink, a grating noise." Tourism is now the mainstay of the economy of Monterey, a city of 30,000; Cannery Row has been reborn with shops, restaurants and an aquarium. The bay is the best place on the West Coast to see playful sea otters in the wild.

Carmel, which developed as an artists' community near the old mission in the early 20C, is a genteel resort town. It is a perfect complement to historic Monterey and rugged Big Sur, whose primeval beauties extend 90mi down the California coast to the imposing hilltop estate known as Hearst Castle.

Sights

Monterey State Historic Park★★

Headquarters at Pacific House, Custom House Plaza. ☎ *831-649-7118. www. parks.ca.gov.*

Monterey's compact central district is ideally explored on the **Path of History Walking Tour**★, a 2mi route blazed by bronze discs embedded in sidewalks, and described in maps and pamphlets available at an information center at **Pacific House.** This two-story adobe, built in 1847 to house US troops, also contains a history museum.

Fisherman's Wharf is lined with shops and cafes. Adjacent is broad **Custom House Plaza**★★. At **Stanton Center,** a theater presents a film outlining Monterey history. The **Maritime Museum of Monterey**★ *(☎831-372-2608, www.montereyhistory.org)* exhibits model ships, navigational devices and nautical paraphernalia from 300 years of seafaring. The adobe **Custom House**★ served port authorities from 1827 to 1867.

The two-story **Larkin House**★★ *(Calle Principal & Pearl St.),* built in 1834, melded New England architecture— high ceilings, a hipped roof and central hallway—with the local adobe motif, giving rise to the Monterey Colonial style of architecture. The **Cooper-Molera Complex**★★ *(Pearl St. at Munras Ave. & Polk St.)* features a large home whose separate wings—an adobe section and a two-story Victorian—contrast Hispanic and Anglo cultures.

Monterey Bay Aquarium★★

Kids ⏱ *West end of Cannery Row.* ☎*831-648-4800. www.mbayaq.org.*

Built out over the water in a revamped cannery building, this modern aquarium presents the rich marine life of Monterey Bay—focal point of the **Monterey Bay National Marine Sanctuary**, North America's largest offshore natural preserve. With more than 300,000 animals and plants of nearly 600 species, the aquarium represents the full range of Monterey Bay habitats, from coastal wetlands and tide pools to deep sea.

The west wing houses the **Nearshore Habitats** exhibits, including a touch pool for fast-gliding bat rays, a group of playful sea otters and the 28ft-high **kelp forest**★ tank, where swaying seaweed provides a rich marine home. **Outer Bay**★ habitats in the east wing showcase the inhabitants of the open ocean, highlighted by an enormous **ocean tank**★★ where sea turtles, sharks, barracudas and other species swim. **Mysteries of the Deep**★★ displays up to 60 species collected from the dark waters of Monterey Canyon, 3,300ft deep.

17-Mile Drive★★

Access via the Carmel Gate (N. San Antonio Ave. off Ocean Ave.) or the Pacific Grove Gate (Sunset Dr., Pacific Grove). ☎*831-624-6669.*

Celebrated for exquisite coastline views, this private toll road winds through exclusive estates and the 8,000-acre Del Monte Forest. Turnouts offer spectacular vistas, including **Lone Cypress,** a classic landmark of the Monterey Peninsula. Golfers from around the world play the renowned links at Pebble Beach and Spyglass Hill.

Carmel★★

Hwy. 1, 5mi south of Monterey. ☎831-624-2522. www.carmelcalifornia.org.

A delightful square mile of carefully tended cottages beneath a canopy of pine, oak and cypress, Carmel began to attract artists and writers in the very early 20C. While strict ordinances preserve residential charm, a painstakingly quaint commercial district of upscale boutiques, galleries, inns and restaurants nestles around Ocean, 6th and 7th Avenues *(between Junipero Ave. & Monte Verde St.).* Steep Ocean Avenue meets the turquoise waters of Carmel Bay at **Carmel City Beach**★★, a wide sweep of white sand bounded on the south by rocky Point Lobos and on the north by the clifftop greens of the Pebble Beach Golf Club.

San Carlos Borromeo de Carmelo Mission★★★

Rio Rd. & Lasuen Dr. ☎ 831-624-1271. www.carmelmission.org.

Headquarters of the mission chain in its expansive early years, the Carmel Mission resonates with the vision of Padre Junípero Serra, whose remains are interred in the sanctuary. Founded in 1771 when Serra moved his neophytes from Monterey, this mission prospered under his care and that of his successor, Padre Fermin Lasuén, who rebuilt the original adobe chapel with sandstone in 1782. Restored in 1931, the chapel preserves original 18C paintings and a statue of the Virgin Our Lady of Bethlehem that Serra brought from Mexico in 1769.

Tor House★★

Stewart Way off Scenic Rd., 1.2mi south of Ocean Ave. ☎ 831-624-1813. www.torhouse.org.

Overlooking Carmel Bay, this enchanting stone complex embodies the spirit of its builder, poet Robinson Jeffers (1887-1962), who settled in Carmel in 1914. Guided tours offer a peek at the rooms, including the whimsical Hawk Tower, with Jeffers' desk and chair.

Point Lobos State Reserve★★

Hwy. 1, 3.5mi south of Carmel. b831-624-4909. www.parks.ca.gov.

This small but dramatic peninsula defines the southern end of Carmel Bay. Early Spanish explorers named the site *Punta de Los Lobos Marinos* ("point of the sea wolves") because of the barking of resident sea lions. Deeded to the state in 1933, the site comprises 1,250 acres, including 750 submerged acres of the first US underwater reserve.

Big Sur★★★

Hwy. 1 between Carmel and San Simeon. ☎831-667-2100. www.bigsurcalifornia. org.

This rugged coastline, extending 90mi south from Carmel, is celebrated for its charismatic, wild beauty. A precipitous coastal wall, plunging 4,000ft to the sea, thwarted settlement by the Spanish, who called it *El Pais Grande del Sur*—"the Big Country to the South." Mid-19C homesteaders trickled into narrow valleys to ranch and log redwoods. Completion of the highway in 1937 opened the area to visitors.

Traveling south from Carmel, the concrete-arch **Bixby Creek Bridge**, built in 1932, is one of the 10 highest single-span bridges in the world. **Point Sur State Historic Park** preserves an 1889 stone lighthouse built 272ft above the surf on a volcanic rock connected to the mainland by a sandbar. Near the **village of Big Sur** *(23mi south of Carmel),* in the forested Big Sur River valley, **Andrew Molera State Park** and **Pfeiffer Big Sur State Park**★ offer coastal vistas and access. Four miles south, the venerable **Nepenthe**★ bar and restaurant boasts sweeping **views**★★★ from its cliffside terraces 800ft above the ocean.

Hearst Castle★★★

Rte. 1, 98mi south of Monterey. Visit by reservation only. ☎805-927-2020. www. hearstcastle.org.

Overlooking the Pacific Ocean from atop a Santa Lucia Mountain crest, this 127-acre estate and the opulent mansion

Brigitta L. House/MICHELIN

Bixby Creek Bridge, Big Sur

crowning it embody the flamboyance of William Randolph Hearst. It was eclectically designed and lavishly embellished with the newsman's world-class collection of Mediterranean art.

Hearst's father, George, purchased this ranch in 1865. In 1919, William hired architect Julia Morgan to create a "bungalow" that over 28 years grew from a modest residence to "The Enchanted Hill." Morgan designed a Mediterranean Revival-style main house, **Casa Grande,** and three guest houses. From twin Spanish Colonial towers with arabesque grillwork and Belgian carillon bells, to Etruscan colonnades that complement the Greco-Roman temple facade of the **Neptune Pool**★, and gold-inlaid Venetian glass tiles of the indoor **Roman Pool**★, the design emerged as a mélange that defies categorization.

The 65,000sq-ft main house contains 115 rooms, including 38 bedrooms, 41 bathrooms, two libraries, a billiards room, beauty salon and theater. All feature Hearst's art holdings, including silver, 16C tapestries, terra-cotta sculpture and ancient Greek vases that line the shelves of a 5,000-volume library.

Five different tours are offered, all lasting 2hrs and departing from a visitor center at the foot of the hill. Shuttle buses climb 10min to the castle, with spectacular views en route. As they wait, visitors may take in a 40min film.

Excursions

National Steinbeck Center★★

1 Main St., Salinas, 17mi east of Monterey. ☎*831-796-3833. www.steinbeck.org.*
Exhibits, written excerpts and film clips depict themes and settings of John Steinbeck's novels, stories, scripts and journalistic dispatches. Born in Salinas, Steinbeck (1902-68) grew up amidst the communities and characters that animated his greatest stories and novels, including *Tortilla Flat* (1935), *The Grapes of Wrath* (1939), *The Red Pony* (1945), *Cannery Row* (1945) and *East of Eden* (1952). Although he won Pulitzer and Nobel prizes, his sympathetic depiction of local brothels, labor organizers and ne'er-do-wells embarrassed and antagonized the Salinas establishment.

Pinnacles National Monument★

Rte. 146, 22mi south of Salinas. ☎*831-389-4485. www.nps.gov/pinn.*
The distinctive ridgetop rock formations of this 37sq-mi park are the remnants of a volcano formed 23 million years ago. **Juniper Canyon Trail**★ (*2.4mi round-trip),* climbs steeply into the Pinnacles.

SANTA FE AREA

Known as the "Land of Enchantment," New Mexico is a cultural mélange of ancient and modern Indian and Spanish, American pioneer and high-technology influences. The chosen home of painter Georgia O'Keeffe and author D.H. Lawrence offers stark adobe architecture in brilliant contrast to strikingly blue skies, towering mountains and precipitous gorges.

Though not its largest city, the state capital of Santa Fe is New Mexico's cultural and tourism hub. The former Spanish capital, founded in 1609, is home to outstanding museums, galleries, restaurants and summer opera.

Santa Fe is an hour's drive north of modern Albuquerque, an hour's drive south of the rustic mountain art town of Taos. East is the historic Santa Fe Trail town

of Las Vegas. West is the domain of the Navajo, Zuni and Jicarillo Apache tribes, where Gallup and Farmington are the largest towns.

A thousand years ago, Ancestral Puebloan civilization spawned a sophisticated trade network. Ruins of their culture can be seen at such far-flung sites as Bandelier, Pecos and Aztec Ruins National Monuments and Chaco Culture National Historical Park. Spanish explorer Francisco Vasquéz de Coronado and his expedition searched for gold from the legendary Seven Cities of Cibola in 1540.

New Mexico entered the modern era in the 1940s, when scientists working in Los Alamos, near Santa Fe, created the atomic bombs that ended World War II and changed the world forever.

Lensic Performing Arts Center, Santa Fe

SANTA FE★★★

MAP P 401
MOUNTAIN STANDARD TIME
POPULATION 67,000

Home to Puebloan Indians for more than 1,000 years, Santa Fe was a Spanish territorial capital at the beginning of the 17C, an American frontier city in the 19C, a state capital and center for high-tech research in the mid-20C. Today it has coalesced into a world-renowned center for the arts, cuisine and shopping, its diverse elements and heritage maintaining their unique characters.

- **Information:** ☎505-955-6200 or www.santafe.org
- ▶ **Orient Yourself:** Virtually all the Santa Fe visitor attractions are within a square-mile area in the center of the city.
- **Parking:** Summer poses parking challenges near the Plaza; several outlying fee lots run shuttles to downtown. There is also a fair amount of on-street parking up Canyon Road.
- **Don't Miss:** The Georgia O'Keeffe Museum
- **Organizing Your Time:** Staying at one of the hotels downtown vastly eases getting around in central Santa Fe--but be sure to save one night for a performance at the Santa Fe Opera.
- **Especially for Kids:** Museum of International Folk Art
- **Also See:** Bandelier National Monument, El Santuario de Chimayo

Distinctive adobe and Territorial-style architecture spreads across the foothills of the Sangre de Cristo Mountains at 7,000ft elevation. There are many museums and a wealth of historic churches and other buildings. Art galleries and shops surround the historic Plaza and wind down Canyon Road, once a trail leading to the Pecos Indian pueblos. The newly restored **Lensic Performing Arts Center** (211 W. San Francisco St.; ☎505-988-1234, www.lensic.com) is a downtown Art Deco treasure dating from 1931. Visitors make special trips for the summer Santa Fe Opera, whose modern amphitheater home dominates a hilltop north of town, and impressive Indian Markets.

A Bit of History

Colonists from Spain, including missionaries, founded the first territorial capital in the Española Valley, north of Santa Fe, in 1598. Eleven years later, Don Pedro de Peralta established Santa Fe as the Spanish seat of power. By 1610, the Plaza and Palace of the Governors had been constructed; the city would become the oldest continuous seat of government in the US. That same year, the Mission Church of San Miguel was built. By 1617, 14,000 Indians had been converted to Catholicism.

With the opening of the Santa Fe Trail in 1821, US westward expansion led adventurous Americans from Missouri to the trade hub of Santa Fe, though many continued to California. Briefly occupied by the Confederacy during the Civil War, Santa Fe rebounded strongly. It was attracting artists as early as 1878-81, when Territorial Governor Lew Wallace scribed his novel, Ben Hur.

Since 1909, the "Palace" has been run as a history museum by the **Museum of New Mexico** (113 Lincoln Ave.; ☎505-476-5100; www.museumofnew-mexico.org). Four other Santa Fe museums are under the same umbrella. The Museum of Fine Arts is downtown near the Palace of the Governors, adjacent to the Plaza. The Museum of Indian Arts and Culture and Museum of International Folk Art are 2mi southeast, on beautiful new Museum Plaza (Camino Lejo), and the Governor's Gallery displays contemporary art within the State Capitol building.

Address Book Santa Fe Area

For price ranges see the Legend on the cover flap.

WHERE TO STAY IN THE SANTA FE AREA

$$$$ The Bishop's Lodge – *Bishop's Lodge Rd, Santa Fe, NM .* ✕♿▣⌷ 🅂🅿🄰 ☎ *505-983-6377 or 800-419-0492. www.bishopslodge.com. 111 rooms.* Built in 1851 as the retreat of Jean-Baptiste Lamy, first bishop of Santa Fe, this resort is hidden in a valley 3.5mi north of downtown. Lamy's chapel and garden are at the heart of 450 acres of piñon-juniper forest harboring 15 guest lodges. Horseback riding and tennis are popular activities. **Las Fuentes ($$$)** restaurant offers fine Nuevo Latino cuisine; the new Shánah Spa has a holistic bent.

$$$$ Inn of the Anasazi – *113 Washington Ave., Santa Fe, NM.* ✕♿▣ ☎ *505-988-3030 or 888.767.3966. www.innoftheanasazi.com. 59 rooms.* With traditional beamed ceilings of peeled log, sculpted stairways and intricately patterned pillows, the inn's design is a rich blend of Southwestern cultures. Indian baskets and cacti adorn a lobby with a warm fireplace. The **Anasazi Restaurant ($$$)** focuses on regional cuisine, including coriander-crusted venison.

$$$ Hotel Santa Fe – *1501 Paseo de Peralta, Santa Fe, NM.* ✕♿▣⌷ ☎ *505-243-2300 or 800-825-9876. www.hotelsantafe.com. 163 rooms.* The only Native American-owned hotel in Santa Fe is characterized by Puebloan artwork and a traditional terrace design. The three-story building features ceremonial dance performances and storytellers who immerse guests in Picuris culture. The **Corn Dance Café ($$)** focuses on indigenous cuisine: bison tenderloin, quail with quinoa.

$$ El Rey Inn – *1862 Cerrillos Rd., Santa Fe, NM.* ♿▣⌷ ☎ *505-982-1931 or 800-521-1349. www.elreyinnsantafe.com. 86 rooms.* Best of the Cerrillos Road motels south of the Plaza, El Rey ("the King") succeeds with its Spanish Colonial architecture and carefully tended grounds. Built in the 1930s, renovated and well maintained, the motel boasts a Southwestern décor of hand-painted tiles and hand-crafted furnishings. Fountains and sculptures adorn the garden areas.

$$ The Historic Taos Inn – *125 Paseo del Pueblo Norte, Taos, NM.* ✕♿▣⌷ ☎ *505-758-2233 or 888-518-8267. www.taosinn.com. 36 rooms.* Beginning in 1895, Dr. T. Paul Martin, Taos County's first physician, rented many small adobes in this complex to artists and writers. Rooms showcase kiva fireplaces and bedspreads loomed by Indian weavers. **Doc Martin's ($$)** restaurant, once his waiting room, serves plates of tamales, blue-corn enchiladas and piñon-encrusted salmon.

$$ The Hotel Blue – *717 Central Ave. NW, Albuquerque, NM.* ✕♿▣⌷ ☎ *505-924-2400 or 877-878-4868. www.thehotelblue.com. 135 rooms.* An Art Deco-style "chic boutique" hotel wedged between downtown and Old Town on Route 66, the Blue brings a Route 66 sensibility into the 21C. Rooms are simple, but display modern frills. **Corvette's Diner ($)** is reminiscent of a 50s soda fountain.

$$ La Posada de Albuquerque – *125 2nd St. NW, Albuquerque, NM.* ✕♿▣⌷ ☎ *505-242-9090. www.laposada-abq.com. 107 rooms.* The only historic hotel in Albuquerque has a two-story lobby of arches and balconies centered on a tiled fountain. New Mexico's tallest building when Conrad Hilton opened it in 1939 on the site of a livery stable, it has been fully restored. Each room boasts Spanish tile and hand-carved furnishings.

$ The El Rancho Hotel – *1000 E. Rte. 66, Gallup, NM.* ✕▣⌷ ☎ *505-863-9311 or 800-543-6351. www.elranchohotel.com. 102 rooms.* Katharine Hepburn, Errol Flynn, Spencer Tracy and even Ronald Reagan made their homes-away-from home at this Navajoland inn while filming in the 1940s and 50s. Built in 1937 by R.E. Griffith, brother of movie pioneer D.W., the hotel is now a National Historic Site. Brick and stone with huge wooden beams, it is decorated in Old West style, with dozens of autographed movie-star photos on its walls.

WHERE TO EAT IN THE SANTA FE AREA

$$$ Geronimo – *724 Canyon Rd., Santa Fe.* ☎ *575-982-1500. www.geronimo-estaurant.com.* **Creative American.** Southwest tradition and 21C innovation merge in this Territorial-style adobe, built in 1748 by Spanish farmer Geronimo Lopes. In the sophisticated and romantic space, chef Eric DiStefano prepares meals of sautéed quail breast with polenta, sea scallops with caviar citrus sauce, and elk medallions with native mushrooms and foie gras.

$$$ La Casa Sena – *125 E. Palace Ave., Santa Fe.* ☎ *505-988-9232. Lacasasena. com.* **Mexican.** An early Santa Fe merchant, Don Juan Sena was as prolific in love as he was in business. He built his hacienda, now Sena Plaza, in the 1830s, and expanded it to 33 rooms to house his wife and 23 children. Today the central patio welcomes overflow diners from the fine restaurant, famous for its red trout baked in clay with poblano chiles and portobello mushrooms. Casual diners at adjacent **La Cantina** ($$) are entertained by wait staff performing Broadway show tunes.

$$$ Rancho de Chimayo – *County Rd. 98, S of Chimayo.* ☎ *505-351-4444. www.ranchodechimayo.com.* **Mexican.** Housed in a restored territorial ranch house, this northern New Mexico institution serves classic specialties such as carne adovada and chiles rellenos. The signature dish is a carne asada composed of a New York steak topped with chile verde. The flan is superb.

$$ The Artichoke Cafe – *424 Central Ave. SE, Albuquerque.* ☎ *505-243-0200. www.artichokecafe.com.* **Mediterranean.** A charming bistro in a historic neighborhood east of downtown, this bright, artsy corner draws lunchtime diners with its sandwiches, salads and pasta entrées. Dinner may begin with a steamed artichoke (with three dipping sauces); main courses include pan-seared duck breast (with pomegranate glaze) and daily seafood specials.

$$ El Farol – *808 Canyon Rd., Santa Fe.* ☎ *505-983-9912. www.elfarolsf.com.* **Spanish.** At this popular Canyon Road outpost, plates of tapas give way to live music—blues, salsa, flamenco— as twilight fades to dark. From puerco asada (pork with figs) to boquerones (marinated white anchovies), El Farol ("the Lantern") serves authentic Iberian "little plates." Enjoy entrées like paella before the music .

$$ Maria's New Mexican Kitchen – *555 W. Cordova Rd., Santa Fe.* ☎ *505-983-7929. www.marias-santafe.com.* **Mexican.** Strolling mariachi troubadours serenade diners as cooks craft handmade tortillas on an open grill. Servers carry platters of burritos, tacos and blue-corn enchiladas with Spanish rice. A Santa Fe institution of 50 years, Maria's offers more than 100 varieties of margaritas.

$$ Orlando's – *1114 Don Juan Valdez Ln. at Paseo del Pueblo Norte, Taos.* ☎ *505-751-1450.* **Mexican.** Orlando's mom still makes the sopapillas and other sweets: How's that for a local family restaurant? Cozy, casual and festive, especially on the crowded patio, Orlando's has won Taoseños' hearts with its chile-smothered enchiladas and burritos, carne adovado and fish tacos.

$ Dave's Not Here – *1115 Hickok St., Santa Fe.* ☎ *575-983-7060.* 🕐 *Closed Sun.* **Mexican & American.** Named for a former owner who, obviously, wasn't there, Dave's has been a Santa Fe standby for more than 20 years. From homemade salsa and chiles rellenos to Greek salads, carrot-rich tuna sandwiches, award-winning hamburgers and chocolate cake, the café is consistently good and easy on the wallet.

$ 66 Diner – *1405 Central Ave. NE, Albuquerque.* ☎ *575-247-1421. www.66diner.com.* **American**. A tribute to the days when Route 66 was the "Mother Road," this white, Art Deco-style diner serves all the meals you'd expect, from blue-plate specials to cheeseburgers with fries and a Coke. Service comes with a bubble-gum smile.

Sights

The Plaza★★

Flanked by Palace Ave., Old Santa Fe Trail, San Francisco St. & Lincoln Ave. ✕ ᚛ 🅿 *www.santafe.org.*

Faced on its north by the Palace of the Governors, this National Historic Landmark was the original center of Santa Fe, the focus of a Pueblo Indian revolt in 1680 and recapture of the city by the Spanish in 1692-93. Later, it was the end of the Santa Fe Trail for 19C American travelers heading west.

Strict laws today protect historic adobe and Territorial-style architecture; these buildings are home to shops, galleries, restaurants and hotels. All downtown structures must abide by a building code that limits their choice of color to "42 shades of brown." Many of Santa Fe's finest shops are located on or near The Plaza; it is hard to top Packards *(61 Old Santa Fe Trail; ☎505-983-9241)* for authentic Native American crafts or Montez *(Sena Plaza Courtyard, 125 E. Palace Ave.; ☎505-982-1828)* for traditional Spanish colonial art.

Palace of the Governors★★

105 W. Palace Ave., north side of Plaza. ✕ ᚛ 🅿 *☎505-476-5100. www.palaceofthegovernors.org.*

This low, flat-roofed hacienda was the original home and seat of power for Spanish, Mexican and, later, Anglo governors. Built in 1610, it is one of the oldest occupied buildings in the US, and has been a museum since 1909. Some of a collection of 17,000 objects is displayed in rooms surrounding a courtyard. Exhibits depict Santa Fe history, from Spanish Colonial through the Anglo frontier era to today. A letterpress print shop still operates, next to a gallery displaying historic hide paintings. Outside beneath the portico, Indian craftsmen and artisans spread wares for sale at the **Indian Market**.

The Museum of Fine Arts★

107 W. Palace Ave., opposite the Palace of the Governors. ᚛ *☎505-476-5072. www.museumofnewmexico.org.*

In a Pueblo Revival-style building a block northwest of the Plaza, the museum harbors a collection of 20,000 pieces. Contemporary and historic New Mexican works, among them many of the Taos Society and Cinco Pintores, are presented in rotating exhibits. A long-term exhibit featuring the museum's Georgia O'Keeffe collection is the highlight. The museum also has an extensive photography collection.

Georgia O'Keeffe Museum★★★

217 Johnson St., three blocks northwest of Plaza. ✕ ᚛ *☎505-946-1000. www.okeeffemuseum.org.*

Here is the largest collection of paintings, pastels, watercolors and sculptures by famed artist Georgia O'Keeffe (1887-1986). O'Keeffe was fascinated by the textures created by light and color in the landscape of New Mexico, her adopted home from 1949 until her death. Among the 130 works displayed are her signature flowers and bleached bones, abstracts, nudes, landscapes, cityscapes and still lifes. An 8min video introduces the collection. In 2001, the museum added an American Modernism gallery, featuring works of such O'Keeffe contemporaries as Marsden Hartley, Willem de Kooning, Robert Motherwell and Andy Warhol.

©iStockphoto.com/Lillis photography

Sample wares, Indian Market

The Cathedral Basilica of St. Francis of Assisi★★

Cathedral Place, one block east of Plaza. ♿ ☎505-982-5619. www.cbsfa.org.

The first church between Durango, Mexico, and St. Louis, Missouri, to attain cathedral status was intended to resemble great cathedrals of Europe. Unlike other local churches, it is not built in adobe style. Archbishop Jean-Baptiste Lamy recruited Italian masons to assist in the 1869-86 construction of the French Romanesque structure, which overlooks the east side of the Plaza.

In a niche in the wall of the north chapel is a 13C wooden statue, "La Conquistadora," believed to be the oldest representation of the Madonna in the US. Brought to Santa Fe in 1625, it was rescued from an earlier church during the 1680 Pueblo Rebellion and returned 12 years later as a symbol of Spain's reconquest.

The Institute of American Indian Arts Museum★

108 Cathedral Pl., opposite St. Francis Cathedral. ♿ ☎505-983-8900. www.iaia.edu.

Home of The National Collection of Contemporary Indian Art, this provocative museum presents works of Native Americans including Alaskan Eskimos. Some 6,500 works—paintings, sculptures, ceramics, jewelry, costumes, graphics and photographs—express modern lifestyles. Many are available for purchase.

Loretto Chapel★★

207 Old Santa Fe Trail, two blocks south of Plaza. ♿ ☎505-982-0092. www.lorettochapel.com.

Modeled after the Sainte-Chapelle church in Paris and dedicated in 1878, this chapel is noted for its famous spiral staircase. Leading to the choir loft, this staircase makes two complete 360-degree turns with no nails or other visible support. Legend claims it was built by a mysterious carpenter who appeared astride a donkey, in answer to the prayers of the Sisters of Loretto.

El Santuario de Guadalupe

100 Guadalupe St at Agua Fria St. ☎505-988-2027.

The church dates from 1776 and is the oldest US shrine to the Virgin of Guadalupe, patroness of Mexico. It now operates as a museum and performing-arts center. A famous oil painting, *Our Lady of Guadalupe*, signed by José de Alzíbar in 1783, is inside.

Mission of San Miguel de Santa Fe★

401 Old Santa Fe Trail at E. De Vargas St. ☎505-983-3974.

Established in 1610, this old church was rebuilt a century later and has since been oft-remodeled. A Mexican sculpture of its patron saint, St. Michael, dating from the 17C, highlights a fine collection of Hispanic religious art.

New Mexico State Capitol★

Paseo de Peralta & Old Santa Fe Trail. ♿ 🅿 ☎505-986-4589. www.legis.state.nm.us.

The only round capitol building in the US was built in 1966 in the shape of a Pueblo zia, or Circle of Life. It symbolizes the four directions, four winds, four seasons and four sacred obligations. Some 6.5 acres of gardens surround the building. Within, operated by the Museum of New Mexico, is the **Governor's Gallery** (☎505-827-3089), a fine contemporary art collection that dominates the spa-

San Miguel Mission of Santa Fe

©iStockphoto.com/Lillis photography

The Eight Northern Pueblos

Ancestral Puebloan people first occupied northern New Mexico more than 1,000 years ago. Today, eight independent pueblos are well known for their distinctive, traditional, handmade arts and crafts. Several offer glimpses of their historic past to visitors; the public is generally welcome to view special feast days, including traditional Indian dances scheduled annually at some pueblos.

The eight pueblos collaborate on a popular annual arts and crafts show in July *(b505-747-1593. www.eightnorthernpueblos.com)*.

Tesuque Pueblo – *US 84/285, 7-10mi north of Santa Fe;* ☎505-983-2667. Listed on the National Register of Historic Places, Tesuque has adobe structures dating from AD 1250. A popular flea market is adjacent to the Santa Fe Opera; the Camel Rock Casino-a venue for rock concerts-is about 3mi further north.

Pojoaque Pueblo – *US-84/285, 12mi north of Santa Fe;* ☎575-455-3460. The new **Poeh Cultural Center and Museum** *(☎575-455-2489)* depicts tribal history and culture. Nearby are the Pojoaque *(po-WAH-kay)* Pueblo Visitor Information Center, with a shop offering crafts by 800 Native American artisans, and the Cities of Gold casino-hotel.

Nambe Pueblo – *1mi east of Rte. 503, 20mi north of Santa Fe;* ☎505-455-2036. Inhabited since 1300, this village is known for its stone sculptures, black-and-red micaceous pottery, textiles and beadwork. Several ancient ruins may be found near the Nambe Falls Lake and Recreation Area.

San Ildefonso Pueblo – *Off Rte. 502, 24mi northwest of Santa Fe;* ☎505-455-3549. The village was the home of famed pottery María Martínez, whose family continues to produce her trademark black-on-black matté pottery, as well as other black, red and polychrome pottery sold by individual artisans.

Santa Clara Pueblo – *Rte. 30, 2mi south of Española;* ☎505-753-7326. Descended from ancestral cliff dwellers, villagers are known for their weaving, black pottery and beadwork. Several structures dating from AD 1250–1577 may be seen 11mi west of here at the **Puye Cliff Dwellings**. A tribal permit is required to approach the site by descending staircases and ladders from a 7,000ft mesa top.

Ohkay Owingeh (San Juan Pueblo) – *US-84/285, 5mi north of Española;* ☎505-852-4400. The largest Tewa-speaking pueblo has over 2,000 members. The village, whose architecture ranges from French Gothic (in two Catholic churches) to traditional Pueblo style, operates the large Ohkay Casino and the **O'ke Oweenge Arts and Crafts Cooperative** *(☎575-852-2372)*.

Picuris Pueblo – *2mi north of Rte. 75, 33mi south of Taos;* ☎505-587-2519. Visitors need a permit to visit restored San Lorenzo Mission and nearby pueblo ruins, including a 700-year-old kiva. Picuris was first known as pikuria, or "those who paint"; works by some of the pueblo's 300-odd residents are on display in the Tribal Museum.

Taos Pueblo – *2mi north of Taos Plaza;* ☎575-758-1028. *www.taospueblo.com*. The oldest and best-known northern New Mexico pueblo is described below *(p 405)*.

Taos Pueblo

©iStockphoto.com/Natalia Bratslavsky

cious lobby, hallways to the Senate and House galleries, and upper floors.

Canyon Road★

Santa Fe's greatest concentration of fine-art galleries—more than 80—may be found along narrow Canyon Road, interspersed with several fine restaurants 1-2mi southeast of the Plaza. Near the road's west end, the Pueblo-style **Gerald Peters Gallery** (1011 Paseo de Peralta; ☎505-954-5700) may be the city's largest private gallery. East, beyond the galleries, is the **Cristo Rey Church** (1120 Canyon Rd. at Camino Cabra; ☎505-983-8528), an imposing adobe edifice built in 1940. A massive stone reredos, or altar screen, dating from 1761, was taken from St. Francis cathedral.

Randall Davey Audubon Center

Kids End of Upper Canyon Rd., 2mi east of Camino Cabra. P ☎505-983-4609. nm.audubon.org.

This surprising 135-acre wildlife refuge abuts the Nature Conservancy's Santa Fe Canyon Preserve.

Museum of Indian Arts and Culture★★

Kids 710 Camino Lejo. ♿ P ☎505-476-1250. www.miaclab.org.

A multimedia exhibit, Here, Now and Alwaysaa, highlights the cultural history and lifestyles of New Mexico's Pueblo, Navajo and Apache tribes and features items from a collection of 70,000 artifacts, including basketry, jewelry, textiles and rugs. The **Buchsbaum Gallery of Southwest Pottery**★ demonstrates traditions and innovations; other galleries have rotating exhibits.

Museum of International Folk Art★★

Kids 706 Camino Lejo. ♿ P ☎505-476-1200. www.moifa.org.

Traditional arts from over 100 countries on six continents represent the largest folk collection in the world—more than 120,000 objects. They include historical and contemporary religious art, folk art, traditional costumes and textiles, silver and gold work, ceramics and glass, and children's toys and dolls. Miniature dioramas in the Girard Wing depict world lifestyles. Visitors may descend to the basement and Lloyd's Treasure Chest, a behind-the-scenes look at new items being prepared for exhibition.

Museum of Spanish Colonial Art★

750 Camino Lejo. ♿ P ☎505-982-2226. www.spanishcolonial.org.

This new museum presents a remarkable collection spanning the centuries since Spain first colonized the American Southwest in the late 16C. Santeros, retablos, textiles, tinwork, ceramics, furniture and many more items are presented and described. The museum in a fomer ambassador's residence faces on charming Milner Plaza at Museum Hill, linking the various museums on Camino Lejo.

Wheelwright Museum of the American Indian★

704 Camino Lejo. ♿ P ☎505-982-4636. www.wheelwright.org.

This small museum is built in the eight-sided shape of a Navajo hogan, its door facing east toward the rising sun. Founded in 1937 by a Boston scholar and a Navajo medicine man to preserve ritual beliefs and practices, the museum focuses on living arts in exhibits.

Old Santa Fe Trail Building

1100 Old Santa Fe Trail. ♿ P ☎505-988-6888.

The Intermountain Support Office of the National Park Service is a masterpiece of Pueblo Revival architecture and one of the largest adobe office buildings in the US. Built in 1937-39 (Cecil J. Doty) by the Civilian Conservation Corps, it was designated a National Historic Landmark in 1987.

Shidoni★

1508 Bishop's Lodge Rd., Tesuque, 5mi north of Plaza. ♿ P ☎505-988-8001. www.shidoni.com.

Established in 1971 in the rural Tesuque Valley, the Shidoni foundry is internationally acclaimed for its lost-wax casting process. Visitors may linger in eight acres of sculpture gardens, visit gallery exhibits by 100 sculptors, or take a self-guided tour of the foundry.

The Santa Fe Opera★★

US-84 & 285, 7mi north of Plaza.
♿ 🅿 ☎505-986-5900. *www.
santafeopera.org.*

Works by European composers like Tchaikovsky, Rossini, Mozart and Richard Strauss follow on the heels of 20C American premieres at this hilltop amphitheater. The opera company, often ranked second in the US only to New York's Metropolitan Opera, was established in 1957. Famed conductors and performers guest-star during a nine-week, 35-performance season, which extends from late June to late August. Year-round tours let visitors appreciate the soaring curves of the 2,128-seat theater.

Excursions

Los Alamos★

Rte. 502, 35mi northwest of Santa Fe. ✕♿🅿 ☎505-662-8105. *visit.
losalamos.com.*

Unique among world cities, Los Alamos perches atop a series of isolated finger canyons lined by the cottonwoods (alamos) for which it was named . The town of 12,000 was founded in 1942 as a top-secret community devoted to the creation of atomic weapons. It is the home of the **Los Alamos National Laboratory,** which employs 7,000 in scientific research for national security and economic strength. Unlike other towns in northern New Mexico, the architecture is not predominantly adobe; most homes are of the simple wood-frame variety.

Bradbury Science Museum★★

15th St. & Central Ave. ♿🅿 ☎505-667-4444. *www.lanl.gov/museum.*

This high-tech museum offers exhibits on the historic development of the atomic bomb. More than three dozen hands-on displays educate visitors on current technology and science development at Los Alamos National Labora-

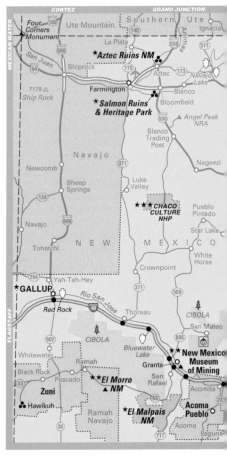

tory, including biomedical and energy research.

Bandelier National Monument★★

Rte. 4, 15mi south of Los Alamos. ⛺♿🅿 ☎505-672-3861. *www.nps.gov/band.*

This 50sq-mi park preserves cliff dwellings and other sites occupied by ancient Puebloans for 500 years starting in AD 1050. From a visitor center and museum, a 1.5mi paved trail along Frijoles Creek leads to the main, partially reconstructed ruins. Wooden ladders allow visitors to climb 140ft to a ceremonial kiva.

Abiquiu★

US-84, 47mi northwest of Santa Fe.

A village that provided scenic inspiration for her work, Abiquiu was home to artist Georgia O'Keeffe for nearly 40 years. Managed by the O'Keeffe Museum, small

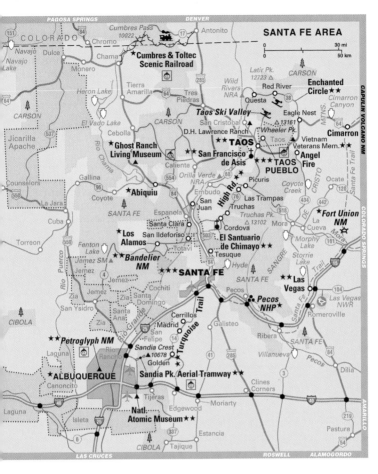

SANTA FE AREA

groups can visit her home and studio, but reservations (☎505-685-4539) are normally required months in advance.

El Santuario de Chimayo★★★

Rte. 76, Chimayo, 25mi north of Santa Fe.
♿ 🅿 ☎505-351-4889. www.archdiocese santafe.org.

A National Historic Landmark, this Spanish adobe church is the most important pilgrimage site in the Southwest. Some 30,000 pilgrims walk here every Good Friday from as far away as Albuquerque. Many enter the anteroom beside the altar to take home soil that is believed to be holy and hold miraculous healing powers. Leg braces , crutches and canes discarded by believers provide testimony. The chapel contains five sacred reredos and a number of religious carvings.

High Road to Taos★★

Rte. 76 east from Chimayo to Rte. 518 near Vadito.

Traditional 19C lifestyles persist in a string of villages along this intriguing and mountainous 25mi route. Beginning in the weaving and chile center of Chimayo, it extends through the wood-carving village of **Cordova**, where crafts are often sold from roadside stalls. The farming hamlet of **Truchas**—where Robert Redford filmed his 1987 movie, *The Milagro Beanfield War*—sits atop a mesa beneath snow-capped 13,102ft Truchas Peak, the state's second-highest elevation. In the village of **Las Trampas,** founded in 1751, is the San José de Gracia Church, an oft-photographed Spanish Colonial adobe structure listed on the National Register of Historic Places.

Pecos National Historical Park★

Rte. 63, 4mi north of I-25 Exit 307, 27mi east of Santa Fe. ♿ 🅿 ☎505-757-6414. *www.nps.gov/peco.*

Coronado, in 1540, wrote that Pecos Pueblo was "feared through the land." Within 300 years, however, the 17 survivors of an original tribe of 2,000 had abandoned their home. This site preserves the ruins of the 14C village and a 1625 mission church.

Las Vegas★★

I-25 Exit 345, 66mi east of Santa Fe. ✕♿🅿 ☎505-425-8631. *www.lasvegasnm.org.*

With 900 buildings listed on the National Historic Register, a classic plaza and no pretensions, Las Vegas—no relation whatsoever to its Nevada namesake—epitomizes old New Mexico. The friendly charm of this city of 14,500 may be discovered in nine historic districts. The campus of New Mexico Highlands Uni-

versity (1893) links downtown, a relic of the Route 66 era, and the Old Town Plaza Park district, surrounded by impressive 19C adobe buildings. Elsewhere, structures represent many Victorian styles.

Fort Union National Monument★

Rte. 161 off I-25 Exit 366, 28mi northeast of Las Vegas. ♿🅿 ☎505-425-8025. *www.nps.gov/foun.*

Established in 1851, Fort Union was a base for military operations on the Santa Fe Trail, the chief quartermaster depot for the Southwest. Campaigns against the Jicarilla Apaches in 1854, the Utes in 1855 and the Kiowas and Comanches in 1860-61 were launched from here. After a railroad replaced the trail in 1879, Fort Union's role decreased, and it was abandoned in 1891. Today's visitors tour its sprawling brick-and-adobe remains and a small museum.

ALBUQUERQUE★

MAP P 401

MOUNTAIN STANDARD TIME

POPULATION 505,000

Albuquerque is an intriguing mix of old and new, of 14C Indian pueblos, 18C Spanish village and 21C high-technology center. Its architecture is liberally sprinkled with reminders of its mid-20C fling as a prime stop on cross-country Route 66, in the days before the interstate highway system. By far New Mexico's largest city, it is one of seven US cities to receive federal funds to preserve its classic roadside architecture; Pueblo Revival architecture, neon-lit cafes and motor courts speckle its cultural corridors, especially Central Avenue east and west of downtown. The restored 1927 KiMo Theatre *(423 Central Ave. NW;* ☎505-768-3522, www.cabq.gov/kimo) **may be the finest example of the Pueblo Deco style of building that fused Art Deco with Native American motifs.**

🛈 **Information:** ☎505-842-9918, www.abqcvb.org
😊 **Don't Miss:** Sandia Peak Tram, Indian Pueblo Cultural Center
Kids Especially for Kids: Rio Grande Zoo
Also See: Rio Grande Nature Center

More than 10 percent of hot-air balloons in the US are registered in Albuquerque. Mornings are generally windless, and on weekend dawns many of the colorful aircraft may be seen floating above the 100sq mi of the city. In October, the city's Balloon Fiesta is the world's largest gathering of hot air.

A Bit of History

Paleo-Indian artifacts ascribed to Sandia Man, discovered in the mountains overlooking Albuquerque, have been dated from 25,000 years ago. Ancestral Indian farmlands, longtime homes of stationary tribes, are still inhabited pueblo communities. Spanish colonists established a villa on the Old Chihuahua Trail in 1706 and named it after the regional governor, the Duke of Alburquerque. Anglos arrived in force in the 1880s when the Santa Fe Railroad bypassed a costly mountain crossing at Santa Fe and came through this site instead. Sleepy Albuquerque was transformed into a rail boomtown, later to become a high-tech hub on the coattails of Los Alamos.

Sights

Old Town★★
Central Ave. NW north to Mountain Rd. NW & Rio Grande Blvd. NW east to 19th St. NW. ✕ ♿ 🅿 www.albuquerqueoldtown.com.
Some 150 shops and galleries face hidden gardens and cobbled walkways around a quiet, tree-shaded 18C plaza. The modern city has grown from this traditional central core. Today, restored adobes share the plaza with Pueblo Revival architecture, some structures painted in bold colors that suggest an adobe-Deco hybrid. The **Church of San Felipe de Neri**★ was built on the west side of the plaza in 1706; reconstructed on the north side in 1793, it has been in continuous use since. Pueblo and Navajo artisans display wares at the small **Indian market** along San Felipe Street, in front of the c.1706 Casa Armijo (now La Placita restaurant).
Old Town walking tours begin 11am most days from The Albuquerque Museum *(below)*. Nearby is the interesting **American International Rattlesnake Museum**★ *(202 San Felipe St. NW; ☎505-242-6569, www.ratlesnakes.com),* just south of the plaza.

The Albuquerque Museum of Art and History★★
2000 Mountain Rd. NW. ♿ 🅿 ☎505-243-7255. www.cabq.gov/museum.
The evolution of the Rio Grande valley, from pre-Columbian tribes through Coronado to the present, is chronicled in the fine Four Centuries★★ exhibit at this Old Town museum. An extensive collection of Spanish Colonial artifacts includes religious tapestries, maps,

coins, arms and armor. Galleries of contemporary art highlight works by New Mexico artists.

New Mexico Museum of Natural History and Science★★
🆔 *1801 Mountain Rd. NW. ✕ ♿ 🅿 ☎505-841-2800. www.nmnaturalhistory.org.*
Four blocks north and east of the Old Town plaza, this lively museum offers a ramble through geologic time, from the formation of the universe to modern times. Interactive exhibits place visitors in the middle of a live volcano and an Ice Age cave. Fossil displays describe the paleontology, zoology and botany of the region from a time when dinosaurs were local residents; a seacoast exhibit covers ocean shores. Other features include the giant-screen Dynamax Theater and the University of New Mexico's **Lodestar Astronomy Center.**

Indian Pueblo Cultural Center★★
🆔 *2401 12th St. NW, 1 block north of I-40. ✕ ♿ 🅿 ☎505-843-7270. www.indianpueblo.org.*
The arts of New Mexico's 19 Pueblo communities are exhibited at this important nonprofit center a mile from Old Town. Modeled after 9C Pueblo Bonito in Chaco Culture National Historical Park, this is the one place to get an overview of cultures as presented by the Indians themselves, not interpreted by Anglos. The Indian Pueblo Cultural Museum exhibits ancient artifacts and contemporary weavings, jewelry, pottery and paintings—each piece individually chosen for display by tribal members—that trace the development of Pueblo cultures. Pottery designs are unique to each pueblo. Traditional dancers perform weekends on an outdoor stage, and artisans demonstrate various crafts.

National Hispanic Cultural Center★
1701 4th St. SW. ✕ ♿ 🅿 ☎505-246-2261. www.nhccnm.org.
Rising south of downtown like a miniature Mayan pyramid, this impressive new complex combines a visual-arts museum with a library, genealogy center, restaurant, meeting areas, per-

forming-arts center and other facilities. Museum exhibits, rotating every 3-6 months, focus on Hispanic art and culture, from 18C-19C retablos to the works of contemporary artists.

Rio Grande Zoo★

Kids *903 10th St. SW.* ✕ ♿ 🅿 ☎*505-764-6200. www.cabq.gov/biopark/zoo.*
Sixty-four acres of riverside cottonwood bosque are home to more than 1,000 animals of various species. Especially strong in regional fauna, the zoo includes a New Mexico prairie ecosystem and a habitat for endangered species of the Southwest. Other highlights include a tropical American rain forest and underwater viewing areas on polar bears and sea lions.

Albuquerque Aquarium & Rio Grande Botanic Garden

Kids *2601 Central Ave. NW.* ✕ ♿ 🅿 ☎*505-764-6200. www.cabq.gov/biopark.*
A 9min film on the Rio Grande biosystem, from source to mouth, introduces the aquarium—which focuses on Gulf of Mexico habitats, from salt marsh to coral reef and sharks in the open ocean. Highlighting the botanic garden are twin climate-controlled conservatories, the aromatic **Mediterranean Pavilion**★ and the sere **Desert Pavilion,** as well as a heritage farm, Japanese garden and children's fantasy garden.

Rio Grande Nature Center★

Kids *2901 Candelaria Rd. NW.* ✕ ♿ 🅿 ☎*505-344-7240. www.rgnc.org.*
Ensconced in 270 acres of cottonwood bosque and riparian wetlands, this state park serves an environmental education function. The **Riverwalk Trail** *(1mi)* and the **Bosque Loop Trail** *(.8mi)* depart from a visitor center whose displays focus on the ecology and geology of the Rio Grande basin.

Petroglyph National Monument★★

Kids *4735 Unser Blvd. NW, 3mi north of I-40 & 4mi west of Old Town.* ♿ 🅿 ☎*505-899-0205. www.nps.gov/petr.*
More than 20,000 petroglyphs, scratched or chipped into basalt along a 17mi lava escarpment beneath five ancient volcanoes, chronicle the lives of countless Native American generations. Paved trails run through **Boca Negra Canyon**, 2.5mi north of the **visitor center** *(Unser Blvd. & Western Trail Rd.).*

University of New Mexico

Yale Blvd. NE at Central Ave. ✕ ♿ 🅿 ☎*505-277-5813. www.unm.edu.*
About 24,000 students attend the main campus of this state institution, 2mi east of Old Town. Though founded in 1889, most of UNM's Pueblo Revival-style buildings were designed by architect John Gaw Meem in the 1930s and 40s. Its interesting museums include the venerable (1932) **Maxwell Museum of Anthropology**★ *(Redondo Dr. at Ash St. NE; ☎ 505-277-4405, www.unm.edu)*, the **University Art Museum** *(Cornell St. north of Central Ave.; ☎505-277-4001, unmartmuseum.unm. edu)*, the **Meteorite Museum** *(☎505-277-2747)*, and the **Geology Museum** *(☎505-277-4204)*, with specimens typical of the New Mexico region.

National Atomic Museum★★

1905 Mountain Rd. ♿ 🅿 ☎*505-245-2137. www.atomicmuseum.com.*
Exhibits trace the development of atomic energy and weaponry, beginning with 4C BC Greek philosopher Democritus, who first proposed the existence of tiny particles as fundamental building blocks. A preponderance of displays is given over to the Cold War era of the 1950s to 80s.

Sandia Peak Aerial Tramway★★

Kids *10 Tramway Loop NE, 6mi east of I-25 via Tramway Blvd. at the Sandia Casino.* ✕ ♿ 🅿 ☎*505-856-7325. www.sandia peak.com.*
The world's longest jig-back aerial tramway covers 2.7mi from the northeastern city limits to 10,678ft **Sandia Crest.** Climbing from urban desert to alpine terrain in just 15min, the tram affords panoramic views of 11,000sq mi, across the entire Albuquerque area and other parts of northern New Mexico. Sandia Crest *(☎505-243-0605)* also can be reached by a 35mi drive from Albuquerque *(east 16mi on I-40, north 6mi to Sandia Park on Rte. 14, then northwest 13mi on Rte. 536).*

Excursions

Turquoise Trail★★

Rte. 14, Tijeras (16mi east of Albuquerque at I-40 Exit 175) to Santa Fe. www.turquoise trail.org.

This 52mi back road avoids I-25 and runs along the scenic eastern edge of the Sandia Mountains, which show a forested side not apparent from the desert-like west slope.

At Cedar Crest *(4mi north of I-40)*, the **Museum of Archaeology and Material Culture** *(Rte. 14; ☎505-281-2005)* has a fine collection on early Native Americans, including Sandia Man, one of North America's earliest fossil-man discoveries. **Sandia Park** *(2mi north of Cedar Crest)*, the turnoff for Sandia Crest, has its **Tinkertown Museum**★ *(Rte. 536; ☎505-281-5233)*, a 22-room folk-art tribute to Ross Ward's life work creating hand-carved, animated dioramas.

Turquoise, gold, silver, lead and coal were once mined in great quantities in **Golden** *(15mi north of Sandia Park)*, **Madrid**★ *(11mi north of Golden)* and **Cerrillos** *(3mi north of Madrid)*. When the last coal mines closed in the mid-1950s, the communities declined until rediscovered by artists and craftspeople, who found them perfect places to make the 1960s live on. Madrid, largest of the three hamlets, invites visitors to descend into the **Old Coal Mine Museum,** *(☎505-438-3780)* and attend melodramas at its **Madrid Opera House**, which boasts a built-in steam locomotive on-stage.

Coronado State Monument★

Rte. 44, Bernalillo, 1mi west of I-25 Exit 242. ☎505-867-5351. www.nmmonuments.org.

The ruins of the Kuaua Pueblo, built about 1325 on the west bank of the Rio Grande, are preserved here.

TAOS★★

MAP P 401
MOUNTAIN STANDARD TIME
POPULATION 5,200

Taos Pueblo has been continuously inhabited for at least 1,000 years. The rustic, Spanish colonial town of Taos is perhaps 300 years old. Built around a cozy plaza that remains the heart of the modern town, it is today a center for the arts, much smaller than Santa Fe but equally alluring to aficionados of Southwest art.

- **Information:**☎575-758-3873, www.taoschamber.com.
- **Don't Miss:** Taos Pueblo
- **Especially for Kids:** Kit Carson Home.

A Bit of History

Taos found its niche in the world of art in 1915 when Joseph Sharp, Ernest Blumenschein, Bert Phillips and friends founded the **Taos Society of Artists.** They focused world attention on the unique light that falls on northern New Mexico; its reputation laid a foundation for today's prolific, tricultural art community.

Taos sits on a plateau between the Rio Grande and the Sangre de Cristo Range. Eleven miles northwest of Taos on US-64, the three-span, continuous-truss Rio

Grande Gorge Bridge, 1,200ft long, crosses the river at a height of 650ft above it.

Sights

Taos Pueblo★★★

2mi north of Taos Plaza via Camino del Pueblo. ☎575-758-1028. www.taos pueblo.com.

The oldest and best-known New Mexico pueblo has been designated a World Heritage Site, of enduring value to mankind, by the United Nations. A visit is a step back in time. Although Pueblo Indian ruins are found throughout the Southwest, here the site is intact, occupied and used daily.

The pueblo contains a multistory mud-and-straw adobe structure with ladders leading to upper floors. Some 150 residents live here year-round without running water or electricity. About 1,100 other pueblo members live in modern homes, but sell mica-flecked pottery, silver and turquoise jewelry, moccasins and drums from homes on the pueblo's ground floor that have been converted to small shops.

Ruins of the **Mission San Geronimo de Taos**★ are near the pueblo entrance.

The pueblo's **Taos Mountain Casino** (Camino del Pueblo, 1.5mi north of Taos Plaza; ☎575-737-0777) offers gaming, dining, shopping and entertainment on the pueblo access road.

The Fechin House and Studio★

227 Paseo del Pueblo Norte. 🅿 ☎575-758-2290. www.fechin.com.

Before he moved to Taos in 1927, Nikolai Fechin (1881-1955) had secured a reputation in his native Russia and in New York as a renaissance man. His paintings, sculptures and drawings are on display inside this Russian-style home.

Kit Carson Home and Museum★★

Kids E. Kit Carson Rd., 1 block east of Taos Plaza. ☎575-758-4945. www.kitcarsonhome.com.

Carson, a famous frontier scout and Indian agent (1809-68), lived in this 1825 house from 1843 until his death. The museum, in a part of the original house, illustrates Carson's career and frontier life of that era through displays featuring guns, clothing, saddles, furniture and period equipment used by mountain men and Indians.

A National Historic Landmark since 1991, the **Mabel Dodge Luhan House** (240 Morada Ln.; ☎575-751-9686; www.mabeldodgeluhan.com), home to Mabel Dodge, darling of the counterculture and patron of the arts, is now a bed-and-breakfast retreat, around a corner

from the Carson Home. Next door is the **Lumina Gallery** (239 Morada Ln.; ☎575-758-7282; www.luminagallery.com), whose two-acre Ridhwan Sculpture Garden is a wildlife habitat with 40 large-scale works.

Ernest L. Blumenschein Home & Museum★

222 Ledoux St., 2 blocks south and west of Taos Plaza 🅿 ☎575-758-0505. www.taoshistoricmuseums.com.

The collection includes works by Taos Society, painter Blumenschein (1874-1960) and his wife.

A few steps east is the **R.C. Gorman Navajo Gallery** (210 Ledoux St.; ☎575-758-3250), home of works by the renowned Native American painter and sculptor.

The Harwood Museum of Art★★

238 Ledoux St. ♿ 🅿 ☎575-758-9826. harwoodmuseum.org.

Works by 20C Taos artists—paintings, drawings, sculptures and photography—are displayed at this museum, a fixture since 1923. There are works by noted American Modernists including Marsden Hartley and Richard Diebenkorn, and a Hispanic folk-art collection with 80 19C retablos (religious paintings on wood), many donated by Mabel Dodge Luhan.

La Hacienda de los Martinez★★

Ranchitos Rd., 2mi west of Taos. 🅿 ☎575-758-0505. www.taoshistoricmuseums.com.

One of the few Spanish Colonial "great houses" open to the public, the fortress-like hacienda was built in 1804 by merchant Don Antonio Severino Martinez. Its windowless adobe walls rise above the west bank of the Rio Pueblo de Taos. Twenty-one spartan rooms, built around two courtyards, provide a look at frontier life.

Millicent Rogers Museum★★

1504 Millicent Rogers Rd., .8mi south of US-64, 3mi north of Taos Plaza. ♿ 🅿 ☎575-758-2462. millicentrogers.org.

Founded by Standard Oil heiress Millicent Rogers (1902-53), this museum exhibits Rogers' own silver and turquoise Indian jewelry, Navajo and Rio Grande weavings. Additional collections include Hispanic religious and domestic arts, and crafts from all over New Mexico, including the María Martínez Family Collection of San Ildefonso pottery, Zuni kachina dolls, basketry and textiles.

Taos Ski Valley★

Taos Ski Valley Rd. (Rte. 150), 19mi north of Taos Plaza. 📖 ☎866-958-7386 *skitaos. org.*

One of the most challenging ski mountains in North America, Taos Ski Valley is an anomaly among major resorts: It doesn't permit snowboarding. The Village, which nestles at the foot of the slopes at 9,207ft elevation, has more than a dozen lodges, numerous restaurants and shops *(www.taosskivalley.com)*. Twelve lifts serve terrain that crests at 11,819ft.

San Francisco de Asis Church★★

Rte. 68, 4mi south of Taos Plaza. ☎575-758-2754.

The exterior of this heavily buttressed adobe church is probably the most painted and photographed in New Mexico. Georgia O'Keeffe and Ansel Adams are among artists who have immortalized its stark, 120ft-long form. The two-story church was built between 1710 and 1755; its few doors and windows are not visible from the highway. In the chapel are images of saints, a large Christ figure and reredos dating to the church's founding.

Excursions

Enchanted Circle★★

Rtes. 522 & 38 and US-64, north and east of Taos. ✕📖 *www.enchantedcircle.org.*

This 85mi US Forest Service Scenic Byway circles 13,161ft **Wheeler Peak,** New Mexico's highest point, and connects Taos with several small resort towns. A first stop for northbound motorists, traveling clockwise around the loop, is the **D.H. Lawrence Ranch and Shrine** *(County Rd. 7, San Cristobal, 6mi east of Rte. 522, 15mi north of Taos;* ☎575-776-2245). Lawrence (1885-1930) lived at this ranch sporadically in the early 1920s; when the author died of tuberculosis in southern France, his ashes were returned for burial.

The town of **Questa** *(Rte. 522, 24mi north of Taos;* ☎575-586-0694) is a starting point for white-water trips on the upper Rio Grande. **Red River** *(Rte. 38, 12mi east of Questa;* ☎575-754-2366; *www.redrivernewmex.com)* and **Eagle Nest** *(US-64 & Rte. 38, 17mi east of Red River & 31mi northeast of Taos;* ☎575-377-2420; *www. eaglenest.org),* both 19C gold-mining towns, are bases for outdoor excursions into pine forests shadowed by Wheeler Peak. Activities include skiing at **Red River Ski Area** *(*☎575-754-2223) and fishing for trout and salmon in Eagle Nest Lake.

Angel Fire *(Rte. 434, just south of US-64;* ☎575-377-6661; *www.angelfirechamber. org),* a tiny village in the Moreno Valley of the Sangre de Cristo Range, is a year-round ski and golf resort. The **Vietnam Veterans Memorial**★ *(US-64, Angel Fire;* ♿📖 ☎575-377-6900), a father's tribute to his martyred son, is a white curved structure perched on a serene hillside, offering broad views of the Moreno Valley and the Sangre de Cristo.

GALLUP-FARMINGTON AREA★

MAP P 400

MOUNTAIN STANDARD TIME

Gallup is a gateway to the Navajo and Zuni reservations and a center for Indian arts and crafts. Free dances are regularly presented, and fine trading posts invite shoppers and browsers. The lucrative native-art market has created many local millionaires among Gallup's 20,200 residents. Farther north, Farmington is the gateway to several of the world's unique and ancient Indian ruins, as well as mountain and desert recreational sites. A business hub for the Four Corners region, the city of 44,000 anchors the northeastern corner of the 250,000sq-mi Navajo Indian Reservation.

- **Information:** ☎505-722-2228 or www.gallupnm.org. ☎505-326-7602, www.farmingtonnm.org, www.indiancountrynm.org
- ▶ **Orient Yourself:** In this part of New Mexico the local landmark is Mount Taylor, halfway between Albuquerque and Gallup. At 11,301 feet it's the tallest thing for hundreds of miles, and sacred to the Navajo.
- ⏱ **Organizing Your Time:** Don't be fooled by the relative proximity of Chaco to Farmington--a trip to Chaco takes a full day.
- **Don't Miss:** Acoma Pueblo; Chaco Culture National Historical Park
- **Especially for Kids:** Cumbres & Toltec RR

Gallup Area

Gallup★

US-666 at I-40 Exit 20, 139mi west of Albuquerque. ✕⟡🅿 ☎*505-722-2228. www.gallupnm.org.*

Gallup is filled with trading posts, Indian shops and galleries along its fabled Route 66 corridor and in its 12-block historic district.

Each August for 80 years, the **Inter-Tribal Indian Ceremonial**★★ (☎*505-863-3896, www.gallupintertribal.com*) has been held at **Red Rock State Park** *(Rte. 66 at I-40 Exit 26, 4mi east of Gallup; 505-722-3829, ww.ci.gallup.nm.us).* Members of 30 tribes—from the area to Mexico and Canada—engage in parades, dances and rodeo events in one of America's largest tribal gatherings.

Zuni Indian Reservation★

Rte. 53, 37mi south of Gallup via Rte. 602. ⟁✕⟡🅿 ☎*505-782-7000. www.ashiwi.org.*

The arts and ambience of an ancient Pueblo community are very much alive in modern Zuni, largest (with 6,367 residents and 259sq mi of land) of New Mexico's pueblos.

A mural at the **Pueblo of Zuni Visitor Information Center**★ *(1222 Rte. 53;* ☎*505-782-5531; www.puebloofzuniarts.com)* depicts the Zuni origin story. The detailed work of silversmiths, carvers and potters is seen at **A:shiwi A:wan Museum & Heritage Center**★★ *(1220 Rte. 53;* ☎*505-782-4403; www.ashiwi.org).* Two dozen kachina murals in **Our Lady of Guadalupe Mission**★, built in 1629, depict a complex spiritual life blending tribal and Catholic traditions.

El Morro National Monument★★

Rte. 53 near Ramah, 54mi southeast of Gallup. ⟁⟡🅿 ☎*505-783-4226. www.nps.gov/elmo.*

For at least 1,000 years, names and messages have been carved into a sandstone monolith that rises 200ft above the valley floor. **Inscription Rock** is in a narrow catchment basin, the only water source for many miles. Pueblo Indians, Spanish explorers and frontier travelers camped here, leaving petroglyphs (AD 1000-1400) and other inscriptions.

El Malpais National Monument and Conservation Area★

Rte. 53, 23mi south of I-40 at Grants. 🅿 ☎*505-783-4774. www.nps.gov/elma.*

A landscape whose name is Spanish for "The Badlands," this park attracts hardy hikers and outdoors lovers. Forty different volcanoes produced a vast lava field, part of it only 2,000 years old.

New Mexico Mining Museum★★

Kids *100 N. Iron Ave., Grants, 61mi east of Gallup and 72mi west of Albuquerque.* ☐ *☎505-287-4802. www.grants.org.* Beneath the office of Grants' city visitor center, accessed via elevator through a small mining museum, is a replica of a uranium mine.

Acoma Pueblo★

Rte. 23, 12.5mi southwest of I-40 Exit 108, 30mi southeast of Grants and 64mi west of Albuquerque. ☐ *☎800-747-0181.* Native Americans say the clifftop **Sky City**★★★ has been inhabited "since the beginning of time." Archaeologists verify that this 70-acre, Medieval-looking, walled adobe village—perched atop a sheer mesa, 367ft above the valley floor—has been lived in at least since the 11C, though the Acoma believe it's longer than that. Between 1629 and 1640, Spanish priests built the **San Esteban del Rey Mission**★★, now (like Sky City itself) a National Historic Landmark. *Photography restrictions are in force in Sky City.* The tribe also operates the **Sky City Casino** *(I-40 Exit 102; ☎505-552-6017).*

Farmington Area

Aztec Ruins National Monument★

84 Ruins Rd., .5mi north of US-550, Aztec. ☐ *☎505-334-6174. www.nps.gov/azru.* Parts of a 400-room Ancestral Puebloan pueblo from AD 1100-1300 remain at this site beside a modern-day trailer park. In its heart is the largest reconstruction anywhere of a great kiva, a round chamber believed to have been used for ceremonies and other gatherings.

Salmon Ruins & Heritage Park★

US-64, 11mi east of Farmington & 2mi west of Bloomfield. ☐ *☎505-632-2013. www.salmonruins.com.* Excavation has partially exposed this 150-room Ancestral Puebloan site

beside the San Juan River. It was originally settled by Chacoans between AD 1088 and 1130, then added onto with Mesa Verde-style techniques around AD 1185, before being abandoned about AD 1250.

Chaco Culture National Historical Park★★★

Rte. 57, Nageezi, 73mi south of Farmington via US-64 & US-550. ☐ *☎505-786-7014. www.nps.gov/chcu.* One of the foremost cultural and historical areas in the US, Chaco Canyon was a major center of ancestral Ancestral Puebloan culture from AD 850-1250. A hub of ceremony, trade and government for the prehistoric Four Corners area—a city of thousands whose trade network extended into Mexico—it was unlike anything before or since.

There are 13 major excavated archaeological sites in Chaco Canyon, and hundreds of smaller sites. **Pueblo Bonito** (c.AD 850-1200) was the largest "great house"—four stories high, with 600 rooms and 40 kivas. Adjacent to it, **Chetro Ketl** (c.AD 1020-1200) contained 500 rooms, 16 kivas and an immense, elevated earthen plaza. **Pueblo del Arroyo** (280 rooms) and **Kin Kletso** (100 rooms) were built in stages in the late 11C and early 12C.

Situated in an isolated desert canyon, Chaco can be reached only by dirt roads. The preferred 21mi route is from the north, via County Road 7900 off US-550, 3mi southeast of Nageezi. An alternative 69mi route from the south begins off Tribal Road 9, 4mi north of Crownpoint. Roads are well maintained but may become impassable during heavy rains, so it's wise to phone ahead.

Cumbres & Toltec Scenic Railroad★

Kids *Rte. 17, Chama, 110mi east of Farmington via US-64.* ☐ *☎575-756-2151. www.cumbrestoltec.com.* The longest remaining example of the original Denver & Rio Grande narrow-gauge line covers 64mi between Chama, New Mexico, and Antonito, Colorado, over trestles and through tunnels in the San Juan Mountains above the Los Piños River.

SEATTLE AREA

Wedged into the far northwest corner of the lower 48 states, the booming metropolis of Seattle has a low-key, youthful flavor. High-tech entrepreneurs mingle easily with rock musicians, and aerospace engineers still sport pocket protectors along with PDAs. A futuristic skyline plays warm-up to snow-draped peaks only a couple of hours' drive away.

The surrounding state of Washington is one of the most geographically diverse in the nation. Its Pacific coast is filigreed by beautiful Puget Sound, surrounded by evergreen forests (most of which have been logged at least once). The volcanic cones of Mounts Baker, Rainier, Adams and St. Helens define the craggy central spine of the sky-scraping Cascade Mountains.

Long before the arrival of Europeans, coastal Indians thrived in the region's riches. Their elaborately carved canoes, totems and masks attested to a culture that took advantage of abundant forests and teeming waterways. British Capt. George Vancouver made detailed charts of the Puget Sound area in 1792. By the early 1800s, the region was included in the vast Oregon Country, hotly contested by British and American fur-trading interests. With the steady arrival of more and more American settlers, the territory became US soil, and towns soon grew along the coast at Seattle and Port Townsend. Today, the global scope of Microsoft, Starbucks and Boeing maintain the area's visibility. While the state struggles to accommodate a burgeoning population, visitors continue to discover scenic splendors and urban pleasures.

©iStockphoto.com/Yanming Di

Mount Rainier National Park

SEATTLE★★★

MAPS P 417 AND P 420
PACIFIC STANDARD TIME
POPULATION 570,000

Blanketing high hills that overlook Puget Sound, Seattle has grown from a hard-working pioneer town into one of the nation's cultural trendsetters. Noted for its livability and natural beauty, the city is surrounded by spectacular vistas—Mt. Rainier and the Cascade Range on the east, the Olympic Mountains on the west. Ubiquitous street-corner coffee bars have encouraged a cafe society, and an abundance of Northwest seafood and produce yields a distinctive regional cuisine and world-class restaurants. In the late 20C, Seattle became a leader in high technology, thanks to local software giant Microsoft. Though light rains fall on the city much of the year, they rarely dampen its youthful spirit.

- **Information:** ☎206-461-5840. www.visitseattle.org.
- ▶ **Orient Yourself:** Mount Rainier is conspicuous south of Seattle; the Cascades are east and the Olympic Mountains west, across Puget Sound. When Rainier is visible, locals say "the mountain's out," and good weather is usually at hand.
- **Parking:** Be sure to snare parking near the waterfront and Pike Place Market before 11 a.m.
- **Don't Miss:** Pike Place Market, the soul of Seattle.
- **Organizing Your Time:** Best to head for Pike Place Market and the aquarium in the morning, and devote the afternoon to Seattle Center.
- **Especially for Kids:** Pacific Science Center; Woodland Park Zoo.
- **Also See:** The Hiram Chittenden Locks in Ballard.

A Bit of History

Though Vancouver sailed into Puget Sound and anchored within sight of Alki Point (now West Seattle) in the late 18C, no serious white settlement arrived until the 1850s, when disappointed 49ers from the California gold fields and homesteaders from the Olympia area filtered north. On a typically chilly, gray November day in 1851, two small pioneer parties—one traveling over-land, the other by schooner—met at Alki. Named for Chief Sealth, respected Duwamish Indian leader, the new town was platted in 1853, with commerce centering upon a sawmill built by Henry Yesler.

By the turn of the 19C, lumber bar-ons Frederick Weyerhaeuser and William Boeing had set up shop in Puget Sound, the latter soon turning to the new technology of flight. These two industrial giants still help fuel the area's economy.

This formerly industrial town has given the country a zest for coffee, rock music and youthful entrepreneurship. And the region's ports continue to thrive on Pacific Rim trade.

Downtown

Pioneer Square★
Generally bounded by Alaskan Way, S. King St., Fourth Ave. S. & Cherry St. ☎206-667-0687. www.pioneersquare.org.

The Pioneer Square National Historic District anchors the south end of downtown with 18 blocks of restored turn-of-the-20C commercial buildings. Site of Seattle's first permanent settle-ment, Pioneer Square has become a sometimes boisterous nightclub district (best avoided after 9 p.m.).

The area is still defined by the long incline of Yesler Way, the original Skid Road down which logs were slid to the sawmill. A great fire destroyed most of downtown in 1889; the town pushed north and east, letting Pioneer Square lapse into a neglected "skid row" of bawdy houses and gambling dens.

Address Book Seattle Area

For prices, see the Legend on the cover flap.

WHERE TO STAY IN THE SEATTLE AREA

$$$$ Alexis Hotel – *1007 First Ave. S., Seattle, WA.* ✗ ♿ 🅿 Spa ☎ *206-624-4844 or 866-356-8894. www.alexishotel. com. 109 rooms.* When the Sultan of Brunei stayed at this century-old hotel for an extended period in 1993, he requested that his suite be redecorated to his desires. Within 48 hours, the Alexis had complied. That's the sort of service you'll get at this luxury boutique property. The **Painted Table ($$$)** offers top-end Northwest cuisine in an artsy atmosphere.

$$$$ Edgewater Hotel– *2411 Alaskan Way, Pier 67, Seattle, WA.* ✗ ♿ 🅿 ☎ *206-728-7000 or 800-624-0670. www. edgewaterhotel.com. 236 rooms.* Ferries, tall ships and sea lions cruise past Seattle's only waterfront hotel, built atop a pier. When the Beatles stayed here back in 1964, they fished from the windows of Room 272. Hand-peeled pine tables create the feeling of a rustic mountain-lake lodge, though the exterior has an industrial cast.

$$$ Inn at the Market – *86 Pine St., Seattle, WA.* ✗ ♿ 🅿 ☎ *206-443-3600 or 800-446-4484. www.innatthemarket.com. 70 rooms.* Within the Pike Place Market complex, the inn's ivied courtyard and fifth-floor deck overlook Puget Sound and the Olympic Range. Room décor features simple lines and soft colors; most rooms have natural-pine furniture and floor-to-ceiling bay windows. Room service arrives from the superb adjacent **Campagne ($$$)** country French restaurant.

$$$ Rosario Resort and Spa – *1400 Rosario Rd., Eastsound (Orcas Island), WA.* ✗ ♿ 🅿 ⛴ Spa ☎ *360-376-2222 or 800-562-8820. www.rosarioresort.com. 127 rooms.* A great base for exploring the San Juan Islands, this historic mansion, with teak-parquet floors and a working pipe organ, occupies eight bayside acres. Guests enjoy whale watching, sailing, yoga, tennis or kayaking. Now owned by Rockresorts, the

lodge has two outdoor pools and a sophisticated spa.

$$$$ Thornewood Castle Inn and Gardens – *8601 N. Thorne Ln. SW, Lakewood, WA.* 🅿 ☎ *253-584-4393. www. thornewoodcastle.com. 6 rooms.* Nestled on four wooded acres at American Lake 10mi south of Tacoma, this 54-room 1911 Gothic Tudor-style manor is the only one of its kind on the West Coast. The current owners have renovated a half-dozen bed-and-breakfast rooms to luxury standards, with old stained-glass panes and antique furnishings.

$$$$ The Willows Lodge – *14580 NE 145th St., Woodinville, WA.* ✗ ♿ 🅿 ⛴ Spa ☎ *425-424-3900 or 877-424-3930. www.willowslodge.com. 88 rooms.* Combining elegance and rusticity, The Willows sits amid five acres of lush gardens at the hub of the cozy Sammamish Valley near Seattle. Century-old Douglas fir timbers and a 30ft, double-sided stone fireplace welcome guests to the main lodge; wood décor and native art carry to the guest rooms. **The Barking Frog ($$$)** bistro shares the grounds with the renowned Herbfarm (below).

$$$ Lake Quinault Lodge – *345 South Shore Rd., Quinault, WA.* ✗ ♿ 🅿 ⛴ ☎ *360-288-2900 or 888-896-3827. www.visitlakequinault.com. 92 rooms.* On the shores of a serene mountain lake in a temperate rain forest, the Lodge—with its grand brick fireplace—has been a haven for rain-soaked travelers since 1926. A totem pole on the wooden porch measures 17ft of annual rainfall. The **Roosevelt Dining Room ($$$)** serves seafood and steaks with an Italian twist.

$$$ The Captain Whidbey Inn – *2072 W. Captain Whidbey Inn Rd., Coupeville, WA.* ✗ ♿ 🅿 ☎ *360-678-4097 or 800-366-4097. www.captainwhidbey.com. 32 rooms.* This 1907 Whidbey Island retreat captures the romance of the sea with feather beds in a weathered log cottage. The rustic dining room affords views of Penn Cove and plates of ginger-steamed mussels. Innkeeper Captain John Colby Stone launches his classic 52ft ketch as guests trim the sails.

$$ Inn at Queen Anne – *505 First Ave. N., Seattle, WA.* &♿ 🅿 ☎ *206-282-7357 or 800-952-5043. www.innatqueenanne. com. 68 rooms.* A garden courtyard and a kitchen in every room are part of the appeal of this c.1930 hotel, in Seattle's Queen Anne neighborhood a couple of blocks from Seattle Center and the monorail to downtown. The sister **MarQueen Hotel** *(600 Queen Anne Ave. N., Seattle, WA;* ☎ *206-282-7407 or 888-445-3076; www.marqueen.com,* $$$) has 53 rooms in a 1918 building just around the corner.

WHERE TO EAT IN THE SEATTLE AREA

$$$$ Rover's – *2808 E. Madison St., Seattle.* ☎ *206-325-7442. www.rovers-seattle.com.* 🕐 *Closed Sun-Mon.* **French.** Thierry Rautureau, fedora-clad chef-owner of this fine restaurant, has created inspired tasting menus worthy of his native France since 1987. From the kitchen of an early-20C frame house, nestled in an off-street courtyard a couple of miles east of downtown, he offers such dishes as partridge with braised cabbage and halibut with a leek ragout.

$$$$ Salish Lodge – *6501 Railroad Ave. SE, Snoqualmie.* ☎ *425-888-2556. www.salishlodge.com.* **Contemporary**. A steady roar persists outside this dramatic restaurant, perched on the crest of 268ft Snoqualmie Falls 30min from Seattle. While famed for its four-course breakfasts, its luxurious hotel and spa facilities, the Lodge also serves fine cuisine like butternut squash-and-lobster bisque, duck confit strudel and hazelnut-crusted venison loin.

$$$ Cascadia Restaurant – *2328 First Ave., Seattle.* ☎ *206-448-8884. www. cascadiarestaurant.com. Dinner only.* 🕐 *Closed Sun.* **Northwest Regional.** Even though he's English, chef-owner Kerry Sear embraces Pacific Northwest lifestyle. He uses only seasonal ingredients found in Cascade Range precincts. He bakes king salmon on cedar fronds, purées fiddlehead ferns with black-trumpet mushrooms, and offers wild-huckleberry sorbets for dessert. A 9ft etched-glass "rain window" separates dining room from kitchen.

$$$ Earth and Ocean – *1112 Fourth Ave. in the W Hotel, Seattle.* ☎ *206-264-6060. www.earthocean.net.* 🕐 *Closed Sun.* **American.** Chef Adam Stevenson has created a tempting menu at this chic restaurant with dot-com appeal. Dinner features vegetarian (sugar-pumpkin soup), seafood (tuna carpaccio) and game dishes (wild-boar ravioli). The wine list focuses on Washington vintages.

$$$ Elliott's Oyster House – *1201 Alaskan Way, Pier 56, Seattle.* ☎ *206-623-4340.* **Seafood.** Fresh Northwest seafood is the raison d'être for this fine restaurant on a pier jutting into Elliott Bay. Oyster selections change daily, and the Pike Place Market provides produce to accompany such dishes as Pacific king salmon cooked on alder planks and Dungeness crab with three dipping sauces.

$$$ Flying Fish – *2234 First Ave., Seattle.* ☎ *206-728-8595. www.flyingfishrestaurant.com.* **Seafood.** Factory-gallery decor is bright and loud: aqua chairs, curvaceous lamps. The menu, which changes daily, puts Pacific Rim accents on fresh seafood. A popular dish is the whole fried snapper platter, sold by the pound and served in lemon-grass marinade with bean sprouts and purple basil.

$$ Primo Grill – *601 S. Pine St., Tacoma.* ☎ *235-383-7000. www.primogrilltacoma.com.* **Mediterranean**. Tacoma News-Tribune readers have voted this the city's best restaurant and owner Charlie McManus the best chef. From an apple-wood grill and wood-burning oven, McManus turns out fire-roasted shrimp, grilled veal chops and Tuscan chicken, along with a variety of creative pizzas and pastas.

$$ Wild Ginger – *1401 Third Ave., Seattle.* ☎ *206-623-4450.* **Asian.** Focal point of this wildly popular restaurant, located opposite Benaroya Hall, is the satay bar, where skewers of lemon-grass chicken, Saigon scallops and Bangkok boar are served across a curving counter. Chefs grind their own spices here; entrées include sea bass with lime juice and fragrant duck with plum sauce.

Proclaimed a historic district in 1969, the area now boasts galleries and restaurants, parks and squares.

The site of the city's first intersection, **Pioneer Place**★★ *(First Ave. & Yesler Way)* holds a 1930s Tlingit Indian totem pole. The six-story **Pioneer Building** *(610 First Ave.)* was completed in 1892 in the Romanesque Revival style; it was once considered the finest building west of Chicago. The popular, humorous **Bill Speidel's Underground Tours**★★ *(b206-682-4646, www.undergroundtour. com)* descend from here into defunct tunnels at the original street level, where visitors learn about Seattle life from the mid-19C through Prohibition.

About two blocks south, the Seattle unit of **Klondike Gold Rush National Historical Park** *(319 Second Ave. S.; ☎206-220-4240, www.nps.gov/klse)* holds artifacts and photographs detailing the Yukon gold rush and its impact on the city. When the steamship *Portland* arrived in Seattle on July 17, 1897, with two tons of gold, gold fever struck the city. Many residents grew rich outfitting prospectors; others shipped out for the Yukon via Skagway, Alaska, where most of this historical park is located.

Pike Place Market★★★

Kids *First Ave. & Pike St.* ✕ P ☎206-682-7453. *www.pikeplacemarket.org.* Often called the soul of Seattle, this "public market center" has been a revered city institution since 1907. Fun, feisty and infinitely appealing, the market maintains its earthy egalitarianism. An abundance of farm-fresh vegetables, seafood and flowers dazzles the eye, and dozens of buskers entertain clapping crowds.

An urban renewal program nearly killed the market in the early 1960s, one plan calling for it to be demolished and replaced by a giant hotel. But Seattleites in 1971 voted overwhelmingly to preserve the market and surrounding blocks. Today a nine-acre parcel and a dozen buildings are protected in a national historic district that extends from First to Western Avenues, Union to Virginia Streets.

Hundreds of food vendors, eateries and small shops line bustling, crowded streets and alleys and fill a multilevel

©iStockphoto./osubuckeye

Pike Place Fish Vendors' Stall

labyrinth of building interiors. The market's original building, the **Main Arcade** *(Pike Place between Pike & Stewart Sts.),* remains the hub of activity, its street-level stalls vibrant and colorful with seasonal vegetables, stands of fresh and dried flowers, and fish shops where salmon, halibut and Dungeness crabs glisten on beds of ice. A crowd often collects around **Pike Place Fish**, where mongers loudly chant the daily specials and throw fish to one another over customers' heads. Nearby **Post Alley**, an Old World-style walkway, offers shops and some top-notch restaurants. Leading down to the waterfront, the **Hillclimb Corridor** is a landscaped series of stairs flanked by shops and cafes.

Seattle Art Museum★★

First Ave. & University St. ✕& ☎206-654-3100. *www.seattleartmuseum.org.* Recently expanded to three times its original size, the Seattle Art Museum's extensive holdings at this well-rounded repository include arts and crafts from Korea, Japan and China; African ceremonial masks and headdresses; and Northwest Coast basketry and wood and stone sculpture. Western art includes works by Rubens, Van Dyck, Lucas Cranach the Elder and Jackson Pollock. The statue out front on First Avenue,

Jonathan Borofsky's Hammering Man, has become a Seattle icon.

Opposite the museum's Second Avenue entrance, **Benaroya Hall**★★ *(Third Ave. & University St.;* ☎*206-215-4800, www. seattlesymphony.org),* is the state-of-the-art home of the Seattle Symphony.

Odyssey: The Maritime Discovery Center

Kids *Pier 66.* ✕ ♿ ☎*206-374-4000. www. ody.org.*

This innovative addition to the Seattle waterfront rises in glass-walled modernism on Bell Street Pier. Its exhibits explore facets of maritime life.

South of Odyssey, the **Seattle Aquarium**★ Kids *(Pier 59;* ☎*206-386-4300, www. seattleaquarium.org)* is home to some 380 species of fish, birds, plants, marine invertebrates and mammals native to the Puget Sound area. The aquarium has its "own" migratory salmon run.

Frye Art Museum★★

704 Terry Ave. at Cherry St. ✕ ♿ 🅿 ☎*206-622-9250. www.fryeart.org.*

A small gem, this facility showcases 19C and 20C representational works by American, French and German artists. The galleries, lit by natural light, offer an appealing, intimate space for the quiet appreciation of art. The core collection of Munich School painters of the late 19C and early 20C - like Franz von Lenbach and Wilhelm Leibl- is the most complete in the US. American paintings in the permanent holdings (not always displayed) include works by Albert Bierstadt, Winslow Homer, John Singer Sargent and Thomas Eakins.

Additional Sights

Seattle Center★★

Kids *Generally bounded by Denny Way, Broad St., Fifth Ave. N., Mercer St. & First Ave. N.* ☎*206-684-7200. www.seattle center.com.*

The location for the 1962 world's fair, this 74-acre campus northwest of downtown now harbors theaters, the city's opera house, museums, an amusement park and a sports arena, the complex drawing more than 8 million visitors a year.

Space Needle★★

Kids *Off Broad St. opposite Fourth Ave. N.* ✕ ♿ ☎*206-905-2100. www.space needle.com.*

Time has not robbed the Space Needle of its modern appearance. Embodying a 1960s vision of the future, the graceful metal tripod (1962, Victor Steinbrueck & John Graham Jr.) rises 602ft, with a revolving, saucer-like observation room and restaurant beneath its acme. Glass-walled elevators whoosh guests to a gift shop and encircling outdoor deck. Panoramic **views**★★ take in the city skyline, Elliott Bay, the Olympic Mountains and the Cascades.

Just north of the Space Needle entrance, the Swedish-designed **Monorail**★ *(departs every 15min;* ☎*206-441-6038, www.seattlemonorail.com)* quietly travels 1.3mi to downtown's Westlake Center in less than 2min.

Experience Music Project★

Kids *325 Fifth Ave. N. at Broad St.* ✕ ♿ 🅿 ☎*206-367-5483. www.emplive.com.*

This psychedelically colored, notoriously unusual building (Frank O. Gehry) pays tribute to the ever-changing dynamic of rock'n'roll with a variety of interactive exhibits. It highlights such Seattle icons as Jimi Hendrix and Kurt Cobain.

Pacific Science Center★★

Kids *Second Ave. N. at Denny Way.* ✕ ♿ 🅿 ☎*206-443-2001. www.pacsci.org.*

The six interconnected buildings with striking arches dominate the south end of Seattle Center. Interactive exhibits range from a virtual meteorology center and a hall of robotic dinosaurs to a tropical butterfly house and a "tech zone," outfitted with computers that enable visitors to compose, create art or try hang gliding.

Olympic Sculpture Park★

Kids *2901 Western Ave. at Broad St.* ✕ ♿ 🅿 ☎*206-654-3100. www.seattleart museum.org.*

The Seattle Art Museum converted 9 acres of vacant industrial ground into this outdoor park in 2007. It holds a representative collection of sculptures by Calder, Serra, Nevelson and Oldenburg. On a hillside overlooking Elliott Bay, the

Seattle Skyline and Space Needle

park offers grand views of Puget Sound and the Olympic Mountains beyond.

Seattle Asian Art Museum★★

1400 E. Prospect St., Volunteer Park. ♿ 🅿 ☎206-654-3100. www.seattleart museum.org.
Ranked as one of the top 10 collections outside Asia, this Art Moderne building (1933, Carl Gould) holds more than 7,000 objects of Asian art, only a quarter of them on display at any one time. Among the artifacts exhibited in the quietly meditative space are South Asian Buddhist and Hindu sculpture, 4,000-year-old Chinese vessels and finely wrought Japanese ceramics and temple art.

University of Washington★

Generally bounded by 15th Ave. NE, NE 45th St., Union & Portage bays. ☎206-543-2100. www.washington.edu.
This major university sprawls across nearly 700 acres above the bank of the Lake Washington Ship Canal. Two excellent museums are located on the campus grounds, designed in the early 20C by landscape architect John Olmsted.

The Burke Museum of Natural History and Culture★★

17th Ave. NE & NE 45th St., ✕♿🅿 ☎206-543-5590. www.washington.edu/burke museum.
The diverse geology, archaeology and ethnology of the Pacific Rim are cel-
ebrated on two floors of exhibits. On the lower level are artifacts and photographs that highlight cultures of the Northwest Coast, the Pacific Islands, and East and Southeast Asia. The main floor examines geologic history through dinosaur skeletons, mineral specimens and an exhibit on plate tectonics.

Henry Art Gallery★★

15th Ave. NE & NE 41st St. ✕♿ ☎206-543-2280. www.henryart.org.
One of the most progressive small museums in the US, the Henry (1927, Carl Gould) is known for embracing adventurous art. Permanent holdings, which may be stored in favor of temporary exhibitions, focus on 20C movements in French and American art. The contemporary collection includes works by Motherwell and Robert Rauschenberg.

Washington Park Arboretum★★

2300 Arboretum Dr. E., between Union Bay & Lake Washington Blvd. E. 🅿 ☎206-543-8800. www.washington.edu/wpa.
Preserving 230 acres of woodlands, the arboretum is the legacy of landscape-architect brothers John Olmsted and Frederick Law Olmsted Jr., who laid out its gardens between 1909 and the early 1930s. Trails wind past 5,500 different trees and other plants, past a Japanese garden and through a rhododendron glen and an avenue of azaleas.

Museum of History and Industry★

2700 24th Ave. E., off Montlake Blvd. NE. ☎206-324-1126. www.seattlehistory. org.

Full-scale displays explore Seattle's colorful past with e.g. a maritime display, the 1889 fire and Klondike gold rush.

Hiram M. Chittenden Locks★★

Kids *3015 NW 54th St. ☎206-783-7059. www.nws.usace.army.mil.*

The US Army Corps of Engineers maintains this site which links Lake Washington, on Seattle's eastern flank, with Puget Sound. It consists of two locks, a dam and spillway, botanical garden and visitor center and opened in 1917. Each year, 100,000 boats—pleasure and fishing craft, freight and research vessels—are "locked through". A **fish ladder** on the south side enables salmon to swim upstream while human visitors watch them through a submarine window.

Woodland Park Zoo★★

Kids *Phinney Ave. N. between N. 50th & N. 59th Sts. ✖🚻Ⓟ ☎206-684-4800. www. zoo.org.*

Highly acclaimed for habitats that reflect the native environments of its 1,100 animals of 280 species, this fine zoo includes 65 acres of savanna, tundra, marshland, tropical rain forest and Northwest habitat. The largest space is an open African savanna; Asian elephants roam through a Thai village as elk graze in an Alaskan taiga. John Olmsted designed most original buildings in 1909; the park has since added many cageless spaces.

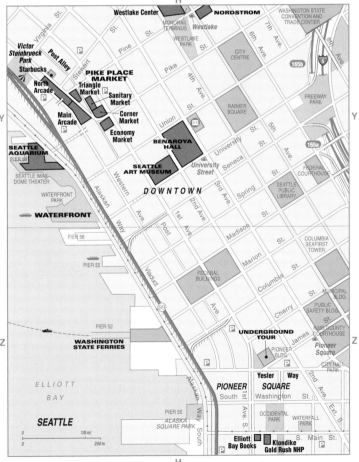

Museum of Flight★★

Kids *9404 E. Marginal Way S. at Boeing Field,* ✕ ♿ 🅿 *☎206-764-5720. www. museumofflight.org. .5mi northwest of I-5 Exit 158.*

The largest air-and-space museum in the western US occupies a steel-and-glass central building that contains a diverse collection of aircraft, from early gliders and space capsules. Highlights include a Concorde and the original 747. One simulator gives visitors a feel for flying and air-traffic control; a theater has a live link to NASA satellite reception. The 1909 "Red Barn" relocated to this site was the hub of William Boeing's original Pacific Aero Products Company.

Excursions

Bloedel Reserve★★

7571 NE Dolphin Dr., Bainbridge Island (35min crossing via Washington State Ferry from Pier 52, Alaskan Way, Seattle). ♿ 🅿 *☎206-842-7631. www.bloedelreserve.org.*

Call for advance reservations & specific directions. This 150-acre reserve encapsulates the meadowlands, forests and glens of the Northwest. Native flora thrives in its own setting, amid deft and subtle landscaping. Trails visit a marsh habitat for migratory and native waterfowl, a wetland forest, a grove of flowering shrubs, a Zen rock garden and a moss garden. The visitor center is housed in **Collinswood**, a classic French château-style home built in 1932.

Tillicum Village★

Kids *Tours (about 4.5hrs) depart Piers 55 & 56, Alaskan Way, Seattle.* ✕ ♿ *☎206-933-8600. www.tillicumvillage.com.*

A commercialized but sincere attempt to celebrate the native cultures of the Northwest, the "village"—actually a single longhouse of Kwakiutl style—was built in the 1960s on small Blake Island in Puget Sound. Visitors are treated to a traditional salmon bake, with the whole fish splayed open on cedar stakes and cooked over an alder-wood fire. Native performers offer a stage presentation based on Northwest myths, then demonstrate such traditional crafts as wood carving. Adjacent **Blake Island Marine State Park** encompasses 476 acres of trees and shrubs, 15mi of trails and 5mi of beaches.

PUGET SOUND AREA★

MAP P 420
PACIFIC STANDARD TIME

Puget Sound funnels through northwest Washington state, spilling around myriad islands and into bays, inlets and straits created by long-gone glaciers. The fingers of water that extend south encompass the ever-expanding Sea-Tac megalopolis. Tacoma, once the preeminent city in Western Washington, now positions itself as a feisty but friendly small city, with a cultural district that rivals Seattle's. Dominated by the grand dome of the state capitol, small-town Olympia lives quietly apart from the hubbub of its northern neighbors.

▶ **Orient Yourself:** The largest inland sea in the US at 16,000 square miles, Puget Sound stretches north-south from the Strait of Juan de Fuca to Olympia. Because the Seattle metro area (and its traffic) is in the middle, driving from Olympia to Bellingham can encompass an entire day, even though it's only 150 miles.

😊 **Don't Miss:** Tacoma's museum district

🕐 **Organizing Your Time:** Plan to devote at least one day just to Tacoma. Visiting the San Juan Islands requires several days to enjoy the low-key island atmosphere.

Kids **Especially for Kids:** Point Defiance Zoo & Aquarium

👣 **Also See:** San Juan Islands

A Bit of History

The commercial center of Bellingham, hard by Canada, also maintains a relaxed, welcoming atmosphere. In the middle of the sound, the main isles of the San Juan archipelago have for decades been the haunt of artists and craftsfolk. Summer visitors now descend upon these enchanting islands to savor their unsullied natural beauty from kayaks, bicycles and hiking trails.

Sights

Tacoma

32mi south of Seattle via I-5 (Exit 133). ☎253-627-2836. www.tpctourism.org.
The 19C port and timber town of Tacoma recently has reinvented itself as a livable modern city of 197,000 people, complete with fine museums, galleries and a new University of Washington branch campus.

Washington State History Museum★★

1911 Pacific Ave. ✕ ♿ 🅿 ☎253-272-3500. www.wshs.org.
In nine thematic exhibit areas, life-size dioramas and voice-overs dramatize the growth of the state from earliest European-Indian encounters, through 19-20C industrialization, to modern high-tech and environmental challenges. Upper-level galleries are devoted to stimulating temporary exhibits.

Tacoma Art Museum★★

1701 Pacific Ave. ✕ ♿ 🅿 ☎253-272-4258. www.tacomaartmuseum.org.
Spiraling upward to a top level devoted to interactive exhibits on creating art, this new facility is a striking addition (Antoine Predock, 2003) to Tacoma's museum district. With a distinct focus on Northwest artists such as Jacob Lawrence and Morris Graves, it offers a regional emphasis that the Seattle Art Museum neglects. The museum's centerpiece is the world's largest collection of **Dale Chihuly works**★★ on permanent display.

Museum of Glass★★

1801 E. Dock St. ✕ ♿ 🅿 ☎253-396-1768. www.museumofglass.org.
This spectacular 2002 museum, designed by Arthur Erickson, reflects the fact Tacoma is Dale Chihuly's hometown. A distinctive 90ft-tall stainless steel cone, inspired by traditional sawmill burners and containing an interactive glass-art studio, rises above the industrial Thea Foss Waterway and connects to a rooftop plaza. An exquisite collection of glass art by **Chihuly**, a driving force behind the museum, is presented on the 500ft-long **Bridge of Glass**★★★, a pedestrian passage to the History Museum and Tacoma Art Museum.

Point Defiance Park★

Pearl St. at N. 54th St., 3mi north of Rte. 16 Exit 132. ☎253-305-1000. www.metroparkstacoma.org.
This 700-acre park rests on bluffs above Puget Sound. In addition to gardens and trails through old-growth forest, Fort **Nisqually Historic Site**★★ *(Five Mile Dr.; ☎253-591-5339, www.metroparkstacoma.org)*—is a living-history museum within a re-created 1855 Hudson's Bay Company fort. The small but well regarded **Point Defiance Zoo and Aquarium**★ (🅺🅸🅳🆂 *5400 N. Pearl St.; ☎253-591-5337, www.pdza.org),* is noted for its belugas and sea otters.

Olympia

60mi south of Seattle via I-5 (Exit 105). ☎360-704-7544. www.visitolympia.com.
Washington's modest capital centers around the striking state capitol building and the workings of state government.

Washington State Capitol★

Capitol Way between 11th & 16th Aves. ☎360-586-3460. www.ga.wa.gov/visitor.
The white-domed capitol makes a grand statement, rising 287ft above its base. Built between 1893 and 1928, the Neoclassical building sports six massive bronze doors embossed with scenes symbolizing state history and industry. Inside, a five-ton crystal Tiffany chandelier is centered above a marble floor

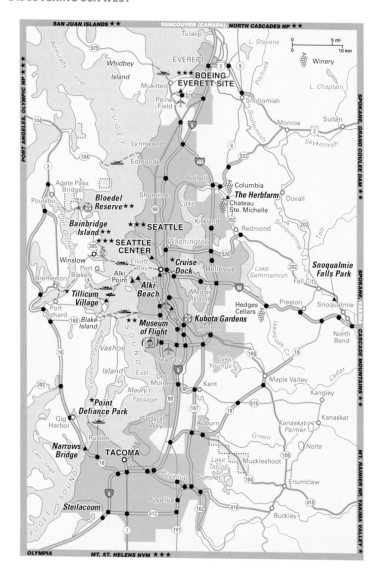

in the vast rotunda. Three blocks away, exhibits at the **State Capitol Museum**★ (*211 W. 21st Ave.; ☎360-753-2580, www. wshs.org/wscm*) focus on construction of the capitol and the area's political and cultural history. The museum is housed in a 1920s Italian Renaissance-style mansion.

Future of Flight Aviation Center★★

Rte. 526, Everett. Take I-5 north 24mi from Seattle to Exit 189; turn west 3.5mi.
♿ 🅿 ☎425-438-8100. *www.futureof flight.org.*

At its plant on the south side of the city of Everett, aerospace giant Boeing assembles its wide-body commercial jets—747s, 777s and 787s. Thousands of people work here in one of the company's largest factories. Free 1hr **tours**★★ take in the cavernous Main Assembly Building, where guides describe the work teams and assembly stations. Just outside, at Paine Field, completed jets are flight-tested.

Whidbey Island

Coupeville, on Rte. 20, is 58mi north of Seattle via I-5 (Exit 182) & Rte. 525. ☎360-675-3535. www.whidbeycamanoislands.com.

A popular weekend getaway for Seattleites, Whidbey Island arcs in a narrow 60mi curve through north Puget Sound, its bucolic tumble of hills, small towns and verdant fields interrupted only by Whidbey Island Naval Air Station. The waterfront town of **Coupeville**★, dating from the 1850s, harbors gift shops and seafood restaurants, as well as Victorian homes built by 19C sea captains. The town is the locus of the sprawling 27-sqmi **Ebey's Landing National Historical Reserve**★, which preserves the land and spirit of an entire rural community. Headquarters are in the **Island County Historical Museum** (23 Front St.; ☎360-678-3310, www.islandhistory.org).

On the north end of the island, **Deception Pass State Park**★ (Rte. 20, 23mi north of Coupeville; ☎ 360-675-2417, www.parks.wa.gov) occupies both sides of Rosario Strait. Turnouts and a pedestrian walkway enable sightseers to cross the 976ft **Deception Pass Bridge**★ and admire the turbulent tidal rapids below.

Skagit Valley

La Conner, on Rte. 534, is 66mi north of Seattle via I-5 Exit 221. ☎360-466-4778. www.laconnerchamber.com.

This lush valley, drained by the Skagit (*SKA-jit*) River flowing west from the Cascades, is especially colorful in spring when thousands of acres of **tulips, daffodils and irises**★★ bloom in farms around Mount Vernon. One of the largest commercial bulb-cultivation districts in the world, the valley hosts special tours and the Skagit Valley Tulip Festival (☎360-428-5959) in April.

The picturesque village of **La Conner**★, on the National Register of Historic Places, edges the Swinomish Channel off Skagit Bay. Founded in the 1860s, the artists' community boasts waterfront galleries, crafts shops, three museums and a charming ambience that make it an attractive weekend destination for urbanites. The **Museum of Northwest Art**★★ (121 S. First St.; ☎360-466-4446, www.museumofnwart.org) has acquired a strong reputation for its focus on Northwest masters, including Guy Anderson, Morris Graves and glass artist Dale Chihuly.

Bellingham★

91mi north of Seattle via I-5 (Exit 256). ☎360-671-3990. www.bellingham.org.

A pleasant, well-heeled city of 71,000 in the Mount Baker foothills, Bellingham wraps itself around a bay of the same name. The town is both a maritime hub, as southern terminus of the Alaska State Ferry System, and a college town focused around **Western Washington University** (south of downtown via Bill McDonald Pkwy.; ☎360-650-3424, www.wwu.edu), noted for its outdoor sculpture.

The **Fairhaven Historic District**★ (between 13th & 20th Sts.) dates to the 1870s but burgeoned in the 1890s during speculation that the Great Northern Railroad would locate its western terminus here. That honor went instead to Tacoma, leaving this neighborhood a delightful mix of red brick storefronts housing cafes, galleries, bookshops and charmingly restored Victorian homes. Preserving the region's cultural and artistic history, the **Whatcom Museum of History and Art**★ (121 Prospect St.; ☎360-676-6981, www.whatcommuseum.org) has collections of West Coast Indian art, pioneer artifacts and natural-history specimens. It is lodged in a distinctive, turreted Victorian city hall, built in 1892 of red brick and topped by a bell tower.

San Juan Islands★★

90–105mi north of Seattle; take I-5 north 65mi to Exit 230 at Burlington, then Rte. 20 west 15mi to Washington State Ferry terminal at Anacortes. ☎360-468-3663. www.guidetosanjuans.com.

This 172-island archipelago was once a range of mountains, covered by glaciers during the ice ages. Lummi Indians hunted on the islands; settlers farmed and tended orchards. Now the quiet San Juans attract artists, craftspeople, writers and summer vacationers who come for bird-watching, whale-watching, beach-combing and general relaxing.

San Juan Island★★

The most westerly of the three islands that offer visitor accommodations is also the most populous. Here the two units of **San Juan Island National Histori-cal Park**★ *(☎360-378-2240, www.nps.gov/sajh)* preserve coastal swatches of land associated with the joint occupation (1859-72) of the island by British and US troops following the Pig War, a tense two-month standoff resulting from the shooting of a swine. In the main town of Friday Harbor, the low-key **Whale Museum**★ *(62 First St. N.; ☎360-378-4710, www.whale-museum.org)* is one of the world's leading institutions devoted to research and education on orcas.

Orcas Island★★

Largest of the San Juans, horseshoe-shaped Orcas bends around long and beautiful East Sound. Its forested low mountains provide panoramas of the San Juans, the Cascade and Olympic Ranges, the Canadian Coast Range and Vancouver Island. More than 5,000 acres of the island are contained within **Moran State Park**★ *(Horseshoe Hwy.; ☎360-376-2326, www.parks.wa.gov)*, which has five lakes and 30mi of hiking trails.

OLYMPIC PENINSULA★★★

MICHELIN MAP 493 B2, 3
PACIFIC STANDARD TIME

Northwestern Washington's Olympic Peninsula extends like a thumb, separating the jigsaw puzzle of Puget Sound islands and waterways from the Pacific Ocean. The glacier-sheathed Olympic Mountains rise in the central part of the peninsula, trapping wet Pacific air and creating a rain shadow to the east. This has made for a remarkable difference in rainfall between the Sequim-Dungeness Valley area on the northeast, which averages 16in a year, and the Pacific coastal valleys, which get 150in or more. Though much of the peninsula's forests have been clearcut, the valleys of Olympic National Park harbor some of the few remaining stands of old-growth rain forest in the contiguous US. Shoreward of the forests lies a strand of wonderfully wild and log-tossed Pacific beach.

- 🚩 **Information:** ☎800-942-4042, www.olympicpeninsula.org.
- ▶ **Orient Yourself:** The peninsula's main highway, U.S. 101, encircles it; driving the entire distance would take a full day, without stops.
- 😊 **Don't Miss:** The Hoh and Quinault rain forests.
- 👣 **Also See:** Port Townsend's beautifully preserved Victorian districts.

A Bit of History

Although early Spanish voyagers first laid claim to these northwestern shores, the Hudson's Bay Company in the early 19C helped firm up Great Britain's dominance of the area. White settlement, mostly concentrated along the Strait of Juan de Fuca, did not begin until the 1850s when farming, logging, fishing and sea trade took hold. Yet the Native American presence remains strong, with much of the shoreline taken up by staunchly protected reservation land.

Sights

Port Townsend★★

Rte. 20, 58mi northwest of Seattle. ☎360-385-2722. www.ptguide.com.
One of the best-preserved 19C seaports in the US, Port Townsend is chockablock with grand houses and commercial buildings with ornate touches and high ceilings. Sited at the entrance to Puget Sound, the town of 9,000 traffics in its maritime flavor and heritage, yet manages to feel sophisticated and authentic rather than commercial. Fine two- and three-story stone edifices cluster along Water Street; many of them house book-

shops, restaurants and boutiques. On the bluff above stands a trove of Victorian homes, some converted to bed-and-breakfast inns.

Port Townsend remains a center for the marine trades: Boat-building, sail-making and rope-making are all practiced and taught here. The entire town is a National Historic Landmark District, and its colorful past is well documented at the **Jefferson County Historical Museum**★ *(210 Madison St. at Water St.; ☎360-385-1003, www.jchsmuseum.org)*. Visitors may partake of both history and scenery at **Fort Worden State Park**★ *(W St. at Cherry St.; ☎360-902-8844, www.parks.wa.gov)*, where the parade ground of a decommissioned fort is lined with a smart row of Victorians (some available for visitor lodging) that once quartered officers. Broad beaches frame views north to the San Juans.

Olympic National Park★★★

Access via US-101 south and west of Port Angeles. △✕⚲🅿 *☎360-452-4501. Visitor center, 600 E. Park Ave., Port Angeles; ☎360-565-3130. www.nps.gov/olym.*

Designated an International Biosphere Reserve and World Heritage Site, the 1,440sq-mi park has exceptional natural beauty and remarkable diversity within its three distinct wilderness ecosystems—glaciated mountain ranges, temperate rain forests and primitive coastal habitats. The park harbors more than 300 types of birds and 70 species of mammals, among them some 5,000 Roosevelt elk, the largest herd in the world.

US Highway 101 runs around the perimeter of the national park on its east, north and west. Among its most accessible attractions is **Lake Crescent**★★ *(18mi west of Port Angeles),* one of three large lakes in the park. Cupped within steep, forested hillsides, the deep glacial lake is popular with outdoor recreation lovers, who often base themselves at the 1915 **Lake Crescent Lodge**★ *(416 Lake Crescent Rd.; b360-928-3211, lakecrescent-lodge.com)*. From here, a 2mi trail leads through old-growth forest to **Marymere Falls**★, a beautiful 90ft cascade. Nearby, Sol Duc Hot Springs offer mineral-rich bathing pools and cabins for rent.

©iStockphoto.com/Natalia Bratslavsky

Port Townsend

Hurricane Ridge★★

17mi south of visitor center on Heart O' the Hills/Hurricane Ridge Rd. ☎*360-457-2879.*

Snowfall may close portions of the road Oct–late Apr. The winding road that climbs to the 5,230ft summit passes through dense forest and skirts lush meadows, unfolding magnificent vistas of crenellated, snow-crusted peaks and the distant sea. Views from the top feature unobstructed perspectives on peaks, ridges and deep valleys. Subalpine meadows are covered in summer with low-lying sedges, grasses and wildflowers.

Hoh Rain Forest★★★

91mi southwest of Port Angeles; entrance station 12mi east of US-101. Visitor center ☎*360-374-6925.*

On the western side of the park, this lush, dripping, primordial world of giant cedar, hemlock and maple is draped with soft green club mosses and floored by shaggy, moldering logs. Shafts of sunlight angle into these ancient woods, casting a mystical glow and creating scenery that is eerily reminiscent of a pre-human earth, rank with life. Three short interpretive trails meander among the arboreal giants, some of them 20 stories tall, 12ft in diameter and 500 years old. The nearby **Quinault rain for-**

©iStockphoto.com/Natalia Bratslavsky

Hoh Rain Forest

est offers a similar experience, slightly less crowded.

Not far west of here, Ruby Beach and several other **beaches**★★ around Kalaloch feature offshore sea stacks and shorelines that vary from narrow and rocky to wide and sandy. The ocean waters are part of the 3,300sq-mi **Olympic Coast National Marine Sanctuary**, where protected animals include sea otters, seals, migrating gray whales and the world's largest species of octopus.

Port Angeles

US-101, about 80mi northwest of Seattle. ☎360-452-2363. www.portangeles.org.

Situated on the Strait of Juan de Fuca about midway along the northern shore of the Olympic Peninsula, Port Angeles functions as a gateway to the national park, with numerous motels and small inns. A ferry service provides a link to Victoria, British Columbia, directly across the strait.

Nearby **Dungeness National Wildlife Refuge**★ *(15mi northeast via Kitchen-Dick Rd.; ☎360-457-8451, www.fws.gov/pacific)* encompasses serene, 6mi-long Dungeness Spit, a sandy hook of land home to a cornucopia of seabirds and marine life.

Neah Bay★

Rte. 112, 70mi northwest of Port Angeles.

Makah Indians have inhabited the Olympic Peninsula's extreme northwestern coastal region for at least 4,000 years. Neah Bay is their modern reservation's only town. The history and culture of the tribe, which in 1999 inspired controversy when it resumed hunting whales after a self-imposed seven-decade moratorium, are brought into focus at the **Makah Museum**★★ *(Bay View Ave.; ☎360-645-2711, www.).*

Seven miles west of Neah Bay, **Cape Flattery**★, named by Captain James Cook in 1788, is the northwesternmost point of the contiguous US. A forest-and-boardwalk trail (.75mi) leads to a crows-nest viewpoint with breathtaking views of the cape and adjacent sea caves.

From Kalaloch south, US-101 zigzags 140mi through timberland and around long marine estuaries. Aberdeen and Hoquiam, on broad Grays Harbor, are logging ports. At the harbor's mouth, 20mi west, Ocean Shores is a thriving small resort town with hotels, restaurant, a new tribal casino and miles of hard, flat beach that invites driving.

Long Beach Peninsula

Rtes. 100 & 103 via US-101, 165mi southwest of Seattle. ☎360-642-2400. www.funbeach.com.

Stretching from the Columbia River to the mouth of Willapa Bay, the Long

Beach Peninsula fronts 28mi of surf-pounded coastline. Originally inhabited by Chinook Indians, the area is famous as the place where Lewis and Clark reached the shores of the Pacific in 1805. The **Lewis & Clark Interpretive Center**★ *(Fort Canby State Park,* *Rte. 100, 2mi southwest of Ilwaco; ☎360-642-3029, www.fortcanby.org/visit/lcic)* outlines their journey of exploration and provides a view of the ironically named Cape Disappointment, where the explorers had their first, awe-inspiring look at the tumultuous Pacific.

CASCADE MOUNTAINS★★

MICHELIN MAP 493 C2,3
PACIFIC STANDARD TIME

Separating the wet coastland from the dry, eastern portion of Washington state, the jagged spine of the Cascades runs the entire length of Washington, from Canada to the Columbia River, and down through Oregon into northern California. Several volcanoes distinguish the Cascades, including its highest peak, Mt. Rainier (14,410ft), and Mt. St. Helens (8,363ft), which blew up as the world watched in 1980. These and other major Washington volcanoes—Mt. Adams (12,276ft), Mt. Baker (10,778ft) and Glacier Peak (10,568ft)—originated only about 1 million years ago, although the Cascades began rising at least 25 million years earlier.

- 🄵 **Information:** ☎360-753-5600, www.experiencewashington.com
- ▶ **Orient Yourself:** Touring the Cascades offers the chance to see one of the most distinct rain shadows in North America--west side valleys hold rainforest, while on the eastern slope, sometimes only miles away, arid conditions prevail.
- 🄳 **Don't Miss:** Mount Rainier and Mount St. Helens
- 🄺🄸🄳🅂 **Especially for Kids:** Northwest Trek
- 🄲 **Also See:** Lake Chelan

A Bit of History

Native Americans and frontier settlers found the Cascades a formidable barrier to east-west travel. Not until 1972, in fact, did the North Cascades Highway (Route 20) traverse the rugged terrain just south of the Canadian border. A patchwork of national park and forest land blankets most of these mountains, helping to protect a rich chain of wildlife and providing myriad opportunities for outdoor recreation.

Sights

Mount St. Helens National Volcanic Monument★★★
164mi south of Seattle. ☎360-449-7800. Main access via Rte. 504, 48mi east of I-5 (Exit 49) at Castle Rock. www.fs.fed.us/gpnf/mshnvm.

One of the world's most famous volcanoes, St. Helens erupted in 1980 with the intensity of several atomic bombs, destroying its northern flank and reducing its elevation more than 1,300ft. Today the eviscerated mountain, surrounded by a 172sq-mi preserve, has become a leading visitor attraction. Youngest of the major Cascade volcanoes, St. Helens was known to ancient Native Americans as Fire Mountain. Quiet through most of the 20C, the conical mountain rumbled slowly awake in spring 1980, for several weeks giving off warning quakes and hisses. The sudden explosion on May 18 sent a column of ash 15mi into the atmosphere; poured hot rock and pumice over the countryside; devastated 250sq mi of forest; caused severe flooding, and left 57 people dead. When the eruption was over, the 9,677ft peak measured only 8,363ft.

The **Mount St. Helens Visitor Center**★★ *(Rte. 504, 5mi east of I-5; ☎360-449-7800)* offers a fascinating live-footage film, a slide show and other worthy exhibits. From here, the 43mi drive along Spirit Memorial Highway leads to the **Johnston Ridge Observatory**★★★ *(Rte. 504; ☎360-274-2140),* within 5mi of the volcano's crater. The devastation is still vividly apparent. Acres of scorched trees, interspersed with newly planted trees, give way to the blowdown zone, where the forest was leveled by the blast.

Mount Rainier National Park★★★

Rtes. 410 & 706, about 70mi southeast of Tacoma. ☎360-569-2211. www.nps. gov/mora.
Highest volcano and fifth-highest peak in the contiguous US, Rainier is a majestic backdrop to the Puget Sound megalopolis. An arctic island in a temperate zone, the summit is covered in more than 30sq mi of ice and snow. Melt-water from its 24 glaciers filigrees the terrain with fast-running rivers and streams, while volcanic steam vents have created a labyrinth of ice caves. Though its last major eruption occurred 2,000 years ago, scientists believe it could come roaring to life again soon.
The **Nisqually-Paradise Road** *(Rte. 706, open all year; other roads closed late Oct–late May, depending upon snowfall)* enters the park at its southwest corner, twisting 19mi past streams, waterfalls and grand viewpoints to the meadows of **Paradise Valley**★★★. A visitor center and observatory at 5,400ft provide overviews of park wildlife and geologic features. Hikes vary from the Nisqually Vista Trail *(1.2mi)* to the challenging Skyline Trail *(5mi).* **Sunrise**★★★ *(14mi from White River entrance, Rte. 410)* is the highest point attainable by car (6,400ft) and boasts breathtaking views of Rainier (west), Sunrise Lake (east) and conical Mt. Adams (south).

Northwest Trek★★

Kids *Rte. 161, 6mi north of Eatonville. ☎360-832-6117.*
This 635-acre wildlife park displays animals native to the Pacific Northwest region. Tram tours (5.5mi, 1hr) enable visitors to see grizzly and black bears, caribou, elk, moose, bison, bighorn sheep, great blue herons, wild turkeys and other creatures. Walk-through habitats, several miles of nature trails and a children's discovery center are additional offerings.

North Cascades National Park★★

Approximately 120mi northeast of Seattle. Main access from Rte. 20, 50–100mi east of I-5 (Exit 230), or from Rte. 542 at Mt. Baker, 55mi east of Bellingham. ☎360-854-7200. www.nps.gov/noca. Old-growth forests, hidden waterfalls, jewellike lakes, alpine meadows and glaciated peaks of 7,000ft to 9,000ft fill this park's 1,069sq mi, most accessible only by foot. Its 300 glaciers account for half the icefields in the US outside Alaska. Endangered animals such as grizzly bears and wolverines inhabit the backcountry, generally far from human eyes. In 1988, Congress designated 93 percent of the park's lands as wilderness, affording the highest degree of federal protection. The 2,600mi **Pacific Crest National Scenic Trail** traverses the park.
Just off Route 20, which divides the park into northern and southern units, the **visitor center** *(Rte. 20, 1mi west of Newhalem)* offers films and information on fishing, hiking and backpacking. A short boardwalk trail ends at a viewpoint looking north to 6,805ft Pinnacle Peak in the Picket Range.

Ross Lake National Recreation Area★

Rte. 20, 50–75mi east of I-5 (Exit 230). ☎360-854-7200. www.nps.gov/rola.
Bordering both sides of Route 20, this 183sq-mi preserve encompasses three dams, three lakes and two small towns. Between 1924 and 1939, Seattle City Light built the dams across the upper Skagit River for hydroelectric power; the largest, Ross Dam, measures 540ft high by 1,300ft long. Since the mid-20C, the power company has conducted popular **tours** outlining the purpose, construction and operation of its dams.

Lake Chelan National Recreation Area★★

Accessible via boat or small plane from Chelan, 182mi east of Seattle on US-97A. ⚠️✕👤 ☎*360-854-7365. www.nps.gov/lach.*

This narrow, 55mi-long fjord lake nestles in a glacially gouged trough in the rain shadow of the Cascades. Its lower end is surrounded by arid hills and apple orchards; its upper end snakes among sawtooth peaks that soar 8,000ft above the water's surface. The recreation area centers on the charming and serene village of **Stehekin**. Shuttle-bus tours ply the gravel Stehekin Valley Road, which follows the Stehekin River north from the head of the lake.

EASTERN WASHINGTON

MICHELIN MAP 493 C,D3,4
PACIFIC STANDARD TIME

Open, dry and rugged, the vast expanse of eastern Washington stretches from the foothills of the Cascades to the Idaho border, and from Walla Walla north to the Okanogan highlands. Rivers cut deep, meandering canyons across the arid land, punctuated by irrigated fruit orchards and vineyards.

- **Information:** ☎360-753-5600. www.experiencewashington.com
- **Don't Miss:** Grand Coulee Dam
- **Also See:** Yakama Nation Cultural Center

Background

Over the centuries, a parade of Plateau Indians, explorers, ranchers and farmers came through and left their respective marks. Modern visitors who explore this grand landscape will find a variety of appealing natural areas, parks, museums and historic sites.

Sights

Spokane★

276mi east of Seattle via I-90. ☎509-624-1341. www.visitspokane.com.

An 1880s transportation and trading center, Washington's second-largest city (198,000 residents) spreads along the wooded slopes of the Spokane River near the Idaho border. Its downtown encompasses dozens of historic buildings and a spectacular stretch of river where waterfalls crash over basalt lava cliffs. Elsewhere, residential neighborhoods line tree-shaded bluffs with well-kept Victorian mansions and Craftsman-style cottages. Exhibits in the **Northwest Museum of Arts and Culture**★ (2316 W. First Ave.; ☎509-456-3931, www.northwestmuseum.org) provide a concise overview of the history of Spokane and eastern Washington.

Riverfront Park★★

Spokane Falls Blvd. between Post & Washington Sts. ✕👤 ☎*509-456-4386. www.spokaneriverfrontpark.com.*

Occupying both banks of the Spokane River, this outstanding park was developed for the Expo '74 world's fair. It offers rolling lawns shaded by ponderosa pines, landscaped walkways, a splendidly restored 1909 **carousel**★, a **gondola ride** to the base of Lower Spokane Falls, a small amusement park and an IMAX theater.

Manito Park★

Grand Blvd. & 18th Ave. 👤🅿️ ☎*509-625-6622.*

This delightful park, 2mi south of downtown, presents a Japanese garden, an immense rose garden, a perennial garden and a European Renaissance-style garden.

Grand Coulee Dam★★

Rte. 155, Coulee Dam, 228mi east of Seattle via US-2. Visit interior of dam by guided tour only. ♿ 🅿 ☎509-633-9265. www.usbr.gov/pn/grandcoulee.

This mammoth, 55-story-high wall of sloped concrete stretches across the Columbia River for nearly a mile, spanning the cliffs of a deep desert canyon. Built by the Civilian Conservation Corps in the 1930s, it is the largest concrete dam in North America and the third largest electric power producer in the world. Lake Roosevelt, its 151mi-long reservoir, is contained within **Lake Roosevelt National Recreation Area** (1008 Crest Dr., Coulee Dam; ☎509-633-9441).

Yakima Valley★

141mi southeast of Seattle via I-90 & I-82. ☎509-575-3010. www.visityakima.com.
A verdant river corridor, the Yakima Valley stretches in a long southeasterly arc nearly 100mi from Ellensburg to the Columbia River.

The city of Yakima itself, a commercial hub of 80,000 people, offers an attractive riverside greenbelt and two interesting museums. The **Yakima Valley Museum** (2105 Tieton Dr.; ☎509-248-0747) focuses on regional history and personalities, including native sons US Supreme Court Justice William O. Douglas (1898-1980) and world-champion skier twins Phil and Steve Mahre (b.1957). The **Yakima Electric Railway Museum** (306 W. Pine St.; ☎509-575-1700) is a depot for vintage electric trolley cars that take passengers on 2hr rides through the city and countryside.

South of Yakima, the history of the Yakama Indian tribe and its modern transformation is presented through dioramas, paintings and petroglyphs at the excellent **Yakama Nation Cultural Center Museum**★ Kids (100 Spilyiy Loop off US-97, Toppenish; ☎509-865-2800, www.yakamamuseum.com). The nearby town of Toppenish is famed for dozens of **murals**★ depicting local history that decorate its buildings.

North, in Ellensburg, the **Chimpanzee and Human Communication Institute**★★ Kids (400 E. 8th Ave.; ☎509-963-2244, www.cwu.edu) is located on the Central Washington University campus. Unique in the world, the facility is not open for drop-in visitors, but does offer workshops that feature chimpanzees trained to converse with humans, and among themselves, in American Sign Language.

Tri-Cities Area

Approximately 220mi southeast of Seattle via I-90, I-82 & I-182. ☎509-735-8486. www.visittri-cities.com.
Including the adjacent communities of Richland, Pasco and Kennewick, poised at the confluence of the Yakima, Columbia and Snake Rivers, this quiet agricultural area came to sudden life in 1942 as a major site for the Manhattan Project. Plutonium produced at the **Hanford Site** north of Richland powered the atomic bomb dropped on Nagasaki in 1945. Production continued until 1988; cleanup of the toxic waste is ongoing.

Today a center for technology industries, the Tri-Cities constitute one of the largest metropolitan areas in Washington state.

Walla Walla

273mi southeast of Seattle via I-90, I-82 & US-12. ☎509-525-0850. www.wwvchamber.com
An appealing agricultural hub and college town, Walla Walla stands amid rolling hills and farmland at the foot of the Blue Mountains.

SIERRA NEVADA

The mountains along California's eastern and northern boundaries historically have been both barriers and magnets. The bulwark of the Sierra Nevada marches 400mi from Tehachapi Pass, south of Bakersfield, to the Cascade Range near Lassen Peak, walling off the fertile Central Valley from the Great Basin. From Lassen north to Mt. Shasta and beyond, the volcanic Cascade Range presents a barrier generally lower, though similarly rugged, punctuated with isolated volcanic peaks of great height. It was the gold in these mountains that inspired the massive influx of prospectors to California during the Gold Rush of 1849.

Mining heritage remains strong in the mountains and foothills, but the Sierra now is better known for its recreational opportunities. Some of the nation's largest and most sublime national parks, wilderness areas and outdoor resorts abound throughout these ranges, preserving landscapes of extraordinary character. Here are the giant forests of Sequoia National Park, the deep canyons and jagged peaks of Kings Canyon, the polished walls and glistening waterfalls of Yosemite. Here, too, are Mt. Shasta's soaring white dome and the deep blue waters of Lake Tahoe, as well as remnants of a recent volcanic past that still smolder at Lassen Peak. West of the Sierra sprawls the Central Valley, created by silt carried in rivers from the mountains over the millennia. The burgeoning state capital of Sacramento is here. To the east, in the rain shadow of the great ranges, lies a high desert of stark mountains and deep valleys. The Great Basin, highly mineralized with ores that spawned their own repeated gold and silver rushes, has left a colorful legacy that epitomizes Nevada.

Emerald Bay, Lake Tahoe

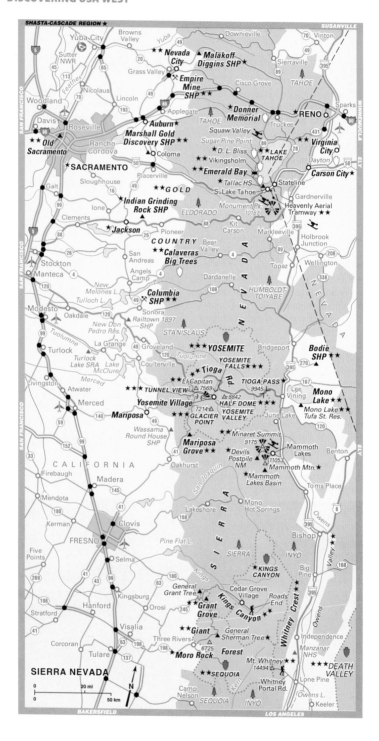

LAKE TAHOE ★★

MAP OPPOSITE

PACIFIC STANDARD TIME

Encircled by a ring of lofty ridges and peaks, this deep blue lake straddling the California-Nevada border at 6,225ft elevation is the most popular resort area in the Sierra. The lake basin was once the summering grounds of the Washoe people. It was rapidly claimed and developed after the 1859 discovery of the Comstock Lode, when its broad surface was used by steamboats that transported timber to shore up the mines.

- **Information:** ☎775-588-5900, www.bluelaketahoe.com
- ▶ **Orient Yourself:** Lake Tahoe is the biggest Western natural lake to straddle two states; the California-Nevada line bisects the lake.
- **Don't Miss:** Squaw Valley Cable Car

A Bit of History

Subsequent developers recognized the lake's rare beauty, staking shoreline claims for early resorts and summerhouses. The federal government set aside most of the hinterlands as national forest in the late 19C; some lakeside properties became California state parks in the 20C. But most of the lakefront remains privately owned. **South Lake Tahoe,** a small city of motels, shops and restaurants, serves vacationers who flock for summer recreation, winter skiing and casino and celebrity entertainment in the adjacent Nevada community of Stateline. Highways encircle the lake, linking numerous ski resorts and smaller, rustic settlements geared for summer visits. Trailheads offer access to excellent hiking, including the 150mi **Tahoe Rim Trail,** which encircles the lake near the ridgeline.

By riding the spectacular cable car at **Squaw Valley** (☎530-583-6985, www.squaw.com), visitors can enjoy splendid views from the 8,200ft-elevation sundeck at **High Camp**★. Skiing and snowboarding provide winter sport at Squaw Valley, site of the 1960 Winter Olympic Games; an ice-skating rink, swimming pool, restaurants and spa are open year-round. Another splendid view of Lake Tahoe, this one from the south, rewards riders who ascend the flanks of 10,167ft Monument Peak on the **Heavenly Gondola**★★ (☎530-586-7000).

Sights

Lake Tahoe Basin Visitor Center

870 Emerald Bay Rd. (Rte. 89), 2.5mi northwest of South Lake Tahoe CA. ⚠ ♿ 🅿 ☎530-265-4531. www.r5.fs.fed.us/tahoe.

This US Forest Service center provides a comprehensive overview of Tahoe's human and natural history. Several trails approach the lakeshore, though only the hardiest swimmers brave its frigid waters. The Rainbow Trail *(.5mi)* follows the fringe of an aspen-ringed meadow to the **Stream Profile Center**★, where subterranean plate-glass windows provide a fish's-eye view of life in a Sierra brook. This walk is most sensational in October, when spawning kokanee salmon fill Taylor Creek with thousands of flaming-red fish.

The trail to **Tallac Historic Site**★ leads to the remains of a fashionable 19C resort hotel and casino built by mining speculator Lucky Baldwin. Other private estates farther east from Baldwin's are now likewise owned by the Forest Service, which maintains the **Pope-Tevis Estate** (1899) and **Valhalla** mansion (1924), and opens the **Baldwin-McGonagle House**★ (1921) in summer as a museum.

Emerald Bay State Park★★

Emerald Bay Rd. (Rte. 89), 8mi northwest of South Lake Tahoe CA. ⚠ ☎530-541-3030. www.parks.ca.gov.

Address Book Sierra Nevada Region

For prices see the Legend on the cover flap.

WHERE TO STAY IN THE SIERRA NEVADA REGION

$$$$$ The Ahwahnee Hotel – *Yosemite Village, Yosemite National Park, CA.* ♿♦️🅿️🏊 ☎559-253-5635. *www.yosemitepark.com. 126 rooms.* This towering timber-and-stone hotel has hosted famous guests from Winston Churchill to Charlie Chaplin since opening in 1927. Nature lovers sit around a granite fireplace and conjure the spirit of John Muir. In winter, great chefs visit The **Ahwahnee Dining Room ($$$)** to teach workshops and prepare gala dinners. The **Yosemite Lodge ($$$)**, **Curry Village ($$)**, the **Wawona Hotel ($$$)** and the **High Sierra Lodges ($)** provide a range of in-park lodging options.

$$$ The Shore House – *7170 North Lake Blvd., Tahoe Vista, CA.* ♿♦️🅿️ ☎530-546-7270 or 800-207-5160. *www.shorehouselaketahoe.com. 9 rooms.* Each room at this bed-and-breakfast has a private entrance that overlooks private gardens and a sandy beach on Lake Tahoe's north shore. The Moon Room has a Tahoe sky painted on the ceiling; the Tree House is framed by ponderosa pines.

$$$ Wuksachi Village and Lodge – *Rte. 198, Sequoia National Park, CA.* ♿♦️🅿️ ☎559-253-2199 or 866-807-3598. *www.visitsequoia.com. 102 rooms.* At the heart of a new park village near Giant Forest, Wuksachi Lodge has its rooms in three beautiful cedar-and-stone buildings. Native granite, oak and hickory furnishings blend with the great trees outside. The restaurant **($$$)** offers a creative blend of Southwestern and Asian fusion cuisines.

$$ Riverboat Delta King – *1000 Front St., Sacramento, CA.* ♿♦️🅿️ ☎916-444-5464 or 800-825-5464. *www.deltaking.com. 44 rooms.* During Prohibition, this "floating pleasure palace" ran from Sacramento to San Francisco. Today the red paddle-wheeler remains in one place, on the Sacramento River in Old Town. Guests stroll on the promenade deck, listen to Dixieland jazz and dine in the **Pilothouse Restaurant ($$)**. Cabins are cozy, with solid oak and polished brass.

WHERE TO EAT IN THE SIERRA NEVADA REGION

$$$$ Erna's Elderberry House – *Rte. 41, Oakhurst, CA.* ☎559-683-6800. *www.elderberryhouse.com. Dinner only.* **Contemporary.** Just 20min south of Yosemite Park, this country manor offers three French-provincial dining rooms and impressive Sierra views. Prix-fixe menus of simple, natural ingredients change daily—perhaps including field greens with nectarine vinaigrette or pan-seared scallops topped by saffron aioli. Elderberry bushes (in French, sureau) surround the estate, which embraces a luxurious inn, the **Château du Sureau ($$$$$)**.

$$$ Louis' Basque Corner – *301 E. Fourth St., Reno, NV.* ☎775-323-7203. **Basque.** Many Basques came to the US from their European homeland in the late 19C, lodging in family boardinghouses. The tradition lives on at Louis', where unacquainted diners share large tables. All-inclusive meals include soup, salad, beans, potatoes and hearty entrées like chicken Basquaise or oxtails bourguignon.

$$$ Sunnyside Restaurant – *1850 W. Lake Blvd., Tahoe City, CA.* ☎530-583-7224. *www.hulapie.com/sunnyside.* **American.** Diners moor their boats at the Sunnyside Marina on Lake Tahoe before grabbing a dinner of barbecued pork ribs with Western "giddy-up" sauce and crispy zucchini. The building doubles as a comfortable mountain lodge, with beautiful views of the surrounding High Sierra.

$ Posh Nosh – *318 Broad St., Nevada City, CA.* b530-265-6064. **Mediterranean.** Local vegetarians love this casual Gold County eatery, but meat eaters are equally delighted with the sandwiches and pastas served indoors or on a garden patio. Try the ratatouille openface sandwich with eggplant, zucchini, bell pepper and tomatoes, topped with feta cheese.

Embracing a glacier-carved fjord acclaimed as the loveliest corner of the lake, this park provides majestic alpine views, beautiful hiking trails and guided tours of a strikingly eccentric mansion, **Vikingsholm**★★ (1929), designed to resemble an AD 9C Nordic castle. The 5.3mi lakeshore Rubicon Trail leads across the northern edge of Emerald Bay to Lester Beach in D.L. **Bliss State Park**★.

Excursion

Donner Memorial State Park★
Off I-80 at Rte. 89, 2.3mi west of Truckee CA. ⚠ 🅿 ☎530-582-7892. www.parks. ca.gov.

Commemorating the Donner Party disaster of 1846-47, the centerpiece of this ironically peaceful park on the shore of Donner Lake is a bronze statue of a family in the desperate straits of starvation. When caught by early snows while attempting to cross the 7,239ft Donner Pass, the party of 87 emigrants, stranded without adequate provisions, erected makeshift cabins and settled in to await rescue as a smaller party set out for help. Before their rescuers returned in mid-February, the survivors were forced to cannibalize their dead; only 47 survived the ordeal. Their story is related in exhibits and film at the park's **Emigrant Trail Museum**★★.

SACRAMENTO AND THE GOLD COUNTRY★★

MAP P 430

PACIFIC STANDARD TIME

California's green and sprawling state capital was founded during the Gold Rush at the confluence of the American and Sacramento Rivers, a port of disembarkation for steamboat passengers. The site lay 2mi west of Sutter's Fort, a spacious rancho founded on a Mexican land grant by Swiss adventurer John Sutter in 1839. Ironically, the stampede sparked by his own workman's discovery of gold ultimately cost Sutter both his property and his mercantile advantages.

- 🔲 **Information:** ☎916-808-7777 or www.sacramentocvb.org
- ⊙ **Don't Miss:** Calaveras Big Trees State Park.
- 🧒 **Especially for Kids:** Panning for gold at Columbia.

A Bit of History

Despite terrible floods and fires, Sacramento's waterfront commercial district thrived as a vital link between trans-Sierra roads and Sacramento River shipping. A protective levee and new brick buildings brought prosperity and stability, prompting California to relocate its capital here in 1854. The city's destiny as a transportation hub was boosted when the Central Pacific line was leveraged eastward across the Sierra Nevada, completing the first transcontinental rail link in 1869. Today sitting astride two major

interstate highways, Sacramento, with a population of 455,000, remains a primary agricultural distribution center in addition to its role as state capital.

The Sierra Nevada foothill region to the east of Sacramento is known as the Gold Country. The region counted nearly 90,000 miners at the peak of the Gold Rush in 1852, and some 106 million troy ounces of gold were extracted before "gold fever" subsided in 1867. While many settlements were quickly depopulated, others developed into commercial centers that today depend more on ranching, tourism and timber production than on mining. Route 49 links the principal communities from Sierra City to Mariposa.

Sights

Sacramento ★

California State Capitol ★★

10th St. between L & N Sts. ✕ ♿ ☎*916-324-0333. www.capitolmuseum.ca.gov.* Surrounded by Capitol Park, a 40-acre rectangle of stately trees and lawn, and crowned by a 210ft Neoclassical dome, the 1860 capitol rises grandly at the head of the Capitol Mall. When the legislature is in session, visitors may observe the Senate and Assembly at work from third-floor balcony seats; both chambers are decorated to appear c.1900.

California Museum for Women, History & the Arts ★

1020 O St. ♿ 🅿 ☎*916-653-7524. www.californiamuseum.org.* Through multimedia exhibits, this sleek treasury of archival documents, artifacts and newsreels attempts to illuminate the qualities of geography, history, politics and population that make California unique. The California Hall of Fame honors icons from John Wayne to Steve Jobs.

Old Sacramento ★★

Kids *I to L Sts., between Sacramento River & I-5. Self-guided walking tour brochure from visitor center (Front & K Sts.).* ✕ ♿ 🅿 *916-442-7644. www.oldsacramento. com*

Sacramento's original downtown is the nation's largest assemblage of Gold Rush-era buildings. Springing up in the early 1850s beside Sutter's embarcadero, the brick and wood buildings, fronted by covered wooden sidewalks, now house a lively collection of souvenir shops, museums and eateries. Permanently docked as a floating hotel along the waterfront levee is the Delta King, a sternwheeler that once shuttled passengers from here to San Francisco. Historic addresses include the **B.F. Hastings & Co. Building** *(2nd & J Sts.),* western terminus of the Pony Express; today it houses Gold Rush paraphernalia in a snug **Wells Fargo History Museum** (☎916-440-4263).

Old Sacramento's high point is the **California State Railroad Museum ★★** Kids *(125 I St.;* ☎*916-445-6645, www.csrmf. org),* where 21 meticulously restored locomotives, a railway post office, a sleeping car, a luxurious private car and other stock illustrate the impact of local and trans-Sierra railroading. Mining and agricultural history, and pioneer domestic life, are dynamically illustrated in exhibits in the **Discovery Museum ★** Kids *(101 I St.;* ☎*916-264-7075, www.the-discovery.org).*

Old Town Sacramento

Sutter's Fort State Historic Park★★

Kids *2701 L St.* [P] *☎916-445-4422. www.parks.ca.gov.*

Founded in 1839 as headquarters of a 76sq-mi land grant known as New Helvetia, Sutter's Fort welcomed early pioneers and explorers with legendary hospitality. John Sutter's prosperity was in sharp decline by the 1850s, however. The state acquired the abandoned and dilapidated fort in 1890, renovating and furnishing it. Visitors may explore the living quarters, bakery, and blacksmith's and other work rooms.

Gold Country★★

Nevada City★★

With scores of handsome Victorian houses on its forested hills above Deer Creek, this picturesque town of 3,500 has long been known as the graceful "Queen City" of the northern mines. Elegant shops and restaurants in the picturesque commercial district today cater to overnight visitors.

Empire Mine State Historic Park★★

Kids *5mi south of Nevada City via Empire St., near Grass Valley.* [P] *☎530-273-8522. www.empiremine.org.*

California's largest and richest mine boasts 367mi of tunnels that produced 5.8 million troy ounces of gold in a century of operation (1856-1956). Visitors may tour the home and gardens of mine owner William Bourn, Jr., and descend 30ft to gaze down the main winze, or diagonal shaft, extending 10,000 feet to a depth of nearly a mile.

Malakoff Diggins State Historic Park★

27mi northeast of Nevada City. Take Rte. 49 north 11mi; turn on Tyler Foote Crossing Rd., left on Cruzon Grade Rd. and follow signs. △ [P] *☎530-265-2740. www.parks.ca.gov.*

California's largest hydraulic mining pit is a lurid example of the disastrous effects on hillsides wrought by miners armed with high-pressure streams of water. The gaping gulch of the Malakoff Pit was eroded from 1855 until 1884, when hydraulic mining was banned by the state because it caused such destructive silting and flooding of downstream farmlands. Gold Rush-era buildings survive in the pleasant, tree-shaded village of North Bloomfield, site of the park visitor center.

Auburn★

The Gold Country's largest town, with 13,000 people, Auburn is a rail and highway junction with a charming 19C Old Town and an informative **Gold Country Museum** *(1273 High St.; ☎530-889-6500).*

Marshall Gold Discovery State Historic Park★★

Rte. 49, 8mi northwest of Placerville. [P] *☎530-622-3470. www.parks.ca.gov.*

This park preserves two-thirds of the historic village of Coloma, built where James Marshall discovered gold on January 28, 1848. A reconstructed sawmill and visitor center commemorate the events that touched off the California Gold Rush.

Jackson★

Founded in 1849, Jackson today displays handsome 19C Main Street architecture. The **National Hotel** (1863) claims to be the oldest continually operating hotel in the state. In a historic brick home (1859) atop a small knoll overlooking downtown, the **Amador County Museum**★ *(225 Church St.; ☎209-223-6386)* displays numerous Gold Rush artifacts.

Indian Grinding Rock State Historic Park★

Kids *Volcano Rd., 12mi east of Jackson via Rte. 88.* △ & [P] *☎209-296-7488. www.parks.ca.gov.*

Pitting a flat limestone outcrop are hundreds of mortar holes once used by native Miwok Indians to grind acorns into meal. Re-created Miwok bark dwellings and a ceremonial roundhouse stand near a small regional museum.

Calaveras Big Trees State Park★★

Rte. 4, 24mi east of Angels Camp. △ [P] *☎530-795-2334. www.parks.ca.gov.*

The first grove of giant sequoias to be developed for tourism was discovered in

1852 by a bear hunter. Visitors see giants along the well-groomed, self-guided nature trail *(1mi)* through the **North Grove.** Fewer hike the more remote trail *(4.7mi round-trip)* to the **South Grove,** although it leads to the park's largest specimens.

Columbia State Historic Park★★

Kids *Rte. 49, 4mi north of Sonora.* ✕ 🅿 ☎*209-532-0150. www.parks.ca.gov.* Founded in 1850, the boomtown of Columbia survived several fires and a lengthy decline before the state acquired it in 1945. Cars are banned from downtown, where costumed park employees re-create daily life in 1850-70 at shops and businesses. Visitors may pan for gold or tour an operating hard-rock tunnel, the **Hidden Treasure Mine**★ *(*☎*209-532-9693).*

Mariposa

A gateway to Yosemite National Park, Mariposa is home to the **California State Mining and Mineral Museum**★★ Kids *(Mariposa County Fairgrounds;* ☎*209-742-7625, www.parks.ca.gov),* one of the West's most informative displays of mining history. With about 20,000 specimens, the collection offers eye-catching displays of California gold, a working model of the 1904 Union Iron Works stamp mill, and a walk-through model of a Gold Country mine.

SEQUOIA AND KINGS CANYON NATIONAL PARKS★★

MAP P 430

PACIFIC STANDARD TIME

The world's largest stands of giant sequoia trees are found in these impressive twin parks, which, together with adjacent national forest, preserve the second-largest roadless area in the continental US.

- 🛈 **Information:** ☎559-565-3341 or www.nps.gov/seki
- 😊 **Don't Miss:** Giant Forest
- ⏱ **Also See:** Kings Canyon

A Bit of History

This is a rugged land of plunging canyons, deep forests, wildlife and mountain crests soaring above 14,000ft. Formed in 1890 to protect uncut sequoia groves, Sequoia National Park was soon tripled in size when Congress established General Grant National Park to protect the Grant Grove. In 1940, the new Kings Canyon National Park absorbed the Grant Grove. Among many superlative features are the Sherman Tree, earth's largest single tree; Kings Canyon, one of the deepest canyons in the US; and Mt. Whitney, highest peak in the continental US.

No road crosses the Sierra here. Visitor facilities lie on the parks' western edge, separated from the east boundary by a broad wilderness open only to hikers and packers. (The eastern slope is accessible by trail from roadheads near the Owens Valley (p 441)). Most visitors arrive by the General's Highway *(Rtes. 198 & 180),* a fine, two-lane loop road that links the Central Valley cities of Fresno and Visalia.

Lodging is available in Sequoia at Wuksachi Village *(*☎*559-565-3301 or 888-252-5757),* or at Grant Grove *(*☎*559-335-5500)* and Cedar Grove Villages *(559-565-0100)* in Kings Canyon. In Sequoia Park, a shuttle bus carries visitors between Wuksachi Village, Lodgepole, the Giant Forest Museum, Moro Rock and Crescent Meadow roughly every half-hour on summer days. Winter brings heavy snows to the parks, but the General's Highway is kept plowed.

Kings Canyon National Park, Kern Valley

Sequoia National Park★★★

Giant Forest★★★
30mi southeast of Big Stump entrance, 16mi northeast of Ash Mountain entrance. 🅿

Containing 8,000 mature sequoias, the sprawling Giant Forest is the second largest of 75 sequoia groves in the Sierra; only the remote Redwood Mountain Grove in the Grant Grove section of Kings Canyon is larger. The largest single tree on earth—the **General Sherman Tree**★—grows near the forest's northern end, adjacent to the General's Highway. With a circumference of 102.6ft and a height of 275ft, it forms a conspicuous starting point for several trails that fan out into the Giant Forest. The **Congress Trail** *(2mi)* loops through some of the forest's largest and most spectacularly homogeneous stands of Sequoiadendron giganteum, including the House and Senate groups.

Crescent Meadow
Described by John Muir as the "Gem of the Sierra," this curving glade—lush with wildflowers and fenced by giant sequoias—lies on the southern edge of the Giant Forest. A .8mi trail winds through meadow and woods to **Tharpe's Log**, a cabin made in the 60ft-hollow of a single log. The 8ft open end was closed off in the 1860s with a chimney, door and window, by a cattleman.

Moro Rock★
South of Giant Forest via Crescent Meadow Road. 🅿

An ingenious trail *(.5mi round-trip)* climbs some 400 steps to the top of this sheer-faced dome, providing spectacular **views**★★ 4,000ft down the Kaweah River Canyon, west to the Central Valley, and 12mi east to the jagged wall of the Great Western Divide. Built in 1931, the stairway was added to the National Register of Historic Places in 1978 in recognition of its harmonious integration with natural rock clefts.

Kings Canyon National Park★

Grant Grove★★
1mi west of Grant Grove Village.

A short loop trail *(.5mi)* passes among several noteworthy giants, including the

General Grant Tree, officially named the "Nation's Christmas Tree" in 1926. The world's third-largest sequoia, this massive specimen is the broadest, with a circumference of 107.6ft.

Kings Canyon★★

Hugging the southern wall of what is claimed to be the deepest gorge in the US (Hells Canyon fans disagree), the Kings Canyon Highway (Rte. 180) winds 30mi and descends 2,000ft from Grant Grove Village to **Cedar Grove Vil-** lage on the canyon floor. At its deepest, 11mi downstream from the park boundary, the gorge is about 8,200ft deep—at 1,850ft elevation, overlooked by 10,051ft Spanish Mountain. Most popular of many canyon-floor trails is **Roads End** *(5mi beyond Cedar Grove),* where lush Zumwalt Meadows lies 3,500ft beneath North Dome, on the north wall, and Grand Sentinel, on the south. Winter snows typically close this highway November to mid-June.

YOSEMITE NATIONAL PARK★★★

MAP P 430
PACIFIC STANDARD TIME

Sheer-walled Yosemite Valley stands at center stage of this sprawling national park, which encompasses 1,170sq mi of pristine forests, groves of giant sequoias, alpine lakes, abundant wildlife and awe-inspiring peaks. Ice Age glaciers grinding down the Merced River canyon scooped out Yosemite's distinctive U-shaped trough, 7mi long and more than 4,000ft deep, sculpting monumental rocks and polishing cliffs where streams now plummet as waterfalls.

- **Information:** ☎209-372-0200 or www.nps.gov/yose
- **Parking:** The main day-use lot at Valley Village is huge; get there early, leave your car and use the park's excellent shuttle bus system.
- **Don't Miss:** Yosemite Falls, El Capitan
- **Especially for Kids:** Tunnel Tree
- **Also See:** The Awahnee Hotel, Tuolumne Meadows

A Bit of History

The native Ahwahneechee people were forced to surrender Yosemite to European and American pioneers in 1851; just 13 years later, the federal government set aside Yosemite Valley and the Wawona Grove as a natural preserve. The effusive writings of naturalist John Muir prompted Congress in 1890 to preserve the surrounding wilderness as Yosemite National Park. Today, millions of visitors a year come to hike, backpack, bicycle, fish, ride horseback, camp, ski or simply drink in the magnificent scenery.

Though it constitutes less than 6 percent of the park's land area, Yosemite Valley remains the principal attraction. Lodging, dining facilities, shops and other amenities are found at rustic Camp Curry, motel-style Yosemite Lodge and at the magnificent hotel **Ahwahnee**★★ *(lodging reservations ☎559-253-5635, www.yosemitepark.com/Accommodations),* perhaps the finest of all national park lodges. Visitors may tour the east end of the valley aboard a free shuttle bus. Outside the valley, a more modest array of park facilities exists at Crane Flat, Tuolumne Meadows, White Wolf and Wawona in summer, and at Badger Pass Ski Resort in winter.

Yosemite Valley

Yosemite Village

The administrative and commercial center of the park includes a post office, the **Ansel Adams Gallery** and a Wilderness Office where hikers obtain backcountry information and permits.

John Anderson/MICHELIN

Half-Dome, Yosemite National Park

Staffed by rangers, the **Visitor Center** presents exhibits on geology and natural history. Evening performances in the adjacent **Yosemite Theater** dramatize the life of John Muir, as impersonated by Lee Stetson. The **Yosemite Museum** houses a collection of native artifacts, changing art exhibits and the snug Yosemite Library. Behind the museum, the reconstructed Ahwahneechee Village displays bark dwellings and a sweat lodge still used for tribal rites.

Yosemite Falls★★★
Plunging 2,425ft in three stages down the valley's north wall, the highest waterfall in North America appears most spectacularly as a billowing plume on windy spring days. It may dry up completely by late summer. From parking lots near Yosemite Lodge, a short path (*.2mi*) leads to the thundering base of the **lower fall**★★ (320ft). The strenuous Yosemite Falls Trail (*7mi round-trip*) switchbacks up a cleft in the north wall, passing above the middle cascade (675ft) to a ledge near the lip of the **upper fall**★ (1,430ft).

Happy Isles★
At the mouth of the Merced River Canyon, a cluster of small islands splits the roaring cataract into smaller channels. A delightful picnic spot at 4,050ft elevation, Happy Isles is the start of the often-spectacular **John Muir Trail.** Very popular is the short, steep jaunt to **Vernal Fall Bridge**★★ (*.7mi*); from here, the Mist Trail climbs to the brink of 317ft **Vernal Fall**★★ (*1.5mi*). Ambitious hikers may proceed to the top of 594ft **Nevada Fall** (*3mi*). A farther trail continues to the summit of **Half Dome**★★★ (*8.2mi*), a massive rock that rises 4,800 vertical feet above its base (to 8,842ft elevation) at the eastern head of the valley. This hike is not for the faint-hearted or weak of limb, as the final assault of the summit mounts a 45-degree granite slab with the aid of an exposed cable ladder.

Tunnel View★★★
From this stupendous viewpoint at the east end of the Wawona Tunnel, visitors gaze eastward into Yosemite Valley. Its portals are framed on the south by **Cathedral Rocks** and on the north by the massive, 3,593ft face of **El Capitan**★★, the world's largest unbroken cliff. Graceful Bridalveil Fall hangs in the foreground, as do ephemeral Ribbon and Silver Strand Falls in early spring. The distinctive, sheer face of Half Dome peers round the shoulder of Glacier Point from the eastern end of the valley.

Excursions

Glacier Point★★★

30mi south and east from Yosemite Village; 0.2mi walk from parking area.
✕&

Road may be closed Nov–late May. Jutting 3,000ft above the valley floor, this majestic clifftop perch offers an unforgettable view of the toy-like Yosemite Valley below. To the northwest, Yosemite Falls hang at full length; to the east, Vernal and Nevada Falls can be seen in one glimpse, while Half Dome looms in the foreground.

Mariposa Grove of Big Trees★★

34mi south of Yosemite Village. ✕& *Tours by foot (loop trips 1mi–7mi) or 1hr tram tour (daily mid-Apr–mid-Nov).*

The largest of the park's three groves of giant sequoias spreads over 250 acres of a steep hillside. Most massive of nearly 400 mature sequoias is the **Grizzly Giant,** a 2,700-year-old specimen with a base circumference of 96ft and a pronounced lean of 17 degrees. The adjacent �🅺ᵢds **California Tunnel Tree**

was bored in 1895 to allow coaches to pass through it, a fashionable novelty of Victorian tourism.

Tioga Road★★

62mi one-way north and east from Yosemite Village to Tioga Pass. Last 45mi (past Crane Flat) closed Nov–late May. Route 120 snakes 14mi through thick evergreen forests before opening to broad views of the high country.

Olmsted Point★ provides striking vistas down Tenaya Canyon to Half Dome and Clouds Rest (9,926ft). Passing subalpine **Tenaya Lake,** the largest natural body of water in the park, the road enters **Tuolumne Meadows**★★, an alpine grassland at 8,600ft elevation. The heart of the high country, Tuolumne Meadows has rustic lodging and dining, a visitor center and access to miles of back-country trails. A marvelous short trail climbs to the glacier-polished summit of 9,450ft **Lembert Dome**★ *(3mi round-trip).* Beyond 9,945ft **Tioga Pass**★, highest point on a continuous roadway in California, Rte. 120 descends 13mi to the junction of US-395 near Mono Lake.

EASTERN SIERRA★

MAP P 430
PACIFIC STANDARD TIME

The eastern escarpment of the Sierra Nevada rises abruptly from the sagebrush flats of the Great Basin, sere by virtue of the rain shadow cast by the Sierra crest. Running parallel, US-395 is among the most spectacular highways in the US, with continuous views of towering granite peaks and awesome volcanic scenery. Side roads probe narrow canyons to lakes and trailheads in rugged alpine regions. The highway reaches its climax in the broad, deep Owens Valley.

▮ **Information:** ☎760-934-2712 www.visitmammoth.com
◉ **Don't Miss:** Owens Valley; Mono Lake
◔ **Also See:** Devils Postpile

Sights

Bodie State Historic Park★★

Rte. 270 east from US-395; final 3mi unpaved. Road may be closed by snow in winter ☎760-647-6445. *www.parks. ca.gov.*

This stark, windswept, unrestored ghost town rambles along dirt streets

in the sagebrush hills of the high desert. Although the discovery of gold in 1859 brought a rush of prospectors, not until 1874 did corporate investment shape Bodie into a mining city of 10,000 people. The town had a nasty reputation, the "bad man from Bodie" being a standard bogey of Western lore. Population dwindled when mining waned in 1882; the

© Jim Kellett, Mammoth Lakes

Tufa Towers at Mono Lake

town was eventually abandoned. It was acquired in 1962 by the state, which has maintained its 150 buildings in a state of "arrested decay" with no restoration. It is often the coldest place in the continental US. The **Miners Union Hall** on Main Street functions as museum and visitor center.

Mono Lake★★

Remnant of a prehistoric lake five times larger than its present 60sq mi, Mono Lake is three times saltier than the ocean and 80 times more alkaline. Dubbed "the Dead Sea of California" by Mark Twain, Mono in fact supports a wealth of brine shrimp and alkali flies that attract migratory birds and waterfowl. The flies were valued by the native Paiutes, who ate the shelled pupae and traded them across the Sierra Nevada to the Yokuts; the Yokut word *mono*, meaning "fly eaters," was attached to the lake itself.

The **US Forest Service Visitor Center** *(north end of Lee Vining, off US-395; ☎760-647-3044)* serves as a museum of the region's natural and human history. The lake is famed as an example of the way urbanization spreads its damage to distant spots: Mono Lake's level dropped dramatically when Los Angeles began running the valley's water south in an aqueduct. Foremost among lakeshore sights are the grotesque limestone spires of **South Tufa**★★ *(6mi south of Lee Vining on US-395, then 4.5mi east on Rte. 120 to gravel access road)*, formed between AD 1100 and 1900 as calcium deposits from submerged springs combined with lake-water carbonates.

Mammoth Region★

A 19C mining town transformed into a four-season resort community, **Mammoth Lakes** *(information ☎760-934-8006)* lies beneath the massive dormant volcano of 11,053ft **Mammoth Mountain**★. Camping, fishing and hiking in the nearby **Mammoth Lakes Basin**★ and the surrounding high country dominate the snow-free season from late May to October. Winter brings skiers to the **Mammoth Mountain Ski Center** *(☎760-934-2571)*; the thaw attracts brash mountain bikers; and a year-round gondola climbs to the summit for magnificent views over the eastern Sierra. Summer trams shuttle hikers over panoramic **Minaret Summit**★★ to **Devils Postpile National Monument**★ *(Rte. 203; ☎760-934-2289, www.nps.gov/depo)*. An easy trail *(.4mi)* leads to the monument's namesake, a 60ft wall of six- to eight-sided basalt columns at the face of a 100,000-year-old lava flow.

The Whitney Crest★★

The 60mi stretch of the **Owens Valley**★★ from Bishop to Lone Pine, bounded by the Sierra Nevada on the west and the White-Inyo Range on the east, ranks among the most dramatic valleys in North America. The valley floor at Lone Pine lies two vertical miles beneath the

14,494ft summit of **Mt. Whitney**★★, highest point in the contiguous US. The most sublime view of the jagged Whitney crest is from the **Alabama Hills**★★, west of Lone Pine; scores of Hollywood films and TV shows have been shot among these fantastic boulder formations. The **Eastern Sierra Interagency Visitor Center** (US-395, *1mi south of Lone Pine; ☎760-876-6222)* provides maps. The steep and winding but well-paved **Whitney Portal Road** climbs to a lovely mountain canyon (8,360ft), trailhead for the rugged **Mt. Whitney Trail** *(21.4mi round-trip; permit required from Inyo National Forest office in Lone Pine; ☎760-876-6200).*

RENO AREA★

MAP P 430

PACIFIC STANDARD TIME

Straddling the Truckee River where the Sierra Nevada meet the Great Basin, Reno enjoys a reputation as a center for outdoor recreation, although casino gaming is its foremost tourism draw. The city was founded around a toll bridge in the 1860s and named for a Civil War general. It achieved an economic boost when Central Pacific rail construction crews passed through in 1868, and grew as a distribution center after the transcontinental line was completed in 1869. The prosperity of nearby Virginia City in the 1870s, and later mining rushes to Tonopah and Goldfield, bolstered its role. Reno became a county seat in 1870 and home of the University of Nevada in 1886.

🛈 **Information:** ☎800-367-7366 or www.visitrenotahoe.com
🚗 **Don't Miss:** Virginia City
📷 **Especially for Kids:** Virginia & Truckee Railroad

A Bit of History

Although gambling and other vices had always thrived in Reno, casino gaming underwent a revolution when Raymond "Pappy" Smith opened **Harold's Club** on Virginia Street in 1935 and began courting a "respectable" clientele through widespread advertising. Attracted by this new image, gambling trips to Reno became a favorite weekend pastime of Californians. They increased in popularity after William Harrah opened **Harrah's** in 1946; by the 1950s, new casinos filled the downtown area with pulsating neon lights, establishing Reno as the supreme gaming destination of Nevada. In the 1960s, however, the Las Vegas Strip wrested that reputation away; by the 1980s, Las Vegas had also surpassed Reno in population.

The Reno area nevertheless experienced unprecedented growth at the end of the 20C. The city, now with a population close to 200,000, offers peerless recreational opportunities—especially with its proximity to Lake Tahoe *(p 431)*—and a broad-based economy as the banking center, transportation hub and entertainment dynamo of northern Nevada.

Sights

Reno★

North Virginia Street★★
Between I-80 & the Truckee River.
✕🚻 ♿ 🅿

This seven-block "Strip" contains Reno's greatest concentration of gambling casinos, flamboyantly celebrated in the **Reno Arch**★ *(Virginia & Commercial Sts.),* which arcs over the street and proclaims Reno "The Biggest Little City in the World."

Rectangular city blocks compel casinos, many of them linked by sky bridges, to conform to regular architectural footprints. Conventional, high-rise facades rely on extravagant **lighting displays**★ and open shopfronts to attract pedestrians to their slot machines and gaming tables. Harrah's, Fitzgerald's, the Cal-Neva, the Eldorado and other casinos established before the 1990s likewise abstain from the fantastic themes that pervade recent casino-hotels of the Las Vegas Strip. The most notable exception is the **Silver Legacy Resort Casino** (407 N. Virginia St.; ☎775-325-7401), where a re-created 120ft mining scaffold ignites an hourly light show, complete with lightning, beneath a central dome that mimics celestial changes. The casino strip ends at the Truckee River, where wooded promenades trace the banks of the cold mountain stream through downtown Reno.

National Automobile Museum (The Harrah Collection)★★

10 Lake St. S. &🅿 ☎775-333-9300. www.automuseum.org.
With more than 200 antique, classic and custom automobiles displayed in imaginative period settings, this collection ranks among the West's most interesting. Visitors watch a high-tech multimedia history of the auto industry, then stroll among indoor "streets" lined by vintage autos and facades that represent the turn of the 20C, the 1930s, the 1950s and contemporary times. Exceptional displays include an 1892 steam-driven Philion carriage, the 1907 Thomas Flyer that won the New York-to-Paris Automobile Race in 170 days, Al Jolson's 1933 Cadillac V-16, and the 1949 Mercury driven by James Dean in Rebel Without a Cause.

W.M. Keck Museum★

1664 N. Virginia St., Mackay School of Mines, University of Nevada. & ☎775-784-6052. www.mines.unr.edu/museum.
The Mackay School of Mines (1908), north of the UN's tree-lined quadrant, is a preeminent school of mining engineering. Specimens of Nevada minerals and fossils line the walls of its Keck Museum, illustrating Nevada's role as a leader in this field. The Mackay silver collection in the basement recalls the role of John Mackay (1831-1902) as one of the Comstock "Bonanza Kings."

Excursions

Carson City★

30mi south of Reno on US-395. ☎775-687-7410. www.carson-city.org.
Founded in 1858, the city was named for the Carson River, itself named by adventurer John C. Frémont for scout Kit Carson. The town became the Nevada territorial capital, then the state capital in 1864, acquiring a US Mint. Today it has a population of 55,000.
The **Kit Carson Trail** winds past historic residences, passing the 1895 home of famed Washoe basket-weaver Datsola-lee, the 1909 Governor's Mansion and a house built in 1864 by Orion Clemens. Clemens, the first and only secretary of the Nevada Territory, accompanied his brother Samuel ("Mark Twain") Clemens from Missouri in a journey described by the author in Roughing It.
The dignified **Nevada State Capitol Complex** (Carson Ave.; ☎800-638-2321) gathers numerous government buildings in a handsome parklike setting. Capped by a silvery cupola, the sandstone capitol (1871) still houses the offices of the governor and other officials; the Senate and Assembly, however, now meet in the Nevada State Legislature (1970) across the adjacent plaza.

Nevada State Museum★★

600 N. Carson St. ☎775-687-4811. dmla.clan.lib.nv.us.
Housed in the 1869 Carson City Mint, this institution provides an engaging overview of Nevada's flora, fauna, geology and human history, with a special emphasis on the state's mining heritage. The **Mint History Gallery**★ surveys the process that produced more than 56 million coins from Nevada gold and silver between 1870 and 1895; workers on occasion still strike medallions on Coin Press No. 1. Beyond an archetypal **ghost town**★, natural-history galleries display mounted birds and mammals from the Great Basin. The **Earth Sciences Gallery** features a walk-through exhibit of Devonian Nevada, 35 to 40 million years ago, when these precincts were on the ocean floor.

Virginia City★★

14mi northeast of Carson City, 23mi southeast of Reno, on Rte. 341. ☎775-847-7500. Preserved as a National Historic Landmark, this bustling old mining town—perched on the steep slopes of Mount Davidson—ranks among the most fascinating in the West.

Visit

Virginia City is built on steep terraces, its downtown concentrated along C Street. Few buildings predate a devastating 1875 fire, but about half were built before 1890. Linked by uneven wooden sidewalks with overhanging roofs and porches, four densely packed blocks of wood and brick buildings are occupied by stores, restaurants, saloons and several private collections of curios optimistically labeled "museums." Among the historic sites is the office of the *Territorial Enterprise*, where young Mark Twain worked in the 1860s. Even children are free to enter any of the colorful saloons on C Street, the **Best and Belcher Mine**★ (☎775-847-0757) behind the Ponderosa Saloon, or the **Choller Mine**★ (☎775-847-0155) on the south edge of town.

Among old mansions seasonally open for tours are **The Castle** (*BStreet;* ☎775-847-0275) and the **Mackay Mansion** (*D Street;* ☎775-847-0336). Built in 1875, **Pipers Opera House**★ (*B& Union Sts.;* ☎775-847-0433, *www.nps.gov/history/nr/travel/nevada*) still offers dramas on the boards where Jenny Lind and Edwin Booth once performed. One of the city's better historical collections occupies the four-story, 1876 **Fourth Ward School**★ (☎775-847-0975). The **Kids** **Virginia & Truckee Railroad** (☎775-885-6833, *www.steamtrain.org*), built to transport silver to Carson City, and Tahoe Basin timber to shore up Virginia City's mines, still offers rides from its F Street station.

SHASTA-CASCADE REGION★

MICHELIN MAP 493 A, B6, 7

PACIFIC STANDARD TIME

At the northern end of the Sierra Nevada, the mountains meet the Cascade, Trinity and Klamath ranges in an arc of peaks arrayed at the head of the Sacramento Valley, with the agricultural center of Redding at its hub.

- **Information:** ☎530-225-4100, www.visitredding.org
- **Don't Miss:** Lassen Volcanic National Park
- **Especially for Kids:** Shasta Lake
- **Also See:** Turtle Bay Exploration Park & Sundial Bridge

A Bit of History

Dominating the landscape for hundreds of miles around is the volcanic cone of Mt. Shasta (14,162ft), which presents an enchanting symbol of this highly volcanic region. Lassen Peak (10,457ft) erupted violently from 1914 to 1917 and today forms the nucleus of a serene, though still smoldering, national park. A trio of large man-made lakes are preserved within **Whiskeytown-Shasta-Trinity National Recreation Areas** (*www.fs.fed.us/r5/shastatrinity*).

Beyond the Cascades, the high Modoc Lava Plateau covers 26,000sq mi of California's northeastern corner, a vast desert upland noted for its lava tubes and stark, craggy scenery.

Sights

Turtle Bay Exploration Park★

Hwy. 44 one mi west of Interstate 5 Exit 678. ⚠♿🅿 ☎530-243-8850. *www.turtlebay.org.*

Highlight of this new park is the **Sundial Bridge**★★, a graceful pedestrian span over the Sacramento River designed by Santiago Calatrava.

Lassen Volcanic National Park★★

47mi east of Redding via Rte. 44. ☎*530-595-4444. www.nps.gov/lavo.*
Lassen Peak erupted May 30, 1914, the first of 298 eruptions over several years. Congress established the 106,000-acre national park in 1916 to allow visitors the opportunity to witness the spectacular effects of volcanism.

The scenic Park Road *(Rte. 89)* makes a winding 30mi arc around Lassen Peak. From the **Manzanita Lake Visitor Center** *(Loomis Museum;* ☎*530-335-7373)*, the road passes through the **Devastated Area**, blasted at the height of Lassen's 1915 eruptions, though now recovering with new forests of aspen and pine. At the road's closest approach to Lassen Peak, at 8,500ft, a strenuous trail *(5mi)* begins climbing to the summit. The highlight of current volcanic activity is **Bumpass Hell**★★. Accessible only by a 3mi round-trip hike from the roadhead, its sulfuric fumaroles, boiling springs and bubbling mudpots are visible from a boardwalk that passes safely over the soft ground.

McArthur-Burney Falls Memorial State Park★

65mi northeast of Redding via Rtes. 229 & 89. ⚠♿🅿 ☎*916-335-2777. www.parks. ca.gov.* Highlight of this popular park is Burney Falls★★, where the combined flows of Burney Creek and an underground stream tumble enchantingly over a 129ft cliff of basalt. Springs amid the ferns in the face of the cliff engorge the falls with ribbons of water, so that the flow is visibly greater at the bottom than the top.

Lava Beds National Monument★★

170mi northeast of Redding via Rtes. 299, 139 & 10. ☎*530-667-8100. www. nps.gov/labe.*
This remote stretch of the Modoc Lava Plateau contains more than 300 lava tubes, several of which penetrate as far as 150ft below the earth's surface, while others extend horizontally for thousands of feet. Rangers provide flashlights, hard hats, books and maps for exploring tubes along **Cave Loop Road** and farther afield.

In 1872, 53 Modoc warriors and their families held off the US Army for five months at a natural fortress now called **Captain Jack's Stronghold**★★. The Modoc leader, Kientpoos (known to settlers as Captain Jack), opted to fight rather than endure exile on a reservation controlled by traditional enemies. Outnumbered as much as 20 times, the Modocs used the crags and caves for hiding and ambushes. Captain Jack finally led the Modocs out of the lava beds after fatally shooting an Army general during peace negotiations. He was later captured and hanged; the remainder of the tribe was exiled to Oklahoma.

Mount Shasta★

Visible for hundreds of miles around northern California, this glacier-clad, 14,162ft volcano is second in height in the Cascades only to Mt. Rainier in Washington. Many hikes start from the **Everitt Memorial Highway**, a scenic route that ascends through Shasta-Trinity National Forest.

YELLOWSTONE REGION

America's first national park, Yellowstone National Park was established by the US Congress in 1872. Much of the park sits astride an ancient collapsed volcanic caldera, 28mi wide and 47mi long. Within the borders of this 3,472sq-mi World Heritage Site (roughly the size of the eastern state of Connecticut) is the largest free-roaming wildlife population in the lower 48 states; the world's greatest concentration of thermal features and its largest petrified forest.

One of the pleasures of a visit to Yellowstone is that it is so accessible. More than 370mi of paved road weave a course through the park, introducing Old Faithful and its surrounding geysers, the travertine terraces of Mammoth Hot Springs and the spectacular chasm of the Grand Canyon of the Yellowstone. Majestic elk, bison, moose and other large animals range widely through this realm of steamy beauty, often visiting campgrounds and lodges, and wandering close to a main road.

Immediately south of Yellowstone is Grand Teton National Park, enclosing a dramatic mountain range that rises high above the Snake River and a series of pristine lakes created by glacial moraines. East of Yellowstone is Cody, founded by William F. "Buffalo Bill" Cody himself in the late 19C. Each of Yellowstone's three Montana entrance routes has a character of its own, from remarkable alpine scenery to outdoor recreation to culture and urbanity.

The Snake River Valley runs west from Yellowstone through southern Idaho, and here, too, are a plethora of worthy stops, including the classic resort facilities of Sun Valley and the roof-of-the-world scenery of Sawtooth National Recreation Area.

MT
Yellowstone NP
ID
WY

Grand Canyon of the Yellowstone

©iStockphoto.com/Aimin Tang

YELLOWSTONE NATIONAL PARK★★★

MAP P 452

MOUNTAIN STANDARD TIME

The earth is a living force in Yellowstone, its dynamic natural features laid bare. Set aside primarily for its geological features—the brilliant, multicolored hot pools and lively geysers, and the dramatic Grand Canyon of the Yellowstone—the park's role as a haven for wildlife has assumed equal importance. This vast wilderness is one of the last remaining strongholds of the grizzly bear; in recent years it has gained additional attention with the reintroduction of wolves into its ecosystem. While visitors can count on Old Faithful to erupt regularly, their chance encounters with the park's large mammals are most endearing—and enduring.

- **Information:** ☎307-344-7381, www.nps.gov/yell
- **Orient Yourself:** Though Yellowstone remains a remote part of the West, scheduled air service reaches Jackson, Idaho Falls and Bozeman, all within a few hours drive of the park.
- **Parking:** The most important parking consideration in Yellowstone is where not to park--not in the roadway, as so many hapless tourists do during the "gawker blocks" that form when animals are near the road.
- **Don't Miss:** Mammoth Hot Springs, Grand Canyon of the Yellowstone
- **Organizing Your Time:** A sketchy Yellowstone experience is possible in one day, starting on the west side at Old Faithful before the tour bus crowds arrive, then circling around to the east. But an entire week can also be devoted to the park, with hikes and side trips.
- **Especially for Kids:** Fountain Paint Pots

Geological Notes

Located on a high plateau bisected by the Continental Divide and bounded to the north, east and south by mountains, Yellowstone occupies the northwest corner of the state of Wyoming, with small portions spilling over into adjacent Montana and Idaho. Five highways (from west, north, northeast, east and south) provide access to its main Grand Loop Road, which dissects the forested landscape in a large figure eight between the principal scenic attractions. Yellowstone boasts more than 10,000 thermal features, the result of a rare, migrating hot spot in the earth's crust that originated near the southern border of Oregon and Idaho, 300mi to the southwest, about 17 million years ago. The lava flows of the Snake River Plain trace the "movement" of this hot spot as the continental plate slides southwesterly above the source of heat, a stationary magma plume only 1- 3mi beneath the earth's surface. The Yellowstone Caldera was created 600,000 years ago by a volcanic blast dwarfing that of Mount St. Helens in 1980.

Park roads are generally open to motor vehicles May through October, and for over-snow vehicles mid-December to early March. Snow may fall at any park elevation any time of year.

Year-round, the Yellowstone Association Institute (☎307-344-2293, www.yellowstoneassociation.org) offers naturalist-led hikes and other activities off the well-traveled roads with access to Yellowstone's fascinating backcountry.

A Bit of History

Nomadic tribes hunted here for thousands of years, but may never have lived in the Yellowstone basin, out of respect for spirits they believed spoke through the rumblings of the earth. They named

Address Book Yellowstone Region

For prices, see the Legend on the cover flap.

WHERE TO STAY IN THE YELLOWSTONE REGION

$$$$$ Jenny Lake Lodge – *Grand Teton National Park, Moran, WY.* ✕ & P ☎ *307-733-4647 or 800-628-9988. www.gtlc.com. Closed Oct-late May. 37 rooms.* Secluded log cabins surround the main lodge, where guests gather in front of a stone fireplace or relax in rockers on the porch. Visitors to this former dude ranch are unburdened by phones, radios or TVs as they repose beneath country-quilt bedspreads. A formal six-course meal is included in the rate. Also in Grand Teton are the **Jackson Lake Lodge ($$$)** and **Colter Bay Village ($$)**.

$$$$** (summer), **$$$ (winter) **Spring Creek Ranch** – *1800 Spirit Dance Rd., Jackson, WY.* ✕ & P Spa ☎ *307-733-8833 or 800-443-6139. www.springcreekranch.com. 120 rooms.* Views of the Teton Range are spectacular from this sprawling 1,000-acre ranch-resort atop East Gros Ventre Butte in the heart of Jackson Hole. Horseback riding, tennis and the gourmet **Granary ($$$)** restaurant tempt guests, whose lodgings come with pine furniture and stone fireplaces.

$$$ Sun Valley Lodge – *1 Sun Valley Rd., Sun Valley, ID.* ✕ & P ⛸ Spa ☎ *208-622-2001 or 800-786-8259. www.sunvalley.com. 148 rooms.* The Union Pacific Railroad opened this majestic hotel in 1936, enabling East Coast society to "rough it" in style alongside Hollywood stars. The oak-paneled lodge still attracts well-heeled visitors to ski and golf. The **Lodge Dining Room ($$$)** serves jazz and regional cuisine, while **Gretchen's ($$)** caters to families. Sun Valley Resort has 510 rooms between the lodge, Tyrolean-style **Sun Valley Inn ($$$)** and condo units.

$$$ The Wort Hotel – *50 N. Glenwood St., Jackson, WY.* ✕ & P ⛸ ☎ *307-733-2190 or 800-322-2727. www.worthotel.com. 60 rooms.* Log beds, plaid blankets and barbed-wire wallpaper are in keeping with the cowboy-rancher atmosphere of Jackson. This Swiss-style hotel, opened in 1941, is famous for its Silver Dollar Bar, an S-curve embedded with 2,032 uncirculated 1921 silver dollars.

$$ The Irma Hotel – *1192 Sheridan Ave., Cody, WY.* ✕ P ☎ *307-587-4221 or 800-745-4762. www.irmahotel.com. 40 rooms.* Cody's founder and namesake, Buffalo Bill, built this basic Victorian, full of tales and personalities, and named it for his daughter in 1902. Some of the high-ceilinged rooms still display bullet holes from past revelry. The cherry-wood bar was a present from Queen Victoria. Mock gunfights are staged outside the hotel each summer evening.

$$ Old Faithful Inn – *Yellowstone National Park, WY.* ✕ & P ☎ *307-344-7311. www.travelyellowstone.com. Closed mid-Oct–early May. 327 rooms.* As the largest log cabin in the world, the Old Faithful Inn was a model for other national-park lodges in the West. Architect Robert Reamer used twisted lodgepole pine in the 85ft-high lobby to create a forest of balconies and stairways under a massive gable roof. Rooms, while small, capture the rustic natural spirit. The newly rebuilt **Old Faithful Snow Lodge ($$)**, nearby, serves winter guests. In all, there are 10 separate lodging properties in Yellowstone Park.

$$ Voss Inn – *319 S. Willson St., Bozeman, MT.* P ☎ *406-587-0982. www.bozeman-vossinn.com. 6 rooms.* An English perennial garden and Victorian rose garden surround this charming 1883 bed-and-breakfast mansion, situated between downtown Bozeman and Montana State University. All rooms are non-smoking, have private baths, and are furnished with antiques.

$ The Hostel X – *3315 McCollister Ave., Teton Village, WY.* P ☎ *307-733-3415. www.hostelx.com. 54 rooms.* "Low end" by ski-resort standards, this bunkhouse—12mi from Jackson at the foot of Rendezvous Peak—has a sense of style. Though rooms are basic, all have one king or four bunk beds, and private baths. There's a fireplace in the guest lounge, a laundry and a game room.

WHERE TO EAT IN THE YELLOWSTONE REGION

$$$ The Gun Barrel Steak and Game House – *862 W. Broadway, Jackson, WY.* ☎ *307-733-3287. www.gunbarrel.com.* **Regional**. This warehouse once was a wildlife museum, but now the game is saved for the plate. Velvet elk with sun-dried tomatoes, venison bratwurst and caribou tortillas head a menu heavy on steaks and chicken. Double Barrel home brew tempts bar patrons.

$$$ Lake Hotel Dining Room – *Yellowstone National Park, WY.* ☎ *307-344-7311. www.travelyellowstone.com. Closed early Oct–mid-May.* **Creative American.** The park's oldest inn may offer its best dining experience. Beyond the sunroom of the bright, wicker-furnished 1891 hotel is the spacious dining room. Hungry park explorers enjoy breakfast buffets, creative lunches (blackened salmon wrap, Montrachet spinach salad) and gourmet steak-and-seafood dinners.

$$$ The Range – *225 N. Cache St., Jackson, WY.* ☎ *307-733-5481.* **Regional**. A stainless-steel exhibition kitchen is the stage for "gourmet theater." The core menu features regional cuisine—homemade wild-game sausage, Rocky Mountain trout with tomatillo-and-corn pico de gallo, elk carpaccio with juniper-garlic aioli. Decor boasts modern lines of leather, rich woods and copper.

$$ Jedediah's Original House of Sourdough – *135 E. Broadway, Jackson, WY.* ☎ *307-733-5671. American.* Housed in one of the oldest log cabins in town, Jedediah's is famous for its sourdough pancake breakfasts. At lunch and dinner, crowds file in for grilled steaks, chicken and trout, served with sourdough bread amid photos of Jackson old-timers and faded newspaper articles.

---

the canyon Mi-tse-a-da-zi, "Rock Yellow River." The first white man to explore the area was probably John Colter, who left the Lewis and Clark party in 1806 to spend several months trapping. His descriptions of Yellowstone's wonders fell on deaf ears back East, where they were regarded as tall tales or the hallucinations of someone who had spent too much time alone in the wilderness. Generations and rumors came and went before the private Washburn-Langford-Doane party braved the wilds in 1870 to finally separate fiction from fact. Stunned to discover there was ample awesome fact, this party convinced the US Geological Survey to investigate. In June 1871, Survey director Ferdinand Hayden explored Yellowstone with 34 men, including painter Thomas Moran and photographer William Henry Jackson; the following year, armed with Hayden's 500-page report and Moran's and Jackson's visuals, Congress proclaimed this wilderness the world's first national park.

Tourists weren't far behind, especially when a rail link from Livingston, Montana, to Gardiner, near the north entrance, eased access. The park's early civilian administrators couldn't handle the poaching and vandalism, so the US Army took over. From 1886 to 1918, 400 soldiers were stationed at Mammoth Hot Springs, enforcing park regulations and guarding primary scenic attractions.

Sights

The following attractions are best seen by driving Yellowstone's 172mi **Grand Loop Road** in a clockwise direction around the park, beginning and ending at any of the five park entrances. The greatest traffic comes through the West Entrance in West Yellowstone, Montana, gateway for this tour.

Norris Geyser Basin★★

Left (west) off the Grand Loop Road at Norris Junction, 14mi north of Madison Junction, then .25mi to parking area. 🅿. The oldest and hottest thermal area in the park is also its most dynamic. The major geysers are in **Back Basin**★, where thermal features are scattered among trees. **Steamboat Geyser** is the world's tallest active geyser. Its rare major eruptions (it is dormant for years at a time) can reach heights of 400ft. **Echinus Geyser**★★, the largest acid-water geyser, puts on an entertaining show every 40-80min, filling, erupting and draining like a toilet bowl.

Just north of the Norris Basin, on the east side of the Grand Loop Road, the **Museum of the National Park Ranger** hosts exhibits on the ranger profession, in a historic early-20C army outpost.

Mammoth Hot Springs★★★

North Entrance & Grand Loop Rds. ♿ 🅿. Perched on a hillside with multicolored terraces above, Mammoth is the park's command post. Headquarters are located in the complex's historic buildings. The green lawns and orderly appearance recall Mammoth's early history as an army post.

Change, constant throughout Yellowstone, is most obvious at Mammoth. Each day, two tons of travertine are deposited by the relatively cool (170ºF) hot springs. The water mixes with carbon dioxide to form carbonic acid, which dissolves underlying limestone to produce the travertine, similar to that found in limestone caves. As this solution reaches the surface, it cools rapidly and releases carbon dioxide, leaving behind deposits of calcium carbonate. Brilliant color is added to this three-dimensional "canvas" by algae and tiny living bacteria.

Elevated boardwalks climb and descend the ornate flows of the Main Terrace and the **Minerva Springs**★★★. Impressive from a distance, this formation is truly remarkable when viewed up close, where the elaborate collection of minute cascades and multicolored terraces resemble a still photo of a waterfall. The most visibly active feature is **Opal Terrace**★★, which sprang to life in 1926 after years of dormancy. Popular with elk, which recline here like living sculptures, it is growing rapidly. A couple of hundred yards north, the distinctive **Liberty Cap**★ juts from the earth like a massive Christmas tree. This extinct hot-spring cone was named for its resemblance to the hats worn by colonial patriots.

Mammoth's red-roofed buildings, many of stone, were built as part of Fort Yellowstone in the 1890s and early 1900s. Today they shelter administration, staff housing and the **Horace M. Albright Visitor Center and Museum**★★ (☎307-344-2263). Named for a longtime director of the National Park Service and early park superintendent, the museum traces the human and natural history of the park, highlighting Thomas Moran paintings and William Henry Jackson photographs from the 1871 Hayden expedition. The facility also serves as the

Mammoth Hot Springs

primary Yellowstone information center and backcountry permit office.

The most interesting aspect of the 1937 **Mammoth Hot Springs Hotel** (☎307-344-7311, www.travelyeloowstone.com) is a US map, assembled on a wall like a large puzzle, the states carefully cut from 15 different woods of nine countries.

Specimen Ridge★

Access by trail 2.5mi east of Tower Junction, 19mi east of Mammoth Hot Springs. P This 8,442ft crest and 40sq mi of surrounding uplands constitute the largest petrified forest in the world. Remnants of more than 100 different plants, including redwoods similar to those of California, are found here. Ash and mudflows buried the trees 50 million years ago; erosion reversed the process.

Tower Fall★★

2mi south of Tower Junction. P.
This impressive waterfall squeezes between namesake stone "towers" and plunges 132ft to join the Grand Canyon of the Yellowstone at its narrowest point. A steep **trail** (.5mi) descends 300ft to the base of the fall. The dramatic **gorge**★★ is best viewed from a turnout at **Calcite Springs,** from which basaltic columns may be seen rimming the 500ft bluffs beneath which the river flows.

Dunraven Pass★

14mi south of Tower Junction. High point of the Grand Loop Road, 8,859ft
Dunraven Pass offers the park's best perspective on the contours of the ancient Yellowstone Caldera, along with spectacular **views**★★ of the Absaroka and Beartooth ranges to the east. Looming over the pass is 10,243ft **Mount Washburn**.

Grand Canyon of the Yellowstone★★★

Canyon Village, 19mi south of Tower Junction. ⚠ ♿ P.
After Old Faithful, this magnificent canyon is probably the park's best-known feature, roughly 20mi long, 800-1,200ft deep and 1,500-4,000ft wide. The brilliant color of its rhyolite rock is due to iron compounds "cooked" by hydrothermal activity. Weathering oxidation of the iron produced the yellow, orange, red and brown colors. At the end of the last ice age, scientists believe ice dams formed at the mouth of Yellowstone Lake. When breached, they released tremendous amounts of water, carving the canyon.

The one-way loop **Inspiration Point Road** visits several canyon viewpoints. **Lookout Point** offers a classic view of the 308ft **Lower Fall**★★—most impressive in spring, when 63,500gal of water cross its crest each second. A little farther west, a trail leads to the brink of the 109ft **Upper Fall**★, where a railing is all that separates viewers from the surging water. Upstream, a 2.5mi spur road crosses the Yellowstone River to the South Rim. **Artist's Point**★★ offers perhaps the best views of the canyon and Lower Fall.

Hayden Valley★★

5–10mi south of Canyon Village. P.
A placid contrast to the dramatic canyon, this lush valley of meadow and marsh is the best place to observe wildlife. Hayden Valley is home to large herds of bison, plus moose and elk, and in spring is a good place to catch a glimpse of grizzly bears. Coming across even a portion of the bison herd is as close as one can come to viewing life in the West before European settlement. Bears are often seen in spring and early summer, when they feed on newborn bison and elk calves.

In summer, traffic backs up for miles when bison decide to cross the road. Turnouts, situated in key positions for viewing, may be occupied by a ranger with a spotting scope happily shared with visitors.

Fishing Bridge

East Entrance & Grand Loop Rds. P.
Until 1973, fishermen stood shoulder-to-shoulder here, angling for abundant cutthroat trout. Fishing was terminated to protect fish spawning and to allow grizzly bears to forage unmolested. **Fishing Bridge Visitor Center**★ (☎307-242-2450) has fine exhibits of the birds of the national park.

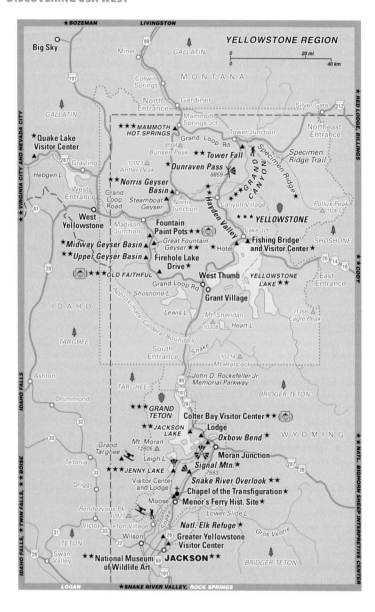

Yellowstone Lake★★

⚠ ♿ 🅿.

At 7,733ft altitude, the largest natural high-elevation lake in North America has 136sq mi of surface area, 110mi of shoreline and depths of nearly 400ft. Although the surface is frozen half the year, lake-bottom vents produce water as warm as 252°F. The Yellowstone River flows into the lake from the southeast, and exits at Fishing Bridge through the Grand Canyon of the Yellowstone, continuing 671mi to its confluence with the Missouri River. It is the longest river still undammed in the lower 48 states.

The stately, three-story **Lake Yellowstone Hotel**★ *(1.5mi south of Fishing Bridge; ☎307-344-7311, www.travelyelloowstone.com)* faces eastward on the lakeshore. Yellow clapboard with white trim, it was built in 1891; the exterior received its first major facelift in 1903 when architect Robert Reamer added Ionic columns and 15 false balconies. At **Bridge Bay** *(3mi south of Fishing Bridge)*, a marina offers 90min boat tours and supplies anglers.

West Thumb

♿ 🅿.

This small collapsed caldera within the big Yellowstone Caldera includes the **West ThumbGeyser Basin**★ on its western shore. It extends beneath Yellowstone Lake where hot springs and even underwater geysers mix their boiling contents with the frigid lake water. A boardwalk winds through the shoreline thermal features, among which are 53ft-deep, cobalt-blue **Abyss Pool**★, and **Fishing Cone Geyser**★.

Grant Village

2mi south of West Thumb. ♿ 🅿.
Named to honor US President Ulysses S. Grant, who signed the legislation that created Yellowstone in 1872, this full-service park community includes the **Grant Village Visitor Center**★ (☎307-242-2650). Exhibits and a 20min film explain the natural benefits of wild fires, such as the conflagration that engulfed the park in 1988.

Old Faithful★★★

🄺🄸🄳🅂 *18mi northwest of West Thumb& 16mi south of Madison Junction.* ♿ 🅿.
The world's most famous geyser has been spouting with uncanny regularity since it was discovered by the Washburn-Langford-Doane party in 1870. Averaging 135ft in height when it erupts, sometimes reaching 180ft, Old Faithful puts on a show approximately every 65- to 91min. Eruptions last 90sec to 5min and spew between 3,700gal and 8,400gal of boiling water.
A semicircular boardwalk with benches surrounds the geyser. During the high season of July and August, thousands of people wait patiently for an eruption, then scurry to other activities, creating a phenomenon locals refer to as a "gush rush." Restaurants fill immediately after an eruption and clear out just before.

Old Faithful

The village flanking Old Faithful is the park's most commercial, with massive parking lots and numerous buildings facing the geyser. Chief among them is **Old Faithful Inn**★★ *(☎307-344-7311, www.travelyeloowstone.com)*, the world's largest log building. This National Historic Landmark was designed by Robert Reamer and constructed in 1903-04. It is the definitive structure of "parkitecture"—six stories high, its massive lobby featuring whole log columns, a stone fireplace and tortured lodgepole-pine railings.
Old Faithful Lodge *(☎307-344-7311, www.travelyeloowstone.com)*, another large log-and-stone building, was completed in 1928. The large plate-glass windows of the **Old Faithful Visitor Center** *(☎307-545-2750)* enable visitors to watch Old Faithful erupt without leaving the building.

Upper Geyser Basin★★

♿ 🅿.
Surrounding Old Faithful is the world's largest concentration of geysers. Among the better known are **Grand Geyser**★, which unleashes a 200ft fountain every 7-15hrs; **Riverside Geyser**★, whose stream spurts up to 80ft over the Firehole River at 5-6hr intervals; and **Castle Geyser**★, which explodes to 90ft twice daily from an ancient 12ft cone.

Geysers

Geysers are created by constrictions in the subterranean plumbing of a hot spring. Steam bubbles, like commuters at rush hour, create immense pressure as they force their way through the water above them, erupting with even more superheated water and steam from the depths.

About 300 of the world's geysers are located in Yellowstone. "So numerous are they and varied," wrote naturalist John Muir, "nature seems to have gathered them from all over the world as specimens of her rarest fountains to show in one place what she can do."

Because no organism can survive in water 161°F or warmer (at this altitude), the Upper Geyser Basin's hottest pools typically reflect the color of the sky. The best-known spring, **Morning Glory Pool**★★, is not as blue as it once was, however: Its hot-water vent has been clogged by coins and other objects thrown into the pool by park visitors, leading to a gradual cooling.

Midway Geyser Basin★

6mi north of Old Faithful. 🅿.
Mist from the wide **Excelsior Geyser** envelops visitors who cross the footbridge and climbpast a multicolored bank of the Firehole River. Runoff from acidic **Grand Prismatic Spring**★★ has created terraced algae mats, often decorated with hoof prints from bison. At 370ft across and 120ft deep, rainbow colored Grand Prismatic is the second-largest hot spring in the world.

Firehole Lake Drive★

8mi north of Old Faithful. 🅿.
A quiet 3mi, one-way circuit east of the Grand Loop Road, this route winds past **Great Fountain Geyser**★★, the White Dome and Pink Cone geysers, and **Firehole Lake**, with runoff in every direction. Between Great Fountain's 45-60min eruptions at intervals of 8-12hrs, the still water of its broad, circular pool mirrors the sky in myriad terraces. Firehole Lake's thermal waters flow through the forest here, giving trees a skeletal appearance of stark white stockings and gray trunks. The absorption of sinter (dissolved minerals) kills the trees but acts as a preservative, delaying their decay.

Fountain Paint Pots★★

Kids *9mi north of Old Faithful.* ♿🅿.
Visitors may view all four types of Yellowstone thermal features on a short tour of this area. A boardwalk leads past colorful bacterial and algae mats, hot pools and the namesake bubbling "paint pots." Adults as well as children revel in the implied messiness, oozing and rotten-egg stench of the spring's hydrogen sulfide gas. The perpetually active **Clepsydra Geyser**★ is especially scenic in winter, when bison wander in front of its plume of steam.

GRAND TETON NATIONAL PARK★★★

MAP P 452

MOUNTAIN STANDARD TIME

The Teton Range rises dramatically above a broad valley near the headwaters of the Snake River, immediately south of Yellowstone National Park. Cresting atop 13,770ft Grand Teton, the Tetons, which extend about 40mi from south to north, are the highlight of the park—485sq mi of rugged peaks, alpine lakes, streams, marshland and sage-and-aspen plains.

- **Information:** ☎307-739-3300, www.nps.gov/grte
- ▶ **Orient Yourself:** Except for experienced wilderness travelers, the Tetons themselves are experienced through vistas from highways that parallel the range on the east and west sides.
- **Parking:** As in Yellowstone, please don't park in the roadway to watch wildlife.

Geological Notes

The Tetons are the result of a continuing cycle of mountain building and erosion. Geologic youngsters at 5 to 9 million years, they are still growing along a north-south fault line. As the valley floor—once a flat layer of sediment left by an ancient inland sea—has subsided, the blocks of rock that form the Tetons have risen, tilting westward. Erosion has shaved soft sandstone from the caps of the peaks, gradually filling the valley several miles deep with sediment.

The high peaks attract significant precipitation, especially as snow in winter. As snowfall rates exceed melting, glaciers form, chiseling singular peaks like the Grand Teton. Twelve active glaciers flow as many as 30ft each year around several of the peaks, especially the Grand Teton and 12,605ft **Mount Moran.** Glacial debris, deposited at the base of the mountains, has formed lateral and terminal moraines that act as natural dams, capturing melt-water to form lakes.

A Bit of History

Known to Native Americans as *Teewinot,* "many pinnacles," the Tetons' modern name came from early-19C French trappers, who saw them as *Les Trois Tétons,* "the three breasts," as they approached from the west.

Although Native Americans used Jackson Hole as a summer hunting ground for thousands of years, few chose to endure the harsh winters. Hardy cattle ranchers were gradually supplanted by tourism following the establishment of Yellowstone Park in 1872.

Grand Teton's transition to national park was not smooth. Early settlers proved as stubborn as the winter weather when it came to turning the land over to federal jurisdiction. Fearing development, philanthropist John D. Rockefeller Jr. secretly bought up ranchland and deeded it to the government. The original 1929 park boundaries expanded to their present margins in 1950. The **John D. Rockefeller Jr. Memorial Parkway,** a corridor linking Grand Teton and Yellowstone parks, was created in 1972.

Sights

Park headquarters are adjacent to the **Moose Visitor Center** (*Teton Park Rd., 0.5mi west of Teton Junction & 12mi north of Jackson, WY;* ☎*307-739-3399),* at the southern end of the park. A driving tour from here is best done in a counterclockwise direction, heading northeast along the Snake River to Jackson Lake, returning south at the foot of the mountain range.

©iStockphoto.com/ Joe McDaniel

Canoeing on Jackson Lake

Snake River Overlook★★
US-26/89/191, 8mi north of Moose Junction. ♿🅿.
Immortalized by photographer Ansel Adams, this is the most popular vista point in the park. Adams created a definitive black-and-white image of the ragged Tetons with the silvery Snake River in the foreground.

Oxbow Bend★
US-89/191/287, 4mi northwest of Moran Junction. ♿🅿.
The Snake River almost doubles back on itself at this bulbous elbow. This is one of the most dependable spots in the park to spy moose, which often feed in the shallows.

Jackson Lake★★
⛺✕♿🅿.
The largest of seven natural morainal lakes in the park, 438ft-deep Jackson Lake—16mi long and 8mi wide—was enlarged by a succession of dams at its Snake River outlet that raised the lake 39ft. **Boat tours** (90min) are offered daily in summer.

Jackson Lake Lodge
US-89/191/287, 6mi northwest of Moran Junction. ⛺✕♿🅿 ☎*307-543-3100. www.gtlc.com.* Designed by Gilbert Stanley Underwood, architect of the Ahwahnee Hotel in California's Yosemite National Park, this concrete, steel and glass structure was built above the beaver ponds of Willow Flats. The lobby features massive, 60ft-tall picture windows framing a classic view of the Tetons.

Colter Bay Visitor Center★★
Kids *1mi west of US-89/191/287, 11mi northwest of Moran Junction.* ⛺✕🅿 ☎*307-739-3594. Open summers only.*
The center holds the **Indian Arts Museum,** whose display of native crafts—beadwork, weaponry, moccasins, shields and pipes—is among Wyoming's best.

Signal Mountain★
Off Teton Park Rd., 16mi north of Moose Junction & 5mi south of Jackson Lake Lodge. ♿🅿.
Rising above **Signal Mountain Lodge** *(Teton Park Rd.;* ☎*307-543-2831)* on the east side of Jackson Lake, 7,593ft Signal Mountain provides great viewsaa of the Tetons and Jackson Hole. The **Signal Mountain Summit Road** is a narrow, winding, 5mi, 800ft climb with few turnouts.

Jenny Lake Scenic Drive★★★
Off Teton Park Rd., beginning 11.5mi north of Moose Junction. ♿🅿.
This 4mi loop weaves along the eastern shore of gem-like **Jenny Lake**★★★ before reconnecting with Teton Park Road. En route are numerous impressive views of the high Tetons. From the **Cathedral Group Turnout**★, the peaks crowd together like church steeples. Little **String Lake** ties Jenny Lake to more northerly **Leigh Lake**. Beyond here, the two-way road becomes a narrow, one-way southerly drive. A cluster of 37 log cabins surrounds rustic **Jenny Lake Lodge** *(*☎*307-733-4647, www.gtlc.com),* the park's premier accommodation. From the **Jenny Lake Overlook**★★, lake waters reflect the Tetons rising abruptly from the water's edge. The **Jenny Lake Visitor Center** at South Jenny Lake has a set of geology exhibits.

Menor's Ferry Historic Site★

Teton Park Rd., 1.5mi north of Moose Junction. ♿ 🅿.

An interpretive trail (.5mi) leads to a replica of a flat-bottomed ferry that Bill Menor operated from 1894 to 1927. Interpreters reenact the Snake River crossing in summer. Menor's white log cabin is decorated as the country store he also ran from the home.

Chapel of the Transfiguration★

0.5mi east of Teton Park Rd., 1.5mi north of Moose Junction. ♿ 🅿.

The window behind the altar of this rustic little chapel, built in 1925, frames the Tetons. Services are offered summer Sundays.

Moose-Wilson Road★

Moose Visitor Center to Rte. 22 (1.6mi east of Wilson). ♿ 🅿.

This scenic drive to the small community of Wilson, at the base of Teton Pass, skirts groves of aspens and a network of willow-clogged beaver ponds. Moose are often spotted from **Sawmill Ponds Overlook.** The road—all but about 2mi of it paved—accesses several popular trailheads, especially to emerald **Phelps Lake** *(2mi).*

JACKSON★★

MAP P 452

MOUNTAIN STANDARD TIME

The resort town of Jackson sits at 6,350ft altitude near the south end of the 45mi-long valley known as Jackson Hole, between the Tetons and the Gros Ventre Mountains. The town's economy has shifted from cattle ranching in favor of tourism and outdoor recreation; it is now a year-round paradise both for wildlife and the wild life. River rafting, fishing, hiking, horseback riding and mountain climbing are among its offerings, and in winter, Jackson is one of the finest ski destinations in the world. Three ski areas, famed for light and ample powder snow, are a short drive away; the Jackson Hole Mountain Resort★★ *(Rte. 390, Teton Village, 12mi west of Jackson; ☎307-733-2292, www.jacksonhole.com)* has the greatest vertical (4,139ft) of any US ski area.

🛈 **Information:** ☎307-733-3316, www.jacksonholechamber.com
☺ **Don't Miss:** National Museum of Wildlife Art
⏱ **Also See:** Teton Village Aerial Tram

Jackson Today

Jackson is crowded with fine restaurants, high-end Western-wear boutiques and fine-art galleries, and its proliferation of modern resort developments has attracted many wealthy part-time residents. But it has retained a firm grip on its Western heritage.

Town Square *(Broadway & Cache Dr.)* is the hub of this community of 8,600. An arch of elk antlers frames each of its four corners—a tiny fraction of what is collected each winter on the National Elk Refuge. Prior to 1957, the antlers

were offered as souvenirs. Today they are auctioned by Boy Scouts in mid-May. Of the $100,000 typically raised, 80 percent goes to augment the elk-feeding program at the refuge.

Summer nights at Town Square, actors re-create a stagecoach robbery and **Jackson Hole Shootout** 🄺🄸🄳🅂—even though no such incident ever took place in Jackson. Facing the Square is the **Million Dollar Cowboy Bar** *(25 N. Cache Dr.; ☎307-733-2207),* with saddles for stools and silver dollars inlaid into its bar.

Sights

Jackson Hole and Greater Yellowstone Visitor Center

532 N. Cache Dr. ♿ 🅿 ☎*307-733-9212. www.fs.fed.us/jhgyvc/.*

This contemporary sod-roofed building, an interagency visitor center, features a platform with spotting scopes for viewing the adjacent elk refuge and marsh, and interpretive exhibits on fire management and wildlife migration.

National Elk Refuge★

Elk Refuge Rd. off E. Broadway. ☎*307-733-9212. www.fws.gov/nationalelkrefuge.*

Between 7,000 and 9,000 elk spend their winters in this 24,700-acre refuge after migrating from higher elevations in the national parks and Bridger-Teton National Forest. The refuge was established after cattle ranching and development disrupted normal migration patterns. **Sled tours**★★ 🅚 *(45min)* are offered daily in winter. Draft horses pull sleighs to herds, where most animals graze sedately—although bull elk may joust with their immense racks. The refuge is also a popular winter range for bighorn sheep, coyotes, deer, wolves and, occasionally, pronghorn and mountain lions. Tickets are sold by the National Museum of Wildlife Art *(below).*

National Museum of Wildlife Art★★

🅚 *2820 Rungius Rd., off US-89, 2.5mi north of Jackson.* ✕♿🅿 ☎*307-733-5771. www.wildlifeart.org.*

Tucked into a hillside overlooking the National Elk Refuge, this sandstone complex (1994) resembles Ancient Puebloan ruins. Covering five centuries, the collection of more than 2,300 works includes John J. Audubon, Robert Bateman, Albert Bierstadt, George Catlin, John Clymer, Bob Kuhn and Charles M. Russell.

The American Bison Collection explores man's relationship with buffalo since the 18C. Also featured is the largest body of work in the US by Carl Rungius.

Teton Village Aerial Tramway★★

Rte. 390, Teton Village. ♿🅿 ☎*307-733-2292. www.jacksonhole.com.*

A gondola whisks sightseers skyward on a brisk ride, climbing over 4,000ft in 12min to the 10,450ft ridge of Rendezvous Peak at the Jackson Hole Ski Area. Spread to the east is Jackson Hole, bisected by the Snake River. Many hikers descend Rendezvous Peak on foot via the steep 10mi **Granite Canyon Trail.**

Excursions

Grand Targhee Ski & Summer Resort

Targhee Rd., Alta, 5mi east of Driggs, Idaho, & 32mi northwest of Jackson via Rtes. 22 & 33. ✕🅿 ☎*307-353-2300. www.grandtarghee.com.*

Nearly 40ft of light, dry snow falls on the "back side" of the Teton Range each winter, making this a mecca for powder hounds. In summer, music festivals and ecology classes complement outdoor recreation and scenic chairlift rides.

National Bighorn Sheep Interpretive Center★★

907 W. Ramshorn St., Dubois, 85mi east of Jackson via US-26/287. ♿🅿 ☎*307-455-3429. www.bighorn.org.*

Visitors here may "manage" a herd of wild sheep, balancing reproduction rates, expected mortality and forage requirements with management techniques including hunting, culling the herd and non-intervention. Nearby **Whiskey Mountain** is home to the largest wintering herd of Rocky Mountain bighorn sheep in the US.

CODY★★

MICHELIN MAP 493 G 6
MOUNTAIN STANDARD TIME

William F. "Buffalo Bill" Cody founded this town as his own in 1896, two decades after he first scouted the region. Cody envisioned a place where the Old and New West could meet; this site, 50mi east of Yellowstone National Park, was ideal. Cody poured the profits from his popular Wild West Show into the town's growth. By 1901, rail service was established; by 1905, construction was under way on the ambitious Shoshone (now Buffalo Bill) Dam.

- **Information:** ☎307-587-2777, www.codychamber.org
- **Don't Miss:** Buffalo Bill Historical Center
- **Especially for Kids:** Cody Nite Rodeo
- **Also See:** Hot Springs State Park

Cody Today

Tourism remains the major industry of the town, whose population now stands at 9,250. Yellowstone-bound guests still drive the economy. The **Cody Country Chamber of Commerce** (836 Sheridan Ave.; ☎307-587-2777) has information on walking tours of the historic town, including **The Irma** (1192 Sheridan Ave.; ☎307-587-4221, www.irmahotel.com). This 1902 hotel, built by Buffalo Bill and named for his youngest daughter, features an ornate cherry backbar hand-crafted in France and shipped to Cody as a gift from Queen Victoria of England. The summer-long **Cody Nite Rodeo**★ (W. Yellowstone Hwy.; ♿🅿 ☎307-587-5155, www.codystampederodeo.com) is a lively introduction to the sport of rodeo. Contestants vie in bronco and bull riding, calf roping, bulldogging and barrel racing; a highlight is the calf scramble, in which children pursue a calf with a yellow ribbon tied to its tail.

Sights

Buffalo Bill Historical Center★★★

720 Sheridan Ave. ✕♿🅿 ☎307-587-4771. www.bbhc.org.

Four internationally acclaimed galleries and a research library, occupying three levels of this fan-shaped complex, explore aspects of the history of the American West. Also on the site is the boyhood home of William F. "Buffalo Bill" Cody, shipped by train from Iowa in 1933.

The **Whitney Gallery of Western Art**★★ presents a broad spectrum of paintings and sculpture, including oils by Catlin, Bierstadt and Russell, and bronzes by Remington. The wing is named for sculptor Gertrude V. Whitney, whose dynamic *The Scout*, north of the complex, depicts a mounted William F. Cody.

The Buffalo Bill Museum★★ chronicles the storied life of "Buffalo Bill," man and myth. Much of the collection focuses on his Wild West Show and its relationship to public perception of the West. Displays include firearms, clothing, silver-studded saddles, and film gathered from Cody's private and public lives.

The Plains Indian Museum★★ interprets the cultural history and artistry of the Arapaho, Blackfoot, Cheyenne, Comanche, Crow, Gros Ventre, Kiowa, Pawnee, Shoshone and Sioux, incorporating modern oral tradition with historical and contemporary artifacts.

The Cody Firearms Museum★, which traces the evolution of guns, is the world's most comprehensive collection of post-16C American and European firearms—nearly 4,000 in all. Exhibits in the **Draper Museum of Natural History**★★ focus on the greater Yellowstone ecosystem and the relationship between man and the natural world.

Trail Town★

1831 DeMaris Dr. off W. Yellowstone Hwy. ☎307-587-5302. ⏲ *Open mid-May–mid-Sept.*
More than 100 wagons and 25 buildings dated 1879-1901, moved from a 150mi radius, are arranged on the original surveyed site for Cody City.

Excursions

Bighorn Canyon National Recreation Are★★★

Via Rte. 37 northeast of Lovell. Visitor center on US-14A, Lovell, 48mi northeast of Cody. ⚠✕♿🅿 ☎307-548-2251. *www.nps.gov/bica.*
Bighorn Lake, a 60mi-long reservoir created by Montana's 525ft-high Yellowtail Dam, is wedged between 2,200ft cliffs. Flanking the national recreation area on its west is the expansive **Pryor Mountain Wild Horse Range**, with 100 to 200 wild horses.

Hot Springs State Park★

Kids *US-20 & Park St., Thermopolis, 83mi southeast of Cody.* ⚠✕♿🅿 ☎307-864-2176. *wyoparks.state.wy.us.*
Shoshone and Arapaho Indians sold these springs to Wyoming in 1896 with the stipulation that they remain free for public use. Today 3.6 million gallons of 135°F water flow daily from Monument Hill, piped through the center of two 20ft travertine terraces. The free Wyoming State Bathhouse sits between two commercial facilities at the foot of the springs.

MONTANA GATEWAYS★

MICHELIN MAP 493 F, G 5

MOUNTAIN STANDARD TIME

Although less than 8 percent of Yellowstone National Park is in Montana, three of its five entrances are in the "Big Sky" state. The West Yellowstone entrance is the busiest, capturing one-third of park visitors. Mammoth Hot Springs is near Gardiner, at the north entrance. The magnificent northeastern-approach road climbs nearly to 11,000ft at Beartooth Pass.

- 🛈 **Information:** ☎406-556-8680, www.yellowstonecountry.net
- 👀 **Don't Miss:** Beartooth Highway
- Kids **Especially for Kids:** Grizzly Discovery Center

Sights

West Yellowstone

US-20 & 287. ⚠✕♿🅿 ☎406-646-7701. *www.westyellowstonechamber.com.*
The Union Pacific Railroad built a spur line to the park's border in 1907. Today this town has 1,200 year-round residents; in winter, it calls itself the "Snowmobile Capital of the World." In the former Union Pacific Depot—designed in "park rustic" style by Gilbert Stanley Underwood—the **Yellowstone Historic Center Museum** (*124 Yellowstone St.; ☎406-646-1100*) offers wildlife dioramas and a highly regarded display of Indian beadwork and quillwork.

Grizzly and Wolf Discovery Center★★

Kids *201 S. Canyon St.* ♿🅿 ☎406-646-7001. *www.grizzlydiscoveryctr.com.*
The habitats and lives of grizzly bears and gray wolves are the focus of this educational facility. A pack of 10 wolves with a clear social hierarchy shares a den in one fenced enclosure. Nearby, eight grizzlies enjoy an enclosure with two ponds and a flowing stream. An interpreter discusses behavior, from eating habits to intelligence and mating.

Quake Lake Visitor Center★

US-287, 25mi northwest of West Yellowstone. ☎406-823-6961. *www.fs.fed.us/r1.*

Just before midnight on August 17, 1959, a magnitude-7.5 earthquake triggered a landslide that buried 19 people at a Madison River campground and destroyed miles of highway. Soon the Madison was backing up behind a natural-earth dam, as cracks developed in the manmade dam at Hebgen Lake. The story of the tragedy, and of how a secondary disaster was averted, is told at this Forest Service visitor center. It is perched on a hillside overlooking the slide scar and natural dam; a quickly engineered spillway; and **Quake Lake,** 190ft deep and 6mi long.

Virginia City and Nevada City★★

Rte. 278, 84mi northwest of West Yellowstone. △✕🅿 ☎*406-843-5555. www.virginiacitychamber.com.*

These sister villages, 1.5mi apart in Alder Gulch, feature Wild West architecture embellished with vigilante legends. Both prospered during an 1863 gold rush; Virginia City survived to become the capital of the Montana Territory, while Nevada City became a ghost town. Today **Nevada City**★★ is a restored mining camp with more than 90 period buildings—some originals, some reconstructions, some moved from other sites. **Virginia City**★★ is a living museum, the entire town listed on the National Register of Historic Places. The Main Street boardwalk is fringed with storefronts that display 19C wares.

Three Forks Area★

I-90, 28mi west of Bozeman. △✕🅿.

Lewis and Clark named the three rivers that merge to form the Missouri—the Madison, Jefferson and Gallatin—for statesmen of their day. **Missouri Headwaters State Park**★ *(Rte. 286, 5mi north of Three Forks; ☎406-994-4042, fwp.mt.gov/parks)* marks the start of North America's longest river system, the Missouri-Mississippi. **Lewis and Clark Caverns State Park**★★ 🅺🅸🅳🆂 *(Rte. 2, 19mi west of Three Forks; ☎406-287-3541, fwp.mt.gov/parks)* boasts 3-million-year-old stalactites and stalagmites as well as a colony of bats.

Bozeman★

Rte. 84 at I-90 Exit 309, 92mi north of West Yellowstone. ✕🅰️🅿 *b406-586-5421. www.bozemanchamber.com.*

Home to **Montana State University**, this town of 29,000 was named for wagonmaster John Bozeman. A railroad spur to West Yellowstone was completed in the early 20C. Today restaurants, bookshops, galleries and boutiques occupy the historic brick buildings on either side of Main Street, and nearby **Willson Avenue**★ is lined with beautiful c.1900 homes.

Museum of the Rockies★★

🅺🅸🅳🆂 *600 W. Kagy Blvd.* 🅰️🅿 ☎*406-994-3466. www.montana.edu/wwwmor.*

Exhibits in this outstanding museum trace the geologic history of the Rockies. In the **Life Sciences Exhibits**★★, a dinosaur display showcases the prominent role played by Montana and Wyoming in modern paleontology. Moving models of the great lizards are popular with children. The Taylor Planetarium features star and laser shows. Outside, the Tinsley Homestead is the venue for living-history demonstrations depicting an early Gallatin Valley farm.

Big Sky

Rte. 64, 3mi west of US-191, 45mi south of Bozeman & 47mi north of West Yellowstone. △✕🅰️🅿 *b406-995-5000. www.bigskyresort.com.*

Developed by TV newsman Chet Huntley, Big Sky is a summer-winter resort with 15 lifts that access 3,650 acres of ski terrain in winter. In summer, there is golf, horseback riding, biking and fishing; gondola rides go part way up 11,150ft Lone Peak and take in wide-ranging views.

Livingston

US-89 at I-90 Exit 332, 60mi north of Mammoth Hot Springs. △✕🅰️🅿 *b406-222-0850. www.livingston-chamber.com.*

Founded in 1882 by the Northern Pacific, Livingston was the point at which rail tourists boarded a spur line to Yellowstone National Park's north entrance. The town of 7,000 has preserved 436 buildings from its heyday.

Red Lodge★

US-212, 115mi east of Mammoth Hot Springs. ✕ ♿ 🅿 *b406-446-1718. www. redlodge.com.*

Red Lodge began as a coal town. After the mines died, tourism brought new life to the community of 2,200. Main Street is lined with brick buildings, most constructed around the turn of the 20C. Oldest is the 1893 Pollard Hotel *(2 N. Broadway; ☎406-446-0001, www.thepollard. net),* a National Historic Register site.

Beartooth Highway★★

US-212 from Red Lodge to Cooke City. 🕐 *Open May–Oct depending upon snow conditions.* ⚠.

CBS correspondent Charles Kuralt called this 67mi route "the most beautiful road in America." Precipitous switchbacks climb from Red Lodge, ascending nearly 4,000ft in 5mi. **Views**★★★ are spectacular from an overlook at 10,947ft **Beartooth Pass**; an interpretive trail is frequented as often by mountain goats as by humans. The broad summit plateau is carpeted with wildflowers in summer; ragged peaks jut upward on every horizon.

Billings

US-87 at I-90 Exit 450. ✕ ♿ 🅿 ☎406-252-4111. www.billingscvb.visitmt.com.
Montana's largest city (90,000 people) spreads across a floodplain of the Yellowstone River. Its most compelling sight is the **Moss Mansion**★ *(914 Division St.; ☎406-256-5100),* a 1903 banker's home built by Henry Janeway Hardenbergh, architect of New York's Waldorf-Astoria Hotel. A castle-like 1901 library of Romanesque design houses the **Western Heritage Center** *(2282 Montana Ave.; ☎406-256-6809),* a history museum. The **Yellowstone Art Museum** *(401 N. 27th St.; ☎406-256-6804),* built around the old county jail, features such Montana figures as cowboy artist Will James and sculptor Deborah Butterfield.

SNAKE RIVER VALLEY★

MICHELIN MAP 493 D, E, F 6
MOUNTAIN STANDARD TIME

Rising in Wyoming and flowing through Yellowstone and Grand Teton National Parks, the Snake River arcs across southern Idaho, carving deep canyons and nourishing rich agricultural lands. A series of dams have turned this high lava plain into productive land, supporting cities and towns of moderate size.

🔢 **Information:** ☎208-334-2470, www.visitid.org
🚗 **Don't Miss:** World Center for Birds of Prey
Kids **Especially for Kids:** Bruneau Dunes State Park

Geological Notes

Once an inland sea that drained westward as the land mass uplifted, the region was covered by lava that oozed through faults to cloak the rich marine silt. To the south, great Lake Bonneville, 340mi long and 140mi wide, covered much of modern Utah and eastern Nevada. When the lake breached a volcanic plug 15,000 years ago, a flood of biblical proportion raged for eight weeks at a rate three times that of the modern Amazon River, sweeping millions of tons of rocks and debris and carving the magnificent Snake River and Hells Canyons.

Sights

Idaho Falls

US-20 & 26 at I-15 Exit 118, 90mi west of Jackson. ✕ ♿ 🅿 ☎208-523-1010. www. idahofallschamber.com.
This agricultural center of 57,000 is the gateway to the **Idaho National Laboratory** *(www.inl.gov).* Spread across 890sq mi of lava rock are scores of nuclear

reactors, the largest concentration on earth. Experimental Breeder Reactor 1 was the first in the US, having operated 1951-64; free tours of the facility, known as **EBR-I**★ *(Van Buren Blvd., Atomic City, 48mi west of Idaho Falls; ☎208-526-0050)* are offered summers.

Twin Falls★

US-93, 6mi south of I-84 Exit 173, 110mi west of Pocatello. ✕ ♿ 🅿 ☎*208-733-3974. www.twinfallschamber.com.*

This town of 40,000 boasts the **Herrett Center for Arts & Science**★ *(315 Falls Ave. W., College of Southern Idaho; ☎208-733-9554; herrett.csi.edu)*, whose anthropology collection, emphasizing Native American cultures, is highly regarded. Interstate 84 travelers enter Twin Falls via the **Perrine Bridge,** 486ft above the **Snake River Canyon** and the longest span bridge in the USA West. The ramp from which motorcycle daredevil Evel Knievel unsuccessfully attempted to leap 1,500ft across the canyon in 1974 can still be seen.

The main attraction here is **Shoshone Falls**★★ *(3300 East Rd., 5mi east of Twin Falls via Falls Ave.; ☎208-733-3974).* Nicknamed "the Niagara of the West," these 212ft falls are 52ft higher than the eastern US cataract. In spring, before upriver irrigation diversions steal much of the thunder, this is an impressive sight, a 1,000ft-wide wall of water that drops into its own cloud of mist.

Thousand Springs Scenic Route★★

US-30 between Buhl (18mi west of Twin Falls) and Bliss (I-84 Exit 141). ♿ 🅿 ☎*208-837-9131. www.hagermanchamber.com.*

The **Thousand Springs**★★ seep or gush from the opposite (north) wall of the Snake canyon, an outflow from the Lost Rivers that disappear into the porous Snake River Plain, emerging through gaps or fractures in the rock. Numerous **fish hatcheries** and trout farms in the valley take advantage of the pristine water.

Perched on a bluff on the southwest side of the Snake is **Hagerman Fossil Beds National Monument**★ *(W. 2700 South Rd.; visitor center at 221 N. State St., Hagerman; ☎208-837-4793, www.nps.gov/hafo).* The richest trove of Pliocene fossils in North America, the beds were first excavated in the 1930s when Smithsonian Institution scientists unearthed a zebra-like horse extinct for more than 3 million years. There are overlooks and trails but no on-site facilities; tours are offered from the visitor center on summer weekends.

Bruneau Dunes State Park★

🄺 *Rte. 78, 18mi south of Mountain Home at I-84 Exit 95.* ⚠ ♿ 🅿 ☎*208-366-7919. www.idahoparks.org.*

These 470ft sand dunes occupy a 600-acre depression in an ancient bend of the

Snake River and the Grand Teton Mountains

©iStockphoto.com/ Steve Geer

Snake. Hiking trails climb the stationary dunes, composed mainly of quartz and feldspar particles. A small observatory attracts weekend stargazers.

Boise★★

US-20/26/30 at I-84 Exit 53, 120mi northwest of Twin Falls. ✕🚻📁 ☎*208-344-7777. www.boise.org.*

The Boise (BOY-see) River lends a unique character to this city of 208,000, Idaho's capital and its commercial and cultural center. High-tech office workers on their lunch hours wade into the stream and cast flies for trout, as Boise State University students drift by on rafts and inner tubes within sight of the Neoclassical **Idaho State Capitol**★ *(700 W. Jefferson St.;* ☎*208-334-5174).* Built of native sandstone in 1905-20 and patterned after the US Capitol in Washington DC, the capitol is the beneficiary of the modern world's first urban geothermal heating system. Since 1892, 700,000gal of 172°F water have been pumped daily from an aquifer adjacent to the **Warm Springs Historic District.** Four hundred private residences and eight government buildings are so heated.

Activity downtown centers around **The Grove** *(8th Ave. & Grove St.),* a broad pedestrian plaza. Nearby, the **Basque Museum and Cultural Center** *(611 Grove St.;* ☎*208-343-2671, www.basquemuseum.com)* reflects the fact that Boise is the largest Basque community outside the group's native Spain and France.

The **Boise River Greenbelt**★★, a mostly paved 35mi network of walking and biking paths, links a series of riverside parks through the heart of the city. Nearest to downtown, **Julia Davis Park** *(Julia Davis Dr. & Capitol Blvd.)* is home to the **Idaho State Historical Museum** 🧒 *(610 Julia Davis Dr.;* ☎*208-334-2120, www.idahohistory.net),* t**he Boise Art Museum** *(670 Julia Davis Dr.;* ☎*208-345-8330, www.boiseartmuseum.org)* and the hands-on **Discovery Center of Idaho** 🧒 *(131 Myrtle St.;* ☎*208-343-9895, www.sciidaho.org).* Also in the park is **Zoo Boise** 🧒 *(355 N. Julia Davis Dr.;* ☎*208-384-4260, www.zooboise.com).* East of the park is the **Morrison-Knudsen Nature Center**★ 🧒 *(600 S. Walnut St.;* ☎*208-334-2225),* which re-creates the life cycle of a mountain stream.

Two miles east, the **Old Idaho State Penitentiary**★ *(2445 Old Penitentiary Rd., off Warm Springs Blvd.;* ☎*208-334-2844, www.idahohistory.net)* is one of only four US territorial prisons still in existence. The fortress-like sandstone edifice was built by convict labor in 1870 and used until 1973.

World Center for Birds of Prey★★

🧒 *5668 W. Flying Hawk Lane off S. Cole Rd., 6mi south of Boise via I-84 Exit 50.* ♿📁 ☎*208-362-3716. www.peregrinefund.org.*

The Peregrine Fund was established in 1970 to save the once-endangered peregrine falcon from extinction. The Fund has now turned its captive-breeding efforts to reestablishing populations of other threatened birds, including the California condor, the South American harpy eagle and the aplamado falcon of the southwestern US. Video cameras and one-way mirrors enable guests to view incubation chambers and birds without disturbing them.

South of Boise, the world's highest concentration of raptors nest on bluffs overlooking the Snake River. The 755sq-mi **Snake River Birds of Prey National Conservation Area** is accessed via Swan Falls Road *(3mi west of Kuna and 23mi south of Boise via I-84 Exit 44;* ☎*208-384-3300, www.birdsofprey.blm.*

©iStockphoto.com/ Andrew Howe

Peregrine Falcon

gov). Best times to visit are late spring, when the young have hatched, and early autumn, when birds congregate to migrate south.

Hells Canyon National Recreation Area★★

Description p 333.

Sun Valley Resort★★

Rte. 75, 83mi north of Twin Falls & 151mi east of Boise. △✕&🄿 ☎*208-725-2111. www.visitsunvalley.com.*

The Wood River Valley was a sleepy back-woods until the 1870s, when the discovery of gold, silver and lead transformed it into a bustling mining district. Sheep ranching later drove the economy, the former tent town of **Ketchum** becoming the second-largest export center in the world. Later, W. Averell Harriman, chief executive of the Union Pacific Railroad, purchased a 4,000-acre ranch and began building a European-style winter resort. When the **Sun Valley Lodge**★★ *(1 Sun Valley Rd., Sun Valley;* ☎*208-622-2001)* opened in 1936, it attracted a Hollywood clientele and set the tone for what then was known as the world's finest ski area, complete with the first chair lift (patterned after a maritime banana hoist). Sun Valley continues to expand and modernize around its core village. With 18 lifts on two mountains—including 9,150ft **Bald Mountain**, whose slopes drop 3,400ft directly into Ketchum—and cross-country runs on the 21mi **Wood River Trail System**, it remains a world-class destination.

Author Ernest Hemingway (1899-1961) spent his later years as a resident of Ketchum, where he is buried; he is remembered with a bust and epitaph at the **Ernest Hemingway Memorial** *(Trail Creek Rd., 1mi northeast of Sun Valley Lodge).*

Sawtooth National Recreation Area★★

Headquarters on Rte. 75, 8mi north of Sun Valley. △✕&🄿 ☎*208-737-3200. www. fs.fed.us/r4/sawtooth.*

Embracing 1,180sq mi of rugged mountains—including 40 peaks of 10,000ft elevation, 1,000 lakes and the headwaters of four important rivers—this is one of the most spectacular yet least-known corners of the continental US. Route 75 climbs up the Wood River to 8,701ft **Galena Summit**★★, then descends the Salmon River drainage. To the east are the magnificent Boulder and White Cloud Mountains, swathed in a carpet of firs. To the west rise the awesome peaks of the Sawtooth Range, a dramatic granite-dominated fault scarp formed 50 million to 70 million years ago. The most developed of four large morainal lakes on the east slope of the Sawtooths is **Redfish Lake**★★, named for the sockeye salmon that traditionally spawned in its waters. A visitor center, log-cabin lodge, marina and beach make this a popular destination.

Tiny **Stanley**★★ *(Rtes. 21 & 75, 61mi northwest of Ketchum & 134mi northeast of Boise;* ☎*208-774-3411. www.stanleycc. org)* is an American Switzerland. Among the 100 or so hardy souls (winter snowfall averages 8ft) who call this gorgeous basin home are 23 outfitters, who specialize in backpacking and horse packing, fishing and white-water rafting.

Craters of the Moon National Monument★

US-20/26/93, 18mi southwest of Arco & 65mi southeast of Sun Valley. △&🄿 ☎*208-527-3257. www.nps.gov/crmo.*

Established in 1924, this 83sq-mi preserve is a jumble of fissures, lava tubes, spatter and cinder cones, an outdoor museum so intimidating, it has yet to be fully explored. This stark landscape was formed when basaltic lava oozed out of cracks in the earth's crust. So moonlike is the terrain that astronauts were trained here for lunar landings. From a newly remodeled **visitor center,** 7mi of paved road thread through the volcanic features. In late spring, the black cinder slopes are transformed into a carpet of wildflowers.

A

INDEX

INDEX

INDEX

WHERE TO EAT

INDEX

WHERE TO STAY

INDEX

MAPS AND PLANS

LIST OF MAPS

THEMATIC MAPS

REGIONAL MAPS

CITY MAPS

MICHELIN COMPANION PUBLICATIONS

MAP 585 WESTERN USA AND WESTERN CANADA

Large-format map providing detailed road systems; includes driving distances, interstate rest stops, border crossings and interchanges.
– Comprehensive city and town index
– Scale 1:2,400,000
  (1 inch = approx. 38 miles)

MAP 761 USA ROAD MAP

Covers principal US road network while also presenting shaded relief detail of overall physiography of the land.
– State flags with statistical data and state tourism office telephone numbers
– Scale: 1:3,450,000
  (1 inch = approx. 55 miles)

NORTH AMERICA ROAD ATLAS

A geographically organized atlas with extensive detailed coverage of the USA, Canada and Mexico. Includes 246 city maps, distance chart, state and provincial driving requirements and a climate chart.
– Comprehensive city and town index
– Easy to follow "Go-to" pointers

LEGEND

★★★ **Worth the trip**
★★ **Worth a detour**
★ **Interesting**

Sight Symbols

⊡─●─────────── Recommended itineraries with departure point

🏛 ⚱ 🕎 Church, chapel – Synagogue ▭ Building described

○ Town described ▭ Other building

AZ B Map co-ordinates locating sights ▪ Small building, statue

■ ▲ Other points of interest ⊙ ⁙ Fountain – Ruins

⚒ ⌒ Mine – Cave 🛈 Visitor information

🌬 ⌖ Windmill – Lighthouse ⊂⊃ ⚓ Ship – Shipwreck

☆ ♠ Fort – Mission ☀ ✹ Panorama – View

Other Symbols

🛡 Interstate highway (USA) 🛡 US highway ⑱⑧⓪ Other route

🍁 Trans-Canada highway 🛡 Canadian highway 🛡 Mexican federal highway

═══ Highway, bridge ═══ Major city thoroughfare

═══ Toll highway, interchange ═══ City street with median

═══ Divided highway ◄─── One-way street

─── Major, minor route ═══ Pedestrian Street

15 (21) Distance in miles (kilometers) ⊁⊰⊱ Tunnel

2149/655 Pass, elevation *(feet/meters)* ═══ Steps – Gate

△6288(1917) Mtn. peak, elevation *(feet/meters)* △ ♜ Drawbridge - Water tower

✈ ✦ Airport – Airfield P ⊠ Parking – Main post office

⛴ Ferry: Cars and passengers ▣ ✚ University – Hospital

⛴ Ferry: Passengers only 🚂 🚌 Train station – Bus station

←⊂ ⊐ Waterfall – Lock – Dam ● ⌂ Subway station

— ·· — ·· — International boundary ❶ ⌂ Digressions – Observatory

- - - - - State boundary ⊥⊤⊥ Cemetery – Swamp

Recreation

■⊶⊶⊶■ Gondola, chairlift ⊙ Stadium – Golf course

🚂 Tourist or steam railway ⊕ ▭ ▣ Park, garden – Wooded area

⛴ ⚲ Harbor, lake cruise – Marina ◉ Wildlife reserve

🏄 ☑ Surfing – Windsurfing ◉ ❦ Wildlife/Safari park, zoo

▨ 🛶 Diving – Kayaking - - - - - Walking path, trail

⛷ 🎿 Ski area – Cross-country skiing 🚶 Hiking trail

Kids Sight of special interest for children

Abbreviations and special symbols

NP	National Park	NMem	National Memorial	SP	State Park
NM	National Monument	NHS	National Historic Site	SF	State Forest
NWR	National Wildlife Refuge	NHP	National Historical Park	SR	State Reserve
NF	National Forest	NVM	National Volcanic Monument	SAP	State Archeological Park

🛡 National Park ⛨ State Park 🌲 National Forest 🌲 State Forest

All maps are oriented north, unless otherwise indicated by a directional arrow.

Michelin Apa Publications Ltd

A joint venture between Michelin and Langenscheidt

Suite 6, Tulip House, 70 Borough High Street, London SE1 1XF, United Kingdom

© 2007 Michelin Apa Publications Ltd
ISBN 978-1-906261-20-7
Printed: November 2007
Printed and bound in Germany

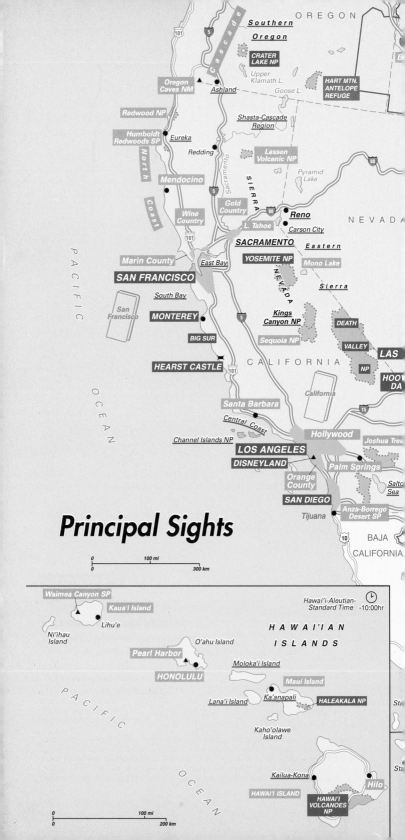

Principal Sights